SENTIENT SEAS

Society and Ecology in Island and Coastal Archaeology

UNIVERSITY PRESS OF FLORIDA

Florida A&M University, Tallahassee
Florida Atlantic University, Boca Raton
Florida Gulf Coast University, Ft. Myers
Florida International University, Miami
Florida State University, Tallahassee
New College of Florida, Sarasota
University of Central Florida, Orlando
University of Florida, Gainesville
University of North Florida, Jacksonville
University of South Florida, Tampa
University of West Florida, Pensacola

Sentient Seas

Archaeologies of Seascapes and Maritime Rituals

Ian J. McNiven

Foreword by Victor D. Thompson
and Scott M. Fitzpatrick

UNIVERSITY PRESS OF FLORIDA

Gainesville/Tallahassee/Tampa/Boca Raton
Pensacola/Orlando/Miami/Jacksonville/Ft. Myers/Sarasota

Cover: Photo by saik20 / Adobe Stock. *Inset:* Mermaid and merman from Ulyssis Aldrovandi's 1642 encyclopedic text *Monstrorum historia: Cum paralipomenis historiae omnium animalium,* page 354 (Source: Smithsonian Library).

Copyright 2026 by Ian J. McNiven

Published in the United States of America

31 30 29 28 27 26   6 5 4 3 2 1

DOI: http://doi.org/10.5744/9780813079615

A record of cataloging-in-publication information is available from the Library of Congress.

ISBN 978-0-8130-7961-5 (cloth)

ISBN 978-0-8130-8154-0 (paperback)

The University Press of Florida is the scholarly publishing agency for the State University System of Florida, comprising Florida A&M University, Florida Atlantic University, Florida Gulf Coast University, Florida International University, Florida State University, New College of Florida, University of Central Florida, University of Florida, University of North Florida, University of South Florida, and University of West Florida.

University Press of Florida
PO Box 140239
Gainesville, FL 32614
floridapress.org

GPSR EU Authorized Representative: Mare Nostrum Group B.V., Doelen 72, 4831 GR Breda, The Netherlands, gpsr@mare-nostrum.co.uk

CONTENTS

FIGURES

FOREWORD

If an archaeologist had to be stuck on a deserted island in the middle of the ocean and could bring along only one book, McNiven's *Sentient Seas* would have to be it. The core strength of the volume is that it forces you to consider the sea from a wholly different point of view. Or, rather, it challenges you to consider the sea from *many* different points of view. Few volumes can claim to have this kind of impact on readers. McNiven accomplishes this by focusing on and unpacking in historical detail the concept of seascape, in the first part of the volume.

Seascape is a relatively recent idea, as McNiven documents, and it is one that has both theoretical and methodological implications. Part of the core thesis of the volume is that the sea is not simply a place to travel upon or a resource to exploit but in all ways connects us to a greater world filled with actors large and small that inhabit the waters around the globe. Indeed, McNiven makes a cogent argument that peoples around the world, throughout history, have actively ascribed sentience to the ocean and seas. This larger point is one of the broader contributions that archaeology, in particular, has engaged with more than many other disciplines and in doing so has made a unique contribution to the study of seascapes more generally.

McNiven takes on some of the most interesting aspects of the histories of people who dwell on and around ocean worlds, or rather, their various seascapes. He pays particular attention to larger cosmological beliefs about the sea and how these define not only lines of travel and features wholly encapsulated by its waters but also how the sea references inland places. Important to this discussion is the nature of liminality, this occupying of a place between worlds, which McNiven points to in his discussions of land, sky, and water as they relate to how space is marked in such environments. These points in particular will provide archaeologists and historians of the world's oceans with much to think about in terms of how we write about coastal peoples.

One of the core strengths of this volume is its largely comparative framework that pulls in case studies and information from around the globe. From Christian Europe to Indigenous peoples of the Pacific, McNiven provides detailed analyses of the various perspectives that people have had on sailing, burial, death, voyaging, shipwrecks, among many others from all over the world. And, while there are many differences, there are also broad underlying themes, all of which point toward a more active role of the sea in the everyday lives of people.

After laying down many of the baseline concepts in the first half of the volume, McNiven then delves deep into the idea that the ocean is full of sentient elements. To illustrate this, he begins by drawing on his own long-term engagement with Torres Strait Islanders to understand dugong bone mounds and hunting rituals. This work sets the stage for his discussion of the more agentive elements of the oceans—from tides to winds and waves. For most people such forces were more than physical occurrences but were embedded in larger belief systems that viewed them as influencing and taking an active role in human life. This active nature is perhaps nowhere more apparent than in McNiven's broader discussion of the fish, whales, seals, and other animals that humans throughout history have relied upon for sustenance—some of which could take human form and even live among us. Even our technologies—fishing nets and lines—are often thought to have agency in our success or failure at sea.

If you were stranded alone on a deserted island with this book, after reading it, you would know that you are not alone. Rather than feeling isolated on a tiny island you would come to realize that you are accompanied by all the denizens of the deep, as well as the sea herself, all of which serve to connect you to the larger world. In sum, this volume is not only filled with a compendium of thoughtful facts and useful information but is an engrossing joy to read.

The next time we're on the beach or in a boat drifting across the ocean swells, we'll be listening to the waves, watching for what the aquatic realm has to offer, and positing how we fit into the larger scheme of things.

Victor D. Thompson and Scott M. Fitzpatrick

Series Editors

PREFACE

Herman Melville's *Moby-Dick* is the world's most famous marine mammal hunting story. D. H. Lawrence (1923:237) described it as "the greatest book of the sea ever written." *Moby-Dick* transcends the familiar trope of "man versus beast" such that emotions of revenge and rage dance with rituals and spiritual forces to stage a duel of epic proportions. Melville, himself a whaler, knew that sperm whale hunting extended well beyond the technological details of harpoons, rigging, and blubber rendering. The hunt begins not with the first steps on the ship *Pequod* but with spiritual engagement at the New Bedford "Whaleman's Chapel" (Melville 1851:37). Here whalers and their families and widows sit before Father Mapple (the self-proclaimed "pilot of the living God") and pray for good hunting and a safe return (Melville 1851:45). "Few are the moody fishermen, shortly bound for the Indian Ocean or Pacific, who fail to make a Sunday visit to the spot" (Melville 1851:37). Surefooted whalers know that the sea—the realm of the leviathans they desire—has the power to swallow into its invisible depths all but those few shipmates who can swim. The sea is a world of fickle forces that they can often skillfully harness and control. It is both a giver and a taker of life. Father Mapple recites the biblical story of Jonah as "a pregnant lesson" to all sailors that through God's hand the sea will punish all those who fail to live a virtuous life (Melville 1851:45). In *Moby-Dick*, the sea is as much a complex lead character and personality as Captain Ahab.

What is the archaeology of *Moby-Dick*? Once the waves and foam settled at the violent death site of the *Pequod*, we can imagine a smashed wreck and her crew coming to rest on the seabed. Yet this shipwreck–grave site is not the enduring legacy of *Moby-Dick*. Melville—the whaler, the author—leaves us with the New Bedford chapel. The chapel, known as the New Bedford Seamen's Bethel, is open to the public, and on a snowy day in January 2005 I entered this place. True to the novel, its walls are lined with marble memorial tablets "sacred to the memory" of dead whalers. You can even sit on the pew where Melville once sat. And just when my romantic fantasies of old whalers felt fulfilled, the reality of this functioning chapel for local seamen hit me as I approached the pulpit. Unlike the weathered nineteenth-century plaques on the side walls, the front wall has shiny ones with names of men killed in recent fishing tragedies.

Fresh flowers were for a group of fishermen who perished the previous week. I was in a sacred place, a place where New Bedford seamen of the past and present (and future) pray for good fishing and a safe trip. It is filled with tablets and widows and painful memories of "beings who have placelessly perished without a grave" (Melville 1851:40). Ironically, this is the place to ensure the continuity of life, for "Faith, like a jackal, feeds among the tombs, and even from these dead doubts she gathers her most vital hope" (Melville 1851:40). The archaeological legacy of *Moby-Dick* is not a shipwreck out to sea but a spiritually charged place for the placeless dead and the faithful living on the land, where the rituals of marine animal hunting and fishing begin and end.

Sentient Seas is about seeing the sea as a central character for encounter and immersion, not as a passive backdrop. Maritime peoples know that the sea—saltwater—not only is populated by sentient beings, both mundane and fantastical, but also has sentience and emotional qualities in its own right. Mariners think about and with the sea and equally know that the sea is aware of them. Yet mariners enter this sentient and fluid realm not as landlubber novices but as highly skilled seafarers whose skill sets extend well beyond the technical to take in a wide range of ritual practices to navigate this social realm of numinous forces. Here the sea is a complex seascape with a cultural imprint of epic cosmological, cognitive, and spiritual dimensions. Luckily, the material correlates of these epic dimensions were frequently expressed on "land" and were central to maintaining a maritime identity. As such, *Sentient Seas* explores the multifaceted dimensions of seascapes expressed both on the sea and on the land. People and their relationship with the sea are far more complex than simply their vista out over the waters.

ACKNOWLEDGMENTS

Sentient Seas took seven years to write, as I endured lockdowns and the COVID-19 pandemic. It was written during innumerable short blocks of time dispersed between my other university duties and fieldwork commitments. In addition to the resources of the Monash University library system, my other major sources of texts were books purchased online, and Archive.org, where digital copies of rare historical texts have been made available for scholarship and research.

Numerous people in Australia and overseas generously provided me with information to help write this book: Chris Ballard, Todd Barlin, John Bradley, John Briggs, Max Friesen, Jan Gjerde, Garrick Hitchcock, Scott Heyes, Erica Hill, Aldona Jonaitis, Madeleine Kelly, Barry McGovern, Paul Memmott, Takuya Nagaoka, Beatrice Nicolini, Patrick Nunn, Kenneth Ruddle, Emanuella de Ruiter, Lynette Russell, Peter Sheppard, Ron Southern, Sean Ulm, and Chris Urwin. Jerome Mialanes kindly translated a number of French texts into English for me.

For assistance with permissions for publication of images, I thank John Bradley (Monash University, Australia) and Yanyuwa Elders Mavis Timothy a-Muluwamara and Dinah Norman a-Marrngawi (Australia); Alex Brown and Esther Rimer (Smithsonian Institution, USA); Maura Coughlin (Northeastern University, USA) and Laurence Prod'homme (Musée de Bretagne, France); Apurba Deb (Department of Sustainable Development, Government of Manitoba, Canada); Jocelyne Dudding, Eona Bell, and Helen Sutton (Museum of Archaeology and Anthropology, Cambridge University, England); James Dunn, Katherine Mager, and Emma Rowles (Sainsbury Centre, University of East Anglia, England); Imelda Miller and Daniel Dow (Queensland Museum, Australia); Patrick Morisson (Alamy Stock Photos); Takuya Nagaoka (Pasifika Renaissance, Japan); Emanuella de Ruiter (Kei Muri Māpara/Methodist Church of New Zealand Archives, Aotearoa/New Zealand) and Peter Sheppard (University of Auckland, Aotearoa/New Zealand); James Shiel (Geographicus Rare Antique Maps, USA); and Pilvi Vainonen (National Museum of Finland) and Jaana Onatsu (Finnish Heritage Agency).

For introducing me to the sea I thank my parents Peter and Glenda McNiven. Endless childhood holidays were spent on the coast of southeast Queensland in the 1960s and 1970s, breathing in the salty air as we sun baked on beaches, surfed the waves, fished and snorkeled deeper waters beyond the breakers, and searched for mud crabs amongst mangrove forests at low tide. Beachcombing was one of my favorite activities, my best finds being intact nautilus shells (including one with the fleshy remains of the cephalopod), Japanese glass fishing buoys, and two bottles containing notes tossed overboard by tourists on passenger ships in the Pacific Ocean. My father also taught me that if I put an empty nautilus shell to my ear I would hear the muffled sound of the sea, wherever I may be.

My entry into the world of maritime cultures and seascapes was a direct result of visiting Torres Strait in northeast Australia in 1996. For this introduction I thank anthropologists John Cordell and Judith Fitzpatrick. For intellectual insight and guidance, I thank Torres Strait Islanders Charles David, Joe David, Mark David, Ned David, Kapua Gutchen, Arthur Kebisu, Sam Kepa, Vic McGrath, Cygnet Repu, Sophie Luffman, Murray George (Mr. George), Falen Passi, and Terrence Whap. A huge thanks goes to my fellow Torres Strait archaeology and anthropology colleagues for numerous fruitful discussions about the sea and seascapes: Jeremy Ash, Liam Brady, Joe Crouch, Bruno David, and Garrick Hitchcock.

Four external reviewers of an earlier version of this book, including Andrej Gaspari and Stefan Claesson, kindly and generously made constructive comments that helped improve the content and format of the book. A special thanks goes to Victor Thompson and Scott Fitzpatrick (series editors) for approaching me to write this book for the University Press of Florida. In particular, I thank Victor for his careful reading and editing skills, which greatly improved the volume's content and readability. Mary Puckett, Acquisitions Editor, University Press of Florida, helped progress the volume from manuscript to a polished book. I thank Mary for her support and encouragement. Marthe Walters, Managing Editor, University Press of Florida, faultlessly oversaw editing and production of the manuscript. Copy editor Billie Smith-Haffener did a great job on polishing the text. Karen Gillen skillfully proofread the text and compiled the index. Financial support for the publication of this book was provided by the Australian Research Council Centre of Excellence for Australian Biodiversity and Heritage (project number CE170100015) and the Australian Research Council Centre of Excellence for Indigenous and Environmental Histories and Futures (project number CE230100009).

Finally, my biggest thanks go to my life partner Lynette Russell, who never doubted I could finish this book. Words cannot express my deep gratitude for her constant support and encouragement. We both share a love of the cultural and historical dimensions of the sea and have spent many hours discussing the sea's endless horizons.

1

Introduction

Seascape Awakenings

How inappropriate to call this planet Earth, when it is clearly Ocean.
Attributed to Arthur C. Clarke

In his 1861 book *The Sea* (*La Mer*), French historian Jules Michelet (1861:19) mused that "On the entire surface of our globe, water is the Generality—land the Exception." Archaeologist Peter Campbell (2023a:343) is not the first person to suggest that "the planet would be better called Oceanus than Earth, as this is a water world." Seas and oceans cover 70% of Earth's surface, with a volume of 1.335 billion cubic kilometers (Eakins and Sharman 2010). Earth's oceans date back at least 3.8 billion years, as evidenced by the age of pillow lava basalt in Greenland that solidified underwater, with the oldest rocks on Earth dated to 4 billion years and the planet's origin put at 4.5 billion years (Genda 2016:31; Jacobsen 2003). It is thought that oceans appeared as part of Earth's formation, possibly enhanced by extraterrestrial water from asteroid impacts (Genda 2016). Indeed, at present, "around 30,000 tonnes of water falls to Earth every year in a fine rain of cometary particles" (Stow 2017:18). Earth's primordial seas were mostly freshwater, gradually accumulating terrestrial salts washed in by rain, albeit remaining relatively stable at around 3.5% salinity for the past 200–300 million years (Stow 2017:44, 46).

The earliest evidence for life on Earth is dated back to 3.4 billion years ago in the form of fossil remnants of a marine stromatolite reef in the Strelley Pool Chert formation in the Pilbara region of Western Australia (Allwood et al. 2007; Javaux 2019). Life spent the first 90% of its history in the sea. Today, it is estimated that around 2.2 million of the estimated 8.7 million species are marine, with 91% of marine species awaiting taxonomic description (Mora et al. 2011). Chris Armstrong (2022:11) adds that because much rain derives from evaporated seawater, "every drop of water you drink will, on average, have been cycled through the ocean more than a million times during the earth's long history." Most extraordinary is the fact that around 50% of the world's oxygen is produced by the photosynthetic activity of phytoplankton (Sekerci and Petrovskii 2015). The sea, in no short order, literally sustains life on Earth.

Around 40% of the oceans are within the territorial waters of nation-states, the remainder is international waters or the "high seas" (Abdulla et al. 2014:60, 72). In 1990, 1.2 billion people representing 23% of the world's population lived within the near coastal zone, defined as areas that are both within 100 km of the coast and elevated within 100 m of sea level (Small and Nicholls 2003:591). That figure rises to 44% for people living within 150 km of the sea (Pungetti 2022:4). This includes over 1,900 "coastal Indigenous peoples" across 87 countries (Cisneros-Montemayor et al. 2016). The vastness of these seas and oceans was represented on maps for hundreds of years, but their scale only became clear for most of us on 7 December 1972, after NASA's Apollo 17 astronauts on the last crewed expedition to the moon took an iconic photo of our spherical blue world at a distance of 29,000 km that "changed the way we visualised our planet forever" (Larsson 2022). Yet most of us have never ventured out on to the sea, and even fewer have voyaged so far from land that the horizon around them for 360 degrees is nothing but water. Few people realize that the first settlers of Australia who voyaged across open seas between the Timor region of eastern Indonesia and Australia's Kimberley coast at least 65,000 years ago may have been the first not to see any land on the horizon (see Bird et al. 2018; Norman et al. 2018). These First Australians not only take the mantle of the world's first known mariners but were also probably the earliest known modern humans who could swim.

Deep Time Mariners: Discovering the Sea

Martin Lewis (1999:208) makes the observation that although today most people conceptualize "oceans" as more encompassing than "seas," the generic term for these global waters is "the sea," with related terms such as the "high seas," "sea level," and "Law of the Sea." An example of oceans encompassing multiple seas is illustrated by the western margins of the Pacific Ocean, which, moving from north to south, includes the Bering Sea, Sea of Okhotsk, Sea of Japan, South China Sea, Philippine Sea, Coral Sea, and Tasman Sea. Yet this classificatory convention is recent and dates to within the past 150 years of the more than 2,000 years of known Western conceptualization of oceans and seas beginning with the ancient Greeks (Lewis 1999). The ancient Greeks saw the terrestrial world as an island taking in the known inhabited world or ecumene (with the Mediterranean at the center) surrounded by a single sea known as Ocean (after Oceanus, the mythological titan) that encircled a spherical globe. This body of water was also referred to as Ocean Sea, Outer Sea, Great Sea,

Oceanus, and the Atlantic (after the Titan Atlas; Lewis 1999:191). Some of the perceived gulfs within the margins of the single ecumenical island continent were variously referred to as the Indian Ocean (adjacent to India) and the Erythraean Sea (Red Sea).

During the 1400s and 1500s, European mariners gave increasing form to continental land masses and named interconnecting oceans. Although usually couched in terms of discovery of new lands, John Parry (1974:xii) makes the point that "the Great Age of Discovery was essentially the age of the discovery of the sea." For example, Spanish explorer Vasco Núñez de Balboa named the Mar del Sur (South Sea) in 1513, but its current name of Pacific Ocean only became common in the 1800s, some 300 years after it was named Mar Pacifico ("peaceful sea") by Portuguese explorer Ferdinand Magellan in 1521 (Bashford 2017; Lewis 1999:198–199). In the late 1500s, Dutch cartographer Abraham Ortelius divided the Atlantic Ocean into Mar del Nort (North Sea) and the Ethiopian Ocean, revealing that the terms "sea" and "ocean" could be used "interchangeably" (Lewis 1999:200). Lewis (1999:211) concludes that the long Western history of dividing, classifying, and naming the seas and oceans is less about geographical discovery and more about "cultural and political outlooks."

Western conceptions of the Pacific Ocean over the past 500 years (and later "Oceania") as a vast expanse of largely empty sea dotted with over 20,000 islands with hundreds of Indigenous societies clumped into equally expansive geocultural zones (Polynesia, Micronesia, Melanesia) clashes with Indigenous explorations and conceptualizations that began at least 50,000 years ago (Papua New Guinea) and expanded dramatically over the past 3,500 years (D'Arcy 2006; Kirch 2000). For example, Māori scholar and poet Alice Te Punga Somerville (2017:26) notes that "where I come from [Aotearoa/New Zealand], Oceania is widely (although not only) known as Te Moananui-a-Kiwa, the great ocean of Kiwa. It is also known as the domain of Tangaroa, one of the many gods of the Māori pantheon, whose realm extends over the sea. This ocean is thus connected to a specific ancestral navigator (Kiwa) and the guardianship of a specific deity (Tangaroa), but also, rather literally, to the Māori language." As this is one perspective (Māori) of the hundreds of Indigenous cultures and societies across Oceania, Somerville (2017:30) adds that "oceans cannot be named, and yet we name them."

Gísli Pálsson (1991:xvi–xvii) makes the interesting observation that European "discovery" of the world's oceans in the late fifteenth and early sixteenth centuries also revealed the world's great cultural diversity. Thus, it was through these voyages that the idea of anthropology was revealed. In this sense, then, "anthropology, the study of humanity, is as much the child of seafaring as of colonialism" (Pálsson 1991:xvii). Indeed, anthropology's foundational paradigm of social evolutionism and its hierarchical ranking of cultures was underpinned by the racist view that sailing to the "ends of the earth" (southern oceans) relative to Europe was akin to traveling back in time where primeval cultures (e.g., Tasmanians) remained extant (Gamble 1992; Jones 1992). On a more substantive front, Alfred Cort Haddon, a key figure in early anthropology, trained initially as a marine zoologist but converted to anthropology after visiting Torres Strait in northeast Australia in the 1880s. His career change followed his realization that local Islanders knew more about coral reef marine biology and ecology than he did and that this embedded knowledge of the sea was far more precious and worthier of documenting and "salvaging" than marine invertebrates (Herle and Rouse 1998; Nakata 2007; Roldán 1992; Urry 1982).

Archaeology reveals that we humans have been engaging with the sea for over 600,000 years. For modern humans, marine mollusk shell and fish bones associated with stone artifacts dating back to 254,000 and 168,000 years ago respectively have been recovered from Benzú rock shelter, Morocco, North Africa (Ramos-Muñoz et al. 2016). In South Africa, the cave site of Pinnacle Point contains the remains of edible marine mollusks dating back to 164,000 years ago (Marean et al. 2007). Evidence for human consumption of marine mammals is much older, with stone tools associated with skeletal remains of two beached whales dating to 614,000–662,000 years ago at Dungo near Baia Farta in southern Angola (Lebatard et al. 2019) and seal bones at Ysterfontein 1 rock shelter in South Africa dating to 46,000–119,000 years ago (Avery et al. 2008). In terms of our Neanderthal cousins, marine shellfish use extends back to 147,000 years at Bajondillo Cave, Spain (Cortés-Sánchez et al. 2011), and consumption of marine mammals (dolphins and seals) dates to at least 42,000 years ago at Vanguard Cave, Gibraltar (Stringer et al. 2008). In these cases, marine animals were obtained through pedestrian access to the intertidal zone, with seals hunted from shoreline colonies and whales and dolphins taken from natural beach strandings. Use of offshore resources from watercraft is more recent, with Sue O'Connor and colleagues (2011) reporting bones of pelagic fish (e.g., tuna) dating back to 42,000 years ago at Jerimalai (now Asitau Kuru) rock shelter in East Timor, Island Southeast Asia.

In some cases, ancient use of marine mollusks is not associated with subsistence but with symbolic behaviors in the form of body adornments. For example, the site of Skhul Cave in Israel contains perforated marine gastropod shells dating to 100,000–135,000 years ago (Vanhaeren et al. 2006). Similar marine shell beads have been found at the Cave of Pigeons in Morocco dating to 82,000 years ago (Bouzouggar et al. 2007; D'Errico et al. 2009), and at Blombos Cave in South Africa dating to 75,000–78,000 years ago (d'Errico et al. 2005; Henshilwood et al. 2004; Vanhaeren et al. 2013). Pleistocene evidence for use

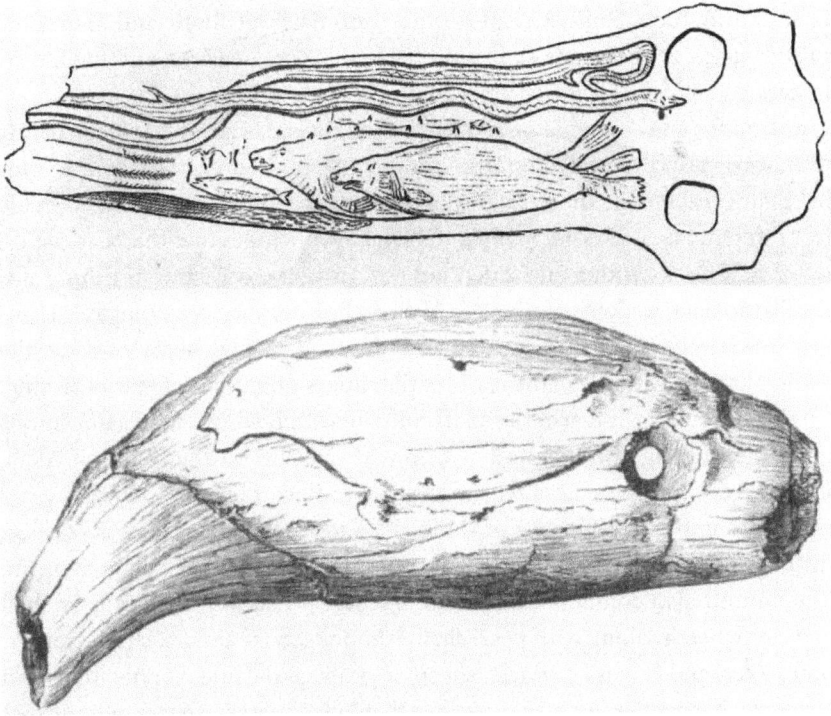

Figure 1. Engraved images of seals from Upper Paleolithic sites, France, associated with the Magdalenian period (12,000–17,000 years ago). *Top:* from Montgaudier site (from de Nadaillac 1888:Figure 35; see also de Sonneville-Bordes and Laurent 1983:Figure 5.1); *Bottom:* from Duruthy site (from de Nadaillac 1888:Figure 39; see also de Sonneville-Bordes and Laurent 1983:Figure 5.4) (Courtesy: Bibliothèque Nationale de France).

of marine mammal bone for adornments is rare and limited to a few perforated seal teeth, and a carved sperm whale tooth from Magdalenian levels (12,000–17,000 years ago) of Upper Paleolithic sites in France (Pétillon 2008:720).

The antiquity of symbolic use of marine shells and marine mammal bone is not matched by ancient archaeological evidence for ritual and spiritual associations with the sea. Pleistocene rock art featuring marine animals is rare and limited to a handful of fish and seal images from Upper Paleolithic Europe (Aura Tortosa et al. 2016:80–81). Monica Hansen (2006:76) lists only four Upper Paleolithic sites with images of seals (engraved and painted) in Europe. Cosquer Cave in southern France has the most recorded marine animal images, with 12% of all paintings representing auks (penguins), seals, fish, and possibly jellyfish or octopus, dating to 22,000–31,000 years ago (Clottes and Courtin 1996:127–139, 163–170). Beautiful naturalistic images of seals engraved onto stone, bone, antler, or tooth plaquettes have also been recorded from Magdalenian levels of 14 sites in Europe (Bosinski and Bosinski 2009; Cleyet-Merle and Madelaine 1995; Hansen 2006; Figure 1). It is probable that these parietal and mobile art images had ritual or spiritual associations.

O'Connor and colleagues (2017) document a burial of an adult woman dating to 11,000–12,000 years ago in Tron Bon Lei rock shelter on the island of Alor in eastern Indonesia. The neck area of the woman features six fishhooks made from trochus shell (*Rochia nilotica*). The team concludes that the "association of the fish-hooks with a burial denotes the cosmological status of fishing" for the Pleistocene residents of Alor and "a direct link between cosmology and fishing" (O'Connor et al. 2017:1466). Indeed, the Tron Bon Lei burial provides the earliest known evidence in the world of the ritual significance of marine fishing.

The oldest known marine animal bone site with obvious ritual associations is a large dugong bone mound at Umm Al Quwain on the island of Akab, United Arab Emirates. This remarkable site radiocarbon dates to 5,300 years ago and comprises hundreds of skull, rib, and forelimb bones of at least 40 dugongs carefully arranged over an area of 2.9 m by 4.7 m to a height of 0.4 m. The mound also contains over 2,000 artifacts, including hundreds of shell and stone beads, along with pearl shell fishhooks, bone points, shell scrapers, flint flakes, and bones of gazelle, sheep or goats, and cattle. Sophie Méry and Vincent Charpentier (2012:76) conclude that "all of these elements indicate that the layout and use of this monument at Akab adheres to precise rules, possibly even instructions. The evidence suggests the presentation of a large marine mammal that is both quite spectacular and very ritualized." In short, it is a site "whose status was very special, was a sanctuary" (Méry and Charpentier 2012:77). The international importance of the Akab dugong bone mound was also clear, with an acknowledgment that it is "the oldest known ritual site in Arabia and the world's oldest known ritual site associated with the dugong" (Méry et al. 2009:705). Indeed, "The monument at Akab has no parallel in the Neolithic elsewhere in the world" (Méry and Charpentier 2012:76).

The Akab dugong bone mound was not initially interpreted as a ritual site and a sanctuary. After the first phase of excavations, the site was interpreted as a place for "slaughtering and butchering activities" (e.g., Jousse et al. 2002:43). Subsequent to this secular interpretation, I published a paper on the results of my work on dugong bone mounds in Torres Strait of northeast Australia (McNiven and Feldman 2013). One of these excavations was on a sandy cay named Tudu where the French navigator and explorer Jules Dumont d'Urville visited and was nearly shipwrecked in 1840. Here Dumont d'Urville observed large mounds of dugong bones, which he thought from his discussions with local Tudulgal people were grave monuments. My excavation of a dugong bone mound on Tudu 160 years after Dumont d'Urville's visit revealed that the site had no obvious association with mortuary practices. The bone mound was a highly structured and ritualized deposit dominated by skull and rib bones and a wide range of artifacts dating to around 1900 CE. It was after reading of the ritual nature of Torres Strait dugong bone mounds in McNiven and Feldman (2003) that the French archaeological team reassessed the Akab dugong bone mound and reinterpreted it as a maritime ritual site.

Unbeknown to the French team, I too underwent a similar interpretative transformation with the Tudu bone mound. When I was first shown the site by local Tudulgal man Mark David in 1999, it was eroding from a creek bank. The erosion face exposed a 6-m-long dense deposit of dugong bones up to 30 cm thick. Careful inspection of this layer and of materials that had eroded out onto the adjacent creek bank revealed fish bones and a wide range of objects such as copper nails, clay tobacco pipes, and flaked bottle glass. Although I was aware of Dumont d'Urville's recordings of dugong bone mounds, I felt that this site was consistent with a midden deposit of domestic refuse associated with a nearby village. In 2000 I led excavations at the bone mound and discovered that the deposit was much more structurally and compositionally complex than a simple midden. All of the objects (mostly of European origin) were either small (e.g., glass beads, clay pipes, nails) or fragments of larger objects such as ceramic plates. Furthermore, numerous isolated dugong ear bones were found scattered throughout; a curious find given that these bones require considerable mechanical force to extract from robust dugong skulls. Finally, the base of the deposit was lined with small pieces of flat metal and fragments of large pearl shells. This was no rubbish dump! After discussions with Torres Strait elders about the finds, eventually I associated the ear bones with dugong hunting rituals and saw dugong bone mounds as mediating ritual engagements between dugong hunters, dugongs, the ancestors, and the sea (detailed in McNiven and Feldman 2003).

Seascape Archaeologies: Epistemological and Ontological Awakenings

The reinterpretation of dugong bone mounds on opposite sides of the world from secular bone dumps to highly structured ritual bone deposits goes to the conceptual heart of *Sentient Seas*. The Akab site dating to 5,300 years ago is the oldest known dugong bone mound in the world, while the Tudu site dating to 120 years ago is the youngest known. Despite separation by considerable time and geography, both sites were created by highly skilled marine mammal hunters from maritime societies. Both also reveal ritual relationships between hunters and dugongs and the importance of spiritual forces in subsistence engagements with the sea. In both cases, ritual interpretations were inspired by historical and ethnographic information on Torres Strait Islanders, a sea people par excellence. Historical and ethnographic information on spiritual and ritual engagements with the marine realm reveals glaring gaps in the conceptual and interpretive frameworks employed by archaeologists. Without such information, the Akab dugong bone mound would remain a "butchering site" and the Tudu dugong bone mound a "domestic dump" within archaeological discourse. However, ritual reinterpretations of both do not deny that the dugong bones they contain are also the result of dugong butchering practices and are the final resting place of bones from animals that were eaten. Indeed, both sites illustrate nicely the point that the division between subsistence and ritual practices is not only arbitrary but also an unhelpful ontological and epistemological dualism to understand the world of maritime peoples in the past.

Rituals and spiritual forces infuse the world of maritime peoples. A central tenet of *Sentient Seas* is that these ritual and spiritual dimensions of *life with the sea* bring us closer to the world of mariners and what it means to identify as a maritime people. Most anthropologists who have worked with maritime peoples would agree with Paul D'Arcy's (2006:84) claim that "superstition and ritual dominated life at sea." However, subsistence and resource use remain the focus of marine management practices and archaeological research on human uses of the sea (McNiven 2025a). Recent histories of the sea focus on political battles for control of the oceans, naval and seafaring empires, trade routes and networks, and European imperialism, commercial exploration, and globalization (e.g., Paine 2013; Redford 2014; Steinberg 2001). It is in this context that Margaret Cohen's (2021) edited series, *A Cultural History of the Sea*, dramatically expands the scope of seascape historiography to be more anthropologically and archaeologically inclusive. The Introduction to Volume 2 of the series makes the important point that published literary and historical approaches to the sea tend to be Eurocentric and based on "*imaginative projections* of a small literate minority who may have had very little experience of the sea and the communities that inhabited it" (Lambourn 2021:2; emphasis added).

Books written on use of the sea from the perspective of mariners open up a whole world of lived experiences, beliefs, and practices labeled variously as maritime or nautical folklore and maritime or nautical superstitions. Examples range from encyclopedic compendiums such as *Legends and Superstitions of the Sea and of Sailors in All Lands and at All Times* by US Navy Lieutenant Fletcher S. Bassett (1885), *Superstitions of Sailors* by Angelo S. Rappoport (1928), and *Folklore and the Sea* by Horace Beck (1999), to localized studies such as *Fisher Folk-Lore: Old Customs, Taboos and Superstitions Among Fisher Folk, Especially in Brittany and Normandy and on the East Coast of Scotland* by Peter Anson

(1965) and *Superstitions: Folk Magic in Hull's Fishing Community* by Alec Gill (1993). And of course, Herman Melville's classic *Moby-Dick; or, The Whale* of 1851 has introduced generations of readers to the otherworldliness of life at sea. Numerous articles on these topics have also appeared over the past 140 years in *The Folk-Lore Journal* (1878–1888) and *Folklore* (1889–present), published by the Folklore Society (London), and *The Journal of American Folklore* (1888–present). I argue that "folklorists come closer than any other disciplinary area in capturing the lived experiences and identity of mariners and fishers across the globe in terms of spiritual beliefs, ritual practices, and cosmological dimensions of seascapes. Indeed, it is only in the past three decades that anthropological and archaeological studies have entered this ontological and epistemological space" (McNiven 2025a:795).

Yet the folkloric literature is not without its problems. A key epistemological issue is "ahistoricity" where cultural practices and beliefs are often essentialized as timeless (Patarino 2002:426; cf. Gill 1993:142–147). A second major problem is that many folkloric works take a pejorative stand on fisherfolk and mariners and what were often considered antiquated and amusing superstitions of uneducated people. Vincent Patarino (2002:78) makes the point that "early folklorists amassed many of the stereotypes about sailors and popularized them among a wide audience, further ingraining the notion of the superstitious sailor into the cultural milieu" (see also Gill 1993:118). For example, Walter Dennison (1893:173) noted that the late nineteenth-century Orkney Islanders of northern Scotland "believed, often correctly, that educated people held [their] lore in contempt." Henning Henningsen (1961:ii) continued these pejorative views: "It is surely superfluous to mention that I have not attempted to give any moral evaluation of the customs we are concerned with, though in the case of many of them readers will probably be surprised by their inhumanity, brutality, silliness and lack of psychological wisdom. Let it be sufficient to say that these are facts which cannot be refuted."

Most of what has been presented by writers as maritime superstitions would in many cases fall under the modern anthropological category of traditional ecological knowledge, and witches better described as ritual specialists. Thus, books on maritime folklore and superstitions collide against more recent historical, anthropological, and archaeological approaches that emphasize ontology, epistemology, belief systems, and rituals, and these minority groups' political struggles for maintenance of cultural identity and autonomy. It is in this connection that Kären Wigen (2006:720; original emphasis) makes the important point that "*investigations into emic conceptions of the sea*—whether articulated by littoral peoples, sailors, merchants, or islanders—form an important counterweight" to imperialist histories. In many cases, historical insights "into emic conceptions of the sea" are hindered by mariners often remaining voiceless in archives. This muteness reflected in part the reticence of mariners to divulge their lore and cultural practices for fear of ridicule.

My epistemological and ontological awaking to the world of maritime peoples occurred once I began undertaking archaeological research with Torres Strait Islanders in the 1990s. I first visited Torres Strait in 1996 at the invitation of two anthropologists—Judith Fitzpatrick, who had been working with Torres Strait Islanders since the 1970s, and John Cordell, who was an expert on coastal peoples and customary marine tenure. Judith and John asked me to join them on a project to record cultural heritage sites in Torres Strait, knowing that I was an archaeologist with experience working on the coastal archaeology of Indigenous Australians. During this trip, John asked me: "Ian, what do you think the archaeology of a totemic seascape would look like?" This seemingly simple question precipitated my own "ontological turn" in archaeology (cf. Alberti 2016). That is, it required me to rethink my approach to the epistemological question of *how* ancient people used the sea because I needed to reconceptualize the more fundamental ontological question of *what* the sea was for peoples of the past (cf. Holbraad and Pedersen 2017:5). The upshot is that I have spent the past 30 years rising to the challenge of creating an archaeology of sentient seas and agentive seascapes. The most important outcome of my epistemological and ontological jolt was that it provided me with new ears and eyes in my many subsequent discussions and interactions with Torres Strait Islanders. *Sentient Seas* is the product of this epistemological and ontological jolt.

Sentient Seas: Seeing Seascapes as Spiritscapes

"Ritually Orchestrated Seascapes" (McNiven and Feldman 2003) brought together my newly acquired knowledge on the spiritual dimensions of Torres Strait Islander ritual relationships with the sea and broadened understandings of the sea as a constructed seascape and spiritscape. That is, "People construct land- or seascapes as anthropomorphized *spiritscapes* to make them comprehensible, and often develop symbolic strategies (rituals and associated magico-religious activities and paraphernalia) to establish the necessary social relations to meaningfully engage with spirits" (McNiven and Feldman 2003:171; original emphasis). These spiritual and ritual engagements with the sea should not be seen as an end in themselves but simply as practices that give form and meaning to the broader cosmological order of the sea as a sentient realm. It is approaching the sea as a *cosmologically constructed sentient realm of spiritual forces with concomitant ritual practices of engagement* that I argue goes to the heart of sea peoples and their maritime identity.

My conceptualization of sentient seas is an extension of anthropological formulations of the theoretical notion of "sentient ecology" (Anderson 1998, 2000:116–117; see also Ingold 2000:10). Traditional Western understandings of ecology separate the social and sacred from the biological. This separation is very much a modern view. For Indigenous peoples and for many Western peoples whose ontologies allow participation in the mutually understood communicative capacity of people and so-called natural phenomena and nonhuman persons and agency, sentience is a characteristic of the world and not the sole prerogative of humans. Mutuality and sentience also concern issues of obligation, respect, reciprocity, and protocol within the broader scope of morality. In this relational ontological guise, humans exist within an interdependent and intersubjective world, where the social world of an individual extends beyond people and encompasses the co-constitutive agency of humans and nonhuman persons. In this expanded social arena, humans and nonhumans have the capacity not only for mutually intelligible communication but also for moral judgment of each other. Jon Anderson (2009:123) states that the "collective agency" of humans and nonhumans in a relational world "is constituted through mutual practical interaction." In this practice-oriented formulation, a research focus on relational ontologies emphasizes co-constitutive processes and "*interactions* rather than the *things* that constitute our world" (Anderson 2009:123; original emphasis; see also Haraway 2007).

Central to academic explorations of sentient ecologies is animism, or at least animistic ontologies, and the conceptualization of what Irving Hallowell (1960:47) coined "other-than-human persons" (Bird-David 1999, 2006; Descola 2013; Ingold 2006). Graham Harvey (2006:xi) states that "animists are people who recognise that the world is full of persons, only some of whom are human, and that life is always lived in relationship with others." Put simply, "Animism is not a set of beliefs but, rather, a relational ontology centered on relationships between human and 'other-than-human' agents" (Harrison-Buck 2012:65). Renewed theoretical interest in animism, or what Harvey (2006) terms "new animism," requires both recognition and critique of Western or Cartesian dualisms such as culture-nature, object-subject, human-animal, mind-body, animate-inanimate, and alive-dead. While the ontological reality of these dualisms is less dichotomous than often presented (Anderson 2009; Latour 1993), emphasis on the deterministic qualities of the "environment" (at least in terms of "hunter-gatherers") and the lack of agency attributed to objects and the inanimate has hindered understandings of the complex relational and mutually constitutive worlds of many non-Western (and Western!) peoples and cultures.

Modernist notions of human exceptionalism underpinned by "anthropocentric narcissism" (Kohn 2013:19) provide an ontological blind spot to the way many peoples relate to the world. Important in this regard is the development of Object-Oriented Ontologies (OOO) as a form of "flat ontology" that holds that all objects, both human and nonhuman, have agency. Campbell (2020:208) points out that with OOO, "the sea is not a passive landscape that humans embed with meaning to form a cognitive 'seascape.' Instead, the sea is a real entity, an actor with agency, which simultaneously operates on multiple scales." Furthermore, just because an object has "agency" and "the capacity to effect change" does not mean that it also possesses "intentionality" underpinned by "sentience" (Campbell 2020:208). This "sea as an actor" OOO approach moves away from the Kantian view that objects and entities (and in this case, constructions such as seascapes) do not exist beyond human mediation and perception. According to Peter Campbell (2020:209), "Since cognitive landscapes rely on human embedded meaning, there is limited explanatory capacity for the sea's agency" beyond interaction with people.

While I appreciate that an OOO approach sees agency of the sea extending beyond anthropocentrism and human perception and comprehension to include nonhuman actors such as marine organisms (e.g., octopuses—Campbell 2023b), my approach focuses on agency of the sea linked to intentionality and sentience. In this ontological guise, agency of the sea is from the perspective of mariners and maritime cultures more broadly, which is only partly human centric. Mariners through the ages have known their seas to be personified with nonhuman spiritual agency and populated with agentive human (e.g., ancestral dead) and nonhuman (e.g., deities) spiritual entities, all with the collective capacity to act independently of people and to selectively respond to human agency and propitiation under special (ritual) circumstances. In this sense, the OOO advocates' focus on agentive relationships between nonhuman entities and sea is overly centered on Western understanding of causal relationships. For example, Campbell (2020:214) discusses the agentive relationship between the sea and the moon to create tides. Yet a number of maritime societies know that tides are the result of breathing by a giant being living in the depths of the ocean. Curiously, Campbell (2020:215) also argues that the "sea as an entity possessing agency better fits ancient perspectives than does a cognitive landscape." He adds: "Practical methods and appeals to the divine demonstrate that the sea was regarded by ancient cultures as possessing agency" (Campbell 2020:215). As is detailed in subsequent chapters of this book, an extensive maritime folklore literature exists on spiritual dimensions of, and ritual relationships with, the sea, along with the centrality of mariners' fear of the fickle and independent agency of the sea. In this light, OOO claims that the sea is not passive but agentive are less novel or revelatory from a folklorist or anthropological perspective.

Critically, Indigenous maritime societies consider spiritual entities of the sea not to be intangible but manifestly tangible and real. For example, the Yanyuwa Aboriginal people of the Gulf of Carpentaria of northern Australia state that "spirits" are "entities that live in the biological world and interact with the animals, birds, plants and humans of this world. They are real and can be interacted with, and have personalities that may be benign or dangerous" (Bradley et al. 2006:111). Yet in keeping with the tenets of OOO, mariners know that the sea exists independent of human thought, and as such people can ever only know part of the sea and what it thinks and how it behaves. In the language of OOO, objects, or in this case the spiritual essences of the sea, forever remain hidden or "withdrawn" from people. As such, people "perceive only the sensual properties" of the spiritual dimensions of the sea when expressed (indirectly) through waves, the elements (e.g., wind), availability of marine animals (e.g., food resources), and so on (see Campbell 2020:210).

Notions of spiritually animate and agentive seascapes have at their heart the non-Cartesian ontological view that seas are anything but passive. The sentient seas worldview is not simply about seas filled with sentient beings but rather is all-encompassing in that it concerns beings in the sea as much as it concerns water itself. For example, Yup'ik peoples of coastal Alaska "believe that because the ocean has a sense of awareness, it will sense a person who is under a circumstance that prohibits them from being down on the ocean [i.e., taboos]; the ocean indeed has always been aware and knowing" (Fienup-Riordan and Carmack 2011:269). The Yolŋu Aboriginal people of East Arnhem Land in northern Australia know that when a large wave rocks their boat on a fishing trip, it is a "message" from the spirit of a close relative in the community who has died (Barber 2005:155, 164). In both examples, understanding of the sentience and animacy of the sea comes through intersubjective and emotional and sensory experiences of the sea. Thus, mariners come to an understanding of the sea possessing animacy, sentience, and life by being on the sea and experiencing the sea's movement (e.g., waves) through their bodies (see Ingold 2000:97). It is in this embodied sense that a flat sea with no wind and movement is referred to as a state of "dead calm," whereby the sea is in a temporary state of lifelessness, or at least asleep.

Eduardo Kohn (2013:21–22) uses the evocative phrase "how forests think" to convey the essence of animistic ontologies of the Runa of Ecuador's Upper Amazon. The concept of sentient seas central to this book similarly gives rise to the active notion of "*how seas think.*" An acknowledgment of sentient seas precludes treating the sea as a passive backdrop and instead elevates the sea as a central actor. Traditionally, researchers have inquired into the multifarious ways people *think about* and act upon the sea. The sentient seas approach of this book extends this view to the varied ways seas in cultural settings around the world *think with* and act upon people. An important caveat in this conceptualization of sentient seas is that the degrees to which different maritime peoples know that "seas think" varies in intensity and complexity. As Hallowell (1960:24) in his original formulation of "other-than-human" persons noted: "I once asked an old [Ojibwe] man: Are *all* the stones we see about us here alive? He reflected a long while and then replied, 'No! But *some* are.'" The lesson here is that animistic ontologies do not embrace a blanket view that all "inanimate" phenomena possess souls, lifeforce, or sentience (as implied in Edward B. Tylor's [1871] original formulation of animism). As Harvey (2006:18) cogently notes, "It is a mistake to see this as a projection or attribution of human-likeness or life-likeness onto 'inanimate' objects." The critical point is that people do not modify the ontological status of phenomena from inanimate to animate but rather experience and identify animacy in phenomena for whom the potential for animacy was ever present. In short, identification of animacy in objects is not about projection but revelation. Istvan Praet (2015:68) makes the point that animate beings and objects are expressions of "positional [relational] qualities rather than [fixed] ontological categories." For people, the identification process invariably encompasses perception of an object's intentionality, a contingent process that often also encompasses mutual acknowledgment and interpersonal communication. As such, my approach explicitly associates agency with intentionality, acknowledging that intentionality is not a prerequisite of all forms of nonhuman agency, even in the context of the sea (see Jones and Cloke 2008; Lehman 2013).

The relational world of sentient seas and agentive seascapes is not a world of people perceiving or engaging with the sea and inscribing or imprinting meaning and sentience upon it. Sentient seas have no prediscursive, inanimate reality. Maritime peoples' relationship with the sea is both the precondition for and outcome of its use. Maritime people's activities *with* the sea are *activations* of existing conditions. In this sense, my sentient seas approach is heavily informed by Tim Ingold's (1993) phenomenological dwelling perspective, which in turn draws on notions of dwelling and Being-in-the-world expounded by the philosopher Martin Heidegger. Focusing on the terrestrial world, Ingold presents landscapes as an enduring record of human dwelling and the cumulative symbolic and material dimensions of generations of people's lives and associated labors. As dwelling by definition is an ongoing process, landscapes are always under construction and works in progress with intrinsic and inherent temporality. In this guise, the sea as a fluid domain may be seen to fall outside of a dwelling perspective, incapable of transformation and the accumulation of generations of human activity. Yet the concepts of sentient seas and seascapes as spiritscapes provide the cosmological and metaphysical framework whereby maritime peoples do modify the sea. Such modification encompasses a board range of ritual practices with the intention of socially engaging with and changing an equally broad range of sentient phenomena such as waves, winds, and marine animals.

Helena Simonett (2016:105) suggests that "human beings . . . have developed a myriad of ritual practices to engage with sentient ecology." Care is needed here not to conflate ritual engagement with operating more broadly within sentient and relational worlds. People's immersion within sentient ecologies is a permanent state of relational being that includes ritual practices. When Yolŋu feel a wave rocking a fishing boat, they are not performing a ritual practice. Feeling the wave through the rocking of the boat and knowing its meaning and message is an act of human–nonhuman communication as a part of everyday life. This said, certain ways of emotional, sensorial, and embodied communication with the nonhuman sentient realm can become more formalized through what Bell (1992) refers to as "ritualization." An important dimension to Bell's practice concept of "ritualization" is that it can apply to any domain of life and culture and not be restricted to the religious or ceremonial. Importantly, the ritualization concept also breaks down the traditional dichotomy between sacred and secular.

Aims and Structure

It is my contention that a sentient seas ontology conceptualized through "seascapes as spiritscapes" and operationalized through ritual practices has broad geographical, cultural, and historical applicability. As such, it has the potential to influence how archaeologists working in coastal regions around the globe come to understand and characterize maritime societies of the past in a way that is more in keeping with the way these maritime peoples not only saw themselves but also saw the sea and indeed thought with and through the sea. This book elaborates an archaeology of sentient seas and agentive seascapes using a broad range of historical, ethnographic, and archaeological examples drawn from across the globe. The ultimate aim of the book is not only to demonstrate the veracity of a sentient seas and agentive seascapes ontology and seascapes as spiritscapes concept but to also illustrate their potential universal application using diverse examples drawn from numerous Indigenous cultures in places such as Australia and North America but also from Western traditions of seafaring and European maritime societies. My chronological sweep is broad and takes in historical and ethnographic information from contemporary societies and societies of the past 1,000 years, along with many examples dating to the past 100,000 years available only through the work of archaeologists.

This book is more ontological than epistemological in that it aims to expose researchers to the multidimensionality of spiritual conceptualizations of, and ritual engagements with, seascapes. In this sense, I do not wish to tell researchers *how* to research seascapes but rather to comprehensively illustrate the range of *what* to think about in terms of seascapes. Here I take inspiration from Martin Holbraad and Morten Pedersen's (2017:16; original emphasis) book *The Ontological Turn: An Anthropological Exposition*, where they state: "For anthropologists to imagine their task as that of explaining *why* people do what they do, they must first suppose that they understand *what* these people are doing. The ontological turn often involves showing that such 'why' questions (explanation) are founded on a misconception of 'what' (conceptualization)."

Sentient Seas is explicitly cross-cultural to shine a light on the diversity of maritime rituals and seascape cosmologies. In numerous cases I provide cross-cultural comparisons to highlight the many extraordinary similarities that exist in the way peoples across the world view the sea and ritually engage with it. These comparisons provide support for the long-standing contention of maritime folklorists that a certain universality exists to maritime cultures. This contention is based on detailed empirical evidence revealed by a strong tradition among maritime folklorists of producing encyclopedic books that contain long lists of facts (e.g., Bassett 1885; Rappoport 1928; Henningsen 1961).

Yet the concept of "maritime culture" exposes itself to criticisms of definition and essentialism. A key definition issue is what exactly is a "maritime culture," "maritime society," or "maritime community"? David Yesner (1980:728) defines "maritime hunter-gatherers" narrowly in subsistence terms as "those for whom marine foods form the largest portion of their intake of either calories or protein in the diet." Jon Erlandson and Scott Fitzpatrick (2006:8–9) expand this definition into the broadened concept of "maritime adaptations . . . where humans regularly used boats for travel and subsistence purposes, where voyaging away from the immediate coastline was possible, and where a majority of nutrition (calories or protein) was derived from marine resources" (see also Marean 2024). Ian Friel (2012:183) posits that "one definition of a maritime society is one in which its members have fairly and regular and direct contact with maritime activities or with people directly engaged in activities related to seafaring—aside from merely consuming the fruits of maritime trade." David Taylor (1992:xii) notes that although defining a "maritime community" is a "difficult question," a "classic maritime community" is one "whose economy is dominated by commercial fishing and other maritime trades, the local culture is full of maritime elements." Jeffrey Fleisher and colleagues (2015:101) more broadly define a "maritime society" as one where "the marine environment influences and is influenced by broader patterns of sociocultural organization, practice, and belief within that society." To avoid going down a reductionist rabbit hole, I use the term "maritime culture" in relation to societies where at least some proportion of the community has a major part of their identity focused on the marine realm.

While a maritime identity does not require direct use of or engagement with the sea, the more a community uses and engages directly with the sea, the more elaborate and embodied will be their maritime identity and conceptualization and ritualization of seascapes. In this sense, it may be more productive to speak of degrees of maritimity and not rigid categorizations of peoples as "maritime" or not. In some situations, coastal peoples may have little to no engagements with the sea (e.g., Falabella and Sanhueza 2019; Hallam 1987), while in other contexts coastal peoples have a deep engagement with the sea and possess an elaborate maritime culture. In the context of ancient Greece, Giorgos Vavouranakis (2011:13) makes the important point that a "maritime way of life may be an obvious option, but it is neither the only nor an inevitable one in the Aegean. There is always room for choice in the relation between people and the sea and this relation may acquire various forms and different degrees of intimacy."

Christopher Nuttall (2021) provides an innovative analytical framework to account for differing degrees of maritimity and concomitant scales of seascape construction for the Ancient Aegean that has broader application. He conceptualizes three heuristically useful categories of "seascape engagement": *coastality* (spatial proximity to the sea, maritime networks, minimal use of marine resources for food and objects, and minimal seascape development), *embedment* (spatial proximity to the sea, maritime networks, moderate use of marine resources for food and objects, and moderate seascape development), and *entanglement* (spatial proximity to the sea, maritime networks, major use of marine resources for food and objects, major seascape development, and maritime social identity; Nuttall 2021:249–252). In short, "Not all coastal peoples construct seascapes to the same degree of cosmological and cognitive complexity" (McNiven 2025a:806). As such, while all of the examples of marine cultural practices presented in *Sentient Seas* relate to coastal peoples, not all relate to people with a "maritime culture."

All cross-cultural comparisons run the risk of arbitrarily finding deductively drawn similarities that ignore historical contingency and verge on stereotyping. Michael Pearson (2006:353–354) makes the important observation that "location on the shore transcends differing influences from an inland that is very diverse, both in geographic and cultural terms, so that the shore folk have more in common with other shore folk thousands of kilometres away on some other shore of the ocean than they do with those in their immediate hinterland." Decades of subsequent scholarship reveals the legitimacy of maritime anthropology, archaeology, and history.

This book is not about rummaging through archaeological literature to identify traces of ritual practices in the past. My focus in part is to expose archaeologists to the scale and scope of ritual practices within sentient sea realms using examples of known ritual practices as observed and documented ethnographically and historically. It is my contention that understandings of past seascape rituals have been hampered by a lack of understanding of what to look for. As Ian Hodder (1999:36) cogently notes, "You cannot see 'what is there' until you know how to look for it." To be sure, archaeologists have made insights into seascape ritual practices, and many of these studies will be highlighted. In many cases, rituals undertaken on and with the sea, usually while on boats, leave few archaeological traces. However, many seascape rituals also occurred within the intertidal zone and often have a long-term materiality with potential for archaeological investigations. Moreover, it is a central thesis of this book that human spiritual and ritual relationships with the sea across the globe also find expression across adjacent lands. In this sense I build on Christer Westerdahl's (1992) concept of "maritime cultural landscapes" and elaborate on what I call "terrestrial seascapes" (McNiven 2025a).

As an anthropological archaeologist who works closely with Indigenous Australians, I am well aware of the strengths and weaknesses of cross-cultural comparisons and the application of ethnographic analogy in archaeological interpretation. Conversely, I am also acutely aware of the limitations of Western views and cultural biases in understanding past cultures. Cross-cultural comparisons provide enormous scope to broaden the ontological and epistemological gaze. Anthropology at its core is a comparative social science. While much of the descriptive content of *Sentient Seas* conforms to this view of anthropology, similarities in ritual practices between different cultures and regions underwritten by similarities in ontology do provide scope for generalizations. Importantly, I emphasize that cross-cultural comparisons found in this book are not meant to provide prescriptive generalizations for archaeologists to use in a simplistic analogical sense. Furthermore, my concept of "ritual orchestration of seascapes," although heavily informed by my research in Torres Strait, is also informed by cross-cultural ethnographic and archaeological data to reveal its potential for wider application in a broad range of archaeological contexts. This book is not about representing in a holistic sense the cultural complexity of any particular maritime culture. It is about showcasing the cultural diversity of maritime cultures across the world, both past and present, and revealing many of the extraordinary similarities that exist in cultural expressions of a maritime identity. As such, writing this book was a constant struggle and trade-off between showcasing cultural diversity at the expense of cultural depth and comprehensiveness and historical contingency.

It is my hope to reveal to archaeologists that any attempt to understand what it meant to be a maritime person in the past must consider cosmological construction of and spiritual engagement with the sea. Through a wide range of examples, this book aims to show how the ethnographically known materiality of many of these spiritual engagements provides tremendous scope for archaeological explorations of such engagements in the past. To achieve these aims I have structured the book into 5 major thematic sections and 12 chapters. The first section introduces the book, its rationale and theoretical underpinnings, and various conceptualizations of seascapes in terms of boundaries and beings (Chapters 1, 2, 3). The second section looks at the ways different maritime societies symbolically and physically structure seascapes at sea (marine seascapes) and on land (terrestrial seascapes) with beings, sites, and places (Chapters 4 and 5). The third section focuses on rituals of marine vessel construction and voyaging and also rituals and spiritual frameworks governing the treatments of shipwrecks and shipwreck victims (Chapters 6 and 7). The fourth section examines a wide range of ritual engagements with the sea related to voyaging, hunting mammals, and fishing that I have more broadly characterized previously as the "ritual orchestration of seascapes" (Chapters 8, 9, 10). The fifth and final section of the book returns to a key issue raised in this Introduction, namely the potential universality and global applicability of a sentient seascapes ontology to archaeologies of maritime societies (Chapters 11 and 12). Chapter 11 introduces the concept of "ontological switching" to help understand why use of the sea is so highly ritualized across the globe. As pollution and climate change impact oceans and threaten the viability of human dependance on the sea, it is hoped that *Sentient Seas* fosters greater understanding and appreciation of traditional knowledge and spiritual connections of maritime peoples with the sea such that we can perhaps turn our collective gaze back to the very being and thing that supports all life on Earth.

2

Cosmological Edges of the Sea

This chapter is based on ethnographic and historical information on conceptualizations of the boundaries of the sea. These understandings have both cosmological (structural) and cosmogonic (origin and developmental) dimensions. The sea has four major geographical boundaries of cosmological significance: sea–land boundary, sea–sky boundary, sea–horizon boundary, and sea–seabed boundary. It is for this reason that Aaron Brody (2008:444) refers to "the literal and psychological boundary of the sea." What emerges from this exploration is that the way post-Enlightenment Westerners view these boundaries is often not how other cultures understand the edges of the sea. Indeed, non-modern views of the edges of the sea bring into sharp focus the subjectivity and ethnocentrism of the view seen in much academic writing that landscapes = land and seascapes = sea. A cross-cultural exploration of cosmological edges of the sea reveals that the world's coastal peoples are varied and complex in the ways they define and engage with the varied dimensional edges of the sea, with some Indigenous communities locating the sea–land boundary more than 10 km "inland." Such variability and diversity have major implications for the way archaeologists theorize on boundaries of the sea in the past, and whether sites should be considered part of the sea or not. Although some researchers have explored seascape definitions that transcend the traditional modernist conception of the sea–land boundary corresponding to the shoreline, deeper cross-cultural and dimensional exploration reveals that transcending the land–sea ontological and epistemological divide also extends to understanding how many maritime societies conceptualize the sea–sky boundary beyond the horizon. Here the critical question becomes defining and understanding the multidimensionality and cosmological complexity of the land–sea–sky boundary.

Liminality and Land-Sea Dualisms

Critical to understanding cross-cultural variability in conceptualizing the sea–land boundary is liminality. The notion of the sea–land boundary as a liminal zone is well-established in European historical and archaeological literature on seascapes and cosmological dimensions of the sea (e.g., Bradley 2000:133; Cunliffe 2017:7; Helms 1988:24–26; Helskog 1999:79–81; Scarre 2002; Van de Noort 2011:24–26; Westerdahl 2005a:11). Barry Cunliffe (2001:9) argues, "If, then, the domains of land and sea were conceived of as separate systems subject to their own very different supernatural powers, the interface between them was a liminal place, and as such was dangerous." Liminality is more process than feature and is associated ontologically with ambiguous and dynamic boundaries between phenomena and entities. Liminal boundaries are considered in-between zones and states that are transitional and unstable (McCay 2008:8). Arnold van Gennep (1960:15) in his 1909 book *Les Rites de Passage* drew attention to the issue of liminality in his discussion of "liminal rites (rites of transition)" and the "magico-religious aspect of crossing frontiers" and "boundaries." Victor Turner (2009) elaborated upon van Gennep's notion of rites of passage and liminality. He noted that "liminal entities are neither here nor there; they are betwixt and between the positions assigned and arrayed by law, custom, convention, and ceremonial" (Turner 2009:95). Significantly, Turner (2009:108) observed "that liminal situations and roles are almost everywhere attributed with magico-religious properties."

The separation between land and sea may seem obvious and fixed to many people. Cunliffe (2017:552) notes that the "sea, in its formless state of perpetual motion, is starkly different from the land. Conceptually it is anti-land, the antithesis. What the land is, the sea is not." In contrast to land, the "sea seems to possess a fundamental autonomy, an oppositional identity that has been construed as anticultural and anarchical" (Patton 2007:11–12). The ontological separation and differentiation between land and sea was actively maintained and expressed in maritime cultural contexts through a broad range of land-sea dualisms. Indeed, a classic structuralist division and opposition exists among all maritime societies between the land and sea. This division is deeply symbolic and operates at "cosmological" (Westerdahl 2011a), ontological, and epistemological levels. Cunliffe (2001:9) makes the point that the "power of the boundary between land and sea must always have been very real in the consciousness of those who inhabited the maritime regions." The following sections indicate differentiation between land and sea is expressed in language, gender, food, materials, animals, and morality.

Many communities employ a "sea language" that is used only while at sea. During the late eighteenth and nineteenth centuries, new recruits to the Royal Navy of England soon learned that "the very language used at sea was completely different from that on land" and that the "sailors' speech . . . was full of curious expressions and slang words" (Adkins and Adkins 2009:18). In northern Europe, use of this language is taken seriously, and those onboard vessels, usually young men new to the fishing game, who inadvertently utter unacceptable (taboo) land words instead of acceptable (noa) sea words are reprimanded. In many cases, taboo word indiscretions also elicit ritual responses to nullify their potential negative impacts, such as grabbing the nearest piece of iron or signing the Christian cross (Gill 1993:114–115). In extreme cases the fishing vessel will return back to port (Westerdahl 2005a:7). The most famous of these sea languages is that used by North Sea fishermen, with an extensive vocabulary of noa words, mostly of Norse origin (Flom 1925:412). The Shetland Islanders of northern Scotland referred to this taboo language as *haaf* language (based on *haf*, the Old Norse term for "sea"; Knooihuizen 2008:108). It had a vocabulary of 300–400 Norse words for "certain objects and persons" that were used while out at sea (Marwick 1975:72). These words were used in place of English or Scottish words used on land (but considered taboo at sea) to ward off "malign forces" and "bad luck" (Marwick 1975:73). Shetland fishermen have 22 noa terms for cats, 18 for horses, 13 for pigs, 11 for sheep, and 7 for cows (Lockwood 1955:11; Westerdahl 2005a:4; see Chapter 10). In Scandinavia, noa words also extend to landforms such as islands and coastal features (Westerdahl 2005a). In the Faroe Islands (between Norway and Greenland) the "sea-language" was termed *sjómál* (Lockwood 1955:1).

Seafaring communities on Indonesian islands such as Lembata, Java, and Sumatra have certain words and phrases whose utterance is prohibited at sea but acceptable when on land (Barnes 1996:295–298). The Sama people of the Togean Islands of central Sulawesi, Indonesia, have certain taboo words (e.g., goat, cat, dog, pig) that must not be uttered while out at sea to avoid bad luck (Lowe 2003:124). Also, spirits of the sea were angered if sailors "ignored prescribed ritual or employed inappropriate words, especially those associated with the land" (Andaya 2006:680). The sacred islet of Lów:a, located 16 km off the east coast of Rossel Island in eastern Papua New Guinea, can only be visited by men using 50–100 noa words "special to the island" (Levinson 2008:282). So common is the "sea language"/"land language" dichotomy that Westerdahl (2005a:7) suggests that "these conceptions should be considered archetypes or common traits of maritime culture" and with a considerable antiquity.

In most coastal areas, maritime communities maintain a broad gender binary between the land as the domain of women (and to a lesser extent men) and the sea as the domain of men (and to a lesser extent women). Classic examples of male-focused sea activities are whaling and fishing, with Icelandic women sealers and fishers and Tasmanian women sealers revealing the complexity of gender divisions (e.g., L. Russell 2012; Willson 2016; see also Kirby and Hinkkanen 2000:231–253). However, defining such a division is complex and depends on whether the measure is at an ontological level or focuses more on practices of use. Ontologically, the gender division can take the form of the gendering of the sea itself in terms of masculine and/or feminine traits. Practices of use concern more the gender of people who use the sea directly, the classic example being the gender of fishers. In a Scandinavian context, Westerdahl (2015:144–145) points out that from a direct practice-based perspective, a general pattern exists of women associated more with land-based activities and men associated more with sea-based activities. Yet as Westerdahl notes, this gender division is relationally interdependent such that men can only operate on the sea because of the support of their women kinfolk and vice versa. Furthermore, while men dominate sea-based activities, the sea itself and associated agentive spiritual forces and beings (e.g., mermaids) were often gendered as feminine. In an Icelandic context, Margaret Willson (2016:58–59) points out the role of "seawomen" on land as "weather-reading" specialists and on whose advice wise fishermen would schedule fishing trips.

In Cornwall, England, the sea is a male domain, while the land is both male and female (Cove 1978:146–147). This gender division was also a feature of coastal fishing villages across Scotland during the nineteenth and twentieth centuries (Nadel-Klein 2000:369). Among the Inuit of Quebec in northeast Canada, the sea is the domain of male hunters and sea mammals and is considered masculine whereas the land is considered feminine. When a son conception was desired, the tents would be set up close to the "tide line" to "cause him to choose a hunter's life" whereas if a daughter was desired the tent would be erected "far from the shore and facing inland" (Saladin d'Anglure 1984:496).

For Lardil people of the Gulf of Carpentaria of northern Australia, the division of "outside country" (marine and adjacent low-lying coastal areas) and "inside country" (inland plateau areas; see below) is mirrored in part by male and female gendered domains. That is, "inside country" and coastal (land) areas to the low-water mark are the "domain of women's gathering" whereas the sea (water) from below the high-water mark is the "zone of male hunting" (Memmott and Trigger 1998:111).

Across Oceania "the association of men with the sea and women with the land" can be defined broadly as a "common element" (Feinberg 1995a:6). Richard Feinberg (1995a:6) continues: "In most island communities, the division of labor between men and women reflects the conceptual division between land and sea. Men usually sail, navigate, engage in deep-sea fishing, and participate in interisland trade. Women's responsibilities involve such pursuits as cooking, gardening, and mat making. The reef flat is a meeting ground where men and women search for shellfish and perform communal fish drives. This division of labor, however, is not universal." Maria Lepowsky (1995:40) concurs, adding that while in Tahitian and Marquesan Polynesian societies "women were forbidden even to travel by canoe," Melanesian women in the Louisiade Archipelago of Papua New Guinea "frequently journey long distances by sailing canoe, as they did in ancient times." In Sikaiana society in the Solomon Islands, the sea (masculine) and land (feminine) distinction holds in general, but "women go to the sea to collect shellfish and sometimes to fish. Men go to the interior bush to clear gardens, plant some crops, and collect coconuts. Some men acquire reputations for being good workers on land but not being adept in salt water; other men are notorious for their lack of interest in working on land but are known for their ability at sea. Sikaiana expect men to be able to do both kinds of work, although more prestige is associated with being capable at sea" (Donner 1995:152).

In many coastal communities it is culturally inappropriate to mix land- and sea-sourced foods. For example, the Lardil state that the most common way of incurring *malkri* (a sickness caused by angering the Rainbow Serpent, Thuwathu, who dwells in the sea) "is to go into the littoral zone or the sea, after eating land-derived food, without having first washed one's hands, face and mouth, and allowed the food to digest. It is said that the smell of land food, especially greasy meat such as snake, goanna, or freshwater turtle (today the cause is more commonly blamed on tinned meat, butter or bullock meat), angers Thuwathu. He can sense the presence of such entities through his energies which somehow pervade throughout the coastal and marine systems" (Memmott 1982:171). People are vulnerable to incurring *malkri* on tidal flats and salt pans, which receive "occasional contact with saltwater" and are considered "particularly dangerous, since the extent of the littoral influence may not be clearly defined" (Memmott 1982:173). Alternatively, "*Malkri* can be induced in an inverse manner by entering fresh-water holes without first removing the smell of seafoods" (Memmott 1982:173). Furthermore, *malkri* can also occur "if land and sea foods are cooked on the same fire. To ensure immunity one should cook these foods on separate fires" (Memmott 1982:174). The Lamalama people of the east coast of Cape York Peninsula of northeast Australia hold that they "should cook and eat mussels, whelks, oysters and other shellfish at the coast, and not take them inland" (Rigsby and Chase 1998:213).

In the Arctic, coastal peoples of the Kamchatka Peninsula of far eastern Russia consider it unnatural to cook land and sea animals in the same pot, as it "damages the chase, and causes boils" (Lean 1903a:156). Among the Copper Inuit of the central Canadian Arctic, "fresh caribou meat must never lie on the side platform of the snowhouse together with seal meat; cod must never be eaten with the blubber of a bearded seal; products of the land and the sea must never be cooked in the same pot at the same time" (Damas 1972:39; see also Jenness 1922:182–183). Among the Iglulik Inuit of northern Canada, "it was forbidden to eat the flesh of walrus, whale or seal on the same day as caribou meat, nor was this allowed to be in the house at the same time" (Rasmussen 1929:193). The Inupiat of Kotzebue Sound in northwest Alaska would never use a dish for beluga meat if it had been used previously to serve bear meat (Lucier and VanStone 1995:58).

The Sama people of central Sulawesi, Indonesia, hold that it is taboo to throw fruit and vegetable peels overboard as "these land species do not belong in the sea" (Lowe 2003:124). These "prohibitions were not so much cultural 'rules' as personal ways of experiencing an agentive and unpredictable nature" (Lowe 2003:124). For Fijians of the South Pacific, "people linked to the sea cannot eat fish in the presence of people linked to the land, but they will eat the land people's pork while the others eat their fish" (Fache et al. 2016:11).

Separation of land- and sea-sourced foods in many coastal communities is also seen in the separation of land- and sea-sourced materials and objects. For example, the Copper Inuit know that "seal blood cannot be used for splicing arrows intended for caribou hunting; sealskin may not be sewn at the fishing creeks while the char are still running. Above all, caribou skin clothing cannot be sewn on the sea ice during the dark period of winter. . . . People hunting the seal while based in snowhouses on the sea ice must not work in soapstone" (Damas 1972:39; see also Jenness 1922:182–184). The Iglulik Inuit hold that "walrus hide, or things made from it, must not be taken inland when hunting caribou, but harpoon lines of bearded seal may be used, if they have not previously been used for walrus hunting" (Rasmussen 1929:193). Alternately, "If women have to sew caribou skins during the sealing season, they must go up inland, if they are living in snow huts built on the ice" (Rasmussen 1929:194).

Lardil people can incur the sickness *malkri* "by wearing into the littoral zone or sea, ochre, blood and/or grease used in body decoration for dance" (Memmott 1982:173). People would rub off the body paint with dry sand if no freshwater was available but never use saltwater for fear of angering the Rainbow Serpent (Memmott 1982:173). The Lamalama "use no saltwater gear or bait when they fish in fresh water, nor do they use freshwater gear or bait in the salt water" (Rigsby and Chase 1998:204).

Archaeological perspectives on the ontological and symbolic dimensions of materiality of the land-sea dualism are rare. An early and insightful analysis is Robert McGhee's (1977) exploration of raw materials used to manufacture hunting technologies of the Thule culture that spread across the Arctic between around 400 and 1,000 years ago. Analysis of hunting equipment from a series of Thule sites reveals a reasonably strong correlation between use of marine mammal bones and ivory to manufacture marine hunting technology (especially harpoons) during winter and terrestrial bone and antler (mostly caribou) for the manufacture of terrestrial hunting technology (e.g., arrows) during summer. McGhee emphasizes that such a division was not based on functional attributes or economic issues of availability and accessibility of raw materials. A more recent analysis of raw material and implement type associations across a range of Arctic archaeological sites spanning the period 300–1,900 years ago by Feng Qu (2017) found a more symbolically complex and less dichotomous picture of associations than presented in McGhee's analysis. In a related sense, Lucy Johnson (2005:43–44) notes that Aleutian (Unangax̂) hunters of southwest Alaska would only remove ballast (terrestrial stones) from a kayak after a seal had been towed ashore, as seals "found things of the land very distasteful, and that the hunter who dumped ballast overboard would not successfully hunt again."

The maintenance of a separation of marine and terrestrial animals seen in food and material culture taboos speaks to broader understandings that these two groups of animals must not mix. For example, the Netsilingmiut (Netsilik Inuit) of northern Canada, at the start of the sealing season after the caribou season, must ritually cleanse their caribou-related items to avoid offending seals. All newly made caribou winter clothing and hunting equipment is smudged over a fire made from the nests of small birds and dry seaweed. "It is supposed that the smoke takes away the smell of the caribou, which would offend the sea-mammals" (Boas 1907:502). Similarly, the "women, before cutting up the meat of the first seal for cooking, wash their hands with a piece of dry skin wetted by their sons. It is believed that this takes away the smell of caribou from their hands" (Boas 1907:502). Yet the separation of land and sea animals was not dichotomous. Frédéric Laugrand and Jarich Oosten (2008:31) point out that, "whereas the necessity to separate land game and sea game is always emphasized in [Inuit] ethnographic literature, the initial gifts required that skins derived from sea game be presented to the owner of the caribou, and skins derived from caribou to the owner of the sea game . . . [reveals that] a connection between land and sea had to be made in order to make hunting successful."

Bengt Nordqvist (2003:538, 540) argues that the land-sea "dualism" during the early Mesolithic of western Sweden was expressed in part by differential processing of terrestrial and marine animal bones found in middens. That is, many marine animal bones were burned whereas none of the terrestrial bone showed signs of burning. Nordqvist (2003:540) suggests that the movement of marine bone from one ontological domain to another, that is from the sea onto the land, necessitated ritual intervention. Specifically, "It seems like the relation to the sea has to be destroyed. The most powerful act has been to use fire as such ritual power" (Nordqvist 2003:540).

Major religions of the world, such as Islam, Christianity, and Hinduism, hold in certain contexts cosmologically ordained negative views of the sea that precipitated considerable ritual intervention in voyaging and in rare contexts induced a moral aversion to the sea that curtailed voyaging altogether. For example, although numerous references can be found to support the general view that Islamic beliefs were incompatible with engagement of the sea (e.g., de Planhol 2000) and the sea was considered the domain of Satan (see below), considerable empirical evidence exists to indicate a long and successful history of Islamic mariners (Conrad 2002). Variants of Christian cosmology similarly hold that the sea is the domain of evil and Satan. The potential for the devil to manifest himself on the seas was a constant fear of Christian mariners. Christian mariners often prayed to maritime saints (Chapters 3, 6, 7) to thwart the malevolent powers of Satan who could raise storms, drown sailors, and wreck ships.

The Christian West has a long tradition of making a dichotomy between land (good) and sea (evil) that continues in certain circles to the present (Corbin 1995:1–9; Gillis 2012:7–13; Lee 1995:3–8; Sackey 2019). Christopher Connery (2006) draws our attention to a range of negative representations of the sea in the Bible, including sea as destroyer of the world and humanity in Noah's Flood (Genesis), sea as destroyer of the Egyptian army in the Red Sea crossing (Exodus), and removal (conquering) of the sea in the wake of the apocalyptic end of the world and Christian persecution prior to a rebirth of Christendom and the Second Coming of Christ (Book of Revelation). Indeed, Revelation 21:1 states that after creation of the new world "there was no more sea." Connery (2006:499) notes that the "sea as disorder and chaos . . . was a primary maritime trope established in the Mesopotamian and Western Semitic texts." Furthermore, the land-sea relationship in a Western Christian guise is less one of "opposites" and more "pure antithesis" (Connery 2006:499). In short, "The sea is portrayed as evil in the Bible" (Lee 1995:109).

Christian negative views of the sea linked to Noah's Flood heavily influenced early Enlightenment (scientific and mechanistic) approaches to understanding the geological evolution of the world. For example, in his 1719 text *The Sacred Theory of the Earth* (first published 1690), theologian Thomas Burnet argued that the biblical Flood destroyed not only humankind through the wrath of God but also transformed the smooth surface of Earth into the ruinous form of canyons and mountains. Furthermore, waters for the Flood emanated from Earth's interior, and much of this water stayed after the Flood in the form of lakes and oceans. In this sense, the world's oceans, seas, and shorelines were a result of a world punished for its human sins by a flood instigated by God. Alain Corbin (1995:9) states, "It was on this shore, more than anywhere else, that Christians could come and contemplate the traces of the Flood, meditate upon that ancient punishment, and experience the signs of divine wrath." Biblically informed views on the origin of the world, the moral corruptness of the sea, and ruination of Earth were popular among early Enlightenment scholars, including Isaac Newton (Cohn 1996:61).

An alternative, biblically informed but wondrous view of the sea emerged in Europe during the late seventeenth and eighteenth centuries. The topographical form of Earth, including coastlines, was now presented as expressing God's creative intentions and design to make the world aesthetically and functionally suitable for human welfare and use. Many early coastal geologists suggested that God had deliberately created the coast, especially rocky and cliffed coastlines, as "indestructible battlements . . . in order to protect the earth from the roaring ocean, which respected this barrier that prevented it from pouring out its waters and causing another flood" (Corbin 1995:105). Furthermore, God was posited to have placed salt into the sea for people to use as a food preservative and to limit development of ice, which menaced fishing boats. Bays were formed for the development of protective harbors, and reefs and rocks were emplaced as a defense for naval strongholds. Tidal currents and sea winds were created to aid voyaging and navigation (Corbin 1995:27–28). These positive views of the sea included the perceived purifying and therapeutic powers and moral virtuousness of immersion in seawater, especially clinically prescribed cold-water bathing among the waves via pedestrian access from the beach (as most people could not swim). Salty sea air was also considered invigorating, contributing to a view that the shoreline, as the dynamic meeting place of air, sea, and land, had restorative powers at a deeper cosmological level. These views and activities were elaborated in the nineteenth century (and indeed continue in various forms today), especially the notion of beachside resorts and holidays, alongside ongoing debates about the morality and decency of swimwear (Corbin 1995:57–96, 164–165; Hassan 2003).

Various Hindu societies of southern Asia similarly had negative attitudes toward the sea in contradistinction to land. For example, the sutra of Baudhāyana, an ancient Hindu Sanskrit text dating to the fifth century BCE, places "sea passage" (*samudra-samyana*) as "at the head of grave sins" (Bindra 2002:34–35). Indeed, the text states that "making voyages by sea" will result in the traveler losing their caste status and three years of punishment (Bindra 2002:35). S. C. Bindra (2002:38) suggests that the "ostensible reasons for this ban were twofold: firstly, the danger of traveler's religion being corrupted by non-Hindu influence, and, secondly, inevitable laxity in keeping with the ritual purity as its observance during a long sea voyage or long stay in a foreign land, would have been well nigh impossible." In addition, Bindra (2002:39) presents the essentialized view that "most human beings have an inherent dislike for sea life and the Hindus are no exception."

Nicholas Polunin (1984:270) notes that the Hindu-dominated Balinese people of Indonesia are terrestrially oriented and look to the mountains as a source of spiritual purity as they "provide water and are the seat of the gods." In marked contrast, "The sea receives the filth of the land" and is seen as a "wilderness beyond the control of human society" (Polunin 1984:270–271). Mark Hobart (1978:23) added that "some of the more philosophically inclined [Balinese] villagers pointed out that the sea is ambivalent. While it is the direction towards which pollution flows, by virtue of this, it can be argued to be capable of absorbing all the impurities of the world."

Sara Rich (2021:91) points out that "conception of the sea as a source of moral corruption can also be found in Graeco-Roman thought, beginning especially with Hesiod's assertion that the sea is evil and that seafaring had resulted in the degradation of humanity from a purer, pre-thalassocratic time." Yet the seashore for the ancient Greeks was where certain statues of gods and deities were taken annually for a purifying bath (Burkert 1985:79; Buxton 1994:102). In this sense the shoreline was "the site for the transition between polluted and pure" (Buxton 1994:102–103). Yet as a result of this purification process, the sea was perceived also as possessing "unclean" properties and as a "repository of the unwanted, the unlucky, the contaminated" (Aston 2009:95; see also Lindenlauf 2004:424). Numerous literary sources document the ancient Greek sea as a place for ritual and permanent disposal of unwanted people and objects, especially spiritually charged objects (see Lindenlauf 2004 for an overview).

According to Kimberley Patton (2007:xi), "Historically, many cultures have revered the sea, and at the same time they have made it to bear and to wash away whatever was construed as dangerous, dirty, or morally contaminating." Patton (2007:xi) argues convincingly that a major consequence of this moral conceptualization of the sea is that "modern marine pollution, now threatening the sea in immeasurable ways, may stem from similar responses." Indeed, she points out the irony that secular scientific views on the inexhaustible capacity of the sea to absorb human toxic waste are founded on a religiously inspired ontology and moral differentiation of the land as virtuous and good and the sea as a realm that mysteriously assimilates evil with a capacity to endlessly store impurity.

In marked contrast, many coastal peoples of southern Africa know the sea to be "an ancestral realm and therefore a giver of life" (Sibeko 2020:16). In addition, the sea is not only a "clean space" but also "a sacred space; a space that holds divine power to heal and cleanse" (Sibeko 2020:16). Oupa Sibeko (2020:22) adds that "the sea is not only a site of the ancestors, it is also a site of memory for those who died at sea before us and they are treated as if they are still alive, they continue as spiritual beings in the ocean." In this sense, seeing the sea in a negative sense is disrespectful to ancestral spirits, especially those people who died at sea.

Sea–Land Boundary

For most Westerners, the sea–land boundary is so obvious that questioning its universality and cross-cultural relevance seems incomprehensible. Patton (2007:22) notes, "What greater line of geophysical demarcation exists than the line that separates the land from the sea . . . ?" All 2-D maps of the coast in the Western cartographic tradition have a dark-colored line delimiting the sea–land boundary. In this connection, Westerdahl (2005b:26) notes that "the transition between land and water" is "the most definite border provided by nature. I have suggested therefore that it is the cognitive border *par préférence* of environmental cosmology." But the world is not that straightforward. Paul Carter (2009:50) posits that "it is not the perception of coasts that is in question but the conception of coast*lines*." In this conception, the coastline was a "graphic symbol" of "Enlightenment epistemology" enacted by state-sponsored maritime explorers of the eighteenth century charged with mapping empire and constructing boundaries between colonizer and colonized (Carter 2009:50, 61; see also Ryan 2012:28–29). As such, a "coastline is an artefact of linear thinking, a binary abstraction that corresponds to nothing in nature" (Carter 2009:9). The arbitrariness of coastlines is revealed also by attempts to measure the length of coastlines, with length increasing as more points and indentations are added in what is known as the "Coastline Paradox" (Caputo 2024:148).

That the sea–land boundary can even be ambiguous to Western science is revealed by studies of estuaries and low-lying deltas where seawater and freshwater mix in spatially complex ways that differ with the seasons and confound cartographic delineation of a coast*line* (see Choi 2022; Krause 2017; Krause and Harris 2021). Ellen Semple (1911:244) made the point that the "old term of 'coastline' has no application to such an intermediary belt, for it is a zone of measurable width . . . showing the interpenetration of sea and land." Similarly, the central sections of many reef islands (sand cays and atolls) feature a lens-shaped freshwater aquifer (rainwater sourced) that sits on top of a lens of brackish water due to mixing from underlying saltwater (seawater sourced). This mixing is due to tidal action with rising tides pushing underlying saltwater upward (Buddemeier 1992). In this sense, the sea–land boundary extends inland and underground from the shoreline. The Kulkalgal of the reef islands of central

Torres Strait of northeast Australia know that rising tides push the freshwater aquifer upward such that it is temporarily accessible via wells (McNiven 2015a).

Maggie Roe (2022:492) argues that the "boundaries between land and sea are in a constant state of flux, are difficult to define and often seem to be more imagined or perceived than real." And how is it possible that the coastal Yolŋu Aboriginal people of East Arnhem Land in northern Australia, who heavily utilize marine resources and have intimate knowledge of their maritime world, possess no words in their language that easily translate "as ocean or sea, no binary opposition 'sea' versus 'land'" (Morphy and Morphy 2009:18)? As such, understanding how peoples of the past ontologically constructed the sea–land boundary is an "empirical question that needs to be demonstrated and not assumed" (McNiven 2008:154). The following digest reveals the cosmological and ontological importance of a range of geographical interfaces between land and sea in terms of shorelines and beaches, intertidal zones and estuaries, islands and inland areas, and freshwater and saltwater.

Few Westerners would disagree with the notion that shorelines and beaches represent "the border between sea and land" (Westerdahl 2011a:294). Indeed, Westerdahl (2015:142) argues that "the general significance of the *liminal area* along the waterline must be accepted, whatever other factors change in the fishing communities together with beliefs therein." In short, conceptualization of the shoreline as delineating and separating land and sea is axiomatic. An example of this view is provided by Shirley Campbell's (2002) work among the Vakuta people of the Trobriand Islands. Campbell (2002:156) notes that Vakutans see the "beach" as "a transitional space between land and sea."

That the beach or shoreline marking the sea–land boundary has long underpinned northern European archaeology is indicated by the pioneering work of Knut Helskog (1999:76), who stated that the "shore is where land meets water. It is a zone that stretches from the dry land immediately above the high-tide mark and into the ocean at the lowest tide mark. It is the area that is the last to be covered by snow when winter returns. In the spring the shore is the first area where the snow disappears and where life associated with land first reappears. As such, the shore . . . connects not only land and water but also the life therein." Kalle Sognnes (1994:39) made the important observation that the "shore is a meeting place for three important elements: sea, land, and air. This border zone between elements is constantly changing because of tides as well as currents and wave action." Following on from Sognnes (1994) and Helskog (1999), Knut Bergsvik (2009:605) hypothesizes that finds of Mesolithic stone adzes and mace-heads within the sea, albeit close to the shore, in Norway may have been "ritually deposited" as votive offerings to spirits at the cosmological meeting place of the three domains of land, sea, and sky. This triadic conception of the cosmological meeting point of land, sea, and air was recognized by the ancient Greeks, who saw the sea as "the meeting point of earth, air, and water" and "the meeting point of different planes of reality" (Beaulieu 2016:188–189).

A range of literature over the past three decades has explicitly identified intertidal zones and estuaries as a liminal boundary zone between the land and sea. It is the physical dynamism of the intertidal zone that has attracted considerable theoretical attention in terms of liminality of the coast and the sea–land boundary. Greg Dening (2004a:16) conceives the intertidal zone at the sea–land boundary as "an in-between space in an in-between space." In a Scandinavian cultural context, Westerdahl (2005b:26) argues similarly that "the liminal zone is the beach or, more specifically, the tidal area, generally between high and low tide" (see also Westerdahl 2010:280). He adds that the "strongest magic possible seems to be applied by transgressing the border between the two elements, land and water" (Westerdahl 2011a:306). Such transgression is applicable both ways in terms of terrestrial things moving onto the sea and marine things moving onto the land (Westerdahl 2010:284).

The dynamics of the intertidal zone conspire to confound easy delineations and demarcations between the land and sea. Mark Busse (2005:449) notes that on the south coast of the Trans-Fly region of southwest Papua New Guinea adjacent to Torres Strait, "the transition from salt water to freshwater is rarely marked, with areas of tidal influence and brackish water often extending considerable distances from the coast." Young Choi (2022:344) notes that "in-betweenness is a definitive characteristic of tidal flats" and that "they are the very border zone that is neither land nor sea, or a simultaneous both." Taking a "slippery ontologies" approach, Choi (2022:342) rightly notes that "the dynamic and ambiguous nature of tidal flats resist placement into stable knowledge systems. They are not merely difficult to understand—they constantly undermine knowledge secured in a fixed form."

As a result of this messiness and ambiguity, different peoples vary on how they use the intertidal zone to define the sea-land boundary. For example, the Yolŋu of East Arnhem Land define the lowest astronomical tide mark as the edge of the seaward limit of "land" but seawater that floods the intertidal zone as part of the sea (Davis 1984:233). Under the United Nations Convention on the Law of the Sea (UNCLOS), territorial lands are considered as areas located above the high-water mark. Indeed, Article 121.1 of UNCLOS defines an "island" as "a naturally formed area of land, surrounded by water, which is above water at high tide." In contrast, UNCLOS defines "territorial sea" as extending from a "baseline" (defined as "the low-water line along the coast"—Article 5) out to "12 nautical miles" (Article 3), and the "Exclusive Economic Zone" as extending from the outer edge of the territorial sea out "200 nautical miles" from the baseline (Article 57). All areas of sea located on the "landward side of the baseline" (i.e., intertidal zone) are considered "the internal waters of the State" (Article 8.1).

Ambiguity in defining the sea–land boundary is complicated further by varying definitions of "sea level" in relation to different parts of the intertidal zone and what is considered areas of land above sea level and areas of seabed below sea level. For example, in Britain in the 1830s, the low-tide mark was taken as the vertical measure of "sea level," while in 1837, "low water at spring tide was adopted as the standard Irish datum" of sea level (von Hardenberg 2021:134). In contrast, sea level was defined as the high-tide mark in Venice, Italy, from the fifteenth through to the nineteenth centuries (von Hardenberg 2021:134).

Over the past 50 years across the globe, sea level has been equated with "mean sea level," whereby tide levels are taken at multiple tide gauge stations (and from satellite recordings in recent years) at multiple locations at various times of the day (e.g., hourly) over a number of years and averaged. Such data averaging can be done for different blocks of time (months and years) at regional and global geographical scales (Woodworth 2017). For example, the US National Oceanic and Atmospheric Administration (NOAA) defines "mean sea level" as the mean of hourly tide height recordings taken at multiple tide gauges around the country for the period 1983 to 2001 (Szabados 2008). In Australia mean sea level (taken as the mean of hourly recordings of tides between 1966 and 1968 for 30 tide gauges around the continent's coastline) was formally used in 1971 to define the Australian Height Datum (i.e., the zero-datum point against which all terrestrial elevations, or height above sea level are measured; Hague et al. 2021; Janssen and McElroy 2021; Roelse et al. 1975; White et al. 2014). In this sense, the highest astronomical tide mark is technically elevated above mean sea level.

In early medieval Britain, "tidal spaces refuse clear definition as either land or sea, and defy human control, exposing the limitations of human authority over the natural environment and assertions of territorial ownership" (Clarke 2011:99). For the medieval church and monasteries in England, the meeting of freshwater and saltwater on the coast was a meeting of good and evil, between God and Satan, respectively. That is, it placed "the coastline, especially intertidal, brackish-water mudflats, at the spiritual battlefront—the literal boundary between 'good' (land, fresh water) and 'evil' (sea, salt water)" (Flatman 2011:315). It was for this reason that "brackish water—the meeting of 'good' and 'bad' water, especially in the intertidal zone—is morally questionable and the intertidal zone an undeniable liminal space of spiritual as well as physical conflict" (Flatman 2011:314).

Semple (1911:244) points out that the "interpenetration of land and sea" across tidal regimes results in "coastal zones" varying considerably in width, extending over 100 km inland from the open sea in some regions. Significantly, she adds that where different maritime communities establish their settlements within such coastal zones varies from place to place and through history. For example, the "inland" extent of colonial "seaport towns" in North America was often determined by the upriver extent of tides, which on the St. Lawrence River was 500 km upstream, near Quebec, and on the Hudson River 200 km upstream, near Albany (Semple 1911:246). Interestingly, the inland extent of seaport towns moved downstream into deeper waters and closer to the sea as the size of vessels increased, such as 40 km from Dordrecht to Rotterdam in The Netherlands (Semple 1911:246). In contrast, dredging of waterways can extend shipping and associated maritime activities inland, such as 290 km from Quebec to Montreal on the St. Lawrence River, and 25 km from Port Glasgow to Glasgow city on the Clyde River (Semple 1911:247).

Islands bring the notion of the liminality of the sea–land boundary into sharp focus. This liminality is accentuated with islets that increase and decrease in size due to the relatively high ratio of intertidal zone to land. In this sense, islets are constantly in a state of ontological flux between land and sea. This ontological flux, when combined with island access requiring crossing the sea–land boundary and a boat journey, bestows islets with "super-liminal" properties within a broadened seascape (Heide 2011). Perhaps it is the characteristics of ontological flux and super-liminality that give islets (both real and mythological) an "Otherworld" (Heide 2011) status in a wide range of maritime cultures as islands of the dead accessed by spirits of the dead using spirit canoes and soul boats (see Chapter 4). Cunliffe (2001:31) makes the observation that islands, "particularly small remote islands, had a special quality. No doubt their isolation and comparative safety provided the conditions desirable for religious and trading communities, but there was surely more to it than that. Perhaps it was the idea of boundedness—the sea serving as the protecting perimeter—that was the attraction. That islands were liminal places, neither entirely of the land nor the sea, would have endowed them with unusual power in the minds of those who lived at the interface between land and ocean."

Another sea–land boundary dimension of islands is the inland extent of seascapes. An innovative approach to mapping the "inland" extent of "seascapes" for the island of Cyprus (80 km by 230 km) in the eastern Mediterranean is provided by Ioannis Vogiatzakis and colleagues (2017). They preface their approach with the view that "islands across the world have evolved at the interface between land and sea, thus comprising landscapes and seascapes" (Vogiatzakis et al. 2017:1). To operationalize this interface, they employ Cyprian Broodbank's

(2000) concept of "islandscapes" and note that "on any island, the importance/ dominance of the seascape over the landscape, or vice versa, usually depends on the size of the island and is manifested by nature and culture" (Vogiatzakis et al. 2017:2). This "importance/dominance" is couched in terms of "cultural imprints" comprising tangible (generally mappable) and intangible (mostly unmappable and therefore "perhaps not informative") elements (Vogiatzakis et al. 2017:2, 8). Despite this admirable constructivist approach to conceptualizing seascapes, Vogiatzakis and colleagues (2017:3) limit delineation of seascapes to the "visual aspect," focusing on "views to the sea only, views to the mainland and the sea, views to one or more neighboring islands, and views to other islands and the mainland." In this GIS viewscapes approach, "the sea/marine component extends well beyond the terrestrial boundary of the island" such that all small islands can be considered seascapes, while seascapes on larger islands will be limited to a peripheral zone such that "inland" areas and people have little to do with the sea (Vogiatzakis et al. 2017:5).

Various Australian Aboriginal groups conceptualize the inland boundary of the sea in a way that undermines the normativeness of seeing the high-water mark as the inland margin of the sea. For example, the Gunditjmara people of southwest Victoria in southeastern Australia map Nyamat Mirring (Sea Country) as extending around 5–10 km inland, taking in coastal wetlands and estuaries (Arundel 2023:11, 22). Similarly, the Ganggalida people of the south-east Gulf of Carpentaria in northern Australia speak of "saltwater country" as extending between 3 km and 10 km inland from the beach (Trigger 1987:72). The area of "saltwater country" inland of the beach comprises a series of long sand ridges (with woodland vegetation) paralleling the beach separated by low flat saline coastal flats or saltpans. During the "wet season," the saltpans are inundated by water originating from inland freshwater creeks and tidal surges. This inundation results in the sand ridges being surrounded by water and the term the Ganggalida use for these ridges is *murndamurra*, which means "islands" in exactly the same way that they refer to islands off shore. It is at the inland extent of saltpans where "saltwater country" ends and the "land" or "mainland" (*wambalda*) starts. The neighboring offshore Lardil people of the North Welles-ley Islands have a similar geographical division in terms of "outside country" (open tidal flats inundated only during high spring tides and storm-induced tidal surges; sand ridges and sand dunes with woodlands; shoreline areas and the sea) and "inside country" (grasslands, woodlands and scrublands of the plateau; Memmott 1983:33–34; Memmott and Trigger 1998:111).

The Yanyuwa of the Sir Edward Pellew Islands and adjacent coast of the southwest Gulf of Carpentaria similarly conceive of the mainland (freshwater country) starting at the inland limit of "saltwater country." This inland limit is defined by the inland limit of coastal saltpans and mudflats which become inundated during spring tides, wet season floods, and tidal surges associated with cyclones (Bradley 1998:131; Bradley with Yanyuwa Families 2010:152). Again, sandy ridges isolated by these flood waters are referred to as "islands." This saltwater country is the domain of the Yanyuwa, who refer to themselves as li-Anthawirriyarra ("those people whose spiritual and cultural heritage comes from the sea" or more simply as "the people of the sea"; Bradley 1998:131). As such, "Proper saltwater country, in a Yanyuwa sense . . . extends for some thirteen kilometres from the sea, inland to a low rise that meets with the savannah grasslands" (Bradley with Yanyuwa Families 2022:35). On this point, John Bradley and Yanyuwa Families (2022:55) are very clear: "saltwater country proper" is the "sea," and what Westerners may consider to be low coastal plains "is not the mainland; that country is the sea, it is sea that country." For the Yanyuwa, the "inland" extent of "sea country" and what may be defined as seascape is also cosmologically defined and legitimated by songlines and the travels of ancestral beings between the "sea" and more than 40 km "inland" in one case (Kearney et al. 2023:107; see Chapter 5). In this sense, the "separation of land and sea is thus not a feature of Yanyuwa comprehension of their sea country" (Kearney 2025:195).

Numerous coastal peoples know that the meeting of freshwater and saltwater, usually at river mouths, has deep cosmological significance for the sea–land boundary. The Yolŋu of East Arnhem Land illustrate well the cosmological complexity of the sea–land boundary from the perspective of the freshwater-saltwater interface. Marcus Barber (2005:9) notes: "Water demonstrates the dynamism and change that constantly occurs between land and sea, indeed, it redefines that division as salt and fresh. In the wet season, the 'rivers' flow kilometres offshore, carrying freshwater, silt and debris from the land out into the deep sea, whilst in the dry season, the salt pushes into the rivers and comes up from beneath until it is found many kilometres inland." Critically, the Yolŋu make "no distinction between seawater and saline groundwater, for they are one and the same, saltwater. Coastal swamps, floodplains, and mangroves are places where land, sea and river merge, where such divisions are much harder to make" (Barber 2005:9). Here, the large-scale interfingering of saltwater and freshwater, land and sea, "erodes a distinction fundamental to the presentation of a map, as the clear black line dividing sea blue from land brown becomes a zone sometimes kilometres wide" (Barber 2005:9).

The seasonal inland movement of sea water is also represented by the Yolŋu in an ancestral (Dreaming) narrative of Mäṉa (shark) who, after being harpooned and injured in coastal waters, "tore through the water" and onto the land, where in his "death throes he gouged" a channel through wetlands and finally came to rest exhausted in a billabong (waterhole). Mäṉa remains beneath the billabong "with the harpoon still piercing him" (Morphy and Morphy 2009:19). Barber (2005:174) reports that the Yolŋu have observed sharks swimming up rivers more than 10 km from the sea. More broadly, the Yolŋu have numerous narratives of ancestral "animals or humans that move between land and sea and or between saltwater and fresh" (Barber 2005:174). Barber (2005:174) adds that "it is noticeable how many of these stories emphasise creatures that live in both salt and freshwater." The constant flow and mixing of freshwater and saltwater is encapsulated in a Yolŋu song as described by Djambawa to Barber (2005:177): "This song is all about the saltwater. The main Saltwater Dreaming going out to the ocean, at low tide, and then to high tide, bringing those things, trees, leaves, all those things going (back) into the river. Those leaves was coming out before from rivers, and they were floating around in the ocean, the sea. Now, when its full tide, the ocean is gathering them again, and bringing them back to the land, to the river or the land."

The cosmological significance of the meeting of freshwater and saltwater is illustrated also by the Maya on the east coast of the Yucatán Peninsula in Mexico facing the Caribbean Sea (Miller 1977:105–114). In the Tulum-Tancah area is a major Postclassic shrine complex on the island of Cozumel associated with Ix Chel, the goddess of the moon and renewal. The shrine's location is associated with the rising of the moon each day over the eastern sea horizon. On the nearby mainland coast are related temples associated with Kukulkán, who takes the form of the cosmologically powerful and dangerous Morning Star (Venus) that similarly rises on the eastern sea horizon and descends in the west. In this sense, both the moon and Venus encapsulate the link between the sea (east) and the land (west) in the cycle of rebirth. This link is further expressed on the mainland coast at a shrine in a large limestone cave with an east–west orientation featuring ritual ceramics and elaborate glyph carvings, including one related to Venus. Significantly, freshwater running through the cave, like other underground water sources in the area, is thought by the Maya to directly link with the sea as part of the cycle of rebirth and what Arthur Miller calls the "Cult of the Sea." That is, it is well known by east coast Maya that underground rivers run west to east and emerge as bubbling springs of cool freshwater from the seabed into warm saltwater. Miller (1977:114) notes: "To the metaphorical Maya mind, the natural phenomenon of underground rivers emerging from the sea was another symbol for the gods' passage in the underworld from the west, where they descend and die, to the east, where they emerge anew, reborn."

Spanish records following their arrival on the coast of Peru in the early 1500s note that Mamacocha/Mama Cocha (Mother Sea) controlled the seas and all water sources given that she also controlled the formation of rain-producing clouds and freshwater in lakes, rivers, and springs (Silverblatt 1987:48). The association between saltwater and freshwater was underpinned by Andean cosmology and two domains. First, the lower part of the world was taken up by the original sea ("cosmic sea") and was the domain of the Mother (Mamacocha). Second, the upper surface of the sea that emerges on the landscape as springs feeding lakes, rivers, and lagoons through a "centrifugal" movement was the domain of Mamacocha's daughters (Cochas; Mazadiego et al. 2009:18). For the Quechua people of Peru, the ocean is referred to as *mamacocha* (motherlake; Stensrud 2020:369). Jeanette Sherbondy (1998:213) notes that across the Andes there "is a widespread belief that large subterranean lakes lie under mountains and that these lakes are the sources of waters that flow from the general direction of these mountains."

The ancient Greeks also held that all terrestrial water derives from the sea. For example, Thales of Miletus (2,650 years ago) proposed that springs and rivers were fed by water from the sea whereby seawater moved inland and underground through pressure to emerge on the surface in the form of springs (Mazadiego et al. 2009:18; see also Irby 2021:21–23). The Roman philosopher Lucretius in his *De rerum natura* (*On the Nature of Things*), written in the first century BCE, advanced that water evaporates from the surface of the land and sea and falls back again as rain (Mazadiego et al. 2009:18). In European Christian cosmology during the Middle Ages through the sixteenth century, all water on land was seen to derive from the sea.

Sea–Sky Boundary

The surface of the sea upon and across which vessels voyage is the product of the meeting of two major cosmological and ontological domains—the sky or atmosphere above and the deep ocean below. Although seemingly two different domains, in many cultural contexts the sea extends into the sky and even into the heavens above to form celestial seascapes.

For the Yolŋu Aboriginal people of northern Australia, large wet season storm clouds forming out on the sea horizon (and the "seaward boundary of the Yolŋu world") are known to gather water from the sea itself (Morphy and Morphy 2006:75). As the clouds move toward the coast, they are literally seen to be transferring freshwater taken from out-to-sea to the land. As such, when the clouds and associated rains finally fall on land, it is the sea connecting with the land via the sky (Buku-Larrŋgay Mulka Centre 1999:56). Importantly, the mixing of waters from the sea and land via rain is a strong metaphor for the close relationships between peoples whose offshore, inshore, coastal, and inland clan estates share the rains (Buku-Larrŋgay Mulka Centre 1999:58). This relationship is a cycle whereby rains fall on the land and run into rivers, which then empty into the sea, where they are taken out to the horizon by currents, whereupon the freshwater is picked up by clouds and brought back to the land (Buku-Larrŋgay Mulka Centre 1999:59). This cycling of freshwater and saltwater articulates with similar mixing of waters with tidal cycles and seasonal cycles (Morphy and Morphy 2006:75–76). Barber (2005:9, 148) makes the critical point that for the Yolŋu it is impossible to conceive of and talk about the sea without engaging with the clouds and the sky—"clouds are integral to the way that coastal country is conceptualised and articulated." In Yolŋu eyes, Western maps of their coasts fail to capture the three-dimensionality of their seas, as they reveal no "clouds, no signs of the sky" (Barber 2005:9).

In numerous cultural contexts, the meeting of the sky and sea was most clearly expressed with vessels voyaging through the skies. For example, Bronislaw Malinowski (1922:40) in his classic text *Argonauts of the Western Pacific* recounts a canoe voyage he joined through the Trobriand Islands where it was pointed out to him that a "narrow gorge" on one of the islands had "been broken through by a magic canoe flying in the air." The phenomenon of boats or ships flying through the air and across the sky is found among a number of maritime cultures in various parts of the world.

When Christopher Columbus anchored off Crocker Island in the Caribbean Sea in October 1492, he was surprised not only by how freely local Indigenous peoples exchanged their gold objects for seemingly mundane objects, but also how their arrival evoked great amazement. A partial reason for the latter is encapsulated by Columbus's observation that "our coming, they considered a great wonder, and believed that we had come from the sky" (quoted in Morison 1963:78). In the late eighteenth century, Hawai'ians knew that between the first and second visits to Hawai'i, the Cook expedition sailed to the horizon and visited the sun. For Hawai'ians, the horizon is where the dome of the sky meets the edge of the earth, "and to voyage beyond is to break into the heavens" (Sahlins 1981:16). Soon after, Tongans of the central Pacific described George Vason of the London Missionary Society as "the man from the sky" (Orange 1840:140). The missionary John Stair (1897:24), who was in Samoa in the 1830s and 1840s, said that Samoans referred to the first European visitors as "sky bursters," as they had "burst through the clouds with their ship" (cf. Tent and Geraghty 2001).

Indigenous understandings of European mariners as peoples from the sky were in many cases informed by the belief that the large white sails of European vessels were clouds. For example, numerous Aboriginal communities initially identified the *Endeavour*, captained by James Cook, as a cloud as it sailed up the east coast of Australia in 1770 (Rix and Cormick 2024). Similarly, Indigenous people of New England noted in the seventeenth century that there initial interpretation of a European sailing ship was as a "walking island" with trees (masts), "white clouds" (sails), and "lightning and thunder" (firing of guns; cited in Hamel 1986:73).

Ships in the sky were a feature of European medieval cosmology. Medieval stories from England and Ireland of sky ships reveal a seascape that is both inland and, perhaps more remarkably, overhead in the sky. For example, *The Annals of Ulster* dated 749 CE mention "ships (naues) with their crews were seen in the air above Clonmacnoise" (quoted in McCaughan 1998:171). At that time, Clonmacnoise, located 60 km inland from the Bay of Galway in the middle of Ireland, was a major religious and trade center and the location of an important monastery (McCaughan 1998:171–172). The poem *De mirabilibus hiberniae*, written by Patrick who was bishop of Dublin 1074–1084 CE, makes mention of the king attending a large festive assembly when "suddenly they see a ship glide through the air, from which someone casts a spear at a fish. It fell to the ground: swimming down, he recovered it" (Carey 1992:17).

Similarly, a French chronicler from 1184 CE notes that a sky ship dropped anchor in the center of London in 1122 (Ross 1998:64). Gervase of Tilbury in his 1211 text *Otia imperialia* refers to a sky ship story involving a church in the Gloucestershire region of southwest England (Oman 1944; cf. Carey 1992:19–20). The day was foggy and churchgoers saw an anchor stuck on a tombstone in the churchyard. They saw tugging on an attached rope and heard men's voices above, suggesting sailors trying to free the anchor. Eventually one of the sailors descended the rope to free the anchor. He was soon swamped by churchgoers and died as if drowned by the dampness of the air. Eventually sailors back on board the presumed ship cut the anchor rope, and the ship and its crew sailed away. According to Gervase, this story "tends to prove that the sea is higher than the land" (Oman 1944:6).

The Norse *Speculum regale* (Royal Mirror) written around 1250 CE refers to a sky ship story whereby Sunday churchgoers at Clonmacnoise were shocked to see an anchor hooked in the arch of the church door (Meyer 1894:312). The anchor was connected to a rope that extended upward to a ship with crew. The next day a crewman, swimming as if underwater, came down the rope to free the anchor. The bishop forbade anyone touching the crewman, fearing he would drown. Unable to dislodge the anchor, the crewman returned to the ship, where the anchor rope was cut, and the ship sailed away. The story of the church and anchor is celebrated in the poem "Lightenings: VIII" by Nobel Prize–winning Irish poet Seamus Heaney (Heaney 1991).

In an equally remarkable story, Gervase reports on a sailor from Bristol in southwest England who while sailing to Ireland had dropped his knife into the sea while washing it after a meal. On his return home, his wife showed him the same knife, which on the same day had fallen through the louvre (smoke outlet) of their house and embedded in a table. Gervase added: "Who after hearing this testimony will doubt that above our habitation is placed the sea, either in the air or on the air?" (Oman 1944:7).

In 1679 a pamphlet was published titled *A True Account of Divers Most Strange and Prodigious Apparitions, Seen in the Air at Poins-Town in the County of Tipperary in Ireland: March the Second, 1678–9. Attested by Sixteen Persons that were Eye-Witnesses* (Anonymous 1679). The account provides basic details of three sky ships with sails and crew observed by a number of people in central southern Ireland. William Hone (1827:281) argues that the account was a fabrication and a piece of either political propaganda or shameless commercialism. Yet the observation of sky ships was a very real phenomenon for many people of the Middle Ages, and the 1679 pamphlet appears to have appropriated such accounts for seventeenth-century purposes.

John Carey (1992) suspects that the various eleventh- to thirteenth-century Irish and English stories of sky ships may be sequentially derivative back, ultimately, to eighth-century Irish accounts. Whatever the case, the fact that such stories had currency over many hundreds of years indicates the pervasiveness of a medieval cosmological mindset of the sea above populated with sky ships and their crews.

Were medieval accounts of ships in the sky indicative of a separate sea world above land or an extension of the known sea? Miceal Ross (1998:65) notes that available evidence indicates that medieval cosmology conceived of the sea extending out from the shore and then curving up overhead. He cites Alan Smith, who informed him that the "ocean was believed to curve somewhat like a Moebius strip. This latter curiosity resembles the fanbelt of a car, except that it has twists in it which impart to it the property that a resolute movement forward from any point inside the lower belt will bring the traveler over the starting point outside the belt and ultimately back to the original position. Put on a cosmic scale, ships sailing westward before the European discovery of America could, by this process, it was believed, 'shoot the gulf' and sail across the sky" (Ross 1998:65). As Michael McCaughan (1998:179) rightly notes, "Clearly the idea of sea or water in the sky, even as a sort of watery black hole, was something the medieval mind could envisage without difficulty." According to Barbara Spooner (1961:323), the English cosmological construction of a looping sea harked back to the Babylonians, who believed that the "sea arched right over the sky's vault, and well underneath the earth."

A recent variant of the sky ship phenomenon comes from oral history about the "Mester Ship" taken from an old man in the Orkney Islands who died in 1840 (Dennison 1890). The Mester Ship was a sailing vessel of colossal size that sailed the North Sea. Such was the size of the vessel that it was not possible to see the stern from the bow, and indeed it was said that once a captain asked a young man at the stern of the vessel to inform men at the bow to weigh anchor, and by the time he returned to the stern he was a white-haired old man. The masts were so tall that once a sailor dropped his new knife from the top of the mast, and by the time it hit the deck it was a "lump of red rust." On one voyage the mast tops collided with the moon, and the "top-gallant mast was left on the moon, and two of the men, who were sitting on the cross trees mending their rivelins (a kind of sandal), were carried away with the mast to the moon. You'll see them in the moon carrying the mast on their shoulders, one at each end; and the cross-trees and top-gallant sail hanging on the middle" (Dennison 1890:69). When asked about the final fate of the Mester Ship, Dennison's "narrator" responded: "They say she sailed away to find the outer edge of the world. Ye know there is a rim of ice about the world. . . . Lord knows what may have happened, for I know not" (1890:70).

William Bottrell (1873:145) reports that Cornish traditions of "phantom-ships sailing overland were common to many places near the Land's End with which no stories were connected; these appearances were merely supposed to forebode tempests and wrecks." Additionally, people of the small coastal village of Parcurno reported that ghost ships "were often seen sailing up and down the valley, over dry land the same as on the sea" (Bottrell 1873:141). These occurrences were "regarded as 'tokens' that enemies were about to make a descent; the number of phantom vessels foreboded the sea robbers' approaching force" (Bottrell 1873:141). In one case, the "ship of the dead, with her ghostly crew" were associated with three known local individuals, two of whom were reputed to have taken the remains of a recently deceased mariner who wished to "rest at the ocean's bottom" (Bottrell 1873:144). This ghost ship was "generally shrouded in mist," with "her keel just skimming the ground, or many yards above it, as she passed over hill and dale" (Bottrell 1873:144).

A possible archaeological expression of sky ships is found in a relief carving on the eighth-century Kilnaruane high cross positioned on a hill overlooking Bantry Bay, County Cork, southwest Ireland (Hourihane and Hourihane 1979; Johnstone 1964; McCaughan 1998:170–171, 2001; Stojanovic 2015). The sandstone cross (only the lower pillar remains) stands approximately 2.3 m high and features an 18-cm-by-88-cm low-relief carved panel with four Christian crosses, and most critically, a boat (probably a *currach*) with four paddlers, a helmsman, and two possible passengers, oriented vertically as if ascending to the sky. The vertical orientation of the boat is considered unique in European medieval art (Stojanovic 2015:19). McCaughan (1998) argues that this relief carving, given its age and iconography, probably fits within the known medieval mindset of "ships

Figure 2. Superior mirage of an inverted ship seen in the sky off the coast of Greenland by William Scoresby in 1822 (from Scoresby-Jackson 1861:Title page).

in the air" and use of ships and the sea by medieval Christians as a symbolic metaphor for spiritual virtuousness and godliness. That is, "Simultaneously and ambiguously it is a Ship of the Church sailing the heavenly seas, which the medieval mind thought of as surrounding the earth, and an aerial Ship of the Church voyaging heavenwards in marvellous flight through the air and the sky" (McCaughan 2001:56).

It is tempting to associate the concept of sky ships with the well-documented meteorological phenomenon of superior mirages. That is, objects and features viewed from a distance (both from land and at sea) appear to be hovering well above the sea horizon as though they are floating in the sky. The optical illusion is caused by a temperature inversion whereby cooler air sitting un-characteristically over warmer air distorts light rays from the viewed object or feature such that it appears to the observer to be hovering above the hori-zon (Blanco-García and Ribas-Pérez 2011; Tape 1985). These superior mirages contrast with inferior mirages, where the mirror image is inverted and can be seen below the original object or feature. Superior mirages over water are rarer than inferior mirages over land (e.g., deserts; Li et al. 2020). A famous early documented example of this superior mirage phenomenon occurred in 1822, when William Scoresby observed a ship floating in the sky off the coast of Greenland. It comprised "the distinct inverted image of a ship in the clear sky, over the middle of the large bay or inlet," that he recognized as his father's ship the *Fame* (Scoresby-Jackson 1861:194). From subsequent discussions with his father, Scoresby calculated that the *Fame* at the time of the mirage was located "entirely beyond the horizon"; that is, a distance of "about seventeen miles" (c. 30 km) over the horizon with a total separation distance of "nearly thirty miles" (c. 48 km; Scoresby-Jackson 1861:194; see also Lehn and Rees 1990; Figure 2).

Seeing mirage objects that are otherwise out of sight over the horizon is a well-understood phenomenon: "If the downward curvature of the light rays is approximately the same as the curvature of the earth, objects beyond the horizon can come into view" (Amery 2020:444). It is improbable that superior mirages of ships floating in the sky resulted in a cosmological tradition of sky ships among observers, given that the atmospheric phenomenon is global and sky ship cosmologies have a restricted occurrence and include incongruous sightings of ships in the sky over land. The considerable nineteenth- and twentieth-century literature on mirage sightings, including ships floating above the sea, never links the phenomena with cosmological traditions of sky ships (e.g., Pinney 2018, 2021).

The linking of seas with skies extends also to the celestial realm and celestial seascapes populated by marine creatures. Many if not all historically known maritime communities reference the sea in the night sky through association of constellations with the marine world. The European constellation tradition owes much of its origins to ancient Greek mythology, as documented by the Greek astronomer Claudius Ptolemy's catalog of 48 constellations written in the second century CE (Simpson 2012; Toomer 1998). Three examples are the Cetus, Argo Navis, and Capricornus constellations (Figure 3). The Cetus (Latin) constellation of Roman times is named after the Ketos constellation of ancient Greek mythology (Hoffmann et al. 2022:315–316; Papadopoulos and Ruscillo 2002:207, 211–212; Simpson 2012:83–89; Toomer 1998:381–382; see Chapter 3). Ancient literary and graphic references to Cetus/Ketos identify it as a "threatening creature of the sea," a sea monster and to a lesser extent a whale, with whale representations becoming dominant with Christian influences after 1600 CE (Hoffmann et al. 2022:336; see also Simpson 2012:40). Ian Ridpath and Wil Tirion's (2006:53) authoritative text *The Monthly Sky Guide* identifies the Cetus constellation as a "sea monster." Capricornus constellation is represented as a hybrid sea creature with the upper body of a horned goat and lower body in the form of a fish's tail (Simpson 2012:507–516; Toomer 1998:375–376; see Chapter 3). The Argo Navis constellation represents the ship *Argo* sailed by Jason and the Argonauts in search of the Golden Fleece

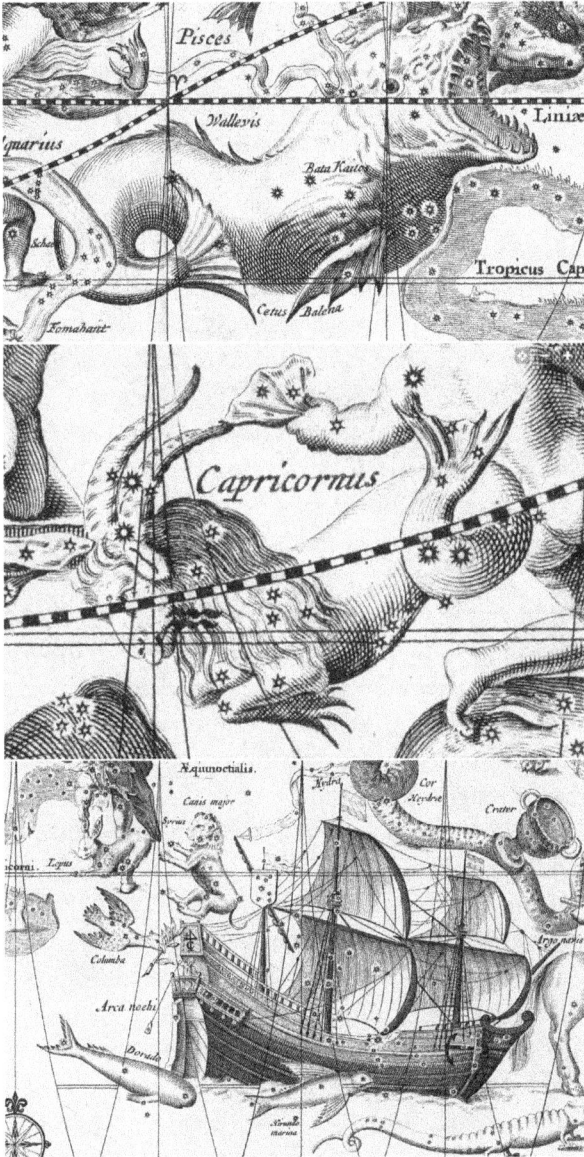

Figure 3. Excerpts from a Dutch constellation/zodiac map titled *Door dit hemels pleyn wert vertoondt den gehelen loop des hemels der vaste sterren met haer beeltenisse* (Backer and Elwe 1792; Courtesy: Library of Congress, Geography and Map Division, G3190 1792.B3). *Top:* Cetus (whale/sea monster) constellation. *Middle:* Capricornus (goat-fish sea monster) constellation. *Bottom:* Argo Navis (ship) constellation.

(Simpson 2012:421–451; Toomer 1998:388–391). The ship evolved through time to take on the form of contemporary sailing vessels.

Peoples of the South Pacific possess arguably the richest corpus of maritime constellations recorded to date. Stephen Chadwick and Martin Paviour-Smith (2017:72) note that "the marine world is reflected above the South Pacific. . . . The stars shining down on the dark ocean are filled with constellations representing fish, fishermen, and their means of transportation. The stories of these constellations remind us of the importance of the sea as a source of food and as a means of travel among the cultures of the South Pacific." The centrality of the sea in Māori culture of Aotearoa/New Zealand is revealed by the term Te Ikaroa ("the long fish"), one of the names for the Milky Way galaxy, which dominates night skies in the Southern Hemisphere (Chadwick and Paviour-Smith 2017: 40).

A wide range of societies and places across the South Pacific and Australia reference marine material culture in constellations, such as canoes (e.g., Groote Eylandt and Torres Strait, North Australia; Malaita, Solomon Islands; Manus Island and New Ireland, Papua New Guinea; and Kiribati), fishhooks (e.g., Kiribati, Marquesas, Hawai'i, and Cook Islands), and fishing nets (e.g., Manus Island; Rennell and Bellona Islands, Solomon Islands; Marshall Islands; Chadwick and Paviour-Smith 2017:72–94). Sharks are among the most common of the diverse array of marine animals in constellations, with Chadwick and Paviour-Smith (2017:95) pointing out that "sharks, it seems, roam the night sky in Oceania."

The celestial seascape of Manus Islanders off the north coast of Papua New Guinea includes the shark (*peo*) and stingray (*pei*) constellations. As both constellations move slowly westward across the sky, the shark moves ever closer to stingray and eventually bites stingray's tail as the two meet on the western sea horizon and descend into the sea. Upset by the biting, stingray hits the sea with its moving tail, producing rough seas and strong winds that mark the start of the northwest (*ai*) season (Hoeppe 2000:31–32). A month after touching the sea (horizon), shark and stingray completely disappear "into the sea" (i.e., below the western sea horizon; in November; Hoeppe 2000:32). Other fish constellations also disappear during the *ai* season, which is also the time of fish abundance in the sea and the fishing season. As the fish constellations reappear with the start of the *kup* season (in April), the availability of fish in the sea decreases (Hoeppe 2000:32). To the Manus, fish seasonally migrate between the sea and the sky (Hoeppe 2000:34). In this sense, the sea–sky boundary on the horizon was "permeable" for "celestial objects" in Manus cosmology (Hoeppe 2000:25).

Nukumanu (atoll) Islanders of far eastern Papua New Guinea have a night sky with an elaborate array of sea-referenced constellations. Examples (with English equivalents) include Te Himu, "Trigger Fish" (Southern Cross), Samomo, "Dolphin" (Big Dipper), Te Manu, "Shark" (Scorpius' Tail), Kaavei, "Octopus Tentacle," Kaipea, "Crab," and Te Ula, "The Crayfish" (Feinberg 1995b:184 –185).

Cook Islanders know the tail of the Scorpio constellation as the "great fish-hook of Tongareva" (Gill 1876a:75). The associated story relates to Vātea, the "father of gods and men," who went fishing with a fishhook and caught a large object from the seabed which he brought to the surface which became the island of Tongareva (Gill 1876a:48). Pleased with his achievement, Vātea "hung up his great fish-hook in the sky" (Gill 1876a:48). This fishhook constellation is known across large areas of Polynesia (Chadwick and Paviour-Smith 2017:81–88).

Māori point out that in the night sky can be seen the *waka* (canoe) of the great warrior Tama-rereti. During a voyage to the "south" the canoe was wrecked, and Tama-rereti and his crew were killed. Tama-rereti's body was placed into the canoe and the whole burned down to embers, whereupon its "spirit or essence was transferred to the sky" (Reed 1967:420). One version is that the *waka* matches the tail of the Scorpion in the constellation of Scorpius (Orbell 1996:176; Reed 1967:28). Another version states that the *waka* is spread over the night sky with the bow (the Pleiades), sternpost (Orion's Belt), and anchor (Southern Cross; Orbell 1996:176, 211). In another version different constellations are identified: pāua shell, which decorated the stern post (Alpha Carinae), bowpiece (Southern Cross), anchor rope (The Pointers), and canoe anchor (Dark Hole; Reed 1967:420).

Tagai is a famous constellation of the Kemer Kemer Meriam of the eastern islands of Torres Strait, northeast Australia. Chadwick and Paviour-Smith (2017:74) describe it as "perhaps one of the largest constellations to be projected into the southern sky." The constellation sits within the Milky Way and includes the culture hero Tagai standing in a canoe (represented by the Scorpius constellation; Chadwick and Paviour-Smith 2017:74–78; Haddon 1908:3–4, 1912:219). His left hand (represented by five stars of the Southern Cross constellation) holds a fishing spear (Haddon 1912:145, 219; Lawrie 1970:304). His right hand is represented by five stars of the Corvus constellation (Hamacher et al. 2022:125). The rest of his body is represented by the constellations of Lupus, Centaurus, and Hydra (Hamacher et al. 2022:126). Intimate empirically based understandings of the movement and phased emergence of Tagai in the sky are used by the Kemer Kemer Meriam and other Torres Strait Islanders to signal the timing of seasons and scheduling of activities. For example, just before the emergence of the right hand of Tagai signals to Kemer Kemer Meriam ritual specialists (Zogo Le) that it is time to perform a ceremony at the sacred stone or shrine (Tagai zogo on the island of Dauar) "that ensures an abundance of turtle" (Haddon 1935:158).

The Goemulgal of Mabuyag in central western Torres Strait recall a legendary narrative of two brothers, Deibui and Teikui, who would spear fish on the reef off the southwest end of the island (Lawrie 1970:87). Sometimes the brothers quarreled, and eventually their spirits ascended to the sky and became two small white star clouds (*kunar*) that are Magellanic Clouds (Chadwick and Paviour-Smith 2017:61; Lawrie 1970:87). The "human forms" of the two brothers became rocks near Burupagaizinga located on the southwest coast of Mabuyag (Lawrie 1970:87).

For Aboriginal Australians, the Maḏarrpa clan of the Yolŋu tell a story of how two ancestral hunters went out fishing when a storm capsized their canoe and one of the men drowned. He appears today in the shape of a rock cod in the Milky Way (Buku-Larrŋgay Mulka Centre 1999:100). Another Yolŋu ancestral narrative similarly tells of two Guwak men who drowned after their canoe was capsized by the wake of a turtle and entered the night sky as part of the Milky Way (Buku-Larrŋgay Mulka Centre 1999:103). Another Yolŋu mythological narrative is the Moon-Bone Song (*'wirmu-'manikai*), which relates how the moon, then a man, died and went out sea, where his bones became the nautilus shell (Berndt 1948). In a repeat cycle of death and rebirth, the moon dives into the sea to die for three days and sheds his bones into the water, which express as nautilus shells that wash up on the beach (Berndt 1948:19, 43, 45). After three days, the "New Moon then emerges from the sea reborn, and again grows his bone, until he regains his full size at Full Moon" (Berndt 1948:45).

The Bugis seafaring peoples of southern Sulawesi in Indonesia identify in their night sky a wide range of named constellations, many of which reference the sea. Examples (with English equivalents) include *bintoéng balé*, shark (Scorpius, south); *bintoéng lambarué*, ray fish/skate (Scorpius, north); *bintoéng kappala'é*, ship (Alpha-Eta Ursa Majoris); and *bintoéng kappala'é*, ship (Alpha-Eta, Uma; Ammarell 1995:205–206, 210).

In 2003–2004, NASA bestowed the name of 2003 VB12 Sedna (after the Inuit female sea spirit—see Chapter 3) to a newly discovered planet that was at the time the furthest-known planet from the sun and the coldest planet in our solar system (Laugrand and Oosten 2008:13).

In some cases, the constellations are referenced in the sea. For example, the sacred site of Lilujulhuwa is a deep hole in the seabed located 1 km off the mainland coast in the southwest Gulf of Carpentaria, Australia, in Yanyuwa Sea Country. The deep hole is the "home to the li-Jakarambirri Dreaming (Seven Sisters)" (Bradley with Yanyuwa Families 2010:156). That is, within the hole dwelled "the powerful Dreamings associated with the star constellation known as the Seven Sisters (also known as the Pleiades), and which has as another representation the Blue-ringed Octopus, both the star and the octopus being called *li-Jakarambirri* in Yanyuwa" (Bradley with Yanyuwa Families 2010:155 –156).

Sea–Horizon Boundary

A related dimension of the sea–sky boundary is where the sea meets the sky on the horizon. While most academic discourse on this topic takes as a natural given that the sea–horizon boundary is easily experienced by looking seaward from the shoreline to where the visible outer edge of the sea meets the sky, geographically conceptualizing the sea–horizon boundary is a different ontological and epistemological question. Just as Epeli Hau'ofa (1994:152) pointed out that the European historiographical tradition of seeing the Pacific as "islands in a far sea" is a "world of difference" to local Islander conceptualizations of "a sea of islands," is it possible that some coastal communities see the sea–horizon boundary as not "out there" but as right here, in an inversion of core and periphery?

The Kaiadilt Aboriginal people of Bentinck Island in the Gulf of Carpentaria of northern Australia illustrate this inversion in their mapping of their 140 km² island and "surrounding" seas. Like all Aboriginal groups of the southern gulf, the Kaiadilt are marine specialists with a subsistence focus on fishing, shellfishing, and turtle and dugong hunting (Best 2012; Tindale 1977). In 1960 anthropologist Norman Tindale (1962) visited the Kaiadilt, mapped around 300 named places across the island and surrounding islets, and plotted these on a base map traced from an aerial photograph using a European cartographic tradition. Tindale (1962:276) claimed that his map is a "view of the native geography of a whole island." But is it? In 1977 Tindale documented Djorangarangati burantant, a 21-year-old Kaiadilt man, and his "concept of his country, together with a sketch map illustrating a few of the place names which he gave when he drew his map" (Tindale 1977:249; Figure 4). The Kaiadilt map has a similar island coastline to Tindale's map but whereas Tindale's map shows the sea surrounding Bentinck Island, the Kaiadilt map shows the sea (*mala*) seemingly inside the island. Yet the Kaiadilt know that the sea is not located inside their island. The map reveals that the Kaiadilt conceive of their Country not as an island surrounded by sea but the sea surrounded by their island. As Paul Memmott and David Trigger (1998:110) observe, in this "powerful representation of the centrality of the sea in Kaiadilt perceptions of their territory," "the perimeter of Kaiadilt territory is the coastline enclosing the sea" and not the sea–horizon boundary as understood by Westerners.

Most discussions on the edges and limits of the sea concern the history of European understandings of the outer margins of the sea on the horizon and conceptualization of the world as either spherical or flat. These discussions tend to start with written records from maritime societies such as the ancient Greeks. For example, the ancient poetic writings of Homer and Hesiod in the

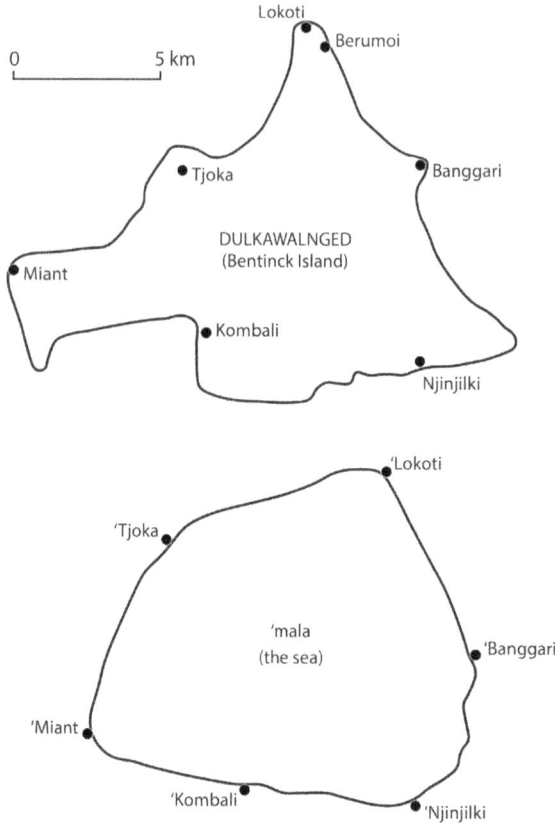

Figure 4. Two cultural maps of Bentinck Island. *Top:* "sketch map" by anthropologist Norman Tindale. *Bottom:* "drawing by Djorangarangati burantant, a 21-year-old Kaiadilt man, showing his concept of his country" (after Tindale 1977:Figure. 1).

eighth and seventh centuries BCE present a flat world with Earth represented as a circular island surrounded by sea known as Ocean after the Titan Oceanus (Romm 1992:13–15; see also Lewis 1999). In this sense, the edge of the Ocean Sea on the horizon was also the edge of the world.

Randall Younker and Richard Davidson (2011:127–128) point out that from at least the sixth century BCE (e.g., Pythagoras), and continuing with the writings of Aristotle (fourth century BCE) and Ptolemy (first century CE), Greek cosmographers also defined a spherical earth suspended inside a nested series of at least eight transparent, hard, rotating spheres (see also Garwood 2008:18–22; Stallard 2010). The first of these outer spheres was heaven, with further rotating spheres variously featuring the sun, moon, planets, and stars. It was Renaissance astronomer Nicolaus Copernicus in his 1543 text *De revolutionibus orbium coelestium* (*On the Revolutions of the Heavenly Spheres*) who argued that the sun and not the earth was the center of the universe.

Aristotle and Ptolemy "provide the classic formulations of the Greek celestial-sphere model that influenced all scholars of the early Christian church and the Middle Ages" (Younker and Davidson 2011:128–129; see also Betten 1923). The celestial-sphere model was also employed by many medieval Islamic scholars (Burnham 2012:50–59). For some medieval Islamic cosmographers, the seas not only were found on the surface of Earth but also formed one of the surrounding spheres (Burnham 2012:54, 67). In the later conceptualization, the outer sea interfaced with the unknowable and infinite abyss of the cosmos and thus separated Earth from the cosmos (Burnham 2012:256). For early Jewish and Christian theological scholars, the surrounding spheres (or domes in the case of the flat-earth advocates) were referred to as *raqia* in the Hebrew Old Testament and "firmament" in the Christian Bible. Whereas ancient Greeks thought of the spheres surrounding Earth as hard, medieval Christian philosophers debated the hardness or softness of these nested spheres (Younker and Davidson 2011:131).

Within Christian cosmology expressed in the Bible, God created a flat earth under a vaulted dome or "firmament" containing the sun, moon, and stars, which move across a stationary earth (Garwood 2008:16–17; Seely 1992:43). The circular earth rests on either water or empty space while the firmament rests on pillars or mountains and what is seen as the "end of the earth" (e.g., Deuteronomy 28:64).

The notion of a flat earth capped by the hemispherical dome was a minority view among Christian scholars and biblical literalists of late antiquity and the early medieval period (300–800 CE; Nothaft 2011). A flat-earth/dome cosmography also continued as a minority view throughout the medieval period (Russell 1989; Simek 1996; Younker and Davidson 2011). While the spherical earth theory was broadly correct, James Allegro (2017) documents a series of fifteenth-century scholars who sought to challenge it on strict empirical grounds. Indeed, "The spherical earth was very much a theory in need of defending during the fifteenth century" (Allegro 2017:77). Some flat-earth advocates argued that Columbus's voyage to the New World in 1492 supported their position as the expedition failed to find evidence of a southern hemisphere. The hypothesis of a spherical earth was only empirically demonstrated and universally accepted by European scholars following the Magellan expedition's circumnavigation of the globe in 1522 (Allegro 2017:63).

The view that the majority of Europeans of the early Christian and medieval eras believed in a flat earth was a nineteenth-century invention (Garwood 2008; Russell 2001). Christine Garwood (2008:34) points out that "a globular earth has been the educated consensus [at least in the West] since at least the fourth century BC." Furthermore, "From the twelfth century onwards, the flat-earth concept is almost a nonissue, so prevalent are written and visual images of a spherical earth" (Garwood 2008:26). Both Russell and Garwood argue that the so-called flat-earth paradigm of medieval thought was invented to denigrate Christianity in an era when biblical understanding of the origins of Earth were in battle with Enlightenment, scientific, and Darwinian evolutionary under-standings. They both point out that it was also during the nineteenth century that the myth associating Columbus with discovery of a spherical earth was developed. As Allegro (2017:69) notes, "Columbus never explicitly credited himself with proving the spherical earth model."

Numerous non-Western cultures hold a flat-earth/sky-dome cosmology such that the horizon out to sea is where the sea and the sky physically meet (Seely 1991, 1992). For example, in Samoan and Tahitian cosmology in Poly-nesia, the earth is seen as endlessly flat but meets up with the sky on the ocean horizon, beyond which is found a series of heavenly levels containing the sun, moon, and stars (Tcherkézoff 1999:419). Despite the perception of a sky–ocean interface on the horizon, Jan Tent and Paul Geraghty (2001:185) argue that given evidence for Polynesian long-distance voyaging and colonizing across the Pacific, "we therefore doubt that the horizon was seen as a conceptual bar-rier; nor is there any evidence to suggest that it was of any great importance in Polynesian culture" (see also Feinberg 2008:81). However, it is clear that the sea horizon was and remains important in Polynesian culture, as indicated by late eighteenth- and early nineteenth-century identification of European ships as celestial vessels of the sky (see above).

Cosmological understandings of the horizon limits of the ocean were more meaningfully expressed by mariners in terms of spiritual entities and meta-physical dangers. Ancient Greek philosophers believed the sun and stars arose from and set into the ocean with the horizon "a terrifying and unapproachable entity" (Romm 1992:16). James Romm (1992:18, 32) notes that according to the ancient Greek poet Pindar in the fifth century BCE, to go beyond the ocean's (Mediterranean or the "Great Sea") threshold at the Pillars of Heracles (Strait of Gibraltar) was the "prerogative of god alone, or mythic figures like Heracles who manage to bridge the human and divine." Indeed, this ocean of the beyond was referred to by the Greeks (e.g., Herodotus) as the Atlantic (Sea of Atlas), in honor of the god Atlas (Roller 2006:2).

Around 500 BCE, the Carthaginian brothers Himilco and Hanno (from the north African coast of the southern Mediterranean) ventured beyond the pillars, exploring to the north (perhaps to the British Isles) and south (perhaps to Cameroon), respectively (Cunliffe 2017:301–307; Roller 2006:27). Accounts of Himilco's voyages mention numerous sailing hazards: an absence of wind, sluggish seas, dense fog, seaweed so dense it stopped ships, shallow waters, and sea monsters (Roller 2006:27). Duane Roller (2006:28) suggests that such negative reports may have been "propaganda designed to frighten Greeks away from areas that the Carthaginians considered their own." The currency of such views on the liminality of a horizon of an ocean considered to be on the cosmological edge of the earth is equally telling. Marie-Claire Beaulieu (2016:9) makes the point that for the ancient Greeks, "sailing on the sea or on the outer Ocean" was never "devoid of religious significance."

Between 320–330 BCE, the Greek explorer Pytheas of the Greek colony of Massalia (now Marseille, France) made his "epic" voyage beyond the pillars to the North Atlantic (Cunliffe 2017:310–317; Roller 2006:60). Whether he actually sailed through the pillars or started his journey from the Atlantic coast of France is the subject of debate (Roller 2006:68–69). In his log titled *Peri ōkeanou* (*Concerning the Ocean*), Pytheas stated: "In these regions [perhaps Iceland—Roller 2006:85–86] obtained neither earth as such, nor sea, nor air, but a kind of mixture of these, similar to the sea-lung, in which . . . earth, sea, and everything else is held in suspension; this substance is like a fusion of them all, and can neither be trod upon nor sailed upon" (Romm 1992:22).

Following earlier views of the Greeks (Beaulieu 2016:7), the consensus among many Romans in the first century CE was "even if the Ocean could be sailed it should not be" (Roller 2006:126). It is telling that the Roman philosopher Seneca stated after a Roman naval disaster in the North Sea in 16 CE: "why do we disturb the peaceful home of the gods?" (Cunliffe 2017:343). Ultimately, "There is no evidence in ancient literature that anyone from the Mediterranean went beyond the Atlantic islands" (Roller 2006:54). Indeed, neither credible literary nor archaeological evidence supports sailing to the furthest of these islands, the Azores located 1,400 km west of Lisbon in Portugal (Roller 2006:49–50, 54; see also Cunliffe 2017:309).

Many medieval mariners looked upon the Atlantic Ocean west of Europe as the "Sea of Darkness" (termed Mare Tenebrosum by European mariners and Bahr al-Zulamat by Islamic mariners) and the metaphysical end of the world populated by all sorts of dangerous and monstrous forces and creatures (Goodrich 1858:137–138; Lunde 1992). For Islamic mariners, the dangerous end point was marked by the Hand of Satan (Bassett 1885:14; Goodrich 1858:15, 137; Figure 5). An eleventh-century Old High German poem, *Merigarto*, describes a trader who traveled to Iceland and saw a "Liver-sea" which was "a fabulous, dangerous coagulated sea in which the ships could not move" (quoted in Simek 1996:68). Matthew Paris's 1250 map of Britain includes an inscription on the left side stating that the western side of Britain "looks out on a vast sea where there is nothing but the abode of monsters" (van Duzer 2013:33). Medieval Islamic scholars similarly theorized that moving outward from familiar coastal waters were seas of decreasing navigability and increasing danger, uncertainty, and liminality known only to God (Burnham 2012:66–67).

Numerous other coastal societies conceptualize the world as an island surrounded by sea. For example, the Maya of Central America saw their world as a giant turtle or crocodile floating in a primordial sea, whereas many contemporary Maya hold the world as a disk or rounded mound surrounded by the sea (Taube 2010:204, 210, 212). In this cosmology, the sea underlies the earth as the underworld, with sinkhole pools (cenotes), lakes, and streams seen as portals into this subterranean realm. Numerous cenotes contain thousands of votive objects in their depths (to the Maya, the sky "is a giant solid bowl atop the earth at the edge of the sea" [Taube 2010:213]). The edge of the sea on the horizon is also the realm of supernatural powers, being the place where the sun rises each day and also the source of destructive hurricanes, gigantic serpents, and nourishing spring and summer rains (Taube 2010:204, 215). In this connection, the west façade of the Temple of Quetzalcoatl (dated to 200 CE) at Teotihuacan, Mexico, located 200 km inland, features the heads of plumed serpents emerging out of flowers in association with relief carvings of marine shells that "denote the sea" (Taube 2010:217). The Warao people of the Orinoco Delta region (Venezuela) see the earth (*hobahi* = "surrounded by water") as a disk supported by an earth monster and surrounded by a ring of sea which is inhabited by "the 'Snake of Being,' a giant serpent" that "devours navigators who dare the sea" (Wilbert 1977:39; see also Wilbert 1993:10).

The Koksoagmyut (Inuit) of the Ungava Bay region of Quebec, northeast Canada, speak of the sky as a huge hard dome over the earth and sea with edges featuring high precipitous sides shelving either inward or outward to prevent any living thing from "going to the region beyond." The sky dome is cold where crystals of ice form and then fall as snow. Clouds are large bags of water carried by two old women, and rain is water that leaks from the bags as they run across the sky. Lightning is their torch and thunder their voices (Turner 1894:267).

For the Marind-anim of southeast Papua (Indonesia), one of the most important *dema* (spirt beings) is Geb, who, along with Sami, are "the first ancestors of the Marind" (van Baal 1966:209). Geb is associated with the beach and with the moon and the sun as the beach connects the place of sunrise and sunset (Geurtjens 1956:401; van Baal 1966:923–924). During the wet season, the sun descends into, and copulates with, the sea on the horizon. Spider-threads floating in air and hanging from coconut trees were said to be the sun's sperm, which blows in from the sea (van Baal 1966:213, 256). Geb is also associated with the Morning Star, which is sometimes called *etob ravos-anoem*, the "sea-inhaler" or "sea-absorber" as it sits close to the horizon above the sea (Geurtjens 1956:403; van Baal 1966:442, 463).

Figure 5. Sailors encountering the malevolent spiritual presence of the "hand of Satan" in the Atlantic Ocean (from Bassett 1885:Frontispiece, cropped).

Tahitians of Polynesia also held that the sun "sank every evening into the sea, and passed, during the night, by some submarine passage, from west to east, where it rose again from the sea in the morning" (Ellis 1832:170). Some peoples of the islands of Bora Bora or Maupiti (French Polynesia) located northwest of Tahiti said that they "had once heard the hissing occasioned by its [the sun] plunging into the ocean" (Ellis 1832:170).

Manus Islanders located 200 km north of the mainland coast of Papua New Guinea similarly hold that the sun sets into the sea. For example, the German missionary Josef Meier recorded that the setting of the sun literally translated to "the sun submerges [into the water]" (Meier 1906, cited in Hoeppe 2000:26). Götz Hoeppe (2000:26–27) adds that for the Manus, "the sun, moon, and stars rise out of the sea and set back into it, this further emphasizes the concept of sea and sky to be permeable to celestial objects." Yet this arrangement is seasonal, as the sun rises and sets over land (Manus Island) during most of the northwest wind (rainy) season (*ai*), and over the sea during most of the southeast wind (dry) season (*kup*). Interestingly, seasonal *ai* and *kup* winds are seen as responsible for seasonal movements of the sun (Hoeppe 2000:29–30). Similarly, the Milky Way was considered to be analogous to clouds in the sky to the extent that seasonal changes in star patterns in the Milky Way were attributed to wind (Hoeppe 2000:33). To the Manus, the sky, sun, moon, stars, clouds, and winds all shared the same elevation above the sea (Hoeppe 2000:25–26, 35).

Sea–Seabed Boundary

While modern scientific thought attributes the form of the ocean floor to plate tectonics and volcanic forces, for some early European scholars such as clergyman Thomas Burnet, the form of the sea with its rugged coastlines and seafloor was indirectly due to humans. In his *The Sacred Theory of the Earth*, Burnet (1719:1:182) described the oceans as "so deep, and hollow, and vast; so broken and confus'd, so every way deform'd and monstrous." Its twisted form, including treacherous rocks upon which ships founder, clearly was inconsistent with the original "Frame of the Earth" by divine design, but a "Ruin" through "great Violence" following the "Deluge" brought on by God to punish a corrupt humanity (Burnet 1719:1:179). For Burnet, the ocean was of an "immeasurable Depth" and "unsearchably deep" (1719:1:176, 178).

For most of human history, the areas of seabed greater than 20 m were directly unreachable due to the limitations of free diving. However, in the fifth century BCE, Herodotus in his *Histories* notes that mariners know they are a day's sailing from the mouth of the Nile River when they bring up mud at 11 fathoms (20 m) using a sounding line (Cunliffe 2017:68). In terms of oceans, Helen Rozwadowski (1996:16) points out that "until the last quarter of the eighteenth century, our [Western] understanding of the ocean's depths derived entirely from the imagination." In many respects the seabed was both literally and metamorphically unfathomable. The seabed beyond the continental shelf and descending down hundreds and even thousands of meters in oceanic expanses only became observable after the advent of crewed deep-sea submersibles in the second half of the twentieth century. Yet various mariners and fishers were aware that the sea was very deep and unreachable through technologies of deep-sea sounding. British and European mariners before the 1750s carried depth sounding lines up to 200 fathoms (366 m) in length (Rozwadowski 1996:38). During the nineteenth century, American whalers reported sperm whales plunging into the depths of the ocean with more than 1,000 fathoms (1,829 m) of rope attached (Rozwadowski 1996:52). In 1851 Captain Samuel Barron of the *John Adams* claimed to have sounded down to 5,500 fathoms (10,058

m) in the Atlantic Ocean while the following year Captain Henry Denham of HMS *Herald* claimed to have sounded down to 7,706 fathoms (14,093 m; Rozwadowski 1996:40, 2005:33).

Before European contact in the eighteenth century, Hawai'ian fishermen were aware that the deep sea extended over 200 m in depth given that some of their sea-bottom fishing hooks and sinkers and octopus lures were attached to strings up to 220 m long (Jokiel et al. 2019; Pfeffer 1995:50–51). Paul D'Arcy (2006:39) cites ethnographic recordings of Hawai'ian fish traps being set at depths of over 130 m and "long lines used for benthic species could reach down 1200 feet [365 m]." Brien Meilleur (2019:313, citing Kamakau 1976) adds that the Hawai'ian terms for deep-sea fishing areas included *kūkaula* (c. 150 m deep) and *pōhākialoa* (c. 370–730 m deep). The currently known deepest part of the ocean is named the Challenger Deep in the Mariana Trench in the Pacific at 10,984 m (Gardner et al. 2014).

Conclusion

Ethnographic and historical accounts from a wide range of maritime cultures surveyed in this chapter indicate that defining the edge of the sea is anything but straightforward. Although the edge of the sea is often discussed in terms of the sea–land boundary, for many maritime societies both past and present, records indicate that conceptualizing the edge of the sea also included the sea–sky, sea–horizon, and sea–seabed boundaries. Each of these boundaries is associated with liminality such that the sea can be conceived as a *poly-liminal* realm. As the following chapters reveal, it is the cosmological complexity of this poly-liminal realm that contributes to the high-level ritualization of mariners' life with the sea.

Many people think that defining the sea–land boundary is an unambiguous exercise. Yet coastal societies with intimate ecological knowledge know that even from a scientific and empirical standpoint, the sea–land boundary is blurred and rarely can be represented as a shoreline. One of the most challenging understandings of the sea–land boundary is provided by Aboriginal societies of northern Australia's Gulf of Carpentaria, where the sea is seen to extend what Western science would describe as 10–13 km "inland." Even though it is generally accepted that the sea is a place that "people cannot (yet) inhabit permanently" (Rozwadowski 2021:139), coastal communities who ontologically extend the sea–land boundary inland of the shoreline are living permanently in the sea and within a "terrestrial seascape" (see Chapter 5). Archaeologists who assume that peoples of the past conceived of the sea–land boundary as the beach or "shoreline" are revealing anthropological naivety. What emerges from the survey of maritime cultures in this chapter is a view that the statements about what defines the sea–land boundary of past societies needs to move away from the axiomatic to the analytical. How societies of the past defined and delineated the sea–land boundary should not be assumed but demonstrated; recognizing the arbitrariness of defining the beach or shoreline as the sea–land boundary is a major step forward. The following chapters illustrate how the "inland" extent of seascapes can be mapped by archaeologists using material culture.

3

Cosmological Beings of the Sea

This chapter explores information on a wide range of the sea beings that typically populate books on maritime mythologies and superstitions. The following account is not comprehensive but illustrative of the breadth and diversity of such beings within seas in selected parts of the world. My sampling of sea beings reveals that they tend to be ontologically unstable, and by extension liminal, entities that invariably represent the fusion of ontologically stable categories of life into new hybrid forms. For heuristic purposes, the following discussion of sea beings is divided into *anthropomorphic and zoomorphic sea gods, deities, and spirits* (sea gods and spirits predominantly of either human or animal form), *human-animal hybrids and transformers* (therianthropic sea beings predominantly of human form combined with animal features), and *animal-animal hybrids and sea monsters* (sea beings of animal form). These categories are sometimes blurred and overlapping, with some sea beings representing more than one category, especially those with the capacity for transformation. As will become evident, whereas sea gods and deities often have shrines and temples as focal points for rituals of veneration and propitiation, human hybrids and monstrous hybrids have few ritual associations. Details on rituals associated with engaging many of these sea gods, deities, and spirits to enhance success in voyaging, fishing, and hunting are presented in Chapters 6–10. The discussion at the end of the chapter explores ontological dimensions of animal-human and animal-animal hybrid beings as expressions of the land-sea dualism/divide and poly-liminality of the sea.

Anthropomorphic and Zoomorphic Sea Gods, Deities, and Spirits

The following discussion is illustrative of the breadth and diversity of such beings that fall within the broad category of gods, deities, and spirits within seas. A detailed global account of sea gods, deities, and spirits would be encyclopedic in scale and well beyond the confines of a single chapter. Yet the enormity of such a comprehensive task tells us that spiritual sea beings are a universal feature of maritime peoples across the globe. Anthropomorphic sea gods, deities, and spirits tend to fuse human form and emotions with cosmic and elemental powers. They are often associated with shrines and temples as focal points for human rituals of veneration and propitiation and tell us much about conceptualization and expression of the land-sea dualism discussed in the previous chapter.

Rituals associated with sea gods, deities, and spirits are associated either with utilizing their powers to create favorable conditions (e.g., weather) through propitiation, or eluding their wrath by avoiding practices that they may consider offensive (e.g., having a priest on board; Beck 1999:310–311). For the most part, sea gods and goddesses are of anthropomorphic form. In many cases, sea deities are hybrid anthropomorphic beings with human and some nonhuman (usually animal) body parts. In many instances, anthropomorphic deities have transformational qualities such that they can also temporarily assume the form of zoomorphic beings. The following survey reveals that marine deities and spirit beings of zoomorphic form are common in many cultural contexts.

The earliest well-documented record of a sea deity is Tiamat, mentioned in the Babylonian *Enūma Eliš* creation myth, which is detailed on a series of cuneiform script clay tablets dating to the twelfth century BCE excavated from Nineveh in northern Iraq. Tiamat is represented as a personification of the sea or as a primordial goddess of the sea who takes human form but also has a tail (Lambert 2007, 2013).

The Phoenicians of the coastal Near East (homeland), but with trade centers across various parts of the Mediterranean between 2,300 and 3,500 years ago, worshipped a sea deity equivalent to the Greek god Poseidon with an associated headland temple on the North African coast (Brody 1998:23–25, 59). Another Phoenician sea deity of unknown name is represented on coins as a winged horse with a serpent's tail for hindquarters (Brody 1998:25–26). Milqart (also Melkarth) was a "tutelary deity of Phoenician sailors" who provided protection on sea voyages, including "vanquishing sea monsters" (Brody 1998:33, 36). He had numerous temples dedicated in his honor (Brody 1998:58, 60; Semple 1927:357). All sea-related Phoenician (and earlier Canaanite) deities were important to mariners because of the "divine protection which they provided during a voyage" (Brody 1998:39). According to Brody (1998:22), none of these sea-related deities should be confused with Yamm (also Jamm or Yam) who was a personification of the sea in the Phoenician-Canaanite world (cf. Connery 2006:500–501).

Wadj-wer (the "great green") was the "god associated with fertility and the sea" for Ancient Egyptians (Morriss 2012:77). In the New Kingdom (3,100–3,500 years ago) papyrus text *The Book of Going Forth by Day* (aka *Book of the*

Dead), Wadj-wer is associated with the words "Sea is his name," suggesting a male gender (Morriss 2012:77). Yet representations of Wadj-wer show an "androgynous form with an emphasised breast and a belly indicative of pregnancy," indicating that they were "clearly associated with procreation and prosperity" (Hart 2005:162). Veronica Morriss (2012:77) notes that "Wadj-wer became a personification of the sea and various other bodies of water, including lakes and regions of the Nile." During the Old Kingdom (4,200–4,700 years ago), Wadj-wer "was the general term for the sea, but it could also refer to branches of the Nile as well as lakes in the Nile Delta and Fayoum" (Morriss 2012:77–78). In this sense, Ancient Egyptian cosmological conceptions of the sea overlapped with the lower (freshwater) reaches of the Nile River. During the Ptolemaic period (2,000–2,300 years ago), Wadj-wer unambiguously became the Egyptian term for the Mediterranean Sea (Morriss 2012:80).

Much diversity and complexity surround ancient Greek deities of the sea. This complexity not only involves the genealogical histories of the deities but also their eventful and epic lives. Oceanus/Okeanos was the primordial personification of the sea which surrounded the terrestrial world. He is often represented as a human with a fish tail instead of legs (Aston 2011:66). He married his sister Tethys (freshwater), and they had 3,000 sons and 3,000 sea nymph daughters known as Oceanids, whose main domain was the western ocean (Atlantic; Dixon-Kennedy 1998:223; Irby 2021:21). Personification of the sea is illustrated more generally by fifth-century-BCE philosopher Empedocles of Acragas in southern Sicily, who observed that the sea becomes saltier when heated by the sun and surmised that the "sea (*thalatta*) is the earth's sweat" (Irby 2021:26).

Pontos was a pre-Olympian sea god (personification of the primordial sea) who through union with his mother Gaia (also Ge; personification of primordial Earth) produced the sea god sons Phorcys and Nereus, both of whom are mentioned in Homer's *Odyssey* from the eighth century BCE (Glynn 1981:121). Phorcys's wife was Ceto, a sea goddess who was turned into a monster by Athene in revenge for intimacy with Poseidon. Early representations of Nereus from the sixth century BCE show him as a fish-tailed man (Glynn 1981). Nereus and his wife Oceanid Doris produced 50 or more sea nymph daughters known as Nereids. Nereids were minor sea deities of the Mediterranean with a friendly disposition toward mariners. Thetis, mother of Achilles, was chief of the Nereids and considered a sea goddess in her own right. Originating from the "depths of the sea" and residing in a submarine "silver-shining cave," her "shape-changing" (transformational) abilities are revealed by a range of incarnations such as human, seal, and cuttlefish (Aston 2009:84, 89–90, 96, 103, 2011:62–63). A Thetis cult, to which mariners may have turned to when in peril, was established at a number of locations in Greece, especially on the Pelion Peninsula (Aston 2009:85, 90, 2011:58, 60, 160).

The most famous and powerful Greek sea god was Poseidon, who was one of the 12 gods in the Greek pantheon on Mount Olympus but also had a submarine palace. He is mentioned in Homer's *Iliad* but his origins (probably not focused on the sea) appear to be much older. His parents were Kronos and his sister Rhea, and he was brother to Zeus (king of the gods and god of the heavens) and Hades (god of the underworld; Simon 2014:37). Poseidon was usually represented as a mature, bearded man holding a trident and was master of other sea deities such as Nereus and Proteus (Dixon-Kennedy 1998:259–261). Although primarily associated with the sea, Poseidon was also linked to the land, specifically agriculture, fertility, freshwater, earthquakes, horses, and bulls (Kokkinou 2014:60–62). In addition to numerous representations of Poseidon in the form of marble and bronze statues, paintings on ceramic vessels and tablets, and coins, he is also associated with numerous temples across the Ancient Aegean (Pevnick 2014). For example, during a fight between Athena and Poseidon for control of Attica (Athens), his trident struck the ground, from which saltwater began flowing, at the current location of the Erechtheion temple at the Acropolis (Hurwit 1999:31–32, 203–204). Located nearly 5 km inland of the sea, this flowing "seawater" is observable today in the form of a saltwater spring (Hurwit 1999; Marx and Gisler 2011). Although creation of a freshwater spring would have benefited the people of Athens, George Elderkin (1941:118–119) makes the point that producing a connection to the sea in the form of a saltwater spring reveals how religious symbolism trumped economic benefit. More broadly, a range of ancient texts point to the special purificatory powers of seawater in ancient Greece, including some sanctuaries where "it could be used for high level cleansings" (von Ehrenheim et al. 2019:21).

Earliest archaeological evidence for Poseidon worship comes from Mycenaean (1100–2000 BCE) sanctuaries on the Greek mainland (Kokkinou 2014:52). Numerous temples and sanctuaries (e.g., featuring only an altar) dedicated to the cults and dating from the tenth century BCE have been documented along the Aegean coasts of Greece and Türkiye, and the coast of Sicily, often on promontories jutting out into the sea (Kokkinou 2014; Paga and Miles 2016:689; Semple 1927). Perhaps the most famous example is the Temple of Poseidon at Cape Sounion located southeast of Athens, which features a Classical marble temple superimposed on a partly constructed Archaic limestone temple destroyed by the Persians, both constructed in the fifth century BCE (Paga and Miles 2016). That the location was an established Poseidon sanctuary before construction of the temples is attested to by archaeological recovery of votive offerings linked to Poseidon dating back to the seventh century BCE (Paga and Miles 2016:686; Theodoropoulou-Polychroniadis 2015:127).

Amphitrite, daughter of Nereus, became Poseidon's wife and as a result became goddess of the sea (Dixon-Kennedy 1998:260). Triton, son of Poseidon and Amphitrite, is sometimes represented with a human upper body and a fish-tailed lower body and had the ability to control waves. Attic vase representations of Triton date back to the sixth century BCE (Glynn 1981). Triton gave his name to a class of minor sea deities known as tritons who are often represented as fish-tailed humans (Vermeule 1979:188–189). Glaukos ("sea-green") was an ancient Greek sea deity who was a mortal fisherman who after eating a magical grass/herb from the shore dived into the sea, "acquiring both divinity and hybrid form" as a fish-tailed human or "merman" form (Aston 2011:163, 2014:367, 380). His transformation site at Anthedon in Boiotia (Greece) is also the location of his cult site, which was used by mariners and called Glaukou Pedêma, Glaukos's Leap (Aston 2011:76, 163). Emma Aston (2014:380) states: "His cult site is therefore a marker of his departure from the land and from the human state, and also, perched as it is on the margin of sea and land, reflects his mixed form, half man half fish, half marine half terrestrial."

The transformational capacity of numerous sea gods and deities is seen by some as a metaphor for the ever-changing qualities of the sea. For example, classicists tend to see "the extreme fluctuations of state to which these shape-changers are given accords with the persona of the sea: restless, in perpetual movement, taking no fixed form"; to which Aston (2011:160) adds that there is "a great deal of truth in this cliché" (see also Shepard 1940:95).

Proteus, son of Okeanos and Tethys, was an ancient sea deity ("Old Man of the Sea") who is also often represented as a bearded man of "merman" form with a fish tail instead of legs whose capacity to shapeshift has become proverbial (Aston 2011:57, 2014:366, 374–375; Brown 2003; Dixon-Kennedy 1998:263). No evidence of Mediterranean cult activity is associated with Proteus (Aston 2011:56). Eurynome was also an Oceanid (daughter of Okeanos and Tethys), a sea goddess who similarly took the form of a mermaid and whose main place of worship was at Arkadia (Aston 2011:65–67). Aston (2011:65) points out that "Eurynome is the only Greek female deity represented as a mermaid" (see also Shepard 1940:23). The mortals Melicertes and his mother Ino leaped into the sea and drowned off Corinth, whereupon they underwent divine transformation into the sea god Palaemon and sea goddess Leucothea, respectively. Leucothea was known to be "benevolent to sailors in distress" (Dixon-Kennedy 1998:191). Aphrodite was one of the 12 Olympian elite deities and goddess of beauty, love, and fertility. According to the Greek poet Hesiod in *Theogony* (700 BCE), Aphrodite was born from the foam of the sea, and for some this elevated her to the status of a sea deity (Dixon-Kennedy 1998:35). This foam was said to represent sperm associated with the penis of Ouranos, which was severed and thrown into the sea by his son Kronus (Andrews 1998:173). Aphrodite's association with the sea is also revealed by epithets such as "Euploia (of Good Sailing), Epilimenia (She at the Harbor), and Pontia (She of the Sea)" (Larson 2007:123).

Even though the Romans borrowed much of their sea cosmology from the Greeks, their sea deities were a poor shadow of the Greeks', due in large part to the fact that the Romans were much less of a seafaring people. For example, the Romans held Oceanus and Tethys as godly personifications and symbols of the sea. The Roman Oceanus was usually depicted as an old man with a long beard and horns in the shape of crab claws (Eraslan 2015). The most famous Roman sea god is Neptune, who was modeled on Poseidon. Numerous Roman mosaics depict Neptune, usually holding his trident, in his marine setting (e.g., Blake 1936:140, 142–143, 145, 148–149, 152, 161; Meiggs 1973:409–412). Triton, as Neptune's son, or at least generic tritons, are also represented in Roman mosaics, as are Nereids (e.g., Blake 1936:141–143, 145–149, 153–154, 161, 184). Castor and Polydeuces (to the Greeks) and Castor and Pollux (to the Romans) were twin brothers known as the Dioscuri and the sons of Zeus. Mariners left votive offerings to the Dioscuri "in fulfillment of their vows when they safely reached harbor" (Atkins 2009:42). The Greek historian Diodorus in 65 BCE and the Roman philosopher Pliny the Elder in the first century CE both noted that Mediterranean mariners associated the appearance of bright lights on a ship, usually at night and often within the mast and rigging (cf. St. Elmo's fire—see below), with the apotropaic presence of the Dioscuri (Carey 1963:29–31; Rich 2013:107). In the mid-sixteenth century, some English mariners continued to ascribe the lights to Castor and Pollux (Carey 1963:33).

Across Scandinavia, Norse mythology of the medieval period held that Rán was the goddess of the sea (Lindow 2001:258–259). In some texts, Rán had a net she used to capture mariners (Lindow 2001:258). In some instances, it is claimed that Rán "takes men into death for her personal [and sometimes 'erotic'] pleasure" (Quinn 2014:86, 88). Her submarine abode was said to be lined with glistening gold known as "flame of the sea," a possible reference to bioluminescent plankton (Guerber 1895:172). Rán's husband was Ægir, the "personification of the sea," who also took anthropomorphic form (Lindow 2001:48). Ægir is similarly considered a "sea-deity," whose name is also a common noun for the sea, and who was known to pull ships below the waves (Quinn 2014:74, 82). He is represented generally as "a gaunt old man, with long white beard and hair, his clawlike fingers ever clutching convulsively" (Guerber 1895:171).

Finnish mythology recorded in the nineteenth century includes reference to Ahto, god of the sea and king of the fishes, who sails around in a boat of water lilies and is represented as an old man with a seaweed beard and a mantle of sea foam. He lives in a castle on the seabed and is very rich owing to his accumulation of treasures from shipwrecks (Bonser 1928:347). For various communities of Ireland, Scotland, and England, Manannán was a sea deity who traveled around in a boat named Scuabtuinne ("Wave Sweeper"). Manannán's father Lir (or Llyr in Welsh mythology) was also a sea deity or perhaps more a personification of the sea (Lurker 2004:112, 118).

It was popularly known among mariners of the Low Countries of northwestern Europe (e.g., Belgium, Germany, The Netherlands) that they would be accompanied by the Klabautermann while sailing the Baltic and North Seas (Buss 1973; Kirby and Hinkkanen 2000:48–49). The Klabautermann were ship spirits often of small human form, smoking a pipe and wearing a red jacket or gray clothes (Buss 1973:41, 44–46). Mariners were known to see Klabautermann on board their vessels, but in many cases their presence on board was known only through "knocking sounds in the hold or walls of the vessel" (Buss 1973:24). They were generally seen to be morally righteous (with Christian values), benevolent guardians of ships, and known to undertake ship repairs at night and to rescue drowning mariners (Buss 1973:49–50, 56, 61–62). Klabautermann were usually invisible, and their "appearance generally signals impending danger, destruction, and even death" (Buss 1973:52). In the early nineteenth century, a Frisian sea captain noted that it was often the case that a dining place for the Klabautermann would be set at the captain's cabin, "with the captain offering the choicest meats and drink to his guest" (Kirby and Hinkkanen 2000:48; see also Buss 1973:54). Experiences of Klabautermann decreased with the introduction of metal ships (Buss 1973:2).

European Christian mariners have a wide range of saints who have the power to provide protection during voyages. In most cases these saints are not deities of the sea per se but holy figures who have privileged proximity to God and the potential capacity, through propitiation, to ensure favorable sailing conditions. In rare cases, maritime saints would manifest themselves during voyages. For example, from at least the Middle Ages, many European mariners associated the appearance of (electrical) lights among the masts and rigging with St. Elmo, who was regarded as their protective patron saint. In the fifteenth century, Columbus and his crew associated these glowing lights with the body of St. Elmo and saw it as foreshadowing success (Bassett 1885:304). In the early sixteenth century, Magellan's crew similarly saw bright lights on the mast, which they associated with St. Anselme (Carey 1963:32). However, Italian mariners in the fifteenth and sixteenth centuries believed that these lights were a "luminous emanation from the body of Christ" (Bassett 1885:304). Other Italian mariners ascribe the lights to the Fires of St. Nicholas (Bassett 1885:79). Portuguese,

British, German, and American mariners associate St. Elmo's lights with fine weather, while for other mariners the lights provide warning of an impending storm (Rappoport 1928:59–60).

Olokun is god of the sea for the Ibo, Bini (Benin), and Yoruba peoples of Nigeria in West Africa. In the Benin Kingdom, Olokun is also associated with the Ethiope (Olokun) River and is "the most widely worshipped deity in the Bini pantheon and is considered the bringer of health, wealth, and fertility" (Ben-Amos 1976:251). Because the souls of the dead and the new born originate from across the sea, Olokun is considered the "bringer of children" (Ben-Amos 1973:28). Olokun lives in a palace of cowrie shells on the seabed with his wives and children, and his two "playmates"—the mudfish and the python (Ben-Amos 1973:28; Rosen 1989:44). Mud shrines to Olokun represent his underwater palace and feature effigies of his wives, children, and chiefs, along with strings of cowries representing his wealth, and other objects of wealth such as cooking pots and European dishes (Ben-Amos 1973:31; Rosen 1989:44). Among Afro-American (enslaved-Yoruba-descended) communities of northeast Brazil, the Nigerian river god Yemanjá has become the god of the sea with associated altar offerings including a range of marine shells, including cowries (*Cypraea* sp.; Alves et al. 2012:Table 1; see also Léo Neto et al. 2012). Agbe-Naete is the deity of the sea for the Fon people of southeast Benin (Ikenga-Metuh 1982:16).

According to Gwen Benwell and Arthur Waugh (1961:266), "Belief in spirits associated with the sea . . . is deep-rooted in many West African tribes." This is most obvious along the Bight of Benin, where the "ancient cult of sea worship" was "widespread" in the countries of Ghana, Benin, and Nigeria (Parés 2005:76). In addition to Christian and Islamic beliefs, Indigenous Ghanaian societies acknowledge a supreme god and a series of lesser gods (e.g., sea deities) who interact with people (Salm and Falola 2002:39–40). In Ga society, for example, Nai is the sea god, who is linked to fishing prosperity (Salm and Falola 2002:40), while in other Ghanaian coastal communities Nana Bosompo is god of the sea (Boaten 1998:47). The Dangme fishers of coastal Ghana contact the sea god Digble through a priest, who becomes "possessed" by the sea god and stands on the altar of the deity (Quarcoopome 1991, 1994:342, 348–349, 355). In the Cape Coast region of Ghana is found Tahbin, "god of the sea," and his wife Tahbi-yin, who takes the form of a mermaid (Benwell and Waugh 1961:266). Both sea beings are feared, as they take lives by drowning (Benwell and Waugh 1961:266).

A number of sea gods have been documented for India. For example, the Vādas of the central east coast of India hold Orusandiamma as the "chief sea goddess." Orusandiamma constantly roams the sea at night and propitiatory offerings are made to her at shoreline shrines to ensure that she does not reap havoc upon fishing vessels (Thurston and Rangachari 1909:7[2]:261–262). Koli fishers of Mumbai of northwest India venerate Dariyadev, a "omnipresent and omnipotent" sea god who is gendered male (Kesarkar-Gavankar and Vicziany 2023:113). Dariyadev personifies the sea, is "formless," and possesses no image and no temples or shrines, with the open sea and shoreline as places of ritual propitiation (Kesarkar-Gavankar and Vicziany 2023:114, 116). More broadly, old Indian Hindu Puranas texts make references to Varuna, god of the sea (Przyluski 1931; Williams 2003:294). In the 1500s numerous Hindu temples around Bali in Indonesia were dedicated to Baruna/Varuna (Andaya 2017:361).

In China, Tianhou (Empress of Heaven, popularly known as Mazu) is a famous goddess of the sea (and procreation) and one of the country's best-known and most revered deities (Irwin 1990:62–64; Ruitenbeek 1999). She is recognized by the Taoist and Buddhist religions and protects devotees during voyages and responds to those in distress. Tianhou was originally a woman from the island of Meizhou off the southeast coast of China who fell into a trance and saved three of her mariner brothers from drowning in the late tenth century. Even after her death she continued to rescue sailors, and by the thirteenth century temples in her honor could be found "in all the maritime provinces of coastal China" (Irwin 1990:63). During the Ming dynasty (fourteenth to seventeenth centuries CE) the cult crossed to Japan, and by the eighteenth century a temple in her honor was operating in Sulawesi, Indonesia. Today, temples dedicated to Tianhou can be found all over the world (e.g., Wak Hai Cheng Bio temple in Singapore—Yeo 2021). Painted and woodblock representations of Tianhou dating back to the eighteenth century show her as an anthropomorphic woman in robes who often appears seated or standing upon a cloud above ships in peril (Ruitenbeek 1999).

Various Chinese myths describe gods for different seas. For example, a narrative describing the divine mandate of King Wu (founder of the Zhou dynasty of the eleventh century BCE) to go to war against the Shang includes reference to meeting the gods of the four seas: The "God of the South Sea is called Chu Yung, the God of the East Sea is called Kou Mang, the God of the North Sea is called Hsuan Ming, and the God of the West Sea is called Ju Shou" (Birrell 1993:263).

In Japan the two main sea deities are Owatatsumi-no-kami (also Watatsumi) and Ryūjin (Ashkenazi 2003:103). Owatatsumi-no-kami is considered the major deity (kami) of the sea (wata) in Shinto mythology. His principal form is a dragon, and he lives in a palace on the seabed and is considered "master of fishes" and "owner" of the jewels that control the tides. Numerous shrines dedicated to the worship of Owatatsumi-no-kami occur across Japan, including in the cities of Osaka, Kobe, and Kitakyushu (Ashkenazi 2003:180, 233). Ryūjin is "lord of the serpents" and according to some lives in a palace in the sea. Although generally seen to take the form of a "giant serpent," he also has the transformational capacity to take human form. He carries the jewels that control the tides, and rough seas are caused by his anger (Ashkenazi 2003:240; Okada 1982:23, 39, 84; Piggott 1969:14–15). Benzaiten (aka Benten) is a sea goddess who is also associated with luck, wealth, romantic happiness, literature, and music. She is often shown with eight arms and accompanied by a "sea serpent or dragon." Although many shrines dedicated in her honor are located "either by the sea or on islands," the most famous is the "floating" red shrine (*torii*) on the northwest coast of Itsukushima Island in Hiroshima Bay (Ashkenazi 2003:126; Piggott 1969:59, 122, 130–133).

In northern Japan, the Ainu have a series of sea deities. For example, Repun-riri-kata inao uk kamui (or simply Repun Kamui) is "the god upon the waves of the sea who receives *inao* [offerings]" and "is the very greatest and most highly esteemed of all the gods of the sea" (Batchelor 1901:533). Presenting himself to people in the form of a large whale, "he is very frequently worshipped by those Ainu who dwell upon the sea-coast" in relation to successful fishing and good weather (Batchelor 1901:533; see also Ashkenazi 2003:187, 238). Rep-un-kontukai ("the servant in the sea") is an intermediary between Repun-riri-kata inao uk kamui and people. He takes the form of a marine turtle. He can be "caught by the fishermen and eaten, but his head is dried, and kept in the hut for worship. Before going to fish, the men themselves, or one of their relatives who happens to possess one, take it from its resting-place, worship it, and offer it *inao*" (Batchelor 1901:533–534). The second most important deity is Kaipe-chupka un guru ("the person who resides in the eastern surf"), whose form is assumed to be a fish (Batchelor 1901:534). Chiwash-ekot-mat ("the female possessor of the places where the fresh and salt waters mingle") receives *inao* in relation to her "duty to watch at the mouths of rivers, and allow the fish, particularly the spring and autumn salmon, to go in and out" (Batchelor 1901:537–538).

The Ainu also know of sea "demons" who possess powers to negatively impact people (Batchelor 1901:540–544). For example, Konoto-ran-guru ("he who descends upon the sea") is thought to take the form of a large fish and is known to cause storms and shipwrecks (Batchelor 1901:540). Kaipokun guru ("the person who resides under the surf") has an "evil disposition" and is known to "swamp the boats as they come to shore." In terms of control, "Any fish caught near his domains unfit for human food are thrown to him to appease his wrath and seek his good will" (Batchelor 1901:543). Otapatche guru ("the person who makes the sand fly") resides "upon the sand close by the edge of the sea, and is supposed to rule over the shore as far up as the waves break and roll" and owns all dead fish washed up on the shore (Batchelor 1901:543). For the most part, *inao* are not made to Ainu sea demons.

In Island Southeast Asia, Nyai Loro Kidul (also Nyai Lara Kidul and Nyai Roro Kidul) is the spirit queen or goddess of the sea south of Java for the peoples of Java in Indonesia (Jordaan 1984). She lives in a palace on the seabed and employs spirits who reside in sea caves (Knappert 1992:210–211). Although she takes the form of a mermaid, her power and influence extend well beyond those normally attributed to mermaids. Some fishing villages in Java hold ceremonies to appease Nyai Loro Kidul through gifts of food, fabrics, and cosmetics. These ceremonies are also about propitiating good catches of fish and shellfish, good weather, and calm seas (see Jordaan 1984:100, 104; Knappert 1992:211). Today, Javanese people make offerings to Nyai Loro Kidul before making contact with the sea to avoid her wrath (Resink 1997:316).

The Orang Laut sea peoples of the Lingga archipelago in western Indonesia assert that Raja Hantu Laut (King Sea Spirit) "reigns over the entire maritime world," along with a Sea Mother Spirit who is "'Mother' to all things," and *anak buah* (follower) sea spirits who are sometimes referred to as *anak hantu laut* (child sea spirits; Chou 2003:62). Cynthia Chou (2003:62) notes further that "as the sea spirits are seen as owning and controlling everything in the maritime world, the Orang Laut believe the relation between the maritime world and the human world must be mediated through an exchange with the spirits."

In the Mettriralma reef complex in eastern Indonesia is a reef named To-ronlawna, which is associated with an old woman who local people consider to be "very evil," especially during a full moon (Pannell 2007:83). Watlawna, another location in the Mettriralma reef complex, is associated with witch- or sorcerer-like beings who on full moons travel across the lagoon to have "bestial sex" with the old woman at Toronlawna (Pannell 2007:83). Local people avoid these two reefs during full moons because of the associated danger "as it is possible for the voracious sexual desires of the beings to be turned upon any humans encountered" (Pannell 2007:83).

The Bajau sea peoples of southeast Sulawesi in central Indonesia have in-corporated their Indigenous beliefs with Islam and hold that the "sea is the home of [seven] mbo madilao (the [guardian] ancestors of the sea), who are believed to be descended from the prophets (nabbi)" (Stacey 2007:31). As one Bajau fisherman explained: "Mbo madilao have control of the universe of the sea and all the creatures in it for Bajo [Bajau] people, for it is their place. Mbo madilao are like the rulers of the sea. . . . Mbo madilao live wherever there is sea, and wherever Bajo people search for a living, even if outside the country of Indonesia, they will be accompanied by mbo madilao" (quoted in Stacey 2007:32–33).

In Melanesia, Thomas Williams (1858:89) recorded that Fijian "sailors are very superstitious." He noted that "certain parts of the ocean, through fear of the spirits of the deep, they pass over in silence, with uncovered heads, and careful that no fragment of food or part of their dress shall fall into the water." More specifically, the Fijian sea god Dakuwaqa took the form of a shark. D'Arcy (2006:42) notes that "Dakuwaqa had a history of fierce retribution against seafarers who did not respect him, but had rescued his worshippers from trouble at sea on a number of occasions."

Solomon Islanders from the island of Makira (San Cristóbal) refer to sea spirits as *adaro* (Codrington 1891:196–197; Fox 1924:124–137; Scott 2013:67–68), and specifically as *adaro ni matawa* (*adaro* = spirits, *matawa* = open sea; Fox 1924:124; Ivens 1927:199–200; cf. *ataro*—Fox and Drew 1915:174–178; *akalo*—Codrington 1891:260; Ivens 1927:199–200). Peoples of Maramasike and Ulawa to the immediate north consider Makira "the home of the Sea Spirits" (Ivens 1927:199–200). *Adaro* are of anthropomorphic form with a fish head and various types of fish (e.g., skipjacks, garfish, flying fish) emanating from their elbows, knees, shoulders, waist, buttocks, and feet (Fox 1924:125–128; Ivens 1927:200; Figure 6). They "move in waterspouts, and the rainbow is their path" (Fox 1924:124; see also Ivens 1927:200). Ngorieru/Ngoriaru is the "chief" of the *adaro* and has his home near Cape Keibeck on the north coast of Makira. Mariners voyaging in canoes past the cape put away their ornaments, talk in hushed tones, and dip their paddles gently into the water in the hope that they do not disturb Ngorieru/Ngoriaru and thus avoid being shot by his giant garfish (*mwanole*) used as arrows (Fox 1924:124; Ivens 1927:200–201). Sea spirits are "malevolent beings" and are known to "shoot" people fishing in canoes or from the shore (Fox 1924:124; Ivens 1927:203). The wound is left in the nape of the neck or just below the chest and unconsciousness soon follows. Flying fox teeth are used as an antidote. In some places fish were never cooked or eaten on the beach for fear of attack by sea spirits (Ivens 1927:203). Offerings in the form of fish ("raw or burnt in sacrifice") placed into the sea or on a special altar are made to appease sea spirits (Ivens 1927:203; see also Codrington 1891:259).

For the Marind-anim of the southeast corner of western New Guinea (Indonesian Papua), the "sea is a *dema*" with the "common name" of *etob* and the "mythical name" of Yorma (van Baal 1966:180). More broadly, *dema* are spirit beings from a mythical creative era who "as personifications of the inner meaning and intention of the world . . . are the personifications of its glory and beauty as well as of its wilfulness" (van Baal 1966:933). The father of Yorma is Desse (Depth) and his mother is Dawena (Groundwater; van Baal 1966:193, 381). Yorma is known for "lashing the coast with his mighty waves" and "acts of violence, such as washing away houses and men by means of his big waves" (van Baal 1966:180, 343). His headgear fluttering in the wind is the foam on the crests of waves, and his drumming is the roaring of the waves (van Baal 1966:383).

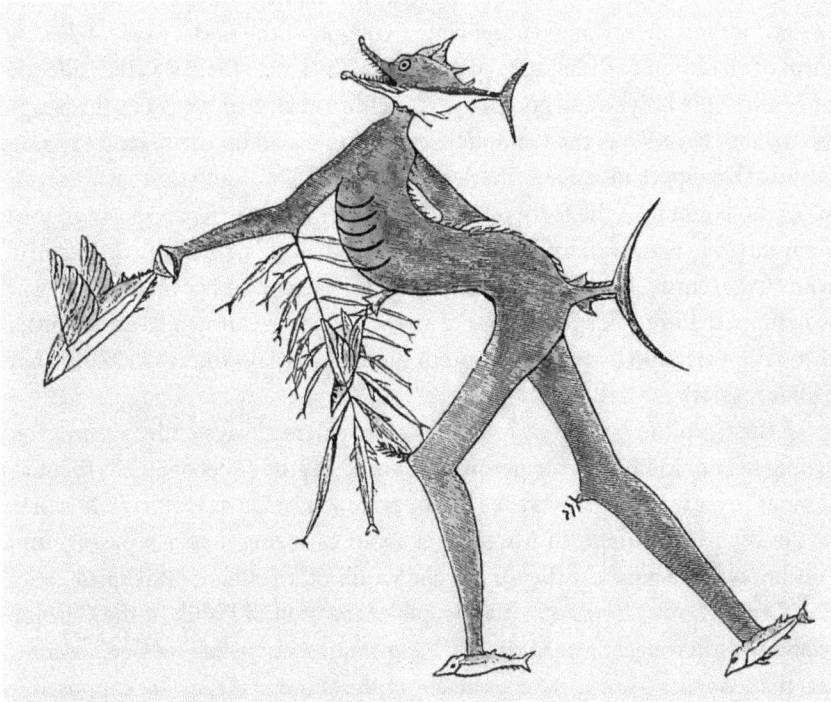

Figure 6. Sea spirit (*adaro ni matawa*), drawn by a young man from Makira (San Cristóbal), Solomon Islands (from Codrington 1891:xiv, 259, 329; see also Fox 1924:124; Fox and Drew 1915:174–175).

Seawater was associated with *nakari dema*, which were "female mythical beings, the companions of the more important male *dema*" (van Baal 1966:188). Waves were the *nakari* of Yorma, with two *nakari* called Karai (Turbid) and Mo (Clear; i.e., "qualities of seawater"; van Baal 1966:189, 383).

In Polynesia the Māori of Aotearoa/New Zealand's North Island see the "personified form of ocean" as associated with different female deities depending on cultural group (Reed 1967:397). In the Hawke's Bay region, she is Hine-moana (Ocean Woman), and she and her husband Kiwa, who is often considered principal guardian of the sea, which is known as Te Moana-nui-a-kiwa (the great ocean of Kiwa), watch over different types of fish, shellfish, octopus, and seaweed, which are their progeny (Orbell 1996:86, 129; Reed 1967:71, 397). In the Bay of Plenty region, she is Wai-nui (Great Waters), while in the Gisborne region she is Moana-nui (Great Ocean; Orbell 1996:129, 182; Reed 1967:397).

Many Hawai'ian gods take the form of marine animals, especially sharks, and even limpet and cowrie shells (Beckwith 1917:506). Joseph Emerson (quoted in Beckwith 1917:512–514) lists 41 "well-known" named shark gods for Hawai'i. In another instance, Kanaloa, the Hawai'ian god of the underworld, takes the form of an octopus (Knappert 1992:147). In Tahiti, the whale was the "Shadow of Ta'aroa," the Polynesian god of the sea (Hilmi et al. 2016:177). For the people of Kiribati, Na Kika is the Octopus-God, who pushed up the seabed to create islands (Knappert 1992:198). Shark gods include Tini Rau (southern Polynesia), who could take the form of either a man or a shark (Knappert 1992:300); Kamohoali'i (Hawai'i); and Tumuitearetoka (Cook Islands), an "evil spirit" who "fed exclusively on human flesh" (Gill 1876a:225). In Hawai'i, people who worshipped and took special care of shark gods were known to be rewarded through protection by the shark god in times of peril on the sea (Titcomb and Pukui 1952:35).

In the Caroline Islands of Micronesia, mariners always endeavor to avoid sailing near to Maihun, a dangerous reef known as the "Reef of Spirits that Eats Canoes" over which waves break (Knappert 1992:174; Lewis 1978:137). Mariners of the island of Fananu in Micronesia avoid canoeing across a passage in a reef known as Lauis lest they incur the wrath of a resident "evil spirit called Sou-Fana" (D'Arcy 2006:47). The people of the atoll of Ifaluk in the Caroline Islands of Micronesia would ritually hang small sections of "blessed" coconut leaf plaited mats from "branches all about the shore" as "they are supposed to keep evil sea-spirits from landing" (Burrows and Spiro 1953:48; see also D'Arcy 2006:49).

Australian Aboriginal cosmologies tend not to feature marine gods and deities but spiritual entities associated with Dreaming creation narratives, imbued with fecundity and spiritual renewal of plants and animals and continuity of elemental forces. Perhaps the best-known and most widespread spiritual being of the Australian Indigenous marine realm is the Rainbow Serpent (see below).

Most references to Indigenous sea deities in North America are from Canada with few recordings known for the coastal United States. In terms of the United States, Paumpágussit was a "sea-god" among Algonquian peoples in the mid-seventeenth century in what is today Rhode Island (Shoemaker 2014:26–27). First Nations coastal peoples of the Northwest Coast of Canada know of an "undersea world" of natural and supernatural creatures and spirit beings, which are considered "coinhabitants" of the sea with humans (Shearar 2000:31–32). The chief of the undersea world is Kumugwe' (the "Rich One") and Taangghwanlaana (the "One in the Sea") in Kwakwaka'wakw and Haida cosmologies, respectively (Shearar 2000:51, 62, 65–66, 103, 109). Taangghwanlaana is associated with Sea Frog, who holds the secrets of wealth and transformation (Shearar 2000:93). Kumugwe' is associated with large rising tides, whirlpools, and numerous sea creatures such as sculpin, octopus, killer whale, and loon, and lives in a seabed house with live sea lions as house posts and guards (Shearar 2000:65, 94). Some say Kumugwe' takes the form of a giant octopus, and wooden mask representations of Kumugwe' sometimes have octopus-like tentacles, in addition to an anthropomorphic face with large features, and gill slit, fish scale, and fish fin motifs in some cases (Shearar 2000:65–66). Some sea spirit beings take a more human form, such as Pugwís of the Kwakwaka'wakw, albeit with a fish-like face (Shearar 2000:85). Other sea beings take on a more obvious hybrid form, such as Sea Bear, who has the head of a bear and the fins and tale of a whale (Shearar 2000:93). According to Cheryl Shearar (2000:81), "Gifts and offerings to supernatural entities of the undersea world are commonly offered from the blade of a paddle." In other contexts, shamans and chiefs had the capacity to undertake spiritual journeys to the seabed villages of the Salmon People to obtain special knowledge and power to enable survival and success of their own villages (Shearar 2000:92).

The existence of a "sea goddess" (or "sea spirit" or "the sea woman") is known among Inuit peoples across the Arctic of North America. She is broadly referred to as Sedna and is considered the creator and controller of many marine animals, especially whales, seals (including walrus), and fish (Laugrand and Oosten 2008, 2013:432; Sabo and Sabo 1985; Swinton 1985). Sedna was feared among many Inuit communities, and her potential wrath was kept in check through strict adherence to taboos and appeasement through respectful behavior toward marine animals, especially seals. As the Iglulik Inuit related to Knud Rasmussen (1929:56), "We fear Takánakapsâluk [cf. Sedna], the great woman down at the bottom of the sea, that rules over all the beasts of the sea."

Nelda Swinton (1985:23) identified 36 names for Sedna used by Inuit groups across the Arctic (see also Laugrand and Oosten 2008:20–24). For example, the Copper Inuit of northwest Canada refer to the "sea goddess" Arnapkap-faaluk ("the big, bad woman"; Damas 1984:407). The Netsilik Inuit of northern Canada know of Nuliayuk, a "goddess" who lives in the depths of the sea and is the mother of all sea and land animals (Balikci 1984:425). Nerchevik is a sea goddess and presides over seals according to the Inuit of the Labrador coast of northeast Canada (Taylor 1984:520). Greenlanders use shamans to contact the Sea Woman, who lives on the bottom of the sea and controls all sea animals and would withhold these animals if offended (Kleivan 1984:619; Petersen 1984:632–634; Sonne 1986:201, 206). In East Greenland she was referred to as Immap ukuua, "mother of the sea" (Petersen 1984:632). Among the Inuit of Arctic central Canada, Sedna is "believed to live in a lower world, in a house built of stone and whale-ribs" (Boas 1901:119).

Human-Animal Hybrids and Transformers

Human-animal sea beings combine human and animal ontological categories. They can take therianthropic form, such that they are part human and part animal, and/or transformational form, such that they shapeshift between human and animal forms or between hybrid human-animal and human forms. Their therianthropic/transformer status is linked directly with the capacity to move between states and transgress the animal-human and sea–land boundary. In this sense, hybrid/transformer sea humans are liminal agents. Some animal-to-human or human-to-animal transformations took place in the primordial past, some take place in the present and are reversible, while others take place after death. The following digest illustrates the range of such beings under the broad labels of seal people, dolphin and porpoise people, whale people, dugong people, shark people, turtle people, and fish people (mermaids and mermen). The transformer/hybrid status of these beings gives rise to fundamental ontological (and by extension epistemological and existential) questions such as What is a whale? What is a seal? and What is a human?

Seal People

In parts of northern Europe and Britain, seals were known to be descended from drowned humans (Black and Thomas 1903:170–193; Clodd 1895; Einarsson 1990; MacGregor 1937:97; Puhvel 1963; Thomson 1996:191). The twelfth-century Norwegian text *Konungs skuggsjá* (King's Mirror) mentions *náselr* (literally "corpse seal") which, according to Ian Whitaker (1986:7, 11), is possibly a reference to the "common seal" but more importantly a reference to the capacity of the seal to assume human form. In Scotland these seal people are popularly known as selkies and were limited to larger seal species (Dennison 1893: 172).

Across Iceland, Scandinavia, and the Baltic states, at least during the eighteenth to twentieth centuries, seals were seen as the reincarnated spirits of the pharaoh of Egypt and his army who drowned in the Red Sea in the wake of the exodus of Moses and the Israelites (Davidsson 1900:314; Puhvel 1963; Willson 2016:66). Evidence for this transformation includes the "resemblance between the bone of a seal and those of a man" and the fact that they have "human figures, natures, and qualities all complete, concealed beneath their coats of seal-skin" (Davidsson 1900:314). Other telltale signs that "seals were the people o' the sea" include their humanlike eyes, ability to weep and shed tears, and vocalizations reminiscent of crying babies (Thomson 1996:154). Seals also have the capacity to operate in the sea and on land, and this "duality" helped draw people to seals (Sanderson 1996:vii). Seals were known on occasion to come ashore and remove

Figure 7. Late nineteenth-century photo of Baubi (Barbara) Urquhart (1814–1893), Shetland Islands of Scotland, the great-great-granddaughter of a selkie (seal-woman) (Bell 2025). Photograph by Rev. Charles Acland (Bell 2025). Glass lantern slide used by Alfred C. Haddon in university lectures and public presentations (Clodd 1895; Courtesy: Museum of Archaeology and Anthropology, Cambridge University, LS.124504.TC1).

their skins to assume human form and lifestyles for short or long periods. Male and female selkies were known to have had sex with humans, to have produced offspring, and even to have married (Darwin 2015; Dennison 1893; Einarsson 1990:37; Powell and Magnusson 1866:xliv; Thomson 1996).

Stories of men marrying seal women and producing children are known from many places, including Norway, Sweden, Denmark, Scotland, and Ireland (Clodd 1895; Darwin 2015:123–124; Figure 7). For example, Clan MacCodrum of the Outer Hebrides of Scotland claim descent from the union of a female selkie and a fisherman. This heredity is signified by MacCodrum descendants' possessing hands resembling flippers due to horny growths between the fingers (Silver 1987:292; Thomson 1996:147–152, 165–171; see also Le Couteur 2015:72–75). In many regions, descendants of seal women also possess special skills in fishing, swimming, and navigation (Darwin 2015:125, 136). Little is recorded concerning ritual engagements between humans and selkies.

Beyond northern Europe and Britain, seal people are little known. A rare exception is the Netsilik Inuit of Canada who know of *to.tale.t*, who are said to be "seal-men" and "spirits that resemble both humans and seals" (Rasmussen 1931:247). Although their origin is unknown, one story relates how the first *to.tale.t* started life as a human boy who developed extraordinary skills at swimming in the sea and capturing seals through holes in the ice (Rasmussen 1931:247–248).

Seals are known to be transformed humans in the Aleutian Islands of south-west Alaska (Black 1998:131). Such transformation may also underpin the Aleut (Unangax̂) conceptualization of sealskin-covered kayaks as male and female forms (distinguished by the shape of the prow). These kayaks "demanded sexual caresses, or even intercourse, from the hunter" (Black 1998:131). The transfor-mational power of seal skins is revealed by an Unangax̂ mythological narrative whereby a number of brothers, after being lured to sea and transformed into sea lions, return home with male and female sea lion skins, which are worn by people who become sea lions and have sea lion children (Black 1998:131). In this sense, most seal people are not physical hybrids, as they morphologically manifest as either seal or human, but spiritual hybrids with the capacity for physical transformation.

Dolphin and Porpoise People

D'Arcy (2006:45) notes that "stories of humans mating with dolphins and por-poises are common throughout Micronesia." Families within clans descended from such unions "refrained from killing or eating" dolphins or porpoises and "often had porpoise tattoo designs on their bodies" (D'Arcy 2006:45). Similar accounts of people descended from the union of human males and women who transformed from dolphins or porpoises are known from the Micro-nesian islands of Yap (D'Arcy 2006:45), Ulithi (Lessa 1961:38–40), Lamotrek (Alkire 1968:284), and the Gilberts (Luomala 1977). In the case of the Gilbert Islanders, "porpoises" are known to live in a village in a section of the sea that is "dry land," known as Mone, "where they look, behave, and live like human beings. By removing their human clothing they assume porpoise shape to swim through the ocean above them" (Luomala 1977:206). In some cases, it is known that drowned Gilbert Islanders transformed into porpoises or dolphins, but only women are known in rare cases to transform back into humans "to live permanently on earth" (Luomala 1977:208).

On the Northwest Coast of western Canada, Killer Whale (orca) clan people are capable of leaving their villages on the seabed and to live as giant humans on the land after they remove their black and white skins (Shearar 2000:63). Furthermore, "Killer Whales are thought to be the reincarnations of great chiefs: when a great chief dies, a Killer Whale customarily comes close to shore to take the chief's spirit" (Shearar 2000:63).

In the mid-nineteenth century, Oswald Brierly recorded that Aboriginal people of Twofold Bay, south coast of New South Wales (Australia), knew orcas to be "the reincarnate spirits of their own departed ancestors—and so firm is their belief that they go so far as to particularise and identify certain individual killer [orca] spirits" (quoted in Clode 2002:157; see also Mead 1992:140). Indeed, local non-Indigenous residents noted that "it was a remarkable coincidence that when one of the local Aboriginal people died a new killer [orca] appeared in the bay shortly after" (Clode 2002:157).

Whale People

In northwest Scotland it was known that witches could shapeshift into whales. In one story, fishermen from Vaternish on the Isle of Skye were having trouble with a whale that kept running into their fishing nets, damaging the nets and allowing the catch to escape. Frustrated, the fishermen successfully killed the whale using a three-pronged potato fork. The next day, a woman in their village was in agony and finally died. Inspection of her body revealed "three ugly wounds" which were seen to indicate that the whale was indeed a witch (MacCulloch 1905:248).

On the Northwest Coast of North America, the Nuu-chah-nulth know that the "human spirit of the whale resides in the area around the dorsal fin . . . [and] stories tell of this spirit being emerging from the whale to come on land and interact with humans, returning to his whale canoe when leaving" (McMillan 2019:317). More broadly, the Nuu-chah-nulth speak of a primordial past "when animals were human beings, to be later transformed into the creatures we know, and the tribes of men had not yet settled in their historic places nor started upon their appointed tasks" (Sapir 1959:106).

Dugong People

The Bardi Aboriginal people of the coast of North West Australia know that "dugongs were once human and ritual songs and stories corroborate this belief" (Green 1988:24). This is one of the reasons that considerable ritual (including taboos) is involved in the hunting, butchering, and consuming of dugongs (Green 1988:24). On the south coast of Papua New Guinea opposite Torres Strait, Gunnar Landtman (1927:293) recorded a story detailing how Kiwai raiders killed men on Daru Island, some of whom transformed into "the shape of dugongs, but with human heads." This transformation was an example of a broader cosmology where "spirits of the dead . . . frequently appear in the shape of animals" (Landtman 1927:441). Across the adjacent islands of Torres Strait, people "when in the state of dying" will often embody their totem and physically move as their totem would move when dying (Laade 1969:34). In the case of members of the dugong totemic clan, the dying person will move as a swimming dugong (McNiven 2013a:111). These "dying movements," known as *lanog digili* by the people of Mer in eastern Torres Strait, are similarly undertaken by members of the shark, whale, and turtle clans (Laade 1969: 34).

The people of Makira (San Cristóbal) in the Solomon Islands attribute the origin of dugongs to a woman. Charles Elliot Fox (1924:272) recorded the following story: "A woman once went out to get sea water, and putting the cup on her head she bent down to wash her hands. Her *mwari'i*, husband's brother, came down to the shore and poked her in the thigh with his comb. She was so ashamed that she dived down and became a dugong (*haihu*), and from her all dugong derive their origin."

For the Lio people of the island of Flores in eastern Indonesia, "myth tells how the first dugong was a human female who, through continuous immersion in the waters of the sea, was transformed into a creature with the lower body of a fish" while maintaining the upper body appearance of a human, specifically a female human, in terms of humanlike nipples, breasts, and genitalia (Forth 2020:57). Another version of the myth from the Sikkanese region to the east of Lio notes that the woman gave birth to twins, one human and the other a dugong (Forth 2020:57). Gregory Forth (2020:57) records that in both versions of the myth, humans and dugongs have a "common ancestry" and as such are termed *ata ruju* ("dugong people") by many Lio. Interestingly, although the Lio consider dugongs of human origin, they are classified as a type of "fish," as through transformation they "acquired the limbless lower body and tail flukes of a fish and, therefore, ceased to be human" (Forth 2020:60). Forth (2020:65) argues that as "humanlike creatures that live entirely in saltwater," Lio conceptualization of dugongs "challenge a major ecological and cosmological opposition, that of land and sea." Furthermore, "The dugong's ambiguity lies explicitly in the way the creature combines human and animal features and attributes of creatures of the sea and the dry land" (Forth 2020:66). Some Lio state that in rare instances, dugongs are known to have temporarily transformed back to a human form to engage with humans (Forth 2021:69–70).

Shark People

In Oceania are numerous communities where the identities of people and sharks overlap in what can be seen as ontological consubstantiation (see Scott 2021:118). For example, on the island of Makira (San Cristóbal) in the Solomon Islands, "shark-men" are the result of either the "life-force" (*adaro*) of a deceased person entering a living shark, such that the shark is "endowed with human understanding, and may aid the living" (see Chapter 4), or living men who have "namesake relations with particular ancestral sharks" (Codrington 1891:259; Fox 1924:109, 231; Scott 2021:118; see also Fox and Drew 1915:162). In terms of the latter, the "shark is said to protect him of its own accord, and if he chose to he could cultivate his power (*mena* [cf. *mana*]) with the shark by making offerings at its shrine. But he is also vulnerable to injuries suffered by the shark. A well-known recent case is that of Mr Ben's brother, Gordon Hidawawa, whose second name is that of a documented pre-Christian shark-man (Fox 1924:232); people told me that the lip cancer Hida developed was owing to his shark having been hooked in the mouth by fishermen" (Scott 2021:118). Fox (1924:231) added that the "descent of the shark-men is from father to son," and if the "shark-child . . . dies the shark will die, if the shark is injured the child will fall sick."

Hawai'ians know that people with spiritual connections to sharks who die at sea will be spiritually transformed into a *aumakua* (ancestral spirit) shark and are "regarded as spirits of half-human beings" (Beckwith 1917:508). One story relates how a "shark-man" had "the power to become a shark the moment he leaps into the sea" (Beckwith 1917:508–509). In some cases, individual sharks could be identified as *aumakua* sharks by living human relatives based on distinctive markings that matched those of deceased family members (e.g., birthmarks and designs on tapa cloth burial shrouds; Beckwith 1917; D'Arcy 2006:43). In one example, an abortive child was buried at sea and the mother identified its *aumakua* when the shark approached her as she was bathing and attempted to be breastfed (Beckwith 1917:504). In Hawai'i, families take care of certain *aumakua* sharks. In one case, a man pointed out that "his shark was rainbow-colored, that it was man before and became shark, and that it acted as protector to his family" (Beckwith 1917:507).

Turtle People

Members of the marine turtle clan (Garohai) on Santa Anna, a small coral island to the southeast of Makira in the Solomon Islands, know the origin story that documents how they are "descendants" of marine turtles (Fox 1924:72). Members of Garohai clan are forbidden to "eat any part of a turtle, and the consequence of breaking this rule, even in ignorance, is death" (Fox 1924:73). As with other totemic clans, Garohai clan members regularly offer "sacrifices and prayers . . . to their animal ancestors" (Fox 1924:72). As seen with "shark-men" of Makira (see above), *adaro* spirit (soul) essences of the human dead can also incarnate as marine turtles (Fox 1924:108, 231).

The western Kamoro of the Mimika coast of southern Indonesian Papua have a mythical narrative that explains how marine turtles are transmogrified humans. That is, a "land serpent" (python) shed its skin and turned into an attractive man so he could seduce a woman he saw bathing in a river. Eventually the two had a child, which was killed by the mother's mother. In anger, the serpent father chopped off his mother-in-law's ears, legs, and arms, leaving only stumps. The mutilated "old woman" entered the sea and turned herself into the first sea turtle "so that my grandchildren will be able to eat me" (Offenberg and

Pouwer 2000:214; Pouwer 2000:51). It is for this reason that Kamoro say that a captured turtle lying on its back "groans like an old woman" (Pouwer 2000:51). Furthermore, when Kamoro men wish to take a turtle for food, they must "approach the grandmother with care . . . not pierce her, but catch her alive" with their hands after they leap from a boat (Pouwer 2000:51).

Fish People

Fish people in the form of mermaids and mermen are the best-known animal-human hybrid sea beings for peoples of European heritage. They are human-animal hybrids and part of what Blind (1881a:207) called the "semi-divine fauna of the sea." All possess the well-known characteristic of a human upper body (head, torso, arms) and fish's lower body (including tail) with a body size comparable to adult or juvenile humans. In a classical Mediterranean siren tradition, mermaids are usually seen as alluring to mariners (essentially all men) because of their feminine beauty (e.g., long hair, conspicuous breasts) coupled with seductive behaviors. Yet encounters were usually seen as potentially treacherous by mariners, foreboding a storm, shipwreck, drowning, and devouring (Bassett 1885:168–201; Beck 1999:227–253; Benwell and Waugh 1961; Rappoport 1928:157–202).

Graphic representations of sea creatures morphologically consistent with mermaids or mermen occur back to the first millennium BCE. For example, an early eighth-century-BCE Assyrian carved stone low-relief frieze in the palace of King Sargon II in Khorsabad in northern Iraq (now in the Louvre) includes two mermen (Albenda 1983; van Duzer 2013:13). These mermen appear next to ships, which Brody (1998:69) interprets as Phoenician sailors towing logs in the Mediterranean (cf. Linder 1986). In ancient Greece, mermen were represented by deities such as Okeanos, Triton, Glaukos, and Proteus, while mermaid deities were comparatively rare, with the single example of Eurynome (Shepard 1940). Ancient Greek artistic representations of fish-tailed men date back to the seventh century BCE (Glynn 1981:122), while a bronze shield blazon of a fish-tailed anthropomorph (probably a female sea serpent known as a gorgon) dates from the sixth century BCE (Vermeule 1979:195–196). Sculptural depictions of sirens transitioning from hybrid bird forms (mostly human-headed birds) to mermaid hybrid fish forms (e.g., female upper body with finned feet) date to the Hellenistic (after 300 BCE) and Roman periods (Benwell and Waugh 1961:46–49). In post-Roman Britain during the second half of the first millennium CE are found numerous literary references to mermaid sirens (Benwell and Waugh 1961:57–66).

During the medieval period the depiction of mermaid sirens and mermen dramatically increases in sculptural form in cathedrals and churches. According

Figure 8. Mermaid and merman from Ulyssis Aldrovandi's 1642 encyclopedic text *Monstrorum historia: Cum paralipomenis historiae omnium animalium,* page 354 (Source: Smithsonian Library).

to Benwell and Waugh (1961:69), this increased representation reflected strategic appropriation of pagan beliefs and beings by the Christian church and increased voyaging and interactions with the sea by Europeans. Yet these representations were not only of classical Greek antiquity but also of local waters. For example, Gervase of Tilbury in Essex, England, in his 1211 text *Otia imperialia*, noted that mermaids and mermen occur in "great numbers" in the "seas of Britain" (Benwell and Waugh 1961:141).

Obvious depictions of mermaids also appear on a number of European medieval nautical maps of the Mediterranean Sea (e.g., late eleventh-century harbor of Brindisi, Italy), the Southern Ocean (San Andrés de Arroyo Beatus dating to 1248), Indian Ocean (Catalan Atlas of 1375), and the Indian Ocean (Catalan Estense *mappa mundi* of 1460; van Duzer 2013:19–20, 25, 43–45). That mermaids were accepted as a "natural" part of the maritime world is revealed in postmedieval and modern era classificatory encyclopedias and treatises on the natural world. Perhaps best known in this regard is Ulyssis Aldrovandi, a late Renaissance naturalist who is often considered "the founder of modern Natural History" (Brito 2016:181). In his 1642 encyclopedic *Monstrorum historia: Cum paralipomenis historiae omnium animalium*, Aldrovandi went to lengths in "normalizing the monstrous" with descriptions of mermaids and mermen, in addition to sea serpents, alongside more commonly accepted marine creatures such as whales (Brito 2016:182; Figure 8). Recorded sightings of mermaids and mermen continued into the eighteenth, nineteenth, and twentieth centuries (Arnold 2013:179–186; Benwell and Waugh 1961).

In Javanese mythology of Indonesia, Kyai Blorong (or Kyai Belorong) was a servant of the sea goddess who had a merman-like form with a human upper body, fish tail lower body, 1,000 arms, and golden scales. He was served by mermaids in his seabed palace (Knappert 1992:163). Fishers of villages on Guimaras Island in the central Philippines know of sea spirits in the form of mermaids. For example, Suclaran villagers call mermaids *serena* who "reside in far and deep places" in the sea (Magos 1994:312). Buntod and Boracay villagers refer to mermaids as *kataw* (Magos 1994:319, 347), as do Igdalaguit villagers, who add that they are "beautiful women with the body of a fish whose sweet singing voice can lure and cause the loss of fishermen out at sea" (Magos 1994:325). Fishers of Suclaran also identify *siyukoy* (sea monsters), one of whom has a "man's body but has fins running down the length of its back and has scales similar to that of a fish" (reminiscent of a merman) and resides in deep water (Magos 1994:312). Fishers of Barangay Igdalaguit also identify a "sea monster" of merman form. Known as *ukoy*, they "are half-man and half-fish with fins running from their heads down to their tails, and considered generous because they provide a bountiful catch to fishermen, though they are also known to snatch men at sea" (Magos 1994:324–325).

Mermaids are also found among the Inuit of Quebec in northeast Canada, where they are known as *iqalunappaa* (Saladin d'Anglure 1984:495). Similarly, the Inuit of Kotzebue Sound in Alaska occasionally come across mermaids (with the tail of a beluga whale or sea lion) during sea mammal hunting expeditions (Burch 1971:153–154). Ernest Burch (1971:154) added that "people who have encountered them have always been afraid and left them alone, although apparently they are harmless."

Few accounts exist of ritual engagements between mariners and mermaids or mermen. This dearth probably reflects the general belief among mariners that mermaids and mermen possess few powers worth either obviating or propitiating. In the west of Scotland, children under the age of 21 days had their right hand "baptised in the waves" to "ward off disaster from the siren [mermaid]," and if done on an incoming tide it "averted death by drowning" (Simpson 1908:119–120). David Thomson (1996:155–175) recounts a story from the island of South Uist in the Outer Hebrides of Scotland, where local fishermen saw a mermaid surface next to their boat. The fishermen knew that to avoid the mermaid casting a fatal spell upon them, they needed to throw at her a "knife, or anything that's made of iron" (Thomson 1996:175). One man failed to throw the right type of object, and he drowned afterward. In other instances, objects such as bottles and casks were thrown into the sea to distract mermen and mermaids, thus allowing mariners to escape potential mishap (e.g., Bassett 1885:170; Benwell and Waugh 1961:169).

Some encounters resulted in rituals that reveal a response to the human side of mermaids. For example, in the early fifteenth century, a mermaid was washed inland near Edam in West Friesland, Holland, after a dike burst. The mermaid was taken in by local women who cared for her for some 15 years before she died and was buried in a Christian cemetery (Benwell and Waugh 1961:81). Some time in the past, a dead merman washed ashore and was buried in the local churchyard of Nissum in Denmark. Subsequently, a severe wind blew sand from the beach over the district. The merman was then exhumed and reburied in nearby sandhills, and the drifting sand ceased (Benwell and Waugh 1961:184; see also Arnold 2013:180–181). Another example dates to around 1830 on the island of Benbecula, in the Outer Hebrides, where a mermaid who had been killed by a stone thrown by a boy was buried by the local community in a coffin close to the shore, near where her body had been found (Waugh 1960:80–81). The killing of mermaids or mermen by people appears to have been rare, owing, it seems, to their humanness.

In rare cases mermaids pass special powers onto humans. For example, in the early nineteenth century, a Welsh fisherman named Pergrin captured a mermaid, and after releasing her was granted three special blessings when needed. After a number of weeks, Pergrin was out fishing with others when the mermaid appeared and shouted to him to pull up his nets and to return to port immediately. This he did, and soon after a storm arose and the rest of the fishing fleet, including 18 men, perished (Benwell and Waugh 1961:150–151). A story from Cornwall relates how a man named Lutey found a mermaid stranded on tidal flats at low tide (Benwell and Waugh 1961:144–145). In payment for carrying the mermaid back into the sea, the mermaid gave Lutey her golden comb with a pearl handle and granted him the power to overcome the spells of witches. However, the mermaid also said she wished to be with Lutey, and nine years later Lutey met up with the mermaid while out fishing and jumped into the sea to swim with her and was never seen again. An Irish fisherman was once granted "immunity from storms" by a mermaid who he had caught accidentally in his fishing net and subsequently released (Benwell and Waugh 1961:156). In some instances, people were cursed by a mermaid whom they ill-treated or killed. Examples include the people of Conway in Wales doomed to always be poor, the villagers of Padstow in Cornwall who had their harbor permanently silted up, and a bay on the west coast of Ireland, which is visited periodically by a large wave known locally as the "avenging wave" caused by a rare conjunction of wind and tide (Benwell and Waugh 1961:143, 151, 158; Hunt 1865:157–158).

Shetland and Orkney Islanders were adamant that mermaids shared the sea with another amphibious hybrid people known as "Finns" or "finfolk" (Blind 1881b:408–409; Dennison 1891a:168, 1892a:115, 1892b). Fin men are described as "well-formed, lithe, sinewy and active . . . with a dark and gloomy visage . . . [and] an austere and gloomy aspect" (Dennison 1891a:168). The relationship of finfolk to human fishers was mostly "unfriendly" and mischievous (Dennison 1891a:169). As finfolk had the "deepest abhorrence" of the Christian cross, fishers would chalk a cross on their boat to frighten away finfolk and carve a cross on sinkers to deter finfolk from stealing fish from hooks (Dennison 1891a:169). Yet fishers could also propitiate finfolk with "white or silver money" (Dennison 1891a:169). For example, Shetland Islanders would throw "silver money" overboard to deter fin folk from doing damage to their boats (Blind 1881b:404).

Animal-Animal Hybrids and Sea Monsters

My use of the category of monstrous hybrid sea beings is limited mostly to animal-animal hybrids, even though some scholars such as Katharine Shepard (1940) designate all hybrid sea creatures (including deities, mermaids, and mermen) as monsters. Whereas most sea monsters and sea serpents of European traditions are monstrous in form and behavior (usually offensively aggressive), in many other cultural contexts sea monsters are monstrous in form and behaviorally amicable and even benign. As such, European sea monster and sea serpent categorizations are not entirely cross-culturally relevant for hybrid animal-animal sea creatures across the world.

Although many coastal Indigenous peoples of the world know of sea monsters, most literature on sea monsters concerns Western traditions of sea serpents in the United Kingdom, Europe, and North America, with early references provided by ancient Greek and Roman writers (Bassett 1885:202–232; Ellis 1995; Heuvelmans 1968, 2006; Jeans 2007:276–294; Lee 1884). Chet Van Duzer (2013:8–9) defines a sea monster as "an aquatic creature that was thought astonishing and exotic (regardless of whether in fact it was real or mythical) in classical, medieval, or Renaissance times." More broadly, David Gilmore (2003:6) defines monsters as "imaginary beings," that is, "supernatural, mythical, or magical products of the imagination" that are "not real." Yet it is clear that those societies and cultures that believe in sea monsters and serpents know that these creatures *are real*. From a European cultural context, Bassett (1885:6–7) makes the point that the "uneducated sailor . . . could know but little of the classical and biblical traditions concerning aquatic monsters, but he could see in the huge forms that sported about him the terrible kraken or the monstrous sea-serpent, or he could imagine the form of the latter in the floating sea weed."

As their categorization implies, sea monsters and sea serpents ranged in size from large to colossal. For example, Jörmungand (aka the Midgard serpent), a sea serpent of Norse mythology, was said to be so huge that it could encircle the (flat) earth (Lindow 2001:229–230). The Hebrew biblical sea monster, the fearsome "Leviathan," described in the Hebrew Bible as "the dragon that is in the sea" (Isaiah 27:1), has since become a term synonymous with giant whales. The Kraken, a sea monster probably based on a giant squid and best known from the Norwegian Sea, was described by Erik Pontoppidan (1755:212) as "about an English mile and an half in circumference" (see also Heuvelmans 2006; Salvador and Tomotani 2014). Although in some cases sea monsters are probably based upon whales and giant squid, in most situations the creatures defy modern Western scientific taxonomic classification.

Western Traditions

The earliest descriptive and graphic accounts of sea monsters and serpents come from literary and archaeological sources for the Ancient Near East and Greece and Rome. Genesis 1:21 in the Hebrew Bible written sometime during the first millennium BCE states: "And God created the great sea-monsters, and every living creature that creepeth, wherewith the waters swarmed, after its kind, and every winged fowl after its kind; and God saw that it was good."

Perhaps the earliest archaeological representation of a sea monster is a 3,000-to-4,000-year-old clay seal from the Minoan settlement of Knossos on Crete showing a canine-headed sea monster "emerging from the waves to devour a Minoan sailor who is standing on the gunwale facing the monster with terror" (Boulotis 1987:32; see also Hopman 2012:24, 58, Figure 2). Archaeological depictions of sea serpents from the subsequent ancient Greek period include engraved gem carvings from the seventh and fifth centuries BCE and vase paintings from the seventh century BCE (Papadopoulos and Ruscillo 2002:218; Vermeule 1979:188, 195). Evidence of early ancient Greek animal-animal hybrids include an engraved gem carving of a fish-tailed goat from the seventh century BCE (Vermeule 1979:188) and dog- and lion-faced creatures with fish-like tails and fins also from the seventh century BCE (Vermeule and Chapman 1971:285, 288). Of these animal-animal hybrids, the most commonly represented is that of the sea horse (horse upper body with a fish/serpent lower body, sometimes with wings) known as a hippocamp with archaeological representations dating back to the fourth and fifth centuries BCE (Shepard 1940:25–27, 39–42, 49–50, 56–58, 68, 77). Poseidon is associated with horses and is often depicted riding the waves with hippocamps. Indeed, the "hippocamp seems to have been invented for Poseidon" (Simon 2014:39). In the Hellenistic age (after 300 BCE) appears the ichthyocentaur, or sea-centaur (an elaborated merman), with a male human upper body, chest and forelegs of a horse, and tail of a fish (Shepard 1940:70). Other innovative sea monsters (animal-animal hybrids) of the Hellenistic age include fish- or serpent-tailed bulls, boars, stags, lions, and panthers (Shepard 1940:78, 94).

A well-known woman-turned-sea-monster is Scylla from Greek mythology, who came from her seabed cave (Strait of Messina in Italy) to sink ships and devour sailors (and dolphins, dogfish, and other sea monsters) according to Homer's *Odyssey* from the eighth century BCE (Hopman 2012, 2024:168, 175; Shepard 1940:43–46, 49, 59, 75–76, 93). Representations of Scylla (e.g., coins, terracotta plaques) date back to the fifth century BCE and present her as a "tri-partite hybrid" with the upper body of a female human, lower body of a fish, and dog heads (usually two or three) extending from her waist (Hopman 2024:169–171; Neils 1995:181; Shepard 1940:43, 60, 93). Scylla has since given her name to the large, fearsome, and highly edible Indo-Pacific mud crab (*Scylla serrata*), which lives in mud burrows in the intertidal zone (Kathirvel and Srinivasagam 1992:127). Ketos (Cetus in Latin) was a sea serpent (or "marine dragon") and is the basis for Cetacea—the Western scientific taxonomic (infraorder) grouping for whales, dolphins, and porpoises (Shepard 1940:28–30, 42–43, 58, 77).

In the fifth century BCE, Herodotus wrote that sea monsters were most prevalent off Mount Athos (Greece) in the northwest Aegean Sea (Vermeule 1979:183). Some Greek vase paintings show gods doing battle with sea monsters, such as the famous Athenian black-figure cup dating to around 520 BCE showing Herakles (known as Hercules by the Romans) battling a wide-mouthed scaly sea serpent (Papadopoulos and Ruscillo 2002:216–217; Vermeule 1979:194). According to John Papadopoulos and Deborah Ruscillo (2002:217), these battles between mythological heroes and sea monsters have "the effect of removing them to an otherworldly realm." In this regard, ancient Greek relationships with sea monsters differed fundamentally from those of later medieval and postmedieval Europeans. That is, whereas in the pre-2,000-year-old ancient Greek world, battles with sea monsters invariably involved anthropomorphic deities, in the past 1,000 years such battles involved mortal mariners. However, meetings between mortals and sea monsters sometimes had dire consequences in the Ancient Aegean, as the Persian Darius learned when his attempt to invade Greece around 490 BCE was dashed when his fleet of 300 ships was scuttled by a storm off the infamous sea monster hotspot of Mount Athos, with Herodotus reporting that many of the 20,000 men lost were devoured by sea monsters (Papadopoulos and Ruscillo 2002:200, 216). Ancient Greek mariners' fear of being eaten by sea monsters may account for their use of the term *laitma* (based on the word for throat, *laimos*) for the sea, which "suggests an image of the deep as a gigantic gullet ready to engulf sailors" (Hopman 2024:168).

The Romans produced numerous extraordinary mosaics depicting elaborate terrestrial and marine hybrid sea creatures. Perhaps the most famous are those found on the floor of the Baths of Neptune within the settlement of Ostia near Rome, commissioned by Hadrian in the late second century CE. Here are found a range of sea creatures with the upper bodies of lions, horses, goats, a ram, and a stag, all with lower bodies of serpent-like tails (Blake 1936:145, Plate 34; van Duzer 2013:9, 120; Meiggs 1973:409–412). Other mosaics depict bulls, cows, birds, dogs, and leopards with serpent-like tails (Blake 1936:141, 144, 146, 149–152).

Medieval understandings of sea monsters are founded upon Christian conceptualizations of the sea and the notion that "all damned creatures dwell in the deep" (Rudolf 2011:45). Some European maps from the medieval and Renaissance periods provide graphic insights into how mariners understood the seas and oceans to be populated by a diverse array of sea monsters and serpents. The earliest surviving European navigational maps, dating from the late thirteenth century, were tools for mariners and, to be affordable, tended not to have graphic illustrations such as sea monsters (van Duzer 2013:40–42). As such, most medieval maps depicting sea monsters would have been expensive to produce and made for wealthy clients such as rulers, royalty, nobles, and the church (van Duzer 2013). The *mappa mundi* (cosmographical world map) in the late eleventh-century St. Sever Beatus illuminated manuscript in Paris (Bibliothèque Nationale) depicts a sea goat and a sea lion swimming within a circumfluent ocean (van Duzer 2013:20–23). Fifteenth-century maps similarly depict sea monsters as hybrids with terrestrial upper bodies and aquatic (fish) lower bodies, such as sea dogs, sea rabbits, sea pigs, sea cows, and sea lions (van Duzer 2013:61–63, 72).

Renaissance map depictions of sea monsters commence in style with the 1539 publication of Olaus Magnus's *Carta marina et descriptio septemtrionalium terrarum ac mirabilium* (*Nautical Chart and Description of the Northern Lands and Wonders*; Starkey 2017; Szabó 2018; van Duzer 2013:81–82). Complementary detailed descriptions of the diverse assembly of depicted sea monsters are found in Olaus Magnus's 1555 book *Historia de gentibus septentrionalibus* (*History of the Northern Peoples*; Starkey 2017; van Duzer 2013:82). Both the map and book document four different types of sea monsters of the Norwegian and North Seas of northern Europe: sea monsters dangerous and even fatal to ships and mariners (e.g., sea unicorn, sea cow, giant crustacean, whale), sea monsters that protected mariners from danger (e.g., rockfish), sea monsters that signaled events to come (e.g., sea pig), and sea monsters that produced products for trade (e.g., beached whales; Starkey 2017:38–51).

In 1544 cosmographer Sebastian Münster published *Cosmographia universalis* in six volumes which went through 35 editions by 1628. It contains a remarkable woodcut plate of sea monsters based on Magnus's *Carta marina* (Figure 9). Gerard Mercator's 1569 world map *Nova et aucta orbis terrae descriptio ad usum navigantium* (*New and Improved Description of the World for the Use of Navigators*) similarly depicts numerous fantastical sea beings and creatures, including Neptune riding a fish-tailed horse in the South Pacific (van Duzer 2013:103–105). Van Duzer (2013:11) states that while "in many cases we do not know the reasons for the presence or absence of sea monsters from medieval and Renaissance maps," their "main roles" may have been to indicate "possible dangers to sailors" and the "vitality of the oceans."

Mariners universally considered sea monsters to be dangerous, a belief reinforced by numerous documented examples of attacks on vessels and ensuing human fatalities. A number of medieval maps provide graphic representations of such attacks. For example, the 1367 nautical chart of the Indian and Atlantic Oceans by Francesco and Domenico Pizzigano depicts two ships in the North Atlantic, one being attacked by a giant octopus and the other by a flying dragon (van Duzer 2013:42). Olaus Magnus's 1539 *Carta marina* shows three ships being attacked by a huge sea serpent and huge whale-like creatures, while his 1555 *Historia* describes a ship under attack from a giant octopus (van Duzer 2013:38, 82, 85). Depictions of sailors attempting to fight off sea monsters are equally rare, and include sounding of a trumpet (Olaus Magnus's 1539 *Carta marina*), thrusting spears (Nikolaos Sophianos's 1545 *Totius Graeciae descriptio*), and ringing of bells (Jan van der Straet's 1630 *Venationes ferarum, auium, piscium*; van Duzer 2013:38–39, 128). In later centuries, vessels fired cannons and rifles at sea monsters and serpents to avoid danger (e.g., Ellis 1995:45; Heuvelmans 1968:173, 240; Jeans 2007:288–289). Icelandic sea monsters, especially those covered in protective mussel shells, "cannot be killed by a leaden bullet, for their shell coat of mail and their demon nature resist any such shot; but he who meets them is lucky if he have a silver button or coin at hand to thrust into his gun; for no monster, however fiendish, can withstand a silver shot" (Powell and Magnusson 1866:lx).

Western depictions of sea monsters on maps rapidly decrease during the seventeenth century, which van Duzer (2013:119) associates with improved "nautical technology" and increased "human confidence in achieving dominion over the seas." In marked contrast, recorded observations continue apace into the seventeenth century and through to the twentieth century and include eyewitness accounts from North America (Bassett 1885:225–227; Heuvelmans

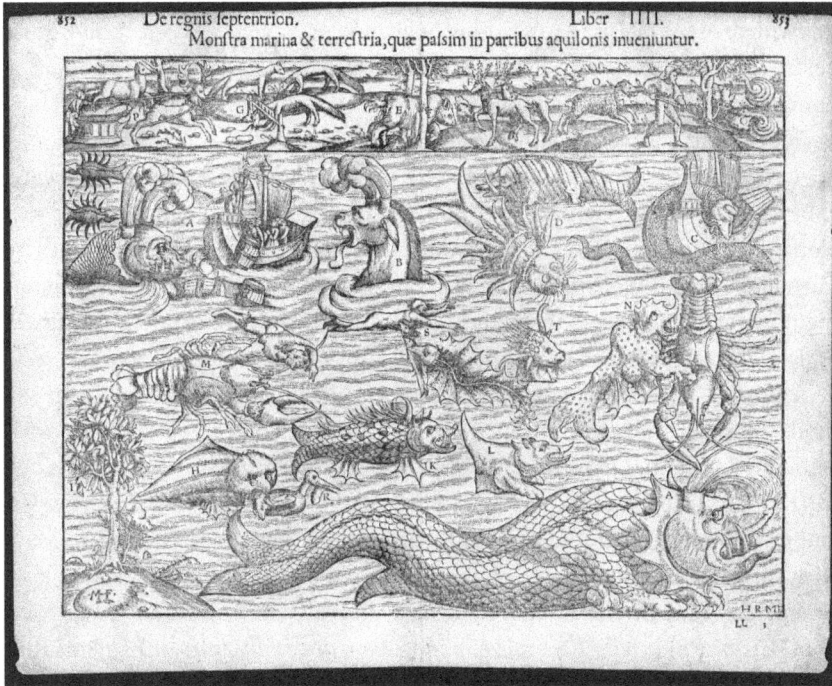

Figure 9. Sea monsters from the 1550 edition of Sebastian Münster's *Cosmographia universalis,* page 852. The woodcut plate shows a sea monster attacking a ship (*top right*), a mariner on a ship shooting at a sea monster (*top left*), and marine birds spontaneously generating from a tree (*lower left;* see Müller 1864:541; Courtesy: Geographicus Rare Antique Maps, http://www.geographicus.com).

1968:34). Similar accounts by settler colonials of British heritage extended to Australian coastal waters in the nineteenth and twentieth centuries (Ellis 1995:314–315; Gilmore 2003:152–153; Smith 1996). Although sea monsters are not considered "real" by modern Western science, Linnaeus included the Kraken (in giant squid form) in the 1735 first edition of *Systema naturae* and his 1746 *Fauna svecica* with the taxonomic name of *Microcosmus marinus* (Salvador and Tomotani 2014:976). Linnaeus subsequently got cold feet and omitted the Kraken from the 1756 edition of *Systema naturae.* However, the Kraken as a giant squid was formerly classified and accepted within Western science as *Architeuthis* sp. following Japetus Steenstrup (1857; Salvador and Tomotani 2014:977–979).

Shetland Islanders of Scotland speak of a sea monster known as the Brigdi, said to be a "huge flat creature with fins fore and aft" (Marwick 1975:21). The Brigdi was known to attack fishing boats and to smash them to pieces using its fins. In some cases, fishermen were able to ward off the Brigdi by chopping at its fins with axes. As late as 1840 a fishing boat crew managed to escape to shore just before the Brigdi destroyed their vessel (Marwick 1975:21). Another sea monster known as Nuckelavee among the Orkney Islanders was described in detail as having a head 1 m wide, with long arms and a body like a misshapen horse, fin-like flippers on its legs, and no skin, exposing raw flesh and yellow veins (Marwick 1975:22–23). Nuckelavee had the capacity to move onto land and was blamed for bad crops, animal diseases, and droughts. Sea monster sightings by European (including United Kingdom) and North American mariners remain regular albeit rare events throughout the nineteenth and twentieth centuries, as do sightings from the shoreline (Arnold 2013:150–178; Faiella 2021).

A limited number of accounts were found of ritual engagements with sea monsters by Europeans. Sightings were a known though rare possibility with associated potential dangers seen largely as beyond ritual prediction or control. If Shetland Islanders saw a Brigdi near their boat they would throw an amber (lammer) bead into the sea to make the sea serpent disappear (Marwick 1975:21). The Nuckelavee could be repelled by the smoke of burning kelp (Marwick 1975:23). The French naturalist Pierre Denys-Montfort in his 1802 book *Histoire naturelle, générale et particuliere des mollusques* documents that a ship sailing off the coast of Angola was attacked and engulfed by the arms of a monstrous cephalopod. The crew sought the assistance of St. Thomas and successfully escaped after attacking the monster with axes and cutlasses. In gratitude, the mariners pledged to make a pilgrimage to St. Thomas's chapel at St. Malo in Brittany, northwest France. Upholding their vow, the sailors visited the chapel, expressing their gratitude by commissioning a painting of the ship being attacked by the monster and presenting it as a votive gift (Ellis 1995:118; Heuvelmans 2006:158–159). Similarly, a votive offering in the form of a plaque giving thanks for escape from an attack by a sea monster off the coast of South Carolina in the USA is found in the church of Our Lady of the Watch in Marseilles, southern France (Faiella 2021:226–227).

Indigenous Traditions

First Nations peoples of the Northwest Coast of Canada and southeastern Alaska cohabit the sea with a range of "dangerous sea monsters" (Shearar 2000:109). For example, Iakim and 'Yagis in Kwakwaka'wakw mythology are known to "capsize and swallow canoes" and cause "storms, waves and dangerous whirlpools" (Shearar 2000:60, 119). Other Northwest Coast sea monsters are friendly to humans, such as Gonakadet, who is known to bestow wealth upon certain individuals among the Tlingit and the Tsimshian (Shearar 2000:50). Wasco or Wasgo is a "giant sea monster" in Haida cosmology who has the hybrid features of the head and tail of a wolf and the fins and blowhole of a killer whale, and is a "favoured spirit guide among Haida fishers" (Shearar 2000:94). In contrast to Europeans, Northwest Coast peoples tend not to fear squid or octopus as sea monsters (Shearar 2000:78, 100). An early example of artistic expressions of Northwest Coast sea monsters is a 3,000-to-3,300-year-old carved antler spoon used for "feeding the ancestors" excavated from near the mouth of the Fraser River within Coast Salish territory. It features a figurative representation of a mask showing a "sea wolf mask confronting a rock fish" (Carlson 2011:644, 2017:350–351). Another example is a carved wooden atlatl recovered from the mouth of the Skagit River, also within Coast Salish territory, and radiocarbon dating to 1,600 years ago (Fladmark et al. 1987). The atlatl features a human head surmounted by a compound (hybrid) "sea-monster or sea-serpent" with serpent-like head and torso with a whale-like dorsal fin and tail that is "probably a variant of the mythological sea-wolf" (Borden 1969:17; Fladmark et al. 1987:357, Figure 1). Knut Fladmark and colleagues (1987:357) add that the sea wolf is a "liminal being that transforms from a land to a sea creature or vice versa as it moves from one dimension to the other."

Qallupilluit (aka Qalupalik) are a class of "sea monsters" (usually gendered female) that take children to the bottom of the sea according to the Central Inuit (Giles et al. 2013:211). Franz Boas (1888:620) described a Qallupilluit as a "fabulous being that lives in the sea" with a body "like that of a human being" and feet that are "very large and look like inflated sealskin floats." The hooded clothing of Qallupilluit is made of duck skin. By the late nineteenth century, their numbers had dwindled. They can be seen swimming rapidly through the sea and basking on rocks in summer and sitting near cracks in the ice and edges of drifting ice in winter. Inuit hunters are known to kill Qallupilluit with walrus harpoons. The flesh of Qallupilluit is poisonous to people but not to dogs (Boas 1888:620).

The Rainbow Serpent is a broad term applied to a diverse class of gigantic serpents and ancestral beings found across Aboriginal Australia (Elkin 1930; Mountford 1978; Radcliffe-Brown 1926, 1930; Taylor 1990). It has also been referred to as a "deity" (Maddock 1978:4; Radcliffe-Brown 1930:342). As their name indicates, Rainbow Serpents are often seen as serpent- or snake-like with manes, beards, and long and sharp teeth, and which "occasionally manifest" as rainbows (Taylor 1990:329; see also Mountford 1978:23). In the southern Gulf of Carpentaria, Rainbow Serpents can physically manifest at sea as waterspouts (e.g., among the Lardil people—Memmott 1982) or waterspouts, whirlpools, or whales (e.g., among the Yanyuwa peoples—Bradley with Yanyuwa Families 2022:53, 150, 269, 272–273). They can be gendered either male or female, inhabit the sea and especially freshwater bodies such as waterholes, lakes, swamps, and rivers, are greatly feared and avoided (and associated with strict laws and taboos), and are often associated with controlling rain. Paul Taçon and colleagues (1996:103) note that the Rainbow Serpent "pervades not only oral history but also ceremony, performance and visual art, and is associated with great acts of creation and destruction." The Rainbow Serpent is visualized in hundreds of rock art sites with Taçon and colleagues (1996) hypothesizing that this tradition may have begun emerging 4,000–6,000 years ago in Arnhem Land. A further link with the sea is the possible early modeling of the form of the Rainbow Serpent on the elongate marine pipefish (Taçon et al. 1996).

Scattered references to the Rainbow Serpent in the sea are known only for the northern half of the Australian continent. Cambridge Gulf in northwest Australia is the residence of Lumiri, a large saltwater snake whose presence is marked by phosphorescence (Elkin 1930:349). Croker Island off the northwest coast of Arnhem Land in the Northern Territory is the domain of a Rainbow Serpent (Peterson and Rigsby 1998:6). On the northeast Arnhem Land coast, Rainbow Serpents (*bilumbira*) are known to live in submerged rocks on the seabed during the dry season and to kill any canoeist who paddles nearby (Mountford 1978:65). Aboriginal people in the southwest Gulf of Carpentaria know that swimming too far off shore from the mouth of the Roper River may result in the Rainbow Serpent making a "rumbling noise" and pulling them down to drown (Mountford 1978:65). In the southeast Gulf of Carpentaria, the Lardil people speak of the "potent presence and powers" of Thuwathu (Rainbow Serpent) "throughout the seas today" as he manifests himself variously as cyclones, waterspouts, and rainbows (Memmott and Trigger 1998:121). The "regular habitat" of Thuwathu is the channel between Forsyth and Andrew Islands (Memmott 1982:170).

In northeast Australia at Cape York in Far North Queensland, the "rainbow" is seen as the reflection of a huge fish which lives "far out at sea" (Roth 1903:10). A little further south, Double Island located immediately off shore north of Cairns is associated with the *kudju-kudju* ("the rainbow"), "who travelled under the sea and came up through a hole in the ground" (McConnel 1930:348). In southeast Queensland, Aboriginal people feared "the rainbow," which they call Thugine (large serpent). One legendary narrative mentions how Thugine "came out of the sea" and took two boys who had mischievously wandered away from camp and turned them into two rocks located off Double Island Point. These rocks are known today as Wolf Rock, located 2 km offshore, which is washed with breaking waves at low tide. According to the "old men," these rocks are "the result of not paying attention to what you are told by your elders" (Howitt 1904:431; see also Miller 1993:38–40).

Despite the size of the Pacific Ocean and hundreds of different island communities, Indigenous accounts of sea serpents are rare. A sea serpent known as Ruki inhabits the waters of Kiribati in the central Pacific (Knappert 1992:251). Yofuné-Nushi is the name of a sea serpent in waters surrounding the Oki Islands of Japan. It was 9 m long with four legs and sharp claws, sharp teeth, a long tail, and shiny white skin, and lived in a cave guarding pearls and a statue of the ruler Hojo Takatoki (Davis 1912:333–336; Knappert 1992:257, 331). In the legendary narrative of Empress Jingo's successful invasion of Korea, the Japanese war fleet was saved from a deadly storm after the sea god commanded "great sea monsters" and "powerful dragon-fishes" to ferry the ships to safety (Davis 1912:331–332).

Various cultural groups in southern Papua New Guinea identify a class of powerful and feared sea monsters known generally as *ma-hevehe* (Williams 1940a:169–182). They are usually conceptualized as "enormous" fish, sharks, whales, and dugongs and are known to cause boat wrecks and drownings (Williams 1932:145, 1940a:169, 171, 1976:79). Francis Edgar Williams (1940a:171) equates some *ma-hevehe* with the Mediterranean sea monster Scylla. Some *ma-hevehe* are thought to have their own ceremonial buildings on the seabed (Williams 1940a:171). *Ma-hevehe* are known by different "personal" names at different locations along the coast (Williams 1932:145). They are seldom seen and people on the sea will probably encounter *ma-hevehe* indirectly as rocks on the seabed, and flotsam debris, drift logs, and sea foam. For example, an encounter with a *ma-hevehe* can be indicated by a fishing net getting caught up on rocks or a canoe taking on water unexpectedly.

In parts of Indonesia, mariners are aware of the *makara*, which is a "hybrid animal that lives in the sea, where it is particularly notorious as a sea monster or sea dragon" (Prajudi 2016:2). It comprises "an elephantine trunk and a crocodile mouth, the body of a snake or fish, and sometimes it has legs like mammals in an addition to having a fish tail" (Prajudi 2016:2). Carved stone representations of *makara* linked to Varuna/Baruna, god of the sea, are found in numerous inland Hindu and Buddhist temples dating to the Mataram era (seventh to eleventh centuries CE; Prajudi 2016). Representations of *makara* do not appear in temples constructed in the subsequent Majapahit Era or Late Classical Era (thirteenth to fifteenth centuries CE), except in water fountains where it is now linked to Gangga, goddess of rivers (Prajudi 2016).

A range of North American, Australian, and Pacific Indigenous societies had rituals aimed at controlling the behavior of sea monsters and serpents. For example, once a year on the night of 13 June the people of the Oki Islands of Japan sacrificed a 14-year-old girl to Yofuné-Nushi (sea serpent) to prevent it from becoming angry and raising storms and destroying the fishing fleet. The need for sacrifices stopped after Tokoyo, an 18-year-old young woman, dived down and killed the serpent (Davis 1912:333–336; Knappert 1992:257, 331). Another Japanese legendary narrative details how Kobo, an eighth-century Buddhist priest, pacified giant sea serpents by spitting into the ocean, as "his saliva was fortified by the radiation of the planet Venus" (Knappert 1992:157). Around Croker Island in Arnhem Land, the Rainbow Serpent is known to have "fearsome power" and is "easily disturbed by things thrown carelessly overboard" such as "meat and fatty substances" (Peterson and Rigsby 1998:6).

The Kwakwaka'wakw of southwest Canada employed a series of ritual activities to avoid contact with "sea monsters" while out porpoise hunting. Blue hellebore root and *Peucedanum* seeds are kept in a wooden box (along with harpoon points, harpoon line, and sinew) in canoes. If a sea monster is seen or suspected to be close, the root and seeds are removed from the box, chewed, and spat into the sea on both sides to the canoe. The sea monster will sink away when it smells the hellebore root (Boas 1921:175, 608–609, 1932:232, 234). Similarly, harpooners wash themselves with hemlock branches at dawn every day as "protection" against sea monsters (Boas 1932:233).

As for many Indigenous groups of North and South American, tobacco is the most important ritual plant of the Warao people of the Orinoco Delta region of eastern Venezuela, who make tobacco smoke offerings to a number of deities and spirits to protect their canoes from being dragged to the bottom of the sea by Hahuba, a sea monster. In addition, the captain-shaman at various times during voyages will attempt to appease Hahuba through chanting (Wilbert 1977:41). Crews know that Hahuba can unleash storms and high waves if she is not propitiated appropriately with "gifts" of tobacco smoke by the shaman-captain (Wilbert 1977:43).

People in southern Papua New Guinea propitiate favorable treatment from *ma-hevehe* sea monsters during voyages by throwing overboard offerings of coconuts, betel nut, and sago (Williams 1932:145). In other cases, the vessel master made attempts to scare off *ma-hevehe* by spitting chewed ginger and scented bark into his hands and mixing this with lime before throwing it into the sea (Williams 1932:155). Similarly, burning odorous leaves and bark in a pot on board the trade vessel is known to keep away *ma-hevehe* (Williams 1932:155). Occasionally, offerings stayed close to the large trading canoe (*bevaia*), which was read as a sign that the *ma-hevehe* had taken hold of the vessel. In one case, the crew abandoned the *bevaia* and were rescued by a missionary boat and taken ashore. The possessed *bevaia* was eventually wrecked, her cargo lost (Williams 1932:146).

In Cook Islands mythology of the South Pacific, Nganaoa is a legendary hero and slayer of sea monsters. Rata, a "renowned chief," agreed to allow Nganaoa to join him on a sea voyage in a newly constructed "great double canoe" after Nganaoa promised "to destroy all the monsters of the ocean which might infest their path" and "Rata wisely reflected that he had entirely forgotten to provide against this emergency" (Gill 1876a:142–146). During the voyage, Nganaoa used his spear to kill a giant "horrid clam," an "octopus of extraordinary dimensions" that attacked their boat, and a "great whale" that also attacked their boat and from which he extracted his "long lost" (alive) parents from its stomach (Gill 1876a:146–147). As such, the "oracle was fulfilled; his voyage was prosperous" (Gill 1876a:147). In Tahitian mythology, the monstrous clam's name is Pua Tu Tahi (Knappert 1992:236).

Discussion

I am unaware of any maritime cultures that do not include all-powerful and often omnipotent sea gods, deities, and spirits in their understanding of, and engagements with, seascapes. In most cases, these sea beings have anthropomorphic form, but many also take hybrid form with zoomorphic features. In other cases, sea beings are more a personification of the sea such that the sea itself is the being and not a separate being who resides in the sea. In this sense, the sea is essentialized as a sentient being. Whether seen as a personification of the sea or as separate beings in the sea, mariners through the ages knew that when they ventured out onto the sea, they were entering the realm of sea gods, deities, and spirits. As such, entering and engaging with the sea came with moral responsibilities necessitating social engagement through ritual with their numinous aquatic hosts.

The anthropomorphic sea deities discussed in this chapter represent an important expression of the ontological divide associated with the land-sea dualism. This divide was most clearly expressed at the shoreline. For example, Aston (2009:91) observes that in ancient Greece, the shoreline "is not a zone in which any sea-divinity is prepared to stay on a permanent basis." It is no coincidence that shorelines, especially sea promontories, are the location of most sea god and deity worship (e.g., at temples) in ancient Greece (Romero Recio 2021; Semple 1927). Aston (2009:91) notes that shorelines for the Greeks and their sea deities were "a liminal space if ever there was one." In contrast, and as subsequent chapters reveal, ritual engagements with sea spirits tend to take place on the sea, as the sea is where these spirits reside and are most meaningfully engaged by people.

It is with hybrid sea creatures that the ontological divide between land and sea is most graphically expressed. As Pálsson (1991:97) points out, such "anomalous water-beings . . . stress the boundary between land and sea." In many respects the compound, hybrid nature of many sea creatures can be seen as a universal dimension of the land-sea dualism explored in Chapter 2. However, whereas this dualism tends to enforce separate land and sea domains expressed through language, gender, and material culture divisions, with sea beings this duality is expressed through hybrid creatures featuring conjoined land and sea domains. Such hybrid beings tend to be unstable, and by extension liminal, entities that invariably represent the fusion of stable categories of life into new (unstable) hybrid forms (see Carroll 1990; Gilmore 2003:9, 21; Kristoffersen 2010). These creatures take two forms: human-animal hybrids and animal-animal hybrids, with essentially all sharing the marine component of the tail of either a fish or a serpent. Ritual engagements with these hybrid sea creatures were rare.

Human-animal and animal-animal hybrids are never seen as a result of cross-breeding. For example, a mermaid is not the result of sex between a human and a fish any more than a sea horse is the result of sex between a terrestrial horse and a marine serpent. Somewhat ironically, these "natural" hybrids are not to be taken literally as part of the natural world. In contrast, they stand as iconographic metaphors for the land-sea duality and the sea's multiplicity of liminal zones. John Boardman (1987:78) makes the important point however that the "parents" of such hybrid creatures do exist as the broader categories of land and sea. Caroline Bynum's (2001:30, original emphasis) comment on hybrid creatures of the Middle Ages is also relevant: "A hybrid is a double being, an entity of parts, two or more. It is an inherently visual form. We *see* what a hybrid is; it is a way of making two-ness, and the simultaneity of two-ness, visible." Furthermore, "Hybrid reveals a world of difference, a world that *is* and is multiple . . . hybrid forces contradictory or incompatible categories to coexist and serve as commentary each on the other" (Bynum 2001:31). As Howard Morphy (1989:5) states: "Composite animals can have a cultural reality that may be more revealing than representations of known species because they create sets of species that cross-cut our categories and force us to ask questions about the relationships between those creatures in the cultures concerned."

Human-animal hybrids are a further expression of the ontological permeability of humans and animals seen in many societies: "Anthropological theorizing informs us that the human-animal duality of Western thought [at least in a modern, metropolitan, and Cartesian sense] is limited in scope for most of humanity and most of human history, where the human-animal divide was more commonly seen as ontologically fluid and permeable and understood in terms of overlapping personhood" (McNiven 2013a:97; see also Guenther 2022). Such overlap extended to transformation and what Eduardo Viveiros de Castro (1998) refers to as "metamorphosis." Philippe Descola (2013:136) makes the point that "conversion from animal to human and from human to animal is a constant feature in animist ontologies." As such, it is not an ontology limited to maritime peoples.

In their human-animal hybrid/transformer form, mermaids' and selkies' amphibiousness is limited to the water's edge (e.g., rocky shoreline or beach) and is neither transferable nor transportable inland. In the case of selkies, the transition from sea to land was only made possible through a corporeal (and less a spiritual) transformation to human form through shedding of their fur coat on the shoreline. Similarly, most human encounters with mermaids take place on the shoreline (and not out at sea) and the shoreline is where mermaids shed their corporeal form (removed their fish tail and fins) but plead for a soul to complete their terrestrial transformation to enter human society. These divisions and boundaries not only express and help enforce the land-sea dualism as an opposition but also express the view that land is the operational domain of humans (both corporeally and spiritually) while the sea is more ontologically ambiguous such that it is the domain of human-animal hybrids. In this sense, hybrid beings are an expression of the poly-liminality and ontological instability of the sea for humans.

All human-animal hybrid beings, because of their compound form, have readily recognizable human and animal body parts. As compound hybrids, the human part of these beings is incapable of living successfully on land. Only humans can live in the terrestrial realm. Mermaids lack two human dimensions that allow them to operate on land. The first limitation is physical and most obvious—an absence of legs to allow locomotion out of water. The second limitation is metaphysical and less obvious—the lack of a soul to allow spiritual expression of humanness. These limitations can be reversed to allow insights into questions of how humans can overcome their limitations to operate successfully in the sea. In terms of physical limitations, humans can train themselves to swim or build boats and ships. In terms of metaphysical limitations, seafaring humans are presented with the challenge of spiritually navigating seas whose ontological status features multiple liminal boundaries and ambiguities as exemplified literally and metaphorically by human-animal hybrid sea creatures. On this metaphysical front, compound human-animal hybrids reinforce to humans that they are not fully equipped to successfully live in the marine realm. In short, *humans must shed part of their terrestrial identity to operate successfully in the poly-liminal realm of the sea.* This shedding involves a form of metamorphosis ("ontological switching"—see Chapter 11) through undertaking a broad range of ritual practices to spiritually buffer humans from the metaphysical instability of the marine realm.

Most animal-animal hybrids (e.g., sea-horses) were of monstrous form and behaviorally benign with few direct human engagements. In contrast, direct engagements with human-animal hybrids and transformers were much more common (e.g., selkies) and complex, ranging from infatuation and intimacy to drowning and devouring. For example, mermaids mix human physical form and beauty (few men can resist their female human charms) with monstrous features (lower body as a fish tail) and monstrous behaviors (they drown and sometimes devour men). Even though some mermaids ask humans, often priests, to grant them a soul so that they can become human, such requests are invariably rejected and it is only in exceptional and rare cases that mermaids have lived successfully with humans (e.g., Bassett 1885:171; Benwell and Waugh 1961:13, 163; Rappoport 1928:195). On the other hand, some selkies (human-seal transformers) were known to have lived successfully with humans (i.e., living on land) and to have produced children.

In many cases, sea monsters were colossal sea serpents who attacked ships and crew. However, most sea monsters were hybrid sea creatures representing the compound fusion of a terrestrial animal with a marine serpent's tail. Terrestrial-marine animal hybrid sea monsters, like sea serpents, further express and reinforce not only the land-sea duality but also that the sea is both ontologically separate from land and metaphysically dynamic. As Harriet Ritvo (1997:186) remarks in relation to nineteenth-century scientific skepticism and even ridicule, sea serpents "embodied alternative modes of understanding the natural world." Thus, sea monsters, like sea gods and deities, defy and even violate "normal" (terrestrial) understandings of the laws of nature (Ritvo 1997:133). Further, in his cross-cultural analysis of the social and psychological roots of sea monsters, Gilmore (2003:189) argues that these creatures "challenge . . . the very foundations of our known world." In this regard, he points out that a universal feature of monsters is that they are seen as omnipotent, malevolent, and largely beyond human control (Gilmore 2003:Chapter 10). This omnipotence is expressed physically with gigantic size; huge mouths, often with large teeth, ready to attack and eat people due to an "obsession with oral aggression"; and extreme aggression (Gilmore 2003:178). In the case of sea monsters, they speak loudly about a domain that even the hardiest and knowledgeable sea people and fisherfolk find deeply challenging, dangerous, and unstable.

The paucity of rituals to help control sea monsters indicates a desire to recognize and acknowledge the sea as possessing uncontrollable dimensions. This dimension is expressed in the saga of *Moby-Dick*, where despite an epic battle between man and beast, the monstrous and malevolent white whale triumphs. In this sense, sea monsters are an acknowledgment that humans can only ever minimally know and control the sea. Perhaps it is for this reason that reported sightings of and interest in sea serpents continue up to the present (Ellis 1995; Heuvelmans 1968, 2006; Ritvo 1997).

4

Emplaced Seascapes

Marking the Sea

Prior to the ontological turn in seascape studies of the past 30 years, it was popularly held in Western academic discourse that the fluid nature of the sea limited its capacity to be historicized with places of cultural meaning (McNiven 2025a). The sea is often considered to be the "antithesis of 'land,' or of 'place'" (Patton 2007:11). Killian Quigley (2021:132) draws our attention to the commonly (mis)understood point that the "sea-surface's remarkable resistance to inscription stands for the limits of human memory, human scrutiny, and, in a distinctly material sense, human culture." Alain Corbin (1995:125) states that "human activities leave no trace upon the sea." Sara Caputo (2024) examines the tracklessness of sea voyaging, and the fleeting materiality of a ship's wake, which placed demands on eighteenth- and nineteenth-century mapmakers to chart with lines the paths of voyages of discovery to legitimate territorial claims on the world's oceans. These lines became "well-beaten tracks" and "common highways" during the nineteenth and twentieth centuries with transoceanic passenger voyages between continents (Caputo 2024:191).

Most archaeologists would agree with Cyprian Broodbank's (2000:70) comment that activities on the sea leave few physical remains in the archaeological record apart from shipwrecks. Tom Gunnar Hoogervorst (2012:249) similarly notes that the "record displays very few traces of 'sea people' [of Southeast Asia], obscuring their prehistoric significance or even presence." In some respects, these views reflect secular engagements with the sea such as technologies of marine resource harvesting and voyaging. Today, we are aware that the world's seas are transforming under the influence of human-induced climate change, including rising sea levels, warming, deoxygenation, and acidification (e.g., Kwiatkowski et al. 2020; Tjiputra et al. 2023). Over the past century, humans have literally changed the nature of sea water across the globe.

But it is not only industrialized humanity that has changed the world's seas; hunter-gatherers both past and present have left their mark on the sea in the form of intentional and unintentional alterations (including domestication) of marine ecologies (Rick and Erlandson 2008; Erlandson and Rick 2010). Examples of environmental engineering include restocking habitats (e.g., movement of fish, including fish eggs, from one waterway to another—Campbell and Butler 2010); extension of fish habitats (e.g., construction of coral and rock shelters on reefs—Hunter-Anderson 1981:86–87; Kikiloi 2003:5–6; construction of fish aquaculture ponds—Kikiloi 2003:6–10; Rogers 2024); extension of shellfish habitats (e.g., sediment accumulation within tidal fish traps—Kemp 2006); extension of protective habitats for fish larvae (e.g., construction of tidal fish traps as artificial rock pools—Pattrick et al. 2022); and sedimentation of the intertidal zone and coastal progradation (e.g., from anthropogenically induced erosion of terrestrial sediments from adjacent slopes—Rowe et al. 2013; Spriggs 1986). Paula Pattrick and colleagues (2022:1) argue that "stone-walled fish traps, an ancient engineering feat in the intertidal region, represent the earliest proof of human manipulation of the coastline in Southern Africa."

From an Indigenous perspective, people's capacity to alter marine ecologies extends well beyond the secular and into the spiritual. Most if not all Indigenous coastal peoples know that they have the capacity to alter the availability of marine resources through manipulation of spiritual forces via a range of ritual practices, especially those associated with increase, maintenance, and hunting success (see Chapters 9 and 10). Many of these rituals have a materiality that is archaeologically visible on the land. But do spiritual and cosmological dimensions of maritime people's engagements and understandings of seascapes have archaeological expressions in the sea itself? Clearly, the dynamic nature of the sea presents challenges for the emplacement of physical sites not found on landscapes and terra firma. An extreme example of this challenge is icescapes of Inuit peoples of the Arctic, where ice flows disappear seasonally, only to be re-formed next winter, albeit always in slightly different forms. The fluid and dynamic physical form of the sea indicates that seascape emplacement is similarly fluid and dynamic.

This chapter uses a wide range of examples to illustrate the diverse array of cultural practices associated with inscribing seas with places of meaning, memory, and significance. Often these marine places are "intangible" to outsiders and relate to culturally specific knowledges of the presence of named places and places inhabited by souls of the dead and spiritual beings. In some cases, people physically enhance the meaningfulness of sea places (intertidal and subtidal zones) through the physical alteration of existing features (e.g., rock art) or the creation of new features through the addition of tangible objects such as stone arrangements (including stone-walled fish traps) and accumulation of animal bones on the seabed.

Seas of Known and Named Places and Features

In his overview of the "anthropology of fishing," James Acheson (1981:276) states that "fishermen are operating on a flat, undifferentiated surface" and that the "sea is a dangerous and alien environment." The Western conception of the seas and oceans as largely great expanses of featureless water spatially comprehensible only through the use of external technology such as celestial (sextant) and satellite (GPS) tracking contrasts with those societies that imbue the sea itself with known features, places, and place-names (toponyms). Although Western mariners also use maps featuring named islands, reefs, and passages for navigation, mariners from small-scale societies, especially those with a subsistence focus on marine resources, have finer-grained and intimate knowledge and toponyms for surface and submarine features of reefs and for the variable nature of open sea waters.

The potential extent of marine place-naming practices is encapsulated in the comment that Polynesia is an "aqueous continent" (Gillis 2007:21) or "blue continent" (Samson 2023) of places. This sentiment can be extended across Oceania. For example, the people of the tiny volcanic island (<1 km²) of Anuta, a Polynesian community in the eastern Solomon Islands, identify more than 300 named "marine features" ("coral heads") in seas and across coral reefs within 5 km of their island (Feinberg 2008; Feinberg et al. 2003). Indeed, Feinberg (2008:74) notes that the 300 recorded places "was just a fraction of the features that Anutans recognize and utilize, but that we had no paper large enough to accommodate them all and still be legible." All of the named features "are invisible from land and only can be seen when hovering directly overhead in a boat or canoe. Most of these features occur at depths of between 30 and 150 feet (c. 9–46 m) below the ocean surface" (Feinberg et al. 2003:245). Saul Riesenberg (1972:20) recorded that for mariners of the Micronesian atoll of Puluwat in the Central Caroline Islands, "the ocean's surface is studded with hundreds, perhaps thousands, of other things, whose names, locations, and relationships he knows, and which function as sea-marks for him." Similarly, Brien Meilleur (2019:308) notes that "saltwater areas of the Hawaiian Islands were overlain by a dense conceptual grid of lexicalised traditional ecotopes, named places and oceanic forms and states" that included "over 1,700 surfing sites, most if not all marked by proper names" (see also Pukui et al. 1974).

Rossel Islanders of eastern Papua New Guinea have a complex system for naming places in the sea. Stephen Levinson (2008:259) points out that "scale plays only a minor role in distinguishing landforms, and motivating toponyms. Single rocks may have proper names, as may small portions of reef, or pools in the Lagoon." Indeed, the language of the Rossel Islanders contains no overarching word for either "ocean" or "sea," despite their being a maritime people with a subsistence (protein) reliance on the sea (Levinson 2008:258, 262, 288). The reefs and lagoonal waters surrounding Rossel Island feature a multitude of named physiographic features. These include 14 named major sections of the barrier reef, 22 named main reef passages, 13 named types of water features, 21 structural features of the lagoon, and 18 named reef structures (Levinson 2008:272–275).

For Torres Strait Islanders of northeast Australia, Haddon (1912:229) recorded that "all the islands, however small, every large sandbank and many coral reefs are named." For example, the Goemulgal of the small island of Mabuyag (6 km²) have more than 100 named places (mostly reefs, channels, and islets) across more than 600 km² of territorial seas (Davis and Prescott 1992; Taranto et al. 1997). Bernard Nietschmann (1989:60) notes that "places used are places named" and that a complex taxonomy of terms is used by the Goemulgal to identify different parts of reefs. Torres Strait Islanders "imbue their marine environment with a density of names far in excess of anything that would be required purely by the logistics of fishing. Territories, subsurface features, rocks, and reef clefts are named after events and mythical characters, providing local people with a constant, visible historical anchor" (Cordell 1989:34).

The Lardil people of northern Australia have numerous place-names along the coastline and also for offshore features. Memmott and Trigger (1998:117) recorded that "prominent features in the sea such as reefs, rocks, oyster banks, sandbars, or sand spits may have a specific name, especially if such a place is of sacred significance." Bradley (1998:128–129) similarly recorded that the nearby Yanyuwa people possess a complex system of place-names for their sea country that includes more than 40 known and named sea grass beds and reefs. Furthermore, Yanyuwa songlines that traverse their islands and sea country also possess their own place-name systems. For example, the songline associated with Dugong Hunters of Excellence Spirit Ancestors features more than 50 pathway sites (Bradley 1998:138; Bradley with Yanyuwa Families 2022).

For the people of the island of Luang in eastern Indonesia, their surrounding reef is known through named places that "include various types of beaches, capes and points, islands, submerged and exposed rocks, spits, sandbars, submerged reefs, areas of deep water, tidal areas, and areas where strong currents and whirlpools are encountered" (Pannell 2007:81). Similarly, the Sama people of the Togean Islands of central Sulawesi, Indonesia, live on boats on the sea for many months of the year and have often been referred to as "sea nomads" (Lowe 2003). To Sama fishers, their "coral reefs and shoals, and even the mid-ocean depths under the water's surface" are "home spaces" that are "intimately known and precisely inventoried" (Lowe 2003:116). Celia Lowe (2003:117) makes the cogent point that "proper names give specificity to an intimately familiar world." Furthermore, "A sense of marine place also develops via the interface between sea creatures and experience—collecting, observing, and telling tales about things found in the sea" (Lowe 2003:115).

The Sami people of the Porsanger fjord of northern Norway are fisherfolk with a strong and long-standing connection to their seascape. Camilla Brattland and Steinar Nilsen's (2011:280) study revealed 1,400 Sami place-names along the fjord (including its western margin). These included 236 place-names for "islands, islets, reefs and underwater grounds and features" and 70 place-names "described more or less shallow bottom features, as well as streams, larger open areas and depths in the body of seawater itself" (Brattland and Nilsen 2011:281).

On the North American continent, a survey of place-names in the Cape Flattery region of Washington State on the Pacific Coast in the early twentieth century revealed 224 place-names known by the Makah people, of which 144 (64%) were "marine" (Reid 2015:141).

An interesting dimension to place-names in the sea is provided by Inuit conceptualizations of, and interactions with, sea ice. Most Inuit groups have around 60–80 terms for "sea ice," with a maximum of 110–120 (Heyes 2011; Krupnik 2011; Krupnik and Müller-Wille 2010:391; Nelson 1969:398–403). More specifically, the Inuit of Igoolik Island in Nunavut territory of northern Canada have a complex mapping and naming system for seasonal sea ice flows that cover local sea waters. For example, Agiuppiniq is the name of a 1-to-3-m-high ice ridge that runs in a line for tens of kilometers to the north and east of the island of Nirlirnaqtuuq (Aporta 2002). Claudio Aporta (2002:341) points out that although "Agiuppiniq is one among hundreds of marks that constitute the topography of the sea ice around Igloolik . . . only a few of these sea ice features can be identified as place-names in a way that is comparable to the naming of geographical features on land." Every spring for at least the past two centuries, the Inuit of Igoolik have established a spring snowhouse settlement at Agiuppiniq focused on hunting of seal and walrus (Aporta 2002:342–343). Indeed, the Inuit of the Igoolik area used to spend up to eight months every year living on sea ice (Aporta 2010:169). Needless to say, all physical evidence of these camps disappears (and sinks to the seabed) each year when the ice melts, leaving open water.

In Micronesian and Polynesian navigational practices, non-instrumental navigation of the seas without the aid of compasses, sextants, clocks, and GPS focuses on intimate ecological knowledge and embodied sensory acuity of features of the sea that augmented the famed star "compasses" (including the sun) and celestial mapping (Akimichi 1996; Strongman 2008). Navigational aids based on indirect features of the sea include following the flight paths of "homing birds" between islands (e.g., Lewis 1970:435, 439) and the distinctive clouds that only form over islands (Lewis 1970:440). Direct features of the sea used as transiting place nodes to guide long-distance voyaging between islands include spatial patterning in reefs, depth-sensitive water colors, currents, swells, flashes of light deep below the surface, waves, movement of specific types of fish, bioluminescence, flotsam, salinity levels, and sea surface temperatures (D'Arcy 2006:72–78; Lewis 1970; Riesenberg 1972). The appearance and movements of certain species of fish and birds are known indicators of the proximity of land (islands; Akimichi 1996:509–510). Subtle wind patterns were felt on the face (D'Arcy 2006:74). Swells were also felt (comprehended) through the body. Such intimate, embodied ecological knowledge contributed in part to what Karin Ingersoll (2016) refers to as "Oceanic literacy." Yet Polynesian navigation was much more than embodied scientific knowledge, it was "a state of being" (Strongman 2008:98). It is for this reason that "it took years of formal training and practical experience to become an accomplished navigator" in Pacific Islander communities (D'Arcy 2006:87). Embodied knowledge enables a Polynesian navigator to not voyage across the sea but to "move through it," to sail "*with* the seascape, not on it, but as part of it" (Ingersoll 2016:133, 151; original emphasis).

North Sea fishermen possess "an encyclopaedic knowledge of the pattern of depths and sea-bed material over a large area of the southern North Sea" (Kemp and D'Olier 2016:695). Spatial patterns in seabed sediments are based upon "types of shell, the colour of deposits, and variations in smell and taste" (Kemp and D'Olier 2016:680). During the Middle Ages, English and French mariners possessed a detailed topographical understanding of their seabeds, cognitively mapped using lead sounding weights (Frake 1985:259). Philip Steinberg (2001:64, 70) points out that whereas ancient Mediterranean sailors navigated primarily using terrestrial landmarks, postmedieval northern Europeans tended to navigate using "site-specific local knowledge of the ocean itself."

Seas of the Living: Spirit Children and Conception

For some coastal peoples, coastal waters are associated with spirit children, conception, and pregnancy. For Trobriand Islanders of southeastern Papua New Guinea, the shoreline is where married women are impregnated with spirit children that become incarnated as their children (Tambiah 1983:172, 197). As originally documented by Malinowski (1916:403–406, 1932:145), spirit children (*waiwaia*) come from Tuma, the island of the dead, and derive from the spirits of dead people (*baloma*). In some situations, spirit children enter women by the assistance of *baloma* spirits, but in other cases the spirit children enter women while they are bathing on their own accord. After leaving Tuma, spirit children are known to float around the sea attached to drift wood, foam, leaves, and branches. Indeed, women who do not wish to become pregnant will resist bathing in the sea if such materials have been washed up onto the beach by the tide (Malinowski 1932:149). A woman can also become pregnant if a maternal relative collects sea water (which may contain a spirit-child) adjacent to the beach in a wooden canoe baler and leaves it in her house overnight (Malinowski 1932:149–150).

Spirit children marine sites are a feature of many Aboriginal groups of the northern tropical coast of Australia. For example, the Yawuru people of the Broome coastal region of northwest Australia hold that spirit children (*rai*) sites are located a little off the coast. Patrick Sullivan (1998:102) notes that "many of these sites are in the sea, usually in coastal reefs and rocks." One such *rai* site is a rock in the sea called Miniriny near Cape Villaret (Sullivan 1998:102). A spirit child enters a woman when she eats food. In the case of marine and terrestrial *rai* sites, the "child is frequently born with the mark of the spear, digging stick, bullet or other implement upon it" (Sullivan 1998:102). The Lardil of the Northern Wellesley Islands of the Gulf of Carpentaria "believe that baby spirits live in the small bubbling holes that can be seen along the seashore at low tide" (Roughsey 1971:17). A Lardil man knows that a big fish, turtle, or stingray easily caught usually indicates that a spirit child has entered one of these marine creatures to seek out a mother. That is, the fisherman takes the animal food home for his wife to eat, whereupon the spirit child enters her body. During her pregnancy she is forbidden to eat turtle, dugong, or large fish.

The Yanyuwa, also in the Gulf of Carpentaria, know that the Tiger Shark Dreaming (cosmological) narrative reveals how the traveling Tiger Shark ancestor being "left spirit children at the sandbar Limabinja" located "in the sea" at the mouth of the Wearyan River (Bradley with Yanyuwa Families 2010:67, 81). The Dugong Hunters of Excellence songline (see below) describes how the eyes of dugong hunters were used to create wells with "spirit children" on islands off the coast (Bradley with Yanyuwa Families 2022:172, 235).

In central northern Australia, Yolŋu (East Arnhem Land) Elder Gawirrin Gumana eloquently describes one such "birth place" in the sea, "marked by submerged rocks," as "a reservoir of souls" (Buku-Larrŋgay Mulka Centre 1999:42). One such site, known as Garapana, is a "spirit reservoir" for the Munyuku clan and also where "the spirit of Munyuku people return after death" (Buku-Larrŋgay Mulka Centre 1999:48–49). Garapana is a rock permanently submerged with its location clearly marked by "swirling waters" and "white foam" (Buku-Larrŋgay Mulka Centre 1999:48). The rock is the transformed knives used by ancestral spirit men of the Munyuku clan after the knives became contaminated from butchering a whale. The bones of the whale have also become part of the rock and are "thought of as the essence of a person" (Buku-Larrŋgay Mulka Centre 1999:49).

Seas of the Dead: Bodies and Souls

The sea, for all maritime societies, is the domain of spirits of the human dead. Unlike gods, deities, spiritual beings, hybrid creatures, and monsters, such spirits of the human dead occur in the sea as a result of human agency. Such agency includes the belief that the sea is the domain of souls of the dead irrespective of whether or not a person died on land or at sea, the belief that the sea is the domain of souls of people who inadvertently died at sea, and the belief that spirits of the dead travel across the sea on their way to the final terrestrial resting place of the dead (e.g., islands of the dead).

Sea Burial

The process of burial at sea usually involves either placing the corpse in a canoe or boat and pushing it out to sea or taking the corpse in a canoe or boat offshore and interring it directly into the sea. In terms of canoe/boat burial on the sea surface, on the Northwest Coast of Canada, shamans often traveled to the spirit world of the dead in spirit canoes, and after death their bodies were placed into canoes and sent off for their "final journey to the spirit world" (Shearar 2000:26). Bodies placed in canoes and set adrift on the sea were part of mortuary practices in various parts of the Pacific such as Ulithi (Caroline Islands), Samoa, Tonga, Fiji, and the Chatham Islands (Moss 1925:10, 16).

Direct interment of corpses (or remains of corpses) into the sea occurred in many coastal communities. Enslaved people in the Haida society of the Northwest Coast of Canada were unceremoniously "cast into the sea at death" (Blackman 1990:255). Walter Roth (1907:398) was informed that some Aboriginal groups of the islands off Broadsound in central Queensland would take "their dead out to sea in a canoe" and place them "over-board." The Kerek peoples of the Russian coastline of the northwest Bering Sea "tie the deceased on a long pole, tow it out into the sea, and then push the body into the water with staffs" (Jochelson 1908:104).

In the Solomon Islands, people from the village of Sa'a on the southeast coast of Maramasike Island use sea burial for certain "chiefs" and "commoners" (for details see Ivens 1927:211–212 and Codrington 1891:262). Two canoes are involved in the process, one with the corpse and a stern paddler and one with "helpers." Bags of sand or stones are attached to the body such that it sinks to the shallow seabed. The body is placed into the water with its head facing the sea. In some cases, mourners will jump into the water and embrace the corpse as it sinks. Solomon Islanders of Makira (San Cristóbal) similarly practiced sea burial for "common people" and "chiefs," who "become incarnate in fish, especially in sharks" (Fox and Drew 1915:161). Bodies were placed into seated, extended, or standing positions on sandy seabed visible from the sea surface (Fox 1924:227). Standing corpses were propped up with branches with the flexibility to "sway gently back and forth [to] keep off the sharks" (Fox 1924:227). Food offerings were made to the spirits of the dead at their sea burial location to propitiate gardening success (Fox and Drew 1915:165). To the immediate north on the island of Ulawa (as with Maramasike), "commoners" and sometimes "chiefs" were interred into the sea and weighed down with stones or a bag of sand (Ivens 1927:208–218). In some cases, it was intended for sharks to eat the corpse (to allow for immediate release of the soul), while in other situations the ritual placement of a fish tooth onto a beach shrine or into the sea enticed sharks to protect the body.

Pororan Islanders off the west coast of Buka Island at the northern end of the Solomon Islands chain (eastern Papua New Guinea) also practiced "sea burial" prior to the impact of Christian missionaries (Schneider 2012:146). Despite this change in body interment, Pororans place the hair of the deceased in a hole in the reef and scatter their possessions nearby (Schneider 2012:157–158). To the immediate south, sea burial (usually at designated burial places) for Mono and Alu Islanders differed for commoners (whole bodies) and people of chiefly rank (cremated remains of bone and ash; Moss 1925:19–20; Wheeler 1914:64, 67, 70–72, 76, 81). In the case of cremated bones, it is desirable that they are eaten immediately by a large fish, presumably a shark (Wheeler 1914:70–77).

In northeast Papua New Guinea on New Hanover (northern end of New Ireland) and the Tabar group (east of New Ireland), mortuary practices took a variety of forms: "cremation, interment, and burial at sea (casting the corpse into the water or setting it adrift in a boat), probably depending on whether the deceased belonged to the snake group (interment) or shark group (casting into the sea)" (Bodrogi 1987:19). Some groups also practiced sea burial as a secondary mortuary rite whereby bones were exhumed and then "thrown into the sea" (Bodrogi 1987:19). Elsewhere on New Ireland, communities inter bodies, but "they bury bodies at sea as well," especially in the case of "chiefs" (Parkinson 1999:123). The Mandak of central New Ireland prior to European contact "buried the dead either within the eantuing yard [special village precinct] or at sea. Each coastal eantuing had an offshore area demarcated as its exclusive burial grounds. With stone weights attached to its feet, the corpse was taken by canoe to deep water and allowed to sink to its watery grave. People could not say what factors determined a sea or land interment. Today all are buried on eantuing grounds, usually in a coffin made from an old canoe" (Clay 1977:114). Sea burials were similarly part of mortuary practices on the nearby Tanga Islands (east of New Ireland) where the "dead bodies of men of little or no social importance were always given a water burial, a feature of which was the quick snatching away of the corpse by a predatory shark. Today this method of water burial is reserved for the corpses of infants up to three years of age" (Bell 1947:323). Sea interments were also undertaken in other parts of Island Melanesia such as New Britain (Papua New Guinea), Tanna and Aneityum (Vanuatu), and Loyalty Islands (New Caledonia; Moss 1925:16–17).

The burial ground of the Cantillon family of Ireland was an island in Ballyheigue Bay in southwest Ireland. Originally burials took place on the island but after the sea washed over the island the church and cemetery were now positioned on the seabed. Since inundation, family funerals consisted of placing the coffin within the tidal zone where it would be "conveyed away by the ancestors" (and tide) to its submarine resting place after mourners had left (Croker 1844:139).

For at least a century it is known that some mariners in the West wished to be buried at sea even if they died on land (Bier 2018:646). In recent decades, this practice has included the sea burial of cremated remains. In the United States, permits for sea burial come under the federal government's Environmental Protection Agency (2025) Marine Protection, Research and Sanctuaries Act 1972. The US Navy also offers a sea burial program to navy personnel, including retirees and veterans. Australian Government regulations under the unceremoniously named Environmental Protection (Sea Dumping) Act 1981, developed to fulfill requirements of the Protocol to the Convention on the Prevention of Marine Pollution by Dumping of Wastes and Other Matter 1972 (the London Protocol), requires that a permit be obtained for burial of bodies in Australian waters but not so for cremated remains. Under the Act and Article 1 and Annex 1 of the London Protocol, permits for sea burial of bodies will only be considered for those individuals "having a demonstrated connection to the sea such as for retired or active navy personnel, fishermen or mariners" (Australian Government 2025). Furthermore, the "body needs to be properly prepared for burial at sea. It is appropriate for the body to be sewn into a shroud made of a very strong, biodegradable material that does not contain plastic fibres or has been chemically treated (e.g., Calico). The shroud should be adequately weighted (all plastics must be removed) to ensure rapid descent and permanent submersion of the body and include slits or openings to minimise flotation" (Australian Government 2025). In addition, "Sea burials are only permitted in waters with a depth greater than 3000 metres [i.e., beyond the edge of the continental shelf]. Sea burial sites must not conflict with other uses of the sea, such as trawling/

fishing grounds. Due to these constraints, sea burial sites are usually located a long distance offshore" (Australian Government 2025).

Little archaeological research has been undertaken on sea burials, largely due to unlikelihood of finding direct evidence of interred human remains on the seabed. However, in an overview of Late Dorset archaeology of the Arctic, Martin Appelt and colleagues (2016:794) state that "one remarkable aspect of the Paleoeskimo period as a whole is the rarity of human remains." They add that the "limited number of specimens as well as their deposition in middens suggests that the bodies of deceased humans may have been 'buried' in the sea directly or on the sea ice, or left unprotected on land."

Most information on burial at sea concerns people who died at sea while on board boats and ships and Christian burial services of the nineteenth century. Prior to this period, sea burial appears to have been associated with little ceremony, at least among Anglo-American mariners of the eighteenth century. Dead mariners were usually wrapped up in their canvas hammock (sometimes old sailcloth), with use of wooden coffins very rare. The cloth shroud was usually stitched up by the "sail-maker," who doubled as "undertaker" with the infamous "last stitch" piercing the deceased's nose (Melville 1855:394). Canon shot were sometimes placed inside the shroud to allow the body to sink after it was thrown overboard. An extraordinary addition to a burial shroud was the damaged right arm of Captain Horatio Nelson, which was surgically removed onboard the HMS *Theseus* during the British Royal Naval siege of Santa Cruz in the Canary Islands in 1797. Nelson requested that his amputated limb be included in the sea burial shroud of the mariner who was killed next to him (Adkins and Adkins 2009:324).

The nineteenth century was a period of unprecedented sea travel and sea burial by migrating peoples across the world. For example, between 1815 and 1914, it is estimated that 22.6 million people emigrated from the British Isles, all in ships (Harper 1999:75). Thousands of people died on these voyages and were buried at sea (Haines and Shlomowitz 1998). Most deaths occurred through disease on board ship during transit, and near immediate burial at sea was the only viable option for the corpse in the absence of embalming fluids and refrigeration. Most of these casualties were women and children, especially lower-class infants in steerage (Jalland 2002:18, 20–21). For example, nearly one-quarter of all infants died on the three-and-half-month sailing voyage between Britain and Australia between 1838 and 1853 (Shlomowitz and McDonald 1991:86). During the voyage of the *Beejapore* to Sydney in 1852–1853, 55 infants and young children died en route (Jalland 2002:30). In many cases, deceased infants were simply wrapped up and unceremoniously thrown overboard (Jalland 2002:31).

Shipboard sea burial services were usually officiated by the captain, an officer, doctor, or chaplain (Jalland 2002; K. Reid 2011). In most cases the formal service was taken from the Church of England's *Book of Common Prayer*, replacing the phrase "we commit his/her body to the ground" with "we commit his/her body to the deep" (K. Reid 2011:39). Many mourners found the sight and sound of the body plunging into the sea and disappearing into the fathomless ocean, and the contemplative silence that followed, somewhat horrifying and distressful (K. Reid 2011:40). For some mourners the distress of sea burial was accentuated by a belief in the wildness of the sea as an undomesticated place where the location of burial remained unmarked and memorialized such that relatives and friends could never return to pay their respects. For others, seas were seen as "naturalised and domesticated seascapes" and a perfect venue for burial (K. Reid 2011:45). For many, sea burial provided the potential for connection to the dead anywhere and everywhere.

In some cases, sea burials were for bodies found floating in the sea after a shipwreck. A famous example is the sea burial of 114 of the 337 bodies recovered in the weeks following the tragic *Titanic* disaster of 1912 (Bier 2018). Another 1,000 bodies were never recovered, with many taken down to the ocean floor within the sinking ship. Most of those buried at sea were third-class passengers and crew, with embalming for land burial limited to first-class passengers (placed in a coffin) and second-class passengers (wrapped in canvas). The class distinction for sea burial appears to have reflected in large part an assumption that first-class passengers probably had life insurance, and beneficiaries required a body as evidence to receive the insurance payout.

Despite the rigid formality of Christian sea burial practices, mourners often did not accept sea burial as a proper Christian burial practice. Such doubts may have fueled a belief among many mariners that the sea was filled with the spirits of the restless dead (Stewart 2011:110–115, 129–131, 165). In a detailed study of English and American maritime mortuary practices during the Age of Sail (fifteenth to early twentieth centuries), David Stewart (2011:115) notes that "fear of the sea's restless dead explains why sailors believed that the burial at sea service was so necessary." Yet the "restless nature of the sea, however, prevented it from being turned into a permanent barrier between the living and the dead. Even after being properly buried, the ghosts of dead mariners sometimes returned to haunt their former shipmates" (Stewart 2005:276).

The Bajau "sea nomads" of southern Sulawesi in Indonesia dispose of a body at sea if the person dies on a boat at sea (Marhadi and La Hatani 2018:631). The body is placed within a "sack" and weighed down with either a "jar" or a "large stone and then drowned in the deep sea." Immediate sea burial is undertaken "because if there is a body on a boat, then the boat cannot sail anymore." It is "believed that the king of the sea" will "hold the boat, so that, it cannot move anymore" (Marhadi and La Hatani 2018:631). In contrast, when a Bajau family member dies at home on an island, "the body will be buried on the beach near the sea" such that it can be "touched by sea water." Indeed, "At least once a year, the cemetery concerned is sprinkled by seawater . . . during a great high tide" (Marhadi and La Hatani 2018:631).

To what extent Anglo-American mariners thought that sea interments saw a body sink to the seabed is difficult to know. Rozwadowski (2005:73) notes that it was generally thought during the nineteenth century that reaching the bottom of the ocean was impossible: "Many sailors believed that wrecked ships, bodies, or other objects thrown overboard did not fall to the bottom, but stopped and floated when they 'found their depth.' If this was true, objects would fall through the water only until the point at which the water's specific density equaled their own, at which depth they would float forever. Such ideas persisted far into the nineteenth century."

In 1850 an English company laid a submarine telegraph cable between Dover (England) and Calais (France) across the bed of the English Channel, only for a fisherman to accidentally cut the cable within a day. The following year another English company laid another cable, this time successful, across the channel (Headrick and Griset 2001). As the first long-distance submarine cables, the English Channel cables generated not only nationalistic and economic interest but also cultural and social interest in terms of the potential disturbance of spiritually charged sites such as shipwrecks. For example, in 1850, London's satirical *Punch* magazine contained a short article and illustration about the severing of the first cable as a metaphor for relationships between England and France. The illustration shows the telegraph cable on the seabed among the scattered and disturbed remains of shipwrecks and human skulls, above which hover two angelic female figures with one holding an olive branch seemingly extending out to France (Figure 10). The illustration was captioned: "Effect of the submarine telegraph; or, peace and good-will between England and France."

A couple of years later in 1857 and 1858, four attempts were made, albeit unsuccessfully, to lay a telegraph cable between Ireland and Newfoundland (Rozwadowski 1996:23). As with the earlier English Channel cable, the transatlantic cable similarly generated concern over potential disturbance of shipwrecks and human remains. Indeed, the 14 August 1858 issue of the American *Harpers Weekly* republished the 1850 *Punch* illustration, replacing the word "France" in the top right corner with "America" (Hanlon 2016:289). Christopher Hanlon (2016) also points out that poems of the time articulate broader community

Figure 10. Satirical illustration associated with the laying of a telegraphic cable across the English Channel in 1850 (from London's *Punch* magazine, Volume XIX, September 1850).

sentiment that the unfathomable seabed, once thought the silent world of the maritime dead, has now been ruptured and disturbed by submarine cables also carrying, somewhat ironically, disembodied voices in Morse code.

Islands of the Dead

Numerous coastal peoples hold that spirits of the dead travel across the sea to the place of the dead "either on their own accord or with the assistance of the living through specially performed (mortuary) rituals" (McNiven 2004:333). Such places of the dead are often conceptualized as islands or lands of the dead but can also be seen as submerged places. In some cases, these islands of the dead can be objectively seen but often they exist in a spiritual sense. Examples of the former include small islands located off the southern coast of Sweden and Norway that are often too small to be inhabited by the living but contain large burial cairns dating to the Bronze Age (Ballard et al. 2004:389). The "souls of the dead" of Ireland are known to inhabit three small islands known as Tech Duinn (House of Duinn, god of death) located in Ballinskelligs Bay, southwest Kerry (Thomson 1996:41).

The people of coastal Gaul (e.g., France) in the first millennium saw England as the island of the dead. The Greek scholar Procopius claimed in the sixth century CE that fishermen of the Gallic coast (eastern shore of the English Channel) acted as ferrymen for souls of the dead. As paraphrased by Wilbur Bassett (1917:122), the "chosen Charon was called to the beach at night where lay vessels empty but deep. The six-day voyage to the isle of souls was made in a night. Names were called and answered from the farther shore, and the awed fisherman returned in his lightened vessel." Bassett (1917:123) suggests that Baie des Trépassés (Bay of the Dead) on the western tip of the Brittany coast may relate to this story. He adds that since the tenth century CE this story has been Christianized such that the "gentle soul-ships of the channel have been changed to wandering hell-ships."

Numerous coastal peoples of Island Southeast Asia possess an islands of the dead concept as part of their spirituality (Moss 1925). For example, Roti/Rote Islander spirits of the dead travel 100 km west to the island of Savu/Sawu, while Savu/Sawu Islander spirits of the dead travel 110 km northwest to the island of Sumba (Moss 1925:4). In Japan, rituals associated with processing the souls of the dead (humans and whales) include conveying whale souls out to "the world of the ancestors," which "exists out beyond the sea" (Boreal Institute for Northern Studies 1988:60). Lamps are floated out to sea as part of giving "whale souls a ceremonial send-off" (Boreal Institute for Northern Studies 1988:60).

In northern Australia, Aboriginal people of Groote Eylandt in the Gulf of Carpentaria ritually ferry spirits of the dead across the sea. As David Turner (2000:43) explains, "The Songpersons take the spirit out into the ocean where it transforms into a fish and from there to the island of Amburrgba, North-East Island, and just beyond and under the sea to Wuragwugwa, a kind of 'gateway' to the 'other side.'" Yet Amburrgba should not be conceived of as a final resting place of the dead geographically separated from the land of the living. The land of the dead "is the 'same' as the land of the living, but in a different dimension and in mirrored image. The physical mediator between them is the source of life itself—water" (Turner 2000:44). The spirits of recent dead Ganggalida of northern Australia dwell in a place "described in English" as "the middle of the sea" (Robins et al. 1998:85). The people of Goulburn Island off Arnhem Land in northern Australia identify Wulurunbu and Lingardji as submerged islands "inhabited by the spirits of the dead" (Cooke and Armstrong 1998:179).

In southwest Australia, Nyungar Aboriginal people of the Swan River area know that the "spirits of the deceased passed into" cormorants that roost on a granite islet (known as Mewstone Rock) located 9 km off the coast. The Aboriginal name of the rock is Gudu Mitch, which is a compound of *gu-urt* (the "heart") and *mit* or *mitch* (the "medium" or "agent"), "signifying that this island is the medium or agent by which the spirit of the departed one enters the body of a cormorant" (Chauncy 1878:269). Large flocks of cormorants move up the Swan River in the morning and return to the islet in the evening. None of these cormorants are taken as food, "lest thereby they should be slaying their ancestors" (Chauncy 1878:269). Yet Ken Macintyre and Barb Dobson (2017) note that the Nyungar term for the Pied Cormorant is *medi* or *meedee* and "translates as 'agent' or 'medium' and possibly refers to its role as an intermediary between the world of the living and the afterlife." That is, the cormorant's "primary role . . . is to deliver the soul safely to its destination" (Macintyre and Dobson 2017). Rottnest Island, located 12 km northwest of Mewstone Rock, is similarly identified by Nyungar people as a place "where the spirits of the dead go" (Draper 2015:240).

Kangaroo Island, located 14 km offshore of South Australia, is known as Karta, the island of the dead, by Ngarrindjeri, Ramindjeri, and Kaurna peoples of the adjacent mainland coast (Draper 2015). According to Norman Tindale and Brian Maegraith (1931:286), a "similar idea is held by the Parnkalla natives, north of Port Lincoln [South Australia], who, according to Schürmann [1846], bury their dead with 'the head towards the west, a custom that . . . is founded on their belief that the soul goes to an island in the east.' This island is called Mungaltanna, and is situated somewhere in Spencer Gulf." Further to the east, the Gunditjmara people of southwest Victoria continue to speak of Deen Maar/ Dhinmar (Lady Julia Percy Island), located 8 km off the coast, as the place where the spirits of the dead travel as their final resting place (Brown et al. 2017:14, 37; Dawson 1881:51; Mathews 1904). Indeed, the Gunditjmara buried their dead with heads facing Deen Maar (Read 2007:69). To the southeast across Bass Strait, Aboriginal people of Cape Portland located on the northeast corner of Tasmania noted in the 1830s that "when black men die they go to the islands" (Robinson cited in Plomley 1966:400).

The island of the dead concept is also found among various peoples of Oceania. For example, the Goemulgal people of Mabuyag island in western Torres Strait of northeast Australia hold that *markai* ("ghost" people) travel across the sea westward to the "mythical" island of Kibu ("land of dead spirits"; Fitzpatrick-Nietschmann 1980:144, 347; see also Haddon 1904:355–356). In New Caledonia, the souls of the dead float down rivers to the sea to their final resting place on the seabed, where they are presided over by a shark god (Knappert 1992:203). The people of Roviana Lagoon on New Georgia Island in the western Solomon Islands hold that the souls of the dead depart from Keru (a cave on the coast at Sibo) on their journey across the sea to Sodo or Sonto (Shortland Islands and Bougainville Island), located over 200 km to the northwest (Waite 1990:59–60). The souls of the dead are escorted by spirits or ghosts in canoes who have come across from Sodo/Sonto (Hocart 1922:91–95). Shrines holding skulls of the dead are located along the edge of the lagoon facing toward passages in the outer reef and the sea to facilitate the souls' journey (Nagaoka 1999:115).

In some cases, spirits of the dead depart from headlands for a realm of the dead that is not identified as an island. For example, the island of Tahiti is conceptualized as a fish with the head located at Taiarapu (southwest), stomach at

Mataeia (west), and tail at Faaa (north). Faaa "is where the spirits of the dead and gods leave the visible world for the invisible world of the gods and ancestors" (Hilmi et al. 2016:175). In addition, Taiarapu is "the primary portal of the gods Taaroa and Tane, and of the spirits of the dead, when they come to visit the visible world of humans" (Hilmi et al. 2016:175). For the Māori of Aotearoa/ New Zealand, Te Rerenga Wairua (Cape Reinga) is "the leaping place of spirits of the dead on their journey to the spirit world of the ancestors" (Hilmi et al. 2016:175).

In many coastal contexts, souls of the dead travel off shore in symbolic soul boats (aka ships of the dead) to an undesignated location. For example, in some parts of Island Southeast Asia and Melanesia, the ritual process of ferrying the souls of the dead across the sea to their final resting place is associated with the carving of model soul boats with people on board. In addition, the cosmological tradition of soul boats in many Southeast Asian coastal communities extends to use of boat coffins. Chris Ballard and colleagues (2004:394) propose that the "concept" of the "ship of the dead" can be extended to rock art in Southeast Asia (e.g., Borneo, Sulawesi, the Moluccas, Timor) and Melanesia (e.g., New Guinea and the Solomon Islands). They add that "a generalized ship of the dead symbolism was a very widespread feature of regional cosmologies, and possibly one of considerable antiquity, pre-dating Austronesian colonization in eastern Indonesia and Melanesia" around 3,500 years ago (Ballard et al. 2004:396). If correct, Southeast Asia and Melanesia provides the earliest known evidence in the world for the concept of maritime ships of the dead.

For the Asmat of the south coast of Papua, eastern Indonesia, the human dead are transferred to "*safan*, the realm of the souls, beyond the sea" and "where the sun sets on the horizon" (de Antoni 2010:205; Zegwaard 1959:1028). The Asmat ancestral dead who reside in *safan* are known as *kavé* (Gerbrands 1967:118). An integral feature of rites associated with assisting the spirits of the dead transfer from their temporary "limbo" existence to *safan* is the carving of *bis* poles for the *bis mbu* or *bis pokumbui*/*bis pokumbu* ceremony (Kjellgren 2014:51; Konrad and Konrad 1996:267). *Bis* poles range in length from 2.5 m to 8 m and are carved from a single mangrove tree trunk (Konrad and Konrad 1996:267). The inverted tree trunk with the root system at the top of the pole is a reference to *safan* where everything is opposite to the earthly realm (de Antoni 2010:205, 220). *Bis* poles exhibit a series of human figures with the lower section known as the canoe (*ci*) sometimes featuring a carving of a canoe vertically oriented and usually with a single passenger representing the deceased (Kjellgren 2014:52, 54). The canoe represents "a supernatural vessel that transports the spirits of the dead to the land of the ancestors" (Kjellgren 2014:54).

Spirits of the dead of the Ngarrindjeri, Ramindjeri, and Kaurna peoples of the mainland coast of South Australia travel to Kangaroo Island (island of the dead) using spirit rafts (Draper 2015:238–239). The triangular-shaped rafts (*kundi*) are the same as used by the living on calm waterways of the lower Murray River. That a strong symbolic link existed between *kundi* used by the living and the dead is revealed by use of these rafts in elevated burial platforms by various Aboriginal groups of the lower Murray River.

Societies with ships of the dead can encounter spirits of the dead while out at sea. For example, the people of the island of Luang in eastern Indonesia say that while out voyaging it is "not uncommon" to encounter the dead as they travel to their final places of rest (Pannell 2007:88). In this instance care is needed, as "the undead are capable of distracting people as they sail through the physically challenging reef environment or of interfering with their fishing activities, cutting fishing lines and anchor ropes, for example" (Pannell 2007:88). For Torres Strait Islanders, *markai* can be seen paddling their spirit canoes on "the open sea on calm nights to catch turtle, dugong or fish" (Haddon 1904:358). The Kwakwaka'wakw of the Northwest Coast of Canada also hold that spirits of the dead travel around in spirit canoes (Boas 1932:216). Similarly, off the coast of Shimbara in the Nagasaki region of southern Japan, "balls of fire" seen at certain times of the year are considered to be the spirits of people who died from an earthquake (Piggott 1969:72).

Marine Inundation: Creation Narratives and Rituals

Many Australian Aboriginal groups associate the present location of inshore waters with inundation by ancestral beings. For example, the Lardil of the southern Gulf of Carpentaria know that ancestral Dreaming beings "submerged parts of the land beneath the sea" (Memmott and Trigger 1998:120). As such, features created on land by these mythic ancestors are now located on the seabed. Examples include channels separating various islands and even the islands themselves (Memmott and Trigger 1998:120). Memmott and Trigger (1998:120) hypothesize that these creation stories of inundation may relate to postglacial sea level rise and island formation "some 6500 years ago" (see also Nunn and Cook 2022). On the southern coast of Australia, Aboriginal people associate the formation of Spencer Gulf with the Kangaroo-man, who used the thigh bone of a mythical ancestor to ritually split open an isthmus to allow seawater to flood into a valley. This action was done to inundate a series of freshwater lagoons which had been the focus of conflict between birds and other animals (Roberts and Mountford 1969:18).

Patrick Nunn (2018, 2020, 2021) has assembled a large corpus of legendary narratives held by Indigenous Australians and coastal communities around Europe (including Great Britain) that he argues are oral histories relating to sea level rise that in many cases may reference postglacial sea level rise at least 7,000 years ago. In some cases, these narratives include references to sunken towns, villages, and gardens (see below), while in other contexts they refer to attempts to mitigate sea level rise, often through ritual. For example, the Gungganyji people of the Cairns region of northeast Australia possess a story of how they rolled fire-heated boulders down a mountainside to stop rising sea levels (Nunn 2020:118–119). The Wati Nyiinyii people of the Nullarbor Plain in South Australia tell a story of how their ancestors stopped sea level rise by building a wall of thousands of wooden spears (Nunn 2020:119–120). A legendary narrative from southwest Scotland documents how the witch Gyre Carline (aka McNeven or Nicneven) used her magic stave to banish the sea from the area that is today the marshland known as Lochar Moss (Kavanagh and Bates 2019; Nunn 2022:82–83). For locals, this legend is consistent with recovery of remains of boats within the marshland (Cromek 1810:293). Nunn (2022) argues that the legend and archaeological remains reference sea level fall associated with coastal emergence due to postglacial isostatic rebound from 6,000 years ago.

Archaeologists have interpreted the creation of a number of shoreline (including intertidal zone) sites in England and Europe as ritual responses to sea level rise. For example, Francis Pryor (2001:431) hypothesizes that the timber alignment and platform at Flag Fen in England in the Bronze Age during the thirteenth century BCE may have been constructed as a ritual response to rising waters and "as a symbolic weir or dam against their inexorable rise." Similarly, Lars Larsson (2003:224) speculates that continued use of cemeteries facing inundation from sea level rise during the end of the marine transgression by late Mesolithic peoples of southern Scandinavia might have been a deliberate strategy to ritually "affect nature and stop or at least reduce the rise of the sea level."

Robert Van de Noort (2011:69) proposes that many votive offering deposits (e.g., polished stone axes and bronze weapons) dating to the Neolithic and Bronze Ages found along coastal margins and associated wetlands of northern Europe "could be understood as offerings or sacrifices to the encroaching sea, or to the expanding wetlands, with the sea or wetlands being attributed other-than-human agency." That is, such votive offerings could be seen as a "convincing way of dealing with extraordinary environmental change" such as the marine transgression and associated sea level rise (Van de Noort 2011:67; see also Bradley 2022:126).

James Leary (2013) similarly suggests somewhat speculatively that a series of Mesolithic deposits of artifacts found in transgressing shoreline contexts in northern Europe may have been ritually related to sea level rise. Furthermore, "The inundating zone may have been deliberately selected for their formal deposition . . . as a way of placating the waters or water spirits that were transgressing onto land" (Leary 2013:211–212). Possible examples include a deposit of around 500 Mesolithic barbed points made from bone and antler recovered from coastal sediments revealed during construction of Europort near Rotterdam, The Netherlands (Verhart 2004:57) and a concentrated (secondary) deposit of ax manufacturing debitage dating to the Mesolithic within the intertidal zone at Vænget Nord, Denmark (Petersen 1989:328). Leary (2013:215) agrees with Pryor's (2001) interpretation of the wooden arrangement at Flag Fen being associated with sea level change and adds that "seahenge" may have been constructed around 4,000 years ago for similar ritual reasons (see Brennand et al. 2003).

Recently, Nunn and colleagues (2022:213) have built on new understandings that the Carnac megalithic site complex "cognitive barrier" at Brittany in France extends into subtidal waters (Cassen et al. 2011:100) and thus "may have been constructed . . . to [ritually] stop the rapid rise of postglacial sea level in the Gulf of Morbihan around 6300 years BP."

Most published references to sunken cities, towns, and gardens concern Europe, including Great Britain (see Nunn 2020, 2021, 2022). Rare examples of such phenomena beyond this cosmological domain include Northwest Coast societies of Canada, who speak of a range of sea beings that reside on the seabed. For example, Haida know that orca "Ocean-People" reside in "towns" that "were scattered along the shores beneath it. These were located at, or rather under, every prominent cape, hill, or reef; and even hills some distance back from the coast had subterranean avenues of approach from the ocean" (Swanton 1905:17). Furthermore, "When travelling about, these Ocean-People appear as killer-whales, but in their submarine towns they are like men" (Swanton 1905:17; see Chapter 3).

European aquatic cosmologies include references to sunken inhabited cities and towns in the depths of the sea replete with buildings, people, and often fantastic and bejeweled gardens. The most famous example is the ancient Greek legend of Atlantis, albeit invented by Plato "as an allegory of what happens when polity [city-state] becomes too large and commercial for its own good" (Gillis 2004:21). Mermaids in European tradition are often associated with bejeweled seabed abodes. Similarly, Orkney Islanders of Scotland identify the town of Finfolkaheem on the bottom of the sea as the permanent home of fin folk. It had gardens with colored seaweeds and huge pearls which were ground to make pearl dust to cover and fluoresce the tails of mermaids. A dance hall of crystal was illuminated by bioluminescence and the Northern Lights (Marwick 1975:25–26).

Off Land's End in Cornwall in southwest England is said to be the sunken city of Lyonesse (sometimes Lethowsow; Nunn and Compatangelo-Soussignan 2024). Legend has it that the 24-km stretch of sea between Land's End and the Scilly Isles to the southwest was once land inhabited by people known as the Silures, who had between 40 and 140 churches. It is said that an "immense number of the inhabitants perished" when waters suddenly inundated this world, perhaps in the eleventh century CE (Hunt 1865:209). Cornish fishermen sometimes bring up windows in their nets and in some cases have seen the remains of houses on the seabed (Hunt 1865:211). Cudden Point, located east of Penzance, is said to be a good place to find artifacts, especially treasure, associated with Lyonesse at very low tides (Hunt 1865:213). Osbert Crawford (1927) documented constructed stone walls exposed at very low tides (some sections remained submerged within the subtidal zone) on the seabed in the area taken in by the legendary Lyonesse. He noted that these walls clearly had been constructed during a period of lower sea level, when what is now seabed was dry land, as "no one makes walls like this below high water mark" (Crawford 1927:6).

Around the coast of England are stories of sunken villages located in the sea where it is claimed the sounds of ghostly residents can be heard. For example, off the coast of the Isle of Man between the mainlands of England and Ireland is sunken land where mariners state that it is possible to hear the submarine sounds of "cattle lowing" and "dogs barking" (Nunn 2021:32). Elderly residents of Dunwich on the east coast of England hear the sound of bells ringing beneath the waves where churches have long succumbed to coastal erosion (Nunn 2021:35–36).

Breton coastal folk of France have legends of the cities of Is and Berbido (Rappoport 1928:147–149). In the case of Is, Bretons state that stone blocks visible at low tide in the Bay of Donarnenez are the remains of the city's foundations (Rappoport 1928:147). Breton sailors see phosphorescence as a result of shimmering jewels associated with the garden of a water demon at the bottom of the sea, which is inhabited by the souls of the pious drowned (Rappoport 1928:52; see also Blind 1881a:197). More generally, Breton mariners note that during their sea voyages and fishing trips that they have seen submarine evidence of sunken walls, castles, and church spires and heard the sound of bells emanating from inhabited sunken towns (Rappoport 1928:148–149).

Numerous examples of inhabited islands that sank beneath the waves are recorded in oral histories of the Southwest Pacific, such as the Solomon Islands, Vanuatu, and Fiji (Nunn 2009, 2021; Nunn et al. 2022). For example, peoples of the southern end of Malaita in the Solomon Islands have oral traditions about an inhabited island called Teonimanu that disappeared beneath the waves as a result of one or a series of giant tsunamis sometime between 200 and 400 years ago (Nunn 2009:152–155). As the island sank, inhabitants fled to nearby islands, where their descendants continue to reside. The location of Teonimanu is known today as Lark Shoal. In one account, the site is referred to as "the land of the sea," where "the ghosts of the dead of Teonimanu dance on the beaches by night among the breakers, and are sometimes seen there by living men" (Fox 1924:169).

Off the northeast coast of Malekula in Vanuatu, oral traditions document the disappearance of the islands of Malveveng and Tolamp in the early nineteenth century (Nunn 2009:161). The location of the two islands is known and is marked by coral reefs. The submerged "surface of Malveveng is said to be 4–5 meters below water level; that of Tolamp is deeper, around 15 meters. When diving it is apparently possible to see a number of signs of the islands' former human occupation, such as stone-ringed meeting places (*nasara*), paths, and stone fences" (Nunn 2009:161).

Archaeological research on artifacts recovered from the continental shelf has resulted in a new form of understanding of sunken abodes. Most relevant is interpretation by archaeologists of numerous ancient artifacts and human remains recovered within fishing nets of professional fishers from the seabed of the North Sea. These objects provide unique insights into Upper Paleolithic, Mesolithic, and Neolithic occupation of what was once dry land prior to inundation from postglacial sea level rise. A famous example is the Upper Paleolithic barbed antler point recovered at a depth of 36 m within a block of peat pulled up in a fishing net by the crew of the trawler *Colinda* from the Leman and Ower Banks, northeast of Norfolk in 1931, and radiocarbon dated to 13,000–14,000 years ago (Clark 1936:15; Housley 1991:30). In 2005 the proximal section of a bovid metatarsal (foot) bone was pulled up in a fishing net southwest of the Brown Bank in the south North Sea (Amkreutz et al. 2018). The bone has been radiocarbon dated to around 13,000 years ago (Upper Paleolithic) and features remarkable decoration in the form of incised zigzag lines. Van de Noort (2011:144) makes the intriguing suggestion that Neolithic stone axes found on the Dogger Bank in the North Sea may have been deliberately placed on relict islands of the final stages of inundation of Doggerland. That is, "The deposition of the polished axes was deliberate and ritually inspired by the social memory of Doggerland, with the islands being attributed special status as the last remnants of the land of the ancestors. In this case, the inundation of the land did not result in a *tabula rasa* of the North Sea, but the memory of the former lands lived on for a considerable period of time."

Marine Features: Creation Narratives and Emplaced Beings

Numerous peoples across the globe hold creation narratives to account for the formation of a wide range of marine features. In terms of waterways, Orkney Islanders have a legend that the 100 km-wide strait that divides Denmark from Norway and Sweden was formed by a gigantic sea monster named Stoor Worm when his tongue fell out and crashed upon the earth (Dennison 1891a:168, 1891b:130–131). The 25-km-wide channel that separates the island of Jersey from the Normandy coast was created by rising seas as God's punishment for blasphemy by a local priest (Bois 2016:60). According to the Lardil people of the Gulf of Carpentaria, northern Australia, channels separating islands in the North Wellesley Group were created by Garnguur (seagull woman) as she dragged her large *walpa* (raft) "back and forth across the peninsula" (Roughsey 1971:20). In another case, the channel separating Mornington Island from Denham Island was created by wurruku (ancestral shark; Kenneth Jacob cited in Ahern and the Mornington Island Elders 2002:54).

Many societies of Oceania possess legendary narratives of islands formed by being "fished-up" from the seabed (Nunn 2003). For example, according to Māori mythology, the North Island of Aotearoa/New Zealand was hauled out of the sea by the demigod Māui (Paulin with Fenwick 2016:110–111). Rennell Island (Solomon Islands) was said to have been hauled to the surface by the culture hero Mautikitiki after being caught on his fishhook (Monberg 1991:23). In the northwest Pacific, Omitsunu, the demigod king of Izumo on the west coast of Japan, and grandson of the storm god Susanowo, is said to have enlarged his kingdom by pulling up islands from the seabed using ropes (Knappert 1992:213). In a similar mythological narrative, an island off the coast of Japan formed as it rose up from the seabed to meet the feet of the goddess Benten, who was descending from heaven (Knappert 1992:73).

In other cases, islands in Oceania were formed through emplacement of sediment or objects (Nunn 2003). For example, the island of Rotuma in the South Pacific is said to have been created by the legendary Raho from Samoa who poured a basket of earth into the ocean (Knappert 1992:250). According to the Erubam Le of Torres Strait of northeast Australia, Maizab Kaur (Bramble Cay) was created by a group of local men led by Rebes using sediment from their residential island of Erub (Lawrie 1970:283–284). The Butchulla Aboriginal people of southeast Queensland, Australia, hold that their ancestral island of K'gari (Fraser Island) formed when K'gari (a female sky spirit) lay down on some rocks in the sea and transformed into a large sandy island (Miller 1993). People of the Polynesian outlier island of Bellona in the Solomon Islands know that their homeland "began as a Nerita shell that rose out of the ocean" (Monberg 1991:23).

According to the Marind-anim, the island of Habé (Habeeke) located 4.5 km off the coast of southeast Indonesian Papua was moved into place by *dema* spirit beings. In one mythological narrative, the sea eagle *dema* Bau moved the island 50 km to its current location from its original location at the mouth of the Bian River to the east (Kooijman et al. 1958:74; van Baal 1966:392). In another narrative, Habé was part of the mainland near the Fly River in southwest Papua New Guinea some 500 km to the southeast before being set adrift by the *dema* Dawi (van Baal 1966:274–278). The northern islands of Kiribati in the central Pacific wandered across the ocean "until one mighty ancestor held them down with an anchor made from strong wood" (Tiata Koriri cited in Nunn 2021:82).

The Haida of the Northwest Coast of Canada have a story of a woman who, after suffering the wrath of her killer whale husband, transformed herself into a reef (Shearar 2000:89). The Larrakia of the Darwin area of northern Australia identify a particular rocky reef located within the intertidal zone of their Saltwater Country as embodying "the spirit of Darriba Nungalinya, a primeval hybrid being (part human and part nonhuman)" (Lobo 2019:398). Darriba Nungalinya is also referred to by the Larrakia as "ancestral Grandfather or Grandfather Rock" (Lobo 2019:398). The site of Darriba Nungalinya must be treated with respect, with Cyclone Tracy, the huge storm which devastated the town of Darwin in 1974, attributed to the wrath of Darriba Nungalinya. In Blue Mud Bay off the coast of Arnhem Land in northern Australia is an elongated coral reef that the Yolŋu know is the "transformed tail" of an ancestral stingray (Morphy and Morphy 2006:70). Another Yolŋu reef, circular in outline, and a connecting sandbar are a transformed ancestral turtle and harpoon rope associated with a turtle hunter (Barber 2005:169; Morphy and Morphy 2006:71).

Aboriginal songlines of northern Australia provide insights into the potential complexity of cosmological narratives associated with formation of marine features. For example, the Bardi and Djawi peoples of the Kimberley coast of northwest Australia know that "ancestral beings travelled the seas and created the islands, reefs, sandbanks and marine species found within the sea. The adventures of these ancestral beings are recalled in song and story. The beings named all the features in the environment including particular places on the seabed where certain ritual activities occurred which, in some cases, resulted in ritual paraphernalia being left behind metamorphosing into particular marine features" (Green 1988:22). The Yolŋu of East Arnhem Land have Dreaming nar-ratives associated with ancestral beings who traveled across the sea and created certain rocks, sandbanks, mud banks, channels, tidal eddies, and reefs (Davis 1989:51; Dhimurru Aboriginal Corporation 2013:23). Some of these places of creation are considered "extremely dangerous and Aboriginal people will avoid them at all times" (Davis 1989:51). On Groote Eylandt in the northwest Gulf of Carpentaria, the Tiger Shark songline records the travels of Tiger Shark, who started on the adjacent mainland (Arnhem Land) and moved across the sea to Groote Eylandt, creating all the features of the coastline (e.g., bays and inlets) through the sweeping action of his tail as he swam (Palmer 1998:149). In the southern parts of the Gulf of Carpentaria, the mainland Ganggalida people are custodians and managers of the Dugong (Bijarrba) Dreaming songline that commences at a freshwater hole located 17 km inland and travels down a watercourse toward the sea and out to offshore islands before turning west toward Yanyuwa country (Memmott and Trigger 1998:120).

Bradley with Yanyuwa Families (2010, 2022) document in detail Dreaming narrative songlines associated with the formation and animation of marine features across the seas of the Yanyuwa people of the southern Gulf of Car-pentaria. Yanyuwa songlines (*kujika*) record the exploits of Dreaming ancestor beings as they traveled across lands and seas creating geographical features, the elements, plants and animals, and people and their clan estates, law, and ceremonies—all intimately connected and interrelated through intricate sys-tems of kinship. This kinship between human and nonhuman kin is agentive, as the creative powers of the Dreaming ancestor beings remain "ever present" (Bradley with Yanyuwa Families 2010:106). That is, the "Dreamings travelled, and they stopped, and they now remain in their respective countries, still sen-tient, active, potent and sometimes very dangerous" (Bradley with Yanyuwa Families 2022:76). Yanyuwa songlines "are never spoken of in the past tense or the future tense" but as "flowing in the country" (Bradley with Yanyuwa Families 2022:131). The recitation of songlines (i.e., singing the verses) by senior knowledgeable Yanyuwa "lifts and holds and animates both country and kin" (Bradley with Yanyuwa Families 2010:xiii). The Dugong Hunters of Excellence songline contains over 300 verses and runs in an east to west direction through the Sir Edward Pellew Islands and associated waters (detailed in Bradley with Yanyuwa Families 2022). As the hunters traveled in their canoes, they named places on islands and in the sea (e.g., reefs) and created various geographical features (including rock outcrops and creeks and emplaced wells and certain food and raw material plants). In one instance a single rock standing in the sea is where one of the hunters stayed and turned into stone.

Rocks in the sea representing emplaced beings are found in numerous places. For example, the Lardil of the south Gulf of Carpentaria have a site known as Ngawilan located offshore from the eastern end of Mornington Island. The site comprises three rocks emerging from the sea which are believed to be "the bodies of their ancestors, the first humans who came into their country" (Memmott and Trigger 1998:119). Off the northwest coast of the South Island of Aotearoa/New Zealand near Westport is a rock pillar known as Wairaka, which represents Tamatea, a woman who drowned herself instead of facing punishment for infidelity (Orbell 1996:49). In the middle of Bonne Nuit Bay on the island of Jersey off the Normandy coast of France is a "water demon" that was turned to stone. The demon had previously emerged from the sea to take a woman named Anna as his bride but was thwarted by the dawn rays of the sun. Afterward the demon disguised himself as a horse and lured the woman's partner Guillaume for a ride into the harbor so as to kill him and hence abduct his "submarine bride." The plan was unsuccessful, and the demon turned into a rock known as Lé J'va (the horse) and La Cheval Guillaume (Bois 2016:9–10).

The Bajau Laut of the Sulu Archipelago between northeast Borneo and the southwest Philippines know of numerous sacred rocks in the sea that are the residence of spirit beings known generically as *saitan*. According to Bruno Bottignolo (1995:42–43), the association of such rocks with potentially dangerous spirits reflects both the danger of such places (especially to navigation) and their solidity (as appropriate dwelling places) in an otherwise fluid, dynamic, and unstable realm. For example, the Bajau Laut of northwest Borneo know of a coral rock within the intertidal zone that is home to a spirit known as Si Bangai-Bangai (Sather 1997:312–313). This spirit moves around the adjacent bay at night in the form of a sea turtle and is known to make people ill. To help reduce the threat to people, flags are placed on the rock in addition to offerings of turmeric rice or rice cakes. Clifford Sather (1997:313) suggests that the location of this harmful spirit on the edge of the land is a "tangible symbol of the danger and unfamiliarity which the Bajau Laut associate with the land."

Emplaced story sites in the sea also include items of material culture associated with legendary beings. For example, within the intertidal surf zone at Moeraki on the east coast of the South Island of Aotearoa/New Zealand is a cluster of spherical and elongated, dome-shaped boulders representing the metamorphosed cargo (eel pots, gourds, and *kumara* sweet potatoes) of the ancestral canoe Āraiteuru from Hawaiki (central Polynesia), which was wrecked nearby and similarly metamorphosed into an offshore reef (Orbell 1996:30–31). According to Aboriginal groups of Cape York Peninsula, northeast Australia, the canoe of Sivirri (culture hero) "turned to stone" and can be seen at low tide at the mouth of Janie Creek (McConnel 1936:71; Thomson 1934a:227). Immediately to the north in the eastern islands of Torres Strait, the canoe of the legendary Tagai transformed into a basalt block exposed at low tide on the island of Mer (Lawrie 1970:304–305). The red- and black-painted arrows fired by a man at his two wives missed and stuck in the ground, where they transformed to red and black stone boulders seen across the intertidal zone on the north coast of Erub, eastern Torres Strait (Teske 1987:10–11). Across the reefs surrounding the island of Luang in eastern Indonesia are numerous "petrified" stone boats (*può*), including one "replete with the fossilized belongings of its occupants" (Pannell 2007:81).

Marking the Seabed: Intertidal

Numerous maritime communities have spiritually important sites located within the intertidal zone. In some cases, these sites are "natural" features, such as freshwater springs and rock outcrops, associated with cosmological narratives of creation (e.g., Lawrie 1970; Smyth 1990). In other situations, people created structures of ritual or ceremonial significance within the intertidal zone. All of these sites were constructed at low tide with the knowledge that they would be inundated during high tide. In some cases, it is difficult to know if the sites were constructed within the intertidal zone or on the adjacent land where they were engulfed by subsequent sea level rise. The following digest reveals that many sites have a materiality conducive to long-term archaeological preservation (e.g., rock art and structures of bone and stone, including fish traps). In other situations, intertidal zones were used for symbolically charged activities that have left few material traces (e.g., public executions).

Rock Art

An extensive petroglyph site located near Wrangell in Alaska consists of numerous boulders with pecked motifs located both within the intertidal zone and just above it, spread over a distance of at least 1 km (Smith 1909). The more than 40 motifs include anthropomorphic faces, whales, salmon, and concentric circles. Similarly, a complex of petroglyph sites located at Cape Alitak on the southern end of Kodiak Island, central southern Alaska, features a range of figurative and nonfigurative (e.g., geometric) motifs; "many of the symbols occur at points where the highest tides and storm waves cover them" (Heizer 1947:284; see also Knebel 2003:40, 81). Figurative motifs include anthropomorphic faces and figures, sperm whales, humpback whales, killer whales (orcas), and possible porpoises or belugas (Heizer 1947:288; Knebel 2003). Neither Harlan Smith (1909) nor Robert Heizer (1947) make any comments on why many petroglyphs are located within the intertidal zone. Woody Knebel (2003:113) speculates that "the Cape Alitak petroglyphs continue to stand a silent vigil, sending out their message with each receding tide." That "message," he hypothesizes, saw "the rock outcrops forming a natural arena for intervention with the spirits of the animals of prey—a receptacle for directing the food supply to enter the more protected waters of Alitak Bay" to be harpooned by hunters (Knebel 2003:112; see also Steffian et al. 2023:7).

Along the Northwest Coast of North America, petroglyphs "are usually between the tide lines" (Hill and Hill 1975:19). Indeed, this section of coast appears to contain the largest complex of petroglyphs found within the intertidal zone anywhere in the world. Beth Hill and Ray Hill (1975:22–23) point out that sea level rise during the Holocene may account for many petroglyph sites on the Northwest Coast now positioned within the intertidal zone. However, they rightly point out, "once we assume that petroglyphs were carved above reach of the tides, would not their altitude have been more random? If the petroglyphs had not been intentionally placed between high and low tide, would we find so many of them confined to this narrow band at the edge of the sea?" (Hill and Hill 1975:23). Remarkably, little ethnographic information is available on the meaning and function of these intertidal sites. However, using this fragmentary information in the broader regional context of known religious and ceremonial practices, Hill and Hill (1975:283) make the plausible conclusion that "an important function" of Northwest Coast petroglyphs was "in gaining supernatural power over the inhabitants of the sea."

The Machias Bay area of Maine is home to Algonquin-speaking peoples and contains the largest concentration of petroglyph sites in Northeast United States. Nine petroglyph sites with pecked motifs, mostly anthropomorphs, dating to the past 3,000 years have been recorded along the shoreline, all within the intertidal zone (Hedden 2004). The deepest petroglyphs are at a site located 12.6 m from the nearest uneroded shoreline and 175–200 cm below the mean high tide level in 1991 (Hedden 2004:330). The shallowest petroglyphs are located within 10 cm of the mean high-tide mark (Hedden 2004:330–331). Informed by local ethnography, Mark Hedden (2004:335) interprets the anthropomorphs featured in the petroglyphs as representing "the interaction between the shaman and the spirits to whom he attributes his powers." Furthermore, "We are never sure whether we are looking at the shaman displaying attributes that express the nature of his powers, at a representation of the spirit who has given the powers, or at some combination of both. The issue is moot. The shaman and the spirit (or spirits) who empower him are, as the shaman is in his trance state, conceived as one, as a fleeting unity. The shaman is spirit. The spirit invests the shaman" (Hedden 2004:336–337).

The extensive Maisabel beach petroglyph site on the north coast of Puerto Rico features more than 30 individual petroglyphs dated mostly to 600–1200 CE (Roe 1991). Motifs include anthropomorphic faces and figures, fish, crabs, marine turtles, and possible woven basketry fish traps (Roe 1991:332–334). Peter Roe (1991:334) concluded that "the Maisabel petroglyphs marked, and mytho-logically validated, the ethnic 'joint' ownership of valuable fishing and marine hunting resources as well as the necessary naturefact aids (local landforms). Moreover, these lithographs were designed to communicate that differential access across competitive ethnic boundaries." This interpretation is consistent with the petroglyphs' location within the intertidal zone, where land meets the sea. Even if the petroglyphs were created on dry land, subsequent submer-sion could have added a new liminal dimension to the site for subsequent generations.

The Keʻekū petroglyph site at Kahaluʻu on the island of Hawaiʻi features more than 60 anthropomorphs located across a *pāhoehoe* (lava) flow that is "submerged at high tide" (Tuggle and Tomonari-Tuggle 1999:6). Stylistic com-parisons with other petroglyph sites across Hawaiʻi suggest that the site is at least 400 years old. This chronology is consistent with oral tradition indicating that one figure represents Kamalālāwalu, king of the island of Maui, who was killed by forces belonging to Lonoikamakahiki, king of the island of Hawaiʻi, around 1600 CE. Kamalālāwalu's body was sacrificed at the nearby *heiau* (temple). Dave Tuggle and Myra Tomonari-Tuggle (1999:10) suggest that the significance may relate to its location at "a place at the sacred boundary of land and sea" as the sea is associated with *pō*, the underworld. Liam Brady and I point out that "while the meaning of the submerged rock art at Kahaluʻu is unknown, the petroglyph of Kamalālāwalu represents at the very least an attempt to inscribe the death of this key person permanently within the marine realm adjacent to the shoreline" (McNiven and Brady 2012:75).

Structures of Stone and Bone

Putting stones into the sea for ritual reasons ranges from informal throwing of pebbles to formal creation of large stone arrangements. For example, before entering the sea for a swim, coastal villagers of Macduff and Rosehearty along the northeast coast of Scotland would first throw three stones (preferably white stones) into the sea. This ritual started with the largest stone and included recitation of special words (Gregor 1884:356).

The largest known stone arrangements within the intertidal zone were con-structed by Aboriginal peoples of central Queensland, Australia. Examples are known from Shoalwater Bay and Mine Island. The Shoalwater Bay stone

arrangements are of curvilinear form and "range in area from less than 100m²
to large complexes covering thousands of square metres" (McNiven 2004:338–
339). All are located within the upper reaches of the intertidal zone, where
inundation occurs only with the highest of tides. As such, these arrangements
would not function as fish traps and are of ritual or ceremonial significance,
perhaps linked to spiritual control of tides (McNiven 2004). The complex of
stone arrangements on Mine Island is of similar curvilinear form, totals 8,347
stones stretching for a total of 2 km, and is probably of ceremonial significance
(Barker et al. 2016). The Shoalwater Bay stone arrangements probably date to
the Late Holocene (McNiven 2004), while Bryce Barker and colleagues (2016)
suggest that the Mine Island sites date mostly to the past 500 years based on
the age of nearby midden sites.

At various locations within the intertidal and adjacent beach zone of the Eyre
Peninsula of South Australia, Sarah Martin (1988) documented a number of
stone arrangements that fell outside of the morphological parameters of stone-
walled fish traps. The site at Fitzgerald Bay consists of two 30-m-long subparallel
lines of stones at right angles to the beach, extending from the "high water mark
to mean low watermark" (Martin 1988:36, 53, Figure 7.1.1). Local Aboriginal oral
history describes the site as "ceremonial," noting also that the area was where
ritual specialists called up sharks and dolphins to "drive the schools of fish in
towards the people waiting on the shoreline who then surrounded the fish and
picked them up" (Martin 1988:36, 83). On the nearby Yorke Peninsula of South
Australia, Amy Roberts and colleagues (2016:15, Figure 8) document a stone-
walled tidal fish trap at Rocky Point that also features circular and star-shaped
stone arrangements inundated at high tide that elders similarly associate with
ritual "singing" and "herding" of fish.

Stone-walled fish traps are found within the intertidal zone in many coastal
regions of the world (e.g., Bradley and McNiven 2019; Connaway 2007; Rowland and Ulm 2011). These sites operate with the rise and fall of tidal waters,
with fish entering traps at higher tides and becoming stranded and available
for collection at low tide. In some cultural contexts, the fish traps are known
to have been made by spiritual beings. For example, the Yapese of Micronesia
attribute the construction of the majority of their tidal fish traps to "spirits"
(Jeffrey 2013:37). On the island of Mer in eastern Torres Strait of northeast
Australia, stone-walled tidal fish traps were built by two legendary or mythical
brothers, Kos and Abob (Lawrie 1970:342–343).

Many stone-walled tidal fish traps of the eastern islands of Torres Strait also
functioned as territorial reef boundary markers (Scott and Mulrennan 1999:161).
As the stone-walled fish traps or territorial boundary markers were constructed

of rock rubble, they could be easily dismantled and moved to other parts of the intertidal zone if desired. In other situations, Torres Strait Islanders visually marked the ownership of reefs and territorial boundaries using long (mostly bamboo) poles (Johannes and MacFarlane 1984:255; Nietschmann 1989:85; Scott and Mulrennan 1999:160). Similar insertion of long bamboo poles into the reef at very low tides to mark reef ownership or boundaries is undertaken by Nila Islanders in the Banda Sea of eastern Indonesia (Pannell 2000:366).

In rare situations, the marking of reefs includes accumulation of bones into structures. For example, the Kiwai of southwest Papua New Guinea opposite Torres Strait know of a class of male and female sea spirits called *óboúbi* that "look like ordinary people" but with "short limbs and stout body" (Landtman 1927:305). Some *óboúbi* live at Kimusu Reef (northern end of Warrior Reef) located 25 km out to sea and beyond the sea horizon visible from land. Here they hunt and eat dugongs, and dugong bones "arranged in circles" on this distant reef at low tide are believed by Kiwai hunters to be the result of such meals (Landtman 1927:305).

Executions

Northwest Coast peoples of Canada were known to execute witches by placing them with tied limbs on the beach such that they would succumb to the next high tide and be cleansed of their evil by seawater (Shearar 2000:114). The *Saga of King Olav Tryggvason* (who lived in the tenth century CE) mentions that "fettered sorcerers" were drowned below the *flomål* (high-tide mark) at Skratteskjær in western Norway (quoted in Westerdahl 2005a:11). Westerdahl (2005b:34) adds that this intertidal zone was "the area where corpses of anonymous outsiders or dangerous evil-doers were buried so they would not walk the earth inland. Ghosts cannot cross water anyway, according to tradition."

The most famous example of executions within the intertidal zone is Execution Dock located at Wapping (London) on the north bank of the lower Thames River tidal estuary. Between 1400 and 1830 CE, Execution Dock was where convicted pirates and other sea criminals were publicly hanged (for details see Frénée 2017). These sea crimes against the state were also considered sins against God and were dealt with by the High Court of Admiralty (held in the Old Bailey), as the Admiralty held jurisdiction over the sea. As such, the gallows at Execution Dock were located both legally and symbolically at the low-tide mark, which was the jurisdictional marine boundary. Hangings were done at low tide to demonstrate that the gallows were within the jurisdiction. The fact that 400–500 pirates were hanged at Execution Dock in the period 1716–1726 reveals the scale of Admiralty executions (Lincoln 2014:34). This peak period of

Figure 11. Intertidal zone hanging execution of the two pirates Purser and Clinton at Wapping, Thames River, London, 1583 (Woodcut from *A True Relation, of the Lives and Deaths of Two Most Famous English Pyrats, Purser, and Clinton who Lived in the Reigne of Queene Elizabeth* by Thomas Heywood 1639).

executions coincided with the peak period of piracy, with some 5,000 pirates, mostly British, operating on the high seas during this period (Rediker 1981:205). The hanging rope was usually short enough to ensure a prolonged and cruel death by strangulation (especially for pirates) but long enough to ensure that corpse's feet were below the upcoming high-tide mark. And once death was complete, wrote John Stow in his 1603 text *A Survey of London*, "there to re-maine, till three tides had ouerflowed them" (Kingsford 1908:2:71). This immersion was, according to some, a symbolic gesture to ensure "ritual cleansing" of sins (Aldersey-Williams 2017:93; Lincoln 2014:37; Figure 11). Triple immersion in water was a well-known baptismal religious rite of purification, particularly among Christians (Aldersey-Williams 2017:93; Henningsen 1961:150; see also Miller 2012:75). Horace Beck (1999:302) makes an unreferenced comment that the hanged bodies from Execution Dock were "buried on the beach between high and low water."

Marking the Seabed (Subtidal)

For the most part, mariners are interested in the nature and location of the seabed to avoid contact and shipwreck. Dangerous shoals and shallows are known through oral history and maritime lore, published navigational charts and sailing directions books, and physical markers such as lighthouses, beacons, and buoys. Often these tangible aids were enhanced through intangible aids such as rituals to help ensure safe voyaging (see Chapter 7). In other situations, mariners use the nature of seabed sediments as a navigational aid. This information was obtained by dropping a lead weight with a sticky substance on the base (e.g., wax) overboard to sample seabed sediments. In rare instances, coastal communities constructed symbolically charged bone and stone features on the seabed below the low tide level in locations that were permanently inundated.

Nuu-chah-nulth whalers of the Barkley Sound area of the west coast of Vancouver Island on the Northwest Coast of Canada created submarine whale bone deposits in passages between islands. For example, Hamota (meaning "bones") is the name of the pass between Clarke and Benson Islands and is associated with stories of Sheshaht/Tseshaht whalers "who attempted to fill in this pass by dumping into it the bones of the many whales they caught" (St. Claire 1991:3, 140; see also Coté 2010:76). Similarly, stories relate how a great whaler named Wi:hswisanʻap (meaning "filling or blocking the pass") attempted to fill up the pass between the two main islands of the George Fraser Islands group "with the bones of all the whales he killed" (St. Claire 1991:157).

Some ceremonial stone arrangements have been recorded on the seabed located below the current low-tide mark. In all cases it is difficult to know if the sites were created underwater or if the sites have been submerged since creation through sea level rise. For example, a megalithic standing stone circle site is located on the shoreline of the islet of Er Lannic in the Gulf of Morbihan, Brittany, northwest France (Flemming 1996:40–41). The site features two near-complete stone circles. The first, with a diameter of around 50 m, is positioned such that its upper sections are above the high-water mark and its lower sections are submerged during high tide. The second circle, with a diameter of around 70 m, is located completely within the subtidal zone.

Conclusion

This chapter reveals that many maritime societies have developed a broad range of strategies and practices to know and engage with a wide range of different types of tangible and intangible places in the sea. This elaborate and complex corpus of places imbues seas with historical meaning and significance that undermines claims that the sea is incapable of inscription and historicizing. For example, Bernhard Klein and Gesa Mackenthun (2004:2) note that prior to the Oceanic turn in history of the past three decades, scholarship supported "the cultural myth that the ocean is outside and beyond history, that the interminable, repetitive cycle of the sea obliterates memory and temporality, and that a fully historicized land somehow stands diametrically opposed to an atemporal, 'ahistorical' sea."

Similar views were held by archaeologists. For example, Cunliffe (2017:2; emphasis added) claimed that "while the land is scarred with human activity—with settlements, field boundaries, burial mounds—reflecting the deep heritage of human interaction, *the sea has no history: it is timeless.* On land one is constantly reminded of how the landscape we see today fossilizes past human activity. The *sea is a place for forgetting.*" In marked contrast, I argue that "for many maritime peoples across the globe, the sea is deeply historicized and a place for remembering, and indeed for deep-time remembering over thousands of years in some cases" (McNiven 2025a:804).

It is encouraging for archaeologists that spiritual and cosmological dimensions of maritime people's engagements and conceptualizations of seascapes have material expressions in the sea. In some cases, such materializations are a direct result of people creating features on the seabed, both within the intertidal zone (e.g., rock art, stone arrangements, fish traps) and within the subtidal zone on the permanently submerged seabed (e.g., bone deposits, sea burials) that also take in shipwrecks and associated dead (see also Chapters 7 and 10). In rare cases, seabed sites are seen to be a result of inundation of terrestrial places, such as sunken settlements.

Sandra Pannell (2007:75) makes the important point that landscapes (and by extension seascapes) are not blank canvases upon which people and culture inscribe names, meanings, and memories. Following Ingold (1993:156–157), the material form of sites and places is an expression of a process of bodily engagement and an existing relationship between people and places. In this sense, the creation of physical sites and features is not an event but part of an ongoing process of place engagement and elaboration. For places in the sea that have a constructed material dimension (e.g., rock art, fish traps), ongoing engagement ensures that such sites are always a work in progress. In addition, the constant dynamic nature of the sea ensures that intertidal and subtidal places are equally dynamic and always in a liminal state of phenomenological and epistemological flux.

5

Terrestrial Seascapes

Inland Referencing of the Sea

It is well known that eighteenth- and nineteenth-century naval personnel from the British Admiralty could spend years at sea on mapping expeditions (e.g., James Cook), with nineteenth-century whalers known to spend up to seven years at sea searching the oceans for their leviathan prey (Beck 1957:169). On a more regular basis, the famous nomadic sea peoples of Southeast Asia spend most of their time on the sea (Hoogervorst 2012). Alain Cabantous (1991:215) calculated that "seafaring people" of northwest France in the eighteenth century spent 45–60% of their "working lives" at sea. Yet in all these cases, these maritime specialists, mostly men, come back to homes on land to reconnect with families and associated community. John Mack (2011:13) makes the important point that "people cannot live entirely at sea without some access to the land and its products." Yet Keith Muckelroy (1978:6) suggests that the "terrestrial settlements" of mariners "will display their maritime connections only marginally. Many of the objects used in seafaring are rarely brought ashore, and any artefact collection made there will represent very poorly the seafaring community itself." Similarly, Anthony Parker (2001:25) notes that "going to sea may be an occasional, temporary activity, depending on other priorities or economic opportunities . . . and leave no distinctive remains in settlements or burials." This chapter uses a wide range of examples to reveal that the pessimism of both Muckelroy and Parker is unfounded on theoretical and empirical grounds.

The process of returning to land from sea-based engagements creates an interesting paradox for maritime peoples, as a maritime identity does not begin and end while out on the sea. A maritime identity is a permanent state of being, which means that it needs to be managed and curated while on the sea *and also* on land. Richard Blakemore (2014:98) rightly points out that "it hardly needs saying, seafarers did not spend their entire lives isolated at sea and other spaces also shaped maritime identities." In the case of mariners returning home to particular parishes of London during the seventeenth century, "the seafaring occupation of the inhabitants of these parishes therefore brought the maritime world home with them" (Blakemore 2014:113).

Pearson (2014:345) aptly notes that "we need to be amphibious, moving easily between land and sea." Such management and curation of a maritime identity operates at a profound ontological level given that the "land" and the "sea" are separate ontological domains. Yet as pointed out in Chapter 2, such ontological separateness does not negate the potential for ontological overlap and blurring. Indeed, curating and managing the ontological overlap and blurring of the sea–land boundary is fundamental to maintaining a maritime identity.

It is in this overlapping context that the potential for material expressions of sea-based activities and marine-based identities on land are considerable. Such potential underpins Westerdahl's "maritime cultural landscapes." Indeed, those maritime cultural landscapes have considerable potential to extend well inland. As Parker (2001) points out, marine boats and ships can travel considerable distances up rivers for either added work or to escape bad weather. Similarly, the houses of mariners may be located many kilometers "up-river" from coastal ports (Parker 2001:31). Westerdahl (2005b:26) notes that "if the contrast between land and sea was important to prehistoric people, as it was in the recent past, we would indeed expect the border, the liminal state, between them to be marked by distinct monuments. As we will see, this is indeed the case: rock carvings, burial cairns/mounds, etc." While largely true, this chapter reveals that such maritime inscription with fixed sites can also extend to areas of "land" well beyond the liminality of the sea–land boundary. It can also include movement of portable marine objects (e.g., shoreline stones, shells, marine animal bones, boats) from the sea to areas tens and even hundreds of kilometers "inland." Such maritime inscription (fixed sites and portable objects) can extend to any areas of "land" considered important to maritime peoples to help express and curate a maritime identity.

How far "inland" maritime inscription or referencing of the sea extends is difficult to predict and as such becomes a question for empirical documentation in differing cultural contexts. As discussed in Chapter 2, in some cultural contexts (e.g., Indigenous northern Australia), the sea–land boundary extends more than 10 km "inland." Relevant here is my concept of "terrestrial seascapes" introduced as a heuristic to help understand inland referencing of the sea and the inland extension of seascapes (McNiven 2025a). I note that the concept of terrestrial seascapes "incorporates Westerdahl's (1992) paradigmatic notion of 'maritime cultural landscapes'; viewshed approaches (seeing the land from the sea) (e.g., Cooney 2004); and sites on land with maritime identities associated with symbolic representations of marine phenomena (e.g., paintings of ships and marine animals in rock art), incorporation of marine objects (e.g., burials and middens with marine animal remains), and ritual engagement and control of the sea (e.g., voyaging and fishing/hunting shrines) (see McNiven 2004, 2008, 2013b; McNiven and Brady 2012)" (McNiven 2025a:777–778). The extent to which terrestrial seascapes feature marine sites and features and marine-related phenomena differs from region to region for a broad range of cultural reasons. One important reason is the degree of maritimity of coastal communities, with maritime communities expected to invest more heavily in cosmological, cognitive, spiritual, and material referencing of the sea on land compared to coastal communities who have little engagement with the sea.

The central tenet of this chapter is that maritime peoples have employed a diverse array of sea referencing strategies to express and curate a maritime identity when residing on land. Although Westerdahl posits that such referencing marks the sea–land boundary, it can also be fundamental to expressing "terrestrial seascapes" more broadly. Furthermore, material and visual markers of a maritime identity on the land are not only about expressing the terrestrial dimension of seascapes but also helping to define and express the sea–land boundary, not simply marking it. The key expression strategy is ceremonial and ritual referencing of the sea on the land. Examples discussed in this chapter include rock art, domestic and ceremonial structures, imported marine animal parts (e.g., shells), and human burials. Although Viking ship burials provide one of the better-known examples of marine-associated interments, more mundane and less theatrical practices included incorporation of marine animal bones and shells within terrestrial burials. Yet, as will become clear, in some circumstances, marine objects located inland have no obvious symbolic association with the sea. Indeed, in some terrestrial cultural contexts, inland marine objects lose their association with the sea.

Rock Art

The creation of marine-themed rock art on "land" represents one of the strongest examples of the capacity of maritime peoples to materially express terrestrial seascapes and a maritime identity inland. In a Scandinavian context, Westerdahl (2010:282) makes the point that rock art "sites farthest from the shore would then express the practical aspect of the distance to which the maritime dichotomy would have been thought to extend on land." In this sense, the distance from the shore of the sea–land boundary as a *"liminal area was re-created by the imposition of figures on rocks"* (Westerdahl 2005b:29; original emphasis). For the Yanyuwa people of northern Australia, rock art associated with ancestral beings and cosmological songlines "expresses a maritime identity inland from the coastline" and aids "transforming terrestrial lived spaces into part of the seascape" (Roos Jacobs et al. 2025:197–198). In many parts of the world, archaeological evidence of rock art sites featuring marine animals are located not only along the coast but also many kilometers inland. Although in numerous cases the function of the rock art remains unknown, at the very least the depiction of marine motifs well away from the coast is an "inland" expression of maritime themes and perhaps a maritime identity. For example, at Namunidjbuk in the Wellington Range of Arnhem Land in the Northern Territory of Australia is a rock art site featuring a red ochre outline painting of a dugong dated stylistically to 6,000–9,400 years ago (Taçon et al. 2020:220–221). Although the painting is currently located ~15 km from the coast, at the time of its creation it would have been located 25–105 km inland due to lower sea levels (Taçon et al. 2020:221).

The Bangudae petroglyph site in southeast South Korea is located adjacent to Daegokcheon Stream some 24 km inland of the coast. It is associated with Neolithic and Bronze Age hunter-gatherers from 2,000 to 6,000 years ago (Jeon 2013; Kang 2020). The site features over 350 motifs across nearly 7 m of cliff face, with images of marine animals (mostly whales) dominating the left half of the panel and images of terrestrial animals (mostly mammals) dominating the right half (Francfort 2013:103; Han 2013; Jeon 2013; Kang 2020). As such, the site expresses marine hunters on the left and terrestrial hunters on the right (Francfort 2013) and may mark the inland boundary of coastal peoples' cosmologically defined seascape.

Benjamín Ballester (2018:145) argues that the depiction of marine motifs (e.g., fish) dating to the past 1,000 years along Izcuña ravine (Atacama Desert, northern Chile) located between 4 km and 9 km inland of the coast reveals that the "painters portrayed a marine activity in a desert setting, in a conscious act of linking the ocean to the desert via rock art." More specifically, Andrés Troncoso and colleagues (2018:281) note that these paintings are "the clearest example of seascape production by communities in the region."

In the arid Skull Valley of Utah, located nearly 1,000 km from the Pacific Ocean, are petroglyphs of a person standing in a canoe, and marine animals such as turtles, fish, a shark, and a whale. The rock art was produced sometime between 1889 and 1917 by Hawai'ians from the central Pacific who moved to Utah to establish the Church of Jesus Christ of Latter-day Saints settlement of Iosepa (Malakoff 2008; Pykles and Reeves 2021). Despite being relocated 4,800 km from their homeland, the Utah-based Hawai'ians inscribed maritime motifs onto rocks in a desert landscape far removed from the islands of Hawai'i. While Hawai'i is well known for its petroglyph rock art tradition, Halley Cox and Edward Stasack (1970:63) point out that "in a land surrounded by the ocean, and which depended upon fish for a substantial part of its subsistence, there are practically no fish or marine life of any kind portrayed by the makers of petroglyphs. Other than a few turtles, crabs, and some other scarcely discernible sea creatures, sea life was largely neglected" (see also Lee and Stasack 1999). As Brady and I commented, "Could it be that these diasporic Hawaiians, as a sea people, were embedding their maritime identity within the harsh Utah desert landscape by inscribing it with marine elements of a more familiar seascape? Is it possible that here, on the desert rocks of Utah, rock art, landscape inscription, seascape ascription, and maritime identity were paradoxically played out a century ago?" (McNiven and Brady 2012:72).

A related dimension of marine animals and maritime identity is totemic rock art—that is, the creation of rock art motifs on land that reference totemic identities associated with the sea. Torres Strait provides a rare ethnographically informed archaeological example of rock art representations of marine totems in rock art. In 1888 Haddon (1901:185, Figure 23) was shown rock paintings in a rock shelter on the island of Kirriri (Hammond Island) in southwest Torres Strait that depicted marine animals that he was informed represented "totems (hammer-head shark, turtle, dugong, and so on)." In 2001 a group of senior clan representatives from the island of Mabuyag in central western Torres Strait visited the major ceremonial (*kod*) site on the sacred islet of Pulu (Brady 2010; McNiven et al. 2009). During the visit, one of the representatives, Cygnet Repu, used locally available red ochre mixed with water to paint a representation of a *kaigas* (shovel-nosed shark), his maternal *awgadh* (totem; see David et al. 2006:cover). Informed by this ethnographic information, Brady (2010:390, 402) considered that 30 out of 44 zoomorphic paintings recorded archaeologically across central and western Torres Strait were "totemic." Support for this conclusion was that "a strong correlation exists between the distribution of totemic animal species recorded across Torres Strait by . . . [Haddon's anthropological team] in 1898, and the depiction of totemic species in Torres Strait rock-art" (Brady 2010:401).

In numerous maritime communities, rock art included depictions of ships. For example, Richard Bradley (2000:141, original emphasis) hypothesizes that the "presence of so many ships" in Scandinavian Bronze Age rock art sites "was not just a reference to their importance in the life of the community; perhaps they were depicted in this particular way *to convey the idea of water itself.* The drawings recreated the sea at the foot of the high ground by depicting the ships on its surface." Furthermore, "The effect of those drawings was to convert the higher ground into another group of islands" surrounded by sea (Bradley 2000:141). In this sense, rock art was used to conceptually and symbolically extend inland (at least on a small geographical scale) not only seascapes but also the sea. In contrast to this view, Johan Ling (2014:232) spatially and conceptually limits Bronze Age "seascapes" to the sea such that associated shoreline rock art sites are seen as being "oriented towards the seascape" (i.e., the sea). Yet this association between sea and seascape is only consistent in part with Courtney Nimura's (2016:46, 65, Table 4.7) detailed study, which reveals that only 16.5% of Scandinavia's more than 19,000 ship motifs are located within 1 km of the current coastline. Significantly, the majority of ship motifs (60.1%) are located 1–6 km from the coastline, though many of these are located near inland waterways and may represent freshwater vessels. Perhaps these "inland" ship motifs hint that some Bronze Age Scandinavians saw seascapes as extending well inland of the shoreline. In this connection, Bradley and colleagues (2020:262) argue that inland rock art sites with ship motifs in Sweden suggest that "some people did move between the sea and the hinterland," perhaps to exchange metal objects imported from overseas (see also Ling 2014; Nimura et al. 2020). At the very least the creation of marine-themed rock art more than 100 km from the coast reveals a desire by some people to inscribe a permanent symbolic maritime presence and marine identity to inland regions. The existence of inland marine-themed rock art in other cultural and geographical contexts around the world provides further hints that seascapes and maritime identities are not always confined to coastal margins.

Between 120 and at least 350 years ago, Indonesian fishers visited Australia's northern shores to work with Aboriginal communities for many months each year to harvest and process trepang (aka sea slug or bêche-de-mer) to take back to Indonesia for the Chinese market (e.g., Macknight 1976; Urwin et al. 2023). Archaeological evidence of these visits includes rock art depictions of Indonesian vessels, mostly *praus* (e.g., de Ruyter et al. 2023; May et al. 2013; Wesley et al. 2012). Rock art paintings of *praus* have been recorded within 20 km of the Arnhem Land coast (Northern Territory), but one example is located around 90 km inland (Chaloupka 1996:136). Anne Clarke and Ursula Frederick (2006:125) note that on Groote Eylandt (Gulf of Carpentaria), rock shelter paintings of *praus* located up to 15 km inland "symbolizes an incorporation" of Makassan sea peoples "deeper within the social landscape" of the island.

Domestic Structures

Elements of the marine realm have been incorporated into the fabric of domestic houses in various coastal regions of the world. In some cases, the elements are raw materials (e.g., bones, skins), material culture (e.g., boat), or symbolic (e.g., boat-shaped houses). Sometimes the elements relate to the superstructure of houses, while in other situations they are restricted to house features, such as windows comprising translucent fish skins in northern Norway (Berg

1984:99). Two well-documented examples of the use of marine objects in the construction of houses are boats (symbolic) and whale bones.

Architectural traditions of the Indonesian archipelago show design elements that have been linked to boats. The classic design element is the saddle-shaped roof lines of houses and barns in various regions of Indonesia (e.g., Sumatra and Sulawesi), which are analogous in form to the extended prows and sterns of marine boats (Gittinger 1976:219; Lewcock and Brans 1975; Manguin 2001; Prajudi 2016). In the Lio district of the island of Flores in eastern Indonesia, houses are viewed as "boats" and posts supporting the roof are referred to as "masts," while the curved sloping roofs are "compared with sails" (Lewcock and Brans 1975:110). Some Flores villages are also organized spatially to represent the plan view of a boat (Lewcock and Brans 1975:113). The "great houses" on the islands of Dawela and Dawelor in eastern Indonesia were "oriented in the direction of a sailing boat voyaging from sunrise to sunset" (Dawson and Gillow 1994:182; see also de Jonge and van Dijk 1995:33–47). In addition, the "rooms were given names that accorded with their position on this sailing boat, the helmsman's part being in the east and the pilot's in the west. Inside the house people would sit with their backs to the eastern part of the house. Right would correspond to north, left to south. The rooms in the eastern part of the house were known as the helmsman's cooking area, flanked by the helmsman's right-hand and left-hand room. To the west were the corresponding pilot's rooms" (Dawson and Gillow 1994:182–183).

Indonesian boat-shaped houses have been linked to the Austronesian roots of many coastal communities of Indonesia, whereupon seafaring peoples from the Taiwan region of Southeast Asia settled across the region perhaps 3,000–4,000 years ago. Rahadhian Prajudi (2016) suggests that use of these boat-shaped houses reflects the movement of coastal peoples to inland regions. That is, the "boat thus became a true icon that was retained when tradition changed into an agrarian one in the hinterland. The visualization of the boat shape remained in use as a representation of sacredness" (Prajudi 2016:7). Moving out into the eastern Pacific Ocean where the Austronesian-speaking ancestors of Polynesians settled over the past 1,000 years, Edwin Ferdon (1979:5) hypothesizes that lenticular-shaped houses used by high-ranking elites on Rapa Nui (Easter Island) were deliberately "boat-shaped" with "symbolic" links to the original vessels used by settlers of the island. As Maia Nuku (2023:135) notes more broadly for Oceania, "a canoe can serve as a metaphor for the clan, memorializing the journey taken to a new island and the establishment of a new line of descendants." Furthermore, "The canoe and the house express ideas relating to ancestry and genealogical connections and demonstrate how they can evolve over time and space. Each is understood to embody ancestors, a founding or clan spirit, providing an important arena for developing visible and material supports that allow interaction with the spiritual realm. Both the canoe and the house signal the continuity of the clan group" (Nuku 2023:135).

Most evidence for use of marine animal bones in domestic structures concerns use of whale bones, especially ribs, as structural supports. In 1555 Olaus Magnus published *Historia de gentibus septentrionalibus* (*History of the Northern Peoples*), in which he describes Scandinavian houses made from the bones (e.g., ribs) of stranded whales (quoted in Küchelmann 2011:212). Magnus (quoted in Szabó 2018:169) notes that "those who sleep inside these ribs are forever dreaming that they are toiling incessantly on the ocean waves or, harassed by storms, are in perpetual danger of shipwreck." Szabó (2018:169) concludes that the "house became an embodiment of the rough northern seas themselves."

Ethnographic and archaeological examples of whale bone domestic structures have been recorded across Arctic and subarctic North America (Alaska and Canada), and temperate California, southern Australia, and southern Africa (Dawson and Levy 2005; Memmott 2007:206–207; Patton and Savelle 2006; Salls et al. 1993; Savelle 1997; Smith and Kinahan 1984). The most detailed ethnographic accounts of whale bone domestic structures come from Alaska, and in particular the Tikigaq Inuit of Point Hope, where bowhead whale bone houses were seasonally animated as whales (Lowenstein 1994:32–33, 42). Tikigaq houses were semisubterranean and featured an entrance hole (*katak*), an entrance tunnel (*qanitchaq*), and a living area with sunlight and ventilation hole. The entrance tunnel was usually made of whale ribs, mandibles, vertebrae, and scapula. During the whaling season, Tikigaq houses "came alive, and brought forth life," such that whale spirits emerged through the *katak*. Made from the bones of dead whales, the houses were "enlivened by women who had themselves 'died' on the ice, returning to animate their 'dead whale iglus'" (Lowenstein 1994:42; Patton and Savelle 2006:143). These women lured live whales to their husband hunters such that the bones of these whales would similarly join the village in a constant cycle whereby "whales became whale-bearing iglus" (Lowenstein 1994:42). A material expression of the house-whale symbolic association was the use of whale crania and mandibles as structural elements of the *katak*, such that entry into the house was literally through the mouth parts of whales (Patton and Savelle 2006:152–153). Debra Corbett (2011:14) notes that in Arctic and sub-Arctic North America, houses were "living persons" and "sentient beings with souls."

A remarkable archaeological example of an early whale bone house is House Pit 2 at the Nursery Site on San Clemente Island off the California coast dated to 4,700–4,900 years ago (Raab et al. 1994:246, 253; Salls et al. 1993:184–189). At Izembek Lagoon on the southwest tip of the Alaskan Peninsula are archaeological remains of a house framed by 32–34 whale mandibles (from 16–17 baleen whales) supported by boulders, which dates to around 1,000 years ago (Dumond 1995:53). On Buldir Island in the Western Aleutian Islands of southwest Alaska, excavations revealed a rectangular, semisubterranean house with "whalebone structural supports" (ribs, mandibles, scapula, vertebra) dating to around 400–500 years ago (Corbett 2011:5). The center of the house featured a fin whale or blue whale skull embedded snout downward into subfloor deposits (Corbett 2011:7). That Aleutian houses were also considered "living beings with bodies," and indeed whale persons, is consistent with use of the term *ang/angi-lix*, which means "smoke hole" and "whale's blowhole" (Corbett 2011:14).

In some cases, marine mammal bones were incorporated into the walls of houses for symbolic reasons. For example, at the Inuit settlement of Wales located on the central west coast of Alaska on the Bering Strait, Thomas Lopp photographed a semisubterranean house with an aboveground roofing structure decorated with numerous walrus skulls (Harritt 2003:47; Smith 1995:42). Roger Harritt (2003:47) notes that the "use of the skulls in this manner suggests that this was the residence of a successful walrus hunter." Andrew Jones (1998:313) notes that "whale and cattle remains are placed at specific junctures within the wall, passage and roof structures at Skara Brae," a Neolithic settlement dating to 4,500–5,200 years ago in the Orkney Islands of northeast Scotland. Whale bone elements include ribs, vertebrae, and a skull (Childe and Patterson 1929; see also Mulville 2002).

Ceremonial Structures

Referencing of the sea in ceremonial structures in terrestrial contexts can take two forms—symbolic referencing of marine themes and material referencing of marine objects. The former is illustrated by Christian churches and construction of stone ship effigies. The latter is most clearly seen in the fabric of ceremonial structures, including stone from the shoreline and the bones and shells of marine animals.

The Christian notion of a church representing a marine ship is an example of a ceremonial structure referencing the sea. The church as a ship metaphor extends back at least to Hippolytus of Rome (170–236 CE), an early Christian theologian, who stated that the "sea is the world. The Church is like a ship, buffeted by the waves but not swamped, for she has with her her experienced pilot, Christ" (quoted in Daniélou 1964:60). Furthermore, the "ladder rising upwards to the sailyard is an image of the sign of Christ's passion leading the faithful to climb up unto Heaven" (quoted in Daniélou 1964:60; cf. Miller

2010:421). Architecturally and etymologically, the church "nave" is derived from the Latin term *navis*, meaning "ship" or "vessel," and is the root of the English word "navigation" (Champion 2015a:89; Corbin 1995:9). Yet as Birgitte Thye (1995) points out, the importance of ship symbolism in churches does not match the importance of ships in the Bible. She notes that "ships, boats and sailing occur on less than a dozen occasions in the Old Testament and the New Testament" (Thye 1995:186). While reference to ships in the Bible may be minimal, there "is no shortage in the New Testament of passages from which to cull maritime metaphors" (Miller 2012:28). Indeed, the Bible contains some 460 references to the sea (Patarino 2002:301). Early Christian congregations referred to themselves as "fishermen" and "Saint Peter's Crew" (Thye 1995:187). Christian parishioners were also aware that the sea was "God's instrument of punishment, as the Flood had shown" (Kirby and Hinkkanen 2000:41). But the story of Noah and the Flood also stands as central to church-ship symbolism given that the Ark, like a church, was a sanctuary for peace and safety (Thye 1995:187).

In some cases, churches incorporate ship features. The internal roof structure of some churches was made to look like the inside of an upturned boat. For example, the roof of the church in Rouen in France is in the shape of an upturned Viking ship. The barrel ceiling of Mortehoe church in Devon, England, was said to be modeled on an upturned ship (Harley 1994:2–3). St. Leonard's Church at St. Leonards-on-Sea in Sussex, England, features a remarkable pulpit in the shape of the bow of a boat made in 1956 (Harley 1994:6–8). Perhaps the best-known example of a ship pulpit feature is the fictional ship's bow pulpit in the New Bedford Seamen's Bethel seen in John Huston's 1956 classic movie *Moby Dick*. Father Maple, played by Orson Welles, stands in the ship pulpit and addresses the congregation as "shipmates." The fictional ship pulpit, from the novel and movie, has become a reality, with installation of a ship pulpit in the bethel in 1961 to fulfill visitor expectations.

On the island of Inishark located off the central west coast of Ireland, archaeological excavation of a medieval monastery dating to 900–1300 CE revealed platform structures thought to have been "hermitages [retreats] for prayer and meditation by individual anchorites or penitents" (Lash 2018a:92, 2018b). The platforms feature pavements of hundreds of water-rolled white quartz pebbles sourced to adjacent beaches. Ryan Lash (2018a:97–98) argues that the pebbles "may have been particularly powerful manifestations of the divine agency controlling the seas." Pilgrims who collected the stones as an "offering" saw similarity "between the watery transportation and transformation of the quartz stones and their own spiritual journey to the island" (Lash 2018a:98–99). That is, the pilgrims were hoping that they might be shaped and transformed by divine agency and the "transformative power of ocean water" on land, analogous to transformation of the pebbles in the sea (Lash 2018b:296).

Torres Strait Islanders of northeast Australia were introduced to Christianity by the London Missionary Society in the 1870s. As a result, most Torres Strait Islander communities took on Christian religious beliefs (and established numerous churches), albeit syncretized with existing religious and spiritual beliefs. All of these churches were constructed of local materials, including coral-lime cement created by burning coral obtained from the sea. For example, archaeological excavation of the ruins of the early London Missionary Society church at Totalai on the island of Mua revealed coral-lime cement rubble footings (Ash 2013:139; Ash et al. 2008:Figure 3). Jeremy Ash (2013:115) concludes that when midden deposits of marine shell and bone are also taken into consideration, the old village site of Totalai is seen to be "awash with saltwater" with "the church fabric itself symbolically and physically connected to its broader maritime context." Most other churches in Torres Strait are similarly constructed of coral-lime cement Torres Strait Islanders manufactured using coral they collected from local reefs (Ash 2013:204; Teske 1987:40).

A recent tradition of constructing stone ships on land comes from the Tanimbar archipelago of the Moluccas in eastern Indonesia (McKinnon 1988, 1991). This practice forms part of a broader tradition where many Indonesians "not only built their houses and ritual centres as great landed boats, they have often constructed their villages and represented their islands as if they, too, were boats" (McKinnon 1988:152). The ritual center of many Tanimbarese villages was a raised earthen platform around 4–5 m across encircled by stones that "were everywhere conceived as boats" (McKinnon 1991:68). In some cases, the boatness of the ceremonial platform was enhanced by addition of boat features, such as the Olilit village on Asutubun Island where the platform featured the anchors and chains "retrieved" from the wreck of a Dutch steamer (McKinnon 1988:160). In other cases, the platform was in the actual shape of a boat, with a hull made of stone blocks and a finely carved stone prow and stern boards. The elaborate prow boards are analogous to elaborately carved wooden prow boards on seagoing Tanimbarese boats (McKinnon 1988). In the bow of the boat was a sacrificial stone altar of the supreme being and deity known as Ubila'a. A fine example of a Tanimbarese stone boat comes from the village of Sangliat Dol, located on the east coast of Yamdena Island. Its prow carving features fish motifs, and the stern carving features birds (Drappe 1940; Ririmasse 2010:249).

Tanimbarese land-based stone boats functioned in a structuralist, dualist, gendered, and relational sense with sea-based wooden boats that ventured out on trading and raiding expeditions. The stone and wooden boats expressed contrasts: immobility and mobility, female and male, and outside and inside, respectively (McKinnon 1991:83). All ceremonies and rituals concerning a village's external affairs (e.g., warfare, alliances) took place at the stone boats. As Susan McKinnon (1991:72) notes, "When the identity of the village as a unit was called into play by outside forces, the internal form of the stone boat became the external form of the village." In short, it was somewhat "paradoxical" that the stone boat was a symbol of the fixed and anchored status of the village. During the ceremony associated with the renewal of intervillage alliances, different dancers at the stone boat assume the status of sails, frigate birds and wind, and captains (McKinnon 1991:76).

Ancient stone arrangements and megalithic structures (including chambered tombs) can be linked to the sea by location along shorelines and by incorporation of beach stones. These megalithic tombs are associated with the Neolithic of western and northern Europe, but not Neolithic central and eastern Europe (Bradley and Phillips 2004:123). In terms of the former, Westerdahl (2010:282) advanced that "the border between liminal and non-liminal states would be within the zone where either the cairn was visible from the water or the sea from the cairn." The issue of intervisibility between stone arrangements and the sea is discussed by various researchers. For example, Chris Scarre (2002) concludes that megaliths located along the coast of Brittany, northwest France, represent symbolic markers of the physical and conceptual boundary between the land and the sea. More specifically, Scarre (2002) associates the liminality of the shore, especially the dynamism of tidal regimes, with mortuary rituals and spiritual transformation of the dead.

In a thought-provoking paper, Chris Fowler and Vicki Cummings (2003:2) document that 65% of the more than 100 Neolithic (4,400–6,000-year-old) megalithic monuments (mostly chambered tombs) located along the eastern side of the Irish Sea have been carefully positioned with "views of the sea" to deliberately create a "connection between the sea and stone-built structures: water and stone." This "metaphorical association between water and stone" was enhanced with the materiality of chambered tombs through the strategic incorporation of marine-sourced objects (i.e., objects "reminiscent of the sea and sea-shore") such as quartz pebbles from the beach, shells, and fish bones (Fowler and Cummings 2003:2, 4; see also Fowler 2001). Furthermore, nearly all of the megalithic stones moved into place at these sites originated within the "inter-tidal zone" and were water worn and modified by marine animals (Fowler and Cummings 2003:5). Fowler and Cummings (2003:10) argue further that "megaliths were orientated towards the shore-line, tides, and the beach as a liminal zone and a permeable membrane between land and sea." The importance of liminality was linked to the ontological and spiritual transformation of dead human bodies into the realm of the dead. Catherine Frieman (2008:139–140, 145) similarly posits that early and middle Neolithic (5,000–6,000-year-old) stone monuments on the Isle of Man in the Irish Sea may not have incorporated beach stones simply to reference the sea but as a symbolic and agentive referencing of liminality in relation to the living and the dead and veneration of the ancestors. Furthermore, "People sensitized to temporal change by the seascape's ebb and flow would have found these temporally enhanced coasts appropriate locations for monuments embodying concepts of time" (Frieman 2008:138; see also Cunliffe 2001).

Arrangements of marine shells focus on large bivalves (e.g., clams) and large gastropods (e.g., trumpet shells). Torres Strait Islanders of northeastern Australia produced perhaps the most elaborate examples of ceremonial shell shrines in the world. In particular, shrines comprising circular arrangements of *bu* (trumpet) shells (*Syrinx aruana*), the world's largest known gastropod, are found across the western and central islands of the Strait, with numbers of *bu* shells at single shrines ranging from fewer than 10 to over 100 (David et al. 2005; McNiven 2015b). In some cases, *bu* shell arrangements are known to be associated with headhunting and culture hero cults (Haddon 1935; Lawrie 1970). *Bu* shell shrines/monuments associated with the culture heroes Kuyam and Sigai are linked to ceremonial *kod* sites and headhunting and have been dated to ca. 200–300 years ago (McNiven 2015b; McNiven et al. 2009). Similar dates from other *bu* shell shrines suggest that ethnographically known practices of headhunting and associated cult practices and shell shrines were elaborated over the past 300 years. The selection of *bu* shells for these shrines is probably associated with their previous function as trumpets to signal the arrival of canoes from headhunting expeditions, and the rarity of the shells due to difficulty of procurement. The Yolŋu of East Arnhem Land know that highly prized trumpet shells (*S. aruana*) are difficult to obtain, as they tend to be found at the lowest astronomical tide mark, which is exposed only a few times of the year (Davis 1984:233). Significantly, the lowest astronomical tide mark is conceived of as marking the seaward limit of "land." In this sense, the ritual significance of trumpet shells may be linked to their status as liminal objects.

A class of ceremonial bone arrangement exists outside of ritual sites related to increase (spiritual renewal) and hunting, and those associated with human burials (see below). In many cases, these sites consist of arrangements of whale bones for which no function can be assigned beyond the hypothesis of ceremonial or ritual. For example, Site PaJs-13 located on Somerset Island in central northern Canada features ceremonial houses (see below) and a circular arrangement of whale skulls that is "probably ceremonial in nature" (Savelle 1997:874; Habu and Savelle 1994).

Across the Bering Sea on the Chukchi Peninsula of northeast Russia are a number of extraordinary whale skull and mandible ritual sites associated with the Punuk cultural phase dated to 800–1300 CE. At Ekven, located on the eastern tip of the Chukchi Peninsula, is archaeological evidence of an extensive whaling settlement that includes a series of whale skulls arranged into circular formations (at least 6 m in diameter in one case) that probably are "ritual structures" (Csonka 2003:120). On the island of Yttygran is the Whale Bone Alley site complex comprising two parallel lines of 50–60 bowhead whale skulls and nearly 30 whale mandibles set upright in the ground running for around 600 m behind the shoreline (Chlenov and Krupnik 1984; Krupnik 1993:191). Mikhail Chlenov and Igor Krupnik (1984:6–7) describe Whale Bone Alley as a "monumental ritual" site that includes a "ring of large boulders," which they refer to as the "Main Sanctuary."

The late Punuk phase site of Masik, located along Mechigmen Bay on the Chukchi Peninsula, was occupied between 1100 and 1700 CE (Bronshtein et al. 2016:483). It is of a similar monumental scale to Whale Bone Alley, with a settlement complex spread over a distance of 1,000 m along a spit featuring the remains of semisubterranean structures (some appearing to be "ceremonial houses" analogous to Inuit *karigis*) and over 1,500 gray whale skulls, 30 bowhead whale skulls, and numerous upright gray whale mandibles (Chlenov and Krupnik 1984:11). Chlenov and Krupnik (1984:12) conclude that Masik is "a large ancient settlement once inhabited by whale hunters who had a rich ritual tradition which included the custom of setting into the ground pairs and fours of bowhead whale skulls."

Across much of the Arctic regions of the Bering Strait, Alaska, northern Canada, and Greenland, various Inuit groups were recorded ethnographically to have constructed semisubterranean ceremonial houses known variously as *qargi, qalgi, karigi*, and nearly 70 other related terms (Larson 1995:208). These houses were used mostly, but not exclusively, by men (Bodenhorn 1990:67). They were the context for whaling rituals (by men and women), and the structures usually incorporated whale mandibles "to insure that all celebrations took place in the presence of the bowhead whale, the community's provider" (Patton and Savelle 2006:144). For example, the Alaskan Inuit community of Inalik (Little Diomede Island) in the middle of the Bering Strait constructed *qagzriq* using a pair of bowhead whale mandibles arching over the entrance (Jolles 2003:334–335).

An excellent example of an archaeologically excavated men's ceremonial house (*karigi*) comes from Site PaJs-13 on Somerset Island in central northern Canada (Habu and Savelle 1994; Patton and Savelle 2006:146). Associated with the Thule culture and dated to 1300–1500 CE, the house features a paved stone floor and six whale crania arranged over the entrance passageway. The walls include whale ribs, vertebrae, and mandibles. Altogether, excavations revealed at least 7 crania, 22 mandibles (distal ends only), 71 ribs, and 77 vertebrae (Habu and Savelle 1994:11, 13–14). The paved floor of the *karigi* was covered with Layer 10 consisting of grease, baleen, and skin fragments. Junko Habu and James Saville (1994:15) hypothesize that Layer 10 may have been "ceremonial" in nature and "served symbolically to separate the whale from the land," informed by Judith Huntsman's (1963:107) ethnographically informed comment that "the whale dislikes things that are associated with or come from the land." In this sense, the *karigi* was constructed to ensure that the sea, as represented by whale bones, maintained its ontological distinction from the land, while the seascape extended onto the land.

Ceremonial Songlines

Australian Aboriginal songlines marking the path of Dreamtime cosmological and mythological narratives of the creation period sometimes reference the sea and marine animals across inland regions. In this sense, these inland regions have a cosmologically ordained hybrid ("amphibious") terrestrial-marine identity (see Kearney 2025). For example, the Yanyuwa people of the Gulf of Carpentaria of northern Australia have a dugong site located many kilometers "inland" that is associated with the King Tide songline (Bradley with Yanyuwa Families 2022:266). The King Tide Dreaming saw a large area inland of Limmen Bight on the mainland flooded by sea water before it retreated to Yumunkuni (Beatrice Island), where it remains today. This flooding was encouraged by the Dugong Hunters Dreaming, who took advantage of the expanded sea to compete against each other to harpoon the first dugong. Physical expression of this flooding is at Wunubarryi (Mount Young) located 3.5 km inland of the current sea. Here is a series of quartzite boulders known to be "metamorphosed dugong and a single dolphin which were stranded on dry land" after the sea receded (Bradley 1991:102; Bradley with Yanyuwa Families 2022:266). Bradley (1991:102) adds that it is "interesting to note that a similar occurrence happened in 1984 during Cyclone Kathy; a number of dugong and sea-turtle were stranded after a storm surge carried them up to eight kilometres inland in the vicinity of the McArthur River delta area." Expression of the competitive hunting is found further inland (46 km from the sea) in the form of rocky outcrops at Kulumbirri, which represent "the wrecked bark canoes of the dugong hunters who lost the competition" (Bradley with Yanyuwa Families 2022:266–267).

The Tiger Shark Dreaming songline of the Yanyuwa (Rrumburriya clan) travels for approximately 55 km from Manankurra (located 9.5 km inland from

Figure 12. Tiger Shark ancestral being traveling 10 km "inland" to Manankurra, where he introduced cycad palm trees that remain the sacred responsibility of the Rrum-burriya clan of the Yanyuwa people, Gulf of Carpentaria, northern Australia. (Still image from animation *The Song of the Tiger Shark at Manankurra [Manankurra Kujika]*, a 2008 production of the Wununguru Awara Animating Indigenous Knowledges project, Monash University. Courtesy of John Bradley. Permission to reproduce from senior Yanyuwa Elders Mavis Timothy a-Muluwamara and Dinah Norman a-Marrngawi.)

the sea) down the Wearyan River to its mouth and then across 20 km of sea to Vanderlin Island (Bradley 2006; Bradley with Yanyuwa Families 2010:58–87). Because of its association with the Tiger Shark Dreaming, Manankurra, with its "crowds" of cycad palm trees next to the Wearyan River, is a profoundly important sacred ceremonial place (Bradley and Kearney 2009:463). The cycad palms were brought to Manankurra by the Tiger Shark spirit ancestor as he traveled up the Wearyan River (Figure 12). The "tessellated patterning of the palm trunks signify wounds the Tiger Shark sustained fighting other sharks" (Bradley with Yanyuwa Families 2010:60). Before arriving at Manankurra, Tiger Shark left "a small bundle of cycad fruit" in the sea at Wurlma, represented today by "a long block of rock on the eastern edge of the reef" (Bradley with Yanyuwa Families 2010:237). The freshwater well at Manankurra is Tiger Shark's eye; "his mouth is located deep in the waters of the river" (Bradley with Yanyuwa Families 2010:60). Despite its location nearly 10 km inland from the sea, Manankurra is considered the "true home" of the Tiger Shark (Bradley with Yanyuwa Families 2010:68). The starchy kernels of the cycad palms were an important food source for people attending ceremonies at Manankurra. Women prepared the starch using large grindstones (averaging around 20 kg) obtained from sandstone outcrops on islands off the adjacent coast (Bradley 2006:174). The grindstone bases are called *rra-walma*, with *walma* the term for "large, flat submerged rocks that surround parts of the coast of the Sir Edward Pellew Islands" (Bradley 2006:174). Indeed, one senior Yanyuwa man described the grindstones as "from the sea" (quoted in Bradley 2006:175).

Amanda Kearney (2025:192, 195) adds that the uninterrupted flow of Yanyuwa songlines and associated pathways of ancestor beings across the "sea" and "land" occurs "irrespective of the land sea interface" and is "one in which the movements of ancestral beings blur the boundaries of land and sea exclusivity." Furthermore, "Ancestral beings move unencumbered by logics of separation and land/sea rationalities, as they hop from land to sea in aquatic or terrestrially adjusted forms, dance on the ocean floor, emerge from the depths of the sea to walk across the land, blow across the surface of the earth, disassemble their body parts and manifest in enduring formations for all to see today" (Kearney 2025:193).

The Wardaman people of the Katherine region of the Northern Territory of Australia, along with their neighbors, are holders of the Dreamtime narrative and associated creation songline or Dreamtime Track of the black-headed python known as Kunukban, an "ancestral snake hero" (Arndt 1965:241). Kunukban originated from the island of Puruyu:nungu:kunian located "far out in the Timor Sea" between northwest Australia and Indonesia (Arndt 1965:249). His inland journey began at Wyndham in the northeast corner of Western Australia, where "he came out of the sea" and continued eastward as he carved out gorges through mountains and corridors for the Ord, Bulla, Baines, and Victoria Rivers. His inland travels ended at Beetaloo Lagoon, located nearly 700 km southeast of Wyndham, where "some say he is still in there, but some say he went underground and came out under the sea" (Arndt 1965:252).

Guugu Yimithirr Aboriginal people of the lower Endeavour River of coastal Far North Queensland have a Dreamtime narrative that connects the sea with Ngurrayin lagoon located 7 km inland (Gordon and Haviland 1979:17; Haviland et al. 1998). A long time ago, Ngurrayin was an interregional gathering place for "different tribes" who all spoke the same language. Freshwater in the lagoon never dried as "sea water comes underground from the ocean and holds the water in that lagoon up." Once, a nhinhinhi (giant grouper) came underground from the sea and swallowed people gathered at Ngurrayin before heading underground back to sea. After two months the grouper returned to Ngurrayin and "vomited all the people out," after which they all spoke different languages.

The linking of marine and terrestrial realms through referencing of a marine animal (grouper) on land by the Guugu Yimithirr also finds expression in another Dreamtime narrative documenting when "all the creatures, from the land and sea, came together to have a great dance" over many days at a large swamp known as Wuyii (Gordon and Haviland 1979:47). At the end of the event, the land and sea animals "exchanged clothing with one another" (Gordon and Haviland 1979:50). For example, goanna (land) traded his "tough hide" with crocodile (sea), sea urchin traded his "hard spikes" with echidna (land), and turtle (sea) traded his "big heavy shell" with tortoise (land; Gordon and Haviland 1979:50). In marked contrast to monstrous animal-animal hybrids discussed in Chapter 3, Guugu Yimithirr composite animals are not monstrous but everyday animals whose hybrid terrestrial-marine form is not obvious to outsiders.

Importing Marine Animal Parts (Shells and Bones)

Marine shells dominate midden sites along many coastal regions of the world. Where those middens relate to foraging practices of hunter-gatherers, additional midden sites, usually of much smaller size, can be found kilometers inland. These inland shell deposits are the result of people either walking inland from coastal residential camps with shellfish while foraging for other foods (e.g., plants) or walking to the coast from inland residential camps to collect shellfish. Archaeological research reveals that inland camps (residential camps or foraging camps) with marine shells dating to the Late Pleistocene and Holocene occur mostly within 6 km of the coast with the vast majority within 3 km (e.g., Bailey and Craighead 2003:184; Godfrey 1989:68, Figure 1; Jerardino 2016:224; Luebbers 1978:301; Marean 2024; McNiven 1992), corresponding to ethnographically documented effective foraging radii of hunter-gatherers (Bigalke 1973:161; Kelly 2013:96–102). People knew their inland camps had direct connections with the sea, with marine shells contributing to the material fabric of sites. In this sense, these inland camps, at least in part, had a marine identity that helped define a broadened terrestrial seascape.

Beyond subsistence practices, people in various parts of the world have traded material culture comprising marine animal parts (e.g., shells, pearls, corals, teeth, bones) to inland regions well beyond 6 km for tens of thousands of years. From a purely archaeological perspective, to what extent the inland recipients of these traded objects associated such marine objects with the sea or even knew of the existence of the sea is difficult to know. In some cases, ethnographic and historical information reveals that possession of marine objects by inland peoples was associated with the sea and indeed was conceptualized as referencing and symbolizing the sea or a particular dimension of the sea.

In many inland regions of the world are found marine shells, often with symbolic, ideological, spiritual, and cosmological significance, located hundreds and in some cases thousands of kilometers from their coastal marine source (e.g., Cattaneo-Vietti et al. 2016; Claassen 1998:203–212; Rybska 2014; Safer and Gill 1982). These shells include small whole shells or pieces of shell incorporated into body adornments (e.g., jewelry), shell decorative elements on material culture (e.g., shell inlay), shell money, and large shells that function as objects in their own right (e.g., trumpets). In many cases these traded shells have been carved with decorative designs, with many shells having a ritual or religious dimension.

Archaeological evidence reveals inland movement of marine shell artifacts during the Pleistocene. The earliest known examples of marine shell body adornments are perforated gastropod (*Tritia gibbosula*) beads dating to at least 142,000 years ago excavated from Bizmoune Cave, Morocco (North Africa), located 12 km from the present coast (Sehasseh et al. 2021). Bar-Yosef Mayer and colleagues (2009:307, 311) document 92,000-year-old *Glycymeris nummaria* bivalves (some with "ochre stains" and "naturally perforated") used as "ornaments" at Qafzeh Cave, Israel, "brought from the Mediterranean Sea shore," then located 40–45 km away. Similarly, 82,000-year-old marine shell beads (*T. gibbosula*) were recovered from Grotte des Pigeons in Morocco, 40 km from the coast (Bouzouggar et al. 2007; Sehasseh et al. 2021:1). The movement of these shells indicates "interlinking exchange systems or of long-distance social networks" (Bouzouggar et al. 2007:9969). Of similar Middle Paleolithic age, the open site of Oued Djebbana, Algeria (North Africa), contains a single perforated *T. gibbosulus* gastropod bead sourced to the coast located at least 190 km away (Vanhaeren et al. 2006).

But do inland-traded shells reference the sea in some way? In most cases it is very difficult to know whether or not inland peoples who obtain marine shells have any sense of the marine origin of the shells or link the symbolic significance of the shells with the sea. Ethnographically, Williams (1940b:139) recorded that the Foi people of Lake Kutubu in Papua New Guinea, located 170 km (straight line) from the coast, had no idea of the sea or the ultimate marine origin of pearl shell valuables. Indeed, the origin of the shells was something of a mystery to the Foi, who stated that the shells originate from the "south" and from a "great reservoir of shell" in highland valleys further inland to the "north" (Williams 1940b:134). Similarly, the Kasere (aka Ikobi; Franklin

1973:266; Franklin and Voorhoeve 1973:Map 4) of the Upper Kikori River to the southeast of the Foi possess a legend that pearlshell (*yaku*) "comes from a sacred spot near the headwaters of the Hawoi River" located to the northwest, where it "grows on a tree and can jump or walk from there into the water and travel southward" toward the sea (Austen 1948:19). Further to the west in Indonesian Papua, the Wodani, who imported cowrie shells from the coast, had no idea of the "existence of the sea" located over 120 km away (Breton 1999:558).

Chank (conch; *Turbinella pyrum*) shells used as ceremonial trumpets and vessels for pouring ritual libations by Hindus across India had symbolic links with the sea (Hornell 1942; Lerner 1984:82–85). According to one legend, the conch shell was the home of Panchajana, a terrible marine demon who lived on the bottom of the sea. Panchajana was attacked by Krishna (an incarnation of Vishnu). Krishna seized the conch shell home of Panchajana as a trophy, and ever since the conch has been one of the emblems of Vishnu and Krishna (Hornell 1914:120, 1942:116). Extremely rare sinistral forms of these conch shells with left-coiling, counterclockwise whorls are accorded great significance and are presented as offerings at Hindu shrines (Hornell 1942:117). Hindu Brahmans who worship the conch would on special holy days recite a prayer that included: "Oh, chank shell, thou wast produced in the sea and art held by Vishnu in his hand. Thou art worshipped by all the gods. Receive my homage" (Hornell 1942:118). The rare sinistral spiral form of these conch trumpets are similarly "objects of adoration" in Buddhist monasteries located 1,000 km inland in Tibet (Hornell 1942:117). In some cases, elaborately decorated conches with relief carvings of Vishnu used in India during the eleventh or twelfth century were eventually traded inland to Tibet and embellished with silver (Lerner 1984:84). Tibetan chanks used as trumpets were commonly adorned with metals (e.g., silver and brass) and semiprecious stones (e.g., turquoise; Lambourn 2021:17; Pal 1969:126).

Oral traditions of the Benin of Nigeria (West Africa) recount how King Oba Eresoyen (reign 1735–1737 CE) "once quarrelled with Olokun, the god of the sea, and closed the way so Olokun could not get water. Through the mediation of a palm wine tapper Eresoyen agreed to release the water. As a reward Olokun heaped up cowries to the sky for Eresoyen and they were packed to the palace. As a result, Eresoyen decorated the walls and floors of his palace with cowries. His appellation then became: Eresoyen who built a house of money" (Ben-Amos 1999:103–104; see also Ogundiran 2002:445). At the same time, the public quarters of the residence of High Chief Ezomo Ekeneza were "elegantly encrusted" with cowrie shells (Ogundiran 2002:446). Although oral tradition attributes the source of cowries to Olokun, the actual source was slave raiders and traders who used cowries imported from the Indian Ocean as money (Ogundiran

2002:441–443, 445). Indeed, during the peak of the Atlantic slave trade in the eighteenth century, Dutch and English traders imported more than 10 billion cowries to the Bight of Benin (Ogundiran 2002:440, 2014:71). Beyond use by royalty as a symbolic link to Olokun and the sea, cowries in Yorubaland (from the coast up to 300 km inland) were incorporated into a wide range of local institutions, "from their use as currency and social payments (e.g., brideprice, tributes, taxes) to their ascribed aesthetic qualities and their embodiment of transformative/ritual potency" (Ogundiran 2002:440, 2014:74). In addition, Yoruba households created shrines and altars used by men and women for "the propitiation of Ori, the deity of fate and destiny, a force that resides in an individual's inner head" (Ogundiran 2014:74). Ori shrines and altars were studded with cowrie shells, incorporating up to 12,000 cowries during the peak supply period of cowries in the late eighteenth and early nineteenth centuries (Ogundiran 2002:448, 2014:75). Ogundiran (2014:78–79) argues that part of the "indexical" value of cowries was their association with the "ocean."

The center of production of ethnographically known Australian Aboriginal pearl (marine) shell (mostly *Pinctada maxima*) objects is a 600-km-long section of coast centering on Broome in the central Kimberley region of northern Western Australia (Akerman 2023; Akerman and Stanton 1994; Edwards and Yu 2018). Many of these objects feature engraved designs (mostly geometric) with red ochre infill. As no archaeological evidence of engraved pearl shells has been recovered, engraved pearl shells are thought to date to after European contact and introduction of metal tools in the second half of the nineteenth century (Akerman 2023:18). In the Kimberley, engraved shells are known mostly as either *riji* or *jakoli*, while *longka-longka* is the most common term used across Central Australia (Akerman 2023:2, Map 1). Both decorated and undecorated shells can have one or more drilled holes for the addition of a suspension chord often made of woven human hair or animal fur. Pearl shells were either suspended around the neck (pendants) or from the waist (pubic covers). They are used by men, women, and children and are "secular in nature" and "not part of the secret-sacred realm" (Edwards and Yu 2018:4).

Ethnographic recordings indicate an extraordinary geographical spread of the inland exchange of Kimberley pearl shell objects, spanning two-thirds of the continent of Australia and extending 1,700 km to Yalata on the southwest coast of South Australia and at least 1,700 km eastward to Lawn Hill in northwest Queensland (Akerman 2023:Map 2, 36; Akerman and Stanton 1994:Map 1; Trigger 1987:76). The Walmadjari, Ngardi, and Kukaja peoples, whose Country in the southeast Kimberley region extends 200–900 km inland of the coast, hold a mythological narrative whereby a bilby (small marsupial) stole pearl shells from inland areas and fled west, pursued by Rain and Lightning beings.

Reaching the coast, bilby deposited the shells back into the sea at a place that is now a spiritual increase place for pearl shells, according to the Ngardi (Akerman 2023:41, Map 6; Akerman and Stanton 1994:27). Daisy Bates noted that pearl shells increased in value as they were traded inland and that they "were broken up into small and yet smaller portions, each shell or portion of shell retaining its coastal name" (Australasian, 1 November 1930:4). Many Pitjantjatjara people of Central Australia, located 1,000 km southeast of the Kimberley coast, know that pearl shells originate in the sea (Akerman 2023:6).

Kimberley Aboriginal cosmology holds that pearl shells are scales of the Rainbow Serpent that have fallen off and settled on the seabed (Akerman 2023; Edwards and Yu 2018:10). For coastal (Saltwater) peoples of the Kimberley coast, the surface luster and shimmer of pearl shells "is considered to be water, the sea and life itself" (Edwards and Yu 2018:36; see also Akerman 2023; Akerman and Stanton 1994:19). As pearl shell objects move inland through exchange partners, they continue to be connected to water (often seen as the "concentrated essence of water") and are used in rain-making ceremonies by desert communities (Akerman 2023:6; see also Akerman and Stanton 1994:23; Edwards and Yu 2018:32; Mountford 1976:53, 275). Similarly, in the broader Kimberley region, publicly shared information reveals that rain-making ceremonies "usually involved the scraping or grinding of the shell, thus releasing particles of its essence" (Akerman 2023:56).

Archaeologically, most studies that discuss the inland movement of marine shells (especially shell beads) focus on the shells as markers of social prestige and social interaction through exchange networks (Trubitt 2003). Few studies discuss the relational symbolism of marine shells that have been moved inland in terms of referencing the sea and maritime identity. Lloyd Weeks and colleagues (2019:21) state that peoples across southern Arabia living hundreds of kilometers inland 2,000–3,000 years ago imported marine shell objects that were "intrinsically associated with the sea." More generally, Mary Trubitt (2003:244) notes that objects made from marine shell that are traded inland are "symbolically linked with water and the sea." Yet ethnographic examples indicate that it is unwise to assume that ancient inland peoples who possessed imported marine shells also imported the symbolic associations of these shells with the sea. Despite these issues, a number of archaeological studies have explicitly explored the broader cosmological implications of the marine identity and source of marine shell objects, especially those objects transported many kilometers inland.

Michelle Langley and colleagues (2016:12, 15; see also Langley et al. 2023) provide a rare archaeological example of the potential marine symbolism of Late Pleistocene shell objects, albeit recovered from a site located only 3 km from the shoreline. They note that nautilus shell beads at Asitau Kuru (previously Jerimalai) were a "social signifier" that reveals "the integration of the coast and its resources into the lives of those who occupied Timor-Leste from 42,000 cal. BP. Not only were these peoples successfully exploiting the ocean for their nutritional needs, but they appear to have intertwined this landscape within their social realm through selecting particular marine raw materials to manufacture items of ornamentation." Jane Balme and Kate Morse (2006:809) go a step further by suggesting that the long-distance inland movement of marine shells in northwest Australia during the Late Pleistocene "implies that it was the marine source of the shell that was of some significance."

Conch shell trumpets made from marine *Strombus* sp. and *Murex* sp. have been recovered archaeologically from a wide range of ceremonial contexts across inland Southwest North America dating to the past 1,200 years (Mills and Fergusson 2008; van Dyke et al. 2024). Most of the shells are thought to have been imported inland from the Gulf of California, located 500–1,000 km to the southwest, with some evidence for direct procurement by ritual specialists undertaking religious pilgrimages (Mills and Fergusson 2008:345, 350–351). Although direct procurement indicates known association between the shells and sea, it is unknown if inland shell trumpets had marine symbolism. More generally, Cheryl Claassen (2008) argues that for inland peoples of the North American Southeast and across various parts of Central America, the significance of imported marine shells was directly connected to the known cosmological importance and power of the sea.

The 3.8 million pieces of shell weighing 500 kg recovered from caches in multiple architectural contexts at the large Puebloan community of Casas Grandes (or Paquimé) in arid northern Mexico comprise the largest inland assemblage of marine shells recovered from an archaeological site in the New World (Whalen 2013:627). Most of the shells are perforated dog whelks (*Nassarius*) sourced to the Gulf of California, 400 km to the west, and date to the Medio Period around 500–900 years ago. Michael Whalen (2013:635–636) argues that the shells, like many imported marine shells used by Native Americans (see Claassen 1998, 2008), were "animate objects" with "powerful" spiritual agency, that participated in the ritual maintenance of Casas Grandes as a "sacred place" linked to water and rain.

In Classic Mayan iconography, marine "shells serve as marine symbolism par excellence" (Zender 2010:84). Mary Miller and Megan O'Neal (2010:35) note that the "common offering of *Spondylus*, copious cinnabar, and a single jade bead or figurine found at Tonina, Copan, and elsewhere may unite notions of deep water, high mountain, and maize, with the jade replacing the pearl or creature that may have once resided within the shell." Furthermore, for those

Maya "who lived far from the sea—and who might never hear the crash of ocean waves or collect a queen conch from the sand—the sea could still be present, invoked and created both through natural resources and the things humans made" (Miller and O'Neal 2010:36). Carvings of royal ancestors on marine shells such as conchs was a symbolic reference to the eastern sea and the realm of supernatural power (Finamore and Houston 2010:125, 130).

Andean societies of highland Peru imported *Strombus* and *Spondylus* shells from the warm waters of Ecuador to the north for use in "rituals associated with assuring adequate water for crops and as offerings to springs" due to their symbolic associations with the sea (i.e., water, rain, purification, earth; Helms 1988:124). More specifically, the ruling elites of the Chimú culture of northern coastal Peru (tenth to fifteenth centuries CE) imported *Spondylus* shells from Ecuador as ritual markers of political status and agricultural fecundity (Pillsbury 1996). Elizabeth Currie (2016:5) suggests that archaeological evidence of "sea shells being sacrificed to springs and flowing waters" is consistent with José de Acosta's (1962:246–247) sixteenth-century observation that Andean peoples considered certain marine shells as "daughters of the sea, mother of all waters." In this sense, "It seems that the sea penetrated the land itself, underpinning the cycles of life, bringing fertility" (Currie 2016:5). As noted in Chapter 2, Mamacocha (Mother Sea), controller of the sea, also was responsible for the formation of rain-producing clouds and freshwater in lakes, rivers, and springs (Silverblatt 1987:48).

The earliest evidence for inland movement of marine bone is projectile points made from whale bone dating to the Magdalenian of the Upper Paleolithic (15,000–17,000 years ago) found in caves in the Pyrenees of southwest Europe, up to 350 km from the coast (Pétillon 2013). To what extent such objects were associated with the sea by inland peoples is difficult to know. In contrast, inland movement of marine bone by Central Americans provide rare and instructive insights into the known and potential cosmological dimensions of the introduction of marine bone to inland regions. Here the movement of marine vertebrate remains focused on elasmobranchs, especially requiem sharks (e.g., tiger sharks) and eagle rays (Myliobatidae). For example, the Maya incorporated shark teeth (including fossil shark teeth) into ritual and spiritually charged (votive offering) contexts in Mesoamerica (de Borhegyi 1961; Newman 2016). Ritual caches of shark teeth (and shark burials) have been recovered from South America in a coastal "temple" complex in Peru (Powell 2020; Prieto 2018). Wyllys Andrews (1969:110) points out that stingray barbs found on inland Mayan sites were not simply imported as sharp-pointed implements, as numerous local plant "thorns" could have served the same piercing function. He concludes that the "fact that they were chosen, despite the difficulty of collection and importation, bespeaks some fundamental identification between the practices and the sea" (Andrews 1969:110). Similarly, Elizabeth Wing (1977:55) asks, "What value, however, was placed on marine fish or their parts used for nonsubsistence purposes? Were they valued as objects or as tangible representations associated with the sea?"

Bodies Buried with Marine Animals

A common terrestrial expression of maritime identity by coastal communities is burial of the dead with parts of marine animals. Examples include marine mammals (walruses, seals, whales, dugongs), reptiles (turtles), fish, and mollusk shells, including burial within midden deposits.

Early examples of human burials with marine mammal remains come from the East and West Coasts of North America. At Rattlers Bight near Nain on the Labrador coast of Canada, William Fitzhugh (1976:125, 1978:66; Rankin 2008:129) excavated a burial containing a walrus skull within a cemetery dating to 3,500–5,000 BP. The Little Beach site on the west coast of Vancouver Island in British Columbia features "whalebones . . . placed over a number of cairn burials dating between 4000 and 3000 B.P." (Monks et al. 2001:65). A rare South American example of a burial with whale bone comes from Panama at the site of El Caño, located 17 km from the coast, where a 1,000-year-old grave of a high-ranking individual contains a large-whale vertebra located under a human skeleton (Cooke et al. 2016:734). However, the majority of the world's evidence for the incorporation of sea mammal remains (essentially all bone) into human burials dates to the past 2,000 years, from the Arctic and Inuit cultures on the Russian and American sides of the Bering Strait.

Remarkable examples of burials with marine mammal bones come from the Uelen cemetery in the remote northeast corner of Russia where the Bering Strait meets the Chukchi Sea. Here an ancient Inuit coastal site contains more than 70 burials from the Old Bering Sea/Okvik cultures, dating to 1,400–1,700 years ago (Arutiunov and Sergeev 2006:35; Hill 2011:413; Mason and Rasic 2019:465). Numerous burials contain marine mammal bones, many of which have been modified in some way, often to form implements. They include whales (mostly jaws and scapula plus a few ribs and vertebrae), walrus (nearly all scapula plus a tooth), and seals (scapula and ribs; Arutiunov and Sergeev 2006:41–69). In some cases, graves are edged by whale jaws (up to 2 m in length), and in others they are capped by a whale scapula (up to 0.8 m long). Immediately to the south at Ekven cemetery, a burial dated to 1,300–1,600 years ago features nine scapulae (40–45 cm in length) from small gray whales (Krupnik 1987:18).

Archaeological excavation of an old Inuit cemetery at Sivuqaq on St. Lawrence Island in the Bering Strait, Alaska, revealed 114 interments, one of which is an adult associated with grave goods (e.g., stone artifacts and bone harpoon heads) and a whale rib radiocarbon dating to 1,000–1,300 years ago (Staley and Mason 2004). The whale rib "was probably a grave marker" (Staley and Mason 2004:127). Other burials at Sivuqaq of similar age feature walrus skulls laid at the feet of the body (Hill 2017:88). At the nearby Mayughaaq cemetery, 16 of the 18 interments dating to 800–1,300 years ago contain whale bone, mostly mandibles and ribs. Two burials also contain walrus ribs (Staley and Mason 2004:128, 132–133). Burials excavated near Gambell on St. Lawrence Island and dating to the early Punuk period (500–1,000 CE) are mostly "framed and/or covered by mandibles, ribs, and skulls" of whales (Bandi 1995:168).

A number of ground interments associated with whale bones, mostly scapula, have been excavated archaeologically across the Eastern Aleutian Islands (Black 1987:35–37; O'Leary and Bland 2013). In the Eastern Aleutians, Aleš Hrdlička (1945:238, 325) documented mummified human burials in a series of caves that also included a whale scapula (Kagamil Island) and a whale skull and three scapulae (Ship Rock islet—see Chapter 9), dating to the past 1,000 years (Coltrain et al. 2006). Lucille Johnson (2019:1023, 1026) documented burials from Asx̂aana-x̂ Cave in the Islands of the Four Mountains, Alaska, dating to the past 600 years that included a wide range of whale bone artifacts (e.g., wedges), large whale bone elements (e.g., ribs, scapulae), and a collapsed "whalebone sepulcher" comprising rocks and two 1-m-long "planks" of whale bone in the rear area (see also Day 2019:204).

In northeast Australia, Torres Strait Islanders included dugong bones in some burials during the nineteenth century. For example, William Wyatt Gill (1876b:202) notes seeing "recent graves" on Mabuyag/Mabuiag with piles of sand and "ornamented with dugong skulls and ribs and large helmet-shells (*Cassis tuberosa*)" (see also Haddon 1904:259–261). To the south, the Kuuku Ya'u "sandbeach people" of the east coast of Cape York Peninsula were recorded in the early twentieth century marking graves with elaborate and structured mounds of dugong ribs and skulls. For example, Donald Thomson (1934b:254, Plate XXXI, Figure 2) documented and photographed a recently created example of such a grave in the 1920s. Remains of these graves were visible up until the 1970s (Rigsby and Chase 1998:207).

The Seri Native Americans of northwest Mexico were recorded in the late nineteenth century as placing two marine turtle carapaces over bodies "as a kind of coffin" before the grave was infilled. In addition, a ceramic bowl containing "a few fresh mollusks" and "portions of turtle-flippers, and, if practicable, a chunk of charred plastron" were placed on the grave as "food for the long journey" (McGee 1898:291). Immediately north of Mexico, "marine turtle shells have been found in funerary situations in various places in Florida, notably in Calusa and Tequesta sites" (Frazier 2003:12).

Fragments of carapace/plastron from green turtle (*Chelonia mydas*) are associated with 80 of the more than 215 burials at Ra's al-Hamra 5 (RH-5) located on a small headland close to the shore of the Batinah coast of Oman, dating to 5,300–5,800 years ago (Frazier et al. 2018:5; Potts 1990:69–71; Salvatori 2007). Turtle crania or parts of crania were recovered from "nearly 13% of excavated graves: as many as 29 skulls have been recovered from a single grave, and as many as 34 lower jaws were found in another grave" (Frazier et al. 2018:5). Two graves are covered by a whole turtle carapace (Salvatori 2007:5). A separate pit above Grave 216 contains 12 turtle crania (Salvatori 2007:26). Many graves are topped with a cluster of white pebbles "which seem to be analogous to turtle eggs" (Salvatori 2007:26). The extraordinary association between marine turtle and human bones at the RH-5 cemetery clearly indicates a deep cosmological, spiritual, social, and symbolic relationship between marine turtles and people in Oman over 5,000 years ago. Peter Magee (2014:77) notes that "it is possible to speculate that the metaphysical transformation of the dead into a turtle marked a symbolic embrace of, or perhaps return to, the sea." At the very least the association is related to "identity" (Charpentier and Méry 2010:20).

Archaeological examples of human bodies buried with marine fish (or parts thereof) as grave goods are rare. Most common are burials found in association with low numbers of shark teeth (including fossil megalodon teeth) in the Americas. Examples include 1,200-to-4,900-year-old graves in São Paulo State, Brazil (Cione and Bonomo 2003:227), 1,000-to-4,300-year-old Late Woodland to Late Archaic burials on the Maritime Peninsula of the US Northeast and southeast Canada (Betts et al. 2012), 3,000-to-4,200-year-old graves on the coast of Rio de Janeiro, Brazil (Cione and Bonomo 2003:226), and 500-to-2,500-year-old Late Postclassic to Preclassic Mayan graves in Central America (de Borhegyi 1961:281–282).

A remarkable example of a burial with fish remains comes from the coast of southern California within the territory of the Chumash people. The burial was located on "the crest of an exposed headland over-looking the ocean" and dates to around 2,000 years ago (Davenport et al. 1993:264). It comprises a male adult in a flexed position wearing a headdress made from the skull with rostra (beak) of a large swordfish (*Xiphias gladius*; Davenport et al. 1993; Rogers 1929:410). Across the back of the head, neck, and shoulders was draped a "cape" made from numerous triangular-shaped sections of abalone (*Haliotis*) shell with hole piercings presumably for string assembly. The overlapping arrangement of the shells "imitate the scales of the fish" (Orr 1944:33). The right eye socket of the swordfish skull was inlaid with shaped sections of mother-of-pearl shell set within asphaltum (bitumen). David Rogers (1929:410), who excavated the site in 1926, interpreted the burial as that of a ceremonial swordfish "dancer," with Demorest Davenport and colleagues (1993:268) adding that the burial was of "a shaman for a cult of the swordfish." Furthermore, the shaman was not buried as an individual but in his "avatar" role as a swordfish shaman, thus permanently fixing him in the transformational state of a swordfish (Davenport et al. 1993:269). In addition to the swordfish bones, marine symbolism was enhanced by inclusion of two types of shell, and possibly also the asphaltum, given that the Chumash obtained much of their asphaltum from fragments of submarine outcrops washed up on local beaches (Brown et al. 2014).

Numerous examples exist of human graves associated with marine mollusk shells. In some cases, these shells appear to be shell artifacts showing signs of deliberate modification or use (see below). In extreme cases, so much shell is present that the bodies appear to have been buried within shell midden deposits (see below). However, in many archaeological contexts, bodies are associated with a small assemblage of marine mollusk shells that appear to be the remains of meals. An early example is two flexed bodies (male and female) buried in close proximity in Raru Mali 2 cave located 500 m inland on the island of Kisar in eastern Indonesia dating to around 14,000–16,000 years ago (Hawkins et al. 2024). Grave fill includes an "abundance" of marine shells (e.g., abalone, chiton) from "funerary rites" and associated "ceremonial feasting" (Hawkins et al. 2024:11).

Many ancient burials across the Aegean Sea are associated with modest amounts of marine shell food remains that were deposited either at the time of interment or subsequently by visitors. For example, marine mollusks were found associated with burials at the Early Bronze Age Minoan cemetery of Archanes Phourni located 11.5 km inland on the island of Crete. Nuttall (2021:146) comments that "these are certainly the remains of funerary cuisine, to which marine invertebrates played an important role. They appear to derive from acts taking place both during the deposition of the body and outside the grave, possibly later and some form of ancestor worship, in which seafood played a significant role." Similarly, the "use of seafood in association with the [Bronze Age] shaft graves at Mycenae and Lerna [on the Greek mainland] is significant and suggests that the sea was referenced by some kin groups as part of funerary ritual and potentially, as an aspect of elite identity. The distance of Mycenae to the coast [15 km] reinforces this notion" (Nuttall 2021:148).

Many coastal regions of the world feature shell middens that contain human burials (e.g., Drak et al. 2020:2; Hardy 2017:261–262, 268; Hellewell 2015; O'Sullivan 2002; Suby and Guichón 2014). These midden burials can be seen as an extreme example of bodies interred with marine shell grave goods. However, in this case the bodies are encased in a matrix of shell. Most published reports on midden burials focus on the skeletal remains as a source of biological data and mortuary practices. Few studies investigate the symbolism of using middens as a burial context and shells as a burial matrix, yet in most cases it is clear that local communities deliberately chose to inter bodies within the shell matrix of the middens for symbolic reasons. As Emily Hellewell (2015:32) points out, the "fact that inhumations have been placed within shell middens points to intentional use of these sites as important, ritually laden places." In some cases, burials took place after midden formation ceased, while in other cases it is clear that further midden accumulation took place after the burials.

In an insightful article, Edward Luby and Mark Gruber (1999:95) note that in the San Francisco Bay Area of California, some of the large "shellmounds sometimes contain thousands of burials," including primary inhumations (especially flexed burials) and cremations. Furthermore, these shell mounds clearly are "long-term repositories for the dead" and "played a central role in mortuary ceremonialism" and associated "mortuary feasting" (Luby and Gruber 1999:97, 100). Of critical importance is the view that "the mingling of human remains with animal bones and shells should not be regarded as indifferent disposal of the dead in places where refuse accumulates, but as interment of one part of the community in the matrix from which the community takes its life" (Luby and Gruber 1999:103). Luby and Gruber (1999:95–96) conclude that San Francisco Bay shell mounds have deep "symbolic" and "cosmological" significance, where "the concepts of 'food' and 'ancestor' join together at shellmounds, so much so that ritual attention to the ancestors was very likely regarded as essential to ensuring a continuing supply of food."

Cunliffe (2001:558) notes that the Western European Mesolithic tradition of burying the dead in shell middens extends along the Atlantic Coast from Scandinavia to Spain. He adds: "Perhaps in this practice we are seeing the desire of the hunter-gatherer communities to lay claim to the liminal territory at the edge of the land, the midden also representing the 'history' of the community going back to its ancestral beginnings. . . . The discovery of shell midden deposits in the chambers of a number of Neolithic burial mounds, most notably on the Channel Islands, is a tantalizing hint that the ancestry of the burial tradition might here be being symbolically acknowledged" (Cunliffe 2001:558).

The most developed cultural tradition of interring bodies within shell middens is associated with the *sambaquis* ("hill of shells") shell mounds of southern coastal Brazil (Klokler 2014:151). So extensive is the presence of burials in some of these sites that they are often considered "cemeteries" (Wagner et al. 2011:57). Jabuticabeira II shell mound, measuring 400 m by 250 m with a height of 9 m, has been the focus of extensive research (Gaspar et al. 2014:97; Klokler

2014:153). Other shell mounds in the area of Jabuticabeira II are "more than 30 meters in height" (Klokler 2014:153). Suzanne Fish and colleagues (2000:Table 4) estimate that around 40,000 burials occur within the Jabuticabeira II shell mound. Daniela Klokler (2008:278) argues that Jabuticabeira II was a specialized "ceremonial site, devoted to mortuary ritual" linked to corporate group identity and territoriality by local marine subsistence specialists. Following the approach of Luby and Gruber (1999), Klokler (2008:279) argues that "Jabuticabeira II served as a special locale for ritual feasting in honor of deceased members of the communities that inhabited the surrounding area. The site's construction occurred simultaneously with and as a result of the mortuary ritual" for around 1,500 years between approximately 1,400 and 2,900 years ago. The source of shells within the mound are meals augmented by quarrying of natural shell beds (Klokler 2008:238).

Archaeological excavations at the Greenville Burial Ground within Nisga territory (Tsimshian language group) of west central British Columbia, Canada, revealed numerous interments dating to between 700 and 1,400 years ago within a matrix of midden shell (Cybulski 1992). Jerome Cybulski (1992:168) notes that the "presence of human remains" is "almost constant in British Columbia shell midden sites" in Canada. Cybulski (1992:168) raises interesting questions in this regard: "Because of the almost ubiquitous presence of human remains, one might wonder whether shell deposits were specifically sought out as cemeteries in the prehistoric past; whether, in some cases, shell mounds may have specifically been built for the interment of deceased individuals; or, whether the construction of shell middens was, in some cases, a by-product of a corpse disposal ritual." Indeed, Cybulski (1992:168) hypothesizes that shell midden matrix at the Greenville Burial Ground "was a secondary deposition from village refuse elsewhere in the area of Greenville, specifically brought to the site for mortuary purposes." In other contexts, Cybulski (1992:167) acknowledges that it is "conceivable that whole village sites were periodically abandoned, during which time the accumulated shell refuse was used as a repository for the dead from neighbouring occupied areas."

In many cases, shell middens contain isolated human bones that do not appear to be disturbed burials or associated singularly with consumption of people (i.e., cannibalism; Arias et al. 2009:654; Hellewell 2015; O'Sullivan 2002). These secondary interments were associated with complex mortuary processes that included defleshing and disarticulation of bones (Hellewell 2015). For example, Christopher Meiklejohn and colleagues (2005) document the apparent purposeful association and clustering of selected small human bones (e.g., mostly hand and foot) and seal flipper bones in the 6,000-year-old Mesolithic shell midden site of Cnoc Coig on Oronsay Island in the Inner Hebrides, Scotland (see also

Mithen 2010:345–346). In this case, the symbolic association between human and seal bones may have been as equally important as the symbolic association between the interred bones and the surrounding shell (midden) matrix.

Bodies Buried with Marine Vessels

The practice of burying people in boats or ships or in boat-like coffins is known archaeologically to extend back to at least 6,000 years ago. When combined with ethnographic information, the tradition is best known for northern Europe, Island Southeast Asia, and Oceania. One of the oldest known sites is the Møllegabet dugout canoe boat burial recovered from an Early Ertebølle culture settlement now submerged off the Danish coast and radiocarbon dated to nearly 6,000 years ago (Skaarup 1995:55–57). However, the largest archaeological corpus of boat burials comes from northern Europe focusing on three periods: the Roman period/Roman Iron Age and Migration period (first to sixth centuries CE), the Merovingian/Vendel period (seventh and eighth centuries CE), and the Viking period (ninth, tenth, and eleventh centuries CE), which represents the most (over 75%; Van de Noort 2011:206).

A remarkable cemetery dating to the Roman Iron Age (first to fourth centuries CE) has been revealed at Slusegaard (Denmark) on the island of Bornholm in the Baltic Sea (Crumlin-Pedersen 1995). The cemetery contains approximately 1,400 graves (interments and cremations), of which at least 43 (3%) are associated with boats (complete or pieces of boats). The boat burials date mostly to between 100 and 250 CE. The stratigraphic shadow remains of the boats indicate most were either 3 m or 5 m in length and of log dugout form. People within the boat burials are divided evenly between male and female. Of the 156 child interments, none were associated with boats. Ole Crumlin-Pedersen (1995:94) sees the boats in these graves as a "religious symbol" and as "offerings" to a "fertility god" who traveled around on a boat. Furthermore, "Only a fraction of the population received such offerings in their graves, and the best explanation for this fact is to consider those buried with boats as persons involved directly in the fertility cult as priests or their helpers and therefore so closely connected to the god—or even to be looked upon as part of the family of the gods—that they are 'authorized' to be marked out with the attribute as an offering in their graves" (Crumlin-Pedersen 1995:94).

The two best-known early boat burials in Anglo-Saxon England are Snape (Filmer-Sankey and Pestell 2001) and Sutton Hoo (Carver 1998) dating to the mid- to late sixth century and early seventh century CE, respectively. The Snape ship and canoe burials site is located 7 km inland of the coast (North Sea) in southeast England and was probably visible out to sea (Filmer-Sankey and

Pestell 2001:1–3). It contains two dugout canoe burials and a ship burial. The dugout canoe coffins are both 3 m in length. The Snape ship burial is located within an earthen mound (possibly 5 m in height) and has a reconstructed length of 26.5 m. No human remains were recovered, but the grave goods point to a male of high status. William Filmer-Sankey and Tim Pestell (2001:233–234, 266) suggest the site location may have been governed by the nearby presence of Bronze Age mounds (links to "predecessors" and possible subversion of "ancestors") and visibility from sea (use as a "navigational" aid). Yet the burial site location involved considerable investment of energy, given that the vessels required transport across 2.5 km of land from the nearest river (Filmer-Sankey and Pestell 2001:263).

The famous early seventh-century-CE Anglo-Saxon ship burial site of Sutton Hoo is located nearly 1 km from the tidal waters of the River Deben, which connects to the sea in southeast England (Carver 1998). The distance from the mouth of the river and the North Sea to the site involves a meandering water journey of approximately 16 km, with the site itself located a straight-line distance of 13 km inland from the sea. Two ship burials (Mounds 1 and 2) have been identified among the large burial mound complex (inhumations and cremations). The most spectacular ship burial is Mound 1. It contains remains of a ship 27 m in length, indicating that the effort required to move the ship from the river across land would have been "formidable" (Carver 1998:122). The burial chamber is located within the ship whereas the Mound 2 burial chamber is located under the vessel. Repairs to the hull of the ship indicate that it was a "working vessel, not one especially built for burial" (Carver 1998:122). Although no physical evidence of a body was recovered, the burial has been gendered male based on associated material culture. From the extraordinary nature of grave goods, it is generally accepted that the Mound 1 burial is for a person of very high status, possibly a king. As such, the Sutton Hoo ship burials are probably as much political as they are ceremonial and religious. Martin Carver (1995:121) notes that the "association of boats with the supernatural world is a likely part of the cosmology for the Bronze Age, if not earlier, for peoples associated with and dependent on the sea" and for whom "travel, both of people and ideas, took place routinely over the North Sea."

Viking boat burials of the ninth to eleventh centuries CE are known in Norway, Sweden, Finland, Denmark, Iceland, Scotland, and Brittany. The number of Viking-age boat burials documented archaeologically in northern Europe ranges from 250 to 300 (Müller-Wille 1974:187; Owen and Dalland 1999:47). Nearly all are located adjacent to the sea with some located inland near lakes. The size of boats used for burials ranges from 2.5 m to 27 m, with most in the 5–15 m range (Müller-Wille 1974:193). Most take the form of a boat buried into the ground surface with the body (or bodies) and grave goods placed within the boat and then buried, often with the addition of an earthen mound. Most boat burials have poorly preserved human remains such that the graves are generally based on what are known to be gender-specific objects. The grave goods gender breakdown of Viking boat burials is male (60%), female (20–30%), and both male and female (10%; Müller-Wille 1974:198). Interpretations of Viking boat burials focus on the significance of the accompanying boat as a marker of personal or group identity in terms of voyaging (e.g., trading, raiding, warfare) and social hierarchy (e.g., power, authority, status) and symbolic transport of the deceased in the afterlife (Halstad-McGuire 2010:167–168).

An intriguing and informative form of boat burial in England is what has been referred to as medieval "pseudo-boat-burials." For example, the Norfolk cemetery at Caistor-on-Sea contains 13 such graves dating to the eighth to early ninth centuries CE. The graves contain between 2 and 37 clench-nails (used in the construction of clinker-planked boats) placed in rows along the interred bodies (Brookes 2007:3). The presence of these clench-nails is usually interpreted as evidence for use of segments of marine boat hull planking as coffins (Brookes 2007:6). Stuart Brookes (2007:7), however, advances that these boat fragments may have been included as "grave-goods in their own right." These grave goods are "likely to have signalled metaphorical associations with a real or imagined maritime heritage imbued with mythological and spiritual significance" (Brookes 2007:15). He adds that "burials containing nautical timbers document a symbolic association with boats and the sea. The use of boat timbers in burial and the occurrence of ship fittings as personal effects attest to the persistence of an older cultural tradition of ship imagery, posthumous maritime voyaging and numinous seascapes" (Brookes 2007:15).

Similar mortuary reuse of boat hull planks is documented archaeologically by Lucy Blue (2006) for two burials (Tombs 1 and 2) dating to 1200–1400 CE within the necropolis at the medieval Islamic port of Quseir al-Qadim on the west coast of the Red Sea, Egypt. For example, Tomb 1 (Burial 61) features a "mudbrick-lined, cist-type grave" of a 35-to-40-year-old woman "that was located c. 1 m below the surface and was sealed with [eight] timber planks" (Blue 2006:280). The timber planks feature drilled holes indicative of sewn boat timbers that originally were fastened together by wooden pegs and coconut husk fiber chord. Blue (2006:280) interprets the planks as an example of "sewn boat timbers . . . reused in a terrestrial context in a region where wood was a rare commodity." Although Blue (2006:282) states that "no grave goods were found in association with the burials, other than traces of cloth wrappings," the inclusion of the boat planks cannot be dismissed simply as nonsymbolic. The boat timbers most probably were grave goods with a marine symbolism linked to the liminal status of boats and the spiritual transformation of the deceased.

The church cemetery at Sebbersund in northern Jutland in Denmark dating to around 1000–1100 CE reveals that boat burials were also a feature of early Christian burials in northern Europe. Excavation of 468 of the approximately 1,000 inhumation graves in the churchyard revealed 210 coffins, of which 31 are "boat-shaped" (Birkedahl and Johansen 1995:162). A further 32 graves revealed rivets strongly suggestive of the presence of "boat parts" (Birkedahl and Johansen 1995:162). As such, 13.5% of all excavated graves are considered to be boat graves. Peter Birkedahl and Erik Johansen (1995) do not attribute any special religious or symbolic value to the boat graves, arguing that the boats were used simply as convenient coffins. That is, the "Christian boat-graves in the churchyard must be understood as a practical solution, and the boat is an easily acquired form of coffin at a large and active market place, where coastal transport and fishing were intensive" (Birkedahl and Johansen 1995:163–164). This secular interpretation is implausible. Use of boats from a marketplace as coffins is not inconsistent with the boats possessing deep symbolic and spiritual meaning. Burial of a person from a maritime fishing village in a boat is saturated with marine symbolism.

In Island Southeast Asia, boat burials have been documented both archaeologically and ethnographically in the Philippines, Borneo, and Malaysia (Ballard et al. 2004). In some cases, these boat-burial sites are located inland and incorporate riverine watercraft. A good example of these inland sites is the extensive boat-burial mortuary site of Kain Hitam cave in Sarawak on the island of Borneo in Malaysia, which dates from 2,300 years ago up to the tenth century CE (Szabó et al. 2008). Peter Bellwood and colleagues (2007) report on excavation of the Dong Xa boat-burial radiocarbon dated to 2,000–2,200 years ago in Hung Yen Province of northern Vietnam. The coffin was a ground interment and comprised a 2.3-m section of a dugout "logboat" sealed at both ends with bulkheads and covered with a large sheet of bark. The boat-coffin contained the remains of a 35-to-40-year-old adult that was double-wrapped in a textile shroud and sedge mat and placed on a bed of leaves. Grave goods included a ceramic pot and Chinese coins.

In Oceania, boat burials are known for high-status individuals from the Solomon Islands and Fiji. Part of the mortuary process for certain chiefs in Sa'a village on the southeast coast of Maramasike Island in the Solomon Islands involved placement within a canoe elevated above the ground on forked sticks (see Ivens 1927:208–210 for details). A range of plant products was included with the corpse, which could remain elevated for a year. A key place for these canoe burials was the beach at either a canoe landing place or canoe harbor.

After decomposition, the skull and jaw were removed from the canoe and placed in a recess within a wooden carving of a swordfish. Other bones may also be placed within a swordfish carving or into a beach altar.

On the Northwest Coast of Canada, certain people were buried in a canoe (sometimes with an inverted canoe as a covering) raised up on stilts (Raffan 2011:140; M. Reid 2011:45). In this form, "the canoe . . . is a liminal vessel—taking its occupants from one world to another" (Raffan 2011:141). Furthermore, the Kwakwaka'wakw also erected mortuary poles in the form of vertically oriented canoes with a large and elaborate carved wooden mask at the top (M. Reid 2011:44).

Westerdahl posits that boat burials were an expression of the ontological duality of land and sea. For example, boats "traverse *liminal states,* tangibly the water surface or the tidal shore, the border between sea and land. However, liminal states work in several cognitive dimensions. Life and death is another. This may be one of the combined reasons for the significance of the ship in burials" (Westerdahl 2010:278; original emphasis). In addition, ship burials further express the land-sea ontological duality in terms of the spiritual and magical power of sea objects on land (as opposed to the complementary magical power of land objects at sea; Westerdahl 2005b:18, 20).

But what about the agency of boat burials in terms of their placement in nearshore contexts? Does the act of creating a boat burial add a new maritime dimension to a nearshore context more than just representing an existing maritime identity? Are boat burials part of a strategy of extending the seascape onto the "land" or at the very least blurring the sea–land boundary? Boat burials illustrate nicely the power of maritime objects as both expressive and generative of a maritime identity "on land." The irony of the sixth- and seventh-century Anglo-Saxon ship burials at Snape and Sutton Hoo in southeast England is that these beacons of maritime identity were located many kilometers inland. Informed by Carver's (1995) insights into the political dimensions of Anglo-Saxon and Viking ship burials in Britain, it is plausible that the marine seascape did not exist independent of the terrestrial seascape in terms of Anglo-Saxon maritime identity, power, and politics. The terrestrial seascape was not relevant simply because options for creating materialized marine-focused sites of identity were limited in the marine seascape. The terrestrial seascape was important to Anglo-Saxon maritime peoples because so much time was spent on the "land." In short, the land needed a maritime identity in its own right, not simply as an adjunct to the sea. It is in this sense that terrestrial seascape sites were not simply representative of a sea-based maritime identity but critical to the creation and maintenance of a maritime identity. The terrestrial seascape had both expressive and generative properties in terms of marine cosmologies, identities, and polities. When alive, powerful leaders expressed their maritime powers by voyaging across the sea. When dead, these leaders expressed their maritime powers by voyaging across the land. That ships used in Viking ship burials were seen to be part of a terrestrial seascape is revealed by the ninth-century-CE Oseberg ship burial in eastern Norway, which has its prow tied by rope to a large mooring stone, despite its location 1 km inland from the shore (Bill 2016a:212). The fact that such voyaging may have been related to traveling to the world of the dead (Bill 2016a) does not negate cosmological construction of the land as a terrestrial seascape and a dimension of the sea for the world of the living.

Van de Noort (2011:203) provides a theoretically nuanced discussion of Scandinavian boat burials and what he describes as "the attribution of other-than-human agency to boats." He supports arguments positing that ships and boats used in burials were not intended to facilitate the journey of the deceased into the next world. Indeed, Van de Noort (2011:215) points out that the place-ment of burial ships and boats under earthen mounds, the apparent pegging of vessels "into place," and the placement of ships over bodies in many cases are inconsistent with the journey hypothesis. Alternatively, he posits seeing these vessels as "liminal agents" (after Westerdahl 2005a, 2005b); that is, "the other-than-human agency attributed to the ships was believed to disconnect on death from the physical body of the ship, just as the human agency was thought to be able to disconnect from the body of the person on dying. Thus, traveling together, the 'soul' of the ship facilitated the journey of the 'soul' of the human" (Van de Noort 2011:215–216).

In Southeast Asia, wooden coffins have been made in the shape of boats. For example, at the Bronze Age site of Ban Non Wat in central Thailand, Charles Higham (2011:369) documents an interment of a young woman with evidence of a "wooden coffin with a boat-like prow" dating to 3,100 years ago. In the Philippines, boat-burial sites are within caves and rock shelters "generally ac-cessible from the sea" (Tenazas 1973:19). A boat-burial cave site on Bantayan Island located off Cebu in the central Philippines contains primary burials in boat coffins averaging 2.25 m in length and "miniature wooden boat-coffins" with secondary burials averaging 90 cm in length (Tenazas 1973:20). Another boat-burial cave site on the island of Marinduque in the northern Philippines contains piles of miniature wooden boat coffins, with secondary burials simi-larly averaging 90 cm in length, behind which are found burials within large stoneware jars of possible Chinese origin dating to the twelfth or thirteenth centuries (Tenazas 1973:20).

In a range of cultural contexts, stone arrangements symbolically representing ships and boats in plan or profile and with mortuary associations have been recorded archaeologically. According to Torsten Capelle (1995), around 2,000 such sites have been recorded across Scandinavia, with some dating back to the Bronze Age (1700 BCE) and most dating to between the sixth and eleventh centuries CE (Skoglund 2008). All the Bronze Age boat and ship stone arrangements in Scandinavia are in coastal or near coastal settings. The sites usually consist of upright stones forming the outline of a boat or ship, with most between 4.5 m and 9 m in length (Figure 13). The two largest known examples are 33 m and 45 m in length. In southwest mainland Scandinavia, Bronze Age ship-shaped stone arrangements dating to 1300–1700 BCE are covered by an earthen mound. Clearly, these stone arrangements were not constructed to be seen directly in the landscape (Skoglund 2008:392). In marked contrast, ship-shaped stone arrangements on the island of Gotland in the Baltic Sea to the east date to 700–1100 BCE and are not buried under mounds but are highly visible in the landscape (Skoglund 2008:393). Interestingly, "no burials have been found in 14 of the 54 properly reported excavations of ship settings on Gotland" (Wehlin 2010:93). For those Gotland ship-shaped stone arrangements with burials, Helene Martinsson-Wallin and Joakim Wehlin (2017:245) argue that they employ the symbolism of the ship as a liminal agent (after Westerdahl) and a "mediator between the living and the dead and the gods." Furthermore, these sites symbolize a new form a relationship between Gotlanders and the sea that became increasingly ritualized through construction of monumental stone structures (many using stones possibly collected from the shore) located close to the shoreline, which was a liminal zone in its own right (Martinsson-Wallin and Wehlin 2017:246–248).

Cassandra Clark (2018:115) posits that Scandinavian stone ships "were perceived of not only as grave markers, but as ancestral touchpoints—places within the landscape that familial or communal ancestors could return to and depart from aboard a ship that could traverse the boundaries between the worlds of living and dead." She adds that such travel took place across a "cosmic sea," where the sea is seen as a "cosmological boundary between the worlds of living and dead" (Clark 2018:122–123). Van de Noort (2011:213) makes the point that the location of boat stone arrangements in association with "cremation patches" in the Viking cemetery at Lindholm Høje in northern Jutland "clearly illustrates that the construction of stone boats and the use of real boats in burials were closely linked practices" (see also Cunliffe 2017:437).

Boat-shaped piles of stones associated with burials are a feature of the Batanes Islands of the northern Philippines. Edwin Valientes (2019) summarizes previous archaeological research on "boat-shaped stone markers" on the small island

Figure 13. Bronze Age Gannarve stone ship, Gotland, Sweden (Courtesy: Patrick Morisson / Alamy Stock Photo).

of Vuhus/Ivuhos in the Batanes archipelago. The low-mounded features range in length from 2.3 m to 8.0 m, and most are "generally oriented on a land-sea axis or northwest-southeast directionality" (Valientes 2019:12). Excavation of 3 of the 19 boat-shaped stone arrangements revealed single interments radiocarbon dating at least back to the sixteenth century CE (and beyond local oral histories), thus confirming that the features were "burial markers" (Valientes 2019:15). Valientes (2019) argues convincingly that the Vuhus boat-shaped graves are part of a broader "cosmological" tradition in Island Southeast Asia of boat coffins and soul boats ferrying the deceased to the land (often an island) of the dead. The low number of Vuhus grave sites suggests that the tradition may have been restricted to high-ranking individuals (Valientes 2019).

Bodies Buried with Marine Shell Artifacts

Artifacts manufactured from marine animals have been used as grave goods in many parts of the world for over 10,000 years (e.g., Deshpande-Mukherjee 2021). Shell grave goods range from heavily modified and carved objects (e.g., fishhooks) to individual shells (some with a perforation). Most discussion of these marine shell grave goods focus on issues of social status, exchange, and mobility. Few studies discuss the broader cosmological and symbolic dimensions of referencing the sea. A rare example of the latter is a burial brought to light by O'Connor and colleagues (2017) through archaeological excavations at Tron Bon Lei rock shelter on the island of Alor in eastern Indonesia. The primary flexed burial is of an adult woman dating to 11,000–12,000 years ago (O'Connor et al. 2017:1459–1460). Around and under the chin were located a perforated bivalve shell (*Vasticardium* cf. *flavum*) and six exquisite fishhooks made from trochus shell (*Rochia nilotica*; O'Connor et al. 2017; Samper-Carro et al. 2022). The polished nacreous surface of the fishhooks gives them a luster that is known ethnographically to attract fish. The site is currently located 160 m inland and probably <1 km inland at lower sea level during the time of the burial. O'Connor and colleagues (2017:1466) rightly note that "in both life and death, the Pleistocene inhabitants of Alor Island were intrinsically connected to the sea. The association of the fishhooks with a burial denotes the cosmological status of fishing in this island environment, probably because of the role that fishing played during daily life for the inhabitants of an island that largely lacked other sources of protein." More specifically, the burial may indicate that "fishing equipment was viewed as essential for the transition to the afterlife in the Wallacean Islands" during the Terminal Pleistocene (O'Connor et al. 2017:1452).

Elaborately carved rings of marine shell have been found on the arms (armbands), wrists (bangles), and lower legs (anklets) of bodies in burials in various parts of the Pacific and Southeast Asia. Perhaps the most remarkable examples come from the Bronze Age cemetery at Ban Non Wat in central Thailand, 250 km from the coast. The most elaborately adorned burials at this cemetery for "outstandingly wealthy men, women, infants and children" date to between 2,700 and 3,000 years ago (Higham 2011:379). While these exotic and imported marine shell objects clearly are associated with status, Ken Ross and Mark Oxenham (2017) remind us that their potential cosmological significance should also be considered.

In the western Solomon Islands, Southwest Pacific, elaborately carved pieces of giant clam shell (*Tridacna gigas*) were deposited into shrines and mortuary contexts. Most shell valuables are made from semifossilized clam shell excavated from raised coralline limestone (ancient reefs) located immediately inland of the current shoreline (Sheppard and Walter 2014:35, 42). Two major types of these clam shell valuables were produced ethnographically: rings (*poata*) and elaborate fretwork plaques (*barava*; Lancrenon and Zanette 2011:198–243; see also Aswani and Sheppard 2003 and Sheppard and Walter 2014 for discussion of these shell valuables and other named types). Archaeological research suggest that these objects were used over the past 500 years (Walter and Sheppard 2000).

Bodies buried with single or multiple marine shell grave goods with minimal modification beyond breakage or perforation have been found dating back to the Terminal Pleistocene. In most cases, these minimally modified shells are considered beads for body adornment, either as jewelry (attached to string) or clothing (attached by sewing). The oldest known burial with grave goods (personal adornments) that also happen to be of marine shell is the 74,000-year-old infant (4–6 months) burial at Border Cave, western coastal South Africa (d'Errico and Backwell 2016). The body was buried with a small gastropod (*Conus ebraeus*) with a perforation made by people and associated wear patterns consistent with use as a body adornment. Border Cave is currently located 82 km from the coast, perhaps around 90 km at the time of the burial. In addition to the 11,000-to-12,000-year-old Tron Bon Lei burial, other Terminal Pleistocene examples include the late Upper Paleolithic child (3–7 years old) burial from the La Madeleine site in southwest France dating to 11,600–12,200 years ago accompanied by 1,314 Dentalium shell beads (Vanhaeren et al. 2004). From the arrangement of the beads, it appears that they were "sewn" onto a garment draped over the body (Vanhaeren et al. 2004:1483). The nearest potential source of the shells is the Atlantic coast, which is currently located 180 km west of the site, but was more than 230 km away during the time of the burial and lower sea levels (Vanhaeren et al. 2004:1486). In the Early Holocene, Burial IIa of an adolescent male at Los Canes cave located 10 km inland on the northern (Cantabrian) coast of Spain contains 65 gastropod shells (*Trivia* sp., *Littorina fabalis*, and Naticidae; "many pendants," so presumably perforated) dating to the Late Mesolithic 7,600–8,000 years ago (Arias et al. 2009:651; Drak et al. 2020:3, Table 1). Barbara Leon (2005:8, 12) documents a Neolithic burial dating to 4,700–5,400 years ago located under a Mesolithic shell midden on Dalkey Island, east coast of Ireland, where the cranium was "filled with periwinkle shells," clearly revealing a "connection with the sea" (Bradley 2022:80).

Across various parts of the United States, a wide range of Native American burials include marine shell beads with minimal modification dating to the past 10,000 years. Examples include the Horn Shelter 2 double burial of a man and adolescent dated to 9,700 years ago located approximately 300 km inland in central Texas. The male adult was buried with two small marine shell beads, including an *Oliva* sp. (gastropod; Claassen 2019:89). The Buckeye Knoll hilltop mortuary site, also in Texas, features 20 burials collectively associated with over 1,700 *Prunum apicinum* (gastropod) marine shells with a ground perforation (for stringing and attachment to clothing) dating mostly to between 6,300 and 7,200 years ago (Claassen 2019:90; Ricklis 2012a:158, 2012b:642–646). The site is currently located 44 km from the nearest coastline and the Gulf of Mexico, the probable source of the *P. apicinum* shells (Ricklis 2012b:642). As burials with marine shells were clustered in the southern part of the cemetery, Robert Ricklis (2012c:661) posits the intriguing hypothesis that these individuals within the broader community "had greater affinity for, or connection to, the coastal (southern sector) of the environment than did others." Furthermore, "Perhaps the two sets of individuals represent two lineages, one with a traditional linkage to the coastline and the other with a similar linkage to the interior" (Ricklis 2012c:661). In this sense, the inland marine shells were an explicit reference to the sea and the maritime culture and identity of coastal peoples.

Numerous people buried at the ancient Native American ceremonial city complex of Cahokia in the US state of Illinois between 800 and 1,000 years ago include large lightning whelks (*Busycon sinistrum*) imported 1,100–1,300 km inland from the Gulf of Florida to the south. Following Thomas Emerson (1989) and Whalen (2013), Sarah Baires (2016:246) advanced that lightning whelks, living in the marine realm, were linked symbolically and potently with the watery underworld of the dead. As such, lightning whelks placed with bundle burials "served to connect the living world of humans with the watery underworld of the dead and to facilitate the release of both the human and gastropod soul" (Baires 2016:248). In this sense, the whelks functioned as liminal agents (sensu Westerdahl 2005a, 2005b), facilitating the transfer of the souls of deceased people from the realm of the living to the realm of the dead.

Conclusion

A key message of this chapter is the proposition that a recursive relationship exists between terrestrial seascapes and marine seascapes such that each helps define the other. Terrestrial seascapes were expressed materially in myriad ways, with intentional inscription in the form of both importing marine objects onto the land (e.g., shells, bones), creating symbolic representations of marine objects (e.g., rock art paintings of marine animals), and burials associated with marine animal parts, ships, and boats. In all cases, it is doubtful that the inscription process was entirely responsible for transforming a terrestrial landscape into a terrestrial seascape. The inscription process was more about maritime peoples giving a material expression to the latent maritime dimension of inland areas as a terrestrial seascape. Importantly, the extent to which peoples with a maritime identity relied on a terrestrial seascape, and the extent to which it extended "inland," differs from community to community.

Although this chapter focused on inland representation of marine themes (e.g., rock art paintings of fish, boat-shaped houses) and inland movement of marine objects (e.g., trumpet shells, whale bones) and marine-themed objects (e.g., ships) in ceremonially, ritually, and spiritually charged contexts, the topic has the potential to embrace a wide array of objects along a spiritual–secular spectrum. In terms of the later, the inland movement of marine or at least coastally linked objects can extend beyond marine animals and embrace objects such as stone (e.g., shoreline stones incorporated into ceremonial structures such as churches and megaliths). Hannah Cobb and Jesse Ransley (2019:24) present a speculative, albeit thought-provoking, hypothesis that Mesolithic microliths made from raw materials from the Ayrshire coast of Scotland may never have lost their association with "the sea and people over the sea," even if used to hunt deer well inland in the forests of the Scottish Southern Uplands.

In a discussion of the iconographic representation of the sea in the material culture of the Ancient Aegean, Nuttall (2021:198) notes that the "depiction of specific features relating to the sea, such as boats, marine animals and the sea can be taken as an index of the significance of this zone toward cognitive processing. The continued mimesis of sea-focused iconography indicates the metarepresentational significance to a community and its continued reproduction through transmission over time. The generation of sea-focused representation is a direct indicator of the imbuement of space with meaning, rendering it a place. It is the creation of a seascape." A key representational issue is that depicting the sea as a concept or entity is iconographically challenging. More often than not, iconographic representation of the sea is what Nuttall (2021:197, 211) refers to as "metarepresentation" through "metonyms for the sea" and use of representations of attributes of the sea, key examples being marine animals such as fish, cephalopods, and mollusk shells. Nuttall's comments on marine iconography are relevant to all aspects of marine referencing on land discussed in this chapter. However, whereas Nuttall (2021:30) associates "creation of a seascape" with conversion of the sea as a "space" to a "place," my "terrestrial seascape" approach sees marine referencing as part of a broader process of helping to define, express, and curate the terrestrial dimension of seascapes.

Finally, a wide range of evidence surveyed in this chapter reveals that numerous societies incorporated objects of marine origin into human burials. Inclusion of boats and even ships in the case of Viking and Anglo-Saxon burials exemplifies this process par excellence. Treatment of the dead can be seen as expressions of maritime identities of both the living and dead within a terrestrial seascape context. In short, terrestrial seascapes further demonstrate the recursive relationship between the land and the sea such that expressions of the maritime identity of the dead are important to expressions of maritime identities of the living, and vice versa.

6

Rituals of Ship Construction and Destruction

Embodiment to Predatorization

Life on the sea was about life on boats and ships and what Edward Ward (1707) dubbed the "wooden world." Yet this world of wood extended well beyond the technological and the utilitarian and into the realms of the animate and spiritual. Many, if not most, maritime peoples considered their vessels, especially large boats and ships, to be living, animate objects. Beck (1999:16) posits that "because of the peculiarities of a ship, her movement, her internal noises, and her vagaries in handling, seamen believed her to be animate or at least quasi-animate." Dening (2004b:25) makes the important point that for mariners, movements of a ship were embodied: "A sailing vessel is a machine energized by natural forces and human vigor. Power so harnessed gives every part of a ship a trembling, beating life that transmits itself to the bodies of the sailors and all their senses. Sailors feel the rhythm, hear it, smell it, see it, have the language to describe it."

This chapter uses a wide range of examples to explore the complex and multiple ways mariners in different cultural contexts, both past and present, relate to boats and ships and what I have referred to as "animate object-beings" (McNiven 2018a, 2025b). The focus is the beginning of vessel lives and the highly ritualized processes of construction and launching through to the end of vessel lives and onto the formal ritual processes of retirement and fragmentation. In this sense, the chapter takes a broadly biographical, life-history approach to vessels from birth to death and even afterlife. The spiritual and symbolic dimensions of the death and afterlife of shipwrecked vessels is discussed in Chapter 7.

Embodiment and Animation

In many societies, boats and ships were conceived of as animate object-beings with agency expressed in two major dimensions: the structure and form of vessels, and the behavior and emotion of vessels. At the outset, it is important not to fall into the dualist trap of seeing animacy as inscribed to vessels after they have been constructed. In most cases, the animacy of vessels goes back to the animacy of the trees used in constructing them. That is, the potential for animacy was always inherent in the wood, with the construction process involving a complex transformation from a tree-person to a ship-person. As such, ship construction was often about expressing latent animacy as an expression of an interpersonal relationship between wood and carver, and ship and mariner. In contrast, Silvia Rodgers (1984:2) posits that twentieth-century launching ceremonies of British naval vessels were less about a "transition rite that accompanies the ship as she passes from land to water" and more a "critical transition . . . from the status of an inanimate thing to that of an animate and social being" with "life essence."

Expressions of animacy often accompanied construction of vessels, whereby assembly of vessel parts was considered analogous to conception, gestation, and finally birth. For example, Bugis boatbuilders of *pinisi* from Ara on the southeast coast of Sulawesi "create a ship as a mother creates a baby in her womb" (Pelly 1977:102). Indeed, the connection of the female central keel section (*sombong*, vagina) with the male front and back sections of keel (*lasso*, penis) is conceptualized as "marriage" or "intercourse" to produce a "baby—the ship" (Pelly 1977:96, 102). As a follow-up ritual, the master boatbuilder "spreads a pool of blood from a male and female chicken over the two connecting points" (Pelly 1977:94). Efficacy of the keel connection/conception process is enhanced by the presence of a pregnant woman (Pelly 1977:96). Furthermore, the launch/ birthing of a *pinisi* is embodied further by the physical and highly ritualized addition of a "navel" drilled into the keel the night before the ship's launch, which is termed *pasorong lopi* ("the pushing out of the ship"; Pelly 1977:99, 102).

In the Greco-Roman ancient world, "the eyes, horns, and figureheads gave the ship an anthropomorphic or zoomorphic identity" (Atkins 2009:107). These hull addenda had the result of "giving it the power to see and move" (Atkins 2009:116). Carrie Atkins (2009:96; emphasis added) states of ancient Greek ships that with such additions "the hull was considered to be more than simply timbers and figureheads; rather it was now a *living creature*." Atkins (2009:124) adds that the "eyes imbued the ship with the capability to watch for danger, while horns likely were apotropaic objects to protect a ship from oncoming evils." In the twentieth century, Tyrrhenian fishermen of the west coast of Italy would attach a pair of ox horns to their fishing vessels to help bring good luck and protection (Baldi 1998:154–155).

To the contemporary communities of the central west coast of Ireland, their traditional carvel-built wooden sail-boat known as a Galway hooker was a living, sentient being with a soul and spirit. One person stated that "the people always believed that the boats were alive" (Ó Sabhain 2019:161). Furthermore, "If it's telling you something, you listen to it" (Ó Sabhain 2019:161). Another boat owner knew his vessel had a soul, saying, "It's something that you can't shout about or people will think that you're mad, but I think it has anyway" (Ó Sabhain 2019:189). One dimension of this animacy was the embedded spiritual presence of ancestors in inherited boats. One local mariner "would often speak with and even stroke the side of the boat as if it was human" (Ó Sabhain 2019:181). Another person noted that he talked with his boat and asked it and his muintir (forefathers) for help and guidance, especially in safe voyaging (Ó Sabhain 2019:181).

Fishing boats of Lamalera village on the island of Lembata in eastern Indonesia are considered "as being alive" and possessing a "soul" with different sections of the boat referred to as the "head, shoulders, and breast" (Barnes 1996:245–246). Furthermore, diagonal holes sometimes bored through the bowsprit were said to represent "ears," while a groove in the bowsprit is its "mouth" (Barnes 1996:208, 245). Whenever a fishing boat is taken from the boat shed and carried or dragged down to the water's edge, seawater is splashed onto the sides of the boat to help it prepare for its imminent immersion into the sea and to make movement down the beach easier (Barnes 1996:272). The process of wetting is explicitly compared to a person bathing in the sea, whereby splashing of seawater on the body helps prepare the body for the "shock" of encountering the cold sea (Barnes 1996:272).

In Melanesia, oceangoing outrigger canoes of the Trobriand Islanders of southeast Papua New Guinea were animate object-beings. Malinowski (1922:105; emphasis added) notes that such canoes were "an object of cult and admiration, a *living thing*, possessing its own individuality." The intentionality and agency of Trobriand canoes is illustrated by a "magical rite" such that "the canoe makes up its mind to run quickly" (Malinowski 1922:133). Nancy Munn (1986:145) adds that Trobriand canoes further express intentions and desires such as "want to drink" (when caulking goes dry), "hungry" (when obtaining *kula* shell valuables), and "smell" (when near land). To the southeast, Wala Island outrigger canoes of northwest Malekula, Vanuatu, took on the form and "soul" of high-ranking men, featuring a metaphorical mouth and eyes (prow figurehead representing a bird), ears (prow tassels), penis sheath (stern tassels), arms and legs (outrigger booms), fingers and toes (outrigger float attachment sticks), palm of hand and sole of foot (outrigger float), and belt (attachment to rim of canoe; Layard 1942:469; Tilley 1999:115). The launching of Murik canoes at the mouth of the Sepik River in Papua New Guinea resulted in transformation of "an inert, man-made object into a cosmic agent of productivity on behalf of the descent group" and creation of a new (nonhuman) "person" and "citizen" in the community (Barlow and Lipset 1997:14, 28, 30). These canoes possessed stomachs, hands, and prow heads (Lipset 2014:32–33). Torres Strait Islander canoes of northeast Australia were "animate object-beings" possessing a head (bow), torso (hull), and tail (stern; McNiven 2015c, 2018a).

Inupiat and Yupiit Arctic peoples of the Bering Strait region, taking in the Bering and Chukchi Seas, constructed elaborate watercraft (*umiaq*) that according to Erica Hill (2022:25) were an "animated 'object-being'" (*sensu* McNiven 2018a). Hill (2022:26) argues that *umiaq* were "attributed" both "agency, and possibly personhood," where in certain circumstances the *umiaq* as a transformed bird or a salmon (through the addition of special amulets) expressed intentionality when "deciding to swim upriver and resting onshore." However, little evidence exists to show that *umiaq* were an assembly of body parts.

Hull Timbers

Rich (2013:5) notes that archaeology focuses on the end life of ships (i.e., shipwrecks) with little consideration given to the start of a ship's life and the symbolic value of wood used in construction. In many contexts, the process of embodiment of a vessel begins with the tree(s) from which the vessel is formed. Often the tree and hence the wood possesses spiritual power. Perhaps the best-known ship timber is the cedar of Lebanon from the ancient Mediterranean world and of Old Testament fame. Indeed, these cedars now form part of the Ouadi Qadisha (the Holy Valley) and the Forest of the Cedars of God (Horsh Arz el-Rab) World Heritage Area in Lebanon. Yet cedar forests and cedar timber for shipbuilding were also used from Türkiye, Syria, and Cyprus (Rich 2013). Rich (2013:178, 181) points out that in "the religious and literary records of the Ancient Near East, cedars are probably the species most frequently venerated" and "the most highly regarded tree in the ancient world" (at least in an eastern Mediterranean sense). Cedar forests and wood were "divine property of the gods, as a tradition of prosperity, and as symbols of power and purity (= immortality). The trees, the forests, the wood, and even its resin, were affiliated with divine essence, and utilizing and controlling such a powerful symbol would have been of utmost importance—especially to those whose lives and livelihoods were susceptible to the whims of the sea" (Rich 2013:181–182). Rich (2013:1) concludes that "the choice to use cedar wood—and from which forest it came—was both a practical and ritual consideration." In short, "Some vestige of ownership by the god remained in the cedar" (Kennedy 1974:8).

In the Shetland Islands of Scotland, wood imported from Norway for boat construction was examined closely for the position and shape of knots, which were known to bring different types of luck. For example, "fishy knots" foretold full nets of fish and were considered desirable, whereas "windy knots," "misforen knots," and "wattery swirls" were considered dangerous and were rejected (Marwick 1975:72). Scottish boatbuilders also examined the form of the first wood shavings produced during the manufacture of a boat for special telltale signs as to whether or not the vessel would be associated with good or bad luck (Anson 1965:91). Similarly, these shipwrights identified male and female wood, with use of female wood conveying to the vessel the capacity to sail faster during the night compared to the day (Anson 1965:91).

In German communities flanking the Baltic Sea it was known that spirits (e.g., Klabautermann) entered vessels through wood used in their construction. These spirits were associated with dead humans and entered wood obtained from trees under which were located graves, especially those of stillborn or murdered children, or trees used by people to hang themselves. Spirits of children also entered the wood of trees used in rituals to help heal children with broken limbs. The spirit of a timberman would also enter wood of a tree that killed the timbermen during its felling (Buss 1973:36, 40). Some German communities of the Baltic coast also held that a protective spirit "comes into being" and enters a vessel when the first chip of wood is produced in its construction (Buss 1973:38).

For the Warao of coastal Venezuela, the process of canoe manufacture is overseen by a master canoe maker and shaman who has the important duty of propitiating spirits and associated metaphysical powers (Wilbert 1977). Warao canoes were invented by the culture hero Haburi, who made all canoes in the image of Dauarani, mother of the forest and goddess of the winter sun. As such, canoe manufacture is a process whereby the spirit of a tree "converts" into a canoe through a "divine service" officiated by the master canoe maker (Wilbert 1977:21, 23). The process of selecting a tree involves ritually propitiating Dauarani through gifts to consent to one of her daughters (the tree maiden) being sacrificed (felled). As the daughter converts to a tree for felling, the tree transforms sexually into anthropomorphic twins—male on one side and female on the other, along with hair (crown), body (trunk), and feet (roots). This bisexualism carries over to the canoe. After felling of the tree, the spirit of the tree reluctantly leaves her stump behind as the trunk is taken away to be shaped into the canoe over the course of months. The femaleness of the tree is materially revealed through carving of a triangle (vagina) at the bow and stern with crossbeams holding the sides apart such that "the canoe takes the shape of the vagina of Dauarani" (Wilbert 1977:36).

Among the Kwakwaka'wakw of the Northwest Coast of Canada, carving of tree trunks into canoe hulls involves taboos and rituals to obviate the negative impact of ancestral spirits. For example, Kwakwaka'wakw canoe makers must not have sexual intercourse with their wives during the canoe manufacturing process, otherwise "the tree from which he makes the canoe would be hollow"

(Boas 1921:615). Similarly, the face of a man is painted on each side of the canoe after adzing is complete to frighten off the spirits (i.e., "the souls of dead canoe-builders") who may come and "tell the canoe to split" (Boas 1921:616). When a dugout canoe hull was manufactured by the neighboring Coast Salish, "every good builder had spirit aid at each crucial step. Furthermore, the tree was 'like a person' and had to be treated circumspectly. The good canoe maker had a 'song' which he sang at the felling, splitting, excavating, and steaming. If the song was omitted, an irreparable crack might result" (Barnett 1955:110).

In the Bugis shipbuilding village of Ara on the southeast coast of Sulawesi, selection of forest trees for construction of a ship (*pinisi*) is undertaken by the master builder. The first wood selected is for the front of the keel known as *bengo* ("confused"; Pelly 1977:92). It is believed that with the cutting of this tree or wood, supernatural powers in the forest who otherwise wish to obstruct tree felling become "confused." The master builder enters into a "dialogue" with the "spirit of the tree" and states the name of the boat owner. The master builder makes the first ax cut into the tree, which must be in an upward direction so that "the fortune of the ship will subsequently continue to rise" (Pelly 1977:92).

Malinowski (1922) describes in detail the process of construction of large seagoing canoes (*waga*) used in the famous *kula* exchange system of the Trobriand Islands of southeastern Papua New Guinea. Malinowski documents the complex ritual process of selecting and felling a tree that forms the basis of the dugout hull of the canoe. Once a tree has been selected, a "small incision is made into the trunk, so that a particle of food, or a bit of areca-nut can be put into it" as "an offering to the *tokway* (wood sprite)" (Malinowski 1922:126). *Tokway* are generally thought of as an anthropomorphic "harmful being" with brown skin and "long, sleek hair, and a long beard" (Malinowski 1922:128). The offering is accompanied by a ritual specialist reciting an "incantation" such that the *tokway* is "invited to leave his abode, and to move to some other place, and there to be at his ease" (Malinowski 1922:126–127). If the *tokway* refuses to leave the tree, then "the wood would be full of knots, and that there would be holes in the canoe, or that it would quickly rot" (Malinowski 1922:127). Once all involved in the ritual process are satisfied that the *tokway* has left the tree, the tree is felled.

The construction of large trading canoes (*bevaia*) along the Gulf of Papua in southern Papua New Guinea involves the vessel master (*bevaia haera*) selecting a tree for the hull and undertaking initial axing. The major job of felling and carving of the hull then falls to others, but the vessel master must ensure that he collects the chips of wood he created and place them in a bag for safekeeping until the end of the trading voyage. It is thought that if these chips stay on the ground and become soggy in the rain, then the canoe hull will become waterlogged (Williams 1932:151).

At Walomo village on the northwest coast of Papua New Guinea, the final stage of hollowing out a canoe hull centered on the bow and involved a ritual specialist who in isolation at dawn removed the final wood chips and placed them on a fire such that the smoke blew over the bow and to the water's edge (Frankel 1978:38). As the smoke blew over the sea, he sang an incantation to the sun (referred to as Ade or ancestor) such that the sun would protect the canoe during its life from heat damage and splitting while drawn up on the beach.

Figural Heads

Although "figurehead" is the general term used to describe carved heads on the prow (i.e., the section of bow located above the waterline) of vessels (e.g., Hansen and Hansen 1990), this chapter uses "figural head" as the encompassing term. Three types of figural heads can be identified: figureheads proper (carvings of heads, often with partial or complete sections of the body, attached to the prow of a vessel), stem heads (a vertical bow extension reminiscent of a long neck terminating in a head), and prow heads (the entire prow of a vessel formed into a head). In some cases, vessels can feature more than one type of figural head; differences between these three types can also be a little arbitrary. Vessels with carved figural heads are known for numerous maritime societies both past and present. As expected, the purpose and meaning of figural heads varies considerably given the range of cultures represented. Most archaeological evidence for early use of figural heads is indirect, in the form of representations in rock art, relief carvings, or clay models.

The earliest known examples of figural heads are vessels with stem heads of zoomorphic form represented in Scandinavian Bronze Age rock art. For example, pecked rock art images of boats at Alta, northern Norway, depict boats with stem heads in the shape of an animal's head (elk) dated to 5,000–7,000 years ago (Gjerde 2020). At Boglösa in southern Sweden is a remarkable 4.2-m-long rock art engraving of a ship crewed by six anthropomorphs and a bow and stern both terminating in a large carved horse head dating to the Late Bronze Age (2,500–3,100 years ago; Ling 2013:66).

Fredrik Fahlander (2019) makes the intriguing observation that images of zoomorphic boats in southern Scandinavian Bronze Age rock art are not representations of actual vessels built and used by living people but a separate category of spiritual "object-being." He adds that it is improbable that Bronze Age boat rituals were associated with rock art images, as ethnographic information for Melanesia indicates that "rituals associated with marine activities are generally centred on the boat itself, not on representations" (Fahlander 2019:197). However, this ethnographic situation is only partly true, given that representations of vessels (large canoes) in some Melanesian coastal communities (e.g., rock art, wooden carvings) have ritual associations (Ballard et al. 2004; Brady 2010; Brady and McNiven 2022). In most of these ethnographic contexts, ritualistic representations of boats are not exact "models" of boats used by living people. As such, the large zoomorphic stem heads of ships represented in Bronze Age rock art may be of exaggerated size for ritual reasons compared to those found on boats made and used by mortal people. In this sense, the existence of zoomorphic vessels in rock art does not preclude the parallel existence of zoomorphic vessels made and used by people.

Representations of Phoenician ships often feature a stem head comprising a vertical prow extension terminating in a carving of a horse's head. Brody (1998:26) notes that this stem head probably represents a Phoenician sea deity known to take the hybrid form of a winged horse with a serpent's tail. He adds that the sea horse stem head "imbued" the ship with the "spirit" of the sea horse deity (Brody 1998:26; see also Woolmer 2012:247–248). A probable representation of these sea horse stem heads on Phoenician ships appears on an early eighth-century-BCE Assyrian-carved stone low-relief frieze recovered from the palace of King Sargon II in Khorsabad in northern Iraq (Brody 1998:69). Strong Phoenician influence is also seen in ship figural heads depicted in bronze ship models excavated from the island of Sardinia in southern Italy and dating to the late Nuragic period between the seventh and ninth centuries BCE (Tiboni 2006). The models have zoomorphic-shaped stem heads representing a range of terrestrial animals, particularly ungulates.

Old Norse literature informs us that the ship *Serpent* used by Olav Tryggvasson (king of Norway, 955–1000 CE) possessed a prow shaped like a serpent's head and neck (i.e., stem head) and a stern shaped like a fish's tail, such that "when the sails were unfurled they became the wings of a dragon" (Eriksson 2020:266). The Bayeux tapestry, dating to the eleventh century CE, shows a series of ships in the war fleet of William of Normandy preparing for his conquest of England in 1066 CE. Some of his ships feature stem heads of dragon form. Lucien Musset (2005:61) points out that of equal interest is depiction in the tapestry of some ships moored on the beach where the stem head has been removed, indicating that the "dragon figureheads [stem head] . . . could be removed when the voyage was over and the ships had been drawn up onto the shore." The Landnámabók (Book of Settlements), a medieval Icelandic text describing the Norse settlement of Iceland in the ninth and tenth centuries, refers to "an old heathen law requiring dragon-heads to be removed from ships on approaching unfamiliar shores, to avoid alarming the spirits of the place" (Bruce-Mitford 1970:146). Musset (2005:60) adds that none of the Viking ship burials excavated archaeologically exhibit dragon stem heads. The closest figurative stem head is the reconstructed spiral (snake-like) carving on the ninth century Oseberg Viking ship burial in eastern Norway. Yet the Oseberg ship burial included five wooden carvings, each around 0.5 m long, featuring zoomorphic heads (variously identified as lions, dogs, wolves) surmounted on slightly curved posts (Bill 2016b:146). The carvings were found lying down within the vessel and were included as grave goods. Jan Bill (2016b:147) argues that the carvings had a ritual (apotropaic) function to protect against evil spirits, and were probably "movable architectural objects that, when in use, were mounted on massive timber structures, for example houses." Yet it is possible that the carved heads had multiple functions, including as detachable stem heads on Viking ships.

In terms of figureheads, the best-known examples are European ships. An early example of a European figurehead dates to the late medieval period and was recovered recently in the waters of southern Sweden from the 1495 wreck of *Griffin* or *Gribshunden* ("griffin hound"), the flagship of King Hans of Denmark-Norway (Eriksson 2020). The carved wooden figurehead features a serpent's head with large teeth biting down on a human head with facial expressions of fear. Niklas Eriksson (2020:268) argues that the figurehead is strongly reminiscent of Viking ships and adds that "there is no doubt that there were several different ways to think of ships as more or less animated or living animals or fantasy beasts in the Middle Ages."

Considerable literature exists on the European tradition of carved wooden figureheads dating from the sixteenth to early twentieth centuries (e.g., Hansen and Hansen 1990; Norton 1976; Pulvertaft 2018). European mariners of the past few hundred years often considered the figurehead to be the symbolic embodiment of a ship's soul (Stammers 2004). It is estimated that around 5,000 figureheads were created for British warships during this period, of which around 200 (mostly nineteenth-century) survive today (Pulvertaft 2018:192). Hans Hansen and Clas Hansen (1990:17) point out that figureheads of the 13 large English warships afloat in the early sixteenth century represented dragons (n = 5), lions (n = 5), and other animals (n = 3). The oldest known lion figurehead attached to a ship comes from the remarkably well-preserved wreck of the royal Swedish warship *Vasa*, which sank on its maiden voyage in 1628. According to David Pulvertaft (2018:192), early figureheads of British warships were "in the form of complex groups of figures or crowned lions while those from the later period [after an Admiralty order of 1727 CE] were carved as single figures; some human, some in the form of beasts or birds, but each in some way related to the name of the ship."

Apart from warships, figureheads also adorned "larger merchant and passenger vessels," and "smaller sailing craft" (Hansen and Hansen 1990:27). The subject matter of nineteenth-century figureheads was greater compared to earlier centuries, and included people of note, with upper body figures (e.g., human busts) increasing in popularity (Hansen and Hansen 1990:27). Figureheads of women became increasingly popular in the late eighteenth century, and during the nineteenth century these represented nearly half of all figureheads (McCarthy 2015:29). Some female figureheads show women partly clothed with one or two breasts exposed. It was strongly believed among mariners that bare-breasted female figureheads would help calm seas.

The front of Torres Strait Islander canoes featured a range of elements such as eyes, mouth, and beard such that the entire prow represented an anthropomorphic head (McNiven 2018a). A similar situation of prow heads is associated with Trobriand canoes used in the famous *kula* exchange, with a prow attachment of a double row of shells (*Ovula ovum*) forming the "mouth of the canoe" (Campbell 2002:159). Red-painted "mouth" shells have the appearance of teeth reddened from chewing betelnut. As betelnut is a mildly addictive psychoactive social drug and is often associated with "love and beauty magic," the reddened shells (teeth) are associated with "attracting and seducing" *kula* exchange partners (Campbell 2002:159).

Murik canoes at the mouth of the Sepik River of northern Papua New Guinea also possess prow head features associated with canoe animacy and sentience. David Lipset (2014) refers to Murik canoes as "canoe-bodies," noting that a complex array of anthropomorphic and zoomorphic spirit prow carvings all look forward with "a multiplicity of eyes deciphering the moral character of space, reckoning whether it harbors, or will harbor, friend or foe" (Lipset 2014:34). This intentionalized and subjective "task of surveillance" also "evokes a human subject, sentient, generative, moving through space, transgressing its boundaries" and expressing a "desire for mastery" of social domains (Lipset 2014:34–35).

All figural head carvings on vessel prows possess eyes. Detlev Ellmers (1990:5) refers to the "relationship" that figureheads have "to the endless horizon of the sea at which they cast their eyes." In the case of prow heads, representations of eyes (*oculi* or *ophthalmoi*) were attached as separate features. In some cases, these eyes are the only recognizable head feature on a vessel's prow. In other cases, eyes are accompanied by attachment of other head elements such as a mouth. The addition of eyes to marine vessels has a long history and is found across the world, including Europe, the Mediterranean, east Africa, southern Asia, Southeast Asia, China, and western Melanesia (Agius 2007:104–105; Bowen 1955, 1957; Carlson 2009; Hornell 1923, 1938; Prins 1970; Quigley 1955, 1958; Van de Noort 2011:203; von Brandt 1984; Wahab et al. 2018).

The earliest possible example of a vessel with eye attachments is a ceramic boat model with painted black circles from Chamber Tomb 79 at Mycenae in Greece, dating to the Late Helladic IIIB–C period (around 3,050 to 3,300 years ago; Johnston 1985:29). The earliest clear example of an ancient Greek ship with *oculi* is found on the Aristonothos krater, dating to the first half of the seventh century BCE (Nowak 2001:88; see also Johnston 1985:53–54). The oldest known archaeological example of *oculi* is the pair of small marble disks (diameter: 14 cm) recovered from a fifth-century-BCE wreck of an ancient Greek trading vessel near Tektaş Burnu, south Türkiye (Carlson 2009:354–356; Nowak 2001; see also Galili and Rosen 2015a:51–53, 91, 2015b). Troy Nowak (2001:91) endorses the view that *oculi* "served to symbolize the presence of a ship's protective deity, similar to the function of figure-heads in antiquity." That is, the "eyes empowered the ship's deity to look forward for the helmsman, protecting the ship, its crew and its cargo" (Nowak 2001:91). In relation to ancient Greek ships, Atkins (2009:78, 97) adds that "the eyes on the bow of a ship were also apotropaic, providing a way for the ship to see its path safely through the dangers of the sea," and to "watch for danger" (see also Carlson 2009). Brody (2005:181) similarly notes that inclusion of *oculi* on Phoenician ships is consistent with the "concept of the hull itself housing a divine spirit." That is, the "deity who looks through these oculi guides the front of the ship and helps to avoid danger" (Brody 1998:70). While an association between *oculi* and protective deity may be true, it is also possible that *oculi* indicate that ancient Greek vessels were animate object-beings in their own right.

On the southeast coast of Bangladesh, fishers often paint eye motifs on the prow of their fishing boats that represent the eyes of Ganga, the deity that cares for fishers (Deb 2018:8). The eyes are painted in black, with red in the eye corners (Figure 14). As Ganga is considered to be "hot tempered," her scary reddened eyes are seen to "push away fish into nets, cool down powerful waves approaching fishing boat, and help fishers in tracing their set bag nets in utter darkness of the night" (Deb 2018:10). The agency of the eye is enhanced or "enlivened" by application of a mixture of coconut oil and vermilion on the pupil (Deb 2018:8). In addition, fishing boats are considered "living entities" in their own right such that the size of the "catch reveals the performance of the boats in the sea" (Deb 2018:5).

According to James Hornell (1923:303), *oculi* on Chinese vessels is due to an understanding "that eyes are necessary to boats and ships to find their way safely over the sea, and this must embody some vague idea of the vessel being sentient and associated with some protective spirit or god." Similarly, the "fisherfolk of Gozo (Malta) have a somewhat similar belief; the older generation

Figure 14. *Oculi* representing the eye of the Hindu deity Ganga painted on the prow of fishing boats, coastal Bangladesh (Courtesy: Apurba Deb).

look upon their boats as animate; to them the oculi are made for the boat or its spirit to see with" (Hornell 1923:303). These vessels are not simply seen as "animate" but as an animate being. They are considered one of the family, and indeed as its most valued member.

Landtman (1927:211) recorded that Kiwai peoples at the mouth of the Fly River in southwest Papua New Guinea immediately northeast of Torres Strait use eyes removed from birds to help intentionalize canoes: the "man provides the bow of the canoe with painted eyes, also gluing on real eyes of a *rúburúbu* or *warío* (two large hawks)." As a result, the canoe had the same capacity as men to see dugongs and turtles while out on hunting trips (Landtman 1927:211). In a related sense, Woodlark Islanders of southeast Papua New Guinea place a representation of the head of a sea eagle (*bunibwan*) "at each end of the keel" as it is "a bird that nests in trees and soars above the land- and seascape to locate resources and find the way to destination islands" (Feinberg 2020:346).

The inclusion of *oculi* painted on the prow of *dhow* sailing vessels was "widespread" in the Red Sea and east Africa up until the late 1970s (Agius 2019:207). In this case, *oculi* provided "talismanic protection against the evil eye (*al-ʿayn*)," as it was believed that "a single glance from a human eye with evil intent can harm or kill the targeted person, or summon up powerful natural forces such as gales that could wreck a ship" (Agius 2019:207). The destructive powers of an evil eye could be thwarted using "amulets . . . decorated with vivid depictions of eyes" (Agius 2019:207). In recent years, depiction of *oculi* on Red Sea *dhow* and their function to ward off evil spirits has been replaced by painting vessels vivid blue and turquoise colors that once featured in painted *oculi* (Agius 2019:208–209).

Speed

In the Pomerania region on the southern shore of the Baltic Sea spanning the German–Polish border, a small piece of stolen wood is incorporated into the construction of the keel to make the ship go faster at night (Bassett 1885:433). Henningsen (1965:209) adds that this practice also occurred in Scandinavia and "was thought to give the ships the nature of a thief: quick-running, especially at night. A stolen nail or a piece of steel would do the same."

Along the Gulf of Papua in southern Papua New Guinea, preparations for voyaging success in newly constructed trading canoes (*bevaia*) involved the vessel master (*bevaia haera*) abstaining from eating certain foods (e.g., meat) and from having sexual intercourse (Williams 1932:148–149). Such abstinence would ensure that the vessel master would be imbued with "lightness" which would be passed onto the trading canoe and make it travel faster. In addition, consumption of two varieties of mullet (known for their "exceptional speed in the water") would similarly imbue the master and vessel with speed (Williams 1932:148). To the east of the Gulf of Papua, Motu voyagers during the construction of their famous *lagatoi* trading vessels employ a ritual specialist to smoke the canoe hulls after they have been lashed together by burning special plants and fragments of cassowary claw and garfish snouts in an *ataga* (potsherd; Barton 1910:102). Cassowaries and garfish "move quickly," and the smoking "process is said to bring good luck and to give the *lakatoi* superior sailing powers" (Barton 1910:102–103). In addition, a parcel of the same special plant is fixed to the gunwale (Barton 1910:103).

Part of the construction process for Trobriand canoes involves ritual transformation of a canoe's symbolic "inanimate" properties of "heaviness" associated with land to the symbolic "animate" properties of "lightness," "slipperiness," and "speed" associated with the sea (Munn 1977:41). Murik canoes from the Sepik River mouth region include carved birds (e.g., sea eagles) and bird motifs to "impart both lightness and speed to the canoe" and to express "the desire that the canoe would 'fly' directly to its destination" (Barlow and Lipset 1997:22). Along the Vanimo coast of the far northwest corner of Papua New Guinea, small elaborately carved prow attachments featuring figurative representations of birds, dolphins, tiger sharks, hammerhead sharks, and sprats (fish) imbue canoes with "forceful speed" and the capacity to sail "straight" (Frankel 1978:30–31, 57; Figure 15).

Figure 15. Canoe prow ornament (*piu*), Vanimo coastal region of northwest Papua New Guinea (Max L = 39.7 cm; Source: Private collection; photograph by Ian J. McNiven). Representations of friar bird (*top right*), black dolphin (*top middle*), red tiger shark (*top left*), sprat fish (*center left*), black dolphin (*center middle*), and red tiger shark (*center right*) imbue the canoe with speed (Frankel 1978:30–31, 57).

Bodily Functions

Fishermen from the village of Lamalerap on the island of Lembata in eastern Indonesia consider their whaling and fishing boats as animate beings (Barnes 1974:150). This animate status is expressed in part by eyes painted on the prow of the boat and ritual feeding of boats through the application of the brains of recently caught manta rays (Barnes 1974:148–149). Application locations tend to be "points of access for spiritual force" (Barnes 1974:149). The Asmat of the south coast of Indonesian Papua ritually feed canoes before the vessels head out on their first sea voyage. According to Clemens Voorhoeve (1986:91), before heading out to sea, the inside of the dugout canoe hull is made slippery by application of the slime of fish (*enet*). The process is referred to as "to feed the canoe *enet*."

An important dimension of the animate status of small watercraft in some Indigenous communities is waking-up rituals. For example, many Melanesian communities had rituals of "waking up" and "putting to sleep" canoes. In Fiji, Williams (1858:199) recorded that during construction of a canoe, it was "awoke[n]" every morning and "put to sleep" at the end of each day by the "carpenters" to the "merry beat of drums." Landtman (1927:211) observed at Mawatta village on the New Guinea coast opposite Torres Strait that people "wake up" a canoe by swinging a bull-roarer close to the bow prior to dugong and turtle hunting expeditions. In what may be a related reference to Torres Strait Islanders, Haddon (1904:331) recorded on Mabuyag that "preparatory to starting out to catch the floating turtles the men took a bull-roarer from the *agu* [turtle shrine] and swung it over the canoe." I point out that the concept of "'waking up' of canoes prior to hunting trips implies some notion of an object-being with a life force and perhaps with sentience" (McNiven 2018a:188). In some Bering Strait Inuit communities, the process of launching boats "may be likened to a rite of passage, 'waking up' the watercraft" (Hill 2022:27).

Naming

A wide range of naming conventions exist for vessels around the world (Clary 1994:Chapter 15; Kennedy 1974; Tent 2023). European traditions of naming oceangoing vessels over the past two millennia have focused on religious "protection" through the use of names of guardian saints and deities (Pasierowska 2022:189; see also Jones 2016; Kennedy 1974:1). For example, the Roman poet Silius Italicus documented a second-century-BCE Punic warship named *Libyan Ammon* (the Latinized name for the Phoenician storm god), which according to Brody (1998:66) reveals that the god's "essence was embodied throughout the vessel." Ancient Greeks and Romans similarly named ships after deities for protection at sea (Atkins 2009:84–86; Bassett 1885:401). Mark Woolmer (2012:248) posits that "although the practice of naming vessels after deities was not unique to Phoenicia and can be identified in a number of Mediterranean communities, it was generally confined to societies which believed that their vessels housed some kind of spirit, or were themselves living creatures" (see below). Rachael Pasierowska (2022:189) documents that numerous ships engaged in the Atlantic slave trade between 1750 and 1755 were named after ancient Greek and Roman sea deities to provide "strength and protection while at sea."

From 1300 to 1600 CE, a strong tradition existed in England to name ships after Christian-venerated individuals and saints (Jones 2000; Vaughan 1922:86). Common examples include the *Virgin Mary*, *St. Nicholas*, *St. Christopher*, *St. Thomas*, *St. Margaret*, *St. John*, *St. Andrew*, *St. George*, and *St. Cuthbert* (Jones 2000:24, 33; Patarino 2002:165, 203; Vaughan 1922:86). A famous late fifteenth-century example is Columbus's ship the *Santa Maria*. Patarino (2002:164) notes that "by providing a designation that recalled God or the saints, shipbuilders, monarchs, and merchant owners hoped to ensure that heaven would oversee the safety of the ship and crew, providing her with divine as well as secular patronage."

In some cases, ships were given names that were intended to confer agentive qualities upon vessels. For example, ancient Greek names for warships include *Okeia* (quick), *Petomene* (flying), *Andreia* (courage), *Sobe* (frightening), *Thraseia* (boldness), *Dynamis* (power), *Nike* (victory), *Nikosa* (winning), and *Eutyches* (lucky; Casson 1971:352). British Admiralty vessels for polar exploration during the nineteenth century had evocative names: *Fury, Hecla, Erebus, Terror, Alert, Investigator, Resolute*, and *Intrepid* (Whitridge 2004:227; see below). Vessel masters along the Gulf of Papua in southern Papua New Guinea often keep the names of their trading vessels (*bevaia*) secret to protect the magic they employ to improve sailing conditions (Williams 1932:157).

For centuries, maritime peoples, especially in the West, have referred to boats and ships using the pronouns "she" and "her" (Conway 1989; Dževerdanović-Pejović 2017; Mellefont 2000). The ancient Greeks only used feminine names for ships up until the fourth century BCE (Casson 1971:351). In contrast, the Romans had an equal mix of feminine and masculine names for ships (Casson 1971:358). More broadly, ships sail on their "maiden voyages" and have "sister ships." Interestingly, use of the pronoun "she" for vessels was not matched by a dominance of figureheads representing women. Rodgers (1984) found that a strong tradition exists in the British Royal Navy of gendering ships as "feminine" through the use of feminine ship names at launches and use of the pronouns "she" and "her." The imbuement of these naval vessels as a "feminine entity" takes place during the official launching ceremony, which is mostly performed by a senior woman from broader society (Rodgers 1984:3). Among fishing communities of eastern England, vessels with male names were also always referred to as "she" (Gill 1993:112). A recommendation by *Lloyd's List* shipping newspaper in March 2002 to use gender-neutral references to ships such as "it" instead of "she" to keep pace with Western trends in social and cultural gender mores failed (Dževerdanović-Pejović 2017:317; Mellefont 2000; Smyth 2023:211).

Predatorization

Predatorization involves more than just embodiment and animation of vessels. It moves to the next step of intentionalizing animate vessels such that they have a desire to work with their human crews to attack people (usually enemies), to intimidate and frighten away evil forces, and to hunt sea creatures for food such as marine mammals (see Chapter 9) and fish (see Chapter 10). Such predatorization usually involves figurative attachments of representations of animal heads to the prow of a vessel, either carvings or painted images. Although Atkins (2009:78) righty points out that "items in the bow were there as help for the ship itself to navigate and protect itself as defensive aids," it is clear that such items also took on a formidable *offense* desire and function.

The best-known early example of predatory (attack) attachments to ships are zoomorphic battering rams on the prows of ships of the ancient Greek and Roman worlds (e.g., Basch 1975; Mark 2008). The earliest known example is a Greek ceramic drinking vessel in the form of a boat with a blunt battering ram featuring painted eyes (*oculi*) dating to the seventh century BCE (Johnston 1985:48, 65–66). Based mostly on painted representations of rams on ancient Greek vases, Hector Williams (1989:293) points out that the heads of boars "are by far the commonest form that these rams take, no doubt because of the similarity in purpose to the slashing tusks of the real animal" (cf. Mark 2008:264). Depictions of boar rams are known from sixth century BCE Greek vases, a fourth-century-BCE bronze lamp from Greece, a second-century-CE temple relief in Rome, and clay models (Casson 1994:58; Göttlicher 2004; Johnston 1985:67–68, 97–98; Williams 1989:293). Herodotus records that after the Aeginetans defeated the Samians in 520 BCE, boar's head rams were removed from captured ships and dedicated to their temple of Aphaia on the island of Aegina (Murray and Petsas 1989:115). Other predatory rams include a secondary ram tipped with a lion's head located above the main trident battering ram in a relief carving of a warship on Poplicola's tomb at Ostia (the old port of Rome) and a wolf's head ram depicted on a funerary plaque from Rome (Williams 1989:293). A life-size marble replica of a trireme battering ram (see below) at Ostia is surmounted by a vertical prow beam featuring a relief carving of a lion's head (Basch 1975:Figure 15).

To date, nearly 20 archaeological examples of ancient bronze battering rams from warships have been recovered from the Mediterranean seabed, and these reveal that another strategy for predatorization was the inclusion of relief images. While relief symbols show variation, all rams feature three horizontal fins that from the side have been made to look like a large trident or in some cases blades of three swords (Buccellato and Tusa 2013:78, 81). The changeover from boar's head rams to dagger rams occurred early in the Hellenistic period in the third century BCE (Johnston 1985:87, 96).

The famous Hellenistic bronze ram recovered from a shipwreck off the Athlit coast of Israel is 2.26 m long, weighs 465 kg, and is dated to the second century BCE (Galili and Rosen 2015a:53–54; Murray 1991:66; Oron 2006). Each side of the ram features a helmet surmounted by an eight-pointed star (the symbol of the Dioscuri brothers of ancient Greek mythology), a large trident (possibly associated with Poseidon), and the head of a bird of prey (probably an eagle, possibly a griffin), while the top bears a relief image of a kerykeion or a caduceus (staff of the Greek god Hermes; Galili and Rosen 2015a:54; Murray 1991; Oron 2006:68; Rich 2013:106–111). Both the Dioscuri and Hermes were engaged by mariners to bring on voyaging success. The trident and bird of prey are more explicit predatory symbols of "raw power" (Rich 2013:108). Based on comparisons with contemporaneous numismatic stylistic conventions, William Murray (1991:54) argues that the bird heads are more consistent with eagles, specifically the eagles of Zeus.

The bronze Acqualadroni Ram recovered off the coast of northeast Sicily similarly dates to the second century BCE (Buccellato and Tusa 2013). It is 1.35 m long and weighs around 300 kg. In addition to the typical trident motif, the Acqualadroni Ram features double swords on each side with elaborate hilts. On similar rams, the hilt "depicts a marine animal with the head of an eagle (*hippocampus*?)" (Buccellato and Tusa 2013:79). The "eagle's powerful beak is half open" (Buccellato and Tusa 2013:79) in what is clearly a predatory pose.

Animal head carvings on some ancient ships are positioned too high to be functional as rams and may be more appropriately considered figureheads. An example is a relief carving from Praeneste (now Palestrina), east of Rome, that shows a Roman warship at the Battle of Actium (31 BCE). The prow of the ship features a figurative carving of a crocodile (Abulafia 2012:Figure 33; Williams 1989:293–294). More common are relief carvings of Roman warships showing a centaur (hybrid creature with the upper body of a human attached to the body and legs of a horse) standing over the prow facing forward. In one case the centaur raises one arm high, holding a stone in what appears to be a threatening pose (Williams 1981). In his description of the Battle of Actium between the Romans and Egyptians off the coast of Greece, the Roman poet Propertius wrote of Roman warships with "prows bearing figures threatening with Centauric stones" (Williams 1981:24). The first-century-BCE Roman poet Virgil in *Aeneid* similarly writes of a Tuscan ship master who "moves the huge Centaur forward with oars; that ship stands over the water and lofty it threatens the waves with an immense stone" (Williams 1981:24).

A variant form of ancient predatory figureheads is the attachment of animal horns to the prow of a ship. Gerhard Kapitän (1989:151) suggests that ancient Greco-Roman mariners believed that the "horns of bulls and other strong animals avert mischief and disasters." It was for this reason that representations of bull horns were attached to ancient ships. Five lead horns have been recovered archaeologically from Mediterranean shipwrecks (Atkins 2009:71–73). For example, a 22-cm-long lead horn was recovered from a third-century-BCE Corinthian shipwreck off the Italian coast (Kapitän 1973). Similarly, the bow section of a mid-second-century-BCE shipwreck near Punta Scaletta, Island of Giannutri, on the coast of Tuscany in Italy, revealed a lead bull's horn with adhering horn indicating it had been formed by pouring molten lead into a real horn (Kapitän 1989:151). At least two of the five horns have nail holes in the lead to assist with attachment to the ship's hull (Atkins 2009:71–73, 76).

Woolmer (2012:238, 250) argues that the attachment of bulls' horns to Canaanite and Phoenician warships was more than apotropaic but rather aimed "to imbue the vessel with the strength, power and virility of a bull" and "to infuse a vessel with bull-like qualities" such that it would "ram" and "gore" an enemy's ship "in a manner reminiscent of a charging bull." More specifically, as the bull was seen to be the "totem animal" of the storm deity Ba'al-Haddu/Sapōn and "often represented symbolically by a pair of horns," the attachment of horns to a warship would thus "imbue the ship with the strength and power of Baal-Haddu/Sapon" (Woolmer 2012:239, 245, 248). Woolmer (2012:249) notes that the inclusion of predatory horns on Phoenician warships in the fifth century BCE is consistent with Mark's (2008) argument that ram technology was introduced to Phoenician warships in the fifth century BCE following its development by the Greeks in the sixth century BCE.

English warships of the seventeenth and eighteenth centuries often featured figureheads in the form of a leaping lion. Hansen and Hansen (1990:17) argue convincingly that the "figurehead lion was regarded as a symbol of the speedy and courageous attacker, it embodied characteristics that were also ascribed to the ship." Similarly, Michael Stammers (2004:180) points out that the "lion, as King of the Beasts, was a symbol of power, domination and fierceness, which are all appropriate qualities for a warship." Another form of predatory figurehead employed by the Royal Navy during at least the late eighteenth and nineteenth centuries featured Zeus, head of the ancient Greek pantheon at Mount Olympus and the god of the sky and thunder. Examples of such figureheads featured on HMS *Seringapatam* (an eagle, the bird symbol of Zeus "whose infallible weapon was the thunderbolt"), HMS *Vengeance* (Zeus with his thunderbolt carved into the adjacent trailboard), HMS *Invincible* (Zeus carrying a thunderbolt in one hand and an eagle-topped staff in the other), and HMS *Foudroyant* (Zeus's eagle carrying a thunderbolt in its talons; Pulvertaft 2022:469).

New Georgia Island in the western Solomon Islands of the Southwest Pacific is the home of famous anthro-zoomorphic figureheads on war canoes. The figureheads are known as *nguzunguzu* (Roviana language, *nguzu* = mouth), *toto isu/ishu* (Marovo language, *toto* = directional pointing, *isu* = nose), and *nujunuju* (Vella Lavella language; Sheppard 2021:236; Thomas 2013:200–201; Waite 2000:119). These distinctive figureheads, ranging in length from 11 cm to 39 cm, were attached to the bow of war canoes (*tomoko/tomako*) near the waterline (Waite 2000:119, 2021:80). *Tomoko* plank-built war canoes of the western

Solomon Islands were "the single most economically valuable item possessed by chiefs and their people, and technically the most complicated. It was also central to the politico-religious complex which underlay head-hunting and formed the cultural focus of the societies of the region" (Sheppard 2021:234). The figureheads feature "exaggerated prognathism," expressing a fusion of a human form with that of either a dog or frigate bird (Thomas 2013:200). In some cases, the figure holds in its hands a carved representation of a frigate bird (for navigational aid, including avoiding sunken rocks) or a human head (for success in headhunting raids; Hviding 1995:100; Richards 2012:213). Edvard Hviding (1995:100) records that the "wide open, staring eyes" of a *toto isu* "were supposed to ward off any troublesome sea spirits" (e.g., Kesoko sea spirit; Waite 2021:81, 93). Legend has it that the anthropomorphic Tiola, a spirit that could take the form of a dog and was associated with raiding and headhunting, told the people of Roviana lagoon how to make a *tomoko*: "Tiola told them to make a canoe icon (*nguzunguzu*) and place it on the bow of the canoe. The dog sat down and folded its legs and said 'like this.' Tiola could now follow them in war expeditions. The *nguzunguzu* conferred upon them the power of Tiola and prevented the Kesoko spirit from traversing the bow of the *tomoko* and jinxing the expedition. Wherever they went they exterminated the people" (Aswani 2000:50).

Tim Thomas (2013:200) posits that frigate birds are renowned for their "predatory behaviour," "excellent vision," "swiftness," and "maneuverability," while dogs have "acute senses of smell and hearing" and are "also known for being ravenous, stealing food, eating anything." As such, *nguzunguzu* figureheads embody the "efficacy and potency" of these predatory behavioral traits and "highlight the exaggerated sensory capacity of the spirit in question and by extension their heightened capacity for action in the world" (Thomas 2013:200). Other exaggerated features of *nguzunguzu* that can be associated with predatory behavior include large nostrils (expressing a heightened sense of smell), exposed teeth and an "aggressive snarl" (expressing shouting and devouring), large, open eyes (expressing "omnipotent vision of the spirits"), and large ears (expressing acute hearing; Thomas 2013:201).

Elaborately carved prow boards on seagoing trading and fishing boats of the Tanimbar Archipelago of the southern Moluccas of eastern Indonesia feature representations of roosters, "monsters with toothy mouths," and "shark-like fish" (McKinnon 1988:158). McKinnon (1988:158, 165) argues that the roosters are symbolic of "the deadly enmity of a cockfight" and "impending attack," while the "toothy monsters" signal "hostile intent." When combined, this prow imagery "reinforces the theme of potential hostility and predation" of the boats (McKinnon 1988:158).

An excellent example of images of a predatory being on a vessel's prow comes from the Northwest Coast of Canada, where canoes were known to have figurative carvings of a "spirit guide" such as Wolf, Killer Whale, or Lightning Snake (Shearar 2000:26). For example, the later takes the form of a feathered sea serpent with a wolf-like head and long tongue and the personification of lightning. The painted version was hidden from view under a layer of paint such that the "hunter or fisher could then benefit from the spirit power of the creature while the intended prey could not see the dangerous predatory images and flee to escape capture" (Shearar 2000:68).

Arctic peoples of the Bering Strait region added amulets (painted or carved representations, or body parts) of birds "proficient at diving and fishing, including ducks, cormorants, loons, and grebes" to *umiaq* watercraft (Hill 2022:26). In the case of the Nunivak, representations of agentive birds were painted on watercraft such that "the spirit-power of the animal will become embodied in the kayak (i.e., *qayaq*) and aid materially in catching game" (Curtis 1930, cited in Hill 2022:26). Hill (2022:26) adds that use of these "amulets blurs distinctions among the agencies of humans, animals and animated objects, creating new hybrid assemblages of traits and behaviours."

Melanesian canoes of the New Guinea region (including Torres Strait) were often predatorized for hunting and warfare by the addition of prow carvings of predatory animals. For example, numerous Trobriand canoes of southeastern Papua New Guinea incorporate a representation of an osprey bird as part of elaborately carved prowboards. The osprey is central to the procurement of large quantities of *kula* shell valuables because of the bird's wisdom and highly successful predatory behavior (Campbell 2002:99, 129–135, 140). Such predatorization is enhanced by the prow corresponding to the top of the original tree used in hull construction, as treetops are where ospreys sit to look out for fish (Campbell 2002:163–164, 177).

Perhaps the most obvious dimension of vessel predatorization is naming, as illustrated by ancient and modern naval vessels. For example, ancient Greek names for warships include agentive qualities such as *Agreuousa* (hunting) and *Kratousa* (conquering), and weapons such as *Aichme* (spear), *Lonche* (lance), *Oistos* (dart), and *Sphendone* (sling; Casson 1971:352–353; Kokkinou 2014:60). Roman warship names include victory terms such as *Triumphus*, *Victoria*, and *Fortuna*, predatory animals such as *Aquila* (eagle), *Crocodilus* (crocodile), and *Lupa* (she-wolf), and weapons such as *Clypeus* (shield) and *Quadriga* (chariot; Casson 1971:357).

Modern naval examples include the HMAS *Vampire* (Royal Australian Navy) and US submarines that are often named after "large voracious fish" (Beck

1999:18). The US Navy had an official policy of naming submarines after fish during the first half of the twentieth century (Alden and Wright 2005), many of which were carnivorous: *Barracuda, Bonito, Moray, Remora, Shark, Swordfish, Stingray,* and *Tuna* (Alden and Wright 2005). US naval ships with predatory names include the *Alligator, Asp, Caesar, Eagle, Falcon, Hannibal, Hornet, Nitro, Prometheus, Revenge, Scorpion, Spitfire,* and *Viper* (Kennedy 1974:69–70; Neeser 1921).

Good Luck Rituals

A well-known ritual practice to imbue a boat or ship with good luck is hiding a coin under the mast base during construction. Numerous examples of mast-step coins have been recovered from Roman shipwrecks (mostly in France and Italy) dating to between 150 BCE and 400 CE, indicating that the practice "ranks among the longest-lived of ancient maritime customs" (Carlson 2007:318). In the modern era, Germans preferred coins "with the three 'crosses' (or 'crutches'), namely coins from the year 1777" (Henningsen 1965:205). A survey of shipbuilders in London in the 1960s revealed that "the custom was known, and that it was commonly practised until about thirty years ago. In large wooden ships, where the mast was a fixture, the general practice was to place a new sovereign in the mast-step of the vessel, the date of the coin being the same as the building of the ship" (Marsden 1965:33). Furthermore, "With one exception, all replies to the questionnaire said that the reason for placing the coin in the construction of a sailing ship, was for luck and to date the construction of the vessel. The exception said that the custom was to date the construction of the vessel only, and that there was no superstition connected with it" (Marsden 1965:34). Deborah Carlson (2007:322) notes that the Roman "custom" of mast-step coins developed as a "secular" marine tradition out of the ancient Greek terrestrial tradition of "foundation coins" used in the consecration of new religious buildings. While the "foundation coin" development hypothesis is compelling, the process of "secularization" is less so if Roman vessels are considered animate object-beings with spiritual agency.

A number of US naval vessels included coins under their masts for good luck during the twentieth century. For example, during construction of the USS *New Orleans* in 1934, "the officers placed 10 pennies beneath the foremast, and 2 dimes, 3 nickels and 28 pennies at the heel of the mainmast" (Henningsen 1965:206). As a silver coin dated 1951 could not be found, a silver coin dated 1950 was placed under the mast of the destroyer *Shelton* during refit in San Francisco in 1951 (Henningsen 1965:206). Four 1993 silver dollar coins and a small box of notes were placed under the foremast of an LHD-4 amphibious assault vessel during vessel construction at Ingalis shipbuilding yards in Pascagoula, Mississippi (Clary 1994:37).

Coins were placed under the mast during construction of *Bluenose II* in 1963, a replica of the famous fishing schooner *Bluenose* (Baker 1979:34). In Scotland in recent times, "it was the duty of the master builder to secrete a gold coin 'for luck' somewhere in the splicing of the keel, its exact whereabouts known only to the owner and himself" (Beck 1999:12). Up until at least the 1960s, Texas fishermen associated the ritual concealment of coins on fishing vessels with the bringing of good luck. The owner of a local boatbuilding yard observed: "They put a silver dollar or a silver fifty cent piece or a dime, something silver, under the mast for good luck. That's the first thing we look for in the schooners; sometimes the imprint is there but not the coin. It had wore out. Most of them still do it. They throw it in right before the masts are put in" (Mullen 1969:222).

Launch Rituals

The land-sea dichotomy and the liminality of crossing the sea–land boundary is central to vessel launching rituals. In many respects, this issue concerns a question in maritime anthropology and archaeology: Are marine vessels (ships, boats, canoes, etc.) living entities? And if so, what is involved in ontologically transitioning a vessel from a terrestrial domain to an aquatic domain, and ontologically transforming a vessel from a terrestrial entity into an aquatic entity? Westerdahl (2011a:293) notes that "it is probable that the boat was originally cognitively identified with land, being built entirely of land materials, and got its particular symbolic (and real) power by way of transfer to the wet element. This transfer is made by way of the launching." As the following discussion reveals, many societies perform special rituals at the initial launch of a vessel as protection from bad omens and often in acknowledgment of the vessel's animate if not sentient properties. For example, just before a ship or boat first enters the water in many parts of the world, it is christened for good luck with the breaking of a bottle of champagne or a glass of beer or whiskey on its bow (Gregor 1885a:307, 1886:10). Similarly, many ships are blessed and even baptized by priests at launching (Bassett 1885:399–402). More extreme are launch rituals involving the sacrifice of animals and even people. Interfering with launch rituals can bring bad luck for a ship. For example, many Irish Catholics believe that the *Titanic* sank because Protestant workmen at the Belfast shipyards chalked on the ship's hull "that famous politico-theological phrase which condemns the Pope to the infernal regions" (Hammerton 1931:304).

The blessing of vessels at their launch by priests was a common practice in the Christian world. For example, a medieval Frankish blessing from northern Europe known as "Blessing When One Boards a Ship" states: "May this your people, Lord, be guided by your aid and protected by the arm of your majesty; may the water of the raging sea not trouble them, nor may they be affrighted by the face of the tempest. . . . Build the ship of their salvation, so that their heart may be filled by the increase of health-giving faith" (quoted in Rivard 2009:220). That God had the power to control the sea was well known to the faithful through the story of God parting the waters of the Red Sea as expounded in the Book of Exodus in the Bible (Rivard 2009:222). Similarly, a thirteenth-century "Blessing of a Ship" states in part: "Deign to be favourable to our supplications, Lord, and with your right hand bless this very ship and all who are carried in it" (quoted in Rivard 2009:224). On the coast of Brittany in the nineteenth century it was understood that a boat lost at sea with the loss of all hands was the result of an improper blessing by a priest (Anson 1965:93). At Boulogne-sur-Mer on the northwest coast of France, the blessing of fishing vessels included a priest sprinkling every part of the boat with holy water, including the rigging (Anson 1965:94).

Tyrrhenian fishermen of the west coast of Italy in the twentieth century spoke of the critical importance of a priest to baptize and bless a new fishing boat in terms analogous to baptizing and blessing a new child (Baldi 1998). One fisherman stated that to not baptize a boat was the same as not baptizing a new child and having it included on the "civil registry." In a similarly way, it is only after a boat has been baptized by a priest that "it becomes a real boat" with what Alberto Baldi (1998:148) refers to as a "halo of protection." Another fisherman stated that the birth of a boat and the birth of a child are "almost the same thing," while another referred to a baptized boat as a "Christian" (Baldi 1998:148). Yet whereas a child is blessed with holy water that is freshwater, boats are blessed with holy water that is seawater (Baldi 1998:150). In this sense, Tyrrhenian fishing boats can be seen as nonhuman persons.

Viking ships were sometimes launched by sliding over the bodies of prisoners according to the thirteenth-century Icelandic *Prose Edda*, which refers to the practice as *hlun-rod* (roller-reddening; Bassett 1885:400). In the seventeenth century, Jesuit priest Father Alcina observed in the Visayan Islands of the Philippines that when newly constructed boats intended for war or raiding expeditions were launched, the place of the last roller was taken by a sacrificial prisoner of war who was pulverized to death by the sliding boat such that all who sailed in the boat would be feared and the boat itself would be more formidable (Horridge 1982:24–25).

In Chennai (Madras), Tamil Nadu, eastern India, animal and human launch sacrifices have been replaced by placing a large pumpkin filled with turmeric and vermilion in front of the vessel. At the time of launching the pumpkin split open to "spray spurts of red and yellow juice over the excited crowd, in simulation of the blood splashes ejected when a human victim was sacrificed beneath the keel of a launched boat" (Hornell 1943:124). As Hornell (1943:124) noted graphically, the "fact that the bows of the masula boat are also daubed with red spots as well as the exterior of the pumpkin, corroborates this inference; both appear to be intended to represent the blood splashes spurted from the victim as the boat lumbers over the quivering body."

On the island of Carriacou in the West Indies, boatbuilders sprinkle the deck of a boat with male goat's blood as part of the launching ceremony (Clary 1994:176). Similarly, in the Red Sea on the coast of Sudan, before a boat is launched, a goat is sacrificed and its blood sprinkled on planks "as a blessing and a sign of prosperity and safety," while the goat's skin is attached to the stern post "as a sign of protection against the evil forces" (Agius 2017:142).

In eastern Indonesia, the launch of fishing and whaling boats from the village of Lamalera included smearing the blood of sacrificed goats and pigs on specific parts of the boat, especially the bow extension and harpooning platform (Vatter 1932, cited in Barnes 1996:246). In addition, before launching, a baby pig would be held up to the prow and its throat squeezed to ensure the boat had success in whaling (Barnes 1996:246–247). The launch of a Bugis *pinisi* in southern Sulawesi, Indonesia, includes sacrificing a goat burned with off-cuts from the boat in a pit under the keel and over which the boat runs as men push it toward the water (Pelly 1977:101; see also Zazzaro et al. 2022). This sacrifice is to give "thanks" (symbolic food) to the "supernatural residents of the shipyard" (Pelly 1977:101). In addition, blood from the head of a buffalo killed to feed the many local villagers who will assist with the launch is smeared across the front of the ship's keel (Pelly 1977:101).

On Guimaras Island in the central Philippines, coastal fishers from the village of Suclaran launch newly constructed boats with a ritual known as *daga sa baroto* (literally, "blood letting for a boat"). The ritual "is supposed to ensure safety at sea as well as a bountiful catch. Some fishermen consider this practice an obligatory rite to appease sea-spirits" (Magos 1994:312). It involves killing either a chicken, or a pig for bigger boats and wealthier boat owners, and smearing the animal's blood from the prow to the stern and back again. Further to the north at the village of Gabi, new boats undergo the *padaga* rite to ensure bountiful catches. This rite also includes either chickens or pigs. In terms of the latter, the pig is taken out to sea in the boat, its head is cut off and thrown into the sea as an offering to sea spirits, and its blood smeared over the boat and fishing equipment (Magos 1994:339).

On small islands off the northeast coast of Malekula in Vanuatu, the launch of a canoe was associated with the sacrifice of 70 tusked boars, many small pigs, and 100 chickens (Layard n.d., cited in Hickey and Yoringmal 2013:257). Francis Hickey and Fidel Yoringmal (2013:257) add that the "canoes were given the spirit and grade of the largest tusked boar sacrificed."

The most widespread and best-known launching ritual involves christening by smashing a bottle of alcohol on one end of the vessel, usually the bow. Bottles of wine are used in Brittany (Rappoport 1928:269), while the Scots use bottles of whiskey on either the prow or stern, depending on which way the vessel entered the water (Gregor 1881:197). Some vessels in the United States were launched with ginger ale during the Prohibition era in the 1920s, and missionary vessels were christened with milk (Clary 1994:179). It was a common belief that launching a vessel without christening it was a bad omen. In Brittany it is difficult to find crews for vessels that have not been christened (Rappoport 1928:268). RMS *Titanic* was launched without a ceremony and without the smashing of a bottle of alcohol on its bow (Eaton and Hass 1986:21–22). It was commonly believed that the clipper *Great Republic* was destroyed by fire less than three months after it was improperly launched with a bottle of water (Clary 1994:180).

End-of-Life Rituals

Stammers (2004:83) notes that "sentiment clouds the end of a ship, particularly if it was a famous liner or a warship with battle honours. Their 'passing' has been mourned as if they were sentient beings." Because many cultures see boats and ships as possessing a life force, it is understandable that such vessels can also be seen to die. For example, a clay tablet dating to 1200 BCE sent by the king of Tyre to the king of Ugarit (Syria) states that a certain merchant vessel belonging to the king of Ugarit had literally "'died in a terrible rain' (Ug. *mītat bi gašmi ꜣaduri*)" (Brody 1998:66; see also Wachsmann 1998:334; Woolmer 2012:247). Brody (1998:66) notes that the "ship was not lost or sunk; it literally died as its spirit perished in the wake of the storm." As Woolmer (2012:247) rightly states, "The document points towards a belief that the vessel had a spirit and was seen as a 'living' entity." In England, mariners believed that old ships would "give forth moaning sounds like wailing" prior to breaking up at sea (Bassett 1885:368).

In the nineteenth century, a Chinese vessel wrecked in Japanese waters had to have its "spirit" carried away before the ship could be officially "condemned"

(Hui 2002:81). As the spirit had "lost its abode," it was carried away in a model boat made from a recently felled tree (Hui 2002:81). Similarly, Japanese ships are known to possess souls that continue after the "death" of a ship. For example, in 1930 members of the Osaka Shipbreakers Guild attended a Buddhist ceremony to pray for the souls of 109 ships broken up in their yards over the previous 7 years and the souls of 10 workers killed during these activities (Hammerton 1931:300–301). Before the luxury French ocean liner SS *Île de France* succumbed to Japanese breakers in Osaka in 1959, a Shinto priest conducted a "purification ceremony which 'cleansed her soul' that she might approach the gods. She was then officially dead" (Baker 1979:51). In 1911 the figurehead of the sailing ship *Mandalay* wrecked on the Western Australian coastline was ritually chopped off to "'kill' the spirit of the ship" (Marshall 2003:4).

The Croatian community of Komiža on the island of Vis in the Adriatic Sea celebrate the animacy and agency of boats through a formal "boat funeral" and dedication (Božanić and Buljubašić 2012:17). The annual ceremony is held on 6 December, the day of St. Nicholas the Traveler, the Protector of Seamen. An old boat (sometimes two or three boats) is dragged a distance of 400 m from the beach to a platform outside of the Church of St. Nicholas, where it is burned "as an offering for the salvation of all boats and as a token of the renewal of the boat which the flames have just swallowed" (Božanić and Buljubašić 2012:17). Joško Božanić and Eni Buljubašić (2012:20) note that "Komižan fishermen and mariners sacrifice a boat as an offering to their patron saint in the hope they will survive storms out in the open sea when they are far from home and at the mercy of the menacing elements." In broader context, Božanić and Buljubašić (2012:24) add that "in maritime culture in which the boat takes part in an individual's life, it cannot be solely an object, a means to an end—it is a person. A boat is baptised, simultaneously given a name, and when its life cycle has come to an end it is sanctified by the act of burning at a sacred place. . . . When a boat comes to the end of its life it is made sacred on the funeral pyre."

At least until the late nineteenth century in Scotland, it was "unlucky to break up an old boat—a fact which accounts for so many useless boats being seen at fishing villages" (Grant 1880:399, 593). In the Orkney Islands of northeast Scotland, some retired fishermen knew that they would die only after their old and disused fishing vessel began to fall apart. That these old boats were seen to possess some transferable life force is revealed by a story of an old Shetland man who began mending an old boat in the belief that it would help his very ill wife recover (Marwick 1975:93).

On Eddystone Island in the western Solomon Islands, Arthur Hocart (1935:102) recorded that "when a large and sacred canoe rots, the parts are sometimes, if not always, left in a sacred place. We saw the fragments of a sacred war canoe (*ṅgeto tambuna*) in the sacred place at Velai." Similarly, on Wala Island in nearby Vanuatu, Christopher Tilley (1999:124; original emphasis) documented that canoes "were considered not only to live like human beings of high rank (in a large house), but also to die, and mortuary rites appropriate to the status of a high-ranking big man were performed for *wrecked* vessels. Those which were not wrecked during their lifetime were allowed to die a 'natural' death, i.e., to slowly rot away in their tabooed boat house. Timber was never taken away for firewood or any other use" (see also Layard 1942:470–472).

Many famous ships have been deliberately saved from what is considered the indignity of the breaker's yards by ceremonial sinking and burial at sea. For example, in 1949 the HMS *Implacable*, formerly *Duguay-Trouin* of the French fleet from the famous 1805 Battle of Trafalgar before she was captured by the British in the same year, was deliberately scuttled by the Royal Navy near the Isle of Wight. Although there were many protests over the scuttling as an act of heritage vandalism, Margaret Baker (1979:51; original emphasis) argues that it was "reverently sunk, amid respectful *vales* from the navies of France and Britain." Yet, "Appalled by what happened to the *Implacable*, Frank Carr, then of the National Maritime Museum at Greenwich, formed the *World Ship Trust* whose motto was to be 'Never again'" (Adams 2013:19). Jonathan Adams (2013:19) adds: "It was the fate of this venerable old hulk that led directly to saving the famous tea clipper *Cutty Sark* from a similar end," currently in dry dock in Greenwich, London. Similarly, Lord Nelson's flagship HMS *Victory* from the Battle of Trafalgar remains intact and currently sits in dry dock in Portsmouth and is considered a "national and naval shrine" (Stammers 2004:23). Ironically, concerted efforts to continuously restore the vessel and replace decayed elements has resulted in "no more than about ten percent of the original ship left" (Stammers 2004:141; see also Aberg 2005).

The Royal Australian Navy, like most navies, performs a formal "Decommissioning Service" when naval vessels reach the end of their formal service as military vessels. The Royal Australian Navy Decommissioning Services are highly religious and Christian affairs. For example, the Decommissioning Service for the HMAS *Vampire* took place on the 13 August 1986, some 27 years after she was launched on 23 June 1959. The service program included a formal "Prayer of Thanksgiving" (Royal Australian Navy 1986). After decommissioning, HMAS *Vampire* was preserved as naval heritage and is a showcase feature of the Australian National Maritime Museum in Sydney where it is moored at Darling Harbour.

Many mariners consider the ship's bell to symbolically embody the "soul" of the vessel (Gill 1993:112; Stammers 2004). This association helps explain why numerous churches display bells from ships, presented ex-voto after a ship had ended its life. Examples include bells from the HMS *Canterbury* in Canterbury Cathedral, England, the HMS *Sussex* in Chichester Cathedral, England, the *Iron Duke* in Winchester Cathedral, England, and the *Hantonia* in St. Mary's Church in Southampton, southern England (Clissold 1972:206, 210–211). The latter is "rung ceremonially on any occasion requiring people to pray for the safety of those at sea: from danger, for victory, or for thanksgiving. It has been rung in memory of the United States submarine *Thresher*, which was lost with all on board on 10 April 1963, off the North American coast and, not long after, on 29 December 1963, when the Greek liner *Lakonia*, outward bound from Southampton on a Christmas cruise, caught fire and ultimately sank with the loss of 123 lives" (Clissold 1972:210).

Conclusion

Ethnographic and historical information provides overwhelming evidence that maritime societies from all parts of the globe conceive of boats and ships as animate object-beings. Furthermore, the lives of boats and ships were shaped by myriad ritual practices and spiritual forces from the vessel construction through to the death of vessels. Archaeological evidence in the form of rock art indicates that conceptions of ships as animate beings extend back at least 7,000 years. The complex animate, spiritual, and ritual status of boats and ships also expressed the ontological position of vessels as a "liminal agent between sea and land" (Westerdahl 2011a:295). That is, all boats and ships began their lives on land in the terrestrial domain and required considerable ritual intervention to metaphysically transfer vessels to the marine realm and life world.

The animacy and concomitant intentionality of marine vessels is expressed in multiple tangible and intangible ways, many with direct and indirect materialities amenable to archaeological investigation. As explored in this chapter, materialities of vessel embodiment and animation have been researched archaeologically through recovery of anthropomorphic and zoomorphic figureheads and stem heads (e.g., rock art, models) and prow eyes or *oculi* (e.g., marble representations of eyes from shipwrecks). Predatorization of ships has successfully been documented through recovery from the seabed of metal battering rams in the form of aggressive animals (e.g., boars, lions, eagles) and featuring representations of offensive weapons (e.g., swords) and deities of war. In other cases, vessels are predatorized by the addition of figureheads and stem heads representing aggressive animals (e.g., crocodiles) and hybrid beings (e.g., dragons, centaurs), and offensive animal body parts (e.g., bull horns). Excavation of well-preserved Roman ships indicates that the well-known ritual of including a coin at the base of the mast in the mast step dates back at least 2,000 years.

Little archaeological research has been undertaken on launch rituals associated with the profound ontological transition of vessels from the terrestrial to the marine realm, largely due to poor understanding of potential material correlates. In contrast, greater potential exists to explore the death of boats and ceremonies of decommissioning. Ritualization of the end lives of ships raises question of the extent to which ship burials (e.g., Viking) signify the death of a person and also the death of the ship. Indeed, lack of human remains at some Viking ship burials may not be due to poor preservation but rather may indicate a specialized ship burial and mortuary practices for a nonhuman person.

7

Rituals of Voyaging and Mishap

Seafaring on Land and at Sea

Most mariners invested heavily in rituals to propitiate spiritual forces to help ensure a safe voyage. The best-documented evidence for elaborate voyaging rituals involving prayers, sacrifices, talismanic amulets, votive offerings, and taboos in the ancient past is associated with ancient Greek and Phoenician mariners of the eastern Mediterranean (Blakely 2017; Brody 1998). In more recent times it is known that Islamic mariners of the Red Sea put their sailing fate in the hands of Allah, knowing that survival at sea was due to the will of God (Agius 2019:127, 130). Chinese mariners knew that "navigating the sea demanded as much religious vigilance as technical competence" (Hui 2002:70). Many Christian mariners knew their "best hopes for survival" were "faith in the saving hand of God" in the face of the known potential dangers of voyaging, especially the threat of storms (Frost 2022:403). Yet Marcus Rediker (1987:185) notes that in the context of Anglo-American mariners of the eighteenth century, little evidence exists to support the view that they made "sacrifices to the sea and its special array of deities, as their pagan ancestors had. Anglo-American men of the sea rarely appealed to saints for protection." However, the first half of this chapter shows that a secularized approach to voyaging was more the exception than the rule (see also Patarino 2002). A wide range of historical, ethnographic, and archaeological examples reveal that seafaring and ocean voyaging was, and in many cases remains, a highly spiritual and ritualized undertaking.

The second half of this chapter discusses voyaging mishap. It uses a wide range of examples to demonstrate the diversity and complexity of rituals concerning drowning at sea, and rituals and spiritual agency associated with the process of shipwreck and shipwrecks themselves, and those castaways that managed to survive such mishaps. Any maritime person who has lived a life with the sea will have stories of death and loss of life on the sea. Yet the experiences of death at sea (e.g., drowning) or near-death at sea (e.g., castaways) are ontologically complex and surrounded by uncertainty and liminality. For the maritime living, dealing with the maritime dead, those who died at sea and slipped beneath the waves, is an ongoing process, as they "remained trapped in a liminal state" (Stewart 2011:165). Indeed, John Flavel (1796:4) noted that "seamen are as it were, a third sort of persons, to be numbered neither with the living nor the dead." In many cases, mariners believed in a fatalism of death at sea, encapsulated by John Spitty, an infamous late nineteenth-century mariner from southeast England who was fond of saying "If you were born to be drowned you wouldn't be hung" (Leather 1977:84).

The notion of mariners as constantly courting death places them in a permanent state of liminality, the nearly dead, as it were. Such liminality also relates to the poly-liminality of the sea itself, whereby mariners maintained a constant relationship with the sea's agency. In many cases, liminality of mariners did not change with death, especially death by drowning, whereby the agency of the sea gained control of the dead such that corpses were somehow caught between the human and marine realms. As such, the living, especially those from coastal settlements, had to deal with, and often fear, the relational ontological instability of the sea's drowned dead. It is for this reason that the process of drowning was enmeshed in complex rituals related to either preventing a person from drowning or avoiding rescuing a drowning person for fear of revenge by the sea. Such rituals also crossed over to castaways from shipwrecks who were often looked upon as having been rejected by the sea and in a liminal state of half dead, half alive.

First Voyagers

Determining when people began sea voyaging, let alone practicing sea voyaging rituals, is no easy task. Archaeological research into the development of human seafaring capacities has traditionally focused on technological developments and diffusion in watercraft design (e.g., Anderson 2000, 2010; McGrail 2010), cognitive developments in the capacity to plan and execute voyages (e.g., Davidson and Noble 1992), and cultural developments in the ability for adaptive flexibility to create new homelands (e.g., Gaffney 2021). Broodbank (2006:200) identifies three stages of sea-crossing capability and complexity: *seagoing* (basic), *seafaring* (moderate), and *voyaging* ("ultra-long-range" and "ideologically charged"). In terms of sea crossing, archaeological evidence ranges from the more direct, such as remains of seagoing vessels (e.g., physical remains of boats) or representations of boats in rock art or figurative models, to the more indirect, such as visits to islands evidenced by occupational remains such as stone artifacts. The oldest known rock art depiction of a boat (northern Norway) that also has seafaring capacity is dated to 10,000–11,000 years ago (Gjerde 2021). It is doubtful that the world's oldest known boat—the Pesse canoe from the

Netherlands dating to the Mesolithic, 9,500–10,000 years ago—was capable of sea travel (McGrail 2010:100; Rybníček et al. 2020:3).

Indirect evidence for ancient sea crossings in the form of stone artifacts on islands that were never connected to the mainland demonstrate planned sea crossings by people in the Pleistocene. All of these water crossings were aided by stepping-stone islands but include at least one uninterrupted open-water crossing (UOWC) of at least 20 km. Examples include stone artifacts dating to 800,000 years ago on the island of Flores in eastern Indonesia with an UOWC of up to 22 km by *Homo erectus*, who Robert Bednarik (2003:45) states was the "world's first seafarer" (see also Broodbank 2006:201), stone artifacts probably dating to at least 100,000 years ago on the island of Crete in the eastern Mediterranean with an UOWC of up to 30 km (Strasser et al. 2011), and stone artifacts dating to at least 65,000 years ago in northern Australia and the island of Sahul, indicating an UOWC of up to 80 km (Bird et al. 2018; see also Clarkson et al. 2017; Davidson and Noble 1992; Norman et al. 2018). These founders of Australia are the first known peoples to voyage off the coast to a point where it was no longer possible to see land on the horizon. It is in this context that we can lock in Noel Butlin's (1993:8) contention that these First Nations Australians can "claim the title of the world's first mariners" (see McNiven and Russell 2023:38).

The settlement of Aotearoa/New Zealand by the ancestors of the Māori during the early fourteenth century CE involved an open-sea voyage of 3,000 km from the mythical homeland of Hawaiiki in East Polynesia and represents the longest transoceanic sea voyage in human migration history prior to the commencement of the European Age of Exploration in the late fifteenth century CE (Walter et al. 2017). As discussed below, the earliest known evidence of the ontological dimensions of seafaring is the animate status of boats represented in Scandinavian rock art dating to 7,000 years ago, with votive offering paraphernalia on Mediterranean shipwrecks dating to 2,000–2,800 years ago representing the earliest known evidence for voyaging rituals.

Voyaging Rituals on Land

Land-based voyaging rituals often relate to propitiating spiritual forces that control winds and waves in order to bring about calm seas and safe passage (see Chapter 8). Here rituals are described in terms of attempting to bring about a safe and successful voyage but not stated specifically in relation to controlling the elements, although many probably were related to both.

Brody (1998:74) makes the important observation that rituals of voyaging are associated with "traversing" a "liminal zone" akin to what van Gennep

(1960) and Turner (2009) refer to as a "rite of passage." Furthermore, "One may view setting out on the sea as entering a doubly liminal zone, since sailors are both away from their home and away from the familiarity of the land" (Brody 1998:74). The range of voyaging rituals undertaken by Canaanite and Phoenician mariners listed by Brody have relevance for a wide range of other cultural contexts, both past and present. These "rituals were conducted on land, both before sailing and after safe arrival; on board ship, while leaving and entering port; and at sea, when passing a promontory shrine, and in times of distress" (Brody 1998:74–75). More recently, Brody (2021:2–3) has elaborated this list to include (1) marine patron deities, (2) seaside temples and shrines, (3) spiritually imbued ships with sacred spaces, (4) protective voyaging ceremonies, and (5) marine mortuary practices. Although Brody (1998:75) links these rituals with "the appeasement and protection of patron gods," the following discussion indicates that rituals in other cultural contexts were linked to a broad range of spiritual beings and forces.

For many mariners, a voyaging life was one of unremitting work to read, harness, and survive the ever-changing elements (wind and waves). This voyaging life also involved mariners using their bodies to constantly modify the rigging and sails within the confined space of a vessel that unceasingly moved beneath their feet in rhythm with the heaving expansive sea. Yet mariners' sailing skills and tools extended well beyond muscles and rigging and into the numinous through a wide range of ritual practices to help ensure a safe passage. As Mark Christian (2013:181) notes in relation to Phoenician mariners, "successful voyages depended on more than knowledge of boats, weather, and sea. They must also curry the favour and protection of the god(dess)." Similarly, Brody (2008:445) makes the point that "two kinds of deities were crucial to ancient Mediterranean mariners: gods and goddesses that controlled winds and storms, and those who could aid in the safety and success of navigation." In some cases, the ritual causality is unrecorded, such as on the small island of Iona in the Inner Hebrides of western Scotland, where there exists a stone in the shape of a "pillar" and for which it is said that a "sailor who stretched his arm along it three times in the name of the Trinity could never err in steering the helm of a vessel" (Jones 1871:239).

Among Christians, St. Nicholas was "pre-eminently the sailor's guardian" (Bassett 1885:78; see also Patarino 2002:191–194). However, numerous other Christian saints were considered to be maritime saints that had special powers to protect mariners and help ensure favorable sailing conditions in different regions, such as St. James (Spain); St. Peter, St. Anne, St. Hermes, and St. Maclou (England); St. Cyric (Wales); St. Columba, St. Ringar, St. Ronald, and St. Ninian (Scotland); St. Sauveur (Normandy); St. Michael and St. George (Sardinia); St.

Rosalia (Sicily); St. Phocas (Greece); and St. Bartholomew (Bavaria; Bassett 1885:81–84).

It is a widespread Christian practice to bless vessels or fleets before setting off on voyages, especially long-term voyages or important ones associated with exploration or battle. For example, prior to setting off on his famous expedition of discovery in 1492, Columbus and his crew went in procession to the Franciscan monastery of La Rábida in the town of Palos de la Frontera in southern Spain to seek absolution for their sins and to receive the Eucharist (Goodrich 1858:140). Similarly, in 1497 Vasco da Gama and his crew, prior to departing on his first famous expedition of discovery, spent the night in a small chapel outside of Lisbon in Portugal "in prayer and rites of devotion, invoking the blessing and protection of Heaven" (Goodrich 1858:171). Some churches in Europe have plaques celebrating where captains came to pray before setting out on famous voyages. For example, St. Malo cathedral in Brittany has a floor plaque marking where Jacques Cartier knelt to receive the blessing of the bishop of St. Malo before his voyage of discovery to Canada in 1535. Patarino (2002:205) notes that for English mariners the "tradition of . . . making vows and traveling on pilgrimages to the shrines of saints was widespread in the medieval period."

The most common pre-voyaging ritual is leaving an offering in a religious structure such as a church or temple. For example, fishermen visiting Caher Island off the west coast of Ireland would "leave a pebble, pin, fishhook, or coin in the basin or stone lamp, in St. Patrick's oratory" (Westropp 1923:339). Along the Croisic coast of Brittany, women dressed in their finest clothes stand on the shoreline and sprinkle flowers onto the waves and say to gulls flying about: "Göelans, Göelans, bring us back our children and our husbands, from the sea" (Bassett 1885:272). In Somerset, England, children of mariners would throw an apple into the Bristol Channel and recite: "Come high tide or low tide whatever it be. Oh, God, bring my father home safely to me" (Clary 1994:216).

Ship graffiti scratched onto the walls of churches was a popular form of pre-voyaging ritual practiced across England, Ireland, Scandinavia, Spain, France, Italy, Malta, Greece, Cyprus, Türkiye, and Israel during the medieval period (e.g., Brady and Corlett 2004; Cassar 1966; Champion 2015a, 2015b; Demesticha et al. 2017; Helms 1975; Meinardus 1996–1997; Michail 2015; Walsh 2008; Westerdahl 2013). More than 300 medieval ship graffiti have been recorded in Scandinavian churches (Westerdahl 2013). In Norway most medieval to recent ship graffiti are found in churches located close to the sea and with a clear view of the sea (Christensen 1995:182). As with votive ship models (see below), Westerdahl (2013:343–344) hypothesizes that ship graffiti was a "simplified" form of votive offering. Westerdahl (2013:344) acknowledges Peter von Busch (1985:366) who proposed that the "sea-faring farmers [of Gotland] may have been trying to put the fate of one's ship, crew and cargo into the hands of our Lord when one made a picture of it on the holy walls of the church" (see also Helms 1975). Furthermore, Westerdahl (2013:344) suggests that ship graffiti was "the poor man's votive ship" in comparison to votive model ships, sometimes made of silver, by the wealthy.

In England the vast majority of the more than 300 individual ship graffiti in churches are found in coastal contexts or its immediate hinterland (Champion 2015b:343). Most medieval ship graffiti in English churches are depicted in full side profile (i.e., not from the waterline up), with a single mast and crow's nest, sails furled or missing, and anchors lowered (Champion 2015b:344). Remarkably, little information can be gleaned from written texts concerning the function of English church ship graffiti. Numerous ship graffiti are located in churches that have an association with St. Nicholas, the patron saint of the sea (Champion 2015a:93–94). Such an association suggests strongly that ship graffiti "were created as an action of devotion" to St. Nicholas, perhaps as "prayers . . . from those whose loved ones were in peril upon the sea" or as a "thank-you for a safe journey undertaken" or as a "plea for safe passage on journeys yet to come" (Champion 2015a:93). In another example, 11 ship images dating to 1290–1530s are scratched onto a series of stone pillars near to a side chapel dedicated to St. Nicholas within St. Thomas's church in Winchelsea in southeast England. Following Matthew Champion (2015a, 2015b), Thomas Dhoop and colleagues (2016:303) interpret the St. Thomas's ship graffiti "as part of a Christian tradition of giving a votive offering in an act of prayer, hoping to assure or give thanks for a safe journey across the sea." Michal Artzy (1999, 2003:244) similarly interpreted archaeologically recovered examples of votive ship graffiti on the walls of Temple I at Kition-Kathari on Cyprus, dating to the Late Bronze Age during the twelfth century BCE, as "some sort of a cultic offering by mariners who either offered thanks for safe arrival or hope for future safe sailing and landing."

For many fishing communities, pre-voyaging rituals also encompass taboos on practices known to precipitate bad luck, including death, on a fishing trip. For example, pre-voyaging ("leaving-home superstitions") taboos from Hull in northeast England include "*never* wave a trawlerman off" or say "goodbye," a fisher "must *never* look back" once he steps outside his home on the way to the dock, and fishermen's wives were "forbidden on the fish dock to see the men off" (Gill 1993:15, 17–18, 40, original emphasis).

In many places, mariners will make post-voyaging offerings to spiritual entities in thanks for providing a safe voyage. While numerous historical examples of such practices have been recorded (see below), archaeological documentation of post-voyaging rituals are rare. For example, Edward Pollard (2008) documents a series of 200-m-long coral-rubble causeways and platforms, dating to between the thirteenth and sixteenth centuries, constructed across a lagoon at Kilwa Kisiwani in Tanzania on the coast of east Africa. He argues that one of the causeways associated with a cave and a mosque may have facilitated mariners gaining access to the low-water mark where offerings were made "to give thanks for safe arrival of vessels" (Pollard 2008:112).

The ancient Greeks used entire ships as votive offerings to temples and sanctuaries to give thanks to gods for successful voyages and naval battles. Most of these votive ships were "captured vessels" (Wescoat 2005:167). Sandra Blakely (2017:366) notes that the Sanctuary of Apollo on the island of Delos was strategically positioned "at the center of the Aegean, and the numerous maritime votive objects in his sanctuary—graffiti, *ex voto* anchors, rudders, and even an entire ship—index his power over the sea." The hall-like Monument of the Bulls near the Temples of Apollo on Delos is thought now to have held a "votive ship." The building also contained an altar and statues of deities: "two bronze statues of Apollo, one of Poseidon, and an Athena with two Nikai" (Wescoat 2005:161). Sacrifice of bulls and votive offerings of clay models of bulls were commonly associated with Poseidon (Kokkinou 2014:61). Ioannis Mylonopoulos (2013:6367) cites historical records mentioning that "horses were drowned in honor of Poseidon" at a sea spring named Dine located off the coast at Genesion in the Argolic Gulf, eastern Peloponnese. On the island of Samothrace, also in the Aegean, the Sanctuary of the Great Gods contains the Neorion, a hall-like temple with "marble blocks shaped to cradle the hull of a ship" (Wescoat 2005:163). The Delos and Samothrace votive ship buildings are thought to date to the late fourth and first half of the third centuries BCE (Wescoat 2005:154). Historical sources record that Jason of the Argonauts offered his ship *Argo* to the sea god Poseidon at his temple on the Isthmus of Corinth (Isthmia) in thanks for a safe voyage (Atkins 2009:93). A warship was offered to the seventh-century-BCE sanctuary to Hera and Poseidon on the island of Samos located in the eastern Aegean Sea (Atkins 2009:94).

On reaching Sri Lanka in 1409, Zheng He, who led the third voyage of the famous Ming expeditions of the early fifteenth century, erected a "tablet in Chinese in honour of the local 'Buddha' who reigned over the sea in this region. Accompanying inscriptions in Tamil venerated Tenavari-nayanar, an avatar of Vishnu, while the Persian version praised Allah and Islamic saints" (Andaya 2017:362). In the late nineteenth century in China, John Gray (archdeacon of Hong Kong) recorded that the crews of junks at the end of a successful voyage would visit temples dedicated to Tien-how (Goddess of the Sea), where votive offerings would be made in the form of "thanks-giving, prayers, and offerings of boiled fowl and pork, or of small portions of the merchandise which the junk has brought to port" (Gray 1878:260–261).

Upon arrival at their island destination after a long voyage, Tahitian mariners of Polynesia would make offerings of small pieces of coral and feather amulets to the "social marae [shrine] of their denomination, where they were met by the priest" (Henry 1928:179). If no marae was available, the mariners "presented" their offerings "on the seaside for the sea gods, as to neglect this duty was supposed to incur dire calamities from the gods such as death by strangulation or some other painful way. They repeated the *marotai* [offerings] on their return home" (Henry 1928:179–180). Māori mariners of Aotearoa/New Zealand would make "offerings of seaweed" to Tangaroa-whakamau-tai (guardian of the ocean) "on reaching land" (Best 1929:2).

Perhaps the best-known post-voyaging ritual is the more than 2,500-year-old European tradition of ex-voto ship models. Maura Coughlin (2020:108) points out that "ex-voto" is short for *ex voto suscepto* ("from the vow made") and that such votive objects "connect communities to broader ecologies of ocean fishing communities." Michel Mollat (1975, cited in Coughlin 2020:112) identifies four major categories of ex-voto ship models: *congratulatory* (offerings to give thanks for a safe voyage), *propitiatory* (offerings made in advance for a safe voyage), *commemorative* (offerings made to remember a tragic event, usually a shipwreck or the drowning of a loved one), and *supererogatory* (offerings where the intention is unknown).

Jaclyn Streuding (2014:70) suggests that "votive offerings given by pious Greeks and Romans who evaded disaster at sea primarily comprised small, somewhat modest objects, such as a model boat or figurine, and these offerings may have functioned as symbols of both gratitude and humility." At least 24 clay model boats and boat fragments and one bronze model boat dating to the late seventh to late sixth centuries BCE have been recovered archaeologically from the Temple of Poseidon at Isthmia (Raban and Kahanov 2003:63; Thomsen 2015:111).

The strongest evidence of ex-voto ship models is with Christianity and churches, particularly over the past 500 years (Baader 2016; Canney 1936; Champion 2015a, 2015b; Coughlin 2020; Greiling 2022; Harley 1994; Henningsen 1952). Basil Harley (1994:5) suggests that whereas in Great Britain the model ships "are usually a focus for prayer and meditation," in Continental Europe "they tend to be thank offerings to the Virgin or the saints for the relief of distress or for favours received." In Denmark more than 900 model ships whose purpose was to help ensure good voyaging have been recorded in churches (Champion 2015b:345; Henningsen 1952). Around 130 churches in Western Europe are known to include ship models (Harley 1994:4). Most of these ship models can be found suspended from church ceilings, floating (sailing) through the air (Figure 16). Some models are mounted on church walls and others are placed within glass cases. Due to their historical significance and fragility, many have been removed from churches for security and conservation reasons and are curated within museums. As museum objects, ex-voto ship models become decontextualized, secularized, and impotent.

The earliest surviving church ex-voto ship models in Europe date to the fifteenth century in Spain and Germany (Cunliffe 2017:509; Westerdahl 2013:338, 340; see also Champion 2015a:90). For example, the Mataro wooden model, reputedly from a chapel in the town of Mataro on the coast of Catalonia in northeast Spain, and currently on display in the Maritime Museum Rotterdam, is dated to the early fifteenth century (Culver 1929), a chronology confirmed by radiocarbon dating (according to the museum's display caption). Further evidence from the fifteenth century is a painting attributed to Vittore Carpaccio of the interior of the Church of Sant'Antonio in Castello dated 1495 and housed in the Gallerie dell'Accademia, Venice, which clearly shows votive model ships suspended from the ceiling (Baader 2016:Figure 3, 224). Written records of these objects date back to the twelfth century in Germany (Baader 2016:224) and the thirteenth century in England, with Henry III in 1227 requesting that a silver model of his ship be made and set up in the Norfolk Abbey of Bromholm (Champion 2015a:90).

Nearly 60% of ship models in Danish churches date to the twentieth century (Henningsen 1952:296). The tradition of presenting model ships to churches continues and includes models of diesel-powered steel ships (Harley 1994). For example, a model of the ocean liner *Mauretania* over 3 m in length was presented to Winchester Cathedral by Sir Thomas Royden of the Cunard-White Star Company in 1935 (Harley 1994:9).

In some cases, votive ship models are linked directly with the original ship. For example, the model of the HMS *Victory* in St. Ann's Church on the naval base at Portsmouth is made from oak and copper from the original ship (Harley 1994:41). The model of the HMS *Canterbury* in Canterbury Cathedral, England, is made from teak planking of the original eighteenth-century ship and was mounted on the wall above the original ship's bell (Harley 1994:44, 48).

Concluding on the spiritual and symbolic significance of ex-voto ship models in churches, Hannah Baader (2016:240) states: "ex-voto ship models are part of a transactional process between the physical and divine worlds. They are intended as vehicles for transfer from the profane to the sacred and vice versa. Because of the metaphorical potential of ship ex-votos, transactions between the material world and the religious sphere can be negotiated in a complex way. This potential lies in the creation of a community of travelers as well as in the

Figure 16. A service in Saint-Maxent church in Billiers, Brittany, northwest France, dated 1900–1902. Note votive ship model suspended from the ceiling. (Photograph by Paul Géniaux, cropped; Courtesy: Musée de Bretagne, Rennes, 2018.37.68. Public Domain image.)

dangers of seafaring and the fragility and resistance of the vessels, which in turn point to the fragility and resistance of the human body." Part of the transactional morality of ex-voto ship models is their intricate detail and miniaturized reality that can be seen as a materialization of respect and devotion to spiritual protectors (God, Jesus, and saints).

Voyaging Rituals at Sea

Voyaging rituals at sea take two major forms: first, *vessel-based* rituals focused on the propitiation of deities, saints, and spiritual forces mediated by shrines, charms, figurines, statues, and other agentive objects, and strict adherence of taboos; and second, *sea-based* rituals focused on propitiatory offerings into the sea.

Vessel-Based Rituals

Archaeological evidence of vessel-based rituals to propitiate safe voyages tend to take the form of incense burners and pedestalled water basins. An early example is a small ceramic incense burner recovered from the deep-water wreck of the Phoenician ship *Elissa* dating to 2,750 years ago and located off the coast of Israel in the southeast corner of the Mediterranean (Ballard et al. 2002:163, 166). Brody (2005:178) adds that this incense burner "would have been used for providing offerings for the guardian deities of the unlucky vessel. Vows or prayers would have been made and incense lit to appease the deities at the stern of the ship, an area considered sacred space along with the prow." Four incense burners of "Punic type" (North African Carthaginians with Phoenician origins) were recovered from a second-century-BCE Hellenistic shipwreck excavated at Pisa in Italy. Two of the incense burners are "terracotta molded in the form of a bust of a female deity," which Brody (2005:178–179) suggests represent the head of Tanit, a Carthaginian goddess. A rare image of use of a marine incense burner is the Torlonia relief carving in marble dating to around 200 CE, which was excavated archaeologically from Ostia, the ancient port of Rome. According to Atkins (2009:102), in the aft section of the ship, which is entering or leaving port, "are two men and one woman, standing around a portable altar with a high flame. The man is throwing incense on the flame while the woman holds an *acerra*, or incense box, and the other man holds a bowl, presumably for purification or a wine libation" (see also Casson 1971:182).

Pedestalled basins filled with sacred water for purification rituals by the ancient Greeks and Romans were known as *perirrhanteria*. Ancient Greek texts record that "it was customary, when setting out on a voyage, to pour into the sea during the sacrifice the water that had been used for the ceremonial washing" (Wachsmuth cited in Kapitän 1979:114). Atkins (2009:49) compiled a list of 14 such basins made from either terracotta or marble from 11 shipwrecks dating from the fifth to first centuries BCE. Although Atkins (2009:50) questions to what extent such basins represent ceremonial (*perirrhanteria*) or secular (*louteria*) washing basins, Kapitän (1979, 1989) argues strongly for a ceremonial function on board ships (see also Radić 1991). Artzy (2003:232) argues that a small dish-shaped "altar" dating to the end of the Late Bronze Age (around 3,200 years ago) and excavated from the coastal site of Tel Acco in Israel "was most likely used aboard a ship." The upper concave surface of the altar features a series of four engraved ships upon which were found ashes and three pebbles, one of which was of nonlocal quartz and features a tiny (2-cm-long) engraved ship (Artzy 2003:232, 239).

During the nineteenth century, mariners of the Malay Peninsula used incense as part of a ritual to prepare vessels for voyaging. Walter Skeat (1900:279) notes: "The ship being a living organism, one must, of course, when all is ready, persuade it to make a proper start. To effect this you go on board, and sitting down beside the well (*petak ruang*), burn incense and strew the sacrificial rice, and then tapping the inside of the keelson (*jintekkan sĕrĕmpu*) and the next plank above it (*apit lĕmpong*), beg them to adhere to each other during the voyage."

Some ancient Greek vessels erected poles (*stylis*) in the stern with a representation of a guardian deity (Atkins 2009:87–88). A fourth century BCE Greek vase shows a *stylis* inscribed with "'*ZEUS SOTER*,' protector of sailors and guardian of the ship. This inscription with Zeus' epithet 'Savior' spells out the purpose of the *stylis*, perhaps reaching up to the heavens and invoking the tutelary deities of the ship" (Atkins 2009:88). In contrast, Roman ships tended not to carry a *stylis* (Casson 1971:346).

Archaeologically, Atkins (2009:61) notes that "figurines may be the best physical representation of the tutelary deity of the ship and are certainly the most common religious object found" in ancient shipwreck sites. One of the earliest known examples of an onboard voyaging deity is a cast bronze female figurine 16.3 cm in height and partly covered in gold leaf that was recovered from the prow area of the Uluburun Bronze Age shipwreck dating to the late fourteenth century BCE in waters off the southwest coast of Türkiye (Brody 1998:68; Pulak 1998:216; Rich 2013:97; Wachsmann 1998:206–208). Brody (1998:68) suggests that this 3,300-year-old figurine represents the Canaanite goddess ʾAšerah (Asherah), who provided divine assistance to marine navigators. It is known that Canaanite sailors drew on the celestial powers of ʾAšerah, the highest-ranking goddess in the Canaanite pantheon, to assist with navigation (Brody 1998:26–30). It was ʾAšerah's link to the moon, an important navigational aid employed by Canaanite mariners, that underpinned her importance. Representations of Phoenician ships show crescent or crescent-and-disk symbols of ʾAšerah mounted on a staff located near the stern (Brody 1998:27, 70).

For protection while at sea and safe voyaging during the famous Ming expeditions of the early fifteenth century led by Zheng He, "incense was constantly burnt before an image of the sea goddess, Tian Fei, commonly known as Mazu (great grandmother)" (Andaya 2017:362). In the early nineteenth century, after a Chinese vessel came to grief in Japanese waters, the crew abandoned ship, taking their onboard Mazu statue ashore as a high priority (Hui 2002:81). In such cases, the preferred option was taking the ship Mazu statue to the nearest Mazu temple, followed by erecting a "makeshift altar" (Hui 2002:81).

The Museu de Marinha (Maritime Museum) in Lisbon, Portugal, has on display a small figure (~60 cm in height) of the archangel St. Raphael that was a figurehead on the *São Raphael*, commanded by Paulo da Gama, who was part of the famous Portuguese expedition of four ships, headed up by his brother Vasco da Gama in the *São Gabriel*, that sailed to India in 1497–1499 (Ravenstein 1898:91). After the wrecking of the *São Raphael*, the figurehead was transferred to the *São Gabriel* for the return trip to Portugal. This figure accompanied Vasco da Gama on his subsequent trips to India and stayed there after his death in 1524, until it was returned to Portugal with his great-grandson in 1600. It was moved to a chapel in Vidigueira in south Portugal in 1628, then to the Jeronimos Monastery in Lisbon in 1880. St. Raphael is often considered a patron saint of travelers, and a special protector of mariners.

In the Roman Catholic cathedral in Antipolo near Manilla in the Philippines is a wooden statue of the Virgin Mary, known as Our Lady of Peace and Good Voyage (also Virgin of Antipolo and the Our Lady of Antipolo). The statue obtained its status as a protector of mariners after it was seen to be responsible for providing safe passage of Governor General Juan Niño de Tabora and the galleon *El Almirante* from Mexico to the Philippines in 1626. Indeed, a series of subsequent seventeenth-century transpacific voyages attributed safe passage to having the statue on board their galleons (Andaya 2017:367).

A related form of deity-based ritual is the European tradition of a "crossing the line" ceremony that extends back at least 500 years. It is performed by ship crews when crossing the equator, but also less commonly for crossing the Tropic of Cancer, and more recently by whalers when crossing the Arctic Circle and American ships crossing the International Date Line in the mid-Pacific (Henningsen 1961:15, 41, 60, 62, 92; Lydenberg 1957; Penny 2016). Similar ceremonies were performed by European mariners over the past few centuries when passing significant coastal landmarks such as the Strait of Gibraltar, Cape Horn, and the Cape of Good Hope (Henningsen 1961:188–193, 215). According to Henningsen (1961:197–198; original emphasis), coastal landmark ceremonies (generally referred to as hønse places), tended to be "conspicuous physical features . . . [such as] *headlands* or capes, or at least high *cliffs or points*. They may have been *rocks, islands or groups of islands*. They were places outstanding for some reason or other, where perhaps a turning point in the journey was reached, or a considerable part of it was over. This factor seems to have played a greater part in choosing hønse places than any danger attached to the place itself, as has often been claimed." The most famous hønse place in northern Europe was Cape Kullen, located in southern Sweden and adjacent to the major shipping channel entering and exiting the Baltic Sea (Henningsen 1961:164–173, 198–199; Westerdahl 2005a:4–6). Its fame also is linked to the known presence of a "being" that inhabited Kullen (Henningsen 1961:199).

Since the eighteenth century, the crossing-the-line ceremony was directed by a crewmember dressed up as Neptune (seen as a "maritime deity" that visits the ship), who sits on his throne often accompanied by members of his court, such as his wife Amphitrite (aka Thetis and Neptunette), son Triton, and daughter Tritonia (Henningsen 1961:25, 141). The ceremony is a public event that takes place on the ship's deck and involves the entire crew. The focus is on men, with women receiving a more restrained baptism, such as a gentle sprinkling of seawater (Henningsen 1961:75, 298). Where novices had the means, they could be initiated and avoid the physical ordeal of baptism (e.g., dunking) by simply paying money to other crewmembers. Examples of crossing-the-line (equator) ceremonies during famous voyages of exploration include the HMB *Endeavour* captained by Lieutenant James Cook on 26 October 1768 (Wharton 1893:14) and HMS *Beagle* of Charles Darwin fame on 17 February 1832 (Barlow 1933:36). From the late 1860s, crossing-the-line initiates were often presented with a formal certificate of completion (Henningsen 1961:59, 151–152).

Beyond figurative carvings of deities and saints, a wide range of agentive objects are taken on board vessels to help ensure a safe and successful voyage either through bringing about good luck or warding off evil. In some cases, these objects are small and portable charms. In other cases, they are large attachments to vessels or functional parts of ships that have agentive qualities. A good example of the latter is Hellenistic and early Roman anchors, where the molded lead stock carries inscriptions indicating that the anchor is under the protective care of one and perhaps two deities such as Isis, Hera, or Hercules (Gianfrotta 1980:103; Kapitän 1989:152). In other cases, the anchor stocks bear relief representations of *astragali* (knucklebones) and marine shells (bivalves) that appear to be related to gaming and a symbolic reference to "good luck" (Galili and Rosen 2015a:77) and "good fortune" (Brody 1998:84). Kapitän (1989:152) notes that "anchor stocks bearing symbols would make clear that good luck, protection, vigilance, power and deterrence, and so safety and victory, were on the side of the anchor and ship."

In Polynesia and Micronesia, some mariners placed a piece of brain coral under the seat of their boat, as it "represents the Sea-God, whose help is invoked for a safe crossing" (Knappert 1992:35). In Ireland, clay taken from the grave of St. Cummin has been used as a good luck amulet on voyages for 1,500 years (Beck 1999:13–14, 304–305). In US New England, mariners use "smooth stones with a ring around them" as "lucky stones" (Beck 1999:305). Mariners from the Elizabeth Islands in the US state of Massachusetts use calcareous parts of male horseshoe crabs as "lucky bones" (Beck 1999:305). Barbara Andaya (2017:361) notes that "it seems safe to assume that many of the small images, seals, and amulets invoking Shiva, Vishnu and other deities discovered in early Southeast Asian sites were carried by Indian traders and sailors as talismans in order to guarantee a propitious voyage." Netsilik Inuit hunters of central northern Canada would attach to their clothing a small sealskin pouch containing a piece of seaweed such that their "kayak will not ship water in a high sea" (Rasmussen 1931:272).

Arguably the best-known good luck charm on boats is a horseshoe. In parts of England, Scotland, and the Baltic Sea, mariners would nail a horseshoe to the mast of their ship to bring good luck during voyages (Bassett 1885:462; Gregor 1881:197). A similar tradition existed among certain coastal fisherfolk in Sicily and Italy (Hornell 1923:316). Recognition of the talismanic properties of horseshoes by mariners was an extension of a broader tradition of using horseshoes as a "safeguard against evil spirits" and as an "anti-witch charm *par excellence*" (Lawrence 1898:88). According to Robert Lawrence (1898:26, 32, 43), the power of horseshoes relates to their association with horses (long considered to have spiritual and ritual importance in Europe), their manufacture from iron (which Europeans have long associated with deterring malevolent spirits), and their crafting by blacksmiths (whose trade of fire and manipulating metal was equally associated with spiritual forces). Horseshoe talismans were mostly placed above house entrances in a terrestrial context, but in a maritime context the most common location for emplacement was nailing to the mast of a fishing boat or ship (Lawrence 1898:88, 103–104, 108–109). The most famous nautical example of a horseshoe is the one that, according to legend, Nelson nailed to the mast of HMS *Victory* for the Battle of Trafalgar in 1805 (Hayes 1999:1). For English blacksmiths, the link with the sea is reinforced by St. Clement, the patron saint of farriers, who in 100 CE was bound to a ship's anchor and thrown into the sea (Lawrence 1898:46–48).

For many Christian mariners, the mast of a vessel was imbued with special, sacred qualities. Baader (2016:233) notes that Christians "considered the ship's mast a particularly sacred place." For example, a painting of a boat with a mast in the shape of a cross dating to the second century CE in the catacombs of Rome is a clear reference to a crucifix (Baader 2016:234; Stuhlfauth 1942). The Pierpont Morgan Library in New York holds a 1480 CE Italian painting of a ship with a mast in the form of a crucifix (with a crucified Jesus; Baader 2016:234, Figure 9). Rich (2021:89) adds that the association of mast and yardarms with the crucifix and Christ ensured that "sailing within the protective hull of the body of Christ translated to all faring of the sea as pilgrimage, all voyages evangelical."

Mariners from many different parts of the world have taboos against certain words while out at sea for fear that their utterance will bring bad luck to a voyage (van Ginkel 1990; see also Chapter 2). For example, off the Normandy coast of France, Jersey fishermen taboo words include "du pain" (bread), "du froment" (grain, wheat), "corde" (rope), and many landmarks (Bois 2016:65–66). Fishermen of northeast Scotland would not mention hare or pig while out at sea for fear of it bringing bad luck (Gregor 1881:129, 201). In Northern Ireland, mariners similarly had a range of taboo animal words that they refrained from uttering onboard: cat, hare, rabbit, salmon, and pig (St. Clair 1971:44). The

Sama sea people of northern Sulawesi in Indonesia have prohibitions (taboos) on mentioning the names of land animals such as goat, dog, cat, or pig while at sea as to do so is considered to bring bad luck (Lowe 2003:124). Mariners from the island of Luang in the southern Banda Sea of eastern Indonesia "avoid wearing red clothing and maintain a respectful silence" to avoid "misfortune and death" when sailing near *keramat* which are the abodes of malevolent sea beings (Pannell 2007:86–87).

Mariners of European heritage believed that it is bad luck to have a pig, cat (especially black), or hare on board a vessel (Holland 1942:13–14). Indeed, a cat on a vessel, having "bad luck," will be thrown overboard (Holland 1942:13). For example, in the late seventeenth century, a sea captain believed that the finding of a black cat on his ship before it sank demonstrated that the vessel had been "bewitched" (Rediker 1987:184). In northeast Scotland, "to have thrown a hare, or any part of a hare, into a boat would have stopped many a fisherman in bygone days from going to sea; and if any misfortune had happened, however long afterwards, it was traced up to the hare" (Gregor 1881:129). The presence of lawyers, women, and priests on board vessels is also considered to bring bad luck on voyages (Gregor 1881:199; Holland 1942:13). The origin of the taboo on priests is a little difficult to understand, given that many European crews, especially from merchant and trading vessels, desired the onboard presence of a priest (or at least a copy of the Book of Common Prayer or the Bible) to help provide divine blessing and protection (Miller 2012:103–109, 124–126). Furthermore, many English ships of the sixteenth and seventeenth centuries desired the presence of a priest or chaplain on board during voyages to administer services, sermons, and prayers (Patarino 2002:262–300, 431).

In northeast Scotland, fishermen believe it is bad luck to use white stones, stones with holes, granite stones, or bricks with adhering mortar as boat ballast (Gregor 1885b:180, 1886:14–15). Fishermen on the Isle of Man believe it is bad luck to go to sea in a boat with white stones, possibly due to an association between white stones and cemeteries (see Moore 1894:218). Between 1890 and 1902, the large sailing vessel *Hinemoa* experienced numerous mishaps and crew deaths, which many said were due to a curse over the ship as a result of using ballast from "an old London burial ground" (Clary 1994:47–48). Beck (1999:304) notes that in both Ireland and Scotland, ballast stones must not be taken from the sea, "for the ocean may rise at any moment and claim it." He adds that this idea of the sea reclaiming its own also extended to avoidance of using clothing dyes made from sea plants. In terms of ballast stones, Beck (1999:304) invokes a speculative, functionalist interpretation, suggesting that "sea stones are usually smooth and round and given to shifting with the rolling of the ship; while stones from inland are more angular and less easily rolled about."

Sea-Based Rituals

According to Herodotus, writing in the fifth century BCE, the Persian king Xerxes made ritual preparations for a successful voyage by praying, burning incense, pouring a libation from a golden *phiale* into the sea, and throwing a sword, the *phiale*, and a golden krater (probably containing a wine libation) into the sea (Atkins 2009:99). Polemon of Athens, writing in the second century BCE, noted that when mariners departed from Syracuse harbor in Sicily they waited until they could no longer see the shield held by Athena in the temple dedicated in her honor on the island of Ortygia and then threw into the sea an offering comprising a cup filled with flowers, honey, lumps of incense, and various other aromatics (Kapitän 1989:147). Remarkably, archaeological exploration of the seabed in the area has recovered numerous isolated terracotta cups up to 65 cm in diameter of Hellenistic age (Kapitän 1989:148).

Ehud Galili and Baruch Rosen (2015a:77–78, 87–88, 101) argue that special symbols engraved onto the surface of lead sounding weights (e.g., herring bone and lozenge patterns, Greek crosses, Maltese crosses, individual letters, and words) recovered archaeologically from the seabed (mostly from shipwrecks) off the coast of Israel had an apotropaic function (i.e., the power to ward off evil influences or bad luck). All the sounding weights date to antiquity, with some known to be from the sixth and seventh centuries CE. A small (10-cm-long) lead tablet with an inscription from the Bible in Hebrew dating to 150–200 years ago and recovered from the seabed off the coast of Israel is considered to be an apotropaic object to "protect a person or a group of people involved with a voyage on the sea" (Galili and Rosen 2015a:85).

Westerdahl (2002:65) questions the extent to which isolated finds of ship cargo on the seabed represent secular jettisoning practices and raises the possibility of ritual offerings, perhaps to propitiate a safe voyage. In this connection, individual finds or groups of finds of bronze artifacts dating to the Late Middle and Late Bronze Age (2,800–3,400 years ago) have been recovered from 18 sites in the North Sea and English Channel, up to nearly 6 km from the nearest shore (Samson 2006). Alice Samson (2006) questions the usual explanation of these finds as mishap (e.g., from shipwrecks) and posits an alternative hypothesis of deliberate deposition (i.e., votive offerings) during Bronze Age voyages. Most of the finds are either bronze tools or weapons (mostly axes, swords, and rapiers), with less than 10% classified as ornaments (e.g., pins and needles; Samson 2006:377–378). Samson (2006:385) concludes by arguing that deliberate deposition of bronze objects into the sea indicates that the sea in the Bronze Age was far from an "outside" domain but rather a cultured seascape that "referenced identities and relationships which were integrated into local cosmologies" (cf. Van de Noort 2011:61).

In the twelfth century, a Chinese fleet crossing the Yellow Sea took ritual precautions against the numerous dangerous shoals associated with silts emanating from the Yellow River (Huang He) and "offered chicken and grain to the Shoals and the spirits of shipwreck victims" (Hui 2002:73). The Mandar fishermen of southern Sulawesi similarly make propitiatory offerings into the sea (e.g., food and cigarettes) to help ensure safe passage when passing promontories known to be home to spirit guardians (Zerner 2003:67, 73–74). The people of Malaita in the southern Solomon Islands will throw coconuts into the sea as a thanks offering to sharks that are considered to be guardian ancestors and to have protected them on sea voyages (Ivens 1930:166). Torres Strait Islanders of northeastern Australia make offerings of food, drink, and cigarettes to the sea while on dinghy voyages to propitiate spirits and to bring good luck.

In the early eighteenth century, Chinese traders in Manila were known to throw beads into the sea as they passed a mountain dedicated to the Virgin Mary to help ensure a "profitable voyage and a safe return home" (Andaya 2017:366). The Sama sea peoples of southern Sulawesi in Indonesia appease Ma' empa' engkah na—a dangerous and spiritually powerful giant octopus with four tentacles whose home is a cave and reef complex named Toro Gagallah, near the island of Binongko—"by way of careful propitiation and observance of appropriate behaviors" (Nolde 2009:19).

As for many Indigenous groups of North and South America, tobacco is the most important ritual plant of the Warao people of the Orinoco Delta region of eastern Venezuela. The Warao use their own cultivated tobacco smoke for spiritual protection on canoe voyages out to the island of Trinidad. Commercial cigarettes are considered inappropriate (Wilbert 1993:116). The smoke comes from the captain-shaman, who offers it to three invisible passengers: Uraro (god of the southern edge of the world), Karoshimo (mountain god on the southern edge of the world), and their servant Himabaka. The deities or spirits protect the canoe from being dragged to the bottom of the sea by Hahuba, a sea monster (Wilbert 1977:41).

Tahitian voyagers of Polynesia commenced sea journeys by taking "strips of 'aute (paper mulberry) cloth, called a *hopu* (bather) or *repu* (sea-rolling), and gradually casting them over the approaching and receding waves of the sea, invoked the ocean gods" with the following chant: "Hearken unto us throughout our voyage. O gods! Lead us safely to land. Let our voyage be propitious, free from evil! leave us not in the ocean. Give us a breeze, let it follow us from behind, let the weather be fine, and the sky clear. Hearken unto us, o gods!"

(Henry 1928:178–179). Following these offerings and chant, the mariners "set out to sea in good faith, free and happy" (Henry 1928:179).

In the Society Islands of Polynesia are found numerous heaps of basalt stones created by people on the seabed near passages through fringing reefs. The best known of these is in Tupapaurau pass on the island of Mo'orea (Guérout and Veccella 2006). The site has an estimated 2,000–3,000 objects over an area of 250 m by 50 m. Most of the objects are canoe anchors (spherical stones with a knob protrusion for attaching an anchor rope) and fishing weights for ballasting lines and nets, along with adzes and pestles. Archaeological excavations recovered nearly 700 basalt objects weighing five tons. Max Guérout and Robert Veccella (2006:96) posit that the site is the result of the "voluntary deposit" of special objects "during some ritual related to navigation or fishing." They note that "the anchor by its nature is highly symbolic of marine activities" and that the morphological similarity of anchors to some *ti'i* ceremonial stones "is likely to strengthen the ritual character of the offering" (Guérout and Veccella 2006:96).

Along the coast of Grande Terre in New Caledonia, southwest Pacific, local Kanak fishers know that after the "soul" detaches from the body of the deceased, it travels from the land, into reef lagoons, then through passages out to sea and the "world of the dead" (Breckwoldt et al. 2022:10). One fisher stated, the "passes [passages through the reef] are sacred; it is the passage to the world of the dead, the spirits of the dead are there, we avoid disturbing them, we have a fear when we fish there, we don't go alone, always a small gesture to ask the old people for forgiveness and to look after us" (Breckwoldt et al. 2022:6). To ensure safe travel and "avoid being shipwrecked," fishers "placate" spirits of the dead in reef passages by making "an offering (e.g., tobacco, fabric, money, or food) . . . to the sea, sometimes accompanied by a few words" (Breckwoldt et al. 2022:6).

First Swimmers

Swimmers and nonswimmers alike can drown through mishap, but nonswimmers will probably drown if they enter an open body of water unassisted. Little information is available on when people began to swim, with historical and archaeological information varying considerably in detail across the globe on the extent to which coastal peoples in different regions swam in the sea. The first modern humans to voyage from Indonesia to Australia over 65,000 years ago were not only maritime specialists but also probably able swimmers (McNiven and Russell 2023:38). A direct biological indicator of prolonged and repeated diving and swimming in cold water is the production of external auditory canal exostoses in people's ears. These exostoses are visible in human skulls in the form of bony growths that constrict the external ear canal in front of the ear drum.

The earliest known example of auditory exostoses for a human associated with a "coastal environment" is the 50,000-to-120,000-year-old Tabun 1 Neanderthal skull from Israel (Trinkaus et al. 2019:11). All other archaeological examples of external auditory exostoses associated with marine contexts are Holocene burials (e.g., Katayama 1998; Standen et al. 1997; Tommaseo et al. 1997:Table 4; Villotte et al. 2014). As such, it is probable that people from maritime coastal communities over at least the past 10,000 years, especially subsistence fishers and foragers, possessed swimming skills. Swimming and diving were not limited to warmer tropical and subtropical waters, as considerable evidence also exists of such activities in cold waters of temperate coastal regions (Carr 2022).

Some coastal communities deliberately avoided learning to swim for a range of cosmological and religious reasons (see below). For example, Eric Chaline (2017:13) notes that swimming fell out of favor in many parts of Europe in the medieval period due to the influence of Christianity and its negative views on the sea (see Chapter 2). This situation was prevalent in the United Kingdom during the dominance of the Catholic church between 1000 and 1500 CE (Orme 1983:22). For many medieval Christians, rescue from drowning was through divine intervention and the actions of Christ, angels, and saints and not a sacrilegious self-rescue through a capacity to swim (Orme 1983:23). Anti-learn-to-swim sentiments carried over to British colonies in North America and Australia during the eighteen and nineteenth centuries and given a racist makeover, such that Indigenous and US African enslaved peoples' excellence in swimming was linked to savagery and inferiority, and Euro-Americans' swimming skills linked to cultural and moral superiority (Carr 2022:Chapter 14; Dawson 2006). Despite improvements in swimming capacity during the twentieth century, "most people today can't swim" (Carr 2022:7).

Drowning Preventative Charms and Taboos

The World Health Organization (2014:3) records that 372,000 people died by drowning across the world in 2012, making it the third most common cause of unintentional injury-related death. Pedro Andrade and colleagues (2022:1) note that most of these drownings occur in the sea and "posit that deaths due to saltwater drowning were similarly a major cause of morbidity among human populations in prehistory, in large part due to the extensive use of coastal locations for settlement, and the use of transport by sea as an early and major source of travel." Considerable research indicates that wearing lifejackets dramatically decreases the chances of drowning while at sea (Peden et al. 2018). Yet in many coastal contexts, people of the recent past invested in a wide range of ritual activities (charms and taboos) to help prevent drowning. Fear of drowning was not simply to avert death but to avert the spiritual dangers associated with death by drowning.

Since at least the Middle Ages in the United Kingdom and Europe, a child born in a caul (amniotic membrane enclosing a fetus or newborn, especially its head) was considered to have good luck in life (Forbes 1953). The most celebrated example of this good luck was belief that possession of a caul brings immunity from drowning (Baines 1950; Brand and Ellis 1849:114–115; Gill 1993:21–25; Hammerton 1931:300). In Iceland, caul charms were known as *fylgia*, and "they fancy that the guardian angel, or a part of the infant's soul dwells in it" (Thorpe 1851:114). Christina Hole (1967:186) adds that the caul must be preserved and held by its owner to ensure against drowning. Furthermore, cauls could also be traded, and their drowning immunity powers were passed on to their new owners. Walter Gregor (1881:25) noted that "many an emigrant has gone to the possessor of such a powerful charm, got a nail's breadth of it, sewed it with all care into what was looked upon as a safe part of the clothes, and worn it during the voyage, in the full belief that the ship was safe from wreck, and would have a prosperous voyage." According to Giles Bois (2010:517), a mariner would keep a caul in a bag around their neck under their shirt.

The sale of cauls to sailors was particularly popular in England during times of war. Such powers also extend to immunity from sinking for ships crewed by sailors with cauls. In 1954 a midwife in Banbury, England, offered a woman £10 for her baby's caul to give to a sailor friend (Hole 1957:413). Cauls are difficult to obtain, given that caul births occur only in approximately one in 80,000 births (Byard 2021:526). According to William Jones (1898:113), "Often these cauls became hereditary, being handed down from father to son (especially if it was born in the family), and were regarded by their respective owners with as much superstition as if the caul-born person was still living."

First Nations Canadians of Queen Charlotte Sound use fish bone amulets for protection against drowning (Bassett 1885:469). Yorkshire and Isle of Man fishermen wear T-shaped hyoid bones of sheep as "safeguards against drowning" (Haddon 1906:39). The Horniman Museum in London has in its collection a carved sheep's hyoid bone said to have been "carried as amulet by a seaman from the Yorkshire coast" (Horniman Museum, online catalog, object #19.110). In England, knee bones (patellas) of sheep or humans were worn as charms to ward off drowning (Bassett 1885:470).

Mariners of Maine in the US Northeast believe that a jasper stone will protect a man from drowning (Beck 1957:68). In Ireland, it has been known for at least 1,500 years that any person who takes clay from the grave of St. Cummin will be protected from drowning, while any boat that has some of this holy clay on board will never sink (Beck 1999:13–14).

Icelandic fishers believe that having the preserved egg case of a skate (known as "Peter's ship" or "Peter's purse") on board a vessel will ensure "the crew are safe from drowning" (Davidsson 1900:327). In Scotland, coastal folk use Molucca bean seeds (also referred to locally as Virgin Mary beans), which are found washed up on beaches (having floated in from South America) as a charm against drowning (Thomson 1996:24). Some European mariners of old believed that wearing a gold earring helped ensure protection against shipwreck and drowning (Clary 1994:161). Such a belief is the basis of popular representations of pirates wearing a single large gold earring (Fowles 1978:63). Beck (1957:66) notes that it is a common belief among mariners that a person born with a hair crown will never drown.

US Navy sailors in the early twentieth century had tattoos as a form of charm to help prevent drowning. Examples include the words HOLD FAST on the back of the fingers on both hands (one letter per finger) to aid gripping onto ropes to prevent falling overboard and drowning (Dye 1989:547; Farenholt 1908:39), and representation of a "pig on dorsum of foot, which among the older men was supposed to shield its possessor from death by drowning" (Farenholt 1908:39).

Northern European fishing communities possess numerous taboos associated with preventing drowning. For example, Icelanders believe that a fisherman will drown if his sea-skin clothes are mended with a needle and thread on Sunday (Powell and Magnusson 1866:633). During the nineteenth century and possibly earlier, Scottish women believed that combing their hair at night or by candlelight would cause their friends at sea to drown (Bassett 1885:144). Scottish women also believed that burning hair clippings would doom a blood relative at sea to drown (Clary 1994:134). Wives of fishers from Hull in northeast England knew that their husbands might drown if they "wave" them off or say "goodbye" prior to a fishing trip (Gill 1993:15). A Hull wife similarly knew that she "must *not* wash clothes the day her man sails; otherwise 'He'll be washed overboard'" (Gill 1993:15, original emphasis). In the coastal town of Rowhedge in southeast England, women similarly never wash clothes on the day their mariner husbands set sail for fear "you would wash them away" (Leather 1977: 55–56).

Treatment of Drowning Victims

A wide range of ritual practices associated with drowning victims, some seemingly inhumane, are practiced by maritime peoples across the world. Examples discussed below include rescue taboos, construction of expedient graves and corpseless graves and monuments, and fear of the spirits and ghosts of drowning victims as the restless dead.

In many places around the world, it is believed that a person who falls into the water (either the sea or inland lakes and rivers) is preordained to drown and must therefore not be saved. As Tylor (1871:1:99) remarked: "From this point of view it is obvious that to save a sinking man is to snatch a victim from the very clutches of the water-spirit, a rash defiance of deity which would hardly pass unavenged." According to Beck (1999:300), across northern Europe, people were reluctant to rescue mariners who had fallen overboard. This reluctance was based on the belief that "what the sea wants, the sea will have." A legendary folk tale from Ireland states: "When God created the sea, he set a king over it and made him promise that he would never drown anyone. It was not long until he broke the promise, and from the day that the first man was drowned the sea must always get its own" (Chadbourne 2012:71). A comparable Irish saying is "the sea must have its own" (Chadbourne 2012:71).

Many Irish knew that "sea-fairies" were responsible for drowning mariners. For example, the "old people of Teelin believed of anyone who was drowned that it was the wee folk who had taken him away and because of that he could not be saved" (quoted in Chadbourne 2012:72). Rescuers were also concerned that they would also become victims of this inevitability. For example, in the Shetland Islands of northern Scotland, fisherfolk were reluctant to rescue a fellow mariner from drowning, believing that a person who saves someone from drowning will soon succumb to drowning themself (Gregor 1885b:184). Indeed, Arthur Laurenson (1872–74:713) suggests that for Shetland fishermen, it "is the belief that it is 'unlucky,' or more correctly, 'forbidden,' to save a person from drowning." This avoidance is based on the belief that the "evil spirit—or the god of the sea, good or evil—must have his sacrifice; if you hinder him, you awake his anger, which another victim alone can appease" (Laurenson 1872–74:713). Usually, the alternative victim is seen as the "rescuer" (Hole 1967:188). In Northern Ireland, "there was a marked reluctance to go to the aid of a drowning man, on the premise that if you deprived the sea of its chosen victim, it would simply claim another as its lawful prey" (St. Clair 1971:45). This understanding of "fatalism" and drowning is encapsulated in the following account from the fishing community of Hull in northeast England: "In the mid-1930s, trawler mate Fred Noble, while getting the catch inboard was swept into the sea by a wave. As he bobbed about helplessly in the foam, the skipper reached out and grabbed him. The mate was pulled back from the edge of a watery grave. The sea gods were cheated of their human sacrifice. On his next voyage that same skipper was washed overboard and disappeared forever. The sea gods got their revenge" (Gill 1993:155). As a corollary, the Hull community also knew of instances where men washed overboard were washed back to their vessel by another wave, as "their time had not yet come" (Gill 1993:156). That is, the "sea had taken its quota, and so these men were given back to their families" (Gill 1993:156).

Reluctance to rescue people from drowning may also relate to a belief among mariners that it was bad luck to learn how to swim, as mariners' "business is to master the sea in another fashion" (Lean 1903a:191).

The notion that drowning was a result of forces beyond human control is also found in societies beyond Great Britain and Europe. The Kamchadals of northeast Russia hold that it was improper for a person who fell into water to rescue themself from drowning. Those who did rescue themselves would be largely ostracized from their community, as they were seen as "reckoned for dead" (Rappoport 1928:239). Chinese avoidance of saving drowning victims is based on the belief that the souls of drowned victims remain in a kind of "ocean purgatory, whence it is released only by finding some one to take its place" (Bassett 1885:469). The Inuit know of Atalit, malevolent spirits that live on the bottom of the sea, that seize the drowned (Rappoport 1928:142). In Norse mythology, the female sea deity Rán was known to pull sailors below the waves and drown them so that they could live with her (Lindow 2001; Quinn 2014). In this sense, drowning was seen as "an embrace by a female personification of the sea" (Quinn 2014:89).

Many fishermen from a village near Rosehearty in northeast Scotland would refuse to bring on board their boat the dead body of a drowned person found at sea, fearing bad luck (Gregor 1885c:55). In many parts of Scotland, mariners and fishermen refuse to pick up the body of a drowned person on the beach for fear of becoming a drowning victim themselves (Bassett 1885:468). According to James Grant (1880:397), coastal Scots believe "that if a person die unseen, they who first discover the body will meet his death in a similar manner. This superstitious belief often prevents seamen and fishermen picking up and taking ashore dead bodies discovered at sea."

In a discussion of UK folklore of the sea, Hole (1967:188) notes that "when a drowned corpse was washed ashore, it used to be buried hastily, then and there, within the tidemarks, that is, within the limits of the sea's kingdom. The sea, it was thought, must be able to recover its own, otherwise it will take another victim. Thus, the drowned were often denied Christian burial." In southwest England, John Fowles (1978:47) reports that "before 1800, the washed-up bodies of the drowned were far more often buried below the tideline than in conse- crated ground. When the sea swallows, it likes to hold for ever." Jan Brendalsmo (2002:54, original emphasis) documents that in Norway during the Middle Ages, any unidentified person, drowned or otherwise, that dies in a coastal setting and whose Christian status is unknown was considered unsuitable for churchyard burial and would be buried on the shore at the high-water mark, "*where sea meets land*." Following on from the notion of the sea gets what the sea wants, Tony Pollard (1999:39) surmises that burial of drowning victims on the shoreline may have been aimed at assisting the sea retrieve her victims and thus avoid her wrath. Fear of the fate of one's soul following drowning indicates why coastal peoples of France during the nineteenth century made a sign of the cross before they entered the sea to swim, believing it would ensure they went straight to heaven if they drowned (Anson 1965:46).

At various locations along the English coast, archaeologists have excavated graves dating to the past 500 years that appear to be drowned shipwreck victims washed up on nearby beaches. For example, Roderick McCullagh and Finbar McCormick (1991) document two grave pits with remains of 11 bodies dating to around 1700 in sands above the beach adjacent to the township of Aignish, Isle of Lewis, northwest Scotland. The graves are associated with shipwreck victims, given that all sexed and aged bodies are males 17–30 years old, and the bodies were in unconsecrated ground and not Aignish's Christian cemetery located only a few hundred meters to the east. It was argued that the latter point "strongly suggests that these were not the remains of local people" (McCullagh and McCormick 1991:86). Pollard (1999:37) points out the "burial of corpses washed ashore in consecrated graveyards only became common practice after 1808." The exclusion of the drowned (especially nonlocals) from cemeteries "may have something to do with the idea that the sea is an abstract entity which does not fit within straightforward categories of place and as such makes the drowned different and more *dangerous* than the average corpse" (Pollard 1999:37, original emphasis).

According to Sarah Tarlow (2011:111), drowning victims washed up on beaches were probably unknown to people who found them in terms of names, religious identities, and nationalities and were thus buried adjacent to the beach in unconsecrated land and not in the local community (Christian) cemetery. Yet historical and ethnographic evidence discussed above on the special treatment of victims of drowning in England and Scotland reveals also that the corpses of shipwreck (drowning) victims may have possessed metaphysical properties incompatible with the terrestrial world, particularly the terrestrial domain of Christianity and Christian burial. That bodies washed up on shores may also have been seen as metaphysically contaminated has expression in a statement by the Roman philosopher Seneca that "it is in the nature of the sea to cast back on its shore every secretion and every impurity . . . and this purging occurs not only when the storm is stirring the waves, but when the deepest calm prevails" (Corbin 1995:13).

In Scandinavia fear of the restless souls of the drowned dead resulted in a continued fear of the graves of drowning victims, even in situations where burial took place in a consecrated church graveyard. Westerdahl (2014) posits that many large and complex maze stone arrangements found along the coast of southern Scandinavia and dating mostly from 1300 to 1850 CE may have been constructed to stop the arrival of corpses of drowning victims washing up on shore or to control the unsettled souls of drowning victims in graves. As Westerdahl (2014:492) notes, the "deceased sailors and fishermen were mostly young and had their life-span cut short. They were accordingly thought to live on as ghosts or wraiths, unblessed, deeply unhappy, and without any roots."

In Newfoundland the Great Hurricane (aka Independence Hurricane) of 1775 is reputed to have killed more than 4,000 mariners and fishermen. The settlement of Conception Bay lost more than 300 men alone in the storm. After the storm abated, the local beach was littered with the remains of many of these men. Surviving locals buried the bodies in a mass grave on a nearby bluff. Soon afterward, "many local inhabitants started to claim that they could hear the cries of the drowning men. The moans and shouts of these tortured souls became known as 'the hollies.' There were those who believed that the mournful cries made by dead fishermen were often multiplied by the same souls wailing old sea shanties. Those left behind amongst the living learned to interpret the ghoulish noises. If the hollies were heard crying out, it was taken to mean that a big breeze of wind was coming" (Jarvis 2004:133).

In another Newfoundland example, Chance Cove Provincial Park features remains of the village of Chance Cove, which was abandoned in the late nineteenth century. One explanation for abandonment is avoidance of the restless ghosts of victims of the steamer SS *Anglo Saxon*, which was wrecked on rocks at nearby Clam Cove in 1863. Of the 444 people on board the vessel, 347 drowned, and of these more than 100 were buried within the bank of a brook at Chance Cove. Within a number of years, a small fishing village became established at Chance Cove, and soon after its residents began hearing "ghostly cries and spectral noises" at night, which were attributed to the *Anglo Saxon* dead (Jarvis 2004:112).

In Japan, the finding of drowned bodies at sea is considered a good omen by fishermen, as they can be included in rituals at sea to help increase fish catches (Ōtō 1963). Floating bodies are often referred to as *nagare-botoke* (floating Buddhas) because they are "believed to have the attributes of deities" (Ōtō 1963:112). However, the bodies are left in the water and only recovered at the end of a fishing trip where they are brought ashore and the body buried "in the special graveyard set apart for drowned persons" (Ōtō 1963:112).

For over 2,000 years, Europeans have created monuments to mariners who died at sea. Cenotaphs (corpseless graves) with an inscription carved in stone for people who drowned and disappeared at sea were created by the ancient Greeks as memorials to the dead (Haussker 2009; Vermeule 1979:187–188) and by the Romans "to provide the soul with a dwelling-place" (Toynbee 1996:54). An early example dating to 600–625 BCE comes from Kastrades, one of the harbors of Corcyra on the northwest coast of Greece (Frischer 1984:81). The corpseless tumulus contains an inscription stating that the grave is for Menecrates, who died at sea (cf. Haussker 2009:30). Interestingly, the tumulus is located 100 m from the shore and was not within the port city's cemetery, which was on an inland hill (Frischer 1984:81). From the port city of Piraeus in the Attica region of eastern Greece is a stone grave marker dating to 360 BCE for a boy "who died at the age of eight in the depths of the sea" and "who possesses this pitiless grave, since he lies in dark sea" (Haussker 2009:31–32). Small statues have been found associated with what appear to be cenotaphs in ancient Greece and may represent symbolic representations of the deceased (Haussker 2009:28). Paul Duffy (2007:110) hypothesizes that Bronze Age bodiless cysts (stone-lined graves) dating to between 3,100 and 4,200 years ago at the coastal cemetery at Ayrshire, Scotland, may have been referencing people who died at sea and "who will never return from its unyielding grasp."

In more recent times, memorials to the maritime dead are state sponsored and found in public places to memorialize major events such as the Battle of Trafalgar (e.g., Nelson's column in London). Most literature on memorials for the marine dead (individuals and groups, including entire crews and passengers) are set up by family members or fellow mariners inside churches (mostly plaques) and out in the open in churchyards and cemeteries (mostly headstones; Stewart 2007, 2011). Stewart's (2007:119) surveys of Anglo-American maritime memorials revealed that 40% of sites are not associated with bodies. That is, the deceased died far from their memorial and for practical reasons their body could not be transported home (e.g., buried in foreign soils or interred at sea) or their body was lost at sea. During the nineteenth century, such memorials and headstones increasingly featured Christian symbolism and biblical verses (Stewart 2007:120–123).

Numerous churches contain memorial tablets erected in honor of mariners who died (mostly through drowning) as a result of shipwreck. A famous example is the memorial plaques found in the Seamen's Bethel in New Bedford, brought to wide attention by Melville's *Moby-Dick* and Huston's 1956 adaptation of the novel in the movie of the same name. Most tablets relate to individuals and small-scale events. In other cases, the individuals memorialized were one of hundreds of people who died from a particular shipwreck tragedy.

One of the most famous shipwreck churches in Australia is Quetta All Souls Memorial Church on Thursday Island in Torres Strait (Foley 1990). The Anglican church, built over a number of years commencing in 1893, is a memorial to the tragic sinking of the *Quetta* and the loss of 134 lives after it hit an unmapped reef (known now as Quetta Rock) 45 km southeast of Thursday Island in February 1890. A range of objects from the wreck have been installed in the church over the past century. First was the ship's bell, salvaged from the wreck site in December 1890, followed by a circular cork lifebuoy (found washed up on a nearby beach), and objects such as a stern riding lamp, a rum jar, and a coral-encrusted porthole salvaged from the wreck in 1906. The lamp became the "sanctuary lamp" hanging above the high altar (Foley 1990:121). A salvaged "piece of teak, probably from the wheelhouse, was engraved with the Diocesan Arms" (Foley 1990:121). The ship's "saloon table top," donated to the church in 1965, "became the High Altar marble mensa" (Foley 1990:121). A font made from a "compass bowl" is from the steamer *Catterthun*, wrecked along the coast of New South Wales with the loss of 55 people in 1895 (Foley 1990:121; Spencer 1992). A range of other memorial objects (not from the wreck) within the church (e.g., lectern, wooden stand, stained glass window) were donated by relatives of wreck victims.

The Yanyuwa of northern Australia had a tradition of memorializing people whose bodies were lost at sea, either through drowning or through fatal attack by a shark or crocodile, through the erection of ceremonial stones (Bradley 1998:133; Bradley and Kearney 2011:36; Bradley with Yanyuwa Families 2022:191–192). These stones, known as *kundawira*, were "erected to mark the death of powerful men and to embody their physical presence on traditional homelands" and are treated with great "reverence" (Bradley and Kearney 2011:31, 41). As such, *kundawira* stones were made for senior men whose body was available for mortuary ceremonies and also for those men lost at sea. They were purposefully made of stone to endure as long-term "symbols of remembrance and memory" (Bradley and Kearney 2011:39). They were always erected in coastal contexts, and even though they have not been made for generations, current generations still find these stones, especially after erosion of coastal dunes. The stones range in size up to 60 cm and stand as "silent sentinels of the past lives of important men" (Bradley and Kearney 2011:36). Each *kundawira* represents an individual and was personalized through the addition of adornments such as the attachment of feathers and white and red pigment designs (Bradley and Kearney 2011:36–38, 40).

The Lamalera sea peoples of the island of Lembata in eastern Indonesia take a nautilus shell and place it in the sea if they are having trouble finding the body of someone who has drowned at sea (Barnes 1996:130). If the shell sinks and reappears it is a sign that the body will be recovered. If the shell sinks and disappears it is a sign that the body will never be recovered. In the latter case, a funeral will be held and a nautilus shell will be buried in place of the body. In one case where a number of people died at sea, the community could not find enough nautilus shells, so instead they threw sections of banana trunk into the sea off the shore, one for each missing person. The banana trunk sections were then retrieved and placed into coffins as a substitute for the bodies and buried in a Christian cemetery (Barnes 1996:130–133). In some cases, it is known that people lost at sea return as moray eels (Barnes 1996:322).

Henry Cheever (1854:35) aptly notes that the mariner is a "profound believer in ghosts," especially those associated with people who have drowned or been murdered at sea (see also Bassett 1885:282–296). In many cases, the ghosts or spirits of drowned mariners are seen as restless and are therefore feared by mariners at sea. For example, Japanese sailors often kept cats on board as protection against the "sad" and restless souls of drowned mariners who desired terrestrial interment (Knappert 1992:42).

The most famous example of encounters with the restless sea dead concerns St. Elmo's lights. For example, eighteenth-century German mariners associated St. Elmo's lights with "the souls of dead comrades" (Carey 1963:35). In more recent centuries, Breton sailors associated the lights with the lost souls of relatives, especially those that had drowned (Rappoport 1928:58). In the late nineteenth century, Greek sailors saw the lights as spirits of the dead whose process to heaven had been impeded by evil demons (Carey 1963:36). Many European and American sailors believe that any sailor working within the rigging whose head is illuminated by the St. Elmo's lights will soon die (Rappoport 1928:58). Sailors of Brittany and northeast Scotland knew that the appearance of the lights foretold imminent death of a crew member (Carey 1963:36). Some fishermen of northeast Scotland believe that they will never step on land again once they sight the lights (Gregor 1886:7). Most accounts of the lights do not mention ritual responses beyond prayers.

Mariners of Brittany state that phosphorescence is sometimes associated with a "muffled plaintive sound," which emanates from the souls of the drowned suffering in hell (Rappoport 1928:51). In the early nineteenth century it was recorded that Bretons knew that the "noise of the sea or the whistling of the wind heard in the night is the lamentation of the spirit of some one who has been drowned complaining for want of burial" (Lean 1903a:335). Les Pierres de Lecq (also known as the Paternosters) are a small group of rocky islets on a reef immediately north of the island of Jersey off the Normandy coast of France. Local mariners note that they can hear "les cris d'la mé" (the laments of the dead) in howling winds preceding a storm as they sail past the rocks (Bois 2016:54). Cornish and East Anglian fishermen of England could hear drowned mariners wailing in storms (Anson 1965:155). In Norway it is believed that the voices of drowned people can be heard wailing during storms (Bassett 1885:471).

In Polynesia, people who have drowned at sea can take the form of living sea creatures. For example, in Tahitian society, according to Teuira Henry (1928:389), "fishes were shadows of the gods and were also said to be possessed of disembodied spirits of persons who died at sea, especially of those who were drowned." Furthermore, the "*mahimahi* (dolphin) was supposed to be possessed with the spirits of persons who died at sea, and its varying color in dying was attributed to those spirits leaving its body" (Henry 1928:390). In Hawai'i, people who died at sea and were from families related to sharks could have their spirit ritually transformed into a *'aumakua* (ancestral spirit) shark. Relatives of the deceased placed the bones of the deceased into the sea, where they were taken into the care of a *'aumakua* shark until transformation was complete. "Not all who died at sea shared this fate. Hawaiians believed that souls without a link to marine *'aumakua* could not transform, and were doomed to drift helplessly, formless on the currents" (D'Arcy 2006:43).

In Ireland, Whitsuntide (the week following Whitsunday, the seventh Sunday after Easter) was a period of danger when the drowned dead attempted to take the living. In particular, "Young men should be very cautious not to be out late at night, for all the dead who have been drowned in the sea round about come up and ride over the waves on white horses, and hold strange revels, and try to carry off the young men, or to kill them with their fiery darts and draw them down under the sea to live with the dead for evermore" (Lady Wilde 1890:108–109).

Among First Nations communities of the Northwest Coast of Canada, drowning with one's body unrecoverable is considered the worst form of death. That is, it is not possible to ritually treat these bodies, resulting in their souls being doomed to wonder the earth "discontentedly" (Shearar 2000:49).

In some cultural contexts, mariners make offerings into the sea near where people have drowned. For example, in the twelfth century CE, Xu Jing recorded that as the ship he was on passed over the Yellow Colored Sea (also the called the "Sand Tail") off the coast where the Yellow River (Huang He) enters the sea, they made an offering of chicken and millet "to the sands" as a "sacrifice" to the many souls of mariners who drowned as a result of shipwreck upon the sands (Ruitenbeek 1999:285). Similarly, in Torres Strait of northeast Australia, people stop in a passage where it is known people have drowned to make offerings of food in order to propitiate good favor.

Treatment of Shipwrecks

UNESCO estimates that the world's oceans hold three million shipwrecks (Rich 2021:82), equating on average to nearly one wreck per 10 km by 10 km of sea. Within maritime archaeology, conceptual and analytical approaches to shipwrecks focus on the technological, social, and economic aspects of ship-building and shipping and more recently on shipwreck formation processes and taphonomy, including salvage and scavenging, and wreck life histories (e.g., Gibbs 2006). Yet for many mariners and associated coastal communities, shipwreck was a traumatic and usually deadly process that had ritual and spiritual dimensions.

Robert Gillis (2012:140) writes, "In the nineteenth century, shipwreck became the symbol of the power of nature and the hopelessness of human efforts to control one's own fate on either land or sea." This point was driven home brutally by the sinking of the *Titanic* in 1912. Yet mariners did not simply hand over their fate to the elements and rely only on human technology to offset shipwreck. Mariners knew that numinous forces were at play to precipitate shipwreck. As such, they drew on an arsenal of rituals to help offset these numinous forces to protect their ships and themselves.

Shipwrecking Spirits and Rituals

Rossel Islanders of the Louisiade Archipelago of southeastern Papua New Guinea know that the goddess Laapî, who lives on the sacred islet of Lów:a 16 km offshore, seizes and wrecks boats on the surrounding reefs (Levinson 2008:283). To the northwest, Trobriand Islanders see canoe wrecks as the work of witches. More broadly across the Louisiade Archipelago, Lepowsky (1995:50) recorded that "witches are said to take bodies of their victims to a witches' cannibal exchange feast as a supernatural form of reciprocity. The witches are mostly, but not all, female. . . . Witches cut off sailors' lips with a pearl shell so that they will 'talk like dogs' and drown, meaning that they will be driven senseless and unable to navigate or save themselves. Witches are also responsible for causing sudden strong winds and storms." Louisiade Islanders also know of "powerful place spirits called *silava* [who] inhabit the sea" (Lepowsky 1995:51). Their preferred abodes are fringing reefs, and passages in the barrier reef and between islands "where currents are treacherous, waves are high, and whirlpools common." They take the form of giant octopi, fish, or floating logs, with those on land (at cliff faces, rock outcrops, and streams) taking the form of snakes or birds (Lepowsky 1995:51). Those in the sea are known to "capsize a canoe and drown its occupants." They can be "placated through magical acts such as chewing ginger root while uttering a spell, then spitting charmed saliva on the surface of the sea" (Lepowsky 1995:51).

In some coastal communities in Great Britain, ships were deliberately wrecked for profit and even revenge through special rituals. In terms of the later, Bassett (1885:113) reported that "Margaret Barclay caused the wreck of a ship by molding a figure of it in wax and casting it into the sea. She sank her husband's brother's ship, in sight of land." Folklore from Northern Ireland describes how the Inver tragedy of the 1880s where more than 60 fishermen drowned was due to sorcery by a witch from near Donegal who placed a wooden bowl (symbolizing the fishing boats) into a washtub filled with water (symbolizing the sea) and stirred the water until the bowl sank (St. Clair 1971:47).

On Inishkea South Island, off the coast of western Ireland, is a cylindrical "stone idol" known as Neevougi or Naomhóg that possesses "immense" power and which "is invoked when a storm is desired to dash some hapless ship upon their coast" (Tennent 1852:121; see also White 1959:96–110). The stone is broken into a number of pieces, weighs 0.9–1.4 kg, and is wrapped in red flannel (White 1959:118). During the nineteenth century the Inishkea Islanders were infamous for their piracy and for attacking, robbing, and wrecking passing boats. Another account documents use of the stone as a "fertility god" and that it was "able to stimulate the growth of potatoes" (White 1959:99, 118). Another account describes a "wooden idol" in the form of a "rudely carved image of a man, about eight feet high, dressed in a long flannel gown" (J. E. M. 1873:448). The figure was kept in a special hut used as a place of worship and was brought down to the edge of the shore to halt gales when fishing vessels were unable to be launched and the community suffered "great privations" (J. E. M. 1873:448).

Shipwreck Avoidance Rituals

Numerous maritime communities possess a range of rituals, including charms, votive offerings, and taboos, to help avoid shipwreck. For example, in Scotland during the Middle Ages, a stone with an engraved ship on one side was used as a charm against shipwreck (Bassett 1885:459). In addition to use as charms against drowning, mariners also used cauls as charms to ward off shipwreck. For example, in the eighteenth century it was common for mariners of southern Europe to "suspend a child's caul in the cabin of a ship to save her from sinking" (Bassett 1885:461). In Sunderland of northeast England, wives provided their husbands with bread baked on Good Friday to "avert shipwrecks" (Henderson 1879:82). In England, charms in the form of human remains, such as hands, were once believed to help ward off shipwreck (Bassett 1885:458). On the Isle of Man, feathers picked up during the wren hunt were used as charms against shipwreck (Bassett 1885:458). Japanese mariners will "appeal" to the sea deity Suitengu to help avoid shipwreck (Ashkenazi 2003:256).

For Islamic mariners of the Red Sea, sea spirits (jinn) are known to have the power to manipulate the minds of mariners such that they wreck their vessels on reefs. Jinn also have the power to "stir up the waves and summon gales" (Agius 2019:211). To avoid such mischievous powers, mariners attempt to appease jinn through offerings into the sea, such as coconuts in model boats and food placed into floating boxes (Agius 2017:150–151, 2019:212). Burning incense on board vessels is also known to keep jinn away (Agius 2019:209). Johann (John) Burckhardt (1829:347) adds that the mariners also throw food into the sea to both feed and appease the "evil spirits [who] dwell among the coral rocks." Hadandiwa of the central west coast of the Red Sea "are aware of the danger of *jinn* living in the sea; therefore, eating seafood is prohibited, while sea shells and fish bones are used as protection from danger and are worn as amulets against evil" (Nicolini 2005:160).

Fishermen in the north of England have a taboo against turning a loaf of bread upside-down for fear that "for every loaf so turned a ship will be wrecked" (Henderson 1879:120). Jersey Islanders off the Normandy coast of France have a similar taboo against placing the cut side of a loaf of bread upward on a table for fear of causing their boat to capsize (Bois 2016:62, 122). In Holland overturning a saltcellar was considered unlucky, with each upturning resulting in a shipwreck (Bassett 1885:438). Jersey mariners would only eat a boiled egg through the side, as "opening an egg from either end may have been symbolic of up-ending the boat and might cause it to be holed or capsize" (Bois 2016:69). In Somerset, England, people poke a hole through an eggshell to ensure that it is not used as a boat by fairies to go out to sea and wreck ships. Similarly, in northeast England, Jersey, Holland, Spain, Russia, and the southeastern United States, egg shells are smashed to ensure that they are not available to witches to be used as boats (Bassett 1885:373–374; Bois 2016:69; Gill 1993:96–98; White and Hand 1970:120). Icelandic fishers will remove the eyes of a blue shark as it is boarded due to a belief that if the shark makes eye contact with each crew member, then either a crew member will soon die or the boat will soon sink (Davidsson 1900:328). Icelanders also believe that if a stone is thrown over a vessel that is "putting to sea" then it "will be lost, or will never return." Furthermore, "If one beckon to boats or ships at sea, or count them, they will all be lost" (Powell and Magnusson 1866:640).

Shipwrecks as Ghosts and Gravesites

Numerous coastal communities of the United Kingdom, Europe, and North America have diverse stories of ghost, spectral, or phantom ships (Arnold

2013:Chapter 2; Bassett 1885:Chapter 10; Rappoport 1928:Chapter 10). In some cases, the ghost ships are ancient, as in the case of Norse (Viking) ships and associated crews seen by Newfoundlanders during the nineteenth and twentieth centuries (Jarvis 2017:98–101). Invariably, these ghost ships are crewed by restless spirits of shipwrecked and drowned mariners and their appearance is considered a bad omen presaging danger. Many ghost ships are not only self-propelled (i.e., moving without wind or sails), but in places such as Ireland and Cornwall they were also seen sailing across the sea and land (Bassett 1885:352–355, 362, 366, 369). Cornish fishermen talk of seeing a phantom ship illuminated by Jack Harry's Lights with drowned sailors on the ship's deck (Hammerton 1931:300; Rappoport 1928:234). The most celebrated example is the famous *Flying Dutchman*, sightings of which foretell a shipwreck (Rappoport 1928:225–236; Stewart 2005:279). Sightings of the *Flying Dutchman* were recorded for many of the world's oceans during the nineteenth and first half of the twentieth century (Clary 1994:131–134).

Melanesian peoples of the Pacific have their own version of ghost ships in the form of ghost canoes. For example, Fijians have a legendry narrative of a ghost canoe sailed by Raluve and his new "bride," who disappeared together during a voyage. Their "phantom ship" can be seen at night sailing "amongst the islands and reefs of Fiji" (Reed and Hames 2023:74). For Torres Strait Islanders, ghosts of the dead (*marki*) are known to sail about in their spirit canoes at night hunting for dugong and turtle (Haddon 1904:356). Whereas ghost ships for Pacific Islanders are a normal part of life, seeing the dead at sea in ghost ships for European mariners is considered a bad omen and something to be feared.

In many cultural contexts, shipwrecks associated with loss of life are considered gravesites. The ceremonial process of placing wreaths on the sea surface above the location of shipwrecks or at memorial shrines to shipwrecks on land can be seen as a form of votive offering. In rare instances, votive offerings to shipwrecks are placed on the actual wreck site. Perhaps the most famous example of such votive offerings is RMS *Titanic* and the two plaques left on the bow (capstan) and stern by Robert Ballard and his team in 1986. Since then, numerous other memorial plaques have been placed on the wreck site. The wreck site also has a glass vial containing a sample of ashes of wreck salvager and treasure hunter Mel Fischer, who died in 1998.

In his internationally best-selling book *The Discovery of the Titanic*, Robert Ballard (1995) included an extraordinary photograph of two boots lying on the seabed near the wreck. These boots clearly came to rest on the seabed with their owner, whose body has since decayed. But the *Titanic* gravesite is not simply a gravesite of the shipwreck dead. The controversy surrounding the survival statistics based on class, gender, and ethnicity and the silencing of deeds of heroism of the anonymous poor, those manning the boilers, and other lower-class workers in contrast to headlines featuring the named rich and famous has ensured that *Titanic*'s dead are also a monument to social stratification and exclusion (Biel 1997; Bier 2018).

The notion of shipwreck as gravesite is exemplified well by attempts to counter justifications for the recovery of objects from the *Titanic* through the NOAA *RMS Titanic* Maritime Memorial Act of 1986. The primary purpose of the act is to "encourage international efforts to designate *RMS Titanic* as an international maritime memorial to those who lost their lives aboard the ship in 1912" and to discourage salvage or disturbance of the site (NOAA 2001:18906). The decision of NOAA (2001:18907) to declare the wreck site a gravesite took into consideration preservation of human remains.

In some respects, the special treatment of sunken warships as gravesites is predicated upon the special treatment extended to the physical remains of service people wherever they may rest. This association has nationalist and religious overtones. As Jason Harris (2001:107) notes, "Dying for one's country is the equivalent of dying for God. The two ideas are intertwined and concepts of religion are inexorably intertwined with a soldier's death." Harris (2001:123) argues that nation-states are morally and duty bound to protect their military dead, and as such "disturbance of a sunken warship is improper when it is the final resting place of deceased military personnel."

One of the most famous and sacred of US military shipwrecks is the USS *Arizona* battleship, which was sunk in Pearl Harbor by the Japanese on 7 December 1941 with the loss of 1,177 officers and crew (the remains of most remain entombed within the wreck). The wreck is listed in the National Register as a national historic landmark, owned by the US Department of the Navy, and managed by the US National Park Service. The wreck is considered a national shrine, with a memorial enclosure above it listing the names of her deceased. Survivors of the disaster are entitled to have their ashes interred within the ship while personnel stationed on the ship before the attack are entitled to have their ashes spread across waters covering the wreck. In this sense the wreck of the USS *Arizona* is an active cemetery. Many visitors to the site see oil leaks from the wreck as "tears," implying the wreck is both animate and sentient.

In some cases, offerings are made to shipwreck sites. Westerdahl (2002:58) notes, "It has been mentioned that coins have been offered to wreck sites or stones have been used to 'stone down' the dead people inside the wreck. This might actually be an explanation to the contamination of ship wrecks with later stray finds." Although a sign at the USS *Arizona* memorial requests visitors not to throw coins onto the wreck, National Park Service personnel periodically dive the wreck to remove coins (Lenihan 1991).

Treatment of Castaways

In a range of coastal contexts, treatment of castaways involved spirits and ritual intervention, ranging from votive offerings of thanks to rejection and even execution. In terms of the former, ancient Greek and Roman shipwreck survivors were known to make votive offerings of their castaway clothes and their hair to the gods in gratitude for escaping death (Bassett 1885:393). On the coast of France, fishers who survive shipwreck would give thanks to God by visiting a church. Anson (1965:69) notes that the survivors "wore the same clothes as when their escape took place. It is recalled that sometimes they jumped into the sea, and walked into the chapel dripping wet."

In many cases, shipwreck castaways attributed their survival to prayer and the divine intervention of God. For example, castaways of Christian faith from the *Centaur*, wrecked during a storm off the coast of Jamaica in 1782, attributed their survival and "salvation" to "prayers," "Divine Providence," and the "loving kindness of the LORD" (Inglefield 1795:4, 9, 12; Figure 17). More recently, in 1955, the Singh family attributed their survival in treacherous seas "empty of humanity" on a makeshift raft following boatwreck during a voyage between the islands of Vanu Levu and Viti Levu in Fiji to constant praying to various Hindu gods such as Vayu (wind god), Yama (god of death), Varuna (god of water and the moon), Brahma (lord of creation), and Vishnu (creator, preserver; Singh 2003:70, 87, 94, 122, 131, 135).

During the process of shipwreck, Trobriand Islander sailors note that they can hear the screams of the *mulukwausi* (spirit witches who feed on castaways) as they fly in with the wind but know they are protected by *kayga'u*, a magical cloaking mist (Malinowski 1922:Chapter 10). Part of this protection also involves reciting the *kaytaria* spell to bring the big fish *iraviyaka*, upon which the castaways hitch a ride back to their island. Yet their ordeal is not over, as the castaways know that the *mulukwausi* will have followed them ashore. They throw ritual stones onto the beach before it is safe to leave the water. On the shore the castaways undertake further rituals of spiritual protection involving placing special leaves and spitting ginger onto the ground where they walk. Waiting until night, the castaways proceed to their village knowing they remain invisible because of the cloaking mist of the *kayga'u* magic. Here they enter the house of a maternal relative. Knowing the smell of saltwater on their skin continues to attract *mulukwausi*, the castaways spend five days inside the house being smoked and finally washed with water and coconut. Only then are they safe to return to their homes.

In northeast Scotland, fishermen who were sole survivors of wrecks were treated poorly by their townsfolk, who believed that singular survival had a bad

Figure 17. Praying to God for divine intervention during a storm to allow survival from the wreck of the *Centaur* off Jamaica in 1782 (from Inglefield 1795).

spiritual association (Guthrie 1889:44–45). Thus, far from considered callous behavior, the belief was underpinned by a "far deeper-seated terror of the sea's vengeance" (Hole 1967:188).

Perhaps the best documented example of ritual rejection of castaways comes from Torres Strait. Haddon (1904:278) was informed by the Goemulgal people of Mabuyag in western Torres Strait that "any stranger or uninvited arrival of whatever colour, condition, or circumstance was killed." Furthermore, "The strangers' cheeks, eyeballs, tongue, ears and heart were eaten" (Haddon 1904:278). Mabuyag people added that canoe and shipwreck castaways, known as *sarup*, were also killed (Haddon 1935:56, 349). In 1870 Henry Chester (1870:3) visited Tudu in central Torres Strait and reported that "Natives of other islands who may have the misfortune to be cast-away are barbarously put to death on landing at Toot [Tudu] if found below high water mark, but should they have strength to crawl into the bush and make themselves known to the first passer by, their lives are spared." Landtman (1927:179) shed further light on the topic of killing castaways based on his work with Kiwai people of the adjacent New Guinea coast: "It is universally believed that shipwrecked people are dangerous to their rescuers. They are thought to be 'wild' and possessed of the craving to cause as many as possible to die with them." A number of traditional stories from Torres Strait (including the adjacent New Guinea coast) similarly incorporate killing of *sarup* castaways (including removal of skulls) associated with canoe mishaps (Lawrie 1970:74–75, 345–346; Haddon 1935:349; Landtman 1917:373–377; see also McNiven 2018b; Scott 2004).

Conclusion

The information presented in this chapter makes it clear that most if not all mariners incorporated ritual practices as a routine part of voyaging. The skills of the mariner extend well beyond the technical dimensions of boat use and navigation to include a wide range of ritual practices associated with propiti-ating or rewarding spiritual entities for safe travel. Voyaging rituals may take place before, during, or after a voyage. In many cases, rituals on land, such as those in churches, have a materiality that is highly conducive to archaeologi-cal documentation and analysis (e.g., ship graffiti). However, archaeologists have also been successful in recovering evidence of voyaging rituals that took place on board vessels (e.g., recovery of effigies of gods and saints, and incense burners, from shipwrecks) and even offerings made into the sea (e.g., recovery of metal, stone, and ceramic votive offerings from the seabed).

Poly-liminality of the sea for most maritime peoples ensures that casualties of death or near-death experiences at sea are classed as ontologically unstable and even metaphysically dangerous. For example, drowned people were seen as victims of the agency of the sea, and indeed possessions of the sea beyond the human realm. Drowning victims lost at sea often transformed into tortured ghosts and restless souls trapped in a liminal state between the corporeal and spiritual realms. In a number of maritime societies, the process of possession commenced with the process of drowning such that onlookers knew rescue attempts would be futile. In other cases, those victims who evaded a drown-ing death, such as shipwreck castaways, were treated as liminal people caught between two ontological domains, that is, partly possessed by the sea and partly beyond the human realm. The liminality of drowning victims helps explain numerous European historical examples of the burial of the anonymous dead found washed up on beaches at the sea–land boundary, either within the intertidal zone or immediately above the high-water mark. In contrast, known and named drowning victims lost at sea were sometimes memorialized by a symbolic representation of the body, such as a gravestone in a cemetery, a wall plaque in a church, or a "relic" from the associated shipwreck. That is, bodies of the anonymous drowned dead were buried outside of community space due to their metaphysically dangerous state, while the known and named dead lost at sea were memorialized inside of community space due to the absence of the metaphysically dangerous corpse.

The liminal and metaphysically dangerous status of the drowned dead extended to the liminal status of shipwrecks. In many cases, the ontological instability of shipwrecks related to an understanding of their animate and other-than-human status as object-beings. That is, in common with drowned people, the process of shipwreck was conceived of as analogous to death by drowning. Expressions of the liminal status of shipwrecks include the existence of cursed shipwrecks and ghost ships, both of which were considered spiritually dangerous and to be avoided. As with the drowned dead, considerable ritual activity surrounded the treatment of shipwrecks and objects associated with shipwrecks. In addition, mariners could draw on an arsenal of ritual practices (including charms and offerings) to help obviate shipwreck.

Archaeological understandings of the spiritual and ritual dimensions of voyaging mishaps are poorly developed. To date, insights have focused on the recovery of anomalous burials of people, either informal burials near the sea–land boundary or bodiless graves within cemeteries. Historical evidence presented in this chapter reveals that such graves should not be considered anomalous but entirely consistent with maritime cultures and the liminal status of the drowned dead. It is in this context that the identification of archaeological biomarkers of drowning hold much promise to see if such victims were treated differently in terms of mortuary practices. For example, it is known that some of the seawater that enters the lungs of marine drowning victims passes into the bloodstream and bone marrow cavities. As such, the presence of microscopic marine organisms (e.g., diatoms, phytoplankton) in bone cavities, especially large limb bones, is indicative of drowning in saltwater (Andrade et al. 2022; Carlie et al. 2014). This investigation technique was applied successfully by Andrade and colleagues (2022) to a 5,000-year-old adult male burial excavated from the Atacama Desert immediately inland of the coast in northern Chile; saltwater microfossils (e.g., phytoplankton and sponge spicules) were recovered from the marrow cavity of the right tibia and left humerus.

8

Sentient Elements

Agentive Tides, Waves, and Winds

Maritime peoples engage with three fundamental and dynamic elemental forces of the sea that influence not only use of the sea but also activities on land—tides, waves, and winds. The critical question is: Who or what controls these elemental forces? For most maritime peoples, such elemental forces are also spiritual, animate, and in many cases sentient to the extent that they can be both socially understood by people but also socially engaged and open to manipulation and control through special ritual practices. This chapter engages with a broad range of literature on the spiritual agency and ritual control of tides, waves, and winds by selected maritime peoples around the world.

Tides

Most published texts on tides focus on the history of Western and Islamic scientific thought and gradual understandings of the causal relationship between tides and astronomical movements of the earth, moon, and sun (Aldersey-Williams 2017; Aleen 1967; Cartwright 1999, 2001; White 2017). The astronomical theory of tides can be documented back to the ancient Greeks (Irby 2021:30–33). Yet many coastal peoples, including Europeans before and during the Middle Ages, developed alternative and reliable understandings of how and why tides operate (Frake 1985). Despite the enormous amount of scholarship on seafaring and maritime communities of the Mediterranean, little has been documented and published about the spiritual and ritual dimensions of its tides. Much of this dearth probably relates to the Mediterranean witnessing little tidal action, with a mean tidal amplitude of less than half a meter, compared to meters in the Atlantic and other oceans of the world. For example, northern Australia has tidal amplitudes of up to 9 m, while the Bay of Fundy in southeast Canada has the world's largest tides at 16.3 m and flow speeds of 15 km per hour (Shaw et al. 2010). In Torres Strait of northeastern Australia, tidal ranges of many meters have a major impact on marine food subsistence practices of local Islanders, while strong tidal currents have a major influence on sea crossings and navigation. The intimate relationship between Torres Strait Islanders and tidal movements is expressed in their "more than 80 terms for different tides and tidal conditions" (Nietschmann 1989:69).

For many coastal communities around the world, tidal flows are seen to exert positive and negative influences on land-based activities, such as subsistence practices (e.g., fishing, farming, hunting), major transformational events in life (e.g., pregnancy, birth, puberty, death), and state of being and health. For example, nineteenth-century fisherfolk of Portessie in northeast Scotland knew that it was good luck to work on fishing nets and the baiting of lines during a rising tide (Gregor 1886:9). Fishermen from Kilkeel in Northern Ireland know it is bad luck to put fishing nets into boats on an ebb tide (St. Clair 1971:44). In the Orkney and Shetland Islands of far northern Scotland, farmers know that it is best to churn butter, dig the soil, dig up turfs for thatching, and weed plants on a flowing (rising) tide (Marwick 1975:78). Mating of cows and bulls on a rising tide was also thought to result in bigger calves that would be born during daylight (Marwick 1975:78). Breton farmers of France only sow clover during incoming tides (Hammerton 1931:300, 303). Sowing clover during an ebbing or low tide will result in crop failure or cows bursting who feed upon it. Milk taken from a cow during a rising tide will boil over in a pot on a stove. These same farmers state that bacon tastes better from pigs killed on an outgoing tide (Rappoport 1928:42). In coastal villages of northeast Scotland, "goodwives . . . set their eggs when the tide was ebbing, so that hen-birds might be produced. Putting the eggs below the mother when the tide was rising secured male birds" (Gregor 1881:141). Icelanders hold that "more blood flows from sheep killed while the sea is running out" (Farrer 1879:306). The coastal people of Maine in the US Northeast understand that one should only boil (prepare) soap on a "coming tide" (Beck 1957:69).

Orkney Islanders of Scotland have an "objection to marrying except with a growing moon, while some even wish for a flowing tide" (Tylor 1871:1:117). They also know that a marriage ceremony performed at low water will bring bad luck in the form of no children (Hole 1967:184). In a related sense, in many parts of Brittany the birth of children is associated with a rising tide or when the tide is nearly high, while in Tréguier (Brittany) it is believed that women tend to give birth with an ebbing tide (Rappoport 1928:41). Bretons associate the birth of boys with an incoming tide and the birth of girls with an ebbing tide (Rappoport 1928:41). They similarly know that a boy born on an ebbing tide will probably eventually drown (Anson 1965:41). Palauans of Micronesia hold that women tend to give birth on falling tides. Indeed, nurses in Palau's hospital are known to say to women in labor that "the tide will turn soon and then the baby will come" (Johannes 1981:35). On Erub in eastern Torres Strait of northeast Australia, local Indigenous Erubam midwives attending a birth ask: "What's the tide? It makes the baby come sooner when the tide is coming in again. Go watch the tide, make the baby go calmer when the tide comes back again" (Mye 2007:59–60). Kwakwaka'wakw women of the Northwest Coast of Canada will have afterbirth buried at either the high- or low-tide mark in order to halt further pregnancies ("drown further births"; Boas 1932:202).

In the first century CE, the Roman Pliny the Elder reflected in his *Natural History* that "Aristotle adds that no animal dies except when the tide is ebbing. This has been widely noticed in the Gallic Ocean, and has been found to hold good at all events in the case of man. This is the source of the true conjecture that the moon is rightly believed to be the star of the breath, and that it is this star that saturates the earth and fills bodies by its approach and empties them by its departure" (quoted in Cartwright 2001:116). The association of an ebbing tide with the death of people was also common belief across various parts of Europe and Great Britain in the Middle Ages and through to at least the early twentieth century (Henderson 1879:58; Rappoport 1928:42). The Spanish held that "all who die of chronic diseases breathe their last during the ebb" (Lean 1903b:576). Thomson (1996:101) recounts an early twentieth-century story from County Mayo on the west coast of Ireland where after a particular woman died on her bed it was said that "she went out with the ebb tide," and indeed a close relative observed, "I was looking from the window when God took her and I never saw the water lower than it was that minute" (Thomson 1996:101). When Thomson (1996:103) inquired "whether death always came at low tide," he was informed: "No. But if a beast or person is anyways weak, then their strength will fail and build with the ebb and flow." In various districts along the coast of US New England, a person on their deathbed will be kept informed of the state of the tide such that they can die on an ebbing tide (Bassett 1885:29; see also Beck 1957:69). In contrast, Palauans of Micronesia believe that people generally die on a rising tide (Johannes 1981:35).

In Tréguier in Brittany in northwest France, people drink seawater as a purgative; the seawater should be obtained during an ebbing tide to be efficacious (Rappoport 1928:31). Similarly, people of Brittany know that washing the skin with seawater to cure erysipelas (skin infection) is best done during an ebbing tide (Rappoport 1928:32). According to Rappoport (1928:41), mariners from Lower Brittany associate rising tides with depositing poison on beaches and ebbing tides with seawater that is "pure and more salty" as the poison is taken away with the froth. Yet in Brittany it is generally believed that a sick man will get better with a rising tide and that his strength decreases with the ebbing tide (Rappoport 1928:41). In contrast, in northeast Scotland, sea water is taken from a rising tide to help cure joint pain and spine disease (Gregor 1884:356). In East Anglia, east England, whooping cough could be cured by exposing sufferers to an incoming tide, with the disease taken away by the ebbing tide (Hole 1967:184). Along the central west coast of Ireland, it is known that heel and hand splinters resulting from inadvertently touching or stepping on a sea urchin in the intertidal zone "cannot be removed with the ebb tide"; extraction using a needle is only possible once the spines soften on a rising tide (Becker 2000:150). The Kaole Islamic community of the Swahili coast of Tanzania, East Africa, know that "if someone wants to get rid of bad luck or bad spirits a ritual is performed as the tide is getting low, so that misfortunes are taken out of the body and spirit and sent away with the receding water" (Uimonen and Masimbi 2021:38). Alternately, "When people want to bring back something they have lost, such as a job, friends or income, losses that can be caused by envy and bad spirits, at high tide they can pray to God [Allah] to bring it back" (Uimonen and Masimbi 2021:38).

In various places around the world, the rise and fall of tides is associated with either the breathing (inhalation and exhalation) or drinking (ingestion and regurgitation) of a monstrous being. The Roman geographer Pomponius Mela in the first century CE posited that the "world is a single animate being" and that tidal movements are caused "by its own breathing" (quoted in Cartwright 2001:113). The ancient Norse knew that the god Thor caused the tides with his powerful breathing (Andrews 1998:205). The Shetland and Orkney Islanders of northern Scotland associate the rise and fall of tides with the breathing of a sea monster or serpent that resides in the depths. It is believed the giant creature takes about six hours to breathe in and about six hours to breathe out (Bassett 1885:28; Rinder 1895:57). People of Brittany and Normandy hold that tides are caused by the "breathing of a great monster that comes up to the surface of the water at regular intervals to breathe" (Anson 1965:46).

The Māori of Aotearoa/New Zealand hold that Tangaroa-whakamau-tai is a key "guardian of the ocean" and "controller of tides" (and controller of fish) who some say takes the form of a "monster" and who breathes twice a day to cause the rise and fall of the tides (Reed 1967:71–72). Tangaroa was known to visually express himself, with the Rev. Johann F. H. Wohlers (1874:5) reporting that "sometimes he might be seen for a few seconds standing on the crest of the waves of the sea, when the sun happened to shine against some misty spray." Other Māori accounts state that Rona-whakamau-tai, who was connected with the moon, also was a controller of tides, as was Te Parata, a giant sea creature who lived far out to sea and who similarly controlled the tides by his breathing (Orbell 1996:204; Reed 1967:398).

Aboriginal people of the Forrest River District of northwest Australia associate the tidal process with Lumiri, a large saltwater snake being who "makes the tides by emitting the water from his inside, and causes them to recede by swallowing the water" (Elkin 1930:349). In northeast Australia, Kaurareg Aboriginal people of southwest Torres Strait speak of Waubin, a legendary warrior being who turned into a stone now known as Hammond Rock located off the northeast coast of Kirriri (Hammond Island). Waubin is associated with creating the strong tidal current that runs through the Prince of Wales Channel (Waubinin Malu or "The Sea of Waubin") on the northern side of Kirriri "to discourage outsiders from venturing further south into the Kaurareg area" (Southon and Kaurareg 1998:221).

Coastal peoples of the Malay Peninsula associate the rise and fall of tides with movements of a huge crab on the seabed. According to Skeat (1900:6–7, 92), in the middle of the ocean grows a huge tree called Pauh Jangi or Pauh Janggi, at the base of which is a "cavern" (often linked to a whirlpool) known as Pusat Tassek or Pusat Tasek (Navel of the Seas or Navel of the Ocean) inhabited by a "gigantic crab." The crab's daily movements in and out of the cavern to feed cause the tides. That is, the crab existing the cavern results in water rushing in and an ebbing tide. The crab's return forces water out of the cavern and a rising tide.

In southeast China, the Qiantang River hosts Silver Dragon, the largest tidal bore in the world (Berry 2015:47). The bore is 4 m high, travels at a speed of 10–20 km per hour, and can be heard 20 minutes before it is seen. One legendary narrative associates the bore with the spirit of a fifth-century-BCE general who was murdered and thrown into the river (Aldersey-Williams 2017:216–217). Numerous "monuments have been built along the river in order to propitiate the dragon, which has claimed many lives down the centuries" (Aldersey-Williams 2017:75). Specifically, George Darwin (1899:71) reported that the "people at Haining [city on the Qiantang River] still continue to pay religious reverence to the bore, and on one of the days when Captain Moore was making observations [1892] some five or six thousand people assembled on the river-wall to propitiate the god of the waters by throwing in offerings."

The Tlingit of the Northwest Coast of Canada and southeastern Alaska have a tradition that the ebb and flow of tides is controlled by an old woman who lives in a cliff beside the sea. Legend holds that the old woman refused to allow tidal action until she was visited by Raven, who forced her to allow the tides to rise and fall after he pricked her buttocks with spines from a sea urchin (Swanton 1909:9–10). "Because Raven did this while he was making the world, nowadays, when a woman gets old and can not do much more work, there are spots all over her buttocks" (Swanton 1909:10).

Strong tidal currents and whirlpools are a feature of the Strait of Messina which separates mainland Italy and Sicily and the Tyrrhenian Sea from the Ionian Sea (Alpers and Salusti 1983). Homer in the *Odyssey* states that the ancient Greeks associated the strait and its navigational dangers with a sea monster (Scylla) and the treacherous Charybdis personified as a whirlpool. According to Homer, Charybdis created the large whirlpool by sucking down water (Hopman 2024:168; Irby 2021:33). The strait is 4 km at its narrowest and mariners needed to carefully avoid the dangers between both rocky cliffs (one with Scylla's cave) which has become a proverbial saying "caught between Scylla and Charybdis" or more commonly "caught between a rock and a hard place." Corbin (1995:13) notes: "Every late eighteenth-century tourist dreamed of visiting the straits of Sicily and confronting the terrifying Homeric creatures to be found there."

A whirlpool known as the Swelkie is located within the Pentland Firth, the strait that separates the Orkney Islands from the northeast tip of mainland Scotland. This strait has some of the strongest tidal currents in the world, reaching speeds of 30 km per hour. The Swelkie, according to legend (probably of Viking origin), is said to be caused by two female giants, Fenia and Menia, as they rotate their "magic quern Grotti" and "grind salt for the ocean" (Marwick 1975:32).

The Gulf of Corrievreckan/Corryvreckan located between the islands of Jura and Scarba off the central west coast of Scotland is a "treacherous tideway of currents and whirlpools" and according to local tradition is "haunted by the fiercest of the Highland storm-kelpies" (MacGregor 1937:117; see also Winchester 2001). In Scottish folklore, kelpies are shape-changing aquatic (freshwater and saltwater) spirit beings that usually take the form of a horse but can also take human form. The "most noted whirlpool of the Corrievreckan is that known as the *Cailleach*, meaning the Old Hag. She is believed to be a female kelpie; and her sinister activities are well recorded in the sea-lore of Western Europe" (MacGregor 1937:118). According to Alasdair MacGregor (1937:119), vessels caught within the "whirlpool of the Corrievreckan" were "saved by the throwing into the vortex of a cap or of a fragment of cork, which appeased the wild waters until they had sailed beyond their influence."

On the Northwest Coast of Canada, the chief of the undersea world in Kwakwaka'wakw cosmology is Kumugwe', who is associated with whirlpools (Shearar 2000:65). More ominously, 'Yagis is a Kwakwaka'wakw sea monster who is capable of causing "dangerous whirlpools" (Shearar 2000:119). A little to the south in the northern part of the US state of Washington, the Samish people associate a strong tidal current that runs through Deception Pass in Puget Sound with a "maiden" who was a mortal but went to live in the sea with a male sea being of human form after he was granted permission from her father to marry him. To successfully navigate the dangerous tidal current, travelers would "think about the maiden; if they did not keep their minds on her, their canoes would get caught in the whirlpool and they would sink" (Clark 1953:199).

In some coastal contexts, people had the capacity to ritually manipulate tidal processes. For example, Owatatsumi-no-kami, the Shinto sea deity dragon of Japan who controls the tides with magical jewels, loaned the tide jewels to the Empress Jingo for an invasion of Korea in the third century (Ashkenazi 2003:103). The tide jewels (one for the rising tide and one for the falling tide) were collected and delivered by Isora, the "Spirit of the Seashore." As the Japanese fleet neared the Korean coast, the Korean army launched a fleet of ships. As the Korean ships got near the Japanese fleet, Empress Jingo threw the ebb tide jewel into the sea and the Korean fleet became stranded on the exposed seabed. After many Korean soldiers died after a volley of Japanese arrows, the empress then threw the flood-tide jewel into the sea, which saw nearly all the remaining Korean soldiers drown. The king of Korea surrendered, and Isora collected the tide jewels and returned them to the sea god (Davis 1912:331).

Hornell (1914:18–19) observed that shark charmers (Kadalkattis) in the Gulf of Mannar between southeast India and Sri Lanka also had the power to control tidal currents. The ritual practice included use of a charm of Hindu origin inscribed with Tamil text: "With the help of the power of Siva and his consort, with the help of his grace, of his strength and of his priests, (I conjure you) Oh Subramanian, Lord of Earth, Oh Hanuman, and Oh Arjuna, supreme Lord, come, with a current from the south towards the shore" (Hornell 1914:19).

Haddon (1904:352) recorded a Kaurareg Aboriginal man from southwest Torres Strait who was a powerful ritual specialist with the capacity to "make the sea advance upon the land by taking a block of coral from the edge of the fringing reef and putting it under a tree and in due time the water would come up to the block of coral. He also could cause the sea to return to its normal level." In recent times, Kaurareg have indicated that tidal "currents can be slowed down by making offerings to the spirits associated with them" (Southon and Kaurareg 1998:224). Up until the early nineteenth century, the Kaurareg would throw the bodies of decapitated victims into the sea between Kiwain (a rock) and Thursday Island, which was seen as "feeding" the tidal current and "slowing it down" (Southon and Kaurareg 1998:224).

The Kaiadilt people of Bentinck Island in the Gulf of Carpentaria of northern Australia "address" the new moon each month, "enumerating their needs for lower than ever tides to expose outer reefs where special shellfish and other foods may be obtained" (Tindale 1977:259–260). In addition, they "appeal for bright moonlight to help them on their way. The greatest neap tides occur during the hours of darkness in the Gulf, emphasising their dependence on the favours of the moon" (Tindale 1977:260). Tindale (1977:260) adds that "it may be significant that on neighbouring Mornington Island it is highly improper for anyone to notice the new moon, or even to look in its direction."

Yanyuwa people of the Sir Edward Pellew Islands and adjacent mainland coast located west of the Kaiadilt have the capacity to ritually manipulate the agentive relationship between people and tides given that tidal forces were set in place by Spirit Ancestors (Bradley 1998:132). Ritual control involves "singing" the waves to form or to be calm or to control the physical well-being of people. A senior Yanyuwa woman informed Bradley (1998:132) that the "old men and women can sing people, they can sing them to the sea, as the tide goes out people become dry, they are tired, listless, not well, then later as the tide comes back up they are refreshed, they feel happy again. Such people have songs which make the sea theirs." Such songs are sung by "jealous" people who are resentful that others, for example, may have better hunting success than them (Bradley 1998:132).

Waves

In various maritime cultures, waves are associated with deities or other spiritual beings and entities. For example, Triton (ancient Greece) and Odin (ancient Scandinavia) had the power to control the waves. For the Irish, sea fairies have the power to create smooth or rough seas for mariners (Chadbourne 2012:72–73). In other instances, waves are seen as the personification or part of the physical expression of anthropomorphized spirit beings. For example, in the Cook Islands of the South Pacific, Tikokura took the form of a "storm-wave" and was considered an "evil spirit" (Gill 1876a:225). In Kiribati in the central Pacific, Te Nao was one of the first ancestral creator beings and was considered "The Wave" (Maude and Maude 1994:34). Aremata-Rorua ("Long-Wave") and Aremata-Popoa ("Short-Wave") are "two ocean demons greatly feared by Polynesian mariners because they were totally at the mercy of their immense power" (Knappert 1992:21). For the Mentawai Islanders off the west coast of Sumatra in Indonesia, the sea is the domain of three kinds of spirits: good, bad, and indulgent. These three spirits "fight" each other to decide on the "fate" of mariners at sea expressed through encounters with good or bad waves (Pakan 2018:73). If a mariner possesses a troublesome "soul" then the bad spirit and big and dangerous waves will prevail. Alternatively, a mariner with a "kind" soul will encounter a good spirit and harmless waves (Pakan 2018:73).

Across Scandinavia, Norse mythology speaks of waves as the nine daughters of Ægir (personification of the sea) and Rán (goddess of the sea). Icelandic poet and historian Snorri Sturluson in the *Prose Edda,* compiled around 1200

CE, lists the daughters (Brodeur 1916:219), whose names have been translated and interpreted by Arthur Brodeur (1916:137, 219) and Lindow (2001:49) as follows: Himinglæfa ("That Through Which One Can See the Heaven" or "Transparent-on-Top"), Dúfa ("The Pitching One" or "Wave"), Blódudhadda ("Bloody Hair"—a possible reference to "reddish foam atop a wave" or a reference to the "man-devouring side of her nature"—Quinn 2014:92), Hefring ("Riser" or "Lifting"), Unn ("Frothing Wave" or "Wave"), Hrönn ("Welling Wave" or "Wave"), Bylgja ("Billow"), Kára ("Powerful"), Dröfn ("Foam Fleck" or "Wave"), and Kólga ("The Cool One" or "Cool-Wave"). In Iceland, death waves (*násjóir*) are known to wreck boats and drown mariners attempting to land on the beach. After such a tragedy, "the sea seems content with its prey" and "other boats can land safely" for "it is said of them, 'They land in the death-calm of those who are drowned.'" Death waves can also be spotted at sea by their different color and by their "death-scream" said by some to be a "wild, wailing, awful cry, like that of a man in his death-agony" (Powell and Magnusson 1866:cxxxiv–cxxxv).

The Yanyuwa Aboriginal people of northern Australia know the sea to be masculine while the waves are feminine (Bradley 1998:132). Bradley with Yanyuwa Families (2022:66) elaborate: the "wave is feminine because the Spine-Bellied Sea Snake, *a-wirninybirniny*, is feminine; the wave is the sea snake and the sea snake is the wave—a powerful Dreaming Ancestor." Different features of waves embody the sea snake: crest of wave, *nanda-rayal* ("her spit"); fine mist-like seaspray of waves, *nanda-minymi* ("her condensation"); and waves hitting rocks, *nanda-ruru* ("her spray"; Bradley with Yanyuwa Families 2022: 66).

For the Burarra and Yan-nhaŋu peoples of northeast Arnhem Land of northern Australia, "the constant crashing of beach surf and of inshore waves is described as saltwater 'habitually speaking.' . . . In like manner, the more distant (and therefore less clearly audible) waters of the open sea are said to perpetually 'rumble' or 'growl.' . . . Finally, laterally flowing bodies of saltwater . . . are usually described as 'habitually walking'" (Bagshaw 1998:159).

The Yup'ik of the Bering Strait on the coast of Alaska identify the "long, high-amplitude waves generated by storms in the open Bering Sea and North Pacific" as *qairvaak* (literally, "two large waves"; Fienup-Riordan and Carmack 2011:270). The smaller of the two waves is identified as *ulcuar* (the wife) and the larger wave as *ulerpak* (the husband). The sounds of stormy waves, including sounds made when these waves lift the shore ice, is said to be associated with the married couple (Fienup-Riordan and Carmack 2011:270). While the liquid sea is associated with sentience, sea ice (frozen sea) sitting on top of the sea is considered "inanimate" by the Inuit (Bravo 2009:172).

In numerous cultural contexts, the sound of waves is equated with either spiritual entities or the dead. In terms of spiritual entities, Malinowski (1932:147) recorded that fishermen from the northern end of Kiriwina Island in the Trobriand Islands of eastern Papua New Guinea can hear spirit children "wailing—*wa, wa, wa*—in the sighing of the wind and the waves" when they are "far out into sea." Along the Cornish coast of southwest England, a sea spirit, Bucca (Puck), was behind "the hollow, mournful sound of the waves," which "foretold a tempest" (Bassett 1885:24). Matthew Maury (1855:96) stated that the "astronomer is said to see the hand of God in the sky; but does not the right-minded mariner, who looks aloft as he ponders over these things, hear his voice in every wave of the sea that 'claps its hands,' and feel his presence in every breeze that blows?"

During the nineteenth century, residents of the coastal town of Elsinore in Denmark knew that waves emitting a moaning sound are "portending death" and that the sea wants someone (Bassett 1885:24). Similarly, waves making a "sighing noise" on the coast of Cork in Ireland foreshadow the death of a "great man" (Bassett 1885:24). In the small fishing village of Portessie, northeast Scotland, residents knew that before any disaster or drowning the sea emits a "waichty (weighty) melody," "a dead groan," or simply "a groan" (Gregor 1886:8). In the small fishing village of St. Combs, northeast Scotland, it is said that you can hear "deed (dead) roar o' the sea" before a drowning or shipwreck (Gregor 1885a:306). Portessie fisherfolk also believe that the sea will not be calm until the body of a drowned person destined to be buried on land has been found (Gregor 1886:8). People of Rosehearty in northeast Scotland say that if a person drowned near the shore, breaking waves emit a "mournful sound" until the body is found (Gregor 1885c:54). The coastal folk of Brittany similarly know that roaring surf is "the cry of the numerous drowned men who are restless and agitated as long as their bodies have not yet been found and buried in consecrated ground" (Rappoport 1928:34). A Norse legend recalls that the noise made by waves breaking on a certain beach is the whispering of a king and queen buried in nearby mounds (Bassett 1885:24). In the nineteenth century, the Makah people of the US state of Washington reported that people who had drowned around Cape Flattery would emit "strange noises" through swells within sea caves on the cape to forewarn the living of an imminent storm (Reid 2015:142).

In West Africa during the late seventeenth century, local slave traders were recorded making flattering speeches to the sea and offerings of oil, cloth, corn, rice, and brandy to help smooth rough seas before a voyage (Bassett 1885:390). On the coast of Benin in West Africa in the late seventeenth century, Barbot observed that people "pray to the fetishes to make the sea favourable" (Parés 2005:76). Olokun, the sea god of Nigeria in West Africa, is considered responsible for "rough seas." Local fishermen attempt to propitiate calm seas through sacrifices of chickens and other animals (and reputedly humans in the past) to Olokun (Parrinder 1961:45).

In the Buka Passage region of the northwest Solomon Islands, local fishers know how to ritually calm the sea before going out for a day's fishing by spitting masticated special plants onto a coconut frond and then placing the frond on the beach just in reach of big waves which will "then go back and calm the sea" (Blackwood 1935:327). Spirits associated with a patch of rough sea between the islands of Kirriri and Mua in Torres Strait can be placated to bring about calmer waters by "throwing bread into the water or by lighting a cigarette and throwing it into the sea" (Southon and Kaurareg 1998:224). The Karadjeri (Karajarri) people of northwestern Australia have a ritual for decreasing wind to calm waves and produce favorable conditions for collecting pearl shell on reefs. The ritual involves cleaning out a hole in the ground, lighting a fire in the hole, covering the fire with bushes, and making a verbal request to the ancestral being who established the ritual to bring on the "calm" (*rauwin*; Piddington 1932:392).

In the seventeenth century on the isle of Westray in the Orkneys it was known that if a man in the possession of iron (including iron nails in his shoes) steps onto a rock known as Less located off Noup Head, that the "sea will instantly swell in such a tempestuous way, that no boat can come near to take him off, and that the Sea will not be settled till the peece [*sic*] of Iron be flung unto it" (Wallace 1693:32–33). In Iceland, throwing a stone into the sea is known to bring forth heavy seas "wherein many ships are lost" (Powell and Magnusson 1866:640). Yap Islanders of Micronesia were known to cast a certain plant into the sea accompanied by incantations to induce heavy seas and storms (D'Arcy 2006:147).

Among the Marind-anim of Indonesian Papua, waves are conjured through the utterance of special words coupled with special offerings (van Baal 1966:878). For example, the sea could be calmed by throwing food over the water and saying "*Wandus! Wandus!* You should lie down!" Alternatively, rough seas could be conjured to reap havoc on a village or drown an enemy by throwing a special offering into the sea and uttering "*Yorma! Yorma!* Kill!" The Marind-anim when canoeing through the Muli Strait refrain from throwing rubbish into the sea and making noise to avoid enraging Yorma (sea *dema* spirit; van Baal 1966:385).

In the early fifth century, the bishop of Rome sent St. Germanus, bishop of Auxerre, and St. Lupus, bishop of Troyes, to Britain to preach Christianity. While crossing the English Channel they were hit by a storm courtesy of the devil. After Germanus "rebuked the sea and poured a few drops of oil into it, the raging of the waves ceased" (Grant 1880:135). In Scotland during at least the nineteenth century, "holy oil" and "holy water" poured onto the sea were known to be "efficacious" to "still the waves in case of a storm" (Grant 1880:578–

579). The Kwakwaka'wakw on the Northwest Coast of Canada make the sea calm by throwing boiling seawater upon it (Boas 1932:231). They also can calm rough seas inhibiting canoe landings on the beach by hanging over the side of the canoe pieces of blue hellebore (herbaceous flowering plant) dipped into bilge water and pieces of cedar bark with menstrual blood (Boas 1932:231). In the late seventeenth century, William Bosman (1907:383) observed that coastal peoples of Ghana in West Africa made "great Offerings" of "all sorts of Goods" to a "Divinity" of the sea to calm rough seas. Up until the 1930s, French sailors were known to cast a rosary with a string attached into the sea to calm the waves (Clary 1994:45). Tyrrhenian fishermen of the west coast of Italy during the twentieth century would remove a sacred icon or statue of a saint from safe storage below deck and hold it on the deck of their fishing vessel in a desperate attempt to calm rough seas (Baldi 1998:153).

The ninth wave is considered to have a "particular virtue" by Welsh mariners yet is feared by English mariners (Rappoport 1928:36). Indeed, English mariners believed that the destructive capacity of the ninth wave could be broken by standing on the deck of a vessel looking toward oncoming waves and making a cross symbol with the fingers (Bassett 1885:26). Beck (1999:101–102) states that an old tradition of Irish and Scottish mariners is to calm rough seas by a three-part process of making a sign of a crucifix with a knife, uttering a prayer, and then throwing the knife overboard. Miceal Ross (1994:84) points out that there are around 150 versions of "the knife against the wave" legendary tale cataloged in the National Folklore Collection of Ireland. In one version, a fisherman in Donegal Bay of northwest Ireland threw his bait knife at a "monstrous" life-threatening wave which resulted in the sea becoming smooth. That night the mariner was visited by a man on a white horse who requested he accompany him such that he could pull the same bait knife from his sister's heart. When the mariner asked why they had attempted to drown him and his crew that day, the "sea-woman" (a probable incarnation of a sea fairy) responded, "Because I am in love with you and would like to have you for myself" (Chadbourne 2012:83–85). In a related story from Inishowen in the far north of Ireland, fishermen were in great danger from a huge wave raised by fairies until one of the boat crew removed a nail from his pocket and threw it into the sea, whereupon it subsided (Ross 1994:87).

Winds and Storms

Rappoport (1928:68) notes that "seamen's tales in ancient and modern times attribute an important role to the winds, imagining them as animate beings, incarnations of lower divinities, of demons and spirits." Indeed, Bassett (1885:36) made the important point that mariners invest heavily in wind control, and "the resources of his arts and prayers were expended to obtain favorable breezes, to allay the storm, or dissipate the calm. His principal deities had most to do with the winds that either brought him good fortune, or wreck and disaster." Wind controlling rituals are undertaken to both increase and decrease the wind. Wind, especially storm, decrease rituals are usually associated with producing calmer seas and for smoother boat travel. Wind increase rituals are used to either produce winds to create favorable sailing conditions, or in extreme situations to bring forth storms to thwart the voyaging capacities of rival fishers or naval enemies.

Numerous deities (and saints in the case of Christians—see below) were propitiated by mariners to bring on favorable winds for voyaging. In some cases, these deities are either the personification of the wind (e.g., wind deities) or simply had powers to control elements such as winds (e.g., certain saints). For example, Canaanite and Phoenician mariners of the eastern Mediterranean knew of a number of Ba'al wind and storm deities, specifically the storm god Ba'al-Haddu and his three epithets Ba'al Šamêm, Ba'al Malagê, and Ba'al Sapōn (Brody 1998:10–19, 95, 2023). The later three deities could be called upon to sink enemy ships according to a seventh-century-BCE treaty between Assyria and Tyre. As such, "appeasement and patronage" of these wind/storm gods was "crucial for successful sailing" (Brody 1998:37). A shrine dating to 1550–1600 BCE and possibly dedicated to Ba'al-Haddu has been excavated in the ancient harbor site of Ashkelon on the coast of Israel (Brody 1998:56). A shrine dating to the Persian period (300–500 BCE) at Makmish, also on the coast of Israel, may be associated with worship of Ba'al Šamêm (Brody 1998:57–58). To many, Yahweh (God of the Israelites) is considered to have taken over the role of storm god from Ba'al-Haddu (Brody 1998:82; cf. Green 2003:246).

A temple dedicated to the worship of Ba'al Sapōn has been identified archaeologically at the ancient city of Ugarit located 3 km inland in northern Syria (Brody 2023:403). Significantly, the Temple of Baal complex at Ugarit features 17 stone anchors incorporated into the temple walls, near the temple entrance, and in the general vicinity of the temple, in contexts dating to between 1,200 and 3,900 years ago (Frost 1969:242). The stone anchors are subrectangular- or subtriangular-shaped tabular blocks of dressed stone with an anchor rope hole near the top. The estimated weights of the anchors fall into three groups: 400–600 kg (n = 4), 100–250 kg (n = 9), and 25–80 kg (n = 4; Frost 1969:244). Honor Frost (1969:235) argues that "it is evident that the anchors grouped in the Temple of Baal are votive." That the anchors were made specifically as votives and never "used at sea" is revealed by a lack of wear marks consistent with use as anchors at sea (e.g., chipped bases and rope marks around the holes) and the incomplete state of manufacture of many of the anchors (Frost 1991:357, 362). Frost (1991:357) makes clear the link between the votive anchors at the Temple of Baal and voyaging conditions and success when she states that "the concentration of anchors in and around a single building, which is not only associated with a storm god, but which navigators (unless blindfolded!) must have used as a land-mark, cannot be fortuitous." In short, these anchors stand as "symbols of salvation" (Frost 1991:367). Brody (1998:48) explicitly links the anchor votives with Ba'al, stating that they "are most likely thank-offerings to the Canaanite storm god." In terms of the wall and foundation stone anchors, Brody (1998:48) adds that they may be "the outcome of a 'foundation' vow since these offerings were made during the construction of the building. In other words, while in distress at sea, a sailor makes a pledge to found a building, or to add on to a sacred precinct, in order to honor a patron god." Furthermore, "Tribute to the storm god's favor continued to be offered by sailors after the completion of the temple, as is evident in the free-standing votive anchors" in the temple precinct (Brody 1998:49).

Numerous wind and storm gods are known for the Pacific. Among Polynesian societies, wind gods include La'a Maomao and Hanui-o-Rangi (Knappert 1992:164, 324), Raka Maomao (Māori, Aotearoa/New Zealand; Knappert 1992:241), Fa'atiu (Samoa; Knappert 1992:75), and Paka'a (Hawai'i) who also invented the sail (Knappert 1992:217). Cook Islanders of the central Pacific hold that running along the entire 360 degrees of the edge of the sea horizon are a series of holes through which Raka (god of winds) and his children blow (Gill 1876a:319–320). Polynesian storm gods include Afa (Samoa; Knappert 1992:15, 279); Awha, Apu Matangi, and Tawhiri-Matea (Māori, Aotearoa/New Zealand; Knappert 1992:20, 25, 279, 295, 324); and Apu-Hau (Hawai'i; Knappert 1992:20, 279). Susanowo is the Shinto god of storms in Japan (Knappert 1992:283, 296). According to Bassett (1885:141), Japanese sailors throw coins into the sea "to propitiate the god of storms." On Rossel Island off the eastern end of Papua New Guinea, the southeast trade winds are under the control of the goddess Laapî (who takes the form of a huge octopus or a crab), while the northwest winds are controlled by her husband Kpiyé (who takes the form of a moray eel; Levinson 2008:282–283).

Wind Conjuring

The following sections reveal that a broad range of ritual practices were employed by maritime peoples to conjure winds. However, it also needs to be pointed out that wind conjuring could be subtle and intangible, such as mariners

Figure 18. Bessie Millie from the village of Stromness on the island of Pomona in the Orkney Islands selling wind to a mariner in the early nineteenth century. Her boiling kettle was associated with the ritual of calling up the wind (from Bassett 1885:121).

who "will often say aloud they want to go in one direction when they intend the opposite, to trick the wind into favoring them" (Beck 1957:67).

Pomponius Mela, writing during the reign of Emperor Claudius in the first century CE, noted that women ritual specialists on the Île de Sein off the central coast of France had the power to conjure winds for mariners (Brand and Ellis 1849:5, 14–15; see also Bassett 1885:110). In the early nineteenth century an old woman named Bessie Millie from the village of Stromness on the island of Pomona in the Orkneys was well known for her power to change the wind, which she would do for mariners for a price. Her ritual involved a boiling kettle (Bassett 1885:119; Figure 18).

Fishermen of Rosehearty in northeast Scotland call up the wind by whistling (Gregor 1885c:54; see also Guthrie 1889:47). Clive Holland (1942:14) notes that "if a calm prevails a sailor-man frequently woos the good graces of St. Nicholas or St. Antonio by whistling in the hope and belief that a breeze will spring up."

T. T. Wilkinson (1869:131) recorded an old Scarborough fisherman of northeast England who stated that "we only whistle when the wind is asleep, and then the breeze comes." Mariners of northern Spain, Brittany, the Baltic Sea, and Norway in Europe (Rappoport 1928:89–90) and Texas in the United States (Mullen 1969:223) also call up favorable winds for sailing by whistling.

During the nineteenth century, German mariners and Rosehearty fishermen in northeast Scotland called up a wind by scratching their fingernails on masts (Gregor 1885c:54; Rappoport 1928:92). Some German mariners believe that scratching an "old nail" on the foremast will also raise a wind (Thorpe 1852:183).

In the first half of the seventeenth century, Italian traveler Pietro della Valle recorded that Portuguese sailors on a ship prayed to a statue of St. Anthony for favorable winds. Having no effect, the sailors bound the statue to the mast and addressed it with insults whereupon a breeze was finally raised. The statue was then untied and taken back to its "niche" on the ship (Rappoport 1928:88–89).

French sailors were aware that certain crew members were capable of controlling the winds "through the possession of a ring, worn on the little finger of the right hand." It was fatal for these ritual specialists to spend more than three months on a single voyage and no more than three days ashore (Bassett 1885:105).

In Northern Ireland, mariners threw coins overboard into the sea in order to "bring on a wind" (St. Clair 1971:47). In 1853 the ship *Lahore* was sailing between Rangoon and Calcutta in India. In order to make the wind stronger so that the ship would travel faster, a number of people on board "collected money among themselves, and had the same deposited as a propitiation, in order to ensure a favourable and stronger breeze" (Jones 1898:63). In more recent times, fisherfolk from Chesapeake Bay on the US East Coast have "buying the wind" rituals whereby a coin (e.g., dime, quarter) is thrown overboard in order to conjure wind (Carey 1977:181).

Scottish mariners of the Hebrides attach a male goat skin to the mast "in the hope of securing a favourable wind" (Grant 1880:432). English mariners would stick a knife into a mast to call up winds (Clary 1994:169). In the Western Islands of Scotland, becalmed mariners (including fishermen) visited an oracle well known as the Tobar Mòr (the Great Well) on the Isle of Gigha (MacGregor 1937:146). MacGregor (1937:146) adds that the "captains of foreign vessels windbound in these waters used to give the natives [of Isle of Gigha] a piece of money, in order that they might be permitted to consult the oracle as to the airt [direction] of the wind; and we read that all strangers were accustomed to leave at the well a coin or a pin as an oblation."

In Normandy, women called up winds to bring back their overdue fishermen husbands by burning a new broom (Rappoport 1928:93). German mariners will throw a broom in front of a ship sailing in the opposite direction in order to conjure a "fair wind" (Thorpe 1852:183). Similarly, Pomeranian fishermen of northern Europe call up favorable winds by either throwing an old broom handle into a fire or throwing an old broom without a handle overboard (Rappoport 1928:92–93).

In Brittany "wind-bound" mariners will send two crew to the chapel of St. Marine at Combrit to sweep the floor and throw the dust in the direction of the desired wind (Bassett 1885:406). Similarly, in the coastal village of Roscoff in Brittany, at least until the early twentieth century, women would call up winds by taking dust obtained from sweeping the floor of the chapel of La Sainte Union after Mass and blowing it in the direction from which favorable winds need to come to assist loved ones sail home (Rappoport 1928:85; see also Grant 1880:396). A similar tradition exists in Sardinia (Bassett 1885:143).

When Kwakwaka'wakw of the Northwest Coast of Canada wish to change winds to the northwest to obviate their canoes being "windbound," they take bundles of specially prepared ferns decorated with dentalia (tusk shells) and painted with red ochre and place these in a row on the ground and pray: "Now take pity on me, you owner of the weather. I come to ask you that you may handle lightly your weather as you are owner of the weather. Now take pity and take hold of this magic power" (Boas 1932:230). After heating the ferns over a fire, a second man prays: "Do not let your weather change too suddenly. Do not let your weather be too strong. Treat well your weather, the weather which you control, owner of the weather. A little good will be your weather. Not too strong will be your weather, owner of the weather. Now we are going to be pitied by you" (Boas 1932:230; see also Boas 1921:623–625). The Kwakwaka'wakw also have a ritual that involves kelp to call up the northwest wind which they perform in their canoes (Boas 1921:629–630). They can also call up the wind by hitting the surface of the water with a canoe paddle (Boas 1932:229).

Another ritual undertaken by the Kwakwaka'wakw to change the wind from a southeasterly to northwesterly for better canoe voyaging conditions involves crabs and clam shells (Boas 1921:620–623). Four small crabs are collected from under stones within the intertidal zone when the tide is half out. Cedar bark strips were tied to the right claw of each crab and then the crabs were suspended from long poles on the beach over a fire. After the crabs turned red, they were untied and each was placed into separate large clam shells, which were tied up with the same cedar strips used on the claws. The clams were taken "into the woods" and placed within a hollow at the base of a tree. Before the fourth clam was placed down, it was told: "Warn your friends to call strongly the northwest wind and the east wind, else you will not go back to the beach" (Boas 1921:621). The ritual operator then goes back to the beach, bathes in the sea, and waits for the wind to change. The efficacy of the crabs relates to a mythological creation period when many different types of animals were "all like men." One of these "Myth people" were crabs who had the power to control the wind. A variant of this wind ritual involves use of four starfish (Boas 1921:622).

William the Conqueror of Normandy had "the body of St. Vallery carried about to obtain favourable winds and a prosperous voyage to England" (Bassett 1885:409). Jones (1898:38) notes that when the Swedish bishop Thorlack was forced to leave Uppsala he stole the "finger-bone" of the holy Erik to "secure a favourable wind." When a "dreadful storm" ensued, Thorlack returned the holy relic to Uppsala whereupon he had fine sailing conditions. Similarly, in the early thirteenth century, a monk named Gualtier stole "a bone of the arm of St. Madélaine" from the Abbey of Fécamp in Normandy to ensure favorable winds for a sailing voyage to Jerusalem. Again, a "violent tempest" arose and after confessing to his sins, Gualtier declared to build a chapel in Jerusalem in honor of the saint. However, the rest of the crew successfully convinced the monk to return the sacred relic to the Abbey of Fécamp (Jones 1898:38–39).

The ancient Greeks had an altar at the Bosporus to Zeus, who was a sender of favorable winds (Bassett 1885:61; see also Blakely 2017:368–369). Herodotus records that during the second invasion of Greece by the Persians under the command of Xerxes in 480 BCE, the Greeks prayed and made a sacrifice to Boreas (god of the north wind) and his wife Oreithyia to conjure a storm to halt the advance of the Persian fleet down the east coast of Greece. The request for divine intervention worked: a huge storm arose and destroyed almost a third of Xerxes's fleet near Cape Sepias. In gratitude, the Greeks built a sanctuary in honor of Boreas on the side of the Ilissus River next to the Acropolis in Athens (Finkelberg 2014; Mikalson 2010:157). Athenian vase paintings from the fifth century BCE represent Boreas as a bearded male human with large wings on his back and often wearing winged sandals (Agard 1966).

To the northwest of Galway Bay in western Ireland are found small stone structures associated with controlling the wind and sea conditions. Known as Cashlān Pleimhinin or Cashlaun Flaineen, they comprise "a broken circle, or heap of stones, constructed formally with charms" with an entrance oriented toward the direction of the wind (Westropp 1922:389). The ritual function of these structures includes raising a storm or favorable winds, and bringing fish into nets (Browne 1900–2:527; Westropp 1911:43, 1922:389–390). On a more sinister note, Caesar Otway (1841:389) states that "when a ship was seen off the coast, the 'Caslaan Pleminhin' were erected to effect the wreck; the calm which generally succeeds a storm was looked to as part of the required effect, affording the opportunity of approaching and plundering the unfortunate vessel and her crew."

At St. Leven in Cornwall in southwest England is a "cubical pile of stones called Madge Figge's chair" where a witch so named would sit and "conjure up storms" (Bassett 1885:116). It is said that a light, sometimes seen hovering over the chair, is the ghost of a woman drowned in a wreck and from whom Madge removed jewelry (Bassett 1885:316). At the Church of St. Nicholas in Liverpool (original church consecrated in 1361), also known as the "sailor's church," was a statue of St. Nicholas where "mariners were wont to present a peace-offering for a prosperous voyage on their going out to sea, and a wave-offering on their return" (Jones 1898:40).

St. Columba's chapel (now ruined) on Fladda Chuan in the Hebrides islands of Scotland contained a wind charm. The altar featured a "a blue stone of a round form on it, which is always moist. It is an ordinary custom, when any of the fishermen are detained in this isle by contrary winds, to wash the blue stone with water, all round, expecting thereby to procure a favorable wind. And so great is their regard for this stone that people swear decisive oaths upon it" (Martin cited in Grant 1880:432; see also Bassett 1885:139).

Lascar (Indian/Southeast Asian) crew members of European-owned ships were known to establish onboard (possibly Hindu) shrines to assist with favorable voyaging winds. For example, a mariner reported that when his ship was becalmed in the Straits of Malacca, the Lascar crew prayed to "their idol, whose shrine, under the top-gallant forecastle, was now adorned with numerous votive offerings" (Anonymous 1900:193). The Lascar crew saw the lack of wind as punishment for the "wickedness" of their captain, who, among other things, cast "all manner of disparaging remarks about the idol."

A range of wind-making shrines were employed by Torres Strait Islanders of northeast Australia to assist with canoe voyaging in the late nineteenth century. In the western islands, "wind-makers" were usually hereditary ritual specialists and men (Haddon 1904:350). On Mabuyag, the "wind-maker painted himself red all over and took some 'bushes' (*wor*) and fixed them firmly at low tide at the edge of the reef in such a way that the flowing tide caused them to sway backwards and forwards. In due course the wind came with a steady blow, and the men went out and obtained their dugong. Should none of the meat be given to the wind-maker, he caused the wind to continue blowing so strongly that no canoes could venture out to sea" (Haddon 1904:351). Further, "To stop the wind the wind-maker painted his head and face and reddened his body in the same manner as when making rain, and also painted the 'bushes' red and dried the latter either over a fire in his house or in a sheltered sunny spot and then the wind would die away" (Haddon 1904:351).

In eastern Torres Strait, Haddon (1908:201–202) recorded a remarkable wind-making shrine known as *wag zogo* where ritual specialists (*zogo le*) conjured southeasterly winds. The shrine comprised "two boulders of a pinkish granite" of foreign origin within a basalt rock pool on the fringing reef of Mer (Haddon 1908:201). The ritual process included four to five men who "took *geribe* plants and fronds of the coco-nut palm, and after repeatedly pointing them at the stones left them there . . . [whereupon] a 'big wind' would immediately arise which lasted until the plants were removed."

The people of Auridh in central Torres Strait used a wind and rain shrine featuring a large stone of foreign origin in a giant clamshell (Haddon 1935:88–89, 361) and a portable and "potent wind charm" of anthropomorphic form made from lead (possibly a sounding weight) obtained from European mariners and painted with red ochre (Haddon 1904:353, Plate XVI.7, 1935:89).

Most of these wind-conjuring rituals were undertaken by mariners themselves. In some cases, propitiating favorable winds for voyaging also involved mariners employing female ritual specialists usually referred to in the pejorative as "witches." For example, the *Polychronicon (A Universal History)* was written in Latin by Ralph Higden (Benedictine monk of the monastery of St. Werburgh in Chester, England) in the fourteenth century and translated into English by John of Trevisa (1387) and printed by John Caxton (1482). Based on his own observations of the Isle of Man, Higden reported that certain women sell to mariners wind charms in the form of knotted thread activated by witchcraft (Babington 1869:x, 43).

In northern Sweden in the seventeenth century were wind-calling specialists who for a price would call up a wind. The process included the client purchasing a handkerchief with three knots which when undone would produce "breeze" (first knot), a "gale" (second knot), and a "hurricane" (third knot; Rappoport 1928:86; see also Bassett 1885:118–119). Knotted "napkin" wind-calling charms made by women ritual specialists ("witches") were sold to mariners in Ireland and Denmark (Bassett 1885:119). While the first two knots were for the benefit of the mariners themselves, the third knot was associated with "wicked motives" against enemies (Grant 1880:98). Similarly, three-knotted string wind-calling charms made by women were also purchased and used by mariners in Scotland and England (Brand and Ellis 1849:5; Bassett 1885:119; Rappoport 1928:84). Three-knotted string wind-calling charms were also used by Norwegian mariners (Brand and Ellis 1849:5). Olaus Magnus's 1555 book *Historia de gentibus septentrionalibus (History of the Northern Peoples)* has a woodblock print of Finnish mariners in a ship in a harbor attempting to call up a wind using a three-knotted length of rope (Westerdahl 2005b:28, Figure 16).

In the Stonehaven district of northeast Scotland during the eighteenth and nineteenth centuries, mariners would invariably consult an "ancient dame" or "wise woman" (aka a "witch") to propitiate spiritual forces to bring on favorable winds (Anson 1965:85, 90). In the nineteenth century on the island of Hoy in the southern Orkney Islands lived Mattie Black (said to have had a Native American mother) who was a well-known wind ritual specialist. One story relates how two young men engaged her services to bring on favorable winds for sailing across the Pentland Firth back to Caithness on the opposite mainland coast at the northeast point of Scotland. Mattie Black provided the mariners with three short sticks of straw, each with a color ribbon of cloth. Two straws were to be thrown overboard during the return voyage to propitiate desired sailing conditions. Also on board was the father of one of the young men who disapproved of such ritual intervention. In protest he threw the third straw overboard, which conjured a storm that blew the vessel back to Hoy (Marwick 1975:53–54).

In the seaside town of Gourock on the west coast of Scotland is a 1.8-m-high standing stone known as Kempock Stone (aka Kempoch Stane and Granny Kempock) that is positioned on top of a low cliff overlooking the Firth of Clyde (Edensor and Brophy 2023; MacRae 1880). Although the standing stone's origins are probably prehistoric, possibly Bronze Age, of interest here is its recent use (Edensor and Brophy 2023). According to David MacRae (1880:7), the stone was associated with a "witch, who for years dwelt beside the mystic stone, dispensing favourable winds to seafaring men, who secured her favour by suitable gifts."

Storm Conjuring

In Iceland, the head of a ling (fish) with its mouth kept wide open by a wooden brace placed on a high clifftop above the sea will result in a "terrible storm" from which "countless lives [will] be lost" (Powell and Magnusson 1866:civ). In Tahiti in Polynesia, certain sea deities who have control over winds could be propitiated through offerings to call up a storm to thwart invasion by a hostile fleet from a neighboring island (Ellis 1859:330). Among the Nuu-chah-nulth of the Vancouver region of southwest Canada, ritual specialists had the power to conjure storms by painting "certain marks" on the exposed beach at low tide after bathing in the sea. When rising tidal waters covered the paintings "storms and rough seas would be caused" (Drucker 1951:174). Although the specific reason for this ritual is unrecorded, Philip Drucker (1951:174) noted that certain chiefs ritually conjured storms to injure or kill whales such that they would wash ashore (see Chapter 9).

Women have been strongly associated within calling up storms in various seaside communities of the United Kingdom and northern continental Europe (Bassett 1885:110, 116). From at least the fifteenth century in Europe, female ritual specialists ("witches") were seen as "supreme over the winds" (Bassett 1885:110). In most instances, the motives behind witches calling up storms were seen as mischievous, as they were aimed at sinking vessels (Bassett 1885:110–120; Rappoport 1912:79–81). Yet in other instances it is clear that certain women were known to be wind- and storm-calling ritual specialists without the pejorative appellation of "witches." In some communities, such as in Iceland, women were weather experts within coastal communities (Willson 2016:58–60).

In 1589 Agnis Tompson and a group of fellow witches raised a tempest off the Scottish coast near Leith. To do so they took a "cat and christened it, and afterwards bound to each part of that cat the chiefest parts of a dead man, and several joints of his body" and then threw the bundle into the sea. This act was done to wreck a vessel containing jewels destined for King James VI's bride-to-be, who had arrived from Denmark (Anonymous 1779:449; see also Brand and Ellis 1849:40). In another version of the story, the head witch was Agnes Sampsoun or Samson, who confessed to raising a storm by throwing into the sea a charm comprising "four joints of dead men's fingers" (taken from a graveyard) attached "to the four feet of the cat" to prolong the stay of King James and his bride in Denmark by many months (Grant 1880:252). Agnes and her accomplices were found guilty in "mock trials" and "burned" (Grant 1880:254).

In the mid-seventeenth century in Dunrossness in the southern Shetlands, the crew of a boat drowned during a major storm sent by a local witch whom they had offended. The witch raised the storm by singing over a tub of water containing a wooden cup that increasingly became agitated to the point the cup overturned and the witch exclaimed, "The turn's done" (Grant 1880:537). Around the same time, Mary Lamont of Scotland was well known for having the power to raise a tempest at sea by throwing "small charmed stones into the flowing tide" (Grant 1880:538). In 1662 Lamont confessed to having plotted with two fellow witches "to cast the long stone" (Kempoch Stane) "into the sea, thereby to destroy boats and ships" (MacRae 1880:11). In the same year, Lamont confessed to a government commission tasked with an inquiry into witches having the power to raise storms, among other powers, and was "burned to death" (MacRae 1880:12). Soon after, Isobel Gowdie confessed that she had conjured a storm by wetting a cloth, beating it upon a stone, and calling upon Satan—a ritual process used by other witches (Bassett 1885:113). In 1716 Mrs. Hicks and her daughter were tried as witches in England for, among other things, conjuring storms and wrecking ships "by pulling off their shoes, and making with them a lather of soapsuds" (Bassett 1885:115).

In mid-nineteenth-century England, the "late Jane Nicholson was a Scarborough witch of great repute, and was much feared. If any sailor met her in the morning he would not go to sea on that day, because she had power over the winds and could raise storms" (Wilkinson 1869:132). In the 1850s in the southern Shetland Islands, two couples sailed from Dunrossness to Lerwick to buy wedding clothes. They refused to provide a lift to a local "witch," who in revenge conjured a storm. Due to the storm, the two women walked more than 30 km home; the two men returned in the boat but perished (Marwick 1975:54–55).

Storm Prevention

A wide range of rituals have been documented among maritime communities that are aimed at preventing storms. The following digest reveals that rituals include prayers to deities and gods, offerings to shrines and temples, offerings into the sea (including human sacrifices), onboard figurines of saints and ancestors, onboard charms and libations, and taboos.

Around 200 CE, the Greek writer Athenaeus recorded an incident where mariners sailing between Cyprus and Naukratis survived a bad storm as a result of praying to a small statue of Aphrodite (Atkins 2009:61). In recent centuries, sailors in Brittany knew that St. Beuzec and St. Houarden had the power to calm a treacherous sea (Rappoport 1928:87). Bretons also knew of Gallizenae, a Virgin druidesses of the Île de Sein, central coast of France, who had the power to "calm the winds" (MacKillop 2004:247). Portuguese mariners would attach an image of St. Anthony to the mast of their ship and prayer in an attempt to quell a storm. If the prayers were ineffectual then the image of St. Anthony would be beaten with sticks "to improve its behaviour" (Jones 1898:55).

According to the Greek historian Diodorus of the first century BCE, Greek mythology relates how the Phoenician prince Cadmus called upon a sea deity (cf. Poseidon) to provide protection from several storms encountered during a voyage from Phoenicia to Greece (Brody 1998:82). Cadmus subsequently built a temple in honor of the sea god on the island of Rhodes (Brody 1998:82). Similarly, in the sixteenth century, during a Ming court-sponsored trip to Japan, a ship was caught in a storm and the crew pledged to the sea goddess Mazu that they would erect a commemorative stele in her honor at one of her temples if she would end the storm. The storm had dissipated by the following morning and the ship headed to the Mazu temple at Guangshi on the nearby Fujian coast, where the crew "refurbished the building, and erected a stele on its grounds" (Hui 2002:76). More generally, Jones (1898:44–45) noted that every large Chinese junk has on board a shrine dedicated to Tien-how (deity of sailors), to which prayers are made daily during voyages for calm sailing conditions and to which Taoist priests come on board to make special chants before each voyage.

Textual records document that after being saved by his consort's prayers from a storm near Cyprus during a voyage to the Holy Land in 1254, Capetian King Louis IX of France (who later became a saint) had the consort donate a silver model of a ship to St. Nicola de Port in Lorraine that also housed a reliquary containing a relic of St. Nicolas of Myra, the well-known mariners' saint (Baader 2016:225–227). Over the past 400 years, numerous mariners have donated ex-voto paintings of their ships to churches after narrowly surviving a storm at sea.

European Christians had a tradition of ex-voto model anchors linked to storm prevention. For example, a wax anchor was hung in St. Edmunds Abbey in southeast England by the crew of a fishing boat from the nearby coastal village of Dunwich in gratitude for safe delivery from a storm by St. Edmund, probably in the late thirteenth century (Miller 2003:144). Around the turn of the twelfth century, some merchants from Bremen in Germany offered a silver anchor to St. Bernward's Church in Hildesheim, also Germany, in gratitude for escaping a storm during a voyage (Baader 2016:225).

In St. Clements Bay on the island of Jersey off the Normandy coast of France is a large granite outcrop known as Rocqueberg. This rock was a meeting place for witches, and markings on the rock were attributed to the devil's hooves and other spirits. The witches were known to dance on the rock "singing up storms" to wreck passing ships. Disaster could be avoided by throwing 13 fish onto the rock as a "tribute" to the witches (Bois 2016:13). In the eighteenth century a witch from Hayle in Cornwall, England, received payment for keeping storms away from vessels (Bassett 1885:116).

Japanese mariners would throw jewels into the sea during storms to pacify the dragon king sea god Sagara (also known as Oho-watatsumi, "sea lord, or sea snake," and Toyo-tama hiko no Mikoto, "Abundant Pearl Prince"; Mackenzie 1923:41). In the eleventh century, crew of a Chinese vessel leaving Japan "read a prayer and made an offering comprising chicken, wine, spirit-money, and some other paper items to propitiate the spirits" in an attempt to ward off unfavorable headwinds (Hui 2002:71).

In the early sixteenth century, the Carniolan diplomat and historian Baron Sigismund von Herberstein traveled through Russia and at one stage his ship was detained at a rocky promontory on the Baltic Sea by a "tempest." A sailor stated: "This rock which you see is called Semes, and unless we appease it with a gift, we shall not easily pass it." In secret, the sailor climbed the rock and made an offering of "oatmeal mixed with butter" and the storm duly abated (Jones 1898:61–62). In the seventeenth century, Greek mariners were known to throw loaves of bread consecrated to St. Nicholas into the sea to ward off storms (Bassett 1885:79, 392). Greek sailors were known to make offerings of "small pieces of bread" to the sea during a storm in an attempt to propitiate calm weather (Jones 1898:61). Similarly, Russian mariners would attempt to appease evil forces behind storms through offerings to the sea in the form of cake made from flour and butter (Jones 1898:61).

A story from Tory Island off the northwest coast of Ireland relates how a boat crew once refused to share their poitín (traditional Irish distilled beverage) with fairies in a nearby sea cliff and as a result the fairies brought on rough seas. It was only after the mariners shared the poitín with the fairies that they calmed the wind and hence the seas (Chadbourne 2012:72–73). In 1822 it was observed that Japanese sailors would throw a barrel of sake (rice wine) and numerous copper coins overboard to propitiate Kompira, a "god of the elements," to ensure favorable weather (Bassett 1885:390).

A seventeenth-century French Jesuit missionary in Vietnam, Alexandre de Rhodes, stated that he was saved from a storm during a voyage by throwing a precious religious relic, "a hair of the Holy Virgin," into the sea (Andaya 2017:366). Lean (1903a:401) noted more generally that "hair cut off and thrown into the sea appeases a storm."

In the Baltic Sea located off the southeast coast of Sweden is the small island of Blå Jungfrun also known as the Blåkulla ("Blue Virgin" or "Blue Mermaid"). The "dangerous" island is "the most prominent meeting place of witches in the North" (Westerdahl 2005a:4). To appease Blåkulla and avoid her wrath in the form of storms, passing mariners made sea offerings of gloves, silk scarves, and sashes (Henningsen 1961:177; Westerdahl 2005a:4).

As noted by Brody (1998:82), one of the most famous examples of a human sacrifice associated with quelling a storm at sea is found in the Hebrew Bible (Old Testament) with the exploits of Jonah, dating to around the eighth century BCE. Jonah is instructed by Yahweh (God) to travel to Nineveh and ask its residents to repent their sins or face the wrath of God. Instead, Jonah boards a ship and sails to Tarshish. Unimpressed, "the LORD hurled a great wind into the sea, and there was a mighty tempest in the sea, so that the ship was like to be broken" (Jonah 1:4). Knowing the dangerous situation, "the mariners were afraid, and cried every man unto his god" (Jonah 1:5) for salvation. To quell the storm the mariners threw Jonah into the sea as a sacrifice "and the sea ceased from its raging" (Jonah 1:16). After the crew made their own sacrifice to God, God saved Jonah from drowning by having him swallowed by a giant fish (often seen to be a whale), who vomited him up on land.

Chinese mariners believed that if the voyage is beset by a storm, then the gods must be angered by the presence on the vessel of a sinful person or persons. As such, crew members or passengers who were thought to be sinful and the cause of the foul weather were thrown overboard as a form of sacrifice in an attempt to appease the gods and bring on calm sailing conditions (Jones 1898:45). James Clary (1994:213) notes that Norse and Scottish mariners were similarly known to throw people overboard to appease gods and calm stormy seas.

Many European mariners in the past were known to have on board their ships figurines of saints for protection during voyages. In most accounts it appears that ensuring safe travel equated with spiritually ensuring calm weather and averting storms. Vasco da Gama on his trip to India in 1497 was reputed to have on board his ship a small gilded wooden figure of St. Mary, which he claimed had "preserved him at sea" (Jones 1898:60). To help bring good luck and fortune on voyages, mariners of Roman Catholic faith were known to carry amulets (e.g., small statues) associated with St. Elmo (patron saint of the sea), St. Christopher (patron saint of travelers), and St. Nicholas (Beck 1999:14, 304). In the case of persistent storms, the statue would be attached to a line and dragged behind the vessel. If the storm became extreme, the line would be cut (Beck 1999:14). In coastal villages in Spain, fishermen would tie a rope to the statue of a local saint and throw it into the sea to help quell a storm that was preventing vessels from going out to fish (Rappoport 1928:88). Portuguese and Spanish sailors also used small crosses blessed by priests as charms against storms (Bassett 1885:456). The term used by Portuguese sailors for these charms was fetiçao which is the route of the English word fetish.

Mariners of the Teluk Cenderawasih (formerly Geelvink Bay) region of northern Indonesian Papua propitiated ancestors to produce favorable winds when voyaging in their large, double outrigger, seagoing dugout canoes, including war canoes up to 15 m in length (for a description of these canoes see Galis 1963; Haddon 1937:318–328; Powell 1958; Smidt 2006:393). The region is known for its "sudden storms of short duration" (Powell 1958:111) with certain spirits, especially the South Wind (Korano Wambrauw), known to possess "evil power" and to create "terrible storms" (van Baaren 1968:15). According to J. L. van Hasselt (1876, quoted in van Baaren 1968:27), "In stormy weather or when the wind is contrary travellers often throw tobacco into the sea to induce the spirits to provide them with a favourable wind." An alternative approach for mariners is to take on board canoes three forms of carved wooden ancestor figures known as korwar (full figures, amulets, and canoe prows), who they propitiate to help negate encountering dangerous winds and storms during voyages (Corbey 2019; van Baaren 1968:24, 30, 39, 42, 46).

According to Blakely (2017:376), the Cyranides, magico-medical works in Greek dating to the fourth century, "report that a man carrying the 'eye of a sparrow' would steer well in tempests, and that a sailor who possessed the heart, eye, scalp or wing tips of an eagle, or the heart of a hoopoe [type of bird], would be protected in storms at sea."

Greek and Turkish mariners hang bunches of garlic about their vessels to ward off storms (Bassett 1885:462; Jones 1898:65). The captain of an Indonesian

Bugis *pinisi* will take coconut oil from a bottle hung on the main mast and rub it on the keel and other parts of his ship to help ensure it is "safe from harm" if it "runs into a storm at sea" (Pelly 1977:100, 104). Wood shavings and chips taken from the drilling of the ship's "navel" in the keel infuse the oil with spiritual agency (Pelly 1977:104). Inuit attach seal skins, fox tails, or eagles' beaks to the bow of kayaks as charms against storms (Bassett 1885:458). The Peterborough Lapidary, a medieval text dating to the late fifteenth century, notes that Cymydia (otoliths or ear bones taken from large fish) held in the mouth will help protect against storms while voyaging (Duffin 2007:81, Table 1; see also Klokler 2020).

Manx herring fishers from the Isle of Man take a dead wren with them to sea to ward off storms (Brand and Ellis 1849:199). According to John MacTaggart (quoted in Brand and Ellis 1849:199, original emphasis), "Their tradition is of a *sea sprit* that hunted the *herring tack*, attended always by storms, and at last it assumed the figure of a wren and flew away. So they think when they have a dead wren with them, all is snug."

Russian Finnish mariners had a reputation for having the capacity to either calm seas or call up a storm by plunging a knife into a mast (Holland 1942:14). Greek sailors also would thrust a knife into a mast to quell storms (Clary 1994:169). In some parts of Scotland, an old horseshoe, often one found by chance, was nailed to the mast of a fishing boat for protection against storms (Gregor 1885a:307; Guthrie 1889:47). On some islands in northern Scotland, holy water was sprinkled on waves to help quell a storm (Bassett 1885:393).

Across the Caroline Islands of Micronesia, canoe navigators employed weather charms (*hos*) to help control storms to avert voyaging mishap. Charms consisted of a carved wooden "handle" with anthropomorphic representations of either two torsos, two faces sharing a single torso, or a single torso, hafted onto two to eight large stingray spines, which are "the true source of the charm's supernatural potency" (Kjellgren 2014:135). As summarized by Eric Kjellgren (2007:272–273), each skilled navigator possessed a *hos*. Before setting out on a voyage, the navigator held the *hos* in one hand and with the other hand blew a trumpet shell to "invoke" sea spirits (*yalulawei*) as a special "chant" was recited "to ensure good weather and safe passage" (Kjellgren 2007:272–273). During the voyage, the *hos* was kept in a special "spirit house" attached to the outrigger boom "accompanied by offerings to the *yalulawei*, such as turmeric (a powdered yellow pigment), coconut oil, and mats and textiles" (Kjellgren 2007:273). If a storm approached during a voyage, the *hos* was removed from its spirit house and held as further chants were recited. On land the *hos* was stored in a canoe house.

Whistling on board vessels is often frowned upon and taboo, given its efficacy in calling up the wind that may easily overextend into a gale (Holland 1942:14). For example, fishermen of Ireland, France, Germany, Sweden, and Yorkshire refrain from whistling as it brings a storm (Bassett 1885:145; Russell 1909:483). T. Rowe (1763:14–15, original emphasis) reported: "Our sailors, I am told, at this very day, I mean the vulgar sort of them, have a strange opinion of the devil's power and agency in stirring up winds, and that this is the reason they so seldom whistle on ship-board, esteeming that to be a *mocking*, and consequently an enraging of the devil." Fishermen in Northern Ireland refrained from whistling on boats as it "could call up the wrong sort of wind and weather" (St. Clair 1971:44).

In Europe and the United Kingdom during the Middle Ages and through to at least the nineteenth century, mariners would avoid having a priest on board a vessel for fear that it would cause a tempest (Bassett 1885:108; de Mareville 1854; Gregor 1881:199; Rappoport 1928:77). The presence of lawyers on board ships was often considered a bad omen for conjuring a storm (Grant 1880:398). Swedish mariners avoided having a black cat on board a vessel, as "it carries storm in its tail" (Rappoport 1928:83; see also Bassett 1885:122–123). The association between cats on board a vessel and storms at sea was widespread in the United Kingdom and Europe such that sailors would throw at cat overboard to offset stormy weather (Bassett 1885:122–125). Yet a concurrent belief was that throwing a cat overboard at sea would "provoke a storm" (Henderson 1879:208). Among European mariners, according to Honoré de Mareville (1854), "an infallible recipe for raising a storm is to throw a cat overboard." Scottish fishermen refrain from mentioning the names of dogs while at sea for fear of conjuring a storm (Bassett 1885:125). In England and France, mariners who find a dead hare on board their vessel will immediately throw it overboard for fear that its presence will conjure a storm (Bassett 1885:122, 429; de Mareville 1854; Lean 1903b:583). Pomeranian mariners will not chase or touch birds that land on their ships while at sea for fear of conjuring a storm (Bassett 1885:449).

Pomeranian fishermen abstain from throwing a burning coal overboard as such an activity is known to conjure a storm (Bassett 1885:436). Dutch mariners believe that avoiding eating fish on Easter will ensure that they will be "safe from storms at sea" (Thorpe 1852:331). Coastal fishermen of Bangladesh know that they will be exposed to greater risk of storms at sea if female family members have long nails, dirty hair, or put household rubbish outside at night. Whistling on land or on a fishing boat is also known to conjure strong winds. Alternately, seeing a snake, sparrow, milking cow, or Vaishnava (pious saint) is a good omen (Deb 2018:9).

Conclusion

Ritual engagements with tidal, wave, and wind forces provide some of the most compelling evidence that many maritime peoples acknowledge the agentive and sentient qualities of the marine realm. For example, a diversity of maritime societies account for the rise and fall of tides and strong tidal currents (including whirlpools) by the actions of a zoomorphic aquatic being of monstrous size (exhalation/regurgitation and inhalation/ingestion of seawater) or powers of an anthropomorphic being who similarly resides in the sea. As tidal actions are most clearly expressed within the intertidal zone at the sea–land boundary, they are similarly associated with liminality and transformation. Many coastal societies link the liminal qualities of tidal processes with transformational processes of human lives (e.g., pregnancy, birth, puberty, marriage, death) and domesticated animals and their produce (e.g., churning cream into butter, pasture preparation and maintenance, pregnancy of cows, killing of stock). Some maritime societies undertook rituals (involving special chants and agentive objects) to temporarily control tidal processes.

As with tides, the physical form and movement of waves are often seen as physical expressions and personifications of the agentive, sentient, and emotional qualities of animate beings. In many cases, these animate beings are sea deities and spirits, while in some cases the sound of waves is associated with the mournful cries of the dead. Mariners are aware that they have the capacity to not only read and understand different types of waves as expressions of the intentions and emotional state of these animate beings, but also engage with and even manipulate these animate beings through rituals of propitiation. Most of these ritual engagements relate to decreasing wave intensity to calm seas for safe voyaging and involve prayers and votive offerings (including sacrifices of animals and people) to the sea (both on land and in the sea). In some cases, the focus of propitiation rituals is shoreline shrines. As expected, these rituals go hand-in-hand with a wide range of idiosyncratic activities that are tabooed because they conjure rough seas.

In terms of elemental forces, it is with winds that mariners have the closest relationship, given that winds not only influence waves but also power sailing vessels. Again, winds for most maritime societies are associated with animate beings such as deities and spirits, with some societies identifying male and female storm gods. A wide range of ritual practices are associated with propitiating these animate beings to either increase or decrease winds to enhance voyaging and sailing conditions. Many wind rituals (involving votive offerings and charms) took place at either permanent or impromptu shrines located on land and on board vessels before and during (propitiation rituals) and after (gratitude rituals) a voyage. In some cases, winds can be called up or pacified by crew undertaking specific vocalizations (including whistling); taking on board charms; attaching objects to masts (e.g., knives and horseshoes); and throwing into the sea certain foods and alcohol, selected objects (e.g., coins, brooms, oil, jewels), sacrificed animals (e.g., cats), and even people. In many regions, mariners would request a ritual specialist (e.g., female witches) to call up winds. While most wind conjuring was associated with enhancing sailing conditions, in some cases rituals were performed to propitiate storms to wreck vessels for profit, sink vessels for revenge, and thwart maritime invaders. In a related sense, certain actions onboard vessels (e.g., whistling, touching a sea bird) and the onboard presence of certain people (e.g., priests, lawyers), animals (e.g., cats), and objects (e.g., human remains) were known to conjure storms and were considered taboo.

Archaeological evidence of wind-related rituals has been more forthcoming than for tide and wave rituals. Most of this evidence relates to shrines (sometimes with figurative representations of deities and saints) as loci for ritual offerings and propitiation excavated from terrestrial sites. In nearly all cases, ritual links between controlling voyaging (wind and weather) conditions and archaeologically documented shrines and associated votive offerings is based on written texts. Perhaps the best (and also the oldest) known examples are Canaanite and Phoenician shrines in Syria and Lebanon dating back to 4,300 years ago.

9

Sentient Prey

Hunting with Agentive Skulls and Technology

This chapter explores the profound and varied relationships that Indigenous hunters have with marine mammals, focusing on whales (from Arctic and subarctic seas) and dugongs (from tropical and subtropical seas). The theoretical focus is conceptualization of marine mammals by human hunters as sentient beings and other-than-human persons. This ontological approach is based on animistic ontologies that challenge Western and Cartesian dualist dichotomies between humans and animals, and culture and nature (Anderson 2000; Berkes 2008; Brightman 1993; Descola 2013; Hallowell 1960; Ingold 2000; Scott 1989; Tanner 1979; Viveiros de Castro 1998; Willerslev 2007). Within animistic ontologies, marine mammals are sentient and self-conscience and possess the capacity to read, understand, and make morally prescribed value judgments on the behaviors and attitudes of hunters and their communities and to exercise intentionality, agency, and choice. As Hill (2011:408) notes, sea mammal "interactions with humans are relational, interpersonal and intersubjective." In relational and identity terms, many marine mammals see and define themselves as marine mammals partly through their intimate and intersubjective hunting relationship with humans, while many humans see and define themselves as humans partly through their intimate and intersubjective hunting relationship with marine mammals. Such definition is dynamic and changes in the context of specific hunting events where rituals of engagement actively and situationally manipulate the permeability of the human–animal divide (McNiven 2010).

Most ethnographic information on marine mammal hunting concerns Arctic and subarctic peoples of Siberia, Alaska, Canada, and Greenland. For these peoples, hunting is not simply about eating marine "animals" but also about entering into a respectful and what is often conceived of as a reciprocal and interdependent and morally prescribed social relationship with these "animals" (Fienup-Riordan 1990; Gadamus and Raymond-Yakoubian 2015; Lowenstein 1994; Pelly 2001; Sabo and Sabo 1985). In short, it is a relationship built around mutual respect and "etiquette" (Hill 2018a:40). Marine mammals exercise their agency and make themselves available to human hunters only if they know hunters have previously treated their kin with respect in terms of skillful hunting, appropriate processing of remains (particularly skulls) to allow reincarnation, and adherence to strict and gendered protocols, taboos, and rituals. Proper treatment extends to appropriate use of meat and fat and morally sanctioned generosity and sharing among the broader community to avoid waste and dishonor. Mistreated and disrespected animals invariably communicate their negative ordeal back to their kin who respond by avoiding future contact with hunters. Indeed, it is a broadly held belief that respectful hunting enhances marine mammal numbers. In this guise, hunting is less a technological act and more a social and moral contract. More broadly, Harvey (2006:99) makes the important point that "respectful engagement is the central moral imperative of animism."

This chapter draws on relevant ethnographic literature to provide context to archaeological explorations of rituals of whale and dugong hunting. A wide range of ethnographic information clearly reveals that animal body parts, and in particular skulls, are a material focus of rituals associated with increasing or ensuring the spiritual renewal of marine animals and helping to ensure hunting success. Spiritual renewal is often, but not always, associated with releasing the soul (or some form of life force) from the hunted animal for reincarnation. Archaeological correlates of these practices vary from underrepresentation of whale skulls in sites (associated with ritual deposition of whale skulls into the sea for spiritual renewal) to huge mounded and curated deposits of dugong skulls representing hundreds and even thousands of dugongs (associated with increasing hunting success).

Marine mammal hunting rituals have taken the methodological lead in recent archaeological investigations on how to identify hunting rituals in the archaeological record. These rituals have also provided important theoretical insights into the role of marine mammal bones in mediating human–animal interactions and relationships, and challenged zooarchaeologists to extend faunal analyses from subsistence practices into the ideational and symbolic spheres of past cultures (N. Russell 2012). Such insights and developments have been made possible by the rich ethnographies associated with marine mammal hunting rituals (especially in the Arctic and subarctic) and the materialization of these rituals in the form of highly visible and agentive bone deposits (especially those associated with whales). As will be seen, material agency also encompasses hunting technology and a range of portable hunting charms.

In terms of sentient seas, rituals of marine mammal hunting encompass not only hunters and prey but also often a range of other spiritual beings and forces of the marine realm. Forces of spiritual renewal and agency often extend beyond the immediacy of living marine mammals and humans and include the ancestral dead (both marine mammals and humans). In this complex social milieu, a "dialogical matrix" encompassing the human and nonhuman, and the living and the dead, infuses an animate marine world situated in both the past, present, and future (McNiven 2013a). Hill (2022:19) makes the fundamental point that hunted marine mammals "were aware of human thought, speech and behaviour." As expressions of this social milieu, ritual bone deposits should not be seen as dimensions of "the religious or the supernatural" but as materialized and generative expressions of cosmology, sociality, and morality (Hill 2011:411).

Marine mammal hunting rituals and associated rituals of renewal reveal the potential of archaeology to reach back in time to understand the long-term history of human spiritual and social relationships with the sea and the cosmological positioning of humans and marine animals. Ritual bone deposits are not only materialized expressions of animistic ontologies and maritime cosmologies but also temporalized entities with generative and ongoing spiritual agency and potency. Although constructed by people, these bone deposits equally belonged to the marine mammals hunted as a materialization of their interdependent relationship with humans and their social, cultural, moral, and spiritual world. Such materializations reached their most spectacular form with the hunting of the largest animals in the world—whales.

Whales

Hunting of whales for a broad range of sociocultural, subsistence, and ideological reasons continues to be undertaken by a number of small-scale Indigenous societies in various parts of the world (Kishigami et al. 2013; Reeves 2002; Whitridge 1999). In terms of deep-time history, part of the problem of dating the antiquity of human use of whales relates to archaeological invisibility stemming from butchering of carcasses on beaches such that only meat and fat are removed to settlement sites, with bones left behind on the beach (Smith and Kinahan 1984). Meat and fat tend not to preserve archaeologically (except for adhering skin barnacles) and beach bones tend to wash away unless some are taken onto land for use as material culture (e.g., incorporation into structures and modification into portable objects). Yet chance preservation does occur: Stone tools in association with beached whale bones at Dungo near Baia Farta on the central coast of Angola, southwest Africa, indicate premodern human scavenging of whale meat and fat 614,000–662,000 years ago (Lebatard et al. 2019), with a whale (skin) barnacle at Pinnacle Point cave in South Africa indicating inland transport of whale blubber scavenged from a beached whale located 4.5 km distant around 164,000 years ago (Marean et al. 2007). Projectile points made from whale bone have been recovered from cave sites in the Pyrenees from Middle and Late Magdalenian levels dating to 15,000–17,500 years ago (Pétillon 2013). Recently, aDNA and ZooMS protein analysis of bones has provided new avenues to detect whale use at sites (e.g., Seersholm et al. 2016; van den Hurk et al. 2023).

Understanding the deep history of whaling is complicated further by the issue of differentiating between passively scavenged beached whales versus use of actively hunted whales and also whether or not archaeological evidence for whale use encompasses dolphins and porpoises (similarly members of the infraorder Cetacea; Clark 1947; McCartney 1980; Rodrigues et al. 2016; Savelle 2005; Savelle and Kishigami 2013:3–4; Whitridge 1999). Archaeological evidence for so-called active hunting of whales is generally accepted to be much more recent than the long history of human use of whales, perhaps only within the past 3,000 years, and around 6,000 years ago if dolphins and porpoises are considered (Fitzhugh 2016:260; Glassow 2005; Monks et al. 2001:66; Savelle 2005:55; Savelle and Kishigami 2013:3). However, as the following discussion indicates, the dichotomy between passive and active attainment of whales is complicated and blurred by the fact that numerous Indigenous groups use rituals to actively beach whales. Furthermore, many whales that washed up on beaches would have died as a result of harpooning out at sea (Monks et al. 2001:65). In the latter case, Koniag whalers of the Kodiak Archipelago of central southern Alaska undertook rituals to ensure that appropriate winds blew to ensure harpooned whales drifted ashore (Desson 1995:111–112).

An extraordinarily wide-ranging literature exists on rituals associated with Indigenous whaling across the North American Arctic/subarctic, especially in relation to bowhead whales (*Balaena mysticetus*) and beluga whales (*Delphinapterus lencas*; see Johnson 2023 for an overview). Indeed, this literature represents the single largest corpus of published information on marine mammal hunting rituals (and in particular whaling rituals) for any region of the globe. Obviously, any detailed overview of this literature would require multiple volumes. This chapter focuses on rituals involving whale remains and where relevant the remains of other animals and also human remains. Other related rituals and taboos are included to help provide context to rituals involving the remains of dead animals and humans. A clear impression gained from reading the extensive literature on whale hunting rituals is that they were extremely complex and time consuming and were as important, if not more important, to the success of whale hunting as technologies such as harpoons. As many of these rituals were kept secret, information is often fragmentary and incomplete. The high-level ritualization of whaling by Arctic/subarctic communities reflected a shared understanding that whales possessed "spiritual powers far superior to that of humans" (Day 2019:85).

Increase Rituals

Kathleen Day (2019:82) makes the important point that the "need to treat the bones of whales and other sea mammals with respect in order to insure their rebirth runs throughout circumpolar mythology." Such mythologies were underpinned by animistic ontologies and given concrete expression in the ritual treatment of the bones of hunted whales. For example, the Tigara Inuit of Point Hope, northwest Alaska, hunt bowhead whales from icepack and as such must butcher hunted and killed whales on the ice and then haul meat, fat, and many bones on sleds to terrestrial settlements on the coast up to 5 km distant. Once butchering is completed, the "skull of the whale was returned to the sea, some said 'to give the crabs their share'; others, because the skull contained the whale's *inyua* (life or soul)" (Rainey 1947:261; see also Turner 1994:72–73 for a detailed account of the return of a whale skull from the ice back into the sea by the Point Hope community in 1988). This ritual practice is based on the belief that "whales did not die, they simply 'took off the outside parka' and the *inyusuq* (spirit-soul) returned to find a new body" (Rainey 1947:259). In recent years in Barrow, northern Alaska, a whaling crew, after spending up to five hours butchering a bowhead whale, returned "the skull of the whale to the sea; the contemporary Inupiat believe that because a whale's soul resides in its skull, they should return it to the sea to ensure its rebirth" (Kishigami 2013:111). Herbert Anungazuk (1995:342) adds that a whale's jawbone is "removed and sunk into the waters of the sea, with the belief that the whale spirit will return to its kind and say he was well treated by the people and that they would enjoy continued success."

The Nuu-chah-nulth of British Columbia, Northwest Coast of Canada, know that when whale spirits leave their seabed homes they use canoes that take the form of whales. As the "human spirit of the whale resides in the area around the dorsal fin" (McMillan 2019:317), hunted whales landed on the beach had the "saddle" area, taking in the dorsal fin and sides (*tsakwaasi*), removed and taken to the chief's house where it was honored (Drucker 1951:55). "This respectful treatment encouraged the spirit being that lived in the *tsakwaasi* to leave it and enter another whale as his canoe" (McMillan 2019:317). Remarkably, the Ozette archaeological site located within Makah territory to the immediate south of the Nuu-chah-nulth in Washington State (USA) revealed a life-size whale fin effigy dating to the early 1700s CE that may be analogous to a *tsakwaasi*. However, Alan McMillan (2019:317) argues that the effigy is of an orca.

Archaeological insights into rituals associated with the release of whale souls for reincarnation are rare. Ritual treatment of whale skulls tends to be associated with hunting activities (see below). Allen McCartney (1980:532) hypothesizes that holes chopped or smashed through relatively thin bone in the area of the foramen magnum of nearly 200 whale skulls examined archaeologically at a large Thule site complex at Cape Garry on Somerset Island, central northern Canada, may have been associated with "symbolically 'releasing' the souls of whales." On the north coast of Alaska, Savelle and Vadnais (2011:97–98) recorded that bowhead whale crania were relatively rare among whale bone assemblages at Point Hope (where ethnographic records indicate "releasing of the soul" through ritual depositing of whale crania into the sea) and common within whale bone assemblages at Barrow (with no ethnographic recordings of ritual disposal of crania). They rightly note that Point Hope provides a "striking" example of spiritual renewal of whales "where the crania were returned to the sea" (Savelle and Vadnais 2011:97, 105).

Hunting Rituals and Whale Remains

Across the Arctic regions of eastern Russia, North America, and Greenland, whales were considered "sentient beings" with whom Inuit whale hunting communities maintained strong social relationships to ensure hunting success (Tyrrell 2007:575). Inupiat (north Alaska) knowledge that "a whale has the capacity to see and hear what is happening in human society from far away" is a common understanding across the Arctic (Kishigami 2013:114–115). In the words of one Inupiat man, "Whales have ears and are more like people. . . . I firmly believe this is true, that whales have ears" (Bodenhorn 2003:280–281). Central to the social relationship between humans and whales is respect for whales and respectful treatment of whale remains. Siberian whalers of Chukotka use the term "wakeful" instead of "to kill" such as "not to offend the soul of the dearest guest, the whale" (Bogoslovskaya 2003:250). Milton Freeman (2005:68) adds the important point that among these Inuit communities existed "the prevailing belief among hunters that food animals must continue to be hunted to remain healthy and abundant, for only by hunting can the hunter demonstrate respect through the exercise of appropriate hunting rituals and food-sharing practices."

The Maritime Koryak of the Kamchatka Peninsula of northeastern Russia treat a recently killed beluga whale as an "honored guest" in their village (Jochelson 1904:420; see also Jochelson 1908:65–77; Watanabe 2013:182). The whale is greeted on the shore by songs, dances, and women carrying firebrands. After a couple of days of entertainment, which included ritual feeding of the whale, and rituals over a hearth that included the whale's head, the whale was symbolically sent back to the sea such that it might tell its relatives of its kind treatment and to induce other whales to visit the village. In one case, a dog was killed on the shoreline "as a sacrifice to the master of the sea" (Jochelson 1908:71). On the island of Yttygran off the coast of the Chukchi Peninsula at the Whale Bone Alley site, "numerous vertical poles made of whale mandibles" were erected, according to local whalers, "so that the ancestors could see us hunting and observing the traditions" (Bogoslovskaya 2003:242).

On St. Lawrence Island (Alaska) in the Bering Strait, resident Inuit had elaborate and complex ceremonies and rituals associated with ensuring successful whaling (Hughes 1984:274–275). One ritual involved trays of specially imported and prepared "sacrificial foods" such as reindeer fat, "greens," tobacco, and fish. These foods were taken a short distance offshore in boats, and at dawn the foods were thrown into the air and into the sea by the whaling captain, who also "recited prayers asking for a successful hunting during the coming season" (Hughes 1984:274). After a successful whale hunt, further elaborate rituals were performed, including taking small pieces of flesh from the tips of the whale's tail and flukes and throwing these into the sea as a "sacrifice" to the supreme god and to the "animal spirits" before bringing the whale ashore (Hughes 1984:275). Similarly, at Cape Prince of Wales on the Alaskan coast of the Bering Strait, local Inuit undertake a ceremonial celebration after a hunted whale has been towed ashore. The ceremony involved the boat owner's wife and children dancing "inside a circle composed of large whale ribs" (Curtis cited in Lantis 1947:49). In addition, the boat owner's wife took a piece of the whale and cooked it "ceremonially" (Curtis cited in Lantis 1947:49).

To the north of Goodnews Bay on the southwest coast of Alaska, Robert Porter (1893:100) reported an Inuit settlement of 49 people and "ample proof" of "the large number of beluga (or white grampus) killed here, in the shape of long rows of beluga skulls laid one by one beside each other. . . . These rows, of which there are between 30 and 40 within a few miles, were begun at the beach, where the skulls are half decayed and moss grown, and continued inland, where the newest specimens are found. I have counted nearly 200 in a single row." The local "Kl-ehangamiut people assert that each row of beluga skulls on that long strip of beach represents the number of animals killed by successive generations of hunters from some village farther up the river, who are always careful to add only to the trophies of their own people" (Porter 1893:100). At a deeper ontological level, ethnographic recordings from other parts of the west coast of Alaska inform Hill's (2012:49) suggestion that "hunters may have been satisfying the beluga desire for a caribou-like terrestrial existence by depositing their bones on land rather than at sea, and they may have been assisting in the process of transforming the animal back into prey" (see also Fienup-Riordan 1994:111). In short, the beluga skull arrangements were "intended to please the animals and ensure that they would return the following season" (Hill 2012:49; see also Lucier and VanStone 1995:57).

Gregory Monks and colleagues (2001:62) state that for the Nuu-chah-nulth, "ethnographic accounts state that no special treatment was accorded to whale bones, which were discarded on the beach." This statement is relevant for the Makah to the immediate south, where "no religious regard was ever paid to the bones, which were left on the beach" (Waterman 1920:47). However, Drucker (1951:55) reported that a Nuu-chah-nulth whaler "usually insisted on bringing his catches to his home villages so that the bones of all he had taken would be assembled in one spot." Furthermore, Nuu-chah-nulth whalers of the Barkley Sound area of the west coast of Vancouver Island created submarine whale bone deposits (Monks et al. 2001:64).

A tradition of mourning the death of whales expressed through special ceremonies and rituals, along with erection of stone memorial shrines and in some cases burial of whale bones and whale fetuses exists across Japan (Arch 2018:Chapter 5; Boreal Institute for Northern Studies 1988; Itoh 2018; Kato 2007; Naumann 1974, 2000). Most of these shrines and burials relate to what is referred to as the "classical whaling" period of Japanese small coastal communities over a span of around 300 years from the late 1500s through to the early 1900s (Itoh 2018:11). Classical whaling was largely inshore and involved small row boats and handheld harpoons and nets. Whale ceremonialism is linked to animism and the belief that all animals and many "inanimate" objects possess immortal souls like humans (see Itoh 2018 for details). This animism is embedded syncretically with Shintoism and Buddhism. The Shinto focus for maritime communities is Hiruko, who was cast into the sea as a child and eventually washed ashore, where he was venerated as Ebisu, god of the sea and god of fisheries (whales were also considered a type of fish in traditional Japanese taxonomy). Since then, all things that wash ashore are considered sacred, and the most sacred of all were washed-up dead whales. The metaphysical significance of washed-up whales also relates to the shoreline as a "liminal space" between the "maritime and terrestrial realms" (Arch 2018:181).

Shinto shrines are the focus of Ebisu worship and prayers are offered by fishermen-whalers for safe sailing and good catches of fish (including whales; Itoh 2018:17, 21). The wives of whalers are also intimately involved in the rituals of whaling. For example, in the Ayukawa area of Shikohu island, wives of whalers visit the Yamadori Inari Shrine every morning to pray for good catches and safety while their husbands are out at sea. The round trip to the shrine involves a 40-minute walk along a winding road along a mountainous coast and takes place after offerings have been made at home shrines (Boreal

Institute for Northern Studies 1988:64). In some areas, whaling vessels also have a shrine on board to which prayers and offerings are made by the crew to help ensure safety and a good catch (Boreal Institute for Northern Studies 1988:64). At the Asuka Shrine in Taiji located south of Osaka on the island of Honshu, an annual ceremony was held involving whalers shooting arrows at a target with three carved wooden whales to help bring success during the next whale hunting season (Arch 2018:177).

Buddhist temples are where whales are mourned and prayers offered to the souls of whales so they can attain the enlightenment of Buddha (Arch 2018:Chapter 5; Itoh 2018:21). In many respects these mourning rituals are identical to those performed for people (Itoh 2018:15). It is the obligation of people through appropriate ceremony and ritual to atone the killing of whales. Since whales, especially washed-up whales, are considered to have given (sacrificed) themselves to people for use, people felt morally obliged to show respect and gratitude and to reciprocate with ceremonial care of souls and erection of shrines, lest they evoke the wrath of the spirits of whales (Itoh 2018:24; Kalland 2004). Many fishermen also "feared punishments of the gods for catching whales that were considered gods of the sea, or messengers of the gods" (Itoh 2018:209). However, the practice of creating whale graves and mourning whales was also undertaken by coastal communities that did not hunt whales but only used whales that had washed ashore (Itoh 2018:211).

Most Japanese whale graves do not contain any remains of whales and are akin to memorials. However, at least 30 temple and shrine complexes contain whale graves with the physical remains of whales. In nearly all cases the remains are bones. Where the type of bone buried is documented it includes either skulls, jawbones, nasal bones, ribs, or vertebrae (Itoh 2018:58, 75–77, 79, 99, 109, 137, 172, 174). Soft tissue interments appear to be rare and include one instance of a whale's heart and two instances of whale's eyeballs (Itoh 2018:58, 175, 177).

Japanese fishers considered it inappropriate to kill a mother whale and her calf or a pregnant whale, and feared the vengeful spirit of mother whales that had been killed (Itoh 2018:90). As such, a strong tradition exists in Japan of elaborate ceremonialism and shrine erection associated with killed mother whales and their fetuses (Itoh 2018:213). In some cases, a fetus is given a full Buddhist funeral similar to that for humans (Kalland 2004:85). Mayumi Itoh (2018:59, 96, 109, 157, 177) reports at least seven shrines with whale fetus burials. Most appear to be isolated fetuses and some are associated with fragments of the mother's body such as skull bones, vertebrae, and eyeballs. Two burials are of whale calves. Most extraordinary is the whale grave located near Koganji temple on the southwest corner of Honshu, which contains 75 whale fetuses dating to before 1868 (Arch 2018:164–165; Itoh 2018:121; Kalland 2004:77). The grave overlooks the sea so that the fetuses could see pods of whales swimming past (Itoh 2018:121).

Fishermen from the village of Lamalerap on the island of Lembata in Indonesia place the "skulls of fish or whale killed in the hunt" at the fourth door of the village, known as *ika kotă*, or fish head (Barnes 1974:151). Andaya (2017:358) adds that "on the island of Lembata (eastern Indonesia), the skulls of whales were once stored in temples and venerated like the skulls of ancestors. The hunting of whales was itself a sacred act, with special rituals conducted near a whale-shaped boulder." More recently on Lembata, whale skulls are burned to produce heat to break apart boulders used in house construction (Barnes 2005:82).

Indigenous Arctic whalers also used a wide range of hunting charms made from a range of materials, including animal body parts, to increase hunting success. These charms were worn by whale hunters or included in whaling boats and functioned primarily to attract whales to hunters and hunters to whales. For example, charms of the Inuit of Point Barrow in northern Alaska included small pieces of amber, wolf skulls, a dried raven, the axis vertebra of a seal, feathers, skin of a golden eagle, and tip of a red fox's tail (Murdock 1892:275, 439). Other charms included small wooden carvings of bowhead whales that were "carried in the boat" (Murdock 1892:403) and whale-shaped objects made by flaking stone (flint, jasper, smoky quartz, and more recently glass) that were "worn habitually by many of the men and boys under the clothes, suspended around the neck by a string" (Murdock 1892:435). Point Barrow and Hope Point Inuit also placed dog-skull and wolf-skull amulets in whaling boats to increase whaling success (Lowenstein 1994:46; Murdock 1892:437), presumably to intentionalize and predatorize the boat such that it would independently seek out whales. For similar reasons, Greenland Inuit placed a "fox's head" in the front of a whaling boat (Crantz 1767:1:216).

Among the northern Alaskan Inuit, Robert Spencer (1959:338) observed a wide range of other charms used in boats "necessary to the success of the whaling expedition," including figures of whales, walrus, and seals carved out of baleen, a wolf's head carved from marine ivory, glass trade beads, and hair of a famous dead whaler. The purpose of whale charms is to "bring the whale close to the boat, to make the animal more tractable and amenable to harpooning, to prevent the lines from slipping and fouling," and so on (Spencer 1959:340).

On St. Lawrence Island in the Bering Strait, a whaling captain kept a "sacred hunting pouch" containing parts of whales—"tip of the nose, tips of the flippers and flukes, the tip of the penis, and crystalline lens of the eye" (Jolles 1995:230). The Chukchi of Siberia used whales' eyes as whale hunting charms, with Waldemar Bogoras (1907:408) noting that the "pupils of the eyes are wrapped in leather and then joined together in pairs, and added to the string of amulets belonging to the boat." In terms of eyes, subterranean men's ceremonial houses (qagzriq) of the Alaskan Inuit community of Inalik (Little Diomede Island, Bering Strait) contained wooden buckets with the dried eye of a whale attached to each side. The "meaning or use" of these buckets is unrecorded (Jolles 2003:335).

Archaeological insights into whale hunting rituals associated with animal (including whale) body parts are limited. For example, McCartney (1980:528) notes that despite considerable ethnographic detail on the so-called Alaskan "whale cult" (see Lantis 1938), "little of this special whale hunting cult behavior can be distinguished archaeologically." While some ethnographic sources refer to ritual use of whale skulls, few archaeological studies have linked whale skull sites with whale hunting rituals. Most archaeological studies of whale skull sites that are clearly not associated with house or meat cache structures conclude simply a "ceremonial" function. For example, the archaeological village site of Ozette in Makah territory in Washington State dates to the early 1700s CE. Next to House 1 were "several whale skulls," which McMillan (1999:134) suggests based on ethnographic information may represent "memorials" of hunting success. Archaeological surveys in the Goodnews Bay area of Alaska in the 1980s and 1990s identified beluga skull arrangements similar to those recorded ethnographically by Porter (1893). The Kegcaqurmiut site revealed a 50 m-long alignment of 97 beluga crania oriented perpendicular to the coast and beginning at the top of the gravel beach (Hill 2012:49).

Very few examples of whale hunting charms have been identified archaeologically. Peter Whitridge (2002:68) hypothesizes that a whale phalanx bone with a drilled hole recovered from a classic Thule house at Port Leopold, central northern Canada, may have been used as a whaling charm following Spencer's (1959:346) ethnographic observation that "the small digital bone at the end of the whale flipper was reserved for use as a whaling charm" in northern Alaska. The 22 extracted and modified "auditory bullae" (ear bones) from humpback and gray whales dating mostly to within the past 400 years from the Ozette site within Makah territory may also be hunting charms mediating communication between whales and hunters (McNiven 2010:220). Use-wear along fractured edges of ear bones is consistent with a scraping function but for what purpose remains unknown (Fisken 1994:375; see also Monks 2001:144). Further examples of deliberately extracted whales' ear bones which have been brought into terrestrial settlements come from a series of midden sites dating to between 900 and 5,000 years ago from the Santa Catarina coast of southern

Brazil, which have revealed ear bones (periotic-tympanic complex) of southern right whales *Eubalaena australis* (family Balaenidae; De Castilho and Simões-Lopes 2008:102, 105).

Hunting Rituals and Human Remains

Inupiat beluga whale hunters of the Kotzebue Sound region of northwest Alaska propitiated spirits in a cave on Choris Peninsula "in order to have long life and success in hunting" (Lucier and VanStone 1995:57). The associated ritual involved hanging objects such as glass beads or wolverine fur on sticks pushed into the cave walls. In addition, a "small, dried child's body (or fetus?) assured a qayaqer success in hunting belugas. The dried corpse was wrapped in a hide bundle that the owner carried in his qayaq while hunting" (Lucier and VanStone 1995:57). The mummified body of a bald eagle was also used as a hunting charm (Lucier and VanStone 1995:57).

During the nineteenth century, Aleutian Islanders (Unangax̂) of southwest Alaska reported the use of human remains in marine mammal hunting rituals (Black 1987; Day 2019). For example, Innocent Veniaminov (1840, quoted in Hrdlička 1941a:8) observed mummified human remains in caves and was informed by local Unangax̂ that "it was from these bodies that the hunters endeavored to cut parts of the flesh and especially some part of the hand and of the small finger, or at least a part of the garments, (for good luck in hunting)." William Dall (1875:439–440) was informed that "the bodies of successful hunters were preserved with religious care by their successors. These mummies were hidden away in caves known only to the possessors. A certain luck was supposed to attend the possession of bodies of successful hunters. Hence one whaler, if he could, would steal the mummies belonging to another, and secrete them in his own cave, in order to obtain success in his profession." Waldemar Jochelson (1925:44) noted that "an old Aleut informed us that not all Aleut were embalmed, this being the privilege of noted hunters, especially whale-hunters." Day (2019:254–255) cogently notes that "Unangax̂ bodies were mummified by whalers at which time the dead were transformed into beings that were more powerful in death than in life." Much of the power (and by extension danger) was metaphysical with Day (2019:287, 297) adding that Unangax̂ mummies were both "feared and revered," being "neither living nor dead, but instead in a state of persistent liminality."

The Sugpiaq/Alutiiq of central southern Alaska to the east of the Aleutian Islands, who include the Kodiak Archipelago (Koniag people) and the Prince William Sound region (Chugach people), used mummified human bodies in secret rituals of whale hunting (Day 2019; Desson 1995; Donta 1993). For example, human remains used in whaling rituals by Kodiak whalers included corpses "stolen" from ground interments (that were subsequently mummified) and mummified whalers, both stored secretly in caves (Dall 1878:27; Day 2019:233). Margaret Lantis (1938:441) added that senior Kodiak whalers would bequeath to their sons the caves containing human corpses (up to 20 bodies in one case) that had been employed in whaling rituals. Dominique Desson (1995:89) describes these caves as "whaling shrines." These corpses were usually of "successful whalers" and were "fed" and "cared for" (Lantis 1938:451, 455). Ritual use included whalers taking the corpses to a stream and drinking the "tainted" water, no doubt to gain spiritual power and strength (Lantis 1938:452).

Edward Curtis (1916:39) reported that Nuu-chah-nulth (British Columbia) whalers used human remains, usually a recently deceased adult male, in some whaling rituals "as a last resort to change continued ill luck" in hunting success. The complex ritual included attachment of a corpse to the back of the whaler. Nuu-chah-nulth whalers also took ritual baths where they mimicked whale behavior by diving underwater and coming to the surface blowing out water (Curtis 1916:20; Drucker 1951:169–170). Drucker (1951:167) added that these long ritual baths could take place in "a lake, a stream, or the ocean," and in rare instances whalers died during such bathing due to "malignant" spiritual forces or hypothermia.

Senior Nuu-chah-nulth whaling chiefs also made use of elaborate whaling shrines with human remains located in the forest. One such shrine contained numerous masks, human skulls, and human corpses. Drucker (1951:172) reported that the whaling chief in charge of this shrine performed the following ritual: "He stood 10 corpses erect in a row, tying them to stakes. In their hands he fastened a rope of dyed cedar bark to which a wooden image of a whale was tied. From time to time he visited the place; when he found the rope broken he knew a whale had beached somewhere in the vicinity, and sent men out to look for it."

Nuu-chah-nulth shamans also made shrines with human remains in secret places to conduct rituals to increase whalers' success. Objects housed in one particular shrine to attract whales included excrement of the shaman's wife, human skulls, human corpses, and corpses of "new-born babies" such "that they would cry and call the whales ashore" (Lantis 1938:461). The most famous of these shrines is the Yuquot whaling shrine, located on a small island in Jewitt Lake near the coastal settlement of Yuquot on Nootka Island off the central west coast of Vancouver Island. When the shrine was dismantled and taken to the American Museum of Natural History in 1905, the collection included 87 anthropomorphic wooden figures, four whale wooden figures, and 16 human skulls (see Jonaitis 1999 for details). The two largest whale figures (137–140 cm) have a large recess in the abdominal area.

Makah whalers (Washington State) similarly undertook ritual baths, where "some harpooners imitated the whale, making slow movements so that it would act this way when hunted" (Reid 2015:150). Makah whalers also plundered the graves of the recently deceased to remove skulls. It was well known that the "body of a successful whaler was considered an especially effective charm" (Gunther 1942:66; see also Curtis 1913:147). In another example, a Makah whaler stated that he used "the body of a small baby" as a whaling charm. "He found out where a newly born infant was buried, dug up the body, disemboweled it and hung it in a smokehouse" (Gunther 1942:66). Eventually the infant's body was reburied back into its grave (Gunther 1942:67).

Mummified bodies hidden away in caves in the Aleutian Islands have received research attention since the nineteenth century (Day 2019; Zimmerman 1998). The Smithsonian Institution in Washington, DC, houses hundreds of mummified individuals, with selective radiocarbon dating suggesting most date to within the past 500 years (Day 2019:186). Early researchers such as Veniaminov (1840, cited in Hrdlička 1941a:8), Dall (1875), and Jochelson (1925) made inferential links between ethnographic information on human mummy hunting charms and the mummified bodies recorded in caves. Inspired by this research, Hrdlička (1941a, 1941b, 1945) "excavated" a series of rock shelters with the remains of over 70 mummified human bodies in association with a wide range of objects on a series of islands in the Aleutians in the late 1930s. On Ship Rock islet, the mummified bodies (all flexed) had been placed on three whale scapula, which were resting on a whale skull. Both human and whale remains were under a driftwood pole structure that appeared to have been covered with sea lion skins. The human remains have been radiocarbon dated to c. 400–700 years ago (Coltrain et al. 2006:544). The base of the whale skull features "lines and curves" painted in red ochre while petroglyphs occur in another part of the rock shelter (Hrdlička 1941b:120; see also Black 1987:36; Hrdlička 1945:336). Remarkably, Hrdlička (1941b) made no comments on these recovered mummified remains and hunting rituals.

Rock art sites recorded archaeologically have been linked with whale hunting rituals and human remains. For example, some rock art sites in the Prince William Sound in southeastern Alaska are associated with human burials (including mummified bodies) and red ochre paintings of a whale, seal, and boats with people (Baird 2006:139–142). John Johnson (2023:203) interprets this rock art as associated with whale hunting rituals. This interpretation matches nearby ethnography of the Chugach, with Kaj Birket-Smith (1953:34) noting that hunters "used to make pictures of all kinds of animals on the rocks in secret places: 'this was their luck.'" Petroglyphs of whales at Cape Alava south of Ozette in Makah territory are similarly associated with whale hunting rituals (Johnson 2023:205–206).

Hunting Rituals and Beach Strandings

Icelanders know that if a "wave-mare" (*våg-meri*) fish washes up and is burned on the beach such that the smoke travels out to sea, then "a whale will strand there before long" (Davidsson 1900:329). Senior Makah whaling chiefs possessed so much spiritual power that they "could get whales to beach themselves" at their village. In some cases, "chiefs guarded their rights to drift whales, even going to war with neighbouring villages over these beached carcasses" (Reid 2015:151).

A dramatic ritual undertaken by Nuu-chah-nulth whaling chiefs to make whales (usually dead drift whales) wash up on beaches involved using the corpse of a recently deceased person. The complex ritual process began at Yuquot whaling shrine, which contained human skulls and brush effigies of spiritual beings and men (Drucker 1951:171–173). Then a corpse was stolen from a recent grave and taken down to a coastal beach. Here a tube was inserted from the back of the neck through to the mouth. As "assistants held the body erect facing oceanward, the chief, standing behind the corpse, shouted through the tube, asking that whales drift ashore" (Drucker 1951:172). Information varies on whether the corpse was then returned to its grave or taken away and smoked and preserved for future ritual use (Drucker 1951:172).

Close to the beach at Te Mahia (Mahia Peninsula) on Aotearoa/New Zealand's North Island is the Ika-whenua whale shrine, which Māori know attracts whales from a long distance. The shrine is a 12-m-long rock formation that in "its general outline bears a decided resemblance to a whale" (Phillipps 1948:41). The shape of the outcrop has possibly been modified by people (Palmer 1961:468). The attractive power of the shrine stems from agentive beach sediment ("sand"—Reed 1967:404 or "earth" and "gravel"—Phillipps 1948:43) which possesses *mauri* (life force) that was placed at or near the shrine by Ruawharo, who brought it over from Hawaiki (central Pacific Polynesian homeland) in Takitumu (one of the founding sacred canoes of the Māori in the fourteenth century; Orbell 1996:118; Phillipps 1948:43–44; Reed 1967:404). Te Mahia is named after a place in Tahiti (Best 1929:50). It is said that a whale was stranded on the beach the first morning after placement of the sand (Reed 1967:404). According to William Phillipps (1948:44), Ika-whenua is a "talismanic object" and "is the largest and probably the most important *mauri* in the North Island.

It is or was highly *tapu* [sacred] and venerated in a way that few of us can appreciate. It is still regarded with awe by the Māori people of Mahia and the immediate mainland." In South Australia, certain coastal Aboriginal men of the Whale totem had the power and "magic" to ritually "sing" whales ashore at their totemic "home Kondilindjarung (place of whales)" (Berndt and Berndt 1993:81; Clarke 2001:20, 24).

Archaeological evidence for whale stranding rituals is limited to charms (and orca petroglyphs—see below). For example, "miniature whale effigies" have been excavated from sites along the Santa Barbara Channel and Channel Islands in southern California dating to the past 2,500 years. Their hypothesized function follows ethnographic recordings of local Chumash shamans using "miniature effigies" of whales "in luring whales ashore" (Johnson 2023:212). Another possible archaeological candidate for a whale stranding charm is a modified whale ear bone with a partly worn surface that was collected from a coastal archaeological site near the Kondilindjarung whale "singing" site in South Australia in the 1940s or 1950s (McNiven 2010:220). I have elsewhere suggested that the ear bone probably related to whale stranding given that neither archaeological nor ethnographic evidence is available to indicate Aboriginal people of southeastern Australia traditionally hunted whales using boats and harpoons prior to European contact (McNiven 2010:220; Clarke 2001:22; L. Russell 2012).

Hunting Rituals and Taboos

Whale hunting rituals involved not only a complex relationship between the living and the dead (humans and whales), but also a complex interplay between the ritualized behaviors of men and women, especially wives and their husband hunters. The significant role of wives in Inuit whale hunting is encapsulated in Barbara Bodenhorn's (1990) paper titled "I'm Not the Great Hunter, My Wife Is." The importance of hunters' wives in whaling is also revealed by the role of women in animating whale bone houses. As a Inupiat resident of Point Hope in Alaska put it in 1980, "The whale comes to the whaling captain's wife" (Bodenhorn 1990:61). A broad range of taboos (and protocols), many expressing husband-wife "gendered interdependence," are associated with whale hunting by Inuit and First Nations peoples across the Canadian Arctic/subarctic (Bodenhorn 1990:64). For example, the wives of Koniag whalers of central southern Alaska "had to remain in a lying position and to refrain from eating for the duration of the hunt" (Desson 1995:118). Neighboring Chugach whalers "keep away from women," and especially "menstruating women," before an expedition. The wives of hunters were required to stay at home while their husbands were out hunting to ensure that the whale would not leave the hunter (Birket-Smith 1953:34, 36).

According to Rasmussen (1927:314), northern Alaskan Inuit knew that the "chief had as a rule several wives, and it was the harpooner's right to be visited by the youngest and prettiest. . . . The soul of the whale also was supposed to be attracted by the idea of being killed by a man coming straight from a woman." Rasmussen (1929:187) added that "when a whale has been harpooned, all the women must lie down on the sleeping place with limbs relaxed, and loosen all tight fastenings in their clothes, laces of kamiks, waistband: teqif-iut. Unless this is done, the whales will run the boat far out to sea, dragging it by the line that is made fast to the harpoon head." Inuit communities of north Alaska, the Labrador coast, and Greenland had to extinguish fires (and the associated light) for the duration of nighttime whale hunts (Crantz 1767:1:216; Taylor 1985:126).

During a whale hunt, the wives of Inuit whalers of the Labrador coast of Canada are required to sit cross-legged on their beds as a form of "imitative magic" such that whales would also remain still and be easier to hunt (Taylor 1985:126). Such immobilization rituals extend also to a whaling crew member tying his feet together during the whale hunt and pairs of children tying their legs together and walking inland out of sight of the sea (Taylor 1985:124–125). Similarly, the wife of a Nuu-chah-nulth whaler must "lie and sleep as long as her husband is out whaling, and she must not move, nor eat any food, nor drink" (Curtis 1916:35; Drucker 1951:168). Lantis (1938:461) made the interesting comment that while it is generally stated that the stillness of wives was to "make the whale quiet," such behavior may have been because the "wife was drawing the animal to her." Similarly, among the Makah to the immediate south, the wives of whalers had the power to affect the behavior of whales and as such "had to remain still in the dark and fast for the duration of the hunt" (Reid 2015:151; see also Gunther 1942:67–68). Wives also refrained from combing their hair during a hunt as it might break hairs, which would result in the harpoon rope snapping (Gunther 1942:67). Makah whalers also "abstained from normal food and sex" before a hunt (Reid 2015:150) and even for the entire whaling season (Gunther 1942:67). Sexual abstinence was also a feature of Nuu-chah-nulth ritual preparations for a whale hunt (Coté 2010:25–26).

Whalers of Lamalera on the island of Lembata in eastern Indonesia possess a wide range of words and phrases that are prohibited among whaling crews for the period of time between harpooning a whale and landing back on shore. According to Robert Barnes (1996:295), these prohibitions are "sacred religious restrictions." Examples include not saying the names of places and people and replacing the words for everyday objects such as harpoon, flensing knife, drinking water, and paddle with other words. Violation of these prohibitions is considered to invite bad luck and danger such as attacks by the whale, stranding at sea, and death of crewmembers (Barnes 1996:295–298). More broadly, if a Lamalera whaling crew is having an unsuccessful trip, they may attribute this situation to bad luck brought on by an indiscretion by a crewmember. If a crewmember admits to such an indiscretion, then he will be required to wash out his mouth with holy water (blood was used in the past; Barnes 1996: 299).

The issue of morally prescribed codes of appropriate behavior in relation to traditional whale hunting in small-scale societies is illustrated nicely by Greenlanders. For the Greenland Inuit, whales were a gift from Sassuma Arnaa ("Mother of the Sea"; cf. Sedna—see Chapter 3). Richard Caulfield (1994:267) notes that Greenland hunters "demonstrated their respect for these gifts through ritual behaviour and right mindfulness." Indeed, L. Dalager (quoted in Caulfield 1994:267) recorded that "when they sail out for whale fishing they dress themselves up in their finest clothes ostensibly because the whale demands respect and no filth will tolerate." Alaskan Inuit "elders view whales as sentient beings endowed with conscience and awareness whose feelings have to be respected" (Laugrand and Oosten 2013:436).

Agentive Hunting Technology

In marked contrast to whaling rituals more generally, few details are available on ritual preparation of whale hunting technology (primarily harpoons) to increase its efficacy. That Arctic whaling communities stored whaling equipment in a special place away from domestic structures indicates associated power and forces that needed to be managed through exclusion from everyday life and activities (Jensen 2012). In some cases, such as among the Point Barrow Inuit of northern Alaska, it is unknown why whaling equipment was ceremonially "consecrated" before a whale hunt (Murdock 1892:272).

Most ethnographic information on the ritual preparation of whale hunting technology relates to the predatorization of harpoons through the attachment of charms, application of spiritually potent substances, and/or addition of agentive carvings. In some cases, the functional line between predatorized harpoons and hunting charms more generally is blurred given that some charms taken on board whaling boats (e.g., body parts of eagles, foxes, wolves) may relate to predatorizing the whaling boat or the whale hunting party more generally (cf. Hill 2022). Ethnographic examples of intentionalizing whaling harpoons include Greenland Inuit attaching an eagle's beak to a whale harpoon (Crantz 1767:1:216), presumably to predatorize the weapon to increase hunting success, and Aleut (Unangax̂) hunters attaching feathers of a rosy finch to harpoon points to "attract whales" (Jochelson 2002:77).

The Koniag and Chugach of central southern Alaska applied human fat to harpoons to increase hunting success (Birket-Smith 1953:33–34). Birket-Smith (1953:34) added that the "whalers were reputed for killing people and secretly boiling out their fat to make 'poison.'" In the 1930s, Frederica de Laguna (quoted in Lantis 1938:452, original emphasis) was informed by a Chugach man that at Cook Inlet "were the secret places where the whalers used to boil out the human fat from which they made poison for their lance blades. Afterwards the bones had to be *reassembled* (with pitch, he hazarded) and fed regularly, otherwise the skeleton would pursue the whaler and devour him." Unangax̂ of southwest Alaska also increased whaling success by applying to harpoons human fat obtained from corpses kept in caves (Veniaminov 1984:223).

Orcas, as other-than-human persons, are the ultimate agentive and sentient whaling "technology." For example, on the south coast of New South Wales (Australia), nineteenth- and twentieth-century records document how orcas herded baleen whales into Twofold Bay where they would be harpooned by whalers rowing out from the local shore-based whaling station (Clode 2002; Mead 1992; Neil 2002:8; Robinson et al. 1997). It is probable that these whalers, which included Aboriginal people, were drawing on the skills of local Aboriginal people who had a long cooperative relationship with orcas, including assisting with driving whales into the bay, where they would allow humans access to carcasses once they had their fill of flesh delicacies (focused on lips and tongue; Clode 2002:148–150; Mead 1992:12; L. Russell 2012:37).

As an act of reciprocity and respect, the Twofold Bay whalers rewarded the orcas for their assistance in hunting whales by allowing orcas time to eat the tongues of the dead whales before towing the carcasses to shore for flensing (Mead 1992:44, 208). In addition, chunks of blubber would be given to the orcas during the processing of whale carcasses on the shore (Robinson et al. 1997:14). The orcas were considered "more or less as pet dogs" (Mead 1992:145; see also Robinson et al. 1997:14). Local Aboriginal oral histories document how the orcas would "put a fin" under whalers in the sea whose boat had been smashed by a whale until a rescue boat arrived (Robinson et al. 1997:22).

When Tom, one of the famed named orcas of Twofold Bay, died and washed up on the shore in 1930, George Davidson, with whom Tom had worked closely, suggested that he be towed "out to sea" and given "the decent burial he deserves" (Mead 1992:3). Eventually it was agreed that Tom's body would be rendered down such that his skeleton could be reassembled and put on public display "as a memorial to Tom and the other killers" (Mead 1992:4). In 1931 the Eden Killer

Whale Museum was established to display Tom's skeleton, where it remains to this day (Mead 1992:232).

Archaeological evidence of agentive whaling technology is limited at present to predatorized harpoons and petroglyph representations of orcas. Elaborately carved harpoon sockets of walrus ivory documented ethnographically and archaeologically for the past 2,000 years provide the best-known and most celebrated example of Inuit (Alaskan and Siberian) agentive whaling (and sealing) hunting technology. Archaeological examples with representations of polar bear or wolf heads with prominent teeth are associated with the Okvik/Old Bering Sea 1 culture of the Chukotka region of far northeast Russia (e.g., Arutiunov and Sergeev 2006:110, 193, Figure 43.4; Chaussonnet 1995:36–37, Figure 18) and St. Lawrence Island in the Bering Strait (e.g., Arutiunov 2009:56, Figure 6; Fitzhugh et al. 2009:301, Object #50; Wardwell 1986:56, Object #45; Figure 19a herein), dating to 300–600 CE (Mason and Rasic 2019:465). These harpoon sockets have ethnographic parallels that "often carried a carved or engraved image of a wolf-like predator with pointed ears and a large mouth that gripped the harpoon socket in its teeth" and into which was inserted the removable harpoon head/point (Fitzhugh 2009:168, Figure 13a; see also Nelson 1899:137, Plate LIV.8; Figure 19b herein). Similarly, "Engraved eyes on harpoon gear helped the harpoon find its quarry" (Fitzhugh 2009:173). The harpoon head itself was also "endowed with spiritual intelligence" and was "carved in the form of a bird of prey whose flight may have been guided by tufted circle-dot sensory organs of sight and touch" (Fitzhugh 2009:176). Sergei Arutiunov (2009:57) adds that "the harpoon acquired a life of its own . . . it became an independent master predator."

An engraved image of an orca was uncovered at the base of a midden deposit dating back to around 400 years ago on Protection Island located off the east side of Vancouver Island, British Columbia, Canada (McMurdo 1979). Petroglyphs with representations of orcas thought to date to around 300–500 years are found also on the shoreline near Ozette to the immediate south in the US state of Washington (Ellison 1979). Jeffrey Ellison (1979:241) hypothesizes that through the Ozette petroglyphs, "the hunter believes that he will charm the animals to shore, and therefore increase his success" (see also Johnson 2023:206). Pecked petroglyphs of whales (including orcas) at Cape Alitak on Kodiak Island in southern Alaska have similarly been linked with whale hunting rituals (see Chapter 4).

Engravings of whales in the Sydney region of eastern Australia have been linked to ritual beaching of whales. Peter Stanbury and John Clegg (1996:22) hypothesize that a 6.4-m-long engraving of a whale with a man inside the whale

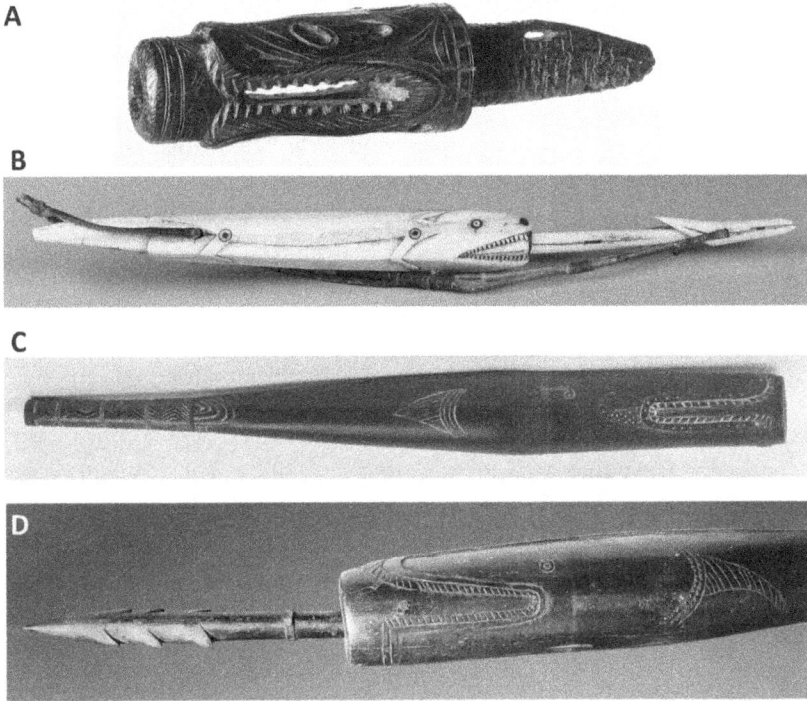

Figure 19. Predatorized harpoon sockets into which were inserted detachable harpoon heads. *A,* Socket section of a harpoon made of walrus ivory, Okvik/Old Bering Sea 1 culture dating to 300–600 CE, recovered archaeologically form St. Lawrence Island, Alaska (L = 14.6 cm; public domain image, Courtesy: Princeton University Art Museum, 1998–482). *B,* Inuit toggling harpoon of walrus ivory with socket, foreshaft, and head (minus point), Alaska, nineteenth century (photograph by James Dunn; Courtesy: Sainsbury Centre, University of East Anglia, UK, 664b). *C,* Socket end of a wooden dugong/turtle harpoon, Mawatta village (Kiwai people), near the mouth of the Fly River, southwest Papua New Guinea, collected by Gunnar Landtman, 1910–12 (photograph by Sakari Kiuru; Courtesy: National Museum of Finland, VK4902:586). *D,* Socket end of a Torres Strait Islander single-piece wooden dugong/turtle harpoon (*wap*) with detachable barbed wooden head. Obtained from the Bogimbah Creek Mission, K'gari (Fraser Island), southeast Queensland in 1897 (Courtesy: Queensland Museum, QE1828).

at Ball's Head directly above the waters of Sydney Harbour may be associated with a ritual specialist "performing a rite to entice a whale to become stranded so that the tribe may feast" (see also Stanbury and Clegg 1996:28–31, 54–55, 80–83). Paul Bahn (2013:64) makes the astute comment that such beaching rituals "could perhaps be seen as a different form of hunting."

Dugongs

Archaeological evidence for hunting and consumption of dugong (*Dugong dugon*) is known back to 6,000–7,000 years ago on Dalma Island (United Arab Emirates), the island of Okinawa (Japan), and Shea's Creek (Australia); and back to at least 4,000 years ago in Torres Strait (Australia; Beech 2000; Crouch et al. 2007; Haworth et al. 2004; Welch et al. 2010:34). A rock art depiction of a dugong in Arnhem Land of northern Australia has been dated stylistically to 6,000–9,400 years ago (Taçon et al. 2020:220–221; see Chapter 5).

Increase Rituals

In eastern Cape York Peninsula of northeast Australia, Thomson (1934b:252) documented a ceremony by the Koko Ya'o (Kuuku Ya'u) people "for the purpose of increasing the number of dugong" that took place at the "dugong totem center," which is marked by a special "dugong stone" at Mosquito Point (see also Rigsby and Chase 1998:207). Men of the dugong clan walked around the stone and "took leaves and struck the stone, spitting and hissing through their lips as they cried: *Ampimbo!* (You come plenty) *Ampi'!* (Come plenty) *Ampi'!* (Come plenty) *Ampi'!* (Come plenty)" (Thomson 1933:501). The ceremony was undertaken at no set time, only when "people notice a falling off in the number of dugong" (Thomson 1934b:252). Similarly, Herbert Hale and Norman Tindale (1933:92–93) recorded "dugong increase charm[s]" in the form of dugong bone "heaps" on the "islands and mainland of Princess Charlotte Bay" of eastern Cape York Peninsula. Some of the piles comprised "only one or two animals," but one large example was "six feet in length, three feet in width, and about three feet in height" and contained "all the major bones" of the dugong. In what is probably a similar increase site, Roth (1903:27) recorded that Princess Charlotte Bay Aboriginal people knew that "if the bones or skulls of the dugong be not put away in a heap or otherwise preserved, no more will be caught. Some of these bone-heaps are of comparatively large size: on the other hand, I have seen dugong skulls hidden singly under bushes on Flinders Island [off Princess Charlotte Bay]."

The Mara Aboriginal people of the Gulf of Carpentaria (west of Cape York Peninsula) perform "dugong increase rituals" at a special dugong Dreaming site to send forth dugongs into the sea (Bradley 1991:102–103). The site consists of a "herd" of "metamorphosed dugong" (quartzite boulders) and the increase ritual includes striking "female dugongs" with hammerstones (see also McNiven 2025a:Figure 6). "Deep grooves and depressions" in some of the dugongs reveal that the "rites of increase are of some antiquity" (Bradley 1991:103). According to the neighboring Yanyuwa, the act of hunting dugongs results in an increase in the number of dugongs, not a decrease (Bradley 1998: 139).

Despite the importance of dugong hunting among Torres Strait Islanders and Kiwai peoples of the adjacent coast of Papua New Guinea, no dugong increase ceremonies have been recorded (McNiven 2016b:204–205; McNiven and Feldman 2003:176). Landtman (1927:127) noted that the lack of increase ceremonies among the Kiwai related directly to their "firm conviction" that "the number of dugong . . . in the sea can never be exhausted."

Archaeological investigations at Princess Charlotte Bay identified "seven discrete clusters" of dugong bones, all dating to the past 200 years given the presence of metal and flaked glass (Minnegal 1984a, 1984b). In total, the seven clusters contained only 239 bones (fragmented skulls and ribs were present in all clusters) representing a total of nine individual dugongs. Cluster 6 contained 115 dugong bones (mandibles and ribs) that "were piled on top of each other in a very small area. . . . It appears that, some time after initial deposition, dugong ribs and mandibles from one or more sites were gathered together and stacked in a heap some distance from other faunal remains. The purpose of this activity must remain a matter for speculation" (Minnegal 1984a:70). The cluster is probably also a ritual installation associated with dugong increase as documented ethnographically in the region (Hale and Tindale 1933; Roth 1903).

Hunting Rituals and Dugong Remains

In Torres Strait of northeast Australia during the late nineteenth century, Haddon recorded a range of dugong hunting charms in the form of dugong body parts and wooden and stone carved figures of dugongs (see McNiven and Feldman 2003 for a detailed overview). In terms of figurative dugong hunting charms, Haddon (1890:352, 1908:217) recorded that "usually a wooden or stone image of a dugong" was hung from a hunting platform (*nat*) "to serve as a charm to ensure the approach of the animal" and to "make him come straight." Some wooden dugong charms collected by Haddon have an abdominal cavity for placement of "chewed" vegetal matter "mixed with dugong grass, dugong fat, and red paint" (Haddon 1890:352–353). A stone charm shaped like a dugong was used by Boigu Islanders to "call up" dugongs. To activate the charm, the ritual specialist pointed the dugong's head north, arranged dugong bones "beside" the stone, and decorated his body with hibiscus leaves (Lawrie 1970:236). Kiwai dugong hunters rubbed their "hands, face and feet" with a small portable figurative dugong stone "to give strength and good luck on the hunt" (Parer-Cook and Parer 1990:23).

A wide range of dugong body parts (soft tissue and bones) were used by Torres Strait Islanders as dugong hunting charms to increase hunting success.

For example, the "nose and anterior part of the face of a dead dugong," and the "larynx and trachea, which were previously stuffed" with a range of plant products (including sea grass), so "dugong he smell him, he come quick" (Haddon 1904:338). In the 1970s, Nietschmann (1977:9) was informed by Torres Strait Islanders that dugongs "don't have good eyes like turtle. They travel with the *aingaizinga*. They know from that compass." The *aingaizinga* is the esophagus of a dugong, and sometimes hunters will extract and eat "a few bits" of it, hoping to "ingest the power of the dugong compass." In the 1980s, Michelle Raven (1990:140) was informed by Boigu Islanders that "dugong skulls were stuffed with plants and used" as hunting charms. In the twenty-first century, senior Mabuyag and Iama/Tudu Islanders refer to dugong ear bones variously as "radar bones" and "wireless bones" that were used to assist communication with dugongs to aid hunting by bringing dugongs closer to hunters (McNiven and Feldman 2003:186).

Senior Elder Father John Manas of Mua in western Torres Strait reported that a "small bag of [raw] dugong meat" can be placed in the front and back of a dinghy to "make the boat go straight to the dugong. The meat steered the dinghy straight to the dugong" (Manas et al. 2008:396). Furthermore, the "brain" and "throat pipe" (trachea) of dugongs were cooked and eaten to assist with dugong hunting (Manas et al. 2008:390–391). The consumption of these organs provides hunters with special knowledge: "you know where they're feeding, and you go there" (Manas et al. 2008:391). More specifically, "That thing leads you. That throat pipe makes you see where the dugongs are, it leads you there, it calls you to there where they are. That throat pipe is a road, when you eat it you know that road. That throat pipe is *yabu* [road], it's the path taken by dugong" (Manas et al. 2008:391). Kiwai dugong hunters of the adjacent coast of Papua New Guinea kept the dried facial skin and windpipe of a dugong in their home under the watchful eye of their wife while out hunting "to bring success" (Landtman 1927:137).

Dugong skull shrines and associated "cult groups" linked to hunting success occur on the paired islands of Shimoji and Kamiji (aka Aragusuku Island) of the Ryukyu Archipelago in the Okinawa Prefecture of southern Japan (Welch et al. 2010:75). According to Akira Arakawa (1978, quoted in Welch et al. 2010:188), "Before leaving the island [Aragusuku] for hunting, the hunters visited the Isho Utaki (isho means sea in Okinawan dialect) and prayed for a successful hunt. As they returned to the island with a catch, they offered its skull to the Isho Utaki to show their gratefulness for divine aid." The "divine aid" related to offerings "to the deity of the sea" and not to dugongs, which are "not a deity" (Welch et al. 2010:73, 80). The shrine on Shimoji Island once featured hundreds of skulls arranged on top of coral-rubble walls (Hoson et al. 2009). The Shimoji dugong shrine is a "sacred place for the local community" (Sudo et al. 2015). Dugong skulls were "buried in the topsoil" and also placed on the top of "stone walls" of the dugong shrine on Kamiji Island (Welch et al. 2010:134, 161).

The ritual placement of dugong skulls at shrines on Shimoji and Kamiji Islands may also reference the transformative and relational ontological status of dugongs and pigs. For example, Iriomote Islanders located immediately northwest of Shimoji and Kamiji Islands state that "the dugong originally lived in the mountains while the wild boar lived in the sea" (Welch et al. 2010:74). Eventually they "decided to swap habitat" such that dugongs were marine and wild boars were terrestrial (Welch et al. 2010:74). This transformation is celebrated during the August Moon Festival, when the skulls of wild boar are ritually deposited ("returned") to the sea and the skulls of dugongs are ritually deposited on land (Welch et al. 2010:74). Andaman Islanders "preserve the skulls of dugongs" to help ensure success in dugong hunting (Radcliffe-Brown 1922:274). More specifically, the Ongee of the Andaman Islands ritually curate the scapula of dugongs and paint these with red ochre and hang them "in rows from the roof as hunters' trophies" (Sarkar 1974:587; see also Ganguly and Pal 1963:560, Figure 4). The Ongee also ritually curate the "skull and lower jaw bone of pigs, turtles and dugongs . . . in their homes" to increase hunting success (Das 2000:6).

Shared caching of dugong, pig, and turtle skulls relates to Ongee ontology and the transformative relationship between the three animals. According to Vishvajit Pandya (1993:31), the Ongee see dugongs as possessing a "shared identity" with turtles and pigs, whereby they are ontologically "positioned between the forest and the sea." A local "myth tells that during the full moon tides, some pigs try to run away from the forest into the sea and some turtles try to run out of the sea into the forest. Because the pigs and turtles move in and out of water, the level of the sea changes and some animals are caught in-between. The animals caught between the forest and sea, in transit, become dugongs" (Pandya 1993:31).

In Torres Strait, ethnographic information on formal ritual installations or "shrines" of dugong bones to increase dugong hunting success are less forthcoming compared to dugong hunting rituals involving wooden and stone figurative charms. Gill (1876b:203) describes a "Devil-tree" on Mabuyag in western Torres Strait, festooned with shells and dugong bones used as "propitiatory offerings" to a "mighty spirit." He also observed a similar tree on Tudu in central Torres Strait that was "completely ornamented with dugong bones, the supposed shrine of a spirit possessing the power of giving or withholding success in dugong-hunting" (1876b:302; see also Haddon 1935:59). Raven (1990:104; see also Haddon 1935:38; Tiley 2023:194) notes a similar

"Tree of Skulls" on Boigu in northern Torres Strait, which was "hung with human heads and dugong skulls as a tribute to the proficiency of hunters and warriors, and as a shrine for hunting success." Haddon (1912:131–132) notes that "dugong and turtle skulls and bones were formerly, and often still are, massed in heaps or placed in rows by the Western Islanders; this was done for ceremonial purposes . . . or merely to keep count of the number of animals caught in any one season, in the latter case they were subsequently distributed and soon crumbled away."

The Kiwai of southern Papua New Guinea opposite Torres Strait know of "three mythical beings called Nágimarkái, Kíbumarkái and Usáraba, who are said to be the 'bosses' of the dugong and turtle" (Landtman 1927:130). The three beings fed on sea foam and lived at a point known as Ganalai and long-ago people "used to lay the bones of the dugong caught by them as an offering there, but nowadays the bones are thrown away anywhere" (Landtman 1927:130).

Considerable archaeological research has been undertaken on ritualized deposits of dugong bones. The dugong bone mound at Umm Al Quwain on the island of Akab, United Arab Emirates, is the oldest known dugong ritual installation and one of the world's oldest known marine mammal ritual shrines (see Chapter 1). Dating to 5,100–5,600 years ago, the mound measures 2.9 m by 4.7 m with a height of 0.3–0.4 m and contains the remains of at least 40 dugongs (Méry et al. 2009:700–701; Méry and Charpentier 2012:73). The mound is "a *structured* accumulation of bones . . . whose layout had been accomplished in stages" (Méry et al. 2009:700; original emphasis). The lower layer of the mound is dominated by dugong mandibles and ribs and red ochre, while the upper layer is dominated by rows of dugong crania and ribs. The crania tend to all be oriented toward the east or northeast. A range of artifacts was found to have been "deposited in or inserted into" the mound, including shell and stone beads, shell fishhooks, bone punches, shell knives, flint flakes, net sinker, and pebbles (Méry et al. 2009:702; see also Méry and Charpentier 2012:74). Bones from sheep, goats, and cattle were also recovered. Originally interpreted as a butchering site, the mound was subsequently seen as a "ritual structure" and even a "sanctuary" (Méry and Charpentier 2012:70, 77) following ethnographically informed interpretations of ritual dugong bone mounds in Torres Strait. However, Méry and Charpentier (2012:77) fall short of inferring a definite association with hunting rituals, stating, "Was it exclusively dedicated to rites linked to the dugong, whose capture was not without risk, or to fishing/sea hunting in general? So far we cannot answer this question."

Torres Strait contains the largest number of dugong bone mounds and ritual installations associated with dugong hunting rituals in the world. Archaeological excavations reveal mounds ranging in length from 5 m to 13 m and in height or thickness from 0.2 m to 0.9 m, and containing the remains of 200 and up to 10,000–11,000 dugongs, dating mostly to the past 400 years (David et al. 2009; McNiven 2010; McNiven and Feldman 2003; McNiven and Bedingfield 2008; McNiven et al. 2009; Skelly et al. 2011; Urwin et al. 2016; Wright et al. 2016). Ricky Feldman and I originally conceptualized Torres Strait Islander dugong bone mounds through the lens of "hunting magic" within the broader context of "Islander ontology and their ritual orchestration of seascapes and spiritual connections to the sea" (McNiven and Feldman 2003:169). These insights focused on the results of excavations of dugong bone mounds on the islands of Tudu and Pulu.

The Pulu bone mound was documented in 1898 by Haddon (1904:5, original emphasis) who was informed by senior members of the nearby residential island of Mabuyag that the site was known as *mŭgi siboi* (now "Moegi Sibuy" or "Small Dugong Head"—McNiven and Feldman 2003:184). The mound, along with other bone mounds, ritual installations made from large trumpet shells, and rock art, formed part of a large totemic ceremonial complex known generally in many parts of Torres Strait as *kod* (see McNiven et al. 2009 for details). Moegi Sibuy measures 3 m by 5.5 m with a height of 0.3 m and contains the remains of at least 250 dugongs. Excavations revealed a lower layer dominated by dugong ribs and an upper layer dominated by dugong crania (fragments and partly complete), with minor inclusions of flaked stone artifacts, shells, and bones of fish and turtle. Radiocarbon dates reveal "phased construction" from around 400 years ago until at least 300 years ago (McNiven et al. 2009:296).

The Tudu bone mound has a diameter of 6 m and thickness of around 0.3 m and contains the remains of at least 200 dugongs. The mound is dominated by dugong ribs and skull fragments with minor amounts of shellfish and bones of fish and bird. In addition, the mound contains a diverse assemblage of material culture of European origin dating to the late nineteenth and early twentieth centuries (e.g., glass trade beads, copper nails, coins, buttons, shotgun cartridges, flaked bottle glass, and clay pipes).

Feldman and I posited that "a broad range of historical, ethnographic and archaeological information associates the Pulu and Tudu Mounds with hunting magic" (McNiven and Feldman 2003:186). In particular, we noted the specialized and structured deposition of dugong bones (especially skulls), the overrepresentation of dugong ear bone hunting "charms," and the "strategic location" of mounds overlooking major dugong hunting grounds. More broadly, the "functional efficacy" and "symbolic meaning" of each of the Pulu and Tudu mounds represent more than the "sum of its parts" (McNiven and Feldman 2003:187). The deposition of dugong bones "incrementally" indicates that mound formation was a process and not necessarily an end in itself. Whatever the case, "as a mound gradually increased in size, so too would its ritual gravity, because of increasing spiritual, social and historical capital" (McNiven and Feldman 2003:188). As long-term cumulative and communal deposits, dugong bone mounds "articulate individual acts of hunting success with collective history and identity" (McNiven and Feldman 2003:188). Furthermore, the materiality of mounds was a constant reminder "that successful dugong hunting depended on successfully-negotiated spiritual and social relationships" (McNiven and Feldman 2003:188).

Dugong ear bones (tympano-periotic complex) excavated from large dugong mounds in Torres Strait have been interpreted as ritual charms associated with increasing dugong hunting success (McNiven and Feldman 2003). I subsequently provided five lines of evidence in support of the ear bones as "hunting charms" hypothesis: (1) the extracted ear bones have all been recovered from dugong bone mounds, which are a "highly specialized ceremonial site type" and spiritually charged depositional context (McNiven and Bedingfield 2008; McNiven and Feldman 2003; Skelly et al. 2011); (2) the ear bones have been "purposefully extracted" from dugong skulls (McNiven and Feldman 2003; Skelly et al. 2011); (3) the ear bones have been "specially arranged" in bone mounds, in some cases set up as left and right pairs in behind dugong skulls (McNiven 2010); (4) the known importance of understanding the "acute hearing of dugongs" to dugong hunting success (McNiven 2010; McNiven and Feldman 2003); and (5) recent ethnographic information on the known use of dugong ear bones to "mediate communication with dugongs" (McNiven and Feldman 2003; McNiven 2010:222–225). In addition, Robert Skelly and colleagues (2011:38) document a "rounded pebble naturally shaped like a periotic bone" uncovered beneath a dugong skull cap within a dugong bone mound on the islet of Koey Ngurtai in western Torres Strait. They argue that the pebble may have had the same ritual function as dugong ear bones.

Hunting Rituals and Human Remains

Torres Strait Islanders and Kiwai peoples also used the ancestral dead to help increase dugong hunting success. Haddon (1935:230) was informed that the "ghosts of successful harpooners" could accompany hunters out to sea to ensure "people lucky along dugong." In preparation for a dugong hunt, Kiwai men may ask an "old man" to call on the "spirit of some famous deceased harpooner" and say, "Boy belong you he go outside to-morrow, he take hand belong you, you no make him miss" (Landtman 1927:131). Bernard Nietschmann and Judith Nietschmann (1981:61) observed that some hunters on Mabuyag would make a "visit to the graveyard to ask ancestors for luck" (see also McNiven and Feldman 2003:Figure 7).

In some cases, Torres Strait Islanders engaged the bones of ancestors to assist with dugong hunting. For example, Gill (1876b:302) recorded that parts of dugong are presented to the "skulls of parents and other relatives" to help in "securing their goodwill" in dugong hunting. A wooden dugong charm collected by Haddon from the island of Mua in 1888 has attached two human fibulae (of the *maidelaig*, sorcery man, who originally made the charm) to "greatly" increase its "efficacy" (Haddon 1904:338; Moore 1984:50).

Hunting Rituals and Taboos

As with whaling, dugong hunting taboos and protocols largely concern gender roles and the critical importance of a hunter's wife to successful hunting. For example, a protocol of sexual abstinence was practiced by the Goemulgal of central western Torres Strait "before dugong-hunting" (Seligmann cited in Haddon 1904:271). Similarly, the leader of dugong hunting expeditions among the Motu community of the Port Moresby region of Papua New Guinea had to abstain from sexual intercourse before heading out to sea (Seligmann 1910:140). The wives of Kiwai dugong hunters keep quiet while their husbands were out hunting lest they risk frightening away dugongs (Landtman 1927:138). Furthermore, sometimes while a hunter is out hunting at night, his wife "lies down naked on her back at the door through which her husband has passed out, holding her feet widely apart, one at each door-post. This causes the dugong to come" (Landtman 1927:138). Landtman (1927:139) concluded that "all the harpooners recognize the important services rendered them by their wives, and for this reason they take care to let their relatives by marriage have a share in the dugong meat."

Agentive Hunting Technology

Torres Strait canoes were intentionalized and predatorized to assist with the hunting of dugongs and turtles (McNiven 2018a:182–186). Strategies included inscribing representations of predatory fish (including remora) onto canoes, attaching carved representations of predatory birds (e.g., frigate birds and sea eagles) and predatory fishes (e.g., kingfish and mackerel) to the stern, attaching figurehead carvings of frigate birds and sea eagles to canoe prows, and giving specific names to canoes (see below). Haddon (1912:216) noted that kingfish and mackerel, and frigate birds and sea eagles, "are voracious catchers of fish, and the representation of them would therefore be obvious to the native mind. Their use would therefore be analogous to that of the canoe [hunting] charms."

Malinowski (1915:656) recorded use of a hunting charm for a dugong hunting net used by the Mailu of the southeast coast of mainland Papua New Guinea. He noted that a hunter named "*Píkana*, was the owner (or, more correctly,

Gubína, master) of the only dugong net in the village . . . [and] also the pos-sessor of a dugong magic which he has inherited from his mother." The charm consisted of three stones "which are put in contact with the net, and then a spell is uttered" (Malinowski 1915:657). The stones were imported from neighbor-ing villages located to the west. Malinowski (1915:657) added that the "dugong net and the dugong charm are inseparable and, from the manner in which the natives looked at things, I felt convinced that the charm was by far the more important element of the two." In the late nineteenth century, the Motu of the Port Moresby region to the west of Mailu charmed dugong nets before use by placing them on top of either the "dried claw of a large raptorial bird" or a small pile of smoldering resin in the canoe (Seligmann 1910:179).

To help increase the efficacy of dugong hunts, Boigu Islanders of northern Torres Strait ensured that their dugong harpoon (*wap*; also used to hunt turtles) touched the dugong stone charm "several times" (see above) and then rubbed their *wap* with coconut oil (Lawrie 1970:236). Ongee dugong hunters of the Andaman Islands rubbed wild ginger on their harpoon for the "hunt to be successful" (Das 2000:8).

Kiwai dugong hunters apply a range of agentive substances to their du-gong harpoons (*wapo*; also used to hunt turtles) to increase hunting success. For example, pig fat and white powder from a sago palm is smeared on the shaft (to ensure the capture of fat dugongs) and a small piece of dog tooth is attached to the harpoon head (which is inserted directly into the socket end of the harpoon) to ensure the harpoon head lodges firmly into the dugong (Landtman 1927:123, 131). Elizabeth Parer-Cook and David Parer (1990:24) added that agentive substances are placed into the socket hole into which the harpoon head is inserted: "He first chews some wild ginger and spits it into the hole. Then he adds a piece of sucker fish so that the harpoon head will simi-larly hold fast to the dugong and not let go. Echidna quills are added so that when the dugong is near the canoe it will curl up and go quiet, like a captured echidna; and an onion root so the dugong will be fat and have tender meat." Kiwai canoes also have agentive additions in the form of "an eye painted on each side of the bow, and in the painted eye is fastened part of the real eye of a fish-hawk" as this "helps the canoe to find the dugong" (Landtman 1927:131).

Kiwai hunters also predatorized dugong harpoons by attaching a wasp to the terminal feather tassel (to help with a surprise attack) and carving the socket end to look like a snake (to help ensure the harpoon has a thrusting attack; Landtman 1927:123–124). The cut-off socket end of a dugong/turtle harpoon from Mawatta village (Kiwai people) on the mainland coast of northern Torres

Strait near the mouth of the Fly River in southwest Papua New Guinea collected by Landtman in 1910–1912 features the carved head of a fish with an open mouth with teeth, eyes, gills, and pectoral fins (cf. Landtman 1933:27, Plate 1; see also Lawrence 2010:144; Figure 19c). The socket end of a dugong/turtle harpoon (L = 4.12 m) sketched by Haddon at Old Mawatta village on the mainland opposite the island of Parama near the mouth of the Fly River (Kiwai people) in 1898 similarly features the carved head of a fish with a mouth (albeit closed), eyes, gills, and pectoral fins (Haddon 1912:376, Figure 369; Herle and Philp 2020:291).

Torres Strait Islander dugong harpoons (*wap*) are functionally identical to Kiwai harpoons and are also predatorized by the addition of figurative carving of predatory animals on the swollen socket end of the harpoon. Examples include a shark's head with a stylized open mouth from Boigu (Lawrie 1970:204) and an eel's head with a stylized open mouth and teeth, gills, and pectoral fins from Dauan (Wilson 1993:70, 72). The Queensland Museum holds a Torres Strait Islander *wap* with the bulbous socket end carved to represent a predatory fish with an open mouth and teeth, eyes, and gills and pectoral fin (Quinnell and Miller 2011:Figure 10; see also Haddon 1912:376, Figures 313, 369; Figure 19d).

Sexual attraction between a Kiwai hunter and his wife is also transferred to a sexual attraction between harpoon and dugong (Landtman 1927; Stasch 1996). In preparation, the hunter inserts special leaves into his wife's vagina, then she inserts these into the harpoon socket hole, and then he "loudly blows out the air through his nose, which sound imitates the snorting (or 'talk') of the dugong" (Landtman 1927:128). Afterward, the wife anoints the barbed harpoon head with vaginal secretions. Then her husband hunter inserts more special leaves into her vagina, removes and chews the leaves, and spits them over his harpoon head. His wife also takes the harpooning hand of her husband and passes it by her vagina (Landtman 1927:129). The swollen socket end of the harpoon was modeled by the harpoon maker on the shape of his wife's breast while the harpoon head "symbolized" her nipple (Landtman 1933:27). In this way, the dugong (personifying the husband hunter) will be sexually attracted to the harpoon (personifying the hunter's wife).

Discussion

Ritual uses of marine mammal remains, particularly bones and especially skulls, reveal geographical and cultural diversity but also numerous commonalities. It is premature at this point to say that it is inevitable that all peoples who hunt marine mammals employ rituals to increase hunting success and rituals of spiritual renewal. In many cases it is difficult to know whether or not the lack of references to such rituals in ethnographic descriptions of marine mammal hunting communities reflects absence of such rituals or simply a lack of recording. However, the fact that such rituals have been documented for a wide range of marine mammal hunting communities in contexts ranging from the Arctic and subarctic (whales) to the tropics and subtropics (dugongs) reveals to archaeologists that they need to be sensitive to the potential presence of such rituals when dealing with ancient marine mammal hunting cultures. To ignore such potential not only has implications for understanding the nature of bone assemblages but also misses opportunities to explore past ontologies and ritual practices that often go to the core of community relationships and identity. This discussion focuses on four issues where archaeology can move exploration of marine mammal skull installations beyond mere identification of ritual or ceremonial sites and behavior. Although this chapter has focused on whale and dugong hunting, many of the ontological and ritual issues discussed are applicable to other marine mammal hunting traditions related to seals (e.g., Hill 2018b), walruses (e.g., Hill 2017), manatees (e.g., Loveland 1976), and dolphins and porpoises (e.g., Naumann 2000).

Skull Installations as Mediating Dialogues with the Dead?

The role of skulls in mediating what I term the "dialogical matrix" between humans and marine mammals takes in both alive and dead animals and alive and dead humans (McNiven 2013a). This dialogical matrix is also gendered with the highly ritualized practices of both men (focused on the hunter) and women (focused on the hunter's wife) integral to hunting success. Ethnographic information for rituals involving the hunting of whales and dugongs reveals that the human dead participated in these dialogues, both in a purely spiritual sense and also through physical remains such as corpses (e.g., Nuu-chah-nulth) and skulls (e.g., Torres Strait Islanders). This information indicates the "importance of the agency of the dead in ritualized hunting dialogues" (McNiven 2013a:100). Depending on the cultural context, dialogue and social engagement is based on hunters and prey ontologically positioned as sharing sentience and personhood and socially positioned as kin with morally prescribed responsibilities of trust and reciprocity. Bradley (1997:9) refers to such communication as a "'killing' dialogue." As a result, "humans and animals cognitively, somatically and spiritually overlap to the point that the human-animal divide is seen as fluid, permeable and mutually intelligible. The degree of permeability is usually situational and negotiable, and open to manipulation through ritual" (McNiven 2010:218). Furthermore, all "killing dialogue" is "interpersonal dialogue" and usually "ritually mediated by material culture that often incorporates animal body parts" (McNiven 2010:217–218). Within a hunting relationship, animal body parts commonly involve eyes and ears and what has been referred to as rituals of "sensory allurement" (McNiven 2010). Dugong ear bone hunting charms provide the best-known example of animal body parts used in rituals of sensory allurement, with circumstantial archaeological evidence available for use of whale and seal ear bones as hunting charms awaiting further testing and scrutiny.

Skull Installations as Hunting Ritual Sites?

In many respects the label of "hunting ritual" is inappropriate as an overarching concept for the diverse array of sites with marine mammal remains, especially skulls, described in this chapter. In some cases, places of skull deposition were related to spiritual renewal or reincarnation (also referred to as increase or maintenance rituals) of animals. Sometimes skull deposition (e.g., of whales) occurred into the sea and the skulls were never seen again by people. In other situations, deposition was on land, resulting in accumulations of skulls that formed sites available for long-term transgenerational engagement by people. Yet even for skull or bone installations containing remains that were related to practices that come under the general appellation "hunting ritual," the sites themselves represent much more. Feldman and I interpreted Torres Strait Islander dugong bone mounds through the dual lenses of hunting ritual and community cohesion. The latter point relates to the fact that "the physicality of mounds would continue to remind observers . . . that successful dugong hunting depended on successfully-negotiated spiritual and social relationships" (McNiven and Feldman 2003:188). Furthermore, dugong bone mounds were equally important to social inclusion and "community welfare and solidarity" (McNiven and Feldman 2003:188). I have elaborated and conceived of the bone mounds as a *community of bones* (McNiven et al. 2009:310, original emphasis). Furthermore, as the "creation of bone mounds was an ongoing process, the structures can be seen as works-in-progress" with "ever-emergent properties" with a robust materiality and temporality conducive to transgenerational engagement (McNiven et al. 2009:291, 310). As such, these ritualized deposits embody "on-going expressive and generative structuring properties in terms of social relationships and identity" (McNiven 2013b:553). The dimensions of social relationships, social inclusion, and community solidarity and identity have potential relevance to understanding other marine mammal bone deposits around the world.

Skull Installations as Shrines and Religious Structures?

Both small and large ritual sites containing marine mammal bones are often referred to in both the ethnographic and archaeological literature as "shrines."

In this regard the term "shrine" is rarely defined and its usage clearly covers a broad range of sites. In essence the critical element is the existence of a special site where people had some form of ongoing spiritual engagement through ritual performance centered on an installation featuring bones, especially skulls. In the *Encyclopedia of Religion*, Paul Courtright (2005:8376) defines "shrines" as "places or containers of religious presence." Furthermore, "Shrines may be seen as sites of condensation of more dispersed religious realities, places where meanings take on specific, tangible, and tactile presence" (Courtright 2005:8376). Despite this definitional focus on what might be seen as a more traditional and religious conception of shrines, Courtright (2005:8376–8377) also discusses a "secular version of a shrine" and a type of shrine that "carries no explicitly religious symbolism," such as some war memorials. Neither of these two views of shrines encompass ritual installations of whale and dugong bones examined in this chapter. Yet ritual installations of marine mammal bones do provide scope for an additional type of shrine related to material and agentive expressions of animistic ontologies.

Marine mammal hunting shrines are not places of worship or pilgrimage but more a material expression of the intimate relationship between hunters and marine animals and the practice of killing as a social and moral contract centered on reciprocity. In many respects, these sites differ to certain terrestrial animal hunting shrines where offerings or sacrifices are indeed made, usually to propitiate a guardian, provider spirit, or deity (e.g., Äikäs et al. 2009; Brown and Emery 2008; Jordan 2003; Salmi et al. 2011). Sites concerning marine mammals are more about ontology and cosmology than the religious and supernatural. As Hill (2011:421) cogently notes, "Relegating offerings, bone caching and the use of amulets to the category of religious ritual obscures the centrality of such acts to daily life and creates a conceptually distinct set of behaviours that risk fundamentally misrepresenting prehistoric ontologies." Furthermore, marine mammal bone deposits "might be more productively interpreted as reciprocal acts of gift giving that materialize the rules of etiquette between human and sea mammal persons" (Hill 2018a:37). The critical point is not to see bone installations as the product of hunting rituals but, alternatively, to see both bone installations and hunting rituals as expressions and materializations of animistic ontologies and the special relationships between people and animals.

Skull Installations as the Shared Archaeology of Humans and Marine Mammals?

Marine mammal bone installations were clearly constructed by people. But it is also the case that these sites are expressions of marine mammal agency given that the sites are materializations of a social and moral contract centered on mutual respect and reciprocity. These sites are as much a part of the sentient, social, and spiritual world of the hunters as they are of the sentient, social, and spiritual word of the animals hunted. Hunters know that unless they treat marine mammal bones with respect and construct formalized and highly structured installations using the bones, especially skulls, of their prey, that their relationship with the marine mammals will break down and result in hunting failure. As Hill (2011:420) states: "These deposits were constructed to accord with hunters' understanding of animals' preferences regarding the treatment of their remains and are indicative of human efforts to honour and maintain good relations with prey." In other words, marine mammal bone installations were constructed by people for people but also, critically, for marine mammals.

Marine mammal bone installations are trans-species sites. While bone installations on land can be seen as archaeological sites that are shared and perhaps even co-owned by hunters and their prey, bone deposits in the sea (seabed) associated with spiritual renewal are out-of-sight and out-of-reach of hunters and are largely the domain of marine mammals. In recent years, archaeologists have begun to explore the archaeology of stone tool use by animals such as chimpanzees, sea otters, and birds (e.g., Dwyer et al. 1985; Haslam et al. 2009, 2019; Luncz et al. 2015). Such animal archaeologies tend to fall outside of the types of archaeologies discussed in this chapter which express intimate codependent and co-constitutive relationships between humans and animals. Marine mammal bone installations blur the boundary between the archaeology of humans and the archaeology of animals. These installations encompass an archaeology of animal agency that extends beyond pushes over the past decade for "multispecies ethnography" (e.g., Kirksey and Helmreich 2010). They also require us to ask the radical anthropological question: "What do marine animals think of the installations comprising the bones of their kin assembled by people?"

10

Sentient Stock

Fishing with Agentive Bones and Technology

This chapter concerns practices of increasing fish stocks and catches through ritual. It also uses a wide range of ethnographic and archaeological examples to explore agentive fishing technologies and rituals associated with increasing the capacity of fishing boats, nets, hooks, and traps to capture fish. Fish are an important source of food for many coastal peoples, with Daniel Moerman (1984:49) stating that "half of the world derives half of its animal protein intake from fish." Although data for this statement is limited to the twentieth century, it is clear that fishing has been important to many coastal communities with increasing stabilization of sea levels over the past 5,000 years. Yet it is known that people have been catching and eating marine fish since the Pleistocene. Archaeological evidence for human use of marine fish extends back to around 168,000 years ago at the cave site of Benzú located in Morocco (North Africa) on the southern shore of the Strait of Gibraltar (Ramos-Muñoz et al. 2016:12; see also Aura Tortosa et al. 2016:73). O'Connor and colleagues (2011) document archaeological evidence for "systematic pelagic fishing" (e.g., offshore fishing for tuna) back to 38,000–42,000 years ago at the site of Asitau Kuru in East Timor, Island Southeast Asia. The oldest known fishhooks in the world come from Okinawa Island in Japan, where two single-piece fishhooks made of trochus shell date to 22,000–23,000 years ago (Fujita et al. 2016:11186–11187). A similar fishhook dating to 16,000–23,000 years ago was recovered from Asitau Kuru in East Timor (O'Connor et al. 2011:1120). The 11,000-to-12,000-year-old burial of a woman with six fishhooks made from trochus shell (*Rochia nilotica*) across her neck excavated from Tron Bon Lei rock shelter on the island of Alor in eastern Indonesia provides the earliest known evidence in the world of the ritual significance of marine fishing (O'Connor et al. 2017).

Increasing Stocks

Many fishing societies employ rituals to renew fish stocks and ensure a plentiful supply of fish. These practices are expressions of an animistic ontology whereby the availability of fish and the maintenance of fish stocks is controlled by spiritual beings and forces reactivated by human ritual intervention. As this discussion reveals, these rituals are associated with propitiating the fecundity powers of spiritual forces (including ancestors and gods) via shrines and votive offerings, and respectful treatment of fish remains. In contrast to rituals to increase fish catches, fish-stock increase rituals rarely employ charms. In some cases, fish-stock increase rituals blur with fish-catch increase rituals.

Spiritual Forces

Many Christian fisherfolk use prayers to help ensure availability of fish stocks. For example, in the nineteenth century a ceremony took place in the strait between the mainland coast and the island of Groix off Brittany in northwest France whereby local fishing boats assembled and priests blessed the sea for an abundance of good quality sardines (Anson 1965:71). Similarly, in northern Scotland between Dunbeath and Clyth Ness in the 1840s, hundreds of fishing vessels were known to assemble off shore with crews singing various psalms to bring fishing success (Anson 1965:118). At Clovelly on the north coast of Devon County, England, fisherfolk attended the Church of England once a year for a special service that included singing Psalm 107 (with the prophetic reference to those "that go down to the sea in ships, that do business in great waters") to ensure God sent an abundance of fish (Anson 1965: 76).

Icelandic fishers entered into a reciprocal relationship with God by returning fish byproduct back to the place of harvesting in the sea to ensure regeneration of fish stocks. That is, fish catches were seen as a "gift of God" (*godsgjöf*) and in a moral economy of reciprocation, fishers would either create or renew fishing spots by throwing bycatch into the sea at such locations. In Icelandic mythology, the seas were governed by the god Njördur, who was known to be "in charge of fishing and sailing" (Pálsson 1991:89–90). As Pálsson (1991:89) explains, "By 'feeding' the fish, humans reciprocate the gift of the fish, thus balancing the exchange with nature as if the act of catching were subject to a formal contract or a mutual agreement." These ritual offerings were also combined with special prayers to help ensure good catches at the start of each fishing season and fishing trip. Importantly, the "ritual and magic associated with fishing did not imply, though, that people thought they had much control over nature, rather it ensured that one did not lose what one already had—for instance the ability to fish" (Pálsson 1991:90).

Hindu fishers of Nambuthalai on the southeast coast of India perform an annual ritual aimed, in part, to "help increase fish stocks" (Bavinck 2015:96). According to Maarten Bavinck (2015:90, 93), the ritual centers on an "image" (effigy) of Gangaiyamman, "one of the deities most clearly associated with the sea," which is set up in a "makeshift temple" located on sand facing the nearby sea. Clay pots filled with turmeric water, coconut water, and milk that were prepared by "married women who themselves represent fertility" are emptied by men into the adjacent sea "to 'cool' the deity's violent nature" (Bavinck 2015:98). In addition, two goats were sacrificed to help "propitiate" Gangaiyamman and other deities "in recognition of the violent and 'hot' nature of these goddesses, and by extension, of the sea itself" to make the sea less "dangerous" and safer to fish (Bavinck 2015:96, 98).

On Bickerton Island in the Gulf of Carpentaria in northern Australia, Ainslie Roberts and Charles Mountford (1971:56) recorded two ritual sites associated with increasing parrot fish stocks and also making the fish easier to catch on fishing lines. Both sites were created by Yambirika, a mythical "parrot-fish man," such that local Aboriginal people would have better access to parrot fish. The first site, at Talimba, is a circular arrangement of stones located above the shoreline. Sand within the circle is "heavily impregnated with the spirits of parrot-fish." At the breeding time of the fish, Aboriginal people take handfuls of the sand and "cast it in all directions" as they chant a song asking for parrot fish to be "everywhere." The second site, at Bartalumba, is where Yambirika transformed into a rock in the sea. The top of the rock projects a meter or so above the water and the associated increase ritual consists of removing small fragments of rock from the site and throwing these in "all directions" while chanting the same song as at the Talimba site.

The Karadjeri (Karajarri) people of the Kimberley coast of northwest Australia have responsibilities for "an increase centre of the parrot fish totem" located near Cape Bossut (Piddington 1932:376). The Karajarri also undertake increase ceremonies for two types of stingrays—one ceremony for the *yubugur* stingray (by the Panaka-Paldjeri moiety) and another ceremony, undertaken simultaneously, for the *dʒaia* stingray (by the Burung-Karimba moiety; Piddington 1932:381–382). The focus of the ceremonies is two holes in the ground, less than a meter apart, immediately above the beach. Mud cleaned out of the holes is molded into "models" of the two types of stingrays and also mixed with human blood and formed into balls "representing the fat" of the stingray (Piddington 1932:381–382). The ritual specialists begin walking with the clay effigies and special vines "to lead the spirit stingarees [stingrays] . . . to the beach" where the balls are buried with pieces of the vines in the intertidal zone such that the smell of the blood will attract stingrays into the shallows to be speared (Piddington 1932:382). An increase ceremony for "rock fish" (*maŋgarabur*) similarly involves cleaning out a hole in the ground in association with "rubbing" a series of surrounding "stones" (Piddington 1932:388). The increase ceremony for "flounder" (*ŋalimarabun*) involves "scrapping" a soft patch in a particular cliff face with a cockle shell and "brushing" nearby flat stones (Piddington 1932:389). The increase ceremony for eels (*irwiliwili*) involves "rearranging" stones in two boomerang-shaped, long linear piles (representing two eels) and "cleaning" the surrounding ground (Piddington 1932:389–390).

The Yanyuwa Aboriginal people of the Gulf of Carpentaria in northern Australia curate the Black Bream Ancestral Dreaming place located on the northwest coast of South West Island. The focus of the site is *mijingu*, an isolated rock monolith standing 50 m out to sea, whose place-name is Rruwarrabar-rarala (Bradley with Yanyuwa Families 2010:180–181). Bradley with Yanyuwa Families (2022:61) note that the "rock is not just a symbol of the black bream; it is the black bream, the ancestor of all future black breams, and it carries inside its own life force and agency."

A rare ethnographic example of a salmon increase ritual performed at Jack's Point by a Coast Salish family from Nanaimo village on the east coast of Vancouver Island (Canada) was documented by Homer Barnett (1955:89). At Jack's Point "there is a rock on which are incised figures of various fish. When the salmon run was late, the ritualist painted over these figures with red ocher; at the same time he also painted bits of four different substances, including goat wool and a grass, and burned them at the foot of the rock" (Barnett 1955:89).

In the estuary of Be-Malai in East Timor, local clans perform a ceremony every four years to "ensure a continuation of an abundant supply of fish" (King 1965:116). The ceremony involved sacrifice of a human but now involves sacrifice of a pig and buffalo and symbolic sacrifice of a man. The ceremony is triggered by the appearance of dead or dying fish and prawns on the surface of the water which is taken as a sign that "the power of the *Lulic* (supernatural influence) in the water is waning and requires rejuvenation" (King 1965:110). A woven fishing net is placed over the male sacrificial victim following his feigned death. Then the small black boar is brought up next to the "sacrificed" man and a knife thrust into the boar's heart and blood made to flow into the estuary in a process known locally as "giving to the water" (King 1965:113). Then follows the sacrifice of the buffalo using a sword thrust into the vaginal passage. Entrails of the buffalo are removed by the male "sacrificial" victim and placed into the estuary (King 1965:116).

In the fishing village of Buckie in northeast Scotland, fisherfolk attempted to increase herring stocks by dressing a cooper "in a flannel shirt, which was stuck all over with burs, and carried on a hand-barrow in procession through the village" (Gregor 1881:145). In the village of Fraserburgh, a ceremony to "raise the herring" entailed "one man, fantastically dressed, head[ing] on horseback the procession. He was followed by a second man on horseback, who discoursed music on the bagpipes. Then came, on foot, a third man, carrying a large flag, and wearing a high-crowned hat, which was hung round with herrings by the tails. A crowd followed the three, and cheered most heartily" (Gregor 1881:145).

In the 1930s, Edward Keithahn (quoted in Hill and Hill 1975:96) documented that a Haida man informed him that the petroglyph located on a boulder "below the low tide line" on the shore of Kulleet Bay on Vancouver Island in British Columbia was associated with the "Rain-god" and salmon availability. That is, Haida would use the site to ritually propitiate rain to make water levels rise in nearby streams which encouraged salmon to migrate upstream where they could be caught.

Archaeological investigations of fish increase and renewal rituals and associated sites are rare and focus on petroglyphs and votive offerings and deposits. Pecked petroglyphs located within the intertidal zone at Wrangell in southeastern Alaska have been associated with increasing local salmon stocks. Keithahn (1940:129) hypothesizes that the location of most petroglyph sites near the mouths of salmon streams plus the seaward-facing aspect of most petroglyphs suggests that they were "meant to be seen by salmon." He noted that Northwest Coast peoples "believed animals could influence their lives either here or hereafter. They believed salmon were people and lived 'in their own country' in community houses in villages under the sea. They were ruled by a 'chief' who each spring dispatched them as 'fish' to the rivers where they became the food of man." Thus, "Through petroglyphs they could supplicate or placate the Salmon Chief or 'Leader' by displaying likenesses or symbols of beings known or at least believed to be in especial favor."

More recently, Amy Steffian and colleagues (2023) document a series of ten Alutiiq/Sugpiaq petroglyph sites with pecked cupules and abraded liner motifs in the Kodiak Archipelago of central southern Alaska. Most of the sites are located at or near Pacific salmon streams and are associated with the Koniag cultural tradition of the past 700 years. They argue that the petroglyphs' "placement at the water's edge, affiliation with anadromous streams, occurrence beside barrier fishing structures, and manufacture during repeated site visits suggest that these carvings helped harvesters maintain relationships with animals to ensure future supplies of fish and game" (Steffian et al. 2023:1). Steffian and colleagues (2023:2, 18) make the intriguing hypothesis that the cupules may have been created by people as portals for the "souls" of salmon to pass into the "spirit world" for "reincarnation." The placement of cupules on riverbanks adjacent to where salmon were caught and butchered by people is unlikely to be coincidental. That is, "At many locations, the rock art is underwater at high tide, visible to ocean creatures. This placement may have enticed animals to give themselves to people by demonstrating the presence of a pathway and the intent of harvesters to support souls in transition" (Steffian et al. 2023:18).

Shrines

The Kemer Kemer Meriam of eastern Torres Strait, northeast Australia, possessed a range of fishing shrines to increase the availability of particular types of fish. For example, at Er on the island of Mer is a "fish shrine" comprising a stone cairn in the intertidal zone from which "projects" a large curved stone. This stone "represents Sorkar," whose "function is to ensure abundance of *tup*, the small fish [sardine] that comes inshore in shoals at certain seasons" (Haddon 1908:217, Plate I.1). According to Haddon (1908:217), "Should boys throw stones at Sorkar the *tup* will be driven away from the shore." On the shore of the island of Waier is a "small shrine" known as *zab zogo* that consists of "one or two clam shells resting against a rounded boulder" associated with abundance of *zab*, a "small fish" (Haddon 1908:217). An ovoid, flat stone in the form of a fish and known as *garom* was kept in a garden at Mei on Mer and "rubbed with coco-nut oil to make fish fat" (Haddon 1908:218).

The Māori of Aotearoa/New Zealand are aware that fish and fishing areas are under the protective care of particular gods. Specifically, "a talismanic object, called a *mauri*, was employed as a form of shrine or resting-place for such gods, and a Maori will tell you that this talisman protects the fish, attracts them to local waters, and so ensures a plentiful supply" (Best 1929:3). However, the talismanic object functioned as the receptacle for the "indwelling *atua*, or spirit, that possesses the power"; the stone itself possesses none (Best 1929:3).

Fishers on 'Anaa atoll in the Tuamotu Islands of French Polynesia used fish-shaped stones known as *puna-ika* ("source-fish") "to promote that species' natural reproduction" (Babadzan 1993, cited in Torrente 2015:24). Efficacy of the stones followed imbuement with *mana* (sacred power) at the *marae* (temple) thereafter they were "pointed in a certain direction . . . to attract the species towards land or to inside the lagoon" (Torrente 2015:24).

In Hawai'i, various gods were responsible for controlling the distribution of fish with individual gods known to be associated with specific types of fish in specific locations (Titcomb and Pukui 1952:45–46). Ku'ula was the god of fishes and fishermen and his wife was Hina-hele (also known as traveling Hina; Titcomb and Pukui 1952:32). According to one legendary narrative, Ku'ula as a mortal man was killed and all the fish in his local area of Maui vanished due to the vengeful actions of the gods. After his death, Ku'ula and his wife assumed the status of gods. However, before his death, Ku'ula passed his fish increase knowledge onto his son Aiai. Aiai established and consecrated the first (small) fishermen's shrines (known as *ko'a ku'ula*) and initiated the practices of offerings being made to these shrines after a good catch to give thanks to Ku'ula for making the fish available (Aluli and McGregor 1992:247; Titcomb and Pukui 1952:32–33). In another legendary narrative, Kaneaukai informed fishers that he was a god of fishes and hence became the focus of worship among many Hawai'ian fishermen (Titcomb and Pukui 1952:33). Since these legendary events, Ku'ula, Hina-hele, Aiai, and Kaneaukai have all assumed the status of Hawai'ian fishing gods, with Ku'ula deemed the "great god of fishermen" (Titcomb and Pukui 1952:33).

Ko'a fishing shrines are a "subclass of *heiau*" shrine or temple dedicated to a particular fishing god, with most occurring in pairs, one dedicated to Ku'ula (male) and the other dedicated to Hina-hele (female; Aluli and McGregor 1992:246–252; Christie 2022; Titcombe and Pukui 1952:35; Weisler et al. 2006:274). The shrines often comprise an "upright" standing stone representing Ku'ula and an adjacent "broader stone" representing Hina-hele (Aluli and McGregor 1992:248). These small shrines are located mostly on the coast adjacent to the sea, often on promontories, and the "first fish of a catch was placed on the *ko'a* as an offering" (McAllister cited in Titcombe and Pukui 1952:36; see also Kikiloi 2003:5). In Hawai'ian language, *ko'a* can translate as "coral," "fishing grounds," and "fishing shrine" (Kirch et al. 2015:167). Some *ko'a* shrines are dedicated to specific types of fish, such the Palielaea shrine for mullet comprising a single stone at the edge of the water near Diamond Head on the island of Oahu (McAllister cited in Titcombe and Pukui 1952:36). Use of coral votive offerings at *ko'a* fishing shrines relates to the spiritual potency of coral in Hawai'ian culture and its cosmological and kinship positioning as "the first organism in the Hawaiian universe" and "the beginning of life, and . . . the most ancient ancestors of all living things" (Gregg et al. 2015:103–104).

The fishing shrine of Kamohio on the small island of Kaho'olawe was collected and placed in the Bishop Museum, presumably in the early twentieth century. It contained two carved wooden figures and 47 "offering bundles," all containing different items, including plants, tapa cloth, grasses, and leaves, with nearly half of all bundles containing the bones of "birds, animals, and fish" (McAllister cited in Titcomb and Pukui 1952:38–39). Another *ko'a* fishing shrine of "recent use" on the small island of Lanai was a walled "enclosure" with a stone-paved floor "littered with pieces of coral, shells, fish-bones, and charcoal" (Emory cited in Titcomb and Pukui 1952:37). Maunupau notes that the *heiau* at Kaupo on the island of Maui "was for the purpose of making fish of all kinds multiply, according to one's desire. It was also called ku'ula for a certain god of fishermen and also a ko'a because fine coral was used to cover the spot for the offerings, coral from the beach" (quoted in Titcombe and Pukui 1952:36, 40). This *heiau* also had a "small shelter" where a "fisherman would sleep . . . and in his dreams would come directions as to where to seek fish" (Titcomb and Pukui 1952:40). In this sense, the function of *ko'a* fishing shrines may have blurred between increasing fish stocks and increasing fish catches (see Christie 2022:387).

As noted, ethnographic information indicates that *ko'a* fishing shrines of Hawai'i are associated with increasing fish stocks. Archaeological surveys of the island of Kaho'olawe have "re-discovered" more than 60 fishing shrines, most occurring around the coast, with a low number located inland elevated 360 m above sea level "overlooking the ocean" (Aluli and McGregor 1992:235, 242, 246, Figure 2). The fishing shrines "mark separate fishing grounds for various species of fish which thrive in the ocean offshore" (Aluli and McGregor 1992:235). For example, the shrines located above Kanapou Bay are associated with sharks, given the waters of the bay are a known "breeding ground for sharks" (Aluli and McGregor 1992:242).

Ko'a fishing shrines have received increased archaeological attention over the past two decades (e.g., Christie 2022; Kirch et al. 2015; Weisler et al. 2006, 2009; Weisler and Rogers 2021). Marshall Weisler and Ashleigh Rogers (2021:53) note that *ko'a* shrines have three "common" features: "1) close proximity to the sea; 2) relatively small size; and 3) presence of coral as offerings, pavement components, or incorporated into walls." Weisler and colleagues (2006) document excavation of fishing shrine sites 18A and 2433A on the island of Moloka'i dating to 1420–1710 CE and 1730 CE, respectively. Shrine 18A contains fish bones, mollusk shell, and coral (Weisler et al. 2006:278–279). Patrick Kirch and colleagues (2015) briefly mention a series of four *ko'a* shrines on the island of Maui where coral votives were dated 1580 to 1760 CE. Weisler and colleagues (2019) and Weisler and Rogers (2021) discuss excavation of *ko'a* shrine site 100C located within the Kealapūpūakiha residential complex on the edge of a peninsula on the northwest corner of Moloka'i. The shrine is marked by "a ring of small cobbles and boulders" and contains fish bones (e.g., sharks, trevally, parrotfish, wrasse, surgeonfish, triggerfish, porcupinefish, pufferfish), sea urchin shell, spiny lobster mandibles, mollusks (limpets), and pieces of branch coral (Weisler and Rogers 2021:54–55). U-series dating of the coral indicates use of the shrine between 1590 and 1640 CE.

Camille Lacorne and colleagues (2024) document votive deposits of fish bones associated with fish "abundance" excavated archaeologically from the settlement of Salango on the coast of Ecuador in South America. The offerings were in the form of multiple layers containing thousands of fish bones buried as "massive" foundational deposits within a perimeter wall of a sacred sanctuary dating to 300–600 CE. The fish bones were associated with a wide range of material culture, including obsidian flakes, marine shells, decorated pottery sherds, and "occasional" fishhooks made from shell and copper (Lacorne et al. 2024). Each offering deposit was capped by a thick layer of ash. The 2.3 kg of excavated fish bones produced a MNI of 337 represented by 49 (mostly pelagic) species and 16 families that mirror known subsistence taxa. Most of the fish were deposited whole with many of large size, weighing more than 2 kg. Lacorne and colleagues (2024:20–21; emphasis added) made three major conclusions. First, "the selection of fish offered at Salango was made to represent the sea and the diversity of fish resources available." Second, the fish deposits "can be seen as offerings to the unseen spirits of the Otherworld to which the sanctuary was itself a point of access." Third, "their sheer numbers point to a concern with *abundance*, both that of the ocean and that, consequently, of the community or communities who maintained the sanctuary and fished off the [nearby] island."

Fish Remains

Most ethnographic information of renewal of fish stocks through special treatment of fish remains (beyond formal ritual deposition at shrines as votives) comes from Indigenous peoples of the Northwest Coast of Canada and to lesser extent neighboring parts of Alaska. In terms of the later, the Chugach of Prince William Sound stated that "fish intestines should be thrown back into the water so that they may turn into new fish. If they drift ashore, the soul of the fish, which remains in the guts, will die and the fish will not come to life again" (Birket-Smith 1953:42).

It is out of respect for the soul of fish and their need to rejuvenate through reincarnation that Northwest Coast groups such as the Bella Coola, Heiltsuk, Gitxsan, Kwakwaka'wakw, Coast Salish, Tsimshian, and Haida all carefully "restored" salmon bones back into the water (Barnett 1955:89, 91; Drucker 1950:284–285). Bella Coola, Haida, Tlingit, and Nuu-chah-nulth also returned salmon offal back to the water for reincarnation (Drucker 1950:284–285). Boas (1932:239) recorded that the Kwakwaka'wakw ensure that "all the bones" of caught salmon are "thrown into the water," whereby "the salmon return to life." It is for this reason that the "bones of the first salmon caught in a weir are also thrown into the water" (Boas 1932:239). Indeed, all the "refuse of salmon is thrown into the water at the mouth of the river. Then the salmon will revive"

(Boas 1932:239). According to the Kwakwaka'wakw, salmon possess "souls" and "are humans who appear in the human-person world in their salmon masks, and they are sentient beings who are aware of the human-person world" (Cullon 2013:11, 21, see also Cullon 2017:105). It was a firm belief among the Kwakwaka'wakw that any "act of ingratitude and disrespect" toward salmon would result in the death of salmon souls and their "refusal to return, which would result in human starvation" (Cullon 2013:32). The cornerstone of salmon resurrection was respectful treatment of salmon remains (e.g., bones and intestines) through replacement back into rivers and the sea. In Kwakwaka'wakw cosmology, the "ocean had a magical effect on salmon, ensuring their resurrection, or rebirth, and enabling them to return to their world beneath the sea . . . located far to the west" (Cullon 2013:28; see also Cullon 2017:109–110, 126, 128–129).

In other contexts, it was inappropriate to throw fish bones from meals into the sea. For example, on Anaa atoll in French Polynesia, Frédéric Torrente (2015: 23) reports that "fish remains were kept in stone structures called *pāfata* or in hanging woven baskets but were never thrown back into the sea, for fear of permanently frightening the species away."

Fish bones were also deliberately burned as an act of ritual reincarnation. For example, the Tsimshian and Gitxsan burned salmon bones out of respect (Drucker 1950:285). Similarly, the Tlingit burn fish bones to enable fish to reincarnate (Langdon 2007:236, 239, 263; Losey 2010:20). Alternately, in Scotland, fisherfolk of Rosehearty avoid burning fish bones to ensure plentiful fish stocks (Gregor 1885b:183). On the east coast of Scotland, fishers do not burn the bones of haddock out of respect, as the "black spots on its skin were the marks left by the finger and thumb of St. Peter when he opened the fish's mouth and took out the piece of silver to pay the tax in the temple" (Anson 1965:24).

The Ainu of northern Japan after catching a large swordfish would bring it ashore for ritual treatment. The head is cut off and stuck into the sand snout first as an "offering to the sea-god" (Batchelor 1901:529). Then "prayers are said to the sea-god and also to the spirit of the slain sword-fish; the sea-god is thanked for the assistance he has given in catching the fish" (Batchelor 1901:529). The "spirit of the dead fish" is also "thanked for having been caught" and "asked to return on some future occasion for the benefit of the people" (Batchelor 1901:527). The head "after being offered and worshipped . . . was divided up and eaten" (Batchelor 1901:529). Hitoshi Watanabe (1972:147) adds that the "head was set on an altar erected out of doors 'so that it might return to the open sea with the *inau* [ritual offering sticks] and regain its original shape.'" At the end of the salmon season, the Hokkaido Ainu also collect all of the jaw bones of dog salmon caught during that year and deposit these into the salmon rivers as a "sending-off" ceremony to ensure salmon renewal for the next season (Watanabe 1994:61; see also Iwasaki-Goodman and Nomoto 2001).

At the southern end of Taiwan, Yami fishers from the island of Botel Tobago (Lan Yu) suspend strings with fish bones from scaffolds for drying fish. Andres von Brandt (1984:524) recorded that "when the success of fishing is decreasing, the bones must be thrown into the sea to have more fish."

After catching a *rou* (gummy shark, *Mustelus antarcticus*) for food, the Bardi Aboriginal people of the Kimberley region of northwestern Australia do not "throw . . . away" its liver but bury it carefully facing down in the ground and mark the location with a standing stone (Rouja 1998:111–112). This ritual appears to be associated with helping ensure their future availability.

Increasing Catches

Increasing fish catches is usually described in terms of "ensuring a good catch," which invariably means making more fish available through appropriate behaviors and ritual practices *in particular areas*, as opposed to increasing fish stock per se (the purview of increase rituals—see above). Rituals (often described in terms of "magic") associated with increasing fish catches are described as propitiating the efficacious powers of gods or spiritual entities or more vaguely where the causal connection between ritual and desired outcome is left undocumented. In the latter case it is assumed that the causal connection is based on spiritual forces responding positively to morally prescribed behaviors by fisherfolk. For example, Ernest Borthwick (1977:66) simply noted that on Lukunor atoll in Micronesia that "considerable ritual and magic once surrounded most fishing techniques, but none more so than the use of coral stone weirs built up along the reef for the capture of large schools of fish." In some cases, causal links remain obtuse. For example, Estonian fishermen of the Baltic Sea know that having an argument with a family member before a fishing trip brings good luck in fishing. Indeed, they are known to deliberately lock storerooms and upturn kettles to upset their wives before a fishing trip (Bassett 1885:434). The following digest of fish-catch increase rituals reveals a focus on propitiating the fecundity powers of spiritual forces (including sea spirits, gods, deities, and ancestors) through votive offerings (often into the sea) and sacrifices, activation of (portable) charms, and offerings at emplaced spiritual centers such as shrines, temples, and churches.

Spiritual Forces

Hindu fishers of coastal Bangladesh who fish in the deep sea "worship the deity *Ganga* with utmost vigor and cordiality" (Deb 2018:6). Ganga is represented in elaborately carved and painted statues as a female deity with four hands who sits on an "imaginary marine animal *Mokor*" (Deb 2018:6). Fishers know that Ganga moves across the sea and can inhabit the front section of fishing boats. She "saves their lives" and "blesses" fishers "with catches" (Deb 2018:6).

Hawaiʻians of Polynesia know they can rely on *aumakua* (ancestral spirit) shark gods to assist with fishing. Martha Beckwith (1917:504) was informed that fishers would be accompanied by their *aumakua* (ancestral spirit) shark gods when out fishing. When that happens, the "*aumakua* obeys the voice of man; name the kind of fish you want and it will bring it. The men give it some of the first catch, then it disappears, and they always come back with full nets. Only when the shark appears do they have luck (hence they recognize the god's intervention). Sometimes the *aumakua* tells them beforehand in a dream that it has gathered the fish together."

Over the past four centuries, observations have been made of fishers from coastal communities of various parts of Europe and the United Kingdom attracting fish to fishers for capture through a process of ritual "singing." For example, in the mid-seventeenth century, Athanasius Kircher (quoted in Sanderson 1973:290) observed that when fishers in northern Sicily in the Messina region head out to fish in boats, one person onboard "summonses, with singular words, the fish which is lying somewhere around; which, as soon as it has heard the words, immediately, strange to say, presents itself as if singled out by them" for spearing by any person onboard. Kircher adds that "not a few have believed that by these words the fish are as it were baited by some magic spell" (quoted in Sanderson 1973:291). In Cornwall, southwest England, in 1746, Nance recorded that "fishermen used to induce this fish [rockling] to allow itself to be caught by whistling to it and calling, no doubt in their most endearing tones" (quoted in Sanderson 1973:294).

At least until the early nineteenth century, fisherfolk from Lewis in the Outer Hebrides of northwest Scotland sacrificed a goat or a sheep either at the start of the fishing season (to propitiate a good fish season) or at the end of a good fishing season (to give thanks for a good season; Abercromby 1895:164–165). The sacrificial ceremony (called Tamnadh or Tamradh) was performed on the surface of the sea where fishing vessels offloaded their catch. The sacrificial act was performed by an aged and revered local fisherman, who would cut off the animal's head. He collected blood in a boat's baler and then "waded into the sea and there poured it out to him whom he considered the ruler of the deep and its numerous inhabitants" (Abercromby 1895:164).

At a place near Yilpara at Blue Mud Bay in Arnhem Land, northern Australia, is located the largest known figurative ground sculpture of a marine animal created by Aboriginal Australians. The site is located within Madarrpa clan lands of the Yolŋu people and has been maintained "for over a hundred years" (Morphy and Carty 2015:99; see also Buku-Larrŋgay Mulka Centre 1999:50). It represents "the ancestral stingray Lulumu" and consists of a cleared area of red sands with the body of the stingray delimited by a low, oval-shaped mound, eyes represented by two shallow pits, and tail "extending into the distance" (Morphy and Carty 2015:99). As documented by Howard Morphy and John Carty (2015:99), "today, before going out fishing, Yolŋu will sometimes place the bones of a previous meal in Lulumu's eyes: a gesture of benediction, simultaneously of thanks and hope." Barber (2005:A53) similarly recorded that "in the past fishers would take some sand from the eyeholes with them in a shell and cast it from the boat into the water to ensure a good catch."

Estonian fishermen of northeast Europe pour beers into the Baltic Sea to help ensure a good haul of fish (Bassett 1885:393). On the east coast of England during the twentieth century, fishermen "having a run of poor hauls" out of desperation would throw money into the sea to "buy" fish (Gill 1993:117). Coastal fishers of Ghana in West Africa were observed in the late seventeenth century making "offerings to the Sea" to ensure large catches of fish (Bosman 1907:153).

The Digo people from the south coast of Kenya perform the *sadaka* ("spirit-appeasing ceremony"), usually at the end of the year, in order to "increase the likelihood of a good supply of fish in the coming year" (McClanahan et al. 1997:110). The ceremony involves making offerings at sacred sites (*mzimu*) on the reef and shore (and also at sites on the land in *kaya* sacred forests). Senior Digo fishers also "convene" a meeting to allow a *sadaka* ceremony to take place in response to a "temporary drop in fish catch" (McClanahan et al. 1997:110).

Fishers of the Kelantan area of the central west coast of Malaysia are aware that "fish are not unconscious of the activities and intentions of the fishermen even at a distance, and evade them if not appropriately treated" and that "the actions of the fish are governed to some extent by the spirits of the sea (*hantu laut*) who have to be placated" (Firth 1946:122). As such, Kelantan fishers are known for "the performance of ritual over both boat and net, and the offering of food and other substances to the sea-spirits to secure their cooperation" (Firth 1946:123). Raymond Firth (1946:123) makes the important point that the "idea as commonly formulated is not that the fish are conjured up by these rites (they are already there out in the sea), but that proper conduct and some sort of mediation are required in order that the fisherman may get into contact with them. . . . People are successful not simply because they are better fishermen than others, but also because they 'meet with fish' when others do not."

Fishers from various coastal villages on the mainland of the large island of Panay and nearby islands in the central Philippines associate fishing success with propitiation of sea spirits. For example, coastal fishers from the village of

Suclaran on Guimaras Island (off the southeast coast of Panay Island) share their seas with sea spirits (*taglawod*) and a "poor catch is commonly interpreted as a manifestation of the sea spirits' envy of the fisherman" (Magos 1994:313). In response, the fishers perform the *panulod* rite in the form of food offerings to the sea spirits with the hope that "they will cease to be envious" (Magos 1994:313). The food offering includes prawns, eggs, fish, crustaceans, coconut water, beer, *tuba* (fermented coconut sap), and cigarettes on a raft of banana trunks, which is towed "toward the middle of the sea and left there" (Magos 1994:313). Fishers also attempt to propitiate good luck in fishing from sea spirits by throwing their first catch of the season back into the sea and also throwing coins into the sea and reciting "*Pabakla ako isda* (Let me buy fish)" (Magos 1994:314).

Fishers from Buntod village (north coast of Panay Island) also throw their first catch (or just the tails of the fish) back into the sea believing that these fish will entice their companions to enter fishing nets (Magos 1994:320). Buntod fishers also throw candles into the sea to attract fish into their nets (Magos 1994:320). At Igdalaguit village (south coast of Panay Island), fishers perform a communal ritual known as Sambayang (also Samba) on the shore to, among other things, "win the favor of sea spirits for a bountiful fish catch" (Magos 1994:326). The ritual includes food offerings consisting of "*tilad* (chewing cud), fish with vinegar, a chicken, a glass of local whiskey, *sinapal* (rice with yeast), coconut meat shaped into rings, fermented coconut sap, thick chocolate drink, a local brand of whiskey, *himugo* (pounded rice with brown sugar), *bagudbud* (rice with refined sugar placed inside a coconut leaf), *alupi* (pounded rice mixed with brown sugar) and seven pieces of toasted bread" (Magos 1994:326–327). Igdalaguit villagers also attempt to garner the favor of sea spirits for good catches through food offerings of fish and rice in their houses (Magos 1994:334).

In most instances, successful fishing relates to the degree to which fishers propitiate a positive relationship with spiritual entities and forces. As Charles Zerner (1994a:27) documented among Moluccan fishermen of Indonesia, success in fishing has less to do with technology and more to do with social relationships and "social interaction between two kinds of communities: one of spirits and one of persons." As such, a "fisherman's fate, as well as his luck in fishing—whether fish cluster about his net or disappear from sight—depends upon his relationship to these fractious spirits of the place" (Zerner 1994b:98). Fishermen attempt to make fish reappear in areas where they have disappeared by propitiating spirits through offerings and sacrifices. For example, on the island of Halmahera in North Maluku, Zerner (1994b:99) was informed that offerings take the form of yellow rice, eggs, and a chicken presented in a small scoop net.

The Sama sea peoples of eastern Indonesia know that if they wish to fish in the area of Toro Gagallah, which is home to a dangerous and spiritually powerful giant octopus, then "it was necessary to make an offering of betel nut, lime leaves and tobacco, as well as avoid using loud or foul language, spitting overboard, or making any aggressive actions, among other taboos, while in the area" (Nolde 2009:31). Similarly, the Orang Laut sea peoples of western Indonesia also know that local sea spirits are easily offended and that successful catches of fish are contingent upon the generosity of these sea spirits propitiated through offerings of food such as chickens and rice in front of their boat (Chou 2003:62–64). After a successful catch, fishers must also make additional offerings such as rice, eggs, and cigarettes either into the sea or rocks jutting out of the sea and also "bathe and cast spells to get the spirits out of their bodies" (Chou 2003:64). Chou (2003:64) adds that the bathing and spells "functions as a boundary weakener, facilitating the exit of the sea spirits from one's inner being." This ritual separation is consistent with the spiritual connection fishers make with sea spirits through dreams and the fact that some fishers possess greater spiritual power in terms of their capacity to communicate successfully with sea spirits.

The Bajau and Mandar sea peoples of the Makassar Strait region in central Indonesia know of places in the sea such as reefs that are the "home" of "sea spirits" who are easily offended and must be acknowledged and shown respect through asking for permission before removing marine life for food and through propitiatory offerings of food (Pauwelussen 2017:62). Indeed, Mandar fishermen note that to take fish without offerings is tantamount to stealing from the spirit guardian (Zerner 2003:74). To help keep the spirits at a safe distance, fishing boats will sprinkle lemon juice on a flagpole or tie bundles of hair to a flagpole (Pauwelussen 2017:64). Fishers who fall ill from diving are said to be influenced by sea spirits, which can be exorcised through food offerings on or near the shoreline (Pauwelussen 2017:136).

The Bajau "sea nomad" people of southern Sulawesi, Indonesia, undertake a series of rituals on the sea to propitiate sea spirits to enhance voyaging safety and fish catches. Akhmad Marhadi and La Hatani (2018:630) note that these sea spirits are the "incarnation of their ancestors," who are "led" by Bombonga di Lao ("king of the sea"). Prophet Khidir, a follower of Bombonga di Lao, is "ruler of the fish" and the focus of fishing rituals (Marhadi and La Hatani 2018:630, 634). The fishing ritual process begins on a fishing boat out at sea and involves preparation of offerings comprising areca palm, betel leaf folded and tied with thread, betel chalk (lime), and tobacco rolled in palm leaves. A shaman (bhisa), following utterance of a "spell," then places the offerings into the sea. Orientation of the betel leaf on the sea surface indicates the direction to where plentiful supplies of fish can be obtained. If no fish are caught, the fishers tap the sea three times as they recite the spell: "Sea king and rulers of fish forgive our mistakes give us easiness to catch fish in the sea" (Marhadi and La Hatani 2018:634).

Charms

Fishermen of the Normandy coast of northwest France know that having a bottle of brandy on board a fishing vessel helps ensure big catches of fish (Anson 1965:130). In the nineteenth century, fishers of the Brittany and Normandy coasts working the Newfoundland banks used bones taken from the gills of cod (said to resemble "curved blades") known as "bone of truth" for fishing divination. The bones were thrown into the air to determine if a catch would be successful or not. The answer depended on how the bones landed on the ground: yes if the extremities of the bones landed touching the ground; or no if the extremities of the bones landed pointing up. Such divination could be associated with a threat: "If you do not tell me that I'll catch (10, 20) fishes, I'll chop you with my knife." The bones could be questioned for months during fishing expeditions (Sébillot 1882:263–264).

Shetland Islanders of northern Scotland were known to insert a certain bone from a halibut into the woodwork of their fishing boat to help conjure fishing success (Marwick 1975:76). They also would "spit into the mouth of the last caught cod; and the consequence, they say, is that it will be followed by a fish equally large or larger" (Sanderson 1973:295).

On Guimaras Island in the central Philippines, fishers from Suclaran village employ a wide range of fishing charms to "protect the bearer from the envy of the sea spirits" (Magos 1994:314). Examples include "hair of a saint's image found in the church, part of a tree where birds often perch, a twig that entertwines with a hole in the middle, or a twig pierced by a vine" (Magos 1994:314). The fishermen know that the more "unique" the charm the greater its efficacious power. Fishers from the village of Buntod on Panay Island employ "dried leaves, palm leaves used and blessed by the priest during Palm Sunday, flowers and clothes of the image of saints paraded during Good Friday" as charms to attract fish into their nets (Magos 1994:320). Fishers from Boracay Island also use "magical charms" (*pangalap*) to help ensure a "bountiful catch," ranging "from leaves to stones or anything that has unique characteristics" (Magos 1994:348).

Fishers in the Buka Passage region of the northwest Solomon Islands employ ritual specialists who hold secret knowledge on "medicines" to be used in "an elaborate ritual directed towards ensuring a good catch" of bonito (Blackwood 1935:331). In order "to bring shoals of bonito into home waters," the ritual specialist prepares a bundle of carefully selected plants, which is placed "into a hole in the reef, at a certain place" (Blackwood 1935:332, 339). After the first lot of bonito are caught, they are cleaned over the bundle hole such that blood of the bonito infuses the bundle and thus "will cause the fish to come in great numbers" (Blackwood 1935:333). Another ritual involved carving a bonito in stone (featuring eyes, a mouth, and tail), washing it in sea water in the fisher's house, and placing it on a bed of specially prepared plant matter facing inland such that "the bonito will come up towards the shore" (Blackwood 1935:334).

A remarkable charm involving a human corpse was used by chief ritual specialists of the Nuu-chah-nulth of the Northwest Coast of Canada to bring on "runs of salmon." The salmon ritual involved the chief and half a dozen or so crew taking a "desiccated" human corpse and placing it in the stern of a canoe. To the hands of the corpse were attached a long length of cedar bark rope which extended out the back of the canoe such that it trailed through the water as the living crew paddled (Drucker 1951:172–173). In a related sense, in parts of Japan, finding on the beach the corpse of a person who drowned at sea was "a premonition of great fishing catches" (Grapard 2018:xxviii).

In Japan, Ebisu is a deity of good luck and fortune and "patron of fishermen" whose anthropomorphic form is known to float about in the sea. Fishermen of the Seto Inland Sea know that when they accidentally catch Ebisu in their nets, he "transforms himself into a curiously shaped stone." These stones are worshipped and provided with offerings of drink and fish to propitiate "fortunate catches" (Ashkenazi 2003:142).

The Māori of Aotearoa/New Zealand employed a wide range of ritual practices to help bring fish toward fishers. For example, fishermen of the Waiongana district of the North Island sprinkled "sea sand" made sacred by a *tohunga* (ritual specialist with skills in communicating with gods) into the sea to attract *kahawai* (sea salmon; Paulin with Fenwick 2016:112).

Shrines

The best-documented example of ancient fishing practices linked to propitiating gods with the powers to enhance the success of fishers at emplaced spiritual sites comes from ancient Greece. Texts from the third and fourth centuries BCE refer to sacrifices at temples and altars associated with the cult of the sea god Poseidon and the first tuna caught every season (Mylona 2015:407). Excavations at the Sanctuary of Poseidon (eleventh century BCE to second century CE) at Kalaureia on the island of Poros in the Saronic Gulf opposite Athens in the western Aegean Sea revealed ritual deposition (votive offerings) of numerous bronze fishhooks and lead net and line weights or sinkers (Mylona 2015:391,

399, 407–408). Sediment analysis also reveals sea algae, indicating transport of sea water to the site over a distance of at least 900 m, perhaps for ritual purification purposes. Faunal deposits of bones (dominated by fish) and marine mollusks at the site appear to be of a ritual nature in terms of feasting (perhaps associated with "cult activities") and possibly in some cases as propitiatory "offerings" by local fishers (Mylona 2015:391, 408). In many respects, the feasting deposits also conform to "ritualized middening practices" (McNiven 2013b). That is, the feasting deposits were also ritualized by the deliberate inclusion of symbolically charged objects such as horse or donkey teeth, dog and puppy bones, purple dye shells, and fishing objects.

It is a common practice for Christian fisherfolk to pray before setting out on fishing expeditions in order to secure good luck in fishing, and to pray in church to give thanks after a successful fishing trip or season. For example, during the nineteenth century, French fishermen from Étretat in Normandy held a special service on St. Sauveur's Day during which they entered the church holding candles and carrying between them a huge loaf of sweetened bread (brioche) under a floral pyramid surmounted by a model of a fishing boat (Bassett 1885:407). In the coastal fishing village of Finisterre in northwest Spain is a church dedicated to Nuestra Señora Santa Maria de las Arenas—Our Lady of the Sands—or La Virgen Santa Maria, the patroness of fishermen (Armstrong 1971:305). Inside the church is a granite statue Virgen de Piedra (the Stone Virgin) embodying the Virgen de las Arenas and dating to the thirteenth or fourteenth century CE. During high Mass on Easter Sunday the Virgin would be ritually turned around to reveal a recess in her back containing a *viril* (phallus) "to assure the congregation they would have a fruitful harvest both of fish and in the fields" (Armstrong 1971:306).

The Cashlaun Flaineen "fishing charm" (i.e., shrine) of Galway Bay in west Ireland comprises an arrangement of stones that functioned "to bring the fish into nets" through utterance of a special "spell" (Browne 1900–2:527; Westropp 1922:390). On the island of Rousay in the Orkney Islands is the Finger Steen, a large stone (glacial erratic) on the cliff edge at the Leean, said to have been thrown into place from the island of Westray to the north by a giant. Local fishermen placed a pebble into the giant's fingermarks on the stone, which "ensured a good haul of fish" (Marwick 1975:59).

In Ga society of coastal Ghana in West Africa, fishers know that successful fish harvests are linked to Nai, the sea god, who is propitiated by priests every Tuesday (Nai's holy day) with "libations" and "gifts of food" at a shrine dedicated to Nai located "near the ocean" (Salm and Falola 2002:40). Steven Salm and Toyin Falola (2002:40) add that "if the harvest of fish begins to decline, then the people know that the sea god must be displeased and additional actions must be taken to seek atonement." Barfuo Boaten (1998:47) also notes that in coastal Ghanaian communities, Tuesday is a taboo day for fishing, as this is the day of rest of Nana Bosompo, god of the sea.

Japanese fishermen (including whalers in the past) worshipped Ebisu as the god of fisheries (including whales and one of the Seven Gods of Fortune) and "prayed for safe sailing and a good catch in the next season" at Ebisu shrines (Itoh 2018:17). Around 3,500 Ebisu shrines are known for Japan, many of them visited by fishermen (Itoh 2018:17).

On the northeast coast of India, Jālāris and Vādas fisherfolk employ clay and wood representations of fishing gods placed on fishing shrines located along the shoreline to enhance fishing success. The clay figurines are "worshipped before fishing expeditions" (Thurston and Rangachari 1909:2:445). Different gods were associated with different aspects of fishing success, for example: Bengali Bābu ("blesses the fishermen, secures large hauls of fish for them, and guards them against danger when out fishing"), Rājamma ("favors her devotees with big catches when they go out fishing"), Yerenamma ("protects fishermen from drowning, and from being caught by big fish"), and Orosondi Ammavāru ("prevents the boats from being sunk or damaged"; Thurston and Rangachari 1909:2:445–446). The chief sea goddess of the Vādas is Orusandiamma, who roams across the sea in a boat at night. Her worship and propitiation involve sacrifice of goats (Thurston and Rangachari 1909:7:261–262).

In eastern Indonesia, fishers from the village of Lamalera on the island of Lembata at the start of each fishing season move "ancestral skulls" and their associated shelf from inside the "boat house" to the front of the structure and wash the skulls with salt water, rub them with coconut skin, and anoint them with coconut oil. In some cases, the skulls were "fed a bit of chicken, rice, or blood." It was said that these practices "assured a good catch" (Barnes 1996:121, 244). Barnes (1996:314) notes that ancestors are known to contact the spirits of fishing places to make fish available to fishers. During the nineteenth century, boat houses were "built from whale jaw bones" and remains of large fish, including sharks (Barnes 1996:121).

At the southern end of Malaita in the Solomon Islands, fishermen associate the availability of bonito fish with the power of ghost sharks (incarnations of successful bonito fishermen and also of priests) and sea spirits (Ivens 1927:137–138). Skulls and jaws of fishermen ghosts were housed in a wooden figure of a swordfish stored in a special shrine (*tawau*) located next to the "canoe house." During bonito fishing expeditions, the human skulls of shark-men ghosts (Chapter 3) were placed on rocks on the shoreline and prayed to with the hope that they, and bonito under their control, would approach the fishing canoes.

Figure 20. Kesoko fishing shrine at Matakota over-looking Roviana Lagoon, New Georgia Island, Solomon Islands, circa 1930s (Courtesy: Kei Muri Māpara/Methodist Church of New Zealand Archives, Christchurch. Sister Lilian Berry Collection, Auckland Photographs O35, Small Drawer 1).

Offerings in the form of almonds and taro (root crop) are made to sea spirits such that they "bring bonito to the fishermen" (Ivens 1927:205).

On Eddystone Island in the western Solomon Islands, fishing shrines are usually located along the shoreline and comprise "a heap of stones with upright stele" (Hocart 1935:104). Offerings are made to these shrines, including the first bonito caught in the fishing season and shell rings (Hocart 1935:107). In one case a rock outcrop on the seabed was also considered a bonito shrine where offerings of shell rings were made (Hocart 1935:105, 108). Hocart (1935:108) adds: "Fishermen throw here a small ring with the words: 'This is the ring for you, the bonito shrine, the manes, be effective, make the bonito rise, and let me catch some.'" Hocart (1937:40) records also that ancestral spirits of the dead at bonito fishing shrines "control the bonito so that it comes to the hook" and are rewarded with offerings of the catch.

Roviana Lagoon on the southwest coast of New Georgia Island in the western Solomon Islands features numerous fishing shrines in the form of low-mounded structures of coral blocks, divided into specialized bonito fishing shrines (*hope inaru*) and more general fishing shrines (*hope Kesoko Bolana*; Nagaoka 1999:65). *Hope* (sacred place) *inaru* (cf. *inaru raqoso* "patron of bonito fishing") are located on the coast and in particular on prominences of offshore islands facing the lagoon (Nagaoka 1999:25; Waterhouse 2005:121). Takuya Nagaoka (1999:116) adds that "offerings to the [bonito] shrines were probably made by fishermen both on the way to fishing points outside the passages and before returning to the villages." *Hope Kesoko Bolana* are named in reference to Kesoko, a male spirit, who is "coupled with a female spirit Bolana" (Nagaoka 1999:65). For example, the Kesoko fishing shrine at Matakota in Roviana Lagoon comprises stacked coral blocks topped by a large wooden statue (*beku*) of Kesoko (Figure 20). The shrine was ritually engaged prior to setting out on various types of fishing expedition: *kuarao* (fish drive using vine and stone wall trap), *valusa* (bonito fishing), or *kura* (fishing for large triggerfish with a basket trap; Nagaoka 2000:4). The "shrine owner" said to Kesoko, "Oh! Kesoko of Matakota. We are going out fishing. Come and guide us to the things which we are aiming for" (Nagaoka 2000:4). Sometimes after fishing expeditions, caught fish are cooked and "offered at the shrine" (Nagaoka 2000:4).

Ethnographically informed archaeological surveys of the margins of Roviana Lagoon have documented large complexes of coral block shrines, including "fishing shrines" located on coastal promontories, dating to the past 500 years (Nagaoka 1999:128, 157; Sheppard et al. 2000:36; Thomas 2014). Shankar Aswani and Peter Sheppard (2003:S66) add that many of these archaeologically documented "fishing shrines" include shell rings (known ethnographically as *hinuili*) made from *Conus*, *Strombus*, *Mitra*, and *Terebra* species. Ethnographically, *hinuili* were "worn as protective amulets, exchanged within families as gifts, and presented to ancestors and fishing and gardening deities at sacred shrines" (Aswani and Sheppard 2003:S66; see also Walter et al. 2004:149). Some fishing shrines exhibit quantities of *Tridacna* "debitage," while some bonito fishing shrines feature human remains and shell valuables (Nagaoka 1999:116).

Taboos and Omens

Different fishers in different parts of Europe consider it bad luck to encounter certain types of animals before a fishing trip. In northeast Scotland, fishers associate encountering a dog on the way to their boat as a bad omen for fishing. Some fishers have been known to kill a dog they encountered for fear of encountering the dog again (Anson 1965:101). Icelandic fishermen also knew that if a dog boarded their vessel or went near their nets or fishing tackle that they would have a poor catch (Bassett 1885:430). In Scotland, if a hare crossed a fisherman's path, then he would not catch fish that day (Bassett 1885:429). Similarly in the US Southeast, fisherman will not go out fishing for the day if they encounter a hare (North Carolina) or rabbit (Kentucky and Illinois) on the way to the boat, as it is a bad luck omen (White and Hand 1970:478). The taboo against hares may relate to an old European belief that witches could transform into hares (Anson 1965:131). Numerous English fishermen will not go out fishing if they see a pig on the way to their vessel (Bassett 1885:279; Wilkinson 1869:131). Galway fishermen in western Ireland will hang up a dead fox near rival fishermen knowing that sighting a fox on the way to their boat will prevent them going out fishing on that day (Bassett 1885:279). Fishermen of Audierne in Brittany would abandon fishing for the day if they found a cat on board their fishing vessel (Anson 1965:116).

Animal taboos also extended to mentioning the names of certain animals while out at sea. For example, it was strictly forbidden on Scottish fishing vessels to make direct verbal reference to pigs, hares, rabbits, dogs, salmon, and trout (Anson 1965:131; Brown 2021:261). The negative impacts of such utterances could be nullified by spitting (Anson 1965:131). Fishermen of the Faroe Islands (between Norway and Greenland) know that "if the fish heard their names mentioned, they would be warned and swim away" (Lockwood 1955:2). Similarly, secret words are used when handling hooks and lines in order to "confuse unfriendly spirits intent on ruining the fishermen's chances" (Lockwood 1955:2). Fishermen of Audierne would even contemplate returning to port if a crewman mentioned a wolf (Anson 1965:131). Yorkshire fishermen had a strong taboo on uttering the name of any quadruped while setting or hauling in lines or nets (Anson 1965:131). Kelantan fishers of Malaysia avoid the use of "animal terms while at sea and substitution for them of other more neutral and more honorific terms" (Firth 1946:122).

In some cultural contexts fishing taboos are associated with women. Fishermen from the port of Kilkeel, County Down, Northern Ireland, knew that if they met a red-haired woman on the way to their boat that "there'd be no luck the day" (St. Clair 1971:43). Some Icelandic fishers consider the presence of a woman on board a fishing boat as good luck while others consider it bad luck (Willson 2016:102–105). On Guimaras Island in the central Philippines, a range of fishing taboos are held by fishers from the villages of Suclaran (e.g., avoidance of talking loud when out at sea, and keeping carnivorous animals and menstruating women away from fishing gear and boats—Magos 1994:314–315) and Igdalaguit (e.g., avoidance of talking loud, menstruating women, and broken needles on boats—Magos 1994:333). Māori fishers from the Bay of Plenty in the North Island of Aotearoa/New Zealand know that their wives must not breastfeed on the first day of the fishing season to ensure good luck in fishing (Paulin with Fenwick 2016:113). In Buka Passage of northwest Solomon Islands, male fishers must abstain from intercourse the night before fishing for bonito to ensure a good catch (Blackwood 1935:331, 341). Fishermen from the island of Yap in Micronesia abstain from sexual intercourse before a fishing trip as the sea, who is a "jealous woman," will pick up the associated scent and vindictively "withhold her favors and fishing will be poor." To circumvent this behavior, fishermen will mask the offending scent by rubbing a special odorous plant over their bodies (Johannes 1981:14).

Fishermen of Scotland, Sweden, and France consider it bad luck for anyone to wish them good luck before setting out to sea (Bois 2016:76; Rappoport 1928:265; Russell 1909:483). As Kilkeel fishermen knew that it was unlucky to be the third vessel to leave the harbor, the first three vessels to leave would be lashed together (St. Clair 1971:44). Jersey fishermen will not take current cake on a fishing trip, as it is thought to bring bad luck (Bois 2016:76). In Iceland fishers consider that a boat containing dirt from the land will endure poor catches (Pálsson 1991:96–97). Cornish fishermen knew that fish "should be eaten from the tail towards the head, to bring the other fishes' heads towards the shore, for eating them the wrong way turns them from the coast" (Tylor 1871:1:107).

Numerous fishing taboos concern particular days when fishing should not take place. Normandy fishermen, especially at Dieppe, know that fishing on All Saints Day will result in nets only pulling up human bones and skeletons (Jones 1898:107–108). Many Christian fishers believe that it is inappropriate to fish on Sunday, the Sabbath (the day of rest). The collapse of the herring industry in Guernsey in the 1830s was said by some fishermen to be the result of certain boats going out fishing on Easter Sunday in 1830 (Anson 1965:112–113). Similarly, the disappearance of herring on the east coast of Scotland in the Dunbar and Stonehaven districts in the mid-nineteenth century was put down to certain fishermen breaking the taboo on Sunday fishing (Anson 1965:113).

Pari fishers of Oyster Bay near Port Moresby on the south coast of Papua New Guinea know that fish are aware of the moral integrity of fishers and will not make themselves available for capture if fishers behave inappropriately in their private lives (Pulsford 1975). For example, "Broken household taboos (*riki*), anger (*badu*) or stealing, adultery or failure to meet obligations (*kerere*), have the effect of causing the fish to keep away from the nets" (Pulsford 1975:111). A similar moral code of conduct exists with fishing in Tonga in Polynesia, where unsuccessful catches may be put down to a death in the family or to inappropriate behaviors by people on land, such as robbery, adultery, or illegal access to land (Bataille-Benguigui 1988:188).

In 1846 a large group of Māori along with a few Europeans went fishing in waters off Ruapapaka Island within the upper reaches of the Hokianga Harbour/ River on the northern tip of Aotearoa/New Zealand. The group was accompanied by a *tohunga* (ritual specialist) to invoke the sea god Tangaroa to ensure a successful catch of fish (Gudgeon 1909:149). Indeed, Walter Gudgeon (1907:68) notes that when undertaking deep-sea fishing, Māori fishermen hold to various restrictions (e.g., no food on board a canoe and no smoking while in a canoe) in order to appease the sea god Tangaroa such that he will not be offended by the taking of fish (i.e., his creations). Ian Barber (2004:444) notes that Māori fishing success related to following mythologically sanctioned fishing rules for specific fishing grounds. Such mythological sanction also relates to reciting formulaic "charms" to "attract fish to the fishing-ground" (Best 1929:208).

Agentive Fishing Technology

In some cases, the agentive capacity of fishing technology rests with spiritual entities that direct fish to be caught either on a hook or in a trap. Often such agency is associated with specific items of fishing technology (e.g., boats, nets, hooks, traps). In addition, a broader agency is morally prescribed and associated with respectful treatment of fishing items to help control spiritual forces that determine fishing success. For example, Hindu fishers of coastal Bangladesh know "that if fishing crafts and gears are sanctified and maintained clean, their catch will be abundant and evil forces/spirits placated down simultaneously" (Deb 2018:4). The following digest of spiritually agentive fishing technologies focuses on boats, nets, hooks, and traps.

Boats

The agentive aspects of many fishing boats in terms of luck in fishing begins with the rituals of construction and launching. In many contexts, associating a fishing vessel with the capacity for successful fishing ventures can be enhanced after launching by further rituals. For example, fishermen of the Windward Islands of the Caribbean know that a fishing boat with good luck means association of the boat with the soul of a dead person, preferably a child (Beck 1977:194). This luck can also be enhanced through the use of *obeah* ("sorcery"). A common form of *obeah* is rubbing boats and fishing gear with special substances, of which the most potent are those containing parts of human corpses, including the heart and genitals of children (Beck 1977:196, 198–199).

Fishers of northeast Scotland refrain from cleaning herring scales off the decks of their boat to ensure that their boat continues to attract fish (Anson 1965:116). In the Shetland Islands, boats were never cleaned after gutting of fish on the deck for fear of washing away good luck. Cleaning was left to the seagulls and the rain (Marwick 1975:77). On the coast of Brittany, fishermen increase fishing luck by smearing the rotten remains of an octopus over their boat. Placing a dead octopus in the bottom of a boat was also thought to enhance fishing success in Brittany (Anson 1865:116). In the Shetland Islands, secreting a dead mouse under the deck of an enemy's fishing boat brought bad luck in fishing (Marwick 1975:76). At Finistère in Brittany, fishers thoroughly smoke fishing boats to rid the presence of the devil to ensure that sardines entered into nets (Anson 1965:120).

Fishers of northeast Scotland and the Shetland and Outer Hebrides Islands to the north knew that a "poor day's fishing" was likely due to their boats being jinxed by bad luck from "some negative supernatural force" such as "a witch, an evil spirit, or an ill omen" (Brown 2021:253, 262). A fire ritual ("burning the Clavie") in the form of moving around the deck with a pole "torch" tipped with an ignited cloth infused with paraffin or diesel fuel "was integral to purifying the boat from evil or negative forces" during a fishing trip (Brown 2021:253–255, 262).

Coastal fishers of Cogtong, central Philippines, sink their fishing vessels periodically to infuse them with salt, which is known to drive out bad "spirits and evil" and associated "bad luck" in fishing. Salt is known to kill "evil and nature spirits" (Torreon and Tiempo 2021:15). In addition, the blood of a sacrificed pig is "smeared in the boat" and the animals' body "thrown to the sea" (Torreon and Tiempo 2021:16). Fishermen stated that the "sea spirits would love to have blood offered because it is a sign that fishermen value the sea and the spirit. It is believed that these supernatural powers are good to human if we are good to them in return" (Torreon and Tiempo 2021:16).

Solomon Islanders of the Santa Ana and Santa Catalina Island groups of Melanesia spiritually embed fishing powers within "sacred" and "specialized" bonito fishing canoes (Davenport 1990:99). These canoes are used to catch bonito and tuna (known collectively as *waiau*) with *waiau* fishing considered "primarily a religious ritual" (Davenport 1990:99). William Davenport (1990:99) records that "most bonito canoes are votive offerings made by important men to their tutelary deities." After a canoe is constructed, "it is sacralised by concealing several teeth from a porpoise, fruitbat, or dog, somewhere inside. These teeth contain special fishing power, injected by a spell. The power and spell came from the deity as part of the original command to build and maintain the canoe" (Davenport 1990:100). The "quantity of bonito caught each year is considered to signal the pleasure or displeasure of the deities" given that "each school of bonito is assumed to be a permanent community under the control of a single tutelary deity" (Davenport 1990:101).

Santa Ana and Santa Catalina bonito fishing canoes also feature a range of carvings to help canoes "seek fish" as a "predator" (Davenport 1990:107). The wooden "up-swept stern piece" of these canoes features a carving of a dog with back-curved tail with a bonito in its mouth that "symbolizes how a bonito canoe and its crew should be poised to catch the sacred fish by being always ready to pounce on its prey" (Davenport 1990:104). Similar predatory features include a carving of a "sea bird holding a fish" on the top of the up-swept stem piece of the prow and an "eye" represented by a circular disk of cone shell inset into the hull behind the prow at the waterline such that the prow is "seen" as a "head" (Davenport 1990:105). In other parts of the Solomon Islands, the "up-swept sterns and low bow sections suggest the profile of a crocodile, head down and tail erect, attacking its prey" (Davenport 1990:105–106). Sandra Revolon (2018:37) adds that fishing canoes of Aorigi (Santa Catalina Island) feature "graphic representation[s]" of sharks ("great predators") as "an explicit desire to attribute the qualities of these remarkable hunters to the watercraft and to the fishers who use them."

Nets

In the European Christian world, the blessing of fishing nets to increase catches is a practice that goes back at least to medieval times. For example, a tenth-century "Blessing of Nets for Catching Fish" states in part: "we pray your goodness, that you might bless with your powerful right hand these nets woven for the capturing of fish, so that when the catch of fish in these nets shall have happened for the use of your servants, we may yield to you, Lord, the granter of good works, deserved thanks for the granted benefits" (quoted in Rivard 2009:225). An old Spanish "Blessing of Nets" similarly states in part: "Grant us, Lord, that by the use of this net we might be refreshed and made to rejoice through the gifts of your grace, just as both refreshed by temporal food we might always express the due abundance of thanks to you in eternal reward" (quoted in Rivard 2009:225).

In the 1940s, John Gillin (1947:33) recorded that fishers from the village of Huanchaco on the Pacific coast of north Peru use 30-m-long fishing nets with upper end projections referred to as a *cabecera* (head) or an *oreja* (ear; see also Grana and Prieto 2021:2). The nets need to be ceremonially treated before they are used at sea. The net owner employs a *brujo curandero* ("curing witch") who "cures" the net. The process involves washing out gourd net floats with special herbal juices and sprinkling the net with special herbs and powders. The net is assigned a *padrino* (godfather) and *madrina* (godmother) who arrange and pay for the *fiesta* ceremony, in which the net is laid out in the form of a cross and sprinkled with holy water blessed by a Christian priest. If the net has a run of not catching any fish, it is considered to have had a spell cast upon it by an enemy who hired a *malero* (evil witch). The spell is reversed by a *brujo curandero*.

During the nineteenth and twentieth centuries, Sicilian and Tyrrhenian fishermen of the west coast of Italy used elaborate and large-scale staked nets and traps to catch tuna (Baldi 1998:155–156). The device consisted of a long net (sometimes over 2 km in length) that extended from the shore out to sea perpendicular to the coast. The net directed schools of tuna into a large rectangular trap structure at its seaward end and operated for a number of months of each year. The capacity of the device to catch tuna and to weather storms was enhanced by the protective power of Christ by use of Christian symbolism. That is, the overall plan of the net/trap system was in the form of a crucifix while the 33 anchors and anchor ropes used to hold the net in place corresponded to the age of Christ at death and were also said to be of crucifix form.

In some cases, spiritually charged objects and materials are added to fishing nets to increase catches. Along the coast of Morbihan, Brittany, sardine fishermen while out in their boats would anoint their fingers with holy water before setting nets. Afterward the rest of the boat and fishing gear were sprinkled with holy water, followed by a prayer (Anson 1965:135). Fishermen of the Tyrrhenian coast of west Italy help ensure the efficacy of their fishing nets by application of holy water (saltwater) blessed by a priest (Baldi 1998:147, 150). In northeast Scotland, newly made fishing nets are splashed with whiskey to help bring good luck in fishing (MacLeod Banks 1939:344). Fishers from Lamalera on the island of Lembata in eastern Indonesia spit chewed garlic and ginger onto fishing nets to ensure that they will catch fish (Barnes 1996:176). In the early seventeenth century, the Spanish recorded on the coast of central Peru that local fisherfolk are known to place "the wings of several little birds" (*cusi*) into their fishing nets "to bring good luck to their fishing" (Rostworowski de Diez Canseco 1977:174). The wings reference the deity Urpay Huachac ("goddess of all marine fish"), which translates to "she who gives birth to doves," after one or two of her daughters turned themselves into doves to either seduce or escape from the god Cuniraya (Marcus 2017:190; Rostworowski de Diez Canseco 1977:173–174).

Salish speakers of the Gulf Islands of northern Washington State in the US Pacific Northwest "attributed personhood to large nets used for taking salmon in saltwater" (Losey 2010:20). Furthermore, the "nets were considered female human beings, and a hole left in the net was known as its vulva. No fish could pass through the vulva without losing its life; the reasons for this are unspecified" (Losey 2010:20; see also Cullon 2017:139–140). According to Diamond Jenness (quoted in Losey 2010:20), the Coast Salish "consider their net to represent a human being with head, body, arms and legs, and they believed that unless it was set in a definite way the leading sockeye [salmon] would turn back disapprovingly and warn those behind."

Hindu fishers of coastal Bangladesh weave four eyes and ears into bag nets (*behundi*) so that the nets can "see and hear" underwater (Deb 2018:10). After undertaking certain rituals, the net becomes "animated" such that it possesses the "innate capacity to see and gather fish underwater" (Deb 2018:10). Although men use the nets for fishing, it is women who weave and undertake the associated animation rituals.

Coastal fishers of Cogtong, central Philippines, ignite a range of special grasses in a coconut shell to create smoke and place it next to a new fishing net "as a way of blessing" and bringing on "good fortune in the fish harvest" (Torreon and Tiempo 2021:15). The ritual was to "remove bad luck," "vanishes the [bad] nature spirits," and "is the best way in helping them to catch more fish" (Torreon and Tiempo 2021:15). A related ritual involves taking a new fishing net down to the edge of the sea, where a "faith healer" utters a Christian prayer in Latin and sacrifices a white chicken such that its blood enters the sea as an "offering" to "supernatural forces at sea . . . in exchange for the abundance of fish caught" in the net (Torreon and Tiempo 2021:15–16).

Motu fishers of the Port Moresby region of Papua New Guinea in the nineteenth century were known to heat up special quartz crystals with fire and then apply these to the corner of a fishing net such that it smoked. This ritual process resulted in the net being "charmed" before it was taken down to the beach for use in the sea (Seligmann 1910:178). On Eddystone Island in the western Solomon Islands, fishing nets can be ritually "charmed" in a two-staged process to help catch fish. First, the floats of a new net are "stroked" with two types of "sea plants" in order "to make plenty of fish run into the net" (Hocart 1937:35). Second, the net is placed on a stone next to a bonito fishing shrine where offerings of shell rings are made to propitiate Mbolana, "a spirit in the net" (Hocart 1937:35). Across Marovo Lagoon on New Georgia Island in the western Solomon Islands, "net fishing (usually for surgeonfish, mullet, and parrotfish) required that sacrifices be made at the shrines called *moru*, dedicated for normal fishing and located at the seashore" (Hviding 1996:268). Marovo shrines comprise "coral stone cairns . . . that were used to enlist the help of ancestral spirits . . . through burnt sacrifice" (Hviding 1996:256).

Fishing net agency in the Solomon Islands also extended to net sinkers. Stone sinkers featured carved anthropomorphic faces, which a man from the island of Malaita explained "symbolize the ancestors" (Solomon Times, 21 February 2008). Furthermore, the "two faces on the carved stone net sinker is a 'guide' for the fishermen to keep them from harm when out at sea, and they also guide the fish right through the net" (Solomon Times, 21 February 2008). The storage of "fishing-nets with stone-sinkers" along with war canoes (*tomoko*) in men's communal houses (*paele*) indicates the spiritually charged status of these objects (Woodford 1890:152). Archaeological research reveals that some fishing shrines at Roviana Lagoon, dating to the past 500 years, are "adorned with net sinkers" in the form of perforated valves of *Tridacna crocea* (Sheppard et al. 2000:36; see also Nagaoka 1999:72, 105, 139).

Hooks

A wide range of marine fisherfolk perform rituals to increase the chances of fishhooks catching fish. For example, the Coast Salish of British Columbia have a story of a man who hooked a magic stone while fishing and thereafter could increase his fishing "luck" by rubbing the "stone fish" on his hook (Barnett 1955:79). Fishers from Pororan Island located off the west coast of Buka Island in eastern Papua New Guinea state that magic was "put on" bonito hooks (made from dolphin or dugong bone with a turtle shell barb) "to ensure a good catch" (Schneider 2012:37). In North Carolina it is believed that "When fishing, spit on your hook and name it. If he loves you you'll catch a fish" (White and Hand 1970:482). An example of imbuing fishhooks with increased capacity to catch fish through spiritual association is provided by certain English and Swedish fishermen who knew that "pins found in church made the best fish-hooks" (Bassett 1885: 435).

The most famous ethnographic example of spiritually agentive fishhooks that operated as liminal agents is halibut figurative hooks from the Northwest Coast of Canada (Cullon 2017:133, 140; Jonaitis 1981; Malindine 2017; Salmen-Hartley and McKechnie 2023). Pacific halibut (*Hippoglossus stenolepis*) is an important marine food of symbolic and spiritual significance to numerous First Nations groups of the Northwest Coast of Canada and adjacent regions of southeastern Alaska (e.g., Haida, Tlingit, Tsimshian, Kwakwaka'wakw, Nuu-chah-nulth) and neighboring US states (Makah; Orchard and Wigen 2016). Most of these groups carved elaborate wooden halibut hooks with three-dimensional representations of a range of anthropomorphic and zoomorphic figures. Aldona Jonaitis (1981) argues that these elaborate fishhooks materialized the process of transcending (crossing the boundary) between the two ontological domains of the air and the sea, particularly the open, deep sea where halibut are found. Furthermore, halibut fishing is "a kind of rite of passage of the hook itself: the hook separates from man when it is thrown into the sea; when it is at the sea-bottom, it is in a liminal state; when it returns to the canoe, with its catch, it is reincorporated into the human domain" (Jonaitis 1981:14). Nearly 80% of halibut hooks have a figurative representation of a land otter, male human, raven, diving bird, halibut, and devilfish, often in combination; all possessing "liminal" qualities and the capacity to transform from one ontological domain to another (Jonaitis 1981:19, Table 3). In the case of diving birds such as mergansers and cormorants, they are proficient fishers and embody the capacity to "transcend cosmic levels" and move between the air and sea and dive to "great depths" (Jonaitis 1981:26).

More recently, Robert Losey (2010:20) emphasizes that halibut "hooks were considered animate and were, with the fisher, socially interacting with halibut." He (2010:20) rightly points out that this view is supported by George Emmons's (1991:117) description of a Tlingit man using a halibut hook: "When he begins to lower hook, he begins to talk to fishhooks, telling them to be watchful and catch his game, and when once caught, not to let it go." As such, "the hooks were acting as social intermediaries between fishermen and fish in a realm (under water) where it was impossible for human persons (shamans being a possible exception) to venture" (Losey 2010:20). The agentive and animate status of halibut hooks was part of "the notion that fishing equipment was also potentially sentient, having 'souls' or living essences, or at the very least was part of the animate world engaged in by both fishes and humans" (Losey 2010:20). Deidre Cullon (2017:153) is quite clear that halibut hooks were considered "sentient." The Yakutat Tlingit of southeastern Alaska "formerly addressed their hooks, lines, and buoys when setting them out to catch halibut. The buoy is said to speak to the fisherman when it has caught a fish" (de Laguna 1972:822).

In northeast Papua New Guinea, fishermen from the Tanga Islands rub turtle shell fishhooks with a particular flower that produces "hooked seed carriers which attach themselves to every passing creature" to "endow" the hook "with similar properties" (Bell 1947:316). Nukumanu fisherfolk of far eastern Papua New Guinea have "prayers" to "cause" fish "to bite the hook" (Feinberg 1995b:180).

Petats language speakers of small islands off the west coast of Buka Island in eastern Papua New Guinea (within the northern Solomon Islands culture area) used bonito fishing lures with shell shanks (e.g., *Tridacna, Conus*) and turtle shell point attached by twine (Bell et al. 1986:50; Blackwood 1935:328–329). Beatrice Blackwood (1935:329) was informed by a fisher that short tassels of glass beads attached to the base of the fishhook below the turtle shell point "were to make it catch many fish" through ritual means. Specifically, "When putting the beads on he spat on the hook and said 'Catch quickly, catch quickly . . . catch fish'" (Blackwood 1935:329). Petats lures were attached by line to a rod and thrown into the sea without bait from a canoe (Blackwood 1935:330–331). Blackwood (1935:331) adds that the "first bonito caught after a period of bad luck is decorated with paint and put back into the sea. This is supposed to attract the other fish to the hook."

More recently, fishers of Pororan Island off the west coast of Buka Island recount that spirits of the dead have the capacity to control whether or not fish go to hooks (Schneider 2012:41). As such, Pororan fishers call out to the spirits of the dead while out fishing in the hope that they will provide a good catch. In some cases, people address spirits of the dead in a general sense while in other situations specific ancestors are called upon. Katharina Schneider (2012:41) provides the example of one fisherman who would take with him in his canoe the remains of his grandfather's fishhook, which had been recovered from his grandfather's grave. This hook had been used successfully by his grandfather to troll for bonito and was considered to provide a conduit to the efficacious spiritual powers of the grandfather.

Fishers of the island of Tikopia located in the southeast corner of the Solomon Islands manufacture elaborate fishing lures to catch bonito. According to Firth (1967:541), bonito are a "prized food resource," and a large catch brought "pride" and "status" to a fisherman. Bonito were considered difficult to catch owing to their "fickleness," and as such, great attention was paid to ritual "formulae," taboos (especially sexual abstinence the night before fishing), and "the technical details of the lure" (Firth 1967:542). The bonito lures (*pa atu*) were notionally owned by chiefs and comprised a shank of clam shell or pearl shell (very rarely whale bone or conch shell) with a turtle shell barb attached by twine (Firth 1951:132; see also Bonshek 2004:42). The white shank "vaguely" looked like a small white fish that was the food of bonito (Firth 1967:544). Ritual attention was paid to the way twine used to attach shank and barb was "crossed at the back of the shank" (Firth 1967:544). Firth (1967:544) notes that "in the Tikopia view the correct lashing was not the invention of men but came from the gods. So the central figure in the invocation was the 'deity of the lashing.'" Success in bonito fishing was said to rest with ritual and spiritual concerns and "not in technical terms" (Firth 1967:546). Charmed bonito lures were capable of working (when combined with strict adherence to taboos) because "fish are sentient beings and free agents" with moral values and capable of understanding ritual prescriptions, according to the Tikopia (Firth 1981:220).

Fishers of Roviana Lagoon of New Georgia Island in the western Solomon Islands also undertake rituals to increase the efficacy of pearl shell bonito lures. For example, pearl shell lures (*gaili*) and associated woven bark twine lines (*taili*) were placed on a famed bonito fishing shrine (*hope inaru*) located on the southeast point of Pukuni Island. The shrine owner then talked to the spirit at the shrine before a fishing expedition, stating: "Let the bonito come out. We are going fishing," in addition to making offerings of tobacco and betel nut (Nagaoka 1999:65–66, 2000:5–6).

The Owa people on the island of Aorigi (Santa Catalina Island) in the eastern Solomon Islands similarly make composite fishhooks with a pearl shell shank. The luster and "iridescence" of the polished pearl shell shank is a visual manifestation of *mana* (spiritual power and agency) that has "efficacy" in engaging with *ataro iesi* "beings of the sea" (Revolon 2018:31; cf. *akalo*—see Chapter 3). Iridescence-imbued *mana* of pearl shell fishhooks helps activate "agency" and efficacy in catching bonito.

The Māori of Aotearoa/New Zealand recited formulaic "charms" over fishhooks to "render them effective" in catching fish (Best 1929:46, 208; see also Taylor 1855:83). One charm (*karakia*) included the line: "Holdfast hooks, hunt your prey, strike true, hook me many fish" (Paulin with Fenwick 2016:79). In various parts of the North Island of Aotearoa/New Zealand, the start of the fishing season was accompanied by ritual activity performed by a *tohunga* (ritual specialist) who ventured out to the fishing grounds in a canoe with a stone bowl (*punga-tai*) containing sediment from a ground oven used to cook the first fish from the previous season. The *tohunga* recited prayers over fishhooks and *punga-tai* before fishing commenced (Paulin with Fenwick 2016:111–112). Māori also used *manea* (stone shanks of composite fishhooks) as "charm-stones (sometimes called *whatu*) to attract fish to fishermen, after the proper incantations had been made over them to *taki*, or draw the fish from the fountains of the sea" (Hamilton 1908:21). *Manea* varied in size from 5 cm to 20 cm and were often highly polished. After a bone barb had been attached with twine, *manea* were towed behind a canoe to attract *kahawai* (sea salmon) and other fish (Hamilton 1908:22).

Māori fishers also used baited hooks and lines (*matau*). Some *matau* feature intricate figurative carvings located on the outer loop (where bait was attached) or the snood end of the shank (where line was attached) that may represent "the god of the sea Tangaroa" (Paulin with Fenwick 2016:114, Figure 54). However, figurative hooks are rare, and rituals associated with fishhooks focused on chants and charms (Paulin with Fenwick 2016:118).

The best-known Māori fishhooks are lures referred to as *pā kahawai* (i.e., *pā* = generic term for fishing lure) used on the North Island of Aotearoa/New Zealand to catch *kahawai* (sea salmon; Beasley 1928:16–18; Best 1929:34–37; Furey et al. 2020:87; Hamilton 1908:30–31; Maaz and Blau 2012:232; Paulin with Fenwick 2016:89–94; Smith 2007). *Pā kahawai* comprised a shank with a section of iridescent abalone or *pāua* (*Haliotis* sp.) carved with a slight "twist" inlaid into a "fish-shaped piece of wood" or sometimes human bone (Best 1929:35; Hamilton 1908:30). An elaborately carved barb, often of human bone, was attached at one end with twine. Usually a few feathers (penguin, kingfisher, kiwi) were attached below the barb "as an additional lure" (Best 1929:36; see also Beasley 1928:16). The lure, attached to flax string, was towed at speed behind a canoe. Augustus Hamilton (1908:30) states that human bone for barbs on *pā kahawai* came from an "enemy." Elsdon Best (1929:31) adds that the incorporation of bone from an enemy in Māori fishhooks was "for the spirit of revenge" (see Best 1924:236;

Bowden 1984:96) and "an act of revenge" (Paulin with Fenwick 2016:72). Yet it seems highly probable that the use of human bone in the manufacture of Māori fishhooks also had cosmological and spiritual significance connected to imbuing hooks with agentive qualities to enhance fish capture efficacy.

Harry Beasley (1928) in his major survey of Pacific Islander fishhooks mentions human bone used in the manufacture of simple, one-piece hooks (Hawai'i and Rapa Nui; and Aotearoa/New Zealand—Skinner 1930:31), the shanks of composite hooks (Hawai'i, Tahiti, Rapa Nui, and Carolines), and the barbs of composite hooks (Aotearoa/New Zealand, Hawai'i, Marquesas, Tuvalu, and Rapa Nui). In the case of the Chamorro of the Mariana Islands of western Oceania, fishers manufactured fishhooks from the clavicles and the long bones of legs and arms of ancestors. The bones "invoked the spiritual strength of their ancestor to increase success" in fishing (McKinnon et al. 2014:68).

Anja Mansrud (2017) argues for the social, cosmological, and ritual significance and agentive qualities of bone fishhooks excavated archaeologically from Middle Mesolithic (8,300–10,300 year old) coastal sites of the northeast Skagerrak area of eastern Norway and western Sweden. Moving beyond basic functionalist descriptions of fishhooks as fishing technology, Mansrud (2017:33) takes a chaîne opératoire ("operational sequence") approach to investigating how "activities related to fishhook manufacture—that is, procurement, manufacture, use, maintenance, repair, and discard—are interconnected processes that highlight relations between humans, their environment, objects and animals." The point is made that raw materials of fishhooks or any other item of material culture are not cosmologically value free or symbolically inert but biographically and agentively loaded. The bone used to manufacture the Middle Mesolithic fishhooks of Skagerrak derived mostly from ungulates (e.g., roe deer, red deer, elks, aurochs) that were hunted for food, and not marine animals. Such raw material leads Mansrud (2017:40) to ask: "When an object was made from a material that was once a living animal, perhaps that animal's 'anima' was retained in the object? Following from this, could it be suggested that fishhooks were animated by certain attributes of the ungulates whose bones were used to make them." Drawing also on local rock art that reveals cosmological relationships between elks and the sea, Mansrud (2017:43) advances that the bone fishhooks of Skagerrak were created as "liminal agents" to transcend the sea-land boundary.

Traps

In an Australian context, many stone-walled intertidal fish traps are associated with the creative acts of ancestral beings. For example, the Lardil of the North Wellesley Islands of the Gulf of Carpentaria know that their first traps "were shaped by the first Lardil people Maarnbil, Jirnjirn and Diwaldiwal who brought culture and language to Mornington Island" (Memmott and Trigger 1998:114). The neighboring Kaiadilt people attribute fish trap construction to Bujuku (Black Crane) and Kaarrku (Seagull; Memmott and Trigger 1998:114). Further to the west, the Yanyuwa people hold knowledge of how certain stone-walled tidal fish traps are associated with the creative acts of ancestral spirit beings. As a result, the "traps are imbued with spiritual potency and agency such that use requires specialized ritual practices (involving ochre and smoke) by senior men who also prescribe who can and cannot use the traps and eat the resulting catch" (Bradley and McNiven 2019:337). Torres Strait Islanders of the eastern strait know that their numerous stone-walled tidal fish traps (*sai*) were initially built by the culture heroes Abob and Kos (Haddon 1935:197; Lawrie 1970:342–343). Abob and Kos morphed into two stones that can be seen on the northwest coast of Erub. Within the nearby intertidal zone is a stone with a hole used by Abob and Kos to moor their canoe (Haddon 1935:197).

Stone-walled tidal fish traps of eastern Torres Strait were associated with special stones linked to ritually enhancing fish catches. For example, the fish trap at Badog Bay on the south coast of Erub has "a large round stone in the centre of the outer wall" called the "Master" of the fish trap that enabled "plenty of fish" when "offered a present of yams, bananas, etc. with singing" that "was carried away at next high tide" (MacFarlane cited in Haddon 1935:197). Similarly, the fish trap opposite Mogot village, also on the south coast of Erub, was once associated with a ~1-m-high "stone figure of a woman" known as Augari or Ogari ("Ugari"—Gutchen 2008:48) that was "master belong that fence" (Haddon 1935:198). Fishers would decorate the agentive figure with coconut palm leaves and offer it "baskets of food" with the verbal request that "you make plenty fish fast in fence" (Haddon 1935:198). In more recent times, a senior man would throw "small rocks towards" these special fish trap stones "to bring more fish" (Gutchen 2008:47–48).

On the island of Mer, also in eastern Torres Strait, ritual stone carvings of fish (*lar*) were painted red and white and arranged into rows on the ground with coconut palm shoots and bushes placed in-between near a house "to ensure that large numbers of fish should be caught in the [tidal] fish-weirs, *sai*" (Haddon 1908:217–218, Plates XX.1, XX.2). Haddon (1908:217) suggested that the placement of the *lar* stones was "a case of homœopathic magic, the man's house being equated to the stone walls of the *sai*."

In the eastern islands of Torres Strait, William MacFarlane recorded strict protocols associated with the repair of stone-walled tidal fish traps, otherwise the fish will not enter the trap. That is, the fish know if the protocols are not followed (quoted in Haddon 1935:197). Other protocols include avoiding making a "loud noise" when moving stones while spearing fish in a trap ("no fish will come again by-and-by; he savee [knows] that noise"), avoidance of pregnant women entering a trap ("the fish will go away and not return for a long time, 'they savee'"), and avoidance of repairs to traps by the husbands of pregnant women (MacFarlane cited in Haddon 1935:197).

The Karadjeri (Karajarri) Aboriginal people of the Kimberley coast of northwest Australia perform a "secret" ceremony "to increase the supply of fish, particularly *paŋanu* (salmon), in the fish traps" (Piddington 1932:392). Close to one of the tidal fish traps (presumably stone-walled) "is a stone, visible at low tide only . . . During the day while the tide is out men clean away the sand from underneath the stone. In the hole so formed they bury a conch shell full of *warbu* (human blood) and also a *kaliguru* (bullroarer) which has been smeared with the same liquid. This will, when the tide comes in, attract the fish to the fish trap where they will be caught" (Piddington 1932:392).

The Yan-nhaŋu of the Crocodile Islands of Arnhem Land of northern Australia must follow strict protocols and site-specific incantations to "increase the number of fish" in tidal fish traps (James 2019:194). As one senior traditional owner noted: "At the fish trap, we speak Yan-nhaŋu language: the language of the spirits of the fish trap and its locality. While we were around the fish trap, we must not call out, laugh, or offend the spirits, because the spirits would not give us any fish. Old people would make an incantation at the fish trap to ensure the spirits gave us lots of fish" (James 2019:193). These fish trap rituals speak to a wider issue of the ethics of reciprocal relationships between people and "ancestral spirits" that go to the heart of "the deep sense of belonging to a place" (James 2019:194–195).

For the Yakutat Tlingit of southeastern Alaska, salmon "fish-traps" with "individual names" possibly "indicate that there was a vague feeling that such inanimate things had a personality or life, similar to that of their owners" (de Laguna 1972:822). Cullon (2017:149) argues that such naming supports the view that fish traps possessed "personhood and sentience." Steve Langdon (2007:236) notes that the Klawock Tlingit of the Prince of Wales archipelago of southeastern Alaska "conceptualized" stake-and-stone fish traps "as 'forts' for the visitors where the salmon could give themselves safely to those (people) they knew would care for them and ensure their opportunity to be reborn." Emmons (1991:106) recorded that for the Tlingit, "carvings, like miniature totem poles representing human figures, fish, etc., were sometimes secured to the barricades overlooking the traps, in the belief that these would encourage or force the fish to enter" (see also Stewart 1977:116). In one case, the figurative carving represented a boy crouched within a salmon, a reference to the Salmon Boy myth (Langdon 2007:266). Langdon (2007:266) notes that the "location of the object is significant in that it was placed on the weir so that it would be seen by a jumping salmon. This placement is designed to interface with Salmon Boy's own account of being directed by the salmon chief to stand up and see where they were, but in his fish form, standing up was actually jumping out of the water. The stake trap could be seen by a jumping salmon but probably not by a swimming salmon."

Cullon (2017:145) reviews ethnographies of First Nations peoples of the Northwest Coast and similarly concludes on the existence of "sentient fish traps." Furthermore, "When considering my argument that sentient fish are in a relationship with humans and that the relationship is based on mutual respect and reciprocity, it no longer makes sense to attempt to understand fish traps as a machine-like object built to catch fish. Instead, options for cooperation, agency and mutual respect should be explored" (Cullon 2017:139). As such, there existed a "*triadic relationship of human-fish-trap*, in which each participant has agency in a relationship that is imbued with reciprocal obligations. In this triad, the fishing structure acts more as an entry point or doorway than a trap. Through this place fish are welcomed into the human world. Through it fish leave the undersea world and enter the human world" (Cullon 2017:140; emphasis added).

Of the little archaeological research that has been undertaken on agentive fish traps, most concerns salmon fishing on the Northwest Coast of Canada and the spiritual relationship between First Nations fishers and salmon. For example, the spatial association between stone-walled tidal fish traps and petroglyphs implies a functional relationship (Ackerman and Shaw 1981; Mobley and McCallum 2001), possibly where the petroglyphs mediated ritual communication with spiritual salmon providers and salmon increase (Keithahn 1940; Lundy 1974:337). On a more sophisticated and ethnographically informed level, Losey (2010:27) found that nearly all wooden tidal traps recorded across tidal flats at Willapa Bay in the US state of Washington, had removed sections indicating that they had been "intentionally dismantled following episodes of fishing." This dismantling was to allow fish to escape capture and unnecessary death during periods of trap disuse (Losey 2010:28). Losey (2010:28) adds that "since fish were seen as sentient and consciously engaging with humans, leaving a trap to capture the fish but then not taking them was the equivalent of refusing gifts or being inhospitable to guests." Furthermore, "From an animistic perspective, this would have significant negative repercussions—fish could choose not to return in the future, might seek vengeance upon the offending party or might find it impossible to regenerate themselves. . . . I suggest that part of the intent in many cases was to manage social relationships between human and other-than-human persons rather than to conserve or manage prey or populations in the modern biological sense" (Losey 2010:28).

Discussion

It is difficult to find ethnographic examples of coastal fishing communities that do not possess rituals associated with increasing fish stocks and increasing the chances of catching fish. For many communities, gods and ancestral beings and spirits have the power to control fish stocks. As such, rituals to *increase fish stocks* are associated with propitiating these spiritual beings and their powers of fecundity. Fish-stock rituals often involve a moral economy of reciprocity whereby fishers undertake behaviors deemed respectful (e.g., returning the first fish caught back to sea, returning fish remains back to the sea, eating fish in a certain way, animal sacrifices). The return of fish remains (e.g., bones) is usually associated with spiritual or soul renewal and rebirth. In some cases, reincarnation requires burning of bones, or not burning bones in other cultural contexts. Rarely do these rituals involve spiritually charged talismanic objects (charms). Most rituals take place at designated sites and shrines (located on land and in the sea) whereby votive offerings are made to spiritual beings or forces. Offerings rarely involve fish but can be marine related (e.g., coral and shells) or of terrestrial origin (e.g., plants, sediment, blood, ochre, fireplace ash).

Finding archaeological evidence of fish-stock renewal rituals as known ethnographically is challenging due to their often ephemeral and intangible nature and wide-ranging form, which together limit the development of material identification criteria. To date, archaeological studies are limited to rock art sites located at the water's edge on the Northwest Coast of Canada and southeastern Alaska linked to spiritual propitiation and reincarnation of salmon, Hawaiʻian *koʻa* fishing shrines and associated votive offerings (e.g., coral) linked to spiritual propitiation, and an ancient Ecuadorian sanctuary with large fish bone votive deposits similarly linked to spiritual propitiation. The Canadian, Alaskan, and Hawaiʻian examples are all founded upon detailed ethnographic information. A critical need exists for ethnoarchaeological studies that focus on the material correlates of fish increase, maintenance, and renewal ceremonies.

In some respects, rituals to *increase fish catches* overlap in form and efficacy with rituals to increase fish stocks. That is, they often involve propitiating spiritual beings and forces through prayers, chants, and votive offerings (e.g., at shrines on land, into the sea, onboard fishing vessels). Offerings include plant foods, seafood, fish bones from a meal, terrestrial sediments, incense, cloth, tobacco, alcohol, money, and the first catch of the season. In rare cases, offerings take the form of animal sacrifices (e.g., goats, sheep). In many cases, fishers employ special objects as charms to help ensure fishing success. As with fish-stock renewal rituals, fish-catch rituals also involve a moral economy of respect and reciprocity toward spiritual beings or forces through votive offerings. Good luck in fishing often involves avoiding activities known to incur bad luck in fishing. In some regions it is bad luck for a fisherman to encounter certain terrestrial animals (e.g., dogs, foxes, cats, hares, rabbits, pigs) before a fishing trip or to have these animals onboard vessels. Avoidance of negative impacts extended to taboos on mentioning these terrestrial animals during fishing trips. The presence of a woman on board a fishing vessel is considered a good luck fishing omen in some cultural contexts and a bad luck omen in other fishing communities. Other fishing taboos, varying from region to region, include fishermen abstaining from sexual intercourse the night before a fishing trip, avoiding wishing fishermen good luck, avoidance of fishing on special religious days, and avoidance of immoral behavior.

As with fish-stock increase rituals, archaeological investigation of fish-catch rituals as known ethnographically is challenging due to their often ephemeral and intangible nature and wide-ranging form which together limit the development of cross-cultural material identification criteria. Archaeological investigations of fish-catch rituals are rare and limited to votive offerings and deposits at ancient Greek temples and at fishing shrines in the Solomon Islands. Again, ethnoarchaeological studies may help develop material correlates of fishing rituals.

A third dimension of fishing rituals is *agentive fishing technology* (boats, nets, hooks, traps). Boats can be imbued with the capacity to attract fish through the ritual application of substances (e.g., derived from human and animal corpses), including not washing away fish residues after a fishing trip. The capacity of woven fishing nets to catch fish can be ritually enhanced through blessings and spells by a religious specialist, application of special substances (e.g., plants, animal body parts, holy water), and symbolic arrangement of the net in the sea (e.g., in the form of a crucifix). The agentive ability of fishhooks to catch fish can similarly be enhanced by contact with spiritually potent charms, blessing by a ritual specialist, and manufacture from spiritually charged animal bone (marine and terrestrial) and human bone. In rare instances, the capacity of fishhooks to catch fish was spiritually enhanced with agentive, animate, and even sentient qualities by the addition of anthropomorphic and zoomorphic figurative carvings of spirit beings and liminally agentive animals. Considerable ethnographic information is available on rituals to increase the capacity of tidal fish traps to catch fish. Rituals of respect and reciprocity include reciting efficacious incantations before trap use, placement of spiritually charged objects and offerings within traps (e.g., shells, human blood, ochre, plant foods, special stones, figurative stone carvings), and taboos (e.g., pregnant women and their husbands must not enter traps).

A low number of archaeological studies have considered the spiritually agentive qualities of fishing technology. Ritual associations with stone-walled tidal fish traps have been inferred by the proximity of petroglyphs and disabling of traps during non-use periods by creation of wall gaps to allow fish to escape as a sign of the morally prescribed respectful relationship between people and fish. The biographical pathway of raw materials used to make fishhooks has been used successfully to explore the symbolic and ontological dimensions of fishing in Mesolithic Norway. This biographical approach holds considerable potential for archaeological explorations of fishing technologies. The approach is analogous to the cosmological and symbolic significance of boats and ships which starts with spiritually imbued trees. This imbuement is an inalienable dimension of the wood used to make vessels and fundamentally defines ritual use of the vessels on the sea. Ethnography also reveals that figurative carvings on fishhooks similarly have spiritual and agentive significance, perhaps analogous to ships' figureheads. Finally, the depositional context of fishhooks can be highly informative of their symbolic significance, such as burials (e.g., O'Connor et al. 2017) and caches (e.g., Leach 2007).

11

Why So Many Maritime Rituals?

This chapter brings together a plethora of views by chroniclers of maritime life over the past two centuries on why the world of mariners (including fishers) is infused with "superstition" in older folkloric terminology and "supernatural agency," "animacy," "ritualization," and "relationality" in contemporary anthropological parlance. The issue of why there are so many maritime rituals is twofold. First, do mariners hold to a larger corpus of spiritual beliefs and employ a wider array of ritual practices compared to peoples whose lives focus on the land? Second, why do mariners across the globe have a shared tradition of spiritual beliefs about the sea and put their faith in a wide range of ritual practices to bring about more favorable engagements with the sea?

In terms of the first question, Raymond Brown, in his 1972 book *Phantoms, Legends, Customs and Superstitions of the Sea*, posits that "sailors are perhaps the most superstitious order of workmen in the world," adding that "the Hindu seaman ranks as the most superstitious of all sailors" (1972:155). While the range of beliefs in spiritual beings and forces connected with the sea is extensive, few studies have specifically addressed the question of whether mariners believe in relatively more spiritual entities and practice more rituals compared to terrestrially based cultures. US Navy Lieutenant Fletcher Bassett (1885:8) in his preface to his monumental 1885 volume *Legends and Superstitions of the Sea and of Sailors in All Lands and at All Times*, stated that "while it is true that the sailor is conservative in his beliefs, I do not believe that he is more superstitious than those of his class who dwell on the land. A comparison of his credulities with the superstitions of the same day and age of the world will not, I believe, result to his disadvantage. Superstition and credulity were rife everywhere when most of the sailor traditions were born, and many of them, as will be shown, are but adaptations of similar beliefs on land—many were first imagined far inland, by people who never saw the sea."

At this juncture in scholarship, empirically informed generalization on the scale and extent of maritime spiritual beliefs, lore, and rituals indicates pervasiveness. As Brody (1998:2) rightly notes, the "impulses behind the religious needs created by venturing at sea appear to be universal." Indeed, such universality helps answer the second question posed above and underpins development of what has been labeled "anxiety ritual theory" and the notion that the inherent risks and dangers of life on the sea, linked to unpredictability of the elements, naturally lend to the development of superstition, spiritual beliefs, and myriad rituals of propitiation. This chapter critically examines anxiety ritual theory (as originally formulated by Bronislaw Malinowski in 1925) and whether danger (as externally generated by the elements) begets superstition and ritualization, or whether danger (as internally generated by ontology) is a social construction that begets superstition and ritualization. This chapter uses the term "superstition" in keeping with its usage in the "anxiety ritual theory" literature.

External Danger Begets Superstition and Ritualization

It is undeniable that life on the sea was, and in many circumstances remains, full of danger, with a high potential for injury and even death. Most of this danger is linked externally to the elements whereby strong winds create large waves and rough seas that claim the lives of many mariners through shipwreck, drowning, and physical injury. The Yanyuwa Aboriginal people of northern Australia are "well aware that a life centred on the sea is far riskier than one based totally upon the mainland, and in the past there was a higher mortality rate associated with the sea" (Bradley 1998:133). Bradley (1998:133) comments that the dangers of life on the sea "are not even called risks: rather they are described simply as, 'that's just the kind of life we have on the sea'" as related one senior Yanyuwa man. As such, the Yanyuwa do not "fear" the sea, but it is certainly "respected" (Bradley 1998:132). Like numerous Aboriginal communities of Australia's tropical northern coastline, the Yanyuwa are expert dugong hunters, and Thomson (1934b:238) observed that hunting of dugongs was "undoubtedly the most dangerous and spectacular occupation" practiced by Indigenous Australians. Among the Nukumanu Islanders of eastern Papua New Guinea, "loss at sea has been a significant cause of death, particularly among the atoll's male population" (Feinberg 1995b:191). In their 1984 edited volume on Indigenous *Maritime Institutions in the Western Pacific*, Kenneth Ruddle and Tomoya Akimichi (1984:1) noted that "people whose livelihood derives either in part or entirely from maritime pursuits, and especially fishermen, are undeniably faced with a more hazardous environment compared with those who make their living by other occupations."

In 1894 the National Amalgamated Sailors' and Firemen's Union of Great Britain and Ireland published data on industrial fatalities associated with a range of occupations. For the first half of 1894, 1,371 "seamen" were killed compared to a combined figure of 1,161 employees killed from a range of land-based industries ("railway servants," "miners," and "factory and workshop operatives"; cited in Miller 2012:202). For the Anglo-American maritime world of the eighteenth century, Rediker (1987:193) writes that the "life cycle of seafaring employment ended, often suddenly and prematurely, with death, which at sea was visible, poignant, commonplace, and never impersonal." "As callous as the seaman appeared toward the death that took so many shapes around him, he could not escape its shadows" (Rediker 1987:194). The use of a mariner's hammock as a shroud for sea burial ensured that death stalked a mariner's sleeping hours (see Rediker 1987:194).

David Stewart (2011:10), in his book *The Sea Their Graves*, provides sobering statistics on the high fatality rates of mariners, remarking that "seafaring is as deadly a profession as any that humans have ever pursued." For example, commercial fishers had the highest occupational death rate in the United States between 1998 and 2007 at 121 per 100,000 compared to the overall average death rate of 4 per 100,000 (Stewart 2011:4). Stewart (2011:4) notes that "this means that fishers are thirty times more likely to die on the job compared to all other U.S. workers." Stewart (2011:5) also cites studies from the UK, where the fatal accident death rate for fishers was 126 per 100,000 for the period 1992–2006. For merchant mariners, the UK fatal accident death rate was >200 per 100,000 in the early twentieth century and declined to 11 per 100,000 in the period 1996–2005. In short, during the twentieth century, "in the United States and the United Kingdom, commercial fishing is consistently the deadliest occupation one can pursue" (Stewart 2011:5). And the death rate during the late nineteenth century was worse, with fatalities in the UK numbering around 1,000–1,400 per 100,000 for the period 1871–1886 (Stewart 2011:7). These figures and others led Stewart (2011:9) to state that during "the Age of Sail, seafaring was anywhere from ten to possibly more than a hundred times as deadly as it is today." As such, the "shadow of death loomed always over mariners and had a great hold on their collective subconscious. Consequently, it influenced their group values and beliefs to a substantial degree" (Stewart 2011:11).

The high death rate of Anglo-American mariners (especially fishers) is often difficult to compare to the death rate of small-scale fishing communities in other parts of the world, especially the developing world, due to poor recordkeeping by government agencies. However, a recent study by the Fish Safety Foundation reveals that across the globe for the period 2000–2020, of the more than 40 million people employed in the fisheries sector (excluding aquaculture), over 100,000 die annually (Willis and Holliday 2022:6–7, 13, 17, 21). Statistics for some African countries from the past 30 years reveal a fisheries death rate 5–10 times greater than the death rate of 120 per 100,000 in the US and UK. Examples include Nigeria (1,000–3,300 per 100,000), West Africa (1,000 per

100,000), and Guinea (500 per 100,000), with an average African rate of around 1,000 per 100,000 (Willis and Holliday 2022:9, 23, 40, Tables 1, 4). In regions where fishing involves lots of deep diving, death rates are very high: Grenada averages 2,700 per 100,000; Thailand, 3,000 per 100,000; and the Philippines, 5,000 per 100,000 (Willis and Holliday 2022:33, Table 6).

Numerous nineteenth-century scholars of maritime lore and culture made a link between the dangerous lives of mariners, their ignorance of scientific knowledge of the elements, and their belief in supernatural forces and what was generally referred to as "superstition." For example, John Brand of the Society of Antiquaries of London and Sir Henry Ellis of the British Museum in their 1849 book *Observations on the Popular Antiquities of Great Britain* wrote that "sailors, usually the boldest men alive, are yet frequently the very abject slaves of superstitious fear" (Brand and Ellis 1849:239).

Henry Buckle (1858:271), in his *History of Civilization in England*, mused that the "credulity of sailors is notorious, and every literature contains evidence of the multiplicity of their superstitions, and of the tenacity with which they cling to them. This is perfectly explicable by the principle I have laid down. Meteorology has not yet been raised to a science; and the laws which regulate winds and storms being in consequence still unknown, it naturally follows, that the class of men most exposed to their dangers should be precisely the class which is most superstitious." Buckle (1858:271–274) equally saw "agricultural-ists" at the mercy of the elements which similarly accounted for their belief in superstition and "supernatural agency," which he contrasted with "soldiers" and "manufacturers." For Buckle it was "ignorance" and risks and dangers as-sociated with the unpredictability of the elements in the absence of knowledge of scientific laws that fostered belief in superstition and "supernatural agency," including propitiation prayers to God in church.

Over the past four decades, maritime scholars from a wide range of dis-ciplines have continued to link danger, fear, and superstition in the lives of mariners. For example, in his well-known book *Between the Devil and the Deep Blue Sea*, Marcus Rediker (1987:183, 199) notes that "early and unnatural death reinforced a belief in spirits and expanded its social function" to "forge occu-pational identity and solidarity." Furthermore, the "uncontrollable vicissitudes of nature, the extreme vulnerability of seamen, and the frequency of death at sea gave a special power to superstition, omens, personal rituals, and belief in luck" (Rediker 1987:186). David Taylor (1992:9) in *Documenting Maritime Folklife* takes a similar view: "Since maritime occupations often place workers in a highly unpredictable, constantly changing, and hazardous environment, it is not surprising that workers hold many beliefs about fortune and misfortune. A primary function of such beliefs is to explain the unexplainable." Horace

Beck (1999:280–281), in his classic text *Folklore and the Sea*, adds: "Perhaps the largest single body of lore concerns the supernatural and, in particular, the dead. Living as he does a hazardous life where no man can be sure of seeing the sun rise on the morrow, it is only natural that the sailor should be inordinately concerned with the spirit world, and this concern is augmented by sea conditions, where fog, ice, mirage, exhaustion, bad food and isolation from normal living enable a man to see, to hear and to feel things not ordinarily experienced by other mortals."

Stewart (2011:96) wrote that a "key function of folklore dealing with danger is that it teaches how to prevent accidents or death from occurring. . . . Superstitions, for example, function as taboos against actions that are thought to bring about disaster. Mariners in the Age of Sail held numerous superstitions, some which survive among their modern comrades." In their book *Lexical Attrition in Scottish Fishing Communities*, Robert Millar and colleagues (2014:24) contend that, "given the perils of their occupation—still dangerous today with technological help; far more so even in the recent past—it was inevitable that superstitions would become an integral part of the everyday routines of the community." And more recently, Mayumi Itoh (2018:17) in *The Japanese Culture of Mourning Whales* similarly theorized that "Japanese were highly superstitious in general, but fishermen were more so because their lives were at the mercy of the vagaries of the weather."

Although much recent maritime scholarship continues to link danger and superstition, discourse has modified subtly such that superstition has been replaced with ritualization, which not only obviates the pejorative overtones of the term "superstition" but also allows more meaningful analysis of mariners' cultural practices both behaviorally and materially. For example, Rediker (1987:181) notes that the "seaman, whose life might be threatened on any given day, made omens central to his outlook, seeking mastery over his surroundings not only through natural observation but also through magic, ritual, and supernatural interpretation." According to Richard Buxton, for the ancient Greek mariner, "it was hard to know when the sea's dark side would burst out: hence the elaborate rituals to invoke divine protection upon a voyage, and the countless offerings made to saviour divinities like the Dioskouroi and the great gods of Samothrace, in return for a voyage successfully accomplished" (Buxton 1994:100). Ina Berg (2011:121) adds: "Due to the dangers and uncertainties encountered by those travelling the seas, it is not surprising to find that societies imagined the sea in general and dangerous locations within it (e.g., whirlpools, fringing reefs, channels) to be the domain of powerful supernatural beings who control wind, currents and waves; these creatures need to be placated with sacrifices, prayers and by upholding certain taboos to insure a safe journey."

Westerdahl (2011b:751) holds similar views: "Nature is experienced as fickle, and ritual produces human magic to avert danger. It was once widely believed, at least in northern Europe, that catching danger in a ritual web of language and vocabulary would render it innocuous."

Despite the "non-material, spiritual" nature of maritime beliefs, Galili and Rosen (2015a:35) also rightly observe that such beliefs were often materiality expressed in maritime rituals and associated practices that are well-suited for archaeological investigation: "Men were always awed by the sea and feared its immense, often unexpected, powers. Terrestrial and underwater archaeological discoveries of material artifacts expose the numerous ways by which those anxieties were remedied and testify to their antiquity."

Links between fear and danger at sea and the development of an extensive maritime lore of superstitions and associated rituals have become formalized into what has come to be known as "anxiety ritual theory." The theory was given an ethnographic reality following Malinowski's research with Trobriand Islanders of southeastern Papua New Guinea between 1915 and 1918 (Symmons-Symonolewicz 1960:38). Results were detailed in his famous 1925 essay "Magic, Science, and Religion," which gained greater readership following reprintings (e.g., Malinowski 1948, 1954). In his essay, Malinowski interpreted the prevalence of magical and ritual practices of the Trobriand Islanders to have developed for cultural activities where elements of unpredictability manifesting in fear of activity failure and danger fell outside of what he labeled "scientific," "*empirical and rational knowledge*" (1925:35–36; original emphasis).

Malinowski's views on magic were a radical departure from nineteenth-century anthropological formulations on magic framed within the colonialist and indeed racist paradigm of social evolutionism. For example, foundation anthropologist at Oxford University, Edward B. Tylor (1871:1:101, 122), in his book *Primitive Culture*, described magic as "pseudo-science," and the "belief in Magic" as "one of the most pernicious delusions that ever vexed mankind." In his famous text *The Golden Bough*, Sir James Frazer (1911:53) saw magic as irreligious and "a spurious system of natural law as well as a fallacious guide of conduct; it is a false science as well as an abortive art." Susan Greenwood (2009:4), in *The Anthropology of Magic*, while not the first person to critique these pejorative and colonialist representations, states the issue succinctly: "Magic has been associated with backwardness and primitivism, a negative trope in constructions of the primitive other."

Moving beyond the essentializing views of his nineteenth-century predecessors, Malinowski elevated to a theoretical level his views on Trobriand Islander magic as separate from, but complementary to, their scientific understandings of the world. His insights were based on observed differences in the relative use of magic by fishers depending on where they fished. He stated famously that "lagoon fishing, where man can rely completely upon his knowledge and skill, magic does not exist, while in the open-sea fishing, full of danger and uncertainty, there is extensive magical ritual to secure safety and good results" (Malinowski 1925:32).

Murray Wax and Rosalie Wax (1963:498) note that the correlation between fishing fear, danger, and anxiety and relative use of rituals in Malinowski (1925) "is so neat that it has been cited numberless times since the publication of the essay." Yet application of Malinowski's anxiety ritual theory to maritime rituals only became commonplace from the 1960s. Indeed, with 6,158 Google Scholar citations (as of 2025), the modern reprint of Malinowski (1954) is one of the most cited publications in anthropology. Many scholars believe the theory has extraordinary explanatory power in terms of understanding the existence of maritime rituals, especially fishing rituals. Popularity of the theory relates to the simple fact that on empirical grounds a strong positive correlation exists between anxiety and ritual in a wide range of contemporary maritime cultural contexts.

Patrick Mullen (1969:216) posits that fishers' superstitious beliefs and rituals operate at a "psychological level of function," as they "relieve some of the anxiety associated with their dangerous occupation." Indeed, he states boldly that "nearly all of the fishermen's superstitious behavior arises as a response to anxiety over their uncertain condition" (Mullen 1969:216). The "major value expressed by the fishermen in their magic is a fear and respect for the sea. Many of the beliefs seek to alleviate the natural hazards of the sea" (Mullen 1969:218). On a more general level, Mullen (1969:217) adds that "anxiety is reduced when a magical practice is followed, the person acts with more confidence in his task, and physical steadiness enables him to perform the task successfully."

Mullen (1969:218–219) argues that his Texas fishers study parallels Malinowski's observations of ritual use by Trobriand Islanders and lends strong support for anxiety ritual theory. That is, Mullen found that Texas fishers who worked the more hazardous waters of the Gulf of Mexico and further out to sea had "over twice as many magic beliefs" as fishers who operated within the bay and closer to shore. In fact, the bay fishers only had a "weak tradition of magic belief" (Mullen 1969:218).

Arguably the most extensive application of Malinowski's anxiety ritual theory to a maritime context is John Poggie and colleagues' study of coastal fishers of southern New England in the United States. Poggie and Carl Gersuny (1972:66) note the theory centers on the issue of "risk" in terms of "certainty or uncertainty of the catch" (risk to "production") and "uncertainty or danger to the fishermen themselves" (risk to "person"; see also Poggie et al. 1976:258).

They found that in a single community that the "hazardous" and sometime fatal work of coastal fishers was highly ritualized (mostly avoidance rituals or taboos associated with personal risks) compared to the "relatively safe" and nonritualized textile milling industry. Further research revealed that length of stay at sea correlated positively with increased perception of risk or danger and ritual activity (Poggie et al. 1976; Poggie and Pollnac 1988:71–72). Poggie and Richard Pollnac (1988:73) concluded that "the principal function of ritual avoidances among fishermen in Southern New England is to reduce anxiety resulting from uncertainty [and risk] with respect to personal safety." They further concluded that "insuring a good catch seems to be secondary to safety. This is like the 'hierarchy of life.' We must satisfy our safety needs before we do anything further!" (Poggie and Pollnac 1988:73).

Trevor Lummis (1985) uses "Malinowski's theory" in his detailed investigation of coastal fishermen and their families in East Anglia, east England. Following Malinowski's Trobriand Island results, Lummis (1985:152–153) found that the "inshoremen were the least superstitious, the trawlermen were a little more so, while the driftermen were the most superstitious of all." This pattern of association matched "capital investment" in boats and fishing equipment, ranging from lowest (inshoremen) to highest (driftermen). In contrast, work-related fatalities were highest among trawlermen, followed by driftermen and inshoremen. As such, contra Poggie and Pollnac (1988), Lummis (1985:153) concluded that "the practice of superstition correlates with economic anxiety but not with personal risk."

Detailed investigation of the maritime culture of Red Sea peoples by Dionisius Agius (2017) revealed that "fear of thunder, lightning, and gales as they blow unpredictably in the Red Sea brings people together to offer gifts; thus propitiation is essential to pacify or appease or expiate" (Agius 2017:152). Citing previous research linking anxiety, superstition, and ritual (Keinan 2002; Malinowski 1954), Agius (2017:144) notes that the "Red Sea is a particularly dangerous arena for securing a livelihood, so it would be understandable that supernatural protection is invoked by prayers, talismanic objects, and tomb visitation." He concludes that while "fear and anxiety" has been allayed to some extent by a "reliance on technology," "it would seem that the turbulent nature of the Red Sea is reflected in the need for beliefs that give positive protective measures against destructive elemental powers" (Agius 2017:152, 154).

Most recently, Apurba Deb (2018) has investigated the relationship between anxiety and ritual among caste-based Hindu coastal fishers of Thakurtala village, Moheskhali Island, southeast Bangladesh. Similarly informed by Malinowski's Trobriand Island research, Deb (2018:1) found that "observances of rituals at both domestic and community ambits are perceived to improve luck, reduce anxiety level associated with marine fishing, and reinforce pre-voyage psychological preparedness of the sea-faring fishers and their family members." As such, "The intensities of rituals and the degrees of risks and uncertainty are linearly correlated; with the increase in the risk level, the observance of rituals escalates" (Deb 2018:9). Deb (2018:11) concludes that "there is insignificant observance of rituals in [the] case of fishers who fish in safe inshore waters or are engaged in ancillary activities. These comparative observations justify well the notion of risk behind observing rituals."

Malinowski's (1925) anxiety ritual theory has only been employed by a few archaeologists in maritime contexts, mostly in a broad fashion of endorsing a link between ritualization and danger, stress, and risk. Examples include Alan Strauss's (1987:127) synthesis of archaeological data on ritualization of the dangerous Native American practice of swordfish hunting in New England, Stewart's (2011:66–69) analysis of Anglo-American grave markers and memorials associated with maritime deaths, and my analysis of ethnographically recorded resource maintenance (increase) ceremonies and shrines across Torres Strait to underpin the archaeologically testable hypothesis that long-term trends in use of these rituals intensified with environmentally induced subsistence stress and risk, especially during extended periods of drought (McNiven 2016b).

Internal Danger Begets Superstition and Ritualization

An alternative theoretical view to anxiety ritual theory is that danger and anxiety are not the cause of mariners' superstitions and rituals but indeed the result of such beliefs and practices. That is, do perceptions of danger and anxiety at sea *produce* superstitions and rituals, or are they the *product* of superstitions and rituals (or a combination of both)? For example, Margaret Lantis, in her celebrated 1938 paper "The Alaskan Whale Cult and Its Affinities," found the theoretical link between danger and rituals wanting in terms of her extensive knowledge of Inuit and Northwest Coast societies. Desson (1995:119) adds that "whaling for the Alutiiq speakers of the Kodiak Archipelago [central southern Alaska] was much more than a search for food. It was an exhilarating, frightening, awesome enterprise intertwined with solitary ritual activity, and replete with danger, which placed the whaler in immediate contact with the spiritual world." In short, whalers feared the spiritual dimensions of whaling more than the physical dangers of the hunt per se. Whales were superior both physically and spiritually, with the liminality of the role of the human dead in hunting adding an extra metaphysical dimension to the danger (see Day 2019:85).

Alfred Kroeber (1948:603), in his 1948 textbook *Anthropology*, critiqued Malinowski's anxiety ritual theory and the underlying proposition that "holds magic and animism to be man's response to his sense of insecurity in the world." Kroeber (1948:604) points to Malinowski's (1935) own extensive research on Trobriand Island gardening, which documents a multitude of magic and ritual practices without fear and anxiety. He concludes that anxiety ritual theory is not applicable to all societies and cultures and that "we cannot predict either the strength or the kind of religion or magic in a given culture from knowing how great the security of life is" (Kroeber 1948:604).

Two issues concern the question of overcoming perceptions of danger and anxiety. First, are danger and anxiety a problem? Second, is the perception of danger and anxiety socially constructed? In terms of the first issue, facing any dangerous situation without comprehension of the danger and risks and their precipitating signs is potentially a recipe for disaster. This sentiment is expressed well by an old man on the island of Aran located off the west coast of Ireland, who noted proverbially that: "A man who is not afraid of the sea will soon be drownded . . . for he will be going out on a day he shouldn't. But we do be afraid of the sea, and we do only be drownded now and again" (Synge 1907:96).

While it is well beyond the scope of this discussion to enter into the considerable anthropological, archaeological, and psychological literature on the management of perceived risk and associated anxiety through ritual, it is clear that at least in terms of the psychological aspect of Malinowski's theory, a balancing act exists to ensure that confidence-inducing and anxiety-reducing rituals achieve some result but not one so great that they create a false and even fatal sense of security. The other balancing act relates to the extent to which dangers are also considered risks that necessitate mitigation behaviors, ritual or otherwise. Similarly, many fishers consider certain dangers and associated risks acceptable out of economic, social, and political desperation (Willis and Holliday 2022). High death rates through drowning among refugees and migrants using overcrowded, leaking boats to seek asylum illustrates how economic and social desperation can induce extreme risk taking. As Mary Douglas (2002:xix) writes in the Preface to the 2002 edition of her classic 1966 text *Purity and Danger*, "Dangers are manifold and omnipresent. Action would be paralysed if individuals attended to all of them; anxiety has to be selective."

The second issue of social construction is the most problematic in terms of the explanatory utility of Malinowski's anxiety ritual theory in maritime contexts. Wax and Wax (1963:499) contend that "explanations of the occurrence of magical rites by an alien observer in terms of risk or hazard are misleading because all activities are risky (uncertain as to outcome) but only some are (immediately) accompanied by rite." Obviously, the extent to which certain risks are considered dangerous and anxiety inducing enough to warrant some form of ritual response can vary from individual to individual and even society to society. A more significant concern is that raised by Alfred Radcliffe-Brown in his 1939 Frazer Lecture titled *Taboo*, in which he critically examined Malinowski's anxiety ritual theory and argued for the exact opposite based on his own extensive fieldwork experiences (Radcliffe-Brown 1958). Radcliffe-Brown (1958:109) argued: "I think that for certain rites it would be easy to maintain with equal plausibility an exactly contrary theory, namely, that if it were not for the existence of the rite and the beliefs associated with it the individual would feel no anxiety, and that the psychological effect of the rite is to create in him a sense of insecurity or danger." Similarly, Simon Bronner (1984:66) notes that a key problem with Malinowski's (1948) theory, and its subsequent application (e.g., Mullen 1969), is: "did risk cause the rise of beliefs or did beliefs perhaps engender the risk?"

The proposition that risks linked to perceptions of danger and anxiety are socially constructed and underpinned by beliefs in some contexts is exemplified by the Bible. Friel (2012) advances that the sea was feared by Anglo-Saxon English because of two negative references in the Bible—Jonah's whale experience and Noah's Flood. In short, the "sea also offered a ready metaphor for the power of evil in the world" and as "a place of danger, violence and devils" (Friel 2012:181–182). The people of Brittany of northwest France once held the view that God made the land but the Devil made the sea (Anson 1965:46). Patarino (2002:335) makes the point that for English sailors of the sixteenth and seventeenth centuries, who wrestled "on a day to day basis with violent, often fickle weather, almost every thing that happened to them, both good and bad, was ascribed to the power of God." In addition, "Many sailors discerned a supernatural power and malevolence in the sea and considered it evil, literally referred to as the devil" (Patarino 2002:422). As such, mariners "needed to rely upon God in order to persevere in the face in extreme adversity" (Patarino 2002:345). Patarino (2002:464) adds that mariners' superstitions were an expression of an understanding that the "sea was not simply a dangerous place to work but was an environment imbued with supernatural character."

Malinowski's anxiety ritual theory posits that areas of sea are considered dangerous by fishers and anxiety inducing because of environmental concerns such as bad weather bringing forth rough seas. But considerable ethnographic information reveals that fishers can also view areas of sea anxiety inducing due to the presence of dangerous spirits and sea monsters. Neil Arnold (2013:10), in *Shadows of the Sea*, writes that British "sailors and other seafaring folk are extremely superstitious. Sea captains and trawlermen will happily chatter over a pint about the rough seas they've conquered, or the mighty fish they've caught in their nets, but the mention of ghosts and the like will send them running for their beds in terror."

According to Alicia Magos (1994:315), fishermen of Suclaran village on Guimaras Island, central Philippines, "have two notions of their fishing grounds. The nearby waters are shallow and, therefore, less dangerous. It is also not considered *mari-it* [dangerous] on the assumption that no sea-spirits live there. Hence, no rituals are performed for fishing in the area. The fishermen could even risk fishing here during bad weather because there are nearby islands. But beyond the nearby waters of Suclaran, the waters become deep and are considered *mari-it*." Magos (1994:349) adds that "fishing areas that are deep . . . are less frequented because they are considered to be spirit-inhabited." For Igdalaguit, Suclaran, and Gabi villagers, "*mari-it* are generally places in the sea which are very deep and are considered to be dangerous because of the presence of malevolent sea-spirits, collectively identified as *puruanon* (malevolent spirit coming from far-flung islands) and the *ukoy*, a sea monster. Deaths are reported in deep waters, and except for divers (Gigantes Sur [island] and Suclaran [village]), they are not frequented by ordinary fishermen" (Magos 1994:351). As such, "Rituals are highly necessary prior to venturing out to those dangerous places" (Magos 1994:315).

In the early nineteenth century, Burckhardt (1829:347) recorded in the northern Red Sea that "Arab sailors are very superstitious; they hold certain passages in great horror; not because they are more dangerous than others, but because they believe that evil spirits dwell among the coral rocks, and might possibly attract the ship toward the shoal, and cause her to founder."

The Ongee of the Andaman Islands associate dangerous areas of sea with the presence of spirit beings. Sabita Sarkar (1974:588) reports: "They believe that the sea spirits live in that part of the sea between South Brother and Passage Islands situated in Duncan Passage in between Little Andaman and Cinque Island which is in general very rough even in normal condition. The Onge[e] consider this portion of the sea most dangerous being the abode of the sea spirits and are, therefore, very cautious in crossing this part while out in their fishing mission in the open sea." In addition, "The Onge[e] do not have any kind of magico-religious beliefs and practices for helping them in their fishing operation and also for the sake of augmenting the supply of marine species in their fishing grounds" (Sarkar 1974:588). However, and of specific relevance to Malinowski's theory, the Ongee undertake rituals to accommodate spiritual dangers of the sea.

The association between areas of dangerous sea and the presence of malevolent sea spirits is not automatic. For example, Pannell (2007:82–83) makes the important observation that the "powerful beings" that inhabit the reef environment and seas of the people of Luang island in eastern Indonesia "contributes to a dangerously unstable and uncertain landscape." Furthermore, "While there is a temptation to posit a functional explanation for this relationship between cosmology and geography, I should point out that the most dangerous features of the reef for shipping, the narrow and shallow passages through the barrier reef, are not associated with either 'libidinous' or 'dangerous' beings" (Pannell 2007:87). Similarly, offshore zones should not be considered naturally more dangerous to fishers compared to inshore zones.

In her study of fishing practices in Tonga, central Pacific, Marie-Claire Bataille-Benguigui (1988) found that associated rituals did not conform to tenets of Malinowski's (1954) anxiety ritual theory. In particular, she notes that "there are also rites for fishing on foot or in shallow water which present no risk such as those involved in the capture of sharks at sea," and "a more dangerous technique, such as that of *fakalukuluku* [swimming offshore to fish and bleeding captured fish that may attract sharks] where the fisherman risks his life each time he goes into the sea, is in no sense accompanied by rituals and taboos to ward off bad luck; this tends to confirm the view that the fishermen, whether anxious or not, do not use magic" (Bataille-Benguigui 1988:193).

In 1918 Malinowski published an article devoted specifically to "Fishing in the Trobriand Islands," focusing on the "coral island" of Boyowa. He documents four types of fishing. First is "lagoon" fishing on the western side of the island, where waters are "almost constantly calm" and "fish are plentiful." Fishing is mostly undertaken using nets and plant-based poison, which is "by far the easiest and most reliable" fishing technique (Malinowski 1918:88). Fishing in the lagoon is carried out "without uncertainty and without risk to the fisher-men" (Malinowski 1918:90). Second is "fringing reef" fishing on the northern, eastern, and southern sides of the island. It is seasonal (during months of low wind), of minor "economic" importance, and is undertaken using "long narrow nets" as "there is no great abundance of fish" (Malinowski 1918:88–89). Third is *kalala* (possibly mullet) fishing on the northern side of the island "during the calm season," when shoals of the fish are netted in "shallow water between the beach and the fringing reef" (Malinowski 1918:89). Fourth is shark fishing on the northern side of the island, "only during the calm spells between the seasons" and "in the open sea, far beyond the fringing reef, in special canoes" using "a large wooden shark-hook" (Malinowski 1918:89).

Malinowski documents different degrees of magic associated with the dif-ferent types of fishing. With lagoon fishing, "there is absolutely no magic in connection with fish poisoning, and very little in connection with the ordinary fishing by means of nets" (Malinowski 1918:90). In contrast, shark fishing is "almost a magico-religious ceremony," with the "bulk" of it "performed in connection with" the construction of new canoes and the maintenance of old canoes (Malinowski 1918:91–92). In this sense, lagoon fishing and shark fishing can be seen as two different types of fishing with different aims. Lagoon fishing is low-risk by design and subsistence focused, whereas shark fishing is high risk by design and seemingly motivated less by maximizing food capture and more by status and prestige. Yet this high risk is not associated with the dangers of the open sea and canoe voyaging conditions, given that shark fishing, like other forms of Trobriand fishing, takes place during calm weather. However, as noted, Malinowski (1925:32) claims that "open sea fishing [is] full of danger and uncertainty" and that the associated "extensive magical ritual [is] to secure safety and good results." Stanley Tambiah (1990:72) made the important observation that "Malinowski fails to inform us that unlike the products of lagoon fishing, deep-sea fishing yields shark, which had a high ritual valuation in the Trobriand scheme of things. And therefore there may be other considerations than sheer danger that may have surrounded deep-sea fishing with ritual."

Liminality and Ontological Switching

The issue of the social construction of perceptions of danger at sea undermine the cross-cultural and universalizing explanatory power of anxiety ritual theory. Indeed, as noted, the ethnographic foundations of the theory in Malinowski (1925) are open to question. The reality of the physical dangers of the sea, expressed clearly with high workplace fatality rates over the past two centuries, is incontestable, and anxiety ritual theory has important explanatory capacity in this regard. Yet the issue of the subjective perception of danger as socially constructed requires deeper theoretical analysis and understanding in terms of liminality and ontology. Much of the following discussion is inspired by Rob van Ginkel's 2013 insightful article "The Cultural Seascape, Cosmology and the Magic of Liminality."

Van Ginkel (2013) reexamines Malinowski's anxiety ritual theory and posits an alternative theoretical approach to understanding maritime rituals. Although van Ginkel focuses on marine fishers, his insights, like Malinowski's, have broader application to mariners in general. Van Ginkel's theoretical approach is underpinned by van Gennep's (1960) and Turner's (1969) concepts of "rites of passage" and liminality, and Douglas's (1966) notion of transitional (liminal) states as dangerous requiring control through ritual. Van Ginkel (2013:46) finds van Gennep's (1960:23) staged formulation of rites of passage in relation to voyaging particularly useful: "the acts of embarking and disembarking [a vessel] . . . are often accompanied by rites of separation at the time of departure and by rites of incorporation upon return" and a period of liminality. Similarly, van Ginkel (2013:45–46) adopts Turner's (1979:465) notion of liminality as a "state or process which is betwixt-and-between the normal."

The act of marine fishing necessitates fishers in their boats not only moving physically from the land to the sea across the sea–land boundary but, critically, also moving metaphysically from one state to another. The latter, van Ginkel (2013) argues, is a liminal transition and as such is associated with considerable dangers, anxiety, and ritualization. Anxiety is associated with movement into the "perilous and unreliable environment" of the sea (van Ginkel 2013:48). Associated rituals, including taboos, are aimed at "coping with potentially hazardous transitions from land to sea" and "rites of separation" (van Ginkel 2013:48–49). During this period of separation from the land, van Ginkel (2013:50–51) posits that "fishermen are liminal *personae*" who "feel particularly exposed to supernatural threats" and as such "tend to be ambivalent and vulnerable." It is for these reasons that fishermen "observe many prohibitions," given that "taboos are about supernaturally controlling the uncontrollable and explaining the inexplicable, filling inevitable knowledge gaps in uncertain and risky pursuits" (van Ginkel 2013:50, 52).

The concept of "liminal *personae*" was developed by Turner (1967:97) out of the foundation research of van Gennep (1960) on rites of passage. Turner (1967:94) rightly notes that van Gennep (1960:11; emphasis added) identified three phases in rites of passage that vary in relative importance and elaboration between cultures: "*preliminal rites* (rites of separation), *liminal rites* (rites of transition), and *postliminal rites* (rites of incorporation)." Turner (1967:93–95) refers to a person who is going through a rite of passage as entering into a "liminal period" and as such can be considered as a "liminal *persona*," that is, a "transitional being" who is transitioning "from one state to another." By "state," Turner (1967:93, 102) is referring to "a relatively fixed or stable condition" such that the liminal *personae* may be said to have undergone "ontological transformation."

Van Ginkel (2013) rightly notes that van Gennep's (1960) and Turner's (1969) conceptualizations of rites of passage and liminality are of fundamental importance in understanding why fishers employ numerous rituals and taboos. Yet despite the fact that Turner (1967) limits the concept of "liminal *personae*" to the period of transition from one state to another, van Ginkel (2013:50) posits that "from the time of their departure until the moment of their return to the shore, fishermen are liminal *personae*." In this sense, van Ginkel seems to be suggesting that fishers exit the stable state of land to become liminal beings associated with rituals and taboos for the duration of their time on the sea and then move back to the stable state of land at the end of their sea work. That is, fishers enter into a liminal state as "liminal *personae*" during transitioning of the sea-land boundary and maintain that liminality while on the sea.

Van Ginkel's (2013) proposition that fishers remain as "liminal *personae*" for the duration of their fishing trip at sea is problematic (see also Brody 2023:399). Following Turner (1967), fishers as "liminal *personae*" should be limited to the period of transitioning of the sea–land boundary as a rite of separation. That is, rather than fixed in a liminal state, fishers undergo a liminal transition as they transition from the ontological state of the land to the ontological state of the sea. In this sense, fishers undergo what Turner refers to as an "ontological transformation" from land to sea such that they become metaphysically in tune with the sea as an ontological domain separate and different to the land. This transition and transformation is a process of "ontological switching" such that fishers, and mariners in general, temporarily alter their ontological status from a person of the land to a person of the sea through elaborate rituals and taboos. In short, mariners when on the sea do not remain in a liminal state but rather have situationally and temporarily transitioned to a different ontological state. This view is in keeping with van Gennep's rites of passage; as van Ginkel (2013:55) rightly observes, "Going to sea implies a rite of separation from the land and family, but also a rite of incorporation into the marine domain and the social configuration of the crew."

Ontological switching helps explain the existence of a vast repertoire of taboos at sea that involve avoidance of references to the land. Land references at sea bring on a sense of anxiety and fear in fishers, and mariners more generally, because it is mixing ontological domains which is seen as inappropriate and metaphysically dangerous. The issue of ontological mixing is similarly discussed by van Ginkel (2013:49), who points out that a number of researchers have touched on the issue of maintenance of "the opposition between land and sea" through taboos on land references while at sea such that associated "symbolism . . . should not be 'mixed up.'" That is, references to land while on the sea could be seen as mixing ontological states and domains and even reversing the liminal transition process such that fishers risk precipitating the dangerous metaphysical situation of becoming out of tune and disharmonious with the marine realm, which might subsequently react negatively. Negative reactions include dangers that risk safety of the crew and vessel from rough seas and risk of poor catches if fish and other marine animals decide to avoid capture.

A potential problem with the theory of ontological switching is why the considerable ritualization of the ontological transition from land to sea is not replicated for the reverse transition of sea back to land. That is, van Ginkel (2013:55) notes rightly that the "rites of separation from the seascape," rites of "(re)incorporation" and "aggregation into the realm of landlubbers would seem to be far less elaborated." He adds that Malinowski's anxiety ritual theory is applicable, as the "fishermen's homeward transition" is a return "to physically less dangerous territory and their uncertainties concerning the catch are over: it has either been plentiful, average or meagre and they cannot change this by performing additional rituals" (van Ginkel 2013:55–56). While the relative under-ritualization of the sea-to-land compared to land-to-sea transition may be applicable for many day-to-day activities (e.g., fishing trips), it is less relevant for sea voyages. For example, pre-voyage rituals of propitiation for safe and successful voyages are often accompanied by post-voyage gratitude rituals. Such gratitude rituals are most poignant for traumatic events such as surviving a life-threatening storm or shipwreck. Such post-voyage rituals often take the form of commemorative (ex-voto) offerings on land at churches and shrines (see Chapter 7).

Two extra metaphysical dimensions can be added to van Ginkel's (2013) arguments for the under-ritualization of the process of "(re)incorporation" of mariners from the sea back to land. The first relates to the ontological distinctiveness and complexity of the sea compared to land. The second concerns the blurred nature of the land-sea dichotomy and conceptualization of terrestrial seascapes. In terms of the ontological distinctiveness of the sea, metaphysical concerns over disharmony with the sea are largely over once a vessel and crew return to port or shore, and metaphysical disharmony with land is relatively and comparatively a minor concern. As discussed in previous chapters of this book, a key issue for many mariners is ensuring that taboos on referencing land while at sea are strictly maintained and enforced, with transgressions swiftly nullified through ritual. Well-documented taboos relate to linguistic references to land (especially terrestrial animals) and use of a distinctive sea language (e.g., noa words; Chapter 2). Taboos on referencing the land at sea (but with no equivalent taboos on referencing the sea while on land) are an explicit expression of the ontological view that the sea is relationally defined in opposition to land. That is, the sea is ontologically oppositional to land and in fact is seen as *non-land*, whereas the land is ontologically defined largely independent of the sea. As such, the "rites of separation" from land to sea are much more ontologically complex and necessitate considerable ritualization compared to "(re)incorporation" from sea to land. Mariners need to ontologically shed their land identity through wide-ranging rituals to ensure metaphysical harmony with the sea. In contrast, shedding a sea identity is not necessary to ensure metaphysical harmony with the land.

In terms of the blurred land-sea dichotomy, "(re)incorporation" from sea to land is also facilitated by the partial maritime identity of coastal zones as terrestrial seascapes. If maritime communities have invested in a range of strategies to extend their seascape inland of the sea–land boundary, then the question of mariners' returning to land is ontologically blurred. As Robert

Smith (1991) notes in relation to Scottish coastal fishing villages: they have "one foot on the land and one in the sea." Thus, mariners returning to land, at least the immediate coastal zone, are not transitioning fully to the land state as it is seen as a terrestrial seascape. Mariners do not need to fully shed their marine ontological state to move from sea to land, as they can metaphysically transition to and harmonize with the marine dimension of land (i.e., terrestrial seascape). In this sense, mariners returning to shore never fully reintegrate or reincorporate into a land-based society, given they never were integrated or incorporated in the first place due to their maritime identity. By extension, mariners never fully transition from a land state to a marine state when going out to sea, as they are never fully in a land state when back on land.

Many coastal fishing communities are socially and even culturally on the margins of mainstream society for a broad range of socioeconomic and sociocultural reasons (Nadel-Klein 2003; Smith 1977). Marginalization also relates to the maritime identity of fisherfolk, who are seen as belonging to the sea and not to the land. At a more profound ontological level, the Othering of fisherfolk by landlubbers may also be an expression of their metaphysical disharmony with land-based society. Yet marginalization and Othering are a two-way process: imposed by landlubbers and self-imposed for solidarity and security. In terms of the latter, in the early seventeenth century, the English Vice Admiral William Monson thought that the different ways of "seafarers" could be due, in part, to "the sea that works contrary effects to the land" (Oppenheim 1913:386).

Jane Nadel-Klein (2003:41) notes that "identifying fisherfolk as different and strange is remarkably common throughout Europe and elsewhere in the world." Furthermore, "Fishing enclaves were held in very low esteem by most non-fishing people. Fishers were marked as a peculiar kind of 'other,' an alien breed of people inhabiting the coast" (Nadel-Klein 2003:40). For example, fishing communities of eastern coastal Scotland have been "stigmatized," "marginalized," and "suffered from pariah status" by landlubbers since the eighteenth century (Nadel 1984:104; Nadel-Klein 2003:22–23). Nadel-Klein (2003:43) adds that "outsiders branded fishers as backward, dirty, inbred, superstitious and intrinsically disreputable." As noted, a key area for derision of fisherfolk was their rich maritime lore of spiritual beliefs and ritual practices, described under the pejorative label of "superstitions" in the extensive folkloric literature of the nineteenth and early twentieth centuries (see Chapter 1).

Many mariners used tattoos to stand out from and to look different from their land neighbors, a signaling strategy to help maintain their maritime identity while back on land. For example, Cori Convertito's (2014) analysis of Victorian Royal Navy records for 30,000 mariners between 1840 and 1870 found that the proportion of men with tattoos ranged from 26% (1845) to 11% (1865). Royal

Navy mariners "preferred that their tattoos be visible," with arms and hands the most preferred locations (Convertito 2014:213). The most common tattoo "theme" was "nautical" (e.g., anchors, ships or brigs, mermaids, stars, sailors, and birds; Convertito 2014:214). The proportion of American mariners (males) with tattoos varied over time: 21% (1796–1803), 6% (1812–1815), and 26–54% (US Navy sailors 1900–1908; Dye 1989:527, 533; see also Newman 1998). These figures contrast markedly with the proportion of the American population with tattoos in 1812–1815 (<1%) and in the mid-1960s (9%; Dye 1989:548–549). For the period 1794–1815, most tattoos were located on the arms (82%) and hands (12%), and in 1900–1908, most tattoos were similarly on arms (Dye 1989:534–535). In 1796–1815, marine motifs were the most popular (Dye 1989:533, 537, 542–543). Ira Dye (1989:553) argues that the "great popularity of tattoos of anchors and mermaids, ships and fish, shows the pride that the early seafarer had in his status as a seaman and adventurer, and shows his wish to have a badge of his seagoing status that identified him to landsmen and other seafarers alike as a member of this group. They were proud to be sailors and wanted people to know that they went to sea. This strongly reinforces the portrait of the seafarer as part of a collective group with shared experiences, dangers and economic tribulations."

That some mariners deliberately resisted integrating back into land-based society (i.e., metaphysically harmonizing with land-based society and the terrestrial world) is illustrated further by the creation of merchant mariners' social enclaves known as "sailortowns" in port cities around the world during the nineteenth century (Beaven 2016; Land 2010). Recently landed and cashed-up sailors gravitated to these enclaves, where they lived a short-term liminal existence of so-called immorality and debauchery. Sailortowns were a "'netherworld' of vice and excess," where mariners "actively flouted middle-class moral conventions" and "cultivated an alternative moral framework" (Beaven 2016:84–85, 94). Gill (1993:132) hypothesizes that "the return-home rituals" of trawlermen from Hull in northeast England during the twentieth century "were submerged in the men's long drinking bouts in the company of other men/ hunters." Significantly, Brad Beaven (2016:86; emphasis added) documents that during the second half of the nineteenth century, observers recorded that the sailortowns of Portsea and Devonport in England had developed "a peculiar land-based maritime culture" that was "steeped in superstition" and "folklore of the sea." Here "the sailors and residents of sailortown looked seaward rather than to their civic fathers for guidance in negotiating their way through port town life" (Beaven 2016:73). In many respects, sailortowns were developed by sailors as specialist liminal enclaves that metaphysically accommodated the ontological transition from sea to land in the form of a strategically constructed (albeit ghettoized) terrestrial seascape.

Conclusion

It is difficult to know if mariners possess a more extensive body of lore, spiritual beliefs, and rituals (for the sea) compared to beliefs and rituals of landlubbers (for the land). Although books on maritime folklore present fishers and mariners more generally as a highly superstitious lot, it is difficult to support this conclusion empirically, given that few researchers have devised appropriate methods to compare people of the sea with people of the land. For example, should comparative criteria focus on the number of superstitious beliefs, rituals, and taboos practiced by marine workers versus terrestrial workers (e.g., Poggie and Gersuny 1972)? Should such quantitative comparisons be undertaken within the same region, or can coastal communities be compared to inland communities located in different regions or even different countries? At one level, even if comparative land-sea quantitative results can be reliably generated, such data explains little, given that deeper analysis at an ontological level is necessary to help understand the occurrence of ritual practices. In this sense, the question of the relative occurrence of sea versus land rituals would be more fruitfully explored by a comparison of the relative ritualization of seascapes (marine and terrestrial) versus landscapes.

Most scholarship on the relative occurrence of maritime rituals concerns inshore fishing versus offshore fishing zones within the same region and exploration of the relative merits of "anxiety ritual theory" (after Malinowski 1925). While a range of studies provide support for Malinowski's contention that heightened anxiety associated with fishing in dangerous offshore waters is associated with greater ritualization compared to fishing in less stressful, calmer inshore waters, the broadscale applicability of this theory is undermined by considerable ethnographic evidence that anxiety of offshore waters is not associated with dangerous elements but with the presence of dangerous spiritual beings. As such, increased ritualization of the sea can be associated with heightened anxiety linked to dangerous elements or dangerous spiritual forces and beings. In this sense, mastery of the sea by mariners is not so much about technological mastery but about spiritual mastery and knowing how to ritually engage and propitiate those spiritual forces and beings who control the marine realm. Such is the pervasiveness of the spiritual dangers of voyaging that Milena Dževerdanović-Pejović (2017:315) observes: "Superstition and maritime beliefs related to the sea have dwelled in seafaring since its beginning, and are so deep-rooted that someone might wonder 'why any sane individual ever ventured out to sea.'"

Maritime rituals and taboos inform us that land and sea are different ontological domains and that moving between each, especially from land to sea, requires ritually activated ontological switching akin to a rite of passage. Ontological switching raises the question of how much of the comradeship among mariners, which in some cases can be seen as a subculture at sea and on land (e.g., tattoos, sailortowns), is a result not only of the common experience of going to sea and working with the sea but also of sharing the periodic and perhaps daily metaphysical experience of liminality and boundary transitioning between ontological zones and states.

12

Summary and Conclusions

It all comes back to the sea. We are all connected by the world's oceans.
Florence Gutchen

Wherever I go, the ocean keeps me connected to Badhu.
Alick Tipoti

Florence Gutchen and Alick Tipoti are artists from Torres Strait in northeast Australia. Gutchen is from Erub in the eastern islands of Torres Strait and is part of a distinctive art movement that creates life-size figurative sculptures of marine animals from "ghost nets" (fragments of old nylon fishing nets that wash up on local beaches) to draw attention to these silent killers of marine turtles and pollution of the world's oceans more generally (Mayer 2020–2021:76). Tipoti's home island is Badhu in the western islands of Torres Strait, and his quote is taken from the award-winning documentary *Alick and Albert*, which follows his visit to see Prince Albert and his family in Monaco 15,000 km away on the other side of the planet. The oneness of the sea collapses differentiating local and nonlocal. In this sense, the sea is far and near all at once. The experience of a marine global connection, expressed by Florence Gutchen and Alick Tipoti, is also seen with the view by relatives of those buried at sea that they can connect with their deceased loved ones by standing on the shoreline at the edge of the sea anywhere in the world.

All mariners know that any patch of sea can transition rapidly from calm waters to life-threatening waves in a matter of hours. As such, all parts of the sea present a potential grave for mariners, and seasoned mariners know that barely a patch of coastal waters exist that have not claimed one or more victims whose bones rest on the seabed. Mariners and fishers know they are potential victims of the sea; they just need to meet the right conditions. And when the sea wishes to claim a victim, mariners of past centuries of places as far distant as northern Scotland in the North Atlantic and Torres Strait in the Southwest Pacific know that rescue is futile—what the sea wants the sea gets. Those people who fall out of metaphysical harmony with the sea are doomed to join the submarine realm. Our relationship with the sea is not one of equals—mariners know that and the sea knows that. It was with humility and resignation that French historian Jules Michelet (1861:20) wrote in his 1861 book *The Sea (La Mer)*: "If we need the Ocean, see ye, my brothers, the Ocean in no wise needs us. Nature, fresh from the hand of Deity, scorns the too prying gaze and the too shallow judgment of finite but presumptuous man."

This book has sampled the extraordinary array of culturally diverse ways that mariners and maritime peoples past and present conceptually conceive of and ritually engage with the marine realm. All maritime peoples know that acknowledging the sea as a sentient domain and treating its omnipresent and omnipotent powers and forces with humility and deference helps keep them alive. Hubris and indifference on the sea means courting death. Far from an alien environment, maritime communities across the world know their seas as *socialized seascapes* of memories, stories, spiritual entities, and meaningful places that operate as mnemonics to embed vast libraries of intimate oceanographic knowledge of the sea and its ways. Yet these processes of knowing and engagement are not simply analogous to landscapes and ways of living on land. The sea is not just physically different to the land (e.g., fluid and endlessly shapeshifting); it is a polyvalent ontological, sentient, and social entity possessing a series of unique and essentialized features that draw attention to the distinctiveness of maritime cultures and maritime ways of being.

This conclusion draws on the chapters of this book to summarize and synthesize the key *ontological dimensions* of the sea that underpin seascapes. These ontological dimensions show varying degrees of overlap and interconnection. Where relevant, known archaeological expressions of these ontological dimensions discussed in previous chapters are highlighted to encourage further archaeological research on a wider range of topics in diverse cultural contexts. In most cases, archaeological investigations and interpretations have been guided strongly by local historical and ethnographic information. As noted in Chapter 1, and following *The Ontological Turn* by Martin Holbraad and Morten Axel-Pedersen (2017), *Sentient Seas* is primarily ontological in that it is less about the epistemological issue of *how* to research seascapes and more about the potential range of *what* to think about in terms of conceptualizing seascapes illustrated by a unique and comprehensive assembly of anthropological, historical, and archaeological examples drawn from across the world. The following discussion focuses on the key dimensions of the sea as hyperobject, sentient, poly-liminal, ontologically separate, and ontologically switchable, and the notions of marine and terrestrial seascapes. To avoid essentialism, it is important to acknowledge that each of these universal dimensions has historically contingent expressions in different coastal regions of the world.

Sea as Hyperobject

An interconnected and unitary view of the oceans is one that resonates with the singular view of oceans and seas by adherents of Object-Oriented Ontology (OOO). For example, Campbell (2020:212) makes the point that the "sea is the defining feature of our planet and an omni-present entity that covers more than two-thirds of its surface." Furthermore, the "sea is the ultimate nonlocal entity. It simultaneously provides the buoyant force to float one ship, its interaction with atmosphere allows a second ship to sail due to wind, while the mixing of waters of different temperatures results in a storm that sinks a third ship" (Campbell 2020:212). More specifically, Campbell (2020:211) makes the insightful observation that the sea, as an agent on a massive temporal and spatial scale, conforms to what OOO philosopher Timothy Morton (2013) calls a *hyperobject*. One side of an ocean connects over vast distances to another side, not simply because each side shares the property of seawater but because the sea itself has a unity and relativity (wormhole-like) quality that collapses spatial and temporal dimensions and physical properties. Objects that fell to the ground from an overhead medieval sky ship that sailed far away from the coast probably did so via what was cosmologically akin to a wormhole. Furthermore, many emigrating Europeans in the nineteenth century felt that a loved one buried at sea after death on a ship belonged to "the *whole* ocean, under all its varied phases of storm or sunshine, as *one* tomb holding their lost treasure" (Polehampton 1862:21; original emphasis).

Interconnectedness of the sea in terms of physical properties is illustrated by long-distance movement of waves. For example, waves generated in the Southern Ocean off Antarctica can travel north for more than 8,000 km to break in diminished form on the beaches of Hawai'i after nearly a week, or further north to the shores of Alaska after 10 days (Stow 2017:62). Wave anomalies generated by the volcanic eruption of Krakatoa in Indonesia in 1883 were detected by tide gauges in the Bay of Biscay of southwest Europe in the Atlantic Ocean, 20,000 km away (Francis and Self 1983). An earthquake in one part of an ocean can create a tsunami wave that travels through the sea at the speed of a passenger jet aircraft to surface with devastating consequences on coastlines thousands of kilometers distant (e.g., Narayana et al. 2005). Aston (2009:90) notes that the speed at which the ancient Greek sea goddess Thetis moved through the sea when summoned reveals that the sea "does not seem entirely to be bound by the usual rules of space and distance," at least as understood on land. Similarly, the ancient Norse conceived of the sea monster Jörmungand as encircling Earth. Nearly all (99%) internet data is transmitted at nearly the speed of light around the globe via more than one million kilometers of submarine cables (Stow 2017:xvii–xviii).

The sea possesses unique long-distance properties of sound and hearing not found on land. For example, the eruption of Krakatoa was heard 4,800 km away by the residents of Rodriguez Island in the Indian Ocean (Francis and Self 1983). Sound travels through seawater nearly five times faster than through air (Stow 2017:53). Dynamite detonated underwater near Australia was heard off Bermuda 25,000 km away (Payne and Webb 1971:129; Stow 2017:53). Before the era of motorized shipping, it is thought that a wayfinding blue whale could propagate a vocalization that traveled for 14 minutes and 650 km underwater to echo off the Bermuda seamount and then return back to the whale (Clark and Ellison 1997). Roger Payne and Douglas Webb (1971:Table 1) calculate that it was theoretically possible for a fin whale to hear the deep-sea vocalization of another fin whale over a distance of 20,000 km in quiet ocean conditions, before industrial noise pollution.

The hyperobject status of the sea supports the view explored in this book of the sea as a separate, cohesive, and indeed singular ontological domain relationally defined in opposition to land with shared ontological dimensions that were invariably ritualized by coastal peoples with maritime cultures in vastly different geographical regions across the globe. That the sea is seen by many people as ontologically singular (and separate—see below) is reflected by the existence of many books on "the sea" and indeed the "blue humanities" more generally. In contrast, few books are written on "the land" as a singular ontological entity.

Archaeological expressions of the sea as hyperobject are not specific but concern the general view that a degree of similarity exists around the world both past and present about shared cultural constructions of, responses to, and ritual engagements with the sea. That maritime cultures and societies share much in common is an epistemological perspective held by many maritime folklorists, historians, anthropologists, and archaeologists.

Sea as Sentient

Socialized seas go to the heart of seascapes and encapsulate the definitional essence of seascapes. Seascapes are the intersubjective way that people understand and engage with the sea. While some ecologists and exponents of Object-Oriented Ontologies may have concerns that defining seascapes as socialized seas is overly anthropocentric and indeed anthropomorphic, my view of "socialized" encompasses animals, humans, and other-than-human persons. In all cases, people engage with seas socially as a relationship between human persons and a vast domain of sentient entities and other-than-human persons manifested variously as spiritual beings (ranging from gods and deities to spirits of the human dead), hybrid creatures (of mixed anthropic and zoomorphic form), animals (e.g., marine mammals and some fish), animate elements (e.g., tides, currents, waves, wind), animate object-beings (e.g., ships, boats), agentive objects (e.g., charms, votive offerings, and procurement technology such as harpoons, fishing nets, and hooks), and ultimately the sea itself (seawater). These social relationships include verbal and nonverbal dialogue and are founded upon mutually understood sentience and personhood such that people know the sea as a realm of intentionalized agency. That is, people understand the sea, and equally of importance, the sea understands people. The sea wants from us what we want from the sea—to be heard, respected, and to conform to the moral obligations of reciprocity. Mariners cannot escape the perceptive and judgmental eyes and ears of the sea.

Mariners are fully aware that the sea and its spiritual and corporeal beings usually reward appropriate and respectful actions, and chastise inappropriate and disrespectful actions. The sea is all pervasive, all knowing, and cognitively aware. Sentience, moral agency, and "personhood of the ocean" are encapsulated nicely by David Martin of the Alaskan Yup'ik community, who noted in 2002 that the "ocean gets mad and becomes angry just like a person. When those who do not follow abstinence practices upset it [i.e., following birth, death, illness, miscarriage, first menstruation], the ocean boils up in anger, and the wind howls" (quoted in Fienup-Riodan and Rearden 2009:234).

The sea's sentience, in its various manifestations, is engaged by mariners socially through dialogue mediated by propitiatory rituals often enhanced by a wide range of agentive objects (e.g., charms that in some circumstances include human and animal remains). People engage ritually with the sea to increase the chances of successful and safe use of the sea in terms of voyaging and procurement of marine resources, especially food. While the causal relationship between ritual performance and outcome is often poorly understand by researchers, in most cases it is not simply a mechanistic causality but a social causality whereby the sea is seen to consciously decide to change or not. Such decisions are often based upon the sea's assessment and judgment of whether or not the behavior of mariners is demonstrably respectful. Expressions of these morally prescribed behaviors include avoiding certain activities (i.e., adhering to taboos) and making propitiatory offerings directly into the sea during a voyage or at shrines located on land either before or after a voyage. Many voyaging rituals focus on propitiating spiritual entities to ensure calm seas and quell rough seas (both linked to controlling waves and winds) for safe voyaging and avoiding shipwreck, and also propitiating winds to propel ships and to bring on rough seas and storms to thwart enemy ships.

In the case of procurement of marine animals such as fish and mammals, rituals linked to shrines incorporating stones or bones aim to increase availability of animals (increase and maintenance ceremonies, and rites of spiritual renewal or reincarnation) and often blur with rituals (usually involving shrines and charms) to increase hunting and fishing success. Rituals usually include propitiatory dialogue with gods and deities (at temples, shrines, churches) and ancestral spirits, often augmented by votive offerings (and animal sacrifices in some cases). Morally prescribed practices include nonverbal dialogue centered on respectful treatment of prey remains, especially bones, as a form of virtue signaling to living fish and marine mammals. Fish renewal rituals included returning bones to the sea or burning bones (e.g., Canada) or not burning bones (e.g., Scotland). Marine mammal (e.g., whales and dugongs) bone rituals include return of skulls to the sea (for reincarnation) and creation of highly structured deposits of bones, especially of skulls (to ensure future hunting success; e.g., in Alaska, Canada, Australia). Other ethnographically documented ritual practices involving mutual recognition of sentience and interbeing dialogue to increase hunting and fishing success include gaining the spiritual assistance of dead hunters or the spiritual agency or power of human corpses and intentionalizing animate objects-beings such as boats and procurement technology (often aided by attached charms) with conscious desires to seek out prey, and vice versa.

Archaeological expressions of sentient seas are dominated by rituals to ensure safe voyages and successful procurement of marine foods. Evidence of voyaging rituals include votive offerings at temples and shrines to propitiate sea deities and spiritual forces that control the elements (e.g., waves and wind). Archaeological evidence of ships and boats as animate object-beings imbued with sentience and intentionality (and predatorization in the case of war ships and marine mammal hunting boats) includes Scandinavian Bronze Age rock art depictions of ships with zoomorphic stem heads, ancient Greek marble *oculi* (eyes) depicted on vases and recovered from shipwrecks, and ancient Greek and Roman battering rams recovered from the seabed featuring representations of swords and predatory animals such as lions, wolves, and eagles.

Archaeological evidence of food procurement rituals focuses on sites linked to increasing availability of prey and increasing hunting and fishing success. *Prey increase rituals* linked to spiritual renewal (reincarnation) include Inuit whale skull sites in Siberia, Alaska, and Canada of the past 1,000 years. *Hunting and fishing success rituals* are more commonly discussed in the archaeological literature, with the earliest known example being a 5,000-year-old dugong bone mound in the United Arab Emirates. Other archaeological expressions of procurement "success" rituals include formal shrines (e.g., Hawai'ian fishing shrines) and charms (e.g., dugong ear bones from Torres Strait) dating to the past 1,000 years.

Sea as Poly-Liminal

Poly-liminality of the sea is associated with cosmologically defining its edges in terms of the sea–land boundary, sea–sky boundary, sea–horizon boundary, and sea–seabed boundary. Each of these boundaries is a liminal interface and underpins the sea as a poly-liminal realm. Even a superficial survey of maritime cultures across the globe reveals that few universals exist in how these boundaries between separate ontological domains (see below) are conceived and defined. What maritime cultures do have in common is that these cosmological boundaries are conceived of as liminal and often require ritual to facilitate crossing. In some cases, ritual crossing is aided by what Westerdahl calls "liminal agents"—that is, certain types of animate objects (e.g., boats, fishhooks) and animals (e.g., sea birds, seals, elks) possess the metaphysical capacity to cross liminal boundaries.

The sea–land boundary is the most ritualized for mariners given that it is crossed daily in most maritime societies (see below). This boundary is also central to the land-sea dualism/dichotomy that is expressed graphically by the phenomenon of hybrid sea creatures and transformational (liminal) beings known by many maritime and seafaring cultures. They include transformational human-marine animals such as seal people (e.g., selkies), dolphin and porpoise people, whale people, dugong people, shark people, turtle people, and fish people (e.g., mermaids); hybrid sea humans representing the fusion of the upper body of a human and the lower body of a fish (e.g., mermaids, mermen, tritons); hybrid sea animals and sea monsters representing the fusion of marine animals (usually the lower body of a fish) with the upper body of a terrestrial animal such as a goat, dog, lion, bull, stag, bird, and horse (e.g., hippocamp); and sea serpents of colossal size (e.g., Kraken). Hybrid and transformational humans and animals, along with sea monsters, reinforce the view that the sea is a domain that defies and even violates the "normal" (terrestrial) understandings of the laws of nature (see Ritvo 1997:133). It is the land-sea duality or dichotomy and sea as a separate ontological domain (see below) that creates the metaphysical conditions for mariners to know and expect to see hybrid and transformational humans and animals, and sea monsters and sea serpents. Ritvo (1997:183) notes perceptively that sea serpents have maintained their status as "the liminal creatures of choice." For many Indigenous maritime communities of North American, Australia, and the Pacific, sea monsters and serpents are expressions of relational ontologies and a spiritual and agentive cosmos of sentient and transformational beings that could be engaged ritually (in this case to avoid harm). In contrast, European maritime traditions had few ritual engagements with hybrid sea creatures and sea monsters and serpents, as they were more metaphysical expressions of the land-sea dualism.

Interestingly, the two sea boundaries that are the most difficult for people to access directly are populated variably by gods, and by hybrid, transformational, and spiritual beings in the form of star constellations (sea–sky boundary) and sunken settlements, including fantastical and often bejeweled abodes and gardens (sea–seabed boundary). Before the development of spacecraft and deep-sea submersibles in the twentieth century, human access to the sea–sky and sea–seabed boundaries was limited to the dead (and shamans in some contexts). That is, the seabed was inhabited by the physical remains and spirits of the marine dead (e.g., victims of shipwreck and those buried at sea), and the sky was inhabited by spirits of the dead (e.g., heaven).

Archaeological expressions of liminality of the sea tend to focus on the sea–land boundary, particularly religious and ritual use of small islands and mortuary rites focused on spiritual transformation and transition of the human dead to the realm of the dead. The relatively high proportion of intertidal zone around small islands makes them liminal places par excellence. Gillis (2004:4, 28) observes that "as liminal places, islands are frequently the location of rites of passage," and "it is not surprising that isles in the Mediterranean were long associated with cults." Island cultic sanctuaries in the Aegean Sea are known for the Late Bronze Age (Melos and Kea—Renfrew 1985) and ancient Greece (Samos and Delos). Christian monasteries of medieval age have attracted considerable archaeological interest on the islands of Iona (Scotland) and Inishark (Ireland; Campbell and Maldonado 2020; Lash et al. 2018). In Torres Strait of northeast Australia, excavations reveal the emergence of large *kod* ceremonial site complexes on the small sacred islets of Pulu and Koey Ngurtai around 300–400 years ago (David et al. 2009; McNiven et al. 2009).

In terms of mortuary rites, archaeological expressions of liminality relate to location of burial sites in or adjacent to liminal zones such as shorelines (sea–land boundary) or inclusion of certain objects and materials in graves as "liminal agents" because of their link to sea boundaries or movement across the sea. Examples include the location of Mesolithic burials within coastal shell middens and Neolithic megaliths (and associated tombs) containing beach-rolled stones along the coasts of western and northern Europe linked to liminality of the sea–land boundary.

Sea as Ontologically Separate

A key dimension of harmonizing with the sea is respecting a wide range of cultural practices that both express and acknowledge the sea as an ontological domain separate and distinct from the land. The *land-sea dualism* is not simply taken for granted by maritime peoples but is activity managed and maintained. Considerable ethnographic and historical information is available to support the view that the sea is relationally defined in opposition to the land. Such relationality extends well beyond the trite comment that the sea is obviously different from land. In many parts of the world, use of the sea is explicitly defined and expressed in opposition to use of the land. Such differentiation and separation can be benign, including the different ways of sea measurement such as distance (nautical miles), depth (fathoms), and speed (knots). In other situations, undertaking land-based or land-associated activities onboard a vessel at sea is seen as culturally and metaphysically inappropriate. For example, many maritime communities maintain a broad gender binary (e.g., land as mostly the domain of women and the sea as mostly the domain of men), food binary (e.g., terrestrial foods cannot be eaten at sea and land and marine foods cannot be cooked in the same pots), material binary (e.g., not mixing land and marine raw materials in objects), animal binary (e.g., objects associated with land animals must not contaminate objects associated with sea animals, and vice versa), and moral binary (e.g., the sea is seen as morally corrupt in comparison to land). In many cases, mixing land and sea-based phenomena and activities is seen as inducing bad luck and danger and is therefore tabooed (see below).

Archaeological expressions of the sea as a separate ontological domain have attracted little attention, and have focused on materiality of the land-sea dualism expressed by structural oppositions. To date, research is limited to Arctic/subarctic sites of the past 2,000 years and the way selected materials of the land were deliberately kept separate from selected materials of the sea. McGhee's (1977) insightful analysis of Thule sites found that marine hunting technology (e.g., harpoons) tended to be made of marine mammal bone and ivory while terrestrial hunting technology (e.g., arrows) tended to be made of caribou bone and antler (cf. Qu 2017).

Sea as Ontologically Switchable

A paradoxical dimension to maintaining the land-sea dualism is the concomitant necessity of developing strategies to accommodate the metaphysically complex issue of moving between the separate ontological domains of land and sea. A common feature of maritime peoples is the use of ritual when physically crossing the liminal interface of the sea–land boundary. Ethnographically and historically recorded examples of ritualized crossing include one-way transitions (e.g., vessel launching ceremonies and transferring spirits of the dead to the realm of the dead) and reversible transitions (e.g., preparations for voyaging and fishing and hunting trips). Interruption of liminal boundary-crossing rituals usually brings forth bad luck. For example, ships and boats can be cursed with bad luck (including shipwreck) if mistakes occur during launching rituals.

A critical dimension of moving successfully from the ontological domain of land to the ontological domain of sea is adherence to *taboo* practices that are taken very seriously by mariners. Certain taboo activities are seen to thwart the capacity of mariners to board their boats (i.e., ontologically transition from land to sea) and to undertake safe and successful activities at sea (e.g., voyaging and fishing). Such thwarting scuttles the capacity of mariners to ontologically switch from land to sea and to enter into a harmonious ontological relationship and metaphysical state with the sea. Many of these taboos are related to terrestrial interventions into preparing for a boating trip, such as seeing a dog, hare, rabbit, fox, or cat on the way to the wharf (e.g., British Isles, France, United States). To ignore such sightings and to head off to sea in a compromised metaphysical state due to incomplete ontological switching invites disharmony with the sea, bad luck, mishap, and sometimes death.

Even after successfully crossing the sea–land boundary and voyaging out to sea, harmonizing with the sea requires vigilance as compromising the land-to-sea ontological switch and falling out of harmony with the sea remains a constant threat. For example, uttering taboo words (often related to terrestrial phenomena) and discovering the presence of certain land animals (e.g., pigs, hares, cats) onboard vessels is seen by many maritime communities as dangerous and inducing bad luck and danger. Numerous rituals can be performed onboard vessels to nullify the potential negative effects of taboo indiscretions (e.g., grabbing the nearest piece of iron, signing the Christian cross, throwing terrestrial animals overboard).

In many coastal cultural contexts, drowning victims are considered permanently trapped in the ontological state of the sea without the means to ontologically switch back to the ontological state of the land. It is for this reason that drowning victims in many parts of Europe (including the UK) found washed up on beaches were buried at the high-water mark at the sea–land boundary in unconsecrated ground and not in local cemeteries. In an analogous sense, castaways in some cultural contexts are considered liminal and metaphysically unstable and dangerous and must be ritually processed before they can reenter terrestrial society, or are executed in the case of Torres Strait Islanders.

Much of the camaraderie documented among communities of mariners and even their social segregation by landlubbers can be seen as an expression not simply of shared identity based on shared work practices on the sea but a shared sense of ritualized liminality associated with ontological switching. In some respects, mariners are Othered by landlubbers because of their regular changing ontological and indeed metaphysical status. Yet in many coastal contexts, maritime peoples endorse their difference to terrestrial peoples. For Islander societies of Oceania, Feinberg (1995a:6) makes the point that the "ocean often provides symbols through which a community constructs and reinforces its sense of cultural identity. Many peoples view themselves as uniquely in tune with the sea and contrast themselves with others whom they see as less adept at dealing with the ocean." Being in tune or in a metaphysical harmonious relationship with the sea encompasses technological and subsistence proficiency but also extends to ontological and epistemological embeddedness and morally prescribed spiritual relationships with the marine realm.

Archaeological expressions of ontological switching have been minimally explored and to date have focused on special treatment of marine animal bone on land and special treatment of victims of drowning. For example, Nordqvist (2003) argues that during the early Mesolithic of western Sweden, movement of marine bone to land required destroying its ontological link with the sea through ritual intervention in the form of burning. Archaeological examples of bodies buried in shoreline deposits dating to the past 500 years at the sea–land boundary in England are probably victims of drowning who were excluded from nearby formal burial grounds, as they were considered metaphysically unstable ("restless souls") due to an inability to ontologically switch from the sea back to land.

Marine Seascapes

Seascapes mean different things to different people and understandings of seascapes vary considerably between ecologists, heritage managers, historians, anthropologists, archaeologists, and more (McNiven 2025a). For many researchers, use of the term "seascapes" has simply become a new way to refer to the sea. Similarly, living along the coast and near the sea does not naturally predetermine a community to be marine oriented or a sea people with well-developed seascapes. While all seascapes with complex tangible and intangible dimensions are expressions of maritime peoples, terrestrial peoples and indeed landlubbers can also conceptualize seascapes, albeit often in negative terms that underpin avoidance of use of the sea.

Sentient Seas takes the view, as expressed by a range of historians, anthropologists, and archaeologists, that a bottom-up approach to seascapes that privileges how maritime peoples themselves conceive of their seas brings us closer to better understanding the ontological dimensions of seascapes. This book, like numerous previous books about the sea, especially the genre of superstition and folklore of the sea and sailors, has taken a comprehensive cross-cultural perspective to reveal that seascapes comprise what Western researchers often refer to as tangible and intangible dimensions. Yet the term "intangible" often misrepresents the spiritual dimensions of seas which for mariners past and present know to be real. Indeed, a key conclusion of this book is that these so-called intangible dimensions have been at the center of conceptualizations of the sea for thousands of years. In many respects, use of the sea, especially voyaging, has been more concerned with dealing with these intangible dimensions, given that they underpin the tangible issues of waves and storms and govern whether a voyage will be successful or not. It is these culturally specific tangible and intangible dimensions of seascapes, underpinned by ontology and epistemology, and comprehended and engaged socially and ritually, that extend seas as seascapes.

Seascapes are seas with a polyvalent cultural identity comprising the features of hyperobject, sentience, poly-liminality, and ontological distinctiveness. This polyvalent identity is on a geographical scale writ large with meaningful places. Christopher Nuttall (2021:17) remarks that marine-oriented peoples understand and engage with the sea (space) as seascape (place). Coastal communities, especially marine subsistence specialists, possess *marine seascapes* populated with places, often named. Most named places appear to be associated with shallow waters and features such as reefs, sandbanks, and channels, many with associated cosmological creation narratives. In addition, those maritime cultures that have embodied systems of navigation, such as across many parts of Micronesia and Polynesia, have hundreds of terms for different parts of the sea based on different surface and subsurface water characteristics (e.g., color, salinity, temperature, currents, swell patterns, bioluminescence, flotsam). Inuit groups of the Arctic/subarctic have hundreds of terms for different types of seasonal ice formations. North Sea fishers have a spatial understanding of the sea based on the texture, color, and smell of seabed sediments. Spiritual geographies of the sea center on places known as the seabed abode of specific deities and spiritual beings.

Historically and ethnographically known ritual engagements with the sea form a critical dimension to the conception and expression of marine seascapes. Although these rituals include a wide range of taboos, most concern propitiating sentient dimensions of the sea in terms of ensuring safe voyaging and an abundance of marine foods, and successful hunting and fishing (see above). As such, the complexity of marine seascapes and associated rituals are defined by degrees of use of the sea. These rituals can be divided into two forms—those that take place within the intertidal (foreshore) zone at the liminal interface and dynamic intersection of land and sea, and those that take place on the more expansive subtidal (open-sea) zone on board ships and boats focused on the water column and its dynamic sea surface and seabed boundaries. *Intertidal zone rituals* usually focus on periodically submerged sites such as fishing and wind shrines marked by specially arranged stones (e.g., Torres Strait), stone-walled fish traps imbued with spiritual agency augmented by charms (e.g., Torres Strait), and burials (e.g., victims of drowning and shipwreck). *Open sea rituals* focus mostly on ensuring safe voyaging (e.g., propitiating spiritual beings and forces to control waves and winds using shipboard shrines and votive offerings into the sea) but also include votive offerings into the sea to bring fishing success (e.g., Solomon Islands) and burials at sea following death on ships and also on land. Indeed, shipwrecks associated with considerable loss of life are considered by many to be sacred sites (e.g., RMS *Titanic*), particularly warships, which in the case of the USS *Arizona* in Pearl Harbor is both an active cemetery and also considered animate and sentient.

Archaeological expressions of the sea dimension of seascapes in the form of objects and sites on the seabed are considerable and take in the intertidal zone and open sea. The *intertidal zone (foreshore)* is often marked with easily accessible sites with physical expressions conducive to long-term preservation. Examples includes sites linked directly with subsistence technologies such as tidal fish traps (organic and stone-walled) and sites of more direct ceremonial and ritual significance such as engraved boulders (rock art) for fish abundance (e.g., Northwest Coast of Canada) and ceremonial stone arrangements linked to tidal regimes (e.g., central coast of Queensland). All of these sites are repeatedly submerged and exposed by tidal waters and in many cases are linked to the metaphysical liminality of the sea–land boundary.

Archaeological research within the *open sea* is more logistically challenging than the intertidal zone due to obvious differences in accessibility. However, open-sea archaeology has attracted considerable attention and often with spectacular results (e.g., shipwrecks). Although archaeological research on the worship and propitiation of sea gods, deities, and saints (often associated with votive offerings) has focused on land sites such as temples and shrines, analogous research, albeit more restricted, has been undertaken at permanently submerged seabed sites, especially shipwrecks which have revealed portable shrines, incense burners, and talismanic charms. More extraordinary has been the recovery of archaeological traces of votive offerings into the open sea beyond shipwrecks, such as Bronze Age metal weapons in the English Channel, Hellenistic age ceramic offering cups off the coast of Sicily, Roman- and Byzantine-age model lead anchors off the coast of Israel, and stone anchors on reefs near canoe passages in the Society Islands of Polynesia. Religious inscriptions on anchors and lead sounding weights (recovered archaeologically from shipwrecks) can be considered a form of sea offering.

Terrestrial Seascapes

The concept of *terrestrial seascapes* centers on three epistemological and onto-logical issues—first, expressions of a maritime identity on land for individuals and communities more broadly; second, conceptualizations of the "inland" extent of the sea or marine-related phenomena; and third, causal relationships between activities at sea and activities on the land, and vice versa. In terms of expressions of maritime identity, a key point argued in this book is that maritime cultures undertake a wide range of strategies to extend seascapes (i.e., social dimensions of the sea) onto the land to help maintain a maritime identity both on and off the sea. That is, extension of seascapes to land relates to the fact that maritime peoples spend considerable time on the "land" such that the land needs a maritime identity in its own right, not simply as an adjunct to that of the sea. As such, terrestrial seascape sites are critical to the creation, expression, and maintenance of maritime identity. While the notion of ter-restrial seascapes has some points in common with Westerdahl's paradigmatic "maritime cultural landscapes," it also differs fundamentally to the view that maritime inscription on land is limited primarily to marine-related activi-ties and infrastructure (e.g., ports and harbors; McNiven 2025a). Terrestrial seascapes encapsulate the dimensions of marine symbolism and marine ritual structures of maritime cultural landscapes but extend ontologically to include the imbuement of land and social practices with a maritime identity that in some circumstances includes cosmologically conceiving the sea–land boundary as located many kilometers "inland." Indeed, the concept of terrestrial seascapes is an acknowledgment that maritime societies cosmologically position the liminal interface of the sea–land boundary well "inland" of the "shoreline." Despite this "inland" positioning, most if not all maritime societies continue to recognize and ritualize the profound ontological importance of moving between land and sea through the process of ontological switching.

Conceptualizations of the "inland" extent of the sea and marine phenomena rupture normative and universalizing understandings of the sea-land boundary. For example, the Yanyuwa and Ganggalida Aboriginal peoples of the Gulf of

Carpentaria of northern Australia conceive of "saltwater country" as extending 10–13 km inland of Western definitions of the coastline. Similarly, the upriver extension of tidal waters often allowed European and North American seaport towns with port facilities and resident mariners to be located tens of kilometers inland of the sea. The extent to which maritime peoples or coastal peoples more generally extend seascapes inland is an empirical question for analytical inquiry. In the case of the ancient Aegean, Nuttall (2021:250; emphasis added) concluded that "not all coastal settlements provide evidence for a deeper interaction with the sea, suggesting that there was an element of *choice* in seascape dialogues." Referencing of the sea across adjacent areas of "land" and terrestrial seascapes will increase in scale and complexity as the extent of maritimity of peoples increases.

Numinous causal relationships between activities at sea and activities on the land (and vice versa) are varied and complex. They include the well-known propitiation of sea gods and deities at temples and shrines on land and propitiation of ritual specialists (e.g., "witches") on land to influence voyaging and fishing at sea, and hunting and fishing rituals at shrines on land to influence the behavior of marine animals (e.g., mammals and fishes). In these cases, people influence behavior of the sea (water and the animals it contains) through ritual and agentive social dialogue between people and spiritual beings or forces and people and animals. More abstract is how independent behavior of the sea can influence activities on land. For example, many coastal communities of Europe (including the UK) and North America know that the rise and fall of tides exert positive and negative influences on terrestrial activities, such as subsistence (e.g., farming and hunting), technology (e.g., maintenance of fishing nets), and major transformational events in life (e.g., marriage, pregnancy, birth, puberty, death). Alternatively, the activities of people on land can influence hunting and fishing success. For example, numerous maritime communities adhere to taboos (e.g., sexual abstinence and strict avoidance of immoral activity) on land prior to venturing out to sea. Similarly, the activities of wives on land (e.g., movements of body) can influence the success of their husband hunters at sea in obtaining whales (e.g., Alaska and Canada) and dugongs (e.g., Papua New Guinea).

Archaeological expressions of terrestrial seascapes beyond marine-oriented temples, altars, and shrines include the inland referencing of the sea through the inland movement of marine-sourced objects and symbolic representations of marine objects. Inland movement of marine objects range from small shells used as body adornments to large objects such as shoreline stones incorporated into churches and megaliths. Marine shells, bones, and teeth (e.g., sharks, whales, dugongs) are incorporated into ceremonial and ritual sites and in rare instances building materials for houses. More dramatic are marine-themed burials, ranging from bodies interred with marine shells and bones (sometimes carved into special objects) to bodies interred into shell middens and most famously in ships buried kilometers inland from the shoreline. Examples include Viking and Anglo-Saxon ship burials, use of boats and canoes as coffins, and inclusion of boat fragments and boat features (e.g., anchors) in graves found variously across northern Europe, Island Southeast Asia, and Oceania; and symbolic boats in the form of boat-shaped arrangements of stones associated with burials (e.g., Scandinavia).

In many cases the inland referencing of the sea is more mundane and part of the normal, daily routines of life, such as the formation of middens with marine food remains at camp sites and houses. In many cases, marine referencing is symbolic, such as figurative representations of ships, marine gods, deities, and marine animals in 3-D (e.g., sculptures and stone arrangements) and 2-D (e.g., rock art, painted walls, painted pots). Often such marine referencing was less about inscribing a maritime identity onto the land and more about giving a material expression to the latent maritime dimension of land as a terrestrial seascape.

Final Comments

My entry point for writing *Sentient Seas* was seeing seascapes as spiritscapes. The notion of spiritscapes emerged primarily from my experiences of working closely and collaboratively with Torres Strait Islanders in northeast Australia. In Torres Strait, I experienced my own ontological turn such that I came to better understand that spiritual and ritual relationships with the sea went to the heart of Torres Strait Islander maritime identity, beyond its usual characterization by outsiders in terms of specialized use of marine resources. As these spiritual and ritual dimensions were cosmologically all pervasive, they encompassed all the fluid and ever-changing daily and seasonal dynamic forms of their seas through tides, winds, and currents on a spatial scale better accommodated collectively by the notion of spiritscape. With new eyes, my reading of maritime ethnographies, histories, and archaeologies across the globe led to my increasing understanding of the universality of the idea of seascapes as spiritscapes. Wherever mariners traveled, the cosmological and spiritual dimensions of the sea traveled with them, as did their ritual engagements with the sea. Indeed, seascape spiritscapes also extended beyond the limits of voyaging, as early European understandings of seas with monsters on the margins of the world attest. Poignantly, all mariners know that the seawater that surrounds their vessels is part of the same seawater that claimed fellow mariners through drowning and other mishaps. Seascapes as spiritscapes is related directly to the notion of the sea as a vast sentient hyperobject where spiritual beings (and spirits of the dead) are never far away.

In the Introduction to this book, I drew attention to the iconic photograph of our spherical blue planet taken by NASA's Apollo 17 astronauts on the last crewed expedition to the moon on 7 December 1972. Chari Larsson (2022) notes that this image "changed the way we visualized our planet forever." Nearly 40 years later, on 14 September 2012, the cremated remains of Neil Armstrong, the first human to step onto the moon, were committed to the Atlantic Ocean during a solemn service onboard the USS *Philippine Sea*. Interestingly, the previous year, on 2 May 2011, the body of Osama bin Laden was buried at sea by selected crew of the USS *Carl Vinson* in the northern Arabian Sea. Here the sea has taken into its realm two of the most famous men in the world—one associated with what many people would consider to be the greatest technological achievement of humanity and the other associated with one of the most audacious violent crimes of the modern era. In this sense, the sea and the world's oceans are far greater than humanity and can easily absorb the best and worst of us. There is certain irony in the sea entombing our dead and the many thousands of mariners who have lost their lives at sea, given that "there is no life on Earth that exists independent of the oceans because they drive our planet's hydrologic, climate, and atmospheric systems" (Campbell 2020:212).

The sea is both giving and unforgiving. But the oceans of the world are changing due to humanly induced global warming. To what extent such changes will alter the ratio of seas as giving and unforgiving has yet to be fully comprehended. History records that for thousands of years, mariners and maritime communities knew that we take the sea for granted at our own peril. Hubris conspired with an iceberg to sink RMS *Titanic* in the early hours of 15 April 1912. Yet in many ways, despite our advanced knowledge and technological might, "the sea of today in many ways is not less but more powerful than the abysmal sea of our ancestors" (Höhler 2021:44). Global warming is threatening human food stocks through destruction of marine ecosystems, the existence of countries such as Tuvalu and Kiribati from sea-level rise, coastal communities through increasing hurricane activity, and perhaps the air we breathe as marine phytoplankton, which produces most of the world's oxygen, succumbs to acidification of the sea.

Global warming is a product of modern industrialization and a resource-raiding ethic by which people and industries take from the sea but give little back to the sea in terms of sustainable management. What is returned is atmospheric carbon pollution coupled with toxic waste dumping, including obsolete chemical weapons and nuclear reactor products (Müller 2021). The sea as a singular and separate ontological domain underpins the industrial world's view that the sea is large enough (as a hyperobject) and distant enough (especially in terms of deep ocean abysses) to "wash away all evils." It is seascape ontology and cosmology, and not marine science, that gives rise to the question of "Why do we continue to assume that it [the sea] can absorb any danger, carry off any blight, dilute any poison, when the evidence to the contrary mounts steadily?" (Patton 2007:27).

Sentient Seas reveals how maritime coastal communities have respected the omnipotent power of the sea and entered into a reciprocal social relationship whereby respect was shown through a multitude of propitiatory ritual engagements that acknowledged human humility, frailty, and gratitude. As the modern world has increasingly abandoned these values, the sea's unforgiving powers over us have steadily and correspondingly increased. Ironically, concomitant abandonment of morally prescribed respectful and reciprocal engagement with the agentive, sentient, and social qualities of the sea has been selective, given that conceptualization of the sea's endless "assimilative capacity" is linked to the one-sided and convenient anthropomorphic perception of its "selfless quality" (Müller 2021:103; Patton 2007:132).

Answering the challenges of global warming extend beyond the knowledge realm of marine and climate scientists who study the sea. Understanding how the impacts of global warming on the world's seas and oceans will change the lives of coastal peoples requires the expertise of maritime humanities (blue humanities) scholars and a broadened seascapes approach. Coastal peoples are embedded in seascapes, not seas per se. In this connection, we need to heed the sage advice of Killian Quigley (2021:133): "If attending to the ocean, in all its forms, is one of the primary ecological and ethical projects of our time, then becoming better seascapists must be a task worth undertaking." *Sentient Seas* shines a light not only on the extraordinary cultural diversity of *what* the sea is ontologically but also *who* is the sea and how maritime peoples over millennia have learned to listen to it and respect and acknowledge its power and authority through ritual. We need the sea a lot more than the sea needs us.

REFERENCES

Abdulla, A., D. Obura, B. Bertzky, and Y. Shi. 2014. Marine World Heritage: Creating a Globally More Balanced and Representative List. *Aquatic Conservation: Marine and Freshwater Ecosystems* 24(S2):59–74.

Abercromby, J. 1895. Traditions, Customs, and Superstitions of the Lewis. *Folklore* 6(2):162–171.

Aberg, A. 2005. Saving the *Victory*. *Mariner's Mirror* 91(2):358–368.

Abulafia, D. 2012. *The Great Sea: A Human History of the Mediterranean*. Penguin, London.

Acheson, J. M. 1981. Anthropology of Fishing. *Annual Review of Anthropology* 10(1):275–316.

Ackerman, R. E., and R. D. Shaw. 1981. Beach-Front Boulder Alignments in Southeastern Alaska. In *Megaliths to Medicine Wheels: Boulder Structures in Archaeology*, edited by M. Wilson, K. L. Road, and K. J. Hardy, pp. 265–277. University of Calgary Archaeological Association, Calgary.

Adams, J. 2013. *A Maritime Archaeology of Ships: Innovation and Social Change in Medieval and Early Modern Europe*. Oxbow, Oxford.

Adkins, R., and L. Adkins. 2009. *Jack Tar: The Extraordinary Lives of Ordinary Seamen in Nelson's Navy*. Abacus, London.

Agard, W. R. 1966. Boreas at Athens. *Classical Journal* 61(6):241–246.

Agius, D. A. 2007. Decorative Motifs on Arabian Boats: Meaning and Identity. In *Natural Resources and Cultural Connections of the Red Sea. Proceedings of Red Sea Project III*, edited by J. Starkey, P. Starkey, and T. Wilkinson, pp. 101–110. Society for Arabian Studies Monographs 5. Archaeopress, Oxford.

Agius, D. A. 2017. Red Sea Folk Beliefs: A Maritime Spirit Landscape. *Northeast African Studies* 17(1):131–161.

Agius, D. A. 2019. *The Life of the Red Sea Dhow: A Cultural History of Seaborne Exploration in the Islamic World*. I. B. Tauris, London.

Ahern, A., and the Mornington Island Elders. 2002. *Paint-Up*. University of Queensland Press, St. Lucia.

Äikäs, T., A.-K. Puputti, M. Núñez, J. Aspi, and J. Okkonen. 2009. Sacred and Profane Livelihood: Animal Bones from Sieidi Sites in Northern Finland. *Norwegian Archaeological Review* 42(2):109–122.

Akerman, K. 2023. *Scales of the Serpent: Kimberley Pearl Shell in Aboriginal Australia*. Hesperian, Carlisle, Western Australia.

Akerman, K., and J. Stanton. 1994. *Riji and Jakuli: Kimberley Pearl Shell in Aboriginal Australia*. Monograph Series 4. Northern Territory Museum of Arts and Sciences, Darwin.

Akimichi, T. 1996. Image and Reality at Sea: Fish and Cognitive Mapping in Carolinean Navigational Knowledge. In *Redefining Nature: Ecology, Culture and Domestication*, edited by R. Ellen and K. Fukui, pp. 493–514. Berg, Oxford.

Albenda, P. 1983. A Mediterranean Seascape from Khorsabad. *Assur* (*Monographic Journals of the Near East*) 3(3):1–34.

Alberti, B. 2016 Archaeologies of Ontology. *Annual Review of Anthropology* 45:163–179.

Alden, J. D., and C. C. Wright. 2005. Nomenclature and Classification of Early United States Submarines. *Warship International* 42(3):283–301.

Aldersey-Williams, H. 2017. *The Tide: The Science and Lore of the Greatest Force on Earth.* Penguin Random House, London.

Aldrovandi, U. 1642. *Monstrorum historia: Cum paralipomenis historiae omnium animalium.* Typis Nicolai Tebaldini, Bononiae.

Aleem, A. A. 1967. Concepts of Currents, Tides and Winds Among Medieval Arab Geographers in the Indian Ocean. *Deep Sea Research and Oceanographic Abstracts* 14(4):459–463.

Alkire, W. H. 1968. Porpoises and Taro. *Ethnology* 7(3):280–289.

Allegro, J. J. 2017. The Bottom of the Universe: Flat Earth Science in the Age of Encounter. *History of Science* 55(1):61–85.

Allwood, A. C., M. R. Walter, I. W. Burch, and B. S. Kamber. 2007. 3.43 Billion-Year-Old Stromatolite Reef from the Pilbara Craton of Western Australia: Ecosystem-Scale Insights to Early Life on Earth. *Precambrian Research* 158(3–4):198–227.

Alpers, W., and E. Salusti. 1983. Scylla and Charybdis Observed from Space. *Journal of Geophysical Research: Oceans* 88(C3):1800–1808.

Aluli, N. E., and D. P. I. Mcgregor. 1992. *Mai ke kai mai ke ola,* from the Ocean Comes Life: Hawaiian Customs, Uses, and Practices on Kahoʻolawe Relating to the Surrounding Ocean. *Hawaiian Journal of History* 26:231–254.

Alves, R., I. L. Rosa, N. A. L. Neto, and R. Voeks. 2012. Animals for the Gods: Magical and Religious Faunal Use and Trade in Brazil. *Human Ecology* 40(5):751–780.

Amery, F. 2020. "An Attempt to Trace Illusions to Their Physical Causes": Atmospheric Mirages and the Performance of Their Demystification in the 1820s and 1830s. *British Journal for the History of Science* 53(4):443–467.

Amkreutz, L., A. Verpoorte, A. Waters-Rist, M. Niekus, V. van Heekeren, A. van der Merwe, H. van der Plicht, J. Glimmerveen, D. Stapert, and L. Johansen. 2018. What Lies Beneath . . . Late Glacial Human Occupation of the Submerged North Sea Landscape. *Antiquity* 92(361):22–37.

Ammarell, G. 1995. Navigation Practices of the Bugis of South Sulawesi, Indonesia. In *Seafaring in the Contemporary Pacific Islands: Studies in Continuity and Change*, edited by R. Feinberg, pp. 196–218. Northern Illinois University Press, DeKalb.

Andaya, B. W. 2006. Oceans Unbounded: Traversing Asia Across "Area Studies." *Journal of Asian Studies* 65(4):669–690.

Andaya, B. W. 2017. Seas, Oceans and Cosmologies in Southeast Asia. *Journal of Southeast Asian Studies* 48(3):349–371.

Anderson, A. 2000. Slow Boats from China: Issues in the Prehistory of Indo-Pacific Seafaring. In *East of Wallace's Line: Studies of Past and Present Maritime Cultures of the Indo-Pacific Region,* edited by S. O'Connor and P. Veth, pp. 13–50. A. A. Balkema, Rotterdam.

Anderson, A. 2010. The Origins and Development of Seafaring: Towards a Global Approach. In *The Global Origins and Development of Seafaring,* edited by A. Anderson, J. H. Barrett, and K. V. Boyle, pp. 3–16. McDonald Institute for Archaeological Research, Cambridge.

Anderson, D. G. 1998. Property as a Way of Knowing on Evenki Lands in Arctic Siberia. In *Property Relations: Renewing the Anthropological Tradition,* edited by C. M. Hann, pp. 64–84. Cambridge University Press, Cambridge.

Anderson, D. G. 2000. *Identity and Ecology in Arctic Siberia: The Number One Reindeer Brigade.* Oxford University Press, Oxford.

Anderson, J. 2009. Transient Convergence and Relational Sensibility: Beyond the Modern Constitution of Nature. *Emotion, Space, and Society* 2(2):120–127.

Andrade, P., J. Goff, R. Pearce, A. Cundy, D. Sear, and V. Castro. 2022. Evidence for a Mid-Holocene Drowning from the Atacama Desert Coast of Chile. *Journal of Archaeological Science* 140:105565.

Andrews, E. W., IV. 1969. *The Archaeological Use and Distribution of Mollusca in the Maya Lowlands.* Middle American Research Institute, Tulane University, Publication 34, New Orleans.

Andrews, T. 1998. *Dictionary of Nature Myths: Legends of the Earth, Sea, and Sky.* Oxford University Press, Oxford.

Anonymous. 1679. *A True Account of Divers Most Strange and Prodigious Apparitions, Seen in the Air at Poins-Town in the County of Tipperary in Ireland: March the Second, 1678–9. Attested by Sixteen Persons That Were Eye-Witnesses.* L.C., London.

Anonymous. 1779. Remarkable Account of Dr. Fian a Noted Sorcerer and of Several Witches in Scotland. *Gentleman's Magazine,* August 49:393–395, September 49:449–452.

Anonymous. [1900]. *The Boy's Own Sea Stories: Being the Adventures of a Sailor in the Navy, the Merchant Service, and on a Whaling Cruise.* Ward, Lock, London.

Anson, P. F. 1965. *Fisher Folk-Lore: Old Customs, Taboos and Superstitions Among Fisher Folk, Especially in Brittany and Normandy and on the East Coast of Scotland.* Faith, London.

Anungazuk, H. O. 1995. Whaling: A Ritual Life. In *Hunting the Largest Animals: Native Whaling in the Western Arctic and Subarctic,* edited by A. P. McCartney, pp. 339–345. Canadian Circumpolar Institute, University of Alberta, Edmonton.

Aporta, C. 2002. Life on the Ice: Understanding the Codes of a Changing Environment. *Polar Record* 38(207):341–354.

Aporta, C. 2010. The Sea, the Land, the Coast, and the Winds: Understanding Inuit Sea Ice Use in Context. In *SIKU: Knowing Our Ice,* edited by I. Krupnik, C. Aporta, S. Gearheard, G. J. Laidler and L. K. Holm, pp. 163–180. Springer, Dordrecht.

Appelt, M., E. Damkjar, and T. M. Friesen. 2016. Late Dorset. In *The Oxford Handbook of the Prehistoric Arctic,* edited by T. M. Friesen and O. K. Mason, pp. 783–806. Oxford University Press, Oxford.

Arakawa, A. 1978. Ningyo to Hitobito no roman. In *Shin Nanto Fudoki.* Daiwa Shobo, Tokyo, Japan.

Arch, J. K. 2018. *Bringing Whales Ashore: Oceans and the Environment of Early Modern Japan.* University of Washington Press, Seattle.

Arias, P., A. Armendariz, R. de Balbín, M. Á. Fano, J. Fernández-Tresguerres, M. R. G. Morales, M. J. Iriarte, R. Ontañon, J. Alcolea, E. Álvarez-Fernández, F. Etxeberria, M. D. Garralda, M. Jackes, and Á. Arrizabalaga. 2009. Burials in the Cave: New Evidence on Mortuary Practices During the Mesolithic of Cantabrian Spain. In *Mesolithic Horizons: Papers Presented at the Seventh International Conference on the Mesolithic in Europe, Belfast, 2005,* edited by S. McCartan, R. Schulting, G. Warren, and P. Woodman, pp. 650–656. Oxbow, Oxford.

Armstrong, C. 2022. *A Blue New Deal: Why We Need a New Politics for the Ocean.* Yale University Press, New Haven.

Armstrong, L. 1971. A Fisherman's Festival at Cape Finisterre, Spain. *Folklore* 82(4):304–311.

Arndt, W. 1965. The Dreaming of Kunukban. *Oceania* 35(4):241–259.

Arnold, N. 2013. *Shadows on the Sea: The Maritime Mysteries of Britain.* History Press, Gloucestershire.

Artzy, M. 1999. Carved Ship Graffiti—An Ancient Ritual? In *Tropis V: 5th International Symposium on Ship Construction in Antiquity,* edited by H. E. Tzalas, pp. 21–30. Hellenic Institute for the Preservation of Nautical Tradition, Athens.

Artzy, M. 2003. Mariners and Their Boats at the End of the Late Bronze and the Beginning of the Iron Age in the Eastern Mediterranean. *Tel Aviv* 30(2):232–246.

Arundel, H. 2023. *Gunditjmara Nyamat Mirring Plan 2023–2033.* Gunditj Mirring Traditional Owners Aboriginal Corporation, Breakaway Creek, Victoria, Australia.

Arutiunov, S. A. 2009. The Eskimo Harpoon. In *Gifts from the Ancestors: Ancient Ivories of Bering Strait,* edited by W. W. Fitzhugh, J. Hollowell, and A. L. Crowell, pp. 52–57. Princeton University Art Museum, Princeton.

Arutiunov, S. A., and D. A. Sergeev. 2006 [1969]. *Ancient Cultures of the Asiatic Eskimos. The Uelen Cemetery,* translated and edited by R. L. Bland. U.S. Department of the Interior, National Park Service, Alaska Regional Office, Anchorage.

Ash, J. 2013. Change and Continuity: An Archaeology of Mualgal Missions, Western Torres Strait, Northeast Australia. PhD dissertation, Monash University, Melbourne.

Ash, J., and B. David. 2008. Mua 22: Archaeology at the Old Village Site of Totalai. *Memoirs of the Queensland Museum, Cultural Heritage Series* 4(2):451–472.

Ashkenazi, M. 2003. *Handbook of Japanese Mythology.* Oxford University Press, Oxford.

Aston, E. 2009. Thetis and Cheiron in Thessaly. *Kernos: Revue internationale et pluridisciplinaire de religion Grecque antique* 22:83–107.

Aston, E. 2011. *Mixanthrôpoi: Animal-Human Hybrid Deities in Greek Religion.* Centre International d'Étude de la Religion Grecque Antique, Liège.

Aston, E. 2014. Part Animal Gods. In *The Oxford Handbook of Animals in Classical Thought and Life,* edited by G. L. Campbell, pp. 366–383. Oxford University Press, Oxford.

Aswani, S. 2000. Changing Identities: The Ethnohistory of Roviana Predatory Head-Hunting. *Journal of the Polynesian Society* 109(1):39–70.

Aswani, S., and P. Sheppard. 2003. The Archaeology and Ethnohistory of Exchange in Pre-Colonial and Colonial Roviana: Gift, Commodities, and Inalienable Possessions. *Current Anthropology* 44:S51–S78.

Atkins, C. E. 2009. More Than a Hull: Religious Ritual and Sacred Space on Board the Ancient Ship. MA dissertation, Texas A&M University, College Station.

Aura Tortosa, J. E., J. F. J. Pardo, E. Álvarez-Fernández, M. P. Ripoll, B. A. Aristu, J. V. Morales-Pérez, M. J. R. García, R. Marlasca, J. A. Alcover, P. Jardón, C. I. P. Herrero, S. P. Gordó, A. Maestro, M. P. V. Currás, and D. C. Salvazar-García. 2016. Palaeolithic-Epipalaeolithic Seapeople of the Southern Iberian Coast (Spain): An Overview. In *Archaeology of Maritime Hunter-Gatherers. From Settlement Function to the Organization of the Coastal Zone*, edited by C. Dupont and G. Marchand, pp. 69–92. Société Préhistorique Française, Paris.

Austen, L. 1948. Notes on the Turamarubi of Western Papua. *Mankind* 4(1):14–23.

Australian Government. 2025. Burial at Sea. Department of Environment and Energy, Canberra. http://www.environment.gov.au/marine/marine-pollution/sea-dumping/burial-sea, accessed 25 January 2025.

Avery, G., D. Halkett, J. Orton, T. Steele, M. Tusenius, and R. Klein. 2008. The Ysterfontein 1 Middle Stone Age Rock Shelter and the Evolution of Coastal Foraging. *South African Archaeological Society Goodwin Series* 10:66–89.

Baader, H. 2016. Vows on Water: Ship-Ex-Votos as Things, Metaphors and Mediators of Communality. In *Ex Voto: Votive Giving Across Cultures*, edited by I. Weinryb, pp. 217–245. Bard Graduate Center, New York City.

Babadzan, A. 1993. *Les dépouilles des dieux: Essai sur la religion Tahitienne au moment de la découverte*. Editions de la Maison des Sciences de l'Homme, Paris.

Babington, C. 1869. *Polychronicon Ranulphi Higden, Monachi Cestrensis: Together with the English Translations of John Trevisa and of an Unknown Writer of the Fifteenth Century*. Volume 2. Longmans, Green, London.

Backer, R. T., and J. B. Elwe. [1792]. *Door dit hemels pleyn wert vertoondt den gehelen loop des hemels der vaste sterren met haer beeltenisse*. [Te Amsterdam, I. B. Elwe]. Map. https://loc.gov/item/2013593225/.

Bagshaw, G. 1998. *Gapu Dhulway, Gapu Maramba*: Conceptualisation and Ownership of Saltwater Among the Burarra and Yan-nhaŋu Peoples of Northeast Arnhem Land. In *Customary Marine Tenure in Australia*, edited by N. Peterson and B. Rigsby, pp.154–177. University of Sydney Oceania Publications, Sydney.

Bahn, P. 2013. The Banggudae Whales in the Context of World Rock Art. In *Bangudae: Petrogyph Panels in Ulsan, Korea, in the Context of World Rock Art*, edited by J. Kim, pp. 37–66. World Petroglyphs Research 1. Hollym, Morgan Hill, California.

Bailey, G. N., and A. S. Craighead. 2003. Late Pleistocene and Early Holocene Coastal Palaeoeconomies: A Reconsideration of the Molluscan Evidence from Northern Spain. *Geoarchaeology* 18(2):175–204.

Baines, C. C. 1950. Children Born with a Caul. *Folklore* 61(2):104.

Baird, M. F. 2006. Frederica de Laguna and the Study of Pre-Contact Pictographs from Coastal Sites in Cook Inlet and Prince William Sound, Alaska. *Arctic Anthropology* 43(2):136–147.

Baires, S. E. 2016. A Microhistory of Human and Gastropod Bodies and Souls During Cahokia's Emergence. *Cambridge Archaeological Journal* 27(2):245–260.

Baker, M. 1979. *Folklore of the Sea.* David & Charles, Devon.

Baldi, A. 1998. Mi-marins, mi-mages: Caractères de l'univers magico-religieux des pêcheurs et des gens de mer du littoral Tyrrhénien. *Material History Review* 48:144–159.

Balikci, A. 1984. Netsilik. In *Handbook of North American Indians, Vol. 5: Arctic*, edited by D. Damas, pp. 415–430. Smithsonian Institution, Washington, DC.

Ballard, C., R. Bradley, L. N. Myhre, and M. Wilson. 2004. The Ship as Symbol in the Prehistory of Scandinavia and Southeast Asia. *World Archaeology* 35(3):385–403.

Ballard, R. D. 1995. *The Discovery of the Titanic.* Orion, London.

Ballard, R. D., L. E. Stager, D. Master, D. Yoerger, D. Mindell, L. L. Whitcomb, H. Singh, and D. Piechota. 2002. Iron Age Shipwrecks in Deep Water off Ashkelon, Israel. *American Journal of Archaeology* 106(2):151–168.

Ballester, B. 2018. El Médano Rock Art Style: Izcuña Paintings and the Marine Hunter-Gatherers of the Atacama Desert. *Antiquity* 92(361):132–148.

Balme, J., and K. Morse. 2006. Shell Beads and Social Behaviour in Pleistocene Australia. *Antiquity* 80(310):799–811.

Bandi, H.-G. 1995. Siberian Eskimos as Whalers and Warriors. In *Hunting the Largest Animals: Native Whaling in the Western Arctic and Subarctic*, edited by A. P. McCartney, pp. 165–183. Canadian Circumpolar Institute, University of Alberta, Edmonton.

Barber, I. 2004. Sea, Land and Fish: Spatial Relationships and the Archaeology of South Island Maori Fishing. *World Archaeology* 35(3):434–448.

Barber, M. 2005. Where the Clouds Stand: Australian Aboriginal Relationships to Water, Place, and the Marine Environment in Blue Mud Bay, Northern Territory. PhD dissertation, Australian National University, Canberra.

Barker, B., L. Lamb, and G. Campbell. 2016. The Mine Island Aboriginal Stone Arrangements: Spiritual Responses to Late Holocene Change on the Central Queensland Coast. *Australian Archaeology* 82(3):232–247.

Barlow, K., and D. Lipset. 1997. Dialogics of Material Culture: Male and Female in Murik Outrigger Canoes. *American Ethnologist* 24(1):4–36.

Barlow, N. (editor). 1933. *Charles Darwin's Diary on the Voyage of H.M.S. "Beagle."* Edited from the MS. Cambridge University Press, Cambridge.

Barnes, R. H. 1974. Lamalerap: A Whaling Village in Eastern Indonesia. *Indonesia* 17:147–159.

Barnes, R. H. 1996. *Sea Hunters of Indonesia: Fishers and Weavers of Lamalera.* Clarendon, Oxford.

Barnes, R. H. 2005. Indigenous Use and Management of Whales and other Marine Resources in East Flores and Lembata, Indonesia. *Senri Ethnological Studies* 67:77–85.

Barnett, H. G. 1955. *The Coast Salish of British Columbia.* University of Oregon Press, Eugene.

Barton, F. R. 1910. The Annual Trading Expedition to the Papuan Gulf. In *The Melanesians of British New Guinea*, edited by C. G. Seligmann, pp. 96–120. Cambridge University Press, Cambridge.

Bar-Yosef Mayer, D. E., B. Vandermeersch, and O. Bar-Yosef. 2009. Shells and Ochre in Middle Paleolithic Qafzeh Cave, Israel: Indications for Modern Behavior. *Journal of Human Evolution* 56(3):307–314.

Basch, L. 1975. Another Punic Wreck in Sicily: Its Ram: 1. A Typological Sketch. *International Journal of Nautical Archaeology* 4(2):201–228.

Bashford, A. 2017. The Pacific Ocean. In *Oceanic Histories*, edited by D. Armitage, A. Bashford, and S. Sivasundaram, pp. 62–84. Cambridge University Press, Cambridge.

Bassett, F. S. 1885. *Legends and Superstitions of the Sea and of Sailors in All Lands and at All Times.* Sampson Low, Marston, Searle and Rivington, London.

Bassett, W. 1917. *Wander-Ships: Folk-Stories of the Sea with Notes upon Their Origin.* Open Court, Chicago.

Bataille-Benguigui, M.-C. 1988. The Fish of Tonga: Prey or Social Partners? *Journal of the Polynesian Society* 97(2):185–198.

Batchelor, Rev. J. 1901. *The Ainu and Their Folk-Lore.* Religious Tract Society, London.

Bavinck, M. 2015. Placating the Sea Goddess: Analysis of a Fisher Ritual in Tamil Nadu, India. *Etnofoor* 27(1):89–100.

Beasley, H. G. 1928. *Pacific Island Records Fish Hooks.* Seeley, Service, London.

Beaulieu, M.-C. 2016. *The Sea in the Greek Imagination.* University of Pennsylvania Press, Philadelphia.

Beaven, B. 2016. The Resilience of Sailortown Culture in English Naval Ports, c. 1820–1900. *Urban History* 43(1):72–95.

Beck, H. P. 1957. *The Folklore of Maine.* J. B. Lippincott, Philadelphia.

Beck, H. P. 1999. *Folklore and the Sea.* Castle, Edison, New Jersey.

Beck, J. 1977. West Indian Sea Magic. *Folklore* 88(2):194–202.

Becker, H. 2000. *Seaweed Memories: In the Jaws of the Sea.* Wolfhound, Dublin.

Beckwith, M. W. 1917. Hawaiian Shark Aumakua. *American Anthropologist* 19(4):503–517.

Bednarik, R. G. 2003. Seafaring in the Pleistocene. *Cambridge Archaeological Journal* 13(1):41–66.

Beech, M. 2000. Preliminary Report on the Faunal Remains from an Ubaid Settlement on Dalma Island, United Arab Emirates. In *Archaeozoology of the Near East.* IVB, edited by M. Mashkour, A. M. Choyke, H. Buitenhuis, and F. Poplin, pp. 68–78. ARC—Publicatie 32. Groningen, The Netherlands.

Bell, C. 1992. *Ritual Theory, Ritual Practice.* Oxford University Press, Oxford.

Bell, D., J. Specht, and D. Hain. 1986. Beyond the Reef: Compound Fishhooks in the Solomon Islands. In *Traditional Fishing in the Pacific: Ethnographical and Archaeological Papers from the 15th Pacific Science Congress*, edited by A. Anderson, pp. 45–63. Pacific Archaeological Records 37. Department of Anthropology, Bernice Pauahi Bishop Museum, Honolulu.

Bell, E. 2025. Who Do You Think You Are? The Seal-Woman of Shetland. Museum of Archaeology and Anthropology, Cambridge University. https://www.maadigitallab.org/blog/2025/04/29/who-do-you-think-you-are-the-seal-woman-of-shetland/.

Bell, F. L. S. 1947. The Place of Food in the Social Life of the Tanga. *Oceania* 17(2):310–326.

Bellwood, P., J. Cameron, N. V. Viet, and B. V. Liem. 2007. Ancient Boats, Boat Timbers, and Locked Mortise-and-Tenon Joints from Bronze/Iron-Age Northern Vietnam. *International Journal of Nautical Archaeology* 36(1):2–20.

Ben-Amos, P. 1973. Symbolism in Olokun Mud Art. *African Arts* 6(4):28–31, 95.

Ben-Amos, P. 1976. Men and Animals in Benin Art. *Man* 11(2):243–252.

Ben-Amos, P. G. 1999. *Art, Innovation, and Politics in Eighteenth-Century Benin.* Indiana University Press, Bloomington.

Benwell, G., and A. Waugh. 1961. *Sea Enchantress: The Tales of the Mermaid and Her Kin.* Hutchinson, London.

Berg, G. 1984. The Use of Fishing Skins in Northern Europe Before the Industrial Era. In *The Fishing Culture of the World: Studies in Ethnology, Cultural Ecology and Folklore,* edited by B. Gunda, pp. 91–104. 2 vols. Akadémiai Kiadó, Budapest.

Berg, I. 2011. Towards a Conceptualisation of the Sea: Artefacts, Iconography and Meaning. In *The Seascape in Aegean Prehistory,* edited by G. Vavouranakis, pp. 119–137. Monograph 14. Danish Institute at Athens, Athens.

Bergsvik, K. A. 2009. Caught in the Middle: Functional and Ideological Aspects of Mesolithic Shores in Norway. In *Mesolithic Horizons: Papers Presented at the Seventh International Conference on the Mesolithic in Europe, Belfast 2005,* edited by S. McCartan, R. Schulting, G. Warren, and P. Woodman, pp. 602–609. Oxbow, Oxford.

Berkes, F. 2008. *Sacred Ecology.* 2nd ed. Routledge, New York.

Berndt, R. M. 1948. A Wɔnguri-Mandʒikai song cycle of the Moon-Bone. *Oceania* 19:16–50.

Berndt, R. M., and C. H. Berndt. 1993. *A World That Was: The Yaraldi of the Murray River and the Lakes, South Australia.* Miegunyah, Carlton, Victoria.

Berry, M. 2015. Chasing the Silver Dragon. *Physics World* 28(7):45–47.

Best, A. 2012. The Aboriginal Material Culture of the Wellesley Islands and Adjacent Mainland Coast, Gulf of Carpentaria: Social and Environmental Factors Affecting Variations in Style. *Queensland Archaeological Research* 15:1–46.

Best, E. 1924. *Maori Religion and Mythology.* Dominion Museum Bulletin 12. W. A. G. Skinner, Government Printer, Wellington.

Best, E. 1929. *Fishing Methods and Devices of the Maori.* V. R. Ward, Government Printer, Wellington.

Betten, F. S. 1923. The Knowledge of the Sphericity of the Earth During the Earlier Middle Ages. *Catholic Historical Review* 9(1):74–90.

Betts, M. W., S. E. Blair, and D. W. Black. 2012. Perspectivism, Mortuary Symbolism, and Human-Shark Relationships on the Maritime Peninsula. *American Antiquity* 77(4):621–645.

Biel, S. 1997. *Down with the Old Canoe: A Cultural History of the "Titanic" Disaster.* W. W. Norton, New York.

Bier, J. 2018. Bodily Circulation and the Measure of a Life: Forensic Identification and Valuation After the *Titanic* Disaster. *Social Studies of Science* 48(5):635–662.

Bigalke, E. H. 1973. The Exploitation of Shellfish by Coastal Tribesmen of the Transkei. *Annals of the Cape Provincial Museums Natural History* 9(9):159–175.

Bill, J. 2016a. Ambiguous Mobility in the Viking Age Ship Burial from Oseberg. In *Materialities of Passing: Explorations in Transformation, Transition and Transience,* edited by P. Bjerregaard, A. E. Rasmussen, and T. F. Sørensen, pp. 207–220. Routledge, London.

Bill, J. 2016b. Protecting Against the Dead? On the Possible Use of Apotropaic Magic in the Oseberg Burial. *Cambridge Archaeological Journal* 26(1):141–155.

Bindra, S. C. 2002. Notes on Religious Ban on Sea Travel in Ancient India. *Indian Historical Review* 29(1–2):29–47.

Bird, M. I., R. J. Beaman, S. A. Condie, A. Cooper, S. Ulm, and P. Veth. 2018. Palaeogeography and Voyage Modeling Indicates Early Human Colonization of Australia Was Likely from Timor-Roti. *Quaternary Science Reviews* 191:431–439.

Bird-David, N. 1999. "Animism" Revisited: Personhood, Environment, and Relational Epistemology. *Current Anthropology* 40(1):67–91.

Bird-David, N. 2006. Animistic Epistemology: Why Do Some Hunter-Gatherers Not Depict Animals? *Ethnos* 71(1):33–50.

Birkedahl, P., and E. Johansen. 1995. The Sebbersund Boat-Graves. In *The Ship as Symbol in Prehistoric and Medieval Scandinavia*, edited by O. Crumlin-Pedersen and B. M. Thye, pp. 160–164. Studies in Archaeology and History. National Museum, Copenhagen.

Birket-Smith, K. 1953. *The Chugach Eskimo.* Nationalmuseets Publikationsfond, Copenhagen.

Birrell, A. 1993. *Chinese Mythology: An Introduction.* Johns Hopkins University Press, Baltimore.

Black, G. F., and N. W. Thomas. 1903. *Orkney and Shetland Islands. Country Folk-Lore Vol. 3.* David Nutt, London.

Black, L. T. 1987. Whaling in the Aleutians. *Études Inuit Studies* 11(2):7–50.

Black, L. T. 1998. Animal World of the Aleuts. *Arctic Anthropology* 35(2):126–135.

Blackman, M. B. 1990. Haida: Traditional Culture. In *Handbook of North American Indians, Vol. 7: Northwest Coast*, edited by W. Suttles, pp. 240–260. Smithsonian Institution, Washington, DC.

Blackwood, B. 1935. *Both Sides of Buka Passage: An Ethnographic Study of Social, Sexual, and Economic Questions in the North-Western Solomon Islands.* Clarendon, Oxford.

Blake, M. E. 1936. Roman Mosaics of the Second Century in Italy. *Memoirs of the American Academy in Rome* 13:67–214.

Blakemore, R. J. 2014. The Ship, the River and the Ocean Sea: Concepts of Space in the Seventeenth-Century London Maritime Community. In *Maritime History and Identity: The Sea and Culture in the Modern World*, edited by D. Redford, pp. 98–119. I. B. Tauris, London.

Blakely, S. 2017. Maritime Risk and Ritual Responses: Sailing with the Gods in the Ancient Mediterranean. In *The Sea in History: The Ancient World*, edited by P. de Souza and P. Arnaud, pp. 362–379. Boydell, Woodbridge.

Blanco-García, J., and F. A. Ribas-Pérez. 2011. Mirages Above the Sea Waters. *Journal of Physics: Conference Series* 274(1):012001.

Blind, K. 1881a. Scottish, Shetlandic, and Germanic Water Tales, Part I. *The Contemporary Review* August 40:186–208.

Blind, K. 1881b. Scottish, Shetlandic, and Germanic Water Tales, Part II. *The Contemporary Review* September 40:399–423.

Blue, L. 2006. Sewn Boat Timbers from the Medieval Islamic Port of Quseir al-Qadim on the Red Sea Coast of Egypt. In *Connected by the Sea: Proceedings of the 10th International Symposium on Boat and Ship Archaeology*, edited by L. Blue, F. Hocker, and A. Englert, pp. 277–284. Oxbow, Oxford.

Boardman, J. 1987. "Very like a Whale": Classical Sea Monsters. In *Monsters and Demons in the Ancient and Medieval Worlds: Papers Presented in Honor of Edith Porada*, edited by A. E. Farkas, P. O. Harper, and E. B. Harrison, pp. 73–84. Philipp von Zabern, Mainz, Germany.

Boas, F. 1888. The Central Eskimo. In *Sixth Annual Report of the Bureau of Ethnology, 1884–1885,* pp. 399–669. Smithsonian Institution, Bureau of American Ethnology, Washington, DC.

Boas, F. 1901. The Eskimo of Baffin Land and Hudson Bay. *Bulletin of the American Museum of Natural History* 15:1–570.

Boas, F. 1907. Second Report on the Eskimo of Baffin Land and Hudson Bay: From Notes Collected by Captain George Comer, Captain James S. Mutch, and Rev. E. J. Peck. *Bulletin of the American Museum of Natural History* 15(2):371–570.

Boas, F. (editor). 1921. Ethnology of the Kwakiutl Based on Data Collected by George Hunt. In *Thirty-Fifth Annual Report of the Bureau of American Ethnology to the Secretary of the Smithsonian Institution, Part I. 1913–1914,* pp. 43–794. Government Printing Office, Washington, DC.

Boas, F. 1932. Current beliefs of the Kwakiutl Indians. *Journal of American Folklore* 45(176):177–260.

Boaten, B. A. 1998. Traditional Conservation Practices: Ghana's Example. *Institute of African Studies Research Review* 14(1):42–51.

Bodenhorn, B. 1990. "I'm Not the Great Hunter, My Wife Is": Iñupiat and Anthropological Models of Gender. *Études Inuit Studies* 14:55–74.

Bodenhorn, B. 2003. Fall Whaling in Barrow, Alaska: A Consideration of Strategic Decision-Making. In *Indigenous Ways to the Present: Native Whaling in the Western Arctic,* edited by A. P. McCartney, pp. 277–306. Canadian Circumpolar Institute Press, Edmonton.

Bodrogi, T. 1987. New Ireland Art in Cultural Context. In *Assemblage of Spirits: Idea and Image in New Ireland,* edited by L. Lincoln, pp. 17–32. George Braziller in association with the Minneapolis Institute of Arts, New York.

Bogoras, W. 1907. The Chukchee: Religion. *Memoirs of the American Museum of Natural History* 11(2).

Bogoslovskaya, L. S. 2003. The Bowhead Whale off Chukotka: Integration of Scientific and Traditional Knowledge. In *Indigenous Ways to the Present: Native Whaling in the Western Arctic,* edited by A. P. McCartney, pp. 210–254. Canadian Circumpolar Institute Press, Edmonton.

Bois, G. J. C. 2010. *Jersey Folklore and Superstitions, Vol. 2: A Comparative Study with the Traditions of the Gulf of St. Malo (The Channel Islands, Normandy and Brittany) with Reference to World Mythologies.* AuthorHouse, Central Milton Keynes, England.

Bois, G. J. C. 2016. *Jersey Maritime Folklore.* 2nd ed. Giles Bois.

Bonser, W. 1928. The Mythology of the Kalevala, with Notes on Bear-Worship Among the Finns. *Folklore* 39(4):344–358.

Bonshek, E. 2004. Ownership and a Peripatetic Collection: Raymond Firth's Collection from Tikopia, Solomon Islands. *Records of the Australian Museum, Supplement* 29:37–45.

Borden, C. E. 1969. Skagit River Atlatl: A Reappraisal. *B.C. Studies* 1:13–19.

Boreal Institute for Northern Studies. 1988. *Small-Type Whaling in Japan: Report of an International Workshop.* Boreal Institute for Northern Studies, University of Alberta, Edmonton.

Borthwick, E. M. 1977. Aging and Social Change on Lukunor Atoll, Micronesia. PhD dissertation, University of Iowa.

Bosinski, G., and H. Bosinski. 2009. Seals from the Magdalenian Site of Gönnersdorf (Rhineland, Germany). In *An Enquiring Mind: Studies in Honor of Alexander Marshack,* edited by P. G. Bahn, pp. 39–50. Oxbow, Oxford.

Bosman, W. 1907 [1705]. *A New and Accurate Description of the Coast of Guinea.* Ballantyne, London.

Bottignolo, B. 1995. *Celebrations with the Sun: An Overview of Religious Phenomena Among the Badjaos.* Ateneo de Manila University Press, Manila.

Bottrell, W. 1873. *Traditions and Hearthside Stories of West Cornwall.* 2nd series. Beare and Son, Penzance.

Boulotis, C. 1987. The Aegean Area in Prehistoric Times: Cults and Beliefs About the Sea. In *Greece and the Sea,* edited by A. Delivorrias, pp. 20–35. De Nieuwe Kerk, Amsterdam.

Bouzouggar, A., N. Barton, M. Vanhaeren, F. d'Errico, S. Collcutt, T. Higham, E. Hodge, S. Parfitt, E. Rhodes, J.-L. Schwenninger, C. Stringer, E. Turner, S. Ward, A. Moutmir, and A. Stambouli. 2007. 82,000-year-old Shell Beads from North Africa and Implications for the Origins of Modern Human Behavior. *Proceedings of the National Academy of Sciences* 104(24):9964–9969.

Bowden, R. 1984. Maori Cannibalism: An Interpretation. *Oceania* 55(2):81–99.

Bowen, R. LeB. 1955. Maritime Superstitions of the Arabs. *American Neptune* 15(1):5–48.

Bowen, R. LeB. 1957. Origin and Diffusion of Oculi. *American Neptune* 17(4):262–291.

Božanić, J., and E. Buljubašić. 2012. The Ritual of Boat Incineration on the Island of Vis, Croatia: An Interpretation. *International Journal of Intangible Heritage* 7:15–30.

Bradley, J. J. 1991. "*Li-Maramaranja*": Yanyuwa Hunters of Marine Animals in the Sir Edward Pellew Group, Northern Territory. *Records of the South Australian Museum* 25(1):91–110.

Bradley, J. J. 1997. *Li-anthawirriyarra*, People of the Sea: Yanyuwa Relations with Their Maritime Environment. PhD dissertation, Northern Territory University, Darwin.

Bradley, J. J. 1998. "We Always Look North": Yanyuwa Identity and the Marine Environment. In *Customary Marine Tenure in Australia,* edited by N. Peterson and B. Rigsby, pp. 125–141. University of Sydney Oceania Publications, Sydney.

Bradley, J. J. 2006. The Social, Economic and Historical Construction of Cycad Palms Among the Yanyuwa. In *The Social Archaeology of Australian Indigenous Societies,* edited by B. David, B. Barker, and I. J. McNiven, pp. 161–181. Aboriginal Studies Press, Canberra.

Bradley, J. J., M. Holmes, D. N. Marrngawi, A. I. Karrakayn, J. M. Wuwarlu, and I. Ninganga. 2006. *Yumbulyumbulmantha ki-Awarawu All Kinds of Things from Country: Yanyuwa Ethnobiological Classification.* Aboriginal and Torres Strait Islander Studies Unit Research Report Series 6. University of Queensland, St. Lucia.

Bradley, J. J., and A. Kearney. 2009. Manankurra: What's in a Name? Placenames and Emotional Geographies. In *Aboriginal Placenames Old and New: Discovering, Inter-*

preting and Restoring Indigenous Nomenclature for the Australia Landscape, edited by H. Koch and L. Hercus, pp. 463–480. Aboriginal History Monographs. ANU E-Press and Aboriginal History, Canberra.

Bradley, J. J., and A. Kearney. 2011. "He Painted the Law": William Westall, "Stone Monuments" and Remembrance of Things Past in the Sir Edward Pellew Islands. *Journal of Material Culture* 16(1):25–45.

Bradley, J. J., and I. J. McNiven. 2019. "Why Those Old Fellas Stopped Using Them?": Socio-Religious and Socio-Political Dimensions of Stone-Walled Tidal Fish Trap Use and Dis-use Amongst the Yanyuwa of Northern Australia. *Journal of Island and Coastal Archaeology* 14(3):337–355.

Bradley, J. J., with Yanyuwa Families. 2010. *Singing Saltwater Country: Journey to the Songlines of Carpentaria.* Allen and Unwin, Crows Nest, New South Wales.

Bradley, J. J., with Yanyuwa Families. 2022. *It's Coming from the Times in Front of Us: Country, Kin and the Dugong Hunter Songline.* Australian Scholarly Publishing, North Melbourne.

Bradley, R. 2000. *An Archaeology of Natural Places.* Routledge, New York.

Bradley, R. 2022. *Maritime Archaeology on Dry Land: Special Sites Along the Coasts of Britain and Ireland from the First Farmers to the Atlantic Bronze Age.* Oxbow, Oxford.

Bradley, R., C. Nimura, and P. Skoglund. 2020. Meetings Between Strangers in the Nordic Bronze Age: The Evidence of Southern Swedish Rock Art. *Proceedings of the Prehistoric Society* 86:261–283.

Bradley, R., and T. Phillips. 2004. The High-Water Mark: The Siting of Megalithic Tombs on the Swedish Island of Tjörn. *Oxford Journal of Archaeology* 23(2):123–133.

Brady, K., and C. Corlett. 2004. Holy Ships: Ships on Plaster at Medieval Ecclesiastical Sites in Ireland. *Archaeology Ireland* 18(2):28–31.

Brady, L., and I. J. McNiven. 2022. The Presence of Absence: Why Does the Post-Contact Rock Art of Torres Strait (Northeastern Australia) Not Include Paintings of European Ships? *Cambridge Archaeological Journal* 32(1):99–115.

Brady, L. M. 2010. *Pictures, Patterns and Objects: Rock-Art of the Torres Strait Islands, Northeastern Australia.* Australian Scholarly Publishing, North Melbourne.

Brand, J., and H. Ellis. 1849. *Observations on the Popular Antiquities of Great Britain.* Vol. 3. Henry G. Bohn, London.

Brattland, C., and S. Nilsen. 2011. Reclaiming Indigenous Seascapes: Sami Place Names in Norwegian Sea Charts. *Polar Geography* 34(4):275–297.

Bravo, M. T. 2009. Sea Ice Mapping: Ontology, Mechanics and Human Rights at the Ice Floe Edge. In *High Places: Cultural Geographies of Mountains, Ice and Science*, edited by D. Cosgrove and V. D. Dora, pp. 162–177. I. B. Tauris, London.

Breckwoldt, A., Y. Dombal, C. Sabinot, G. David, L. Riera, S. Ferse, and E. Fache. 2022. A Social-Ecological Engagement with Reef Passages in New Caledonia: Connectors Between Coastal and Oceanic Spaces and Species. *Ambio* 51(12):2401–2413.

Brendalsmo, J. A. 2002. The Landscape of the Dead: Was Burial in the Parish Churchyard Obligatory in the Middle Ages. In *Kulturminneforskningens Mangfold. NIKU 1994–1999*, edited by G. Gundhus, E. Seip, and E. Ulriksen, pp. 53–60. NIKU, Oslo.

Brennand, M., M. Taylor, T. Ashwin, A. Bayliss, M. Canti, A. Chamberlain, C. A. I. French, V. Fryer, R. Gale, F. M. L. Green, C. Groves, A. Hall, N. Linford, P. Murphy, M. Robinson, J. Wells, and D. Williams. 2003. The Survey and Excavation of a Bronze Age Timber Circle at Holme-next-the-Sea, Norfolk, 1998–1999. *Proceedings of the Prehistoric Society* 69:1–84.

Breton, S. 1999. Social Body and Icon of the Person: A Symbolic Analysis of Shell Money Among the Wodani, Western Highlands of Irian Jaya. *American Ethnologist* 26(3):558–582.

Brightman, R. 1993. *Grateful Prey: Rock Cree Human-Animal Relationships.* University of Regina, Canadian Plains Research Centre, Regina.

Brito, C. 2016. The Monstrous in Aldrovandi and the Natural Order of Marine Animals in the 16th and 17th Centuries. In *Natureza, Causalidade e Formas de Corporeidade,* edited by A. Cardoso, M. S. Marques, and M. Mendonça, pp. 177–192. Edições Húmus, Famalicão.

Brodeur, A. G. 1916. *The Prose Edda by Snorri Sturluson.* Translated by A. G. Brodeur. American-Scandinavian Foundation, New York.

Brody, A. 2021. Sail, Pray, Steer: Aspects of the Sacred Beliefs and Ritual Practices of Phoenician Seafarers. *Advances in Ancient, Biblical, and Near Eastern Research* 1(2):1–30.

Brody, A. 2023. Maritime Viewscapes and the Material Religion of Levantine Seafarers. In *The Bloomsbury Handbook of Material Religion in the Ancient Near East and Egypt,* edited by N. Laneri and S. R. Steadman, pp. 339–412. Bloomsbury Academic, London.

Brody, A. J. 1998. *"Each Man Cried Out to His God": The Specialized Religion of Canaanite and Phoenician Seafarers.* Harvard Semitic Monograph Series 58. Scholars Press, Atlanta.

Brody, A. J. 2005. Further Evidence of the Specialized Religion of Phoenician Seafarers. In *Terra Marique: Studies in Art History and Marine Archaeology in Honor of Anna Marguerite McCann on the Receipt of the Gold Medal of the Archaeological Institute of America,* edited by J. Pollini, pp. 177–782. Oxbow, Oxford.

Brody, A. J. 2008. The Specialized Religions of Ancient Mediterranean Seafarers. *Religion Compass* 2(4):444–454.

Bronner, S. J. 1984. The Early Movements of Anthropology and Their Folkloristic Relationships. *Folklore* 95(1):57–73.

Bronshtein, M. M., K. A. Dneprovsky, and A. B. Savinetsky. 2016. Ancient Eskimo Cultures of Chukotka. In *The Oxford Handbook of the Prehistoric Arctic,* edited by M. Friesen and O. Mason, pp. 469–488. Oxford University Press, Oxford.

Broodbank, C. 2000. *An Island Archaeology of the Early Cyclades.* Cambridge University Press, Cambridge.

Broodbank, C. 2006. The Origin and Early Development of Mediterranean Maritime Activity. *Journal of Mediterranean Archaeology* 19(2):199–230.

Brookes, S. 2007. Boat-Rivets in Graves in Pre-Viking Kent: Reassessing Anglo-Saxon Boat-Burial Traditions. *Medieval Archaeology* 51(1):1–18.

Brown, A. L. 2003. Proteus. In *The Oxford Classical Dictionary,* edited by S. Hornblower and A. Spawforth, p. 1265. 3rd rev. ed. Oxford University Press, Oxford.

Brown, F. J. 2021. The Fishermen's Luck: The Maritime Clavie and Its Variants. *Folklore* 132(3):246–267.

Brown, K. M., J. Connan, N. W. Poister, R. L. Vellanoweth, J. Zumberge, and M. H. Engel. 2014. Sourcing Archaeological Asphaltum (Bitumen) from the California Channel Islands to Submarine Seeps. *Journal of Archaeological Science* 43:66–76.

Brown, L. A., and K. F. Emery. 2008. Negotiations with the Animate Forest: Hunting Shrines in the Guatemalan Highlands. *Journal of Archaeological Method and Theory* 15(4):300–337.

Brown, R. L. 1972. *Phantoms, Legends, Customs and Superstitions of the Sea.* Patrik Stephens, London.

Brown, S., D. Rose, I. McNiven, and S. Crocker. 2017. *Australia's Nomination of Budj Bim Cultural Landscape. World Heritage Nomination for Inscription in the UNESCO World Heritage List.* Department of Environment and Energy, Canberra.

Browne, C. R. 1900–1902. The Ethnography of Carna and Mweenish, in the Parish of Moyruss, Connemara. *Proceedings of the Royal Irish Academy* 6:503–534.

Bruce-Mitford, R. 1970. Ships' Figure-Heads in the Migration Period and Early Middle Ages. *Antiquity* 44(174):146–148.

Buccellato, C. A., and S. Tusa. 2013. The Acqualadroni Ram Recovered near the Strait of Messina, Sicily: Dimensions, Timbers, Iconography and Historical Context. *International Journal of Nautical Archaeology* 42(1):76–86.

Buckle, H. T. 1858. *History of Civilization in England.* Volume 1. D. Appleton, New York.

Buddemeier, R. W. 1992. Climate and Groundwater Resources on Atolls and Small Islands. *Weather and Climate* 12(1):9–16.

Buku-Larrŋgay Mulka Centre. 1999. *Saltwater People: Yirrkala Bark Paintings of Sea Country. Recognising Indigenous Sea Rights.* Jennifer Isaacs Publishing in association with Buku-Larrŋgay Mulka Centre, North Sydney.

Burch, E. S. Jr. 1971. The Nonempirical Environment of the Arctic Alaskan Eskimos. *Southwestern Journal of Anthropology* 27(2):148–165.

Burckhardt, J. L. 1829. *Travels in Arabia.* Vol. 2. Henry Colburn, London.

Burkert, W. 1985. *Greek Religion: Archaic and Classical.* Blackwell, Oxford.

Burnet, T. 1719. *The Sacred Theory of the Earth.* 2 vols. John Hooke, London.

Burnham, E. 2012. The Edges of the Earth: An Epistemology of the Unknown in Arabic Geographies from the 5/11th—7/13th Centuries. PhD dissertation, New York University.

Burrows, E. G., and M. E. Spiro. 1953. *An Atoll Culture: Ethnography of Ifaluk in the Central Carolines.* Human Relations Area Files, New Haven.

Buss, R. J. 1973. *The Klabautermann of the Northern Seas.* Folklore Studies 25. University of California Press, Berkeley.

Busse, M. 2005. Wandering Hero Stories in the Southern Lowlands of New Guinea: Culture Areas, Comparison, and History. *Cultural Anthropology* 20(4):443–473.

Butlin, N. G. 1993. *Economics and the Dreamtime: A Hypothetical History.* Cambridge University Press, Cambridge.

Buxton, R. 1994. *Imaginary Greece: The Contexts of Mythology.* Cambridge University Press, Cambridge.

Byard, R. W. 2021. The Caul and Its Relation to Drowning, Lawyers and Sorcerers. *Forensic Science, Medicine and Pathology* 17(3):526–528.

Bynum, C. W. 2001. *Metamorphosis and Identity.* Zone, New York.

Cabantous, A. 1991. On the Writing of the Religious History of Seafarers. *International Journal of Maritime History* 3(1):213–218.

Campbell, E., and A. Maldonado. 2020. A New Jerusalem "at the Ends of the Earth": Interpreting Charles Thomas's Excavations at Iona Abbey, 1956–63. *Antiquaries Journal* 100:33–85.

Campbell, P. B. 2020. The Sea as a Hyperobject: Moving Beyond Maritime Cultural Landscapes. *Journal of Eastern Mediterranean Archaeology and Heritage Studies* 8(3–4):207–225.

Campbell, P. B. 2023a. If on a Winter's Night a Ship Wrecks. In *Contemporary Philosophy for Maritime Archaeology: Flat Ontologies, Oceanic Thought, and the Anthropocene,* edited by S. A. Rich and P. B. Campbell, pp. 335–350. Sidestone, Leiden.

Campbell, P. B. 2023b. Octopodology and Dark *Amphorae*: Alien Archaeologies, Reflexivity, and non-Human Afterlives of Objects in the Sea. In *Contemporary Philosophy for Maritime Archaeology: Flat Ontologies, Oceanic Thought, and the Anthropocene,* edited by S. A. Rich and P. B. Campbell, pp. 205–230. Sidestone, Leiden.

Campbell, S. F. 2002. *The Art of Kula.* Berg, Oxford.

Campbell, S. K., and V. L. Butler. 2010. Archaeological Evidence for Resilience of Pacific Northwest Salmon Populations and the Socioecological System over the Last ~7,500 Years. *Ecology and Society* 15(1):17.

Canney, M. A. 1936. Boats and Ships in Temples and Tombs. In *Occident and Orient: Gaster Anniversary Volume,* edited by B. Schindler and A. Marmorstein, pp. 50–57. Taylor's Foreign Press, London.

Capelle, T. 1995. Bronze-Age Stone Ships. In *The Ship as Symbol in Prehistoric and Medieval Scandinavia,* edited by O. Crumlin-Pedersen and B. M. Thye, pp. 71–75. Studies in Archaeology and History. National Museum, Copenhagen.

Caputo, S. 2024. *Tracks on the Ocean: A History of Trailblazing, Maps and Maritime Travel.* Profile, London.

Carey, G. 1963. The Tradition of St. Elmo's Fire. *American Neptune* 23:29–38.

Carey, G. 1977. *A Faraway Time and Place: Lore of the Eastern Shore.* Robert B. Luce, Washington, DC.

Carey, J. 1992. Aerial Ships and Underwater Monasteries: The Evolution of a Monastic Marvel. In *Proceedings of the Harvard Celtic Colloquium,* Vol. 12, pp. 16–25. Department of Celtic Languages and Literatures, Faculty of Arts and Sciences, Harvard University.

Carlie, A., C. Arcini, H. Druid, and J. Risberg. 2014. Archaeology, Forensics and the Death of a Child in Late Neolithic Sweden. *Antiquity* 88(342):1148–1163.

Carlson, D. N. 2007. Mast-Step Coins Among the Romans. *International Journal of Nautical Archaeology* 36(2):317–324.

Carlson, D. N. 2009. Seeing the Sea: Ships' Eyes in Classical Greece. *Hesperia* 78:347–365.

Carlson, R. L. 2011. The Religious System of the Northwest Coast of North America. In *Oxford Handbook of the Archaeology of Ritual and Religion,* edited by T. Insoll, pp. 639–655. Oxford University Press, Oxford.

Carlson, R. L. 2017. Figurines and Figural Art of the Northwest Coast. In *Oxford Handbook of Prehistoric Figurines*, edited by T. Insoll, pp. 345–365. Oxford University Press, Oxford.

Carr, K. E. 2022. *Shifting Currents: A World History of Swimming*. Reaktion, London.

Carroll, N. E. 1990. *The Philosophy of Horror, Or Paradoxes of the Heart*. Routledge, New York.

Carter, P. 2009. *Dark Writing: Geography, Performance, Design*. University of Hawai'i Press, Honolulu.

Cartwright, D. E. 1999. *Tides—A Scientific History*. Cambridge University Press, Cambridge.

Cartwright, D. E. 2001. On the Origins of Knowledge of the Sea Tides from Antiquity to the Thirteenth Century. *Earth Sciences History* 20(2):105–126.

Carver, M. 1995. Boat-Burial in Britain: Ancient Custom or Political Signal? In *The Ship as Symbol in Prehistoric and Medieval Scandinavia*, edited by O. Crumlin-Pedersen and B. M. Thye, pp. 110–124. Studies in Archaeology and History. National Museum, Copenhagen.

Carver, M. 1998. *Sutton Hoo: Burial Ground of Kings?* University of Pennsylvania Press, Pennsylvania.

Cassar, P. 1966. The Nautical Ex-Votos of the Maltese Islands. *Maltese Folklore Review* 1(3):226–231.

Cassen, S., A. Baltzer, A. Lorin, J. Fournier, and D. Sellier. 2011. Submarine Neolithic Stone Rows near Carnac (Morbihan), France: Preliminary Results from Acoustic and Underwater Survey. In *Submerged Prehistory*, edited by J. Benjamin, C. Bonsall, C. Pickard, and A. Fischer, pp. 99–110. Oxbow, Oxford.

Casson, L. 1971. *Ships and Seamanship in the Ancient World*. Princeton University Press, Princeton, NJ.

Casson, L. 1994. *Ships and Seafaring in Ancient Times*. British Museum Press, London.

Cattaneo-Vietti, R., M. Doneddu, and E. Trainito. 2016. *Man and Shells: Molluscs in the History*. Bentham Science, Sharjah, United Arab Emirates.

Caulfield, R. A. 1994. Aboriginal Subsistence Whaling in West Greenland. In *Elephants and Whales: Resources for Whom?*, edited by M. M. R. Freeman and U. P. Kreuter, pp. 263–292. Gordon and Breach Science, Basil.

Chadbourne, K. 2012. The Knife Against the Wave: Fairies, Fishermen, and the Sea. *Béaloideas* 80:70–85.

Chadwick, S. R., and M. Paviour-Smith. 2017. *The Great Canoes in the Sky*. Springer, Cham, Switzerland.

Chaline, E. 2017. *Strokes of Genius: A History of Swimming*. Reaktion, London.

Chaloupka, G. 1996. Praus in Marege: Makassan Subjects in Aboriginal Rock Art of Arnhem Land, Northern Territory, Australia. *Anthropologie* 34(1/2):131–142.

Champion, M. 2015a. *Medieval Graffiti: The Lost Voices of England's Churches*. Ebury Press, London.

Champion, M. 2015b. Medieval Ship Graffiti in English Churches: Interpretation and Function. *Mariner's Mirror* 101(3):343–350.

Charpentier, V., and S. Méry. 2010. On Neolithic Funerary Practices: Were There "Necrophobic" Manipulations in 5th–4th Millennium BC Arabia? In *Death and Burial in*

Arabia and Beyond: Multidisciplinary Perspectives, edited by L. Weeks, pp. 17–24. BAR International Series 2107. Archaeopress, Oxford.

Chauncy, P. 1878. Appendix A: Notes and Anecdotes of the Aborigines of Australia. In *The Aborigines of Victoria*, Vol. 2, edited by R. B. Smyth, pp. 221–288. John Currey, Government Printer, Melbourne.

Chaussonnet, V. 1995. *Crossroads Alaska: Native Cultures of Alaska and Siberia*. Arctic Studies Center, National Museum of Natural History, Smithsonian Institution, Washington, DC.

Cheever, H. T. 1854. *The Sea and the Sailor*. A. S. Barnes, New York.

Chester, H. H. 1870. Account of a Visit to Warrior Island in September and October 1870 with a Description of the Pearl Fishery on the Warrior Reef. Report Accompanying a Letter to the Colonial Secretary Dated 20th October 1870.QSA, Col/A151, 3425 of 1870. Queensland State Archives, Brisbane.

Childe, V. G., and J. W. Paterson. 1929. Provisional Report on the Excavations at Skara Brae, and on Finds from the 1927 and 1928 Campaigns. *Proceedings of the Society of Antiquaries of Scotland* 63:225–280.

Chlenov, M. A., and I. I. Krupnik. 1984. Whale Alley: A Site on the Chukchi Peninsula, Siberia. *Expedition* 26(2):6–15.

Choi, Y. R. 2022. Slippery Ontologies of Tidal Flats. *Environment and Planning E: Nature and Space* 5(1):340–361.

Chou, C. 2003. *Indonesian Sea Nomads: Money, Magic and Fear of the Orang Suku Laut*. Routledge Curzon, London.

Christensen, A. E. 1995. Ship Graffiti. In *The Ship as Symbol in Prehistoric and Medieval Scandinavia*, edited by O. Crumlin-Pedersen and B. M. Thye, pp. 180–185. Studies in Archaeology and History. National Museum, Copenhagen.

Christian, M. A. 2013. Phoenician Maritime Religion: Sailors, Goddess Worship, and the Grotta Regina. *Die Welt des Orients* 43(2):179–205.

Christie, J. 2022. Re-Reading Gendered Space at K'oa and Household Shrines on Hawai'i Island and O'ahu. *Archaeologies* 18(2):370–400.

Cione, A. L., and M. Bonomo. 2003. Great White Shark Teeth Used as Pendants and Possible Tools by Early-Middle Holocene Terrestrial Mammal Hunter-Gatherers in the Eastern Pampas (Southern South America). *International Journal of Osteoarchaeology* 13(4):222–231.

Cisneros-Montemayor, A. M., D. Pauly, L. V. Weatherdon, and Y. Ota. 2016. A Global Estimate of Seafood Consumption by Coastal Indigenous Peoples. *PLoS ONE* 11(12):e0166681.

Claassen, C. 1998. *Shells*. Cambridge Manuals in Archaeology. Cambridge University Press, Cambridge.

Claassen, C. 2008. Shell Symbolism in Pre-Columbian North America. In *Early Human Impacts on Megamolluscs*, edited by A. Antczak and R. Cipriani, pp. 231–236. British Archaeological Reports 21865. Archaeopress, Oxford.

Claassen, C. 2019. Shells Below, Stars Above: Four Perspectives on Shell Beads. *Southeastern Archaeology* 38(2):89–94.

Clark, C. 2018. There and Back Again: Ancestor Veneration and Necromancy in Ship-Themed Scandinavian Burials. *International Journal of Student Research in Archaeology* 4:109–125.

Clark, C. W., and W. T. Ellison. 1997. Low-Frequency Signaling Behavior in Mysticete Whales. *Journal of the Acoustical Society of America* 101(5):3163.

Clark, E. E. 1953. *Indian Legends of the Pacific Northwest.* University of California Press, Berkeley.

Clark, J. G. D. 1936. *The Mesolithic Settlement of Northern Europe.* Cambridge University Press, Cambridge.

Clark, G. 1947. Whales as an Economic Factor in Prehistoric Europe. *Antiquity* 21(82):84–104.

Clark, G. 1957. *Archaeology and Society.* 3rd ed. Methuen, London.

Clarke, C. A. M. 2011. Edges and Otherworlds: Imagining Tidal Spaces in Early Medieval Britain. In *The Sea and Englishness in the Middle Ages: Maritime Narratives, Identity and Culture,* edited by S. I. Sobecki, pp. 81–101. D. S. Brewer, Cambridge.

Clarke, P. A. 2001. The Significance of Whales to the Aboriginal People of Southern South Australia. *Records of the South Australian Museum* 34(1):19–35.

Clarkson, C., Z. Jacobs, B. Marwick, R. Fullagar, L. Wallis, M. Smith, R. G. Roberts, E. Hayes, K. Lowe, X. Carah, et al. 2017. Human Occupation of Northern Australia by 65,000 Years Ago. *Nature* 547(7663):306–310.

Clary, J. 1994. *Superstitions of the Sea.* Maritime History in Art, St. Clair, Michigan.

Clay, B. J. 1977. *Pinikindu: Maternal Nurture, Paternal Substance.* University of Chicago Press, Chicago.

Cleyet-Merle, J.-J., and S. Madelaine. 1995. Inland Evidence of Human Sea Coast Exploitation in Palaeolithic France. In *Man and Sea in the Mesolithic: Coastal Settlement Above and Below Present Sea Level,* edited by A. Fischer, pp. 303–308. Oxbow, Oxford.

Clissold, P. 1972. Ships and Monuments in Churches in the Solent Area. *Mariner's Mirror* 58(2):205–215.

Clodd, E. 1895. Proceedings at Meeting of Wednesday, April 24, 1895. *Folklore* 6(3):221–224.

Clode, D. 2002. *Killers in Eden.* Allen and Unwin, Crows Nest, New South Wales.

Clottes, J., and J. Courtin. 1996. *The Cave Beneath the Sea: Paleolithic Images at Cosquer.* Harry N. Abrams, New York.

Cobb, H., and J. Ransley. 2019. Moving Beyond the "Scape" to Being in the (Watery) World, Wherever. In *At Home on the Waves: Human Habitation of the Sea from the Mesolithic to Today,* edited by T. J. King and G. Robinson, pp. 16–33. Berghahn, New York.

Codrington, R. H. 1891. *The Melanesians: Studies in their Anthropology and Folk-Lore.* Clarendon, Oxford.

Cohen, M. (editor). 2021. *A Cultural History of the Sea.* 6 vols. Bloomsbury Academic, London.

Cohn, N. 1996. *Noah's Flood: The Genesis Story in Western Thought.* Yale University Press, New Haven.

Coltrain, J. B., M. G. Hayes, and D. H. O'Rourke. 2006. Hrdlička's Aleutian Population-Replacement Hypothesis: A Radiometric Evaluation. *Current Anthropology* 47(3):537–548.

Connaway, J. M. 2007. *Fishweirs: A World Perspective with Emphasis on the Fishweirs of Mississippi.* Archaeological Report N33. Mississippi Department of Archives and History, Jackson.

Connery, C. 2006. *There Was No More Sea:* The Supersession of the Ocean, from the Bible to Cyberspace. *Journal of Historical Geography* 32(3):494–511.

Conrad, L. I. 2002. Islam and the Sea: Paradigms and Problematics. *Al-Qanṭara* 23(1):123–154.

Convertito, C. 2014. Defying Conformity: Using Tattoos to Express Individuality in the Victorian Royal Navy. In *Maritime History and Identity: The Sea and Culture in the Modern World*, edited by D. Redford, pp. 205–229. I. B. Tauris, London.

Conway, T. M. 1989. When Is a Ship a He? *Mariner's Mirror* 75(1):96–97.

Cooke, P., and G. Armstrong. 1998. Ownership and Resource Use on Islands off the Liverpool River, Northern Territory. In *Customary Marine Tenure in Australia*, edited by N. Peterson and B. Rigsby, pp. 178–191. University of Sydney Oceania Publications, Sydney.

Cooke, R. G., T. A. Wake, M. F. Martínez-Polanco, M. Jiménez-Acosta, F. Bustamante, I. Holst, A. Lara-Kraudy, J. G. Martín, and S. Redwood. 2016. Exploitation of Dolphins (Cetacea: Delphinidae) at a 6000 Yr Old Preceramic Site in the Pearl Island Archipelago, Panama. *Journal of Archaeological Science: Reports* 6:733–756.

Cooney, G. 2004. Introduction: Seeing Land from the Sea. *World Archaeology* 35(3):323–328.

Corbett, D. G. 2011. Two Chiefs' Houses from the Western Aleutian Islands. *Arctic Anthropology* 48(2):3–16.

Corbey, R. 2019. *Korwar: Northwest New Guinea Ritual Art According to Missionary Sources.* C. Zwartenkot Art Books, Leiden.

Corbin, A. 1995. *The Lure of the Sea: The Discovery of the Seaside in the Western World 1750–1840.* Penguin, London.

Cordell, J. 1989. Introduction: Sea Tenure. In *A Sea of Small Boats*, edited by J. Cordell, pp. 1–32. Cultural Survival, Cambridge, Massachusetts.

Cortés-Sánchez, M., A. Morales-Muñiz, M. D. Simón-Vallejo, M. C. Lozano-Francisco, J. L. Vera-Peláez, C. Finlayson, J. Rodríguez-Vidal, A. Delgado-Huertas, F. J. Jiménez-Espejo, F. Martínez-Ruiz, et al. 2011. Earliest Known Use of Marine Resources by Neanderthals. *PloS ONE* 6(9):e24026.

Coté, C. 2010. *Spirits of Our Whaling Ancestors: Revitalizing Makah and Nuu-chah-nulth Traditions.* University of Washington Press, Seattle.

Coughlin, M. 2020. Votive Boats, Ex-Votos, and Maritime Memory in Atlantic France. In *Cultures of Memory in the Nineteenth Century*, edited by K. H. Grenier and A. R. Mushal, pp. 97–122. Palgrave Macmillan, Cham, Switzerland.

Courtright, P. B. 2005. Shrines. In *Encyclopedia of Religion,* edited by L. Jones. Vol. 12. 2nd ed., pp. 8376–8378. Macmillan Reference, Detroit.

Cove, J. J. 1978. Ecology, Structuralism, and Fishing Taboos. In *Adaptation and Symbolism: Essays on Social Organization*, edited by K. A. Watson-Gegeo and S. L. Seaton, pp. 143–154. University of Hawai'i Press, Honolulu.

Cox, J. H., and E. Stasack. 1970. *Hawaiian Petroglyphs.* Bishop Museum Press, Honolulu.

Crantz, D. 1767. *The History of Greenland: Containing a Description of the Country and Its Inhabitants.* 2 vols. Brethren's Society for the Furtherance of the Gospel among the Heathen, London.

Crawford, O. G. S. 1927. Lyonesse. *Antiquity* 1(1):5–14.

Croker, T. C. 1844. *Fairy Legends and Traditions of the South of Ireland*. New ed. Lea and Blanchard, Philadelphia.

Cromek, R. H. 1810. *Remains of Nithsdale and Galloway Song: With Historical and Traditional Notices Relative to the Manners and Customs of the Peasantry*. T. Cadell and W. Davies, London.

Crouch, J., I. J. McNiven, B. David, C. Rowe, and M. Weisler. 2007. Berberass: Marine Resource Specialisation and Environmental Change in Torres Strait over the Past 4000 Years. *Archaeology in Oceania* 42(2):49–64.

Crumlin-Pedersen, O. 1995. Boat-Burials at Slusegaard and the Interpretation of the Boat-Grave Custom. In *The Ship as Symbol in Prehistoric and Medieval Scandinavia*, edited by O. Crumlin-Pedersen and B. M. Thye, pp. 86–99. Studies in Archaeology and History. National Museum, Copenhagen.

Csonka, Y. 2003. Ekven—A Prehistoric Whale Hunters' Settlement on the Asian Shore of Bering Strait. In *Indigenous Ways to the Present: Native Whaling in the Western Arctic*, edited by A. P. McCartney, pp. 109–136. Canadian Circumpolar Institute Press, Edmonton.

Cullon, D. 2013. A View from the Watchman's Pole: Salmon, Animism and the Kwakwaka'wakw Summer Ceremonial. *BC Studies: The British Columbian Quarterly* 177:9–37.

Cullon, D. S. 2017. Dancing Salmon: Human-Fish Relationships on the Northwest Coast. PhD dissertation, University of Victoria, BC, Canada.

Culver, H. B. 1929. A Contemporary Fifteenth-Century Ship Model. *Mariner's Mirror* 15(3):213–221.

Cunliffe, B. 2001. *Facing the Ocean: The Atlantic and Its Peoples, 8000 BC–AD 1500*. Oxford University Press, Oxford.

Cunliffe, B. 2017. *On the Ocean: The Mediterranean and the Atlantic from Prehistory to AD 1500*. Oxford University Press, Oxford.

Currie, E. J. 2016. The Shoreline: Conceptual Boundaries Between Land and Sea in Pre-Columbian Andean Cosmologies. Paper presented at the American Society for Ethnohistory Annual Conference: "Ethnohistories of Native Space," Nashville, Tennessee.

Curtis, E. S. 1913. *The North American Indian, Vol. 9: Salishan Tribes of the Coast, Chimakum, Quilliute, Willapa*. Plimpton, Norwood, Massachusetts.

Curtis, E. S. 1916. *The North American Indian, Vol. 11: Nootka, Haida*. Plimpton, Norwood, Massachusetts.

Curtis, E. S. 1930. *The North American Indian, Vol. 20: The Alaskan Eskimo*. Plimpton, Norwood, Massachusetts.

Cybulski, J. S. 1992. *A Greenville Burial Ground: Human Remains and Mortuary Elements in British Columbia Coast Prehistory*. Archaeological Survey of Canada, Mercury Series Paper 146. Canadian Museum of Civilisation, Quebec.

Dall, W. H. 1875. Alaskan Mummies. *American Naturalist* 9(8):433–440.

Dall, W. H. 1878. *On the Remains of Later Pre-Historic Man Obtained from Caves in the Catherina Archipelago, Alaska Territory, and Especially from the Caves of the Aleutian Islands*. Smithsonian Contributions to Knowledge 318. Smithsonian Institution, Washington, DC.

Damas, D. 1972. The Copper Eskimo. In *Hunters and Gatherers Today*, edited by M. G. Bicchieri, pp. 3–50. Waveland, Prospect Heights, Illinois.

Damas, D. 1984. Copper Eskimo. In *Handbook of North American Indians, Vol. 5: Arctic*, edited by D. Damas, pp. 397–414. Smithsonian Institution, Washington, DC.

Daniélou, J. 1964. *Primitive Christian Symbols*. Translated by Donald Attwater. Burns and Oates, London.

D'Arcy, P. 2006. *The People of the Sea*. University Press of Hawai'i, Honolulu.

Darwin, G. 2015. On Mermaids, Meroveus, and Mélusine: Reading the Irish Seal Woman and Mélusine as Origin Legend. *Folklore* 126(2):123–141.

Darwin, G. H. 1899. *The Tides and Kindred Phenomena in the Solar System*. Houghton, Mifflin, Boston.

Das, H. S. 2000. *Ongés* and Their Vanishing Mermaids. *Hornbill, Bombay Natural History Society* January–March 2000:4–8.

Davenport, D., J. R. Johnson, and J. Timbrook. 1993. The Chumash and the Swordfish. *Antiquity* 67(255):257–272.

Davenport, W. 1990. The Canoes of Santa Ana and Santa Catalina Islands, Eastern Solomon Islands. In *Art as a Means of Communication in Pre-Literate Societies*, edited by D. Eban, E. Cohen, and B. Danet, pp. 97–125. Israel Museum, Jerusalem.

David, B., B. Barker, and I. J. McNiven (editors). 2006. *The Social Archaeology of Australian Indigenous Societies*. Aboriginal Studies Press, Canberra.

David, B., J. Crouch, and U. Zoppi. 2005. Historicizing the Spiritual: *Bu* Shell Arrangements on the Island of Badu, Torres Strait. *Cambridge Archaeological Journal* 15(1):71–91.

David, B., I. J. McNiven, J. Crouch, Mura Badulgal Corporation Committee, R. Skelly, B. Barker, K. Courtney, and G. Hewitt. 2009. Koey Ngurtai: The Emergence of a Ritual Domain in Western Torres Strait. *Archaeology in Oceania* 44(1):1–17.

Davidson, I., and W. Noble. 1992. Why the First Colonisation of the Australian Region Is the Earliest Evidence of Modern Human Behaviour. *Archaeology in Oceania* 27(3):135–142.

Davidsson, O. 1900. The Folk-Lore of Icelandic Fishes. *Scottish Review* 36:312–332.

Davis, F. H. 1912. *Myths and Legends of Japan*. George G. Harrap, London.

Davis, S. 1984. Aboriginal Claims to Coastal Waters in North-Eastern Arnhem Land, Northern Australia. In *Maritime Institutions of the Western Pacific*, edited by K. Ruddle and T. Akimichi, pp. 231–251. Senri Ethnological Studies 17. National Museum of Ethnology, Osaka.

Davis, S. 1989. Aboriginal Tenure of the Sea in Arnhem Land, Northern Australia. In *A Sea of Small Boats*, edited by J. Cordell, pp. 37–59. Cultural Survival, Cambridge, Massachusetts.

Davis, S. L., and J. R. V. Prescott. 1992. *Aboriginal Frontiers and Boundaries in Australia*. Melbourne University Press, Carlton.

Dawson, B., and J. Gillow. 1994. *The Traditional Architecture of Indonesia*. Thames and Hudson, London.

Dawson, J. 1881. *Australian Aborigines: The Languages and Customs of Several Tribes of Aborigines in the Western District of Victoria, Australia*. George Robertson, Melbourne.

Dawson, K. 2006. Enslaved Swimmers and Divers in the Atlantic World. *Journal of American History* 92(4):1327–1355.

Dawson, P. C., and R. M. Levy. 2005. A Three-Dimensional Model of a Thule Inuit Whale Bone House. *Journal of Field Archaeology* 30(4):443–445.

Day, K. 2019. Unangax̂ Mummies as Whalers: A Multidisciplinary Contextualization of Human Mummification in the Aleutian Islands. PhD dissertation, University of Wales Trinity Saint David.

de Acosta, J. 1962 [1590]. *Historia natural y moral de las Indias.* Edited by Edmundo O'Gorman. Fondo de Cultura Económica, Mexico.

De Antoni, A. 2010. *Dugout to the Other Side: Social Structures Inscribed in Mythic Tales and Cosmological Concepts of the Asmat.* Cuvillier Verlag, Göttingen.

Deb, A. K. 2018. "Surrender to Nature": Worldviews and Rituals of the Small-Scale Coastal Fishers of Bangladesh. *Marine Policy* 92:1–12.

de Borhegyi, S. F. 1961. Shark Teeth, Stingray Spines, and Shark Fishing in Ancient Mexico and Central America. *Southwestern Journal of Anthropology* 17(3):273–296.

De Castilho, P. V., and P. C. Simões-Lopes. 2008. Sea Mammals in Archaeological Sites on the Southern Coast of Brazil. *Revista do museu de arqueologia e etnologia* 18:101–113.

de Jonge, N., and T. van Dijk. 1995. *Forgotten Islands of Indonesia: The Art and Culture of the Southeast Moluccas.* Periplus, Hong Kong.

de Laguna, F. 1972. *Under Mount Saint Elias: The History and Culture of the Yakutat Tlingit,* parts 1 and 2. Smithsonian Contributions to Anthropology 7(1) and 7(2). Smithsonian Institution Press, Washington, DC.

de Mareville, H. 1854. Naval Folk Lore. *Notes and Queries* Series 1, 10(245):26.

Demesticha, S., K. Delouca, M. G. Trentin, N. Bakirtzis, and A. Neophytou. 2017. Seamen on Land? A Preliminary Analysis of Medieval Ship Graffiti on Cyprus. *International Journal of Nautical Archaeology* 46(2):346–381.

de Nadaillac, Le M. 1888. *Mœurs et monuments des peuples préhistoriques.* G. Masson, Paris.

Dening, G. 2004a. *Beach Crossings: Voyaging Across Time, Cultures and Self.* Miegunyah, Carlton.

Dening, G. 2004b. Deep Times, Deep Spaces: Civilizing the Sea. In *Sea Changes: Historicizing the Ocean,* edited by B. Klein and G. Mackenthun, pp. 13–35. Routledge, New York.

Dennison, W. T. 1890. Orkney Folklore: Sea Myths. *Scottish Antiquary* 5(18):68–71.

Dennison, W. T. 1891a. Orkney Folklore: Sea Myths. *Scottish Antiquary* 5(20):167–171.

Dennison, W. T. 1891b. Orkney Folklore: Sea Myths. *Scottish Antiquary* 5(19):130–133.

Dennison, W. T. 1892a. Orkney Folklore: Sea Myths. *Scottish Antiquary* 6(23):115–121.

Dennison, W. T. 1892b. Orkney Folklore: Sea Myths. *Scottish Antiquary* 7(25):18–24.

Dennison, W. T. 1893. Orkney Folklore. *Scottish Antiquary* 7(28):171–177.

Denys-Montfort, P. 1802. *Histoire naturelle, générale et particuliere des mollusques, animaus sans vertèbres et a sang blanc.* Vol. 2. De L'Imprimerie de F. Dufart, Paris.

de Planhol, X. 2000. *L'Islam et la mer: La Mosquée et le Matelot, VIIe–XXe siècle.* Librairie Académique Perrin, Paris.

d'Errico, F., and L. Backwell. 2016. Earliest Evidence of Personal Ornaments Associated with Burial: The *Conus* Shells from Border Cave. *Journal of Human Evolution* 93:91–108.

d'Errico, F., C. Henshilwood, M. Vanhaeren, and K. van Niekerk. 2005. *Nassarius kraussianus* Shell Beads from Blombos Cave: Evidence for Symbolic Behaviour in the Middle Stone Age. *Journal of Human Evolution* 48(1):3–24.

d'Errico, F., M. Vanhaeren, N. Barton, A. Bouzouggar, H. Mienis, D. Richter, J.-J. Hublin, S. P. McPherron, and P. Lozouet. 2009. Additional Evidence on the Use of Personal Ornaments in the Middle Paleolithic of North Africa. *Proceedings of the National Academy of Sciences* 106(38):16051-16056.

de Ruyter, M., D. Wesley, W. van Duivenvoorde, D. Lewis, and I. Johnston. 2023. Moluccan Fighting Craft on Australian Shores: Contact Rock Art from Awunbarna, Arnhem Land. *Historical Archaeology* 57:14–31.

Descola, P. 2013. *Beyond Nature and Culture*. University of Chicago Press, Chicago.

Deshpande-Mukherjee, A. 2021. Lingering Traditions: Molluscan Shells and Objects as Grave Goods in Human Burial Context at Protohistoric Settlements in India. In *Culture, Tradition and Continuity: Disquisitions in Honour of Prof. Vasant Shinde,* Vol. 2, edited by P. Shirvalkar and E. Prasad, pp. 329–343. B. R. Publishing, Delhi.

de Sonneville-Bordes, D., and P. Laurent. 1983. Le phoque a la fin des teps glaciaires. In *La faune et l'homme préhistoriques*, edited by François Poplin, pp. 69–80. Mémoires de la Société Préhistorique Française 16. Société Préhistorique Française, Paris.

Desson, D. 1995. Masked Rituals of the Kodiak Archipelago. PhD dissertation, University of Alaska, Fairbanks.

Dhimurru Aboriginal Corporation. 2013. *Dhimurru IPA Sea Country Management Plan 2013 to 2015*. Published by Dhimurru Aboriginal Corporation, Nhulunbuy, Northern Territory.

Dhoop, T., C. Cooper, and P. Copeland. 2016. Recording and Analysis of Ship Graffiti in St Thomas' Church and Blackfriars Barn Undercroft in Winchelsea, East Sussex, UK. *International Journal of Nautical Archaeology* 45(2):296–309.

Dixon-Kennedy, M. 1998. *Encyclopedia of Greco-Roman Mythology*. ABC-CLIO, Santa Barbara.

Donner, W. 1995. From Outrigger to Jet: Four Centuries of Sikaiana Voyaging. In *Seafaring in the Contemporary Pacific Islands. Studies in Continuity and Change*, edited by R. Feinberg, pp. 144–158. Northern Illinois University Press, DeKalb.

Donta, C. 1993. Koniag Ceremonialism: An Archaeological and Ethnohistoric Analysis of Sociopolitical Complexity and Ritual Among the Pacific Eskimo. PhD Dissertation, Bryn Mawr College, Bryn Mawr, Pennsylvania.

Douglas, M. 1966. *Purity and Danger: An Analysis of Concept of Pollution and Taboo*. Routledge and Kegan Paul, London.

Douglas, M. 2002. *Purity and Danger: An Analysis of Concept of Pollution and Taboo*. With a new preface by the author. Routledge Classics. Routledge, London.

Drak, L., M. D. Garralda, and P. Arias. 2020. Los Canes Mesolithic Burials: Archaeothanatology. *Journal of Archaeological Science: Reports* 32:p.102381.

Draper, N. 2015. Islands of the Dead? Prehistoric Occupation of Kangaroo Island and Other Southern Offshore Islands and Watercraft Use by Aboriginal Australians. *Quaternary International* 385:229–242.

Drappe, P. 1940. *Het leven van den Tanémbarees: Ethnografische studie over het Tamém-bareesche volk.* Internationales Archiv für Ethnographie. Supplement to Vol. 38. E. J. Brill, Leiden.

Drucker, P. 1950. Culture Element Distributions: XXVI Northwest Coast. *Anthropological Records* 9(3):157–294.

Drucker, P. 1951. *The Northern and Central Nootkan Tribes.* Smithsonian Institution Bureau of American Ethnology Bulletin 144. US Government Printing Office, Washington, DC.

Duffin, C. J. 2007. Fish Otoliths and Folklore: A Survey. *Folklore* 118(1):78–90.

Duffy, P. R. J. 2007. Excavations at Dunure Road, Ayrshire: A Bronze Age Cist Cemetery and Standing Stone. *Proceedings of the Society of Antiquaries of Scotland* 137:69–116.

Dumond, D. E. 1995. Whale Traps on the North Pacific? In *Hunting the Largest Animals: Native Whaling in the Western Arctic and Subarctic,* edited by A. P. McCartney, pp. 51–61. Canadian Circumpolar Institute, University of Alberta, Edmonton.

Dumont d'Urville, J. 1846. *Voyage au Pole Sud et dans l'océanie: Atlas pittoresque.* Vol. 2. Gide et J. Baudry, Paris.

Dwyer, P., M. Minnegal, and J. Thomson. 1985. Odds and Ends: Bower Birds as Taphonomic Agents. *Australian Archaeology* 21:1–10.

Dye, I. 1989. The Tattoos of Early American Seafarers, 1796–1818. *Proceedings of the American Philosophical Society* 133(4):520–554.

Dževerdanović-Pejović, M. 2017. Linguistic Facts as a Reflection of Changes in Seafaring: Is a Ship Still a "She"? *Mariner's Mirror* 103(3):313–322.

Eakins, B. W., and G. F. Sharman. 2010. *Volumes of the World's Oceans from ETOPO1.* NOAA National Geophysical Data Center, Boulder, Colorado.

Eaton, J. P., and C. A. Hass. 1986. *Titanic: Triumph and Tragedy.* W. W. Norton, New York.

Edensor, T., and K. Brophy. 2023. The Potent Urban Prehistory of an Ancient Megalith: The Kempock Stone, Gourock, Scotland. *International Journal of Heritage Studies* 29(1–2):81–96.

Edwards, T., and S. Yu. 2018. *Lustre: Pearling and Australia.* Western Australian Museum, Perth.

Einarsson, N. 1990. Of Seals and Souls: Changes in the Position of Seals in the World View of Icelandic Small-Scale Fishermen. *Maritime Anthropological Studies* 3(2):35–48.

Elderkin, G. W. 1941. The Cults of the Erechtheion. *Hesperia: The Journal of the American School of Classical Studies at Athens* 10(2):113–124.

Elkin, A. P. 1930. The Rainbow Serpent Myth in North-West Australia. *Oceania* 1(3):349–352.

Ellis, R. 1995. *Monsters of the Sea: The History, Natural History, and Mythology of the Oceans' Most Fantastic Creatures.* Doubleday, New York.

Ellis, W. 1832. *Polynesian Researches During a Residence of Nearly Eight Years in the Society and Sandwich Islands.* Vol. 3. 2nd ed. Fisher, Son, & Jackson, London.

Ellis, W. 1859. *Polynesian Researches.* Vol. 1. Henry G. Bohn, London.

Ellison, J. 1979. The Ozette Petroglyphs: An Approach to the Study of Petroglyphs. In *CRARA '77: Papers from the Fourth Biennial Conference of the Canadian Rock Art Re-*

search Associates, edited by D. Lundy, pp. 219–243. Heritage Record 8. British Columbia Provincial Museum, Victoria BC.

Ellmers, D. 1990. Foreword. In *Ships' Figureheads,* by Hans J. Hansen and Clas B. Hansen, p. 5. Schiffer, Pennsylvania.

Emerson, T. E. 1989. Water, Serpents, and the Underworld: An Exploration into Cahokian Symbolism. In *The Southeastern Ceremonial Complex: Artifacts and Analysis*, edited by P. Galloway, pp. 45–92. University of Nebraska Press, Lincoln.

Emmons, G. T. 1991. *The Tlingit Indians.* Edited and additions by Frederica de Laguna. University of Washington Press, Seattle.

Eraslan, Ş. 2015. Oceanus, Tethys and Thalssa figures in the Lights of Antioch and Zeugma Mosaics. *Journal of International Social Research* 8(37):454–462.

Eriksson, N. 2020. Figureheads and Symbolism Between the Medieval and the Modern: The Ship *Griffin* or *Gribshunden*, One of the Last Sea Serpents? *Mariner's Mirror* 106(3):262–276.

Erlandson, J. M., and S. M. Fitzpatrick. 2006. Oceans, Islands, and Coasts: Current Perspectives on the Role of the Sea in Human Prehistory. *Journal of Island and Coastal Archaeology* 1(1):5–32.

Erlandson, J. M., and T. C. Rick. 2010. Archaeology Meets Marine Ecology: The Antiquity of Maritime Cultures and Human Impacts on Marine Fisheries and Ecosystems. *Annual Review of Marine Science* 2:231–251.

Fache, E., S. Pauwels, and J. Veitayaki. 2016. Introduction: Pacific Islanders, "Custodians of the Ocean" Facing Fisheries Challenges. In *Fisheries in the Pacific: The Challenges of Governance and Sustainability*, edited by E. Fache and S. Pauwels, pp. 7–18. Pacific-Credo, Marseille, France.

Fahlander, F. 2019. Fantastic Beings and Where to Make Them: Boats as Object-Beings in Bronze Age Rock Art. *Current Swedish Archaeology* 27:191–212.

Faiella, G. 2021. *Mysteries and Sea Monsters: Thrilling Tales of the Sea.* Vol. 4. The History Press, Gloucestershire.

Falabella, F., and L. Sanhueza. 2019. Living on the Coast Without Depending on Coastal Resources: Isotopic Evidence in Central Chile. *Journal of Archaeological Science: Reports* 26:p.101890.

Farenholt, A. 1908. Tattooing in the Navy, as Shown by the Records of the U.S.S. *Independence. United States Naval Medical Bulletin* 2(2):37–39.

Farrer, J. A. 1879. *Primitive Manners and Customs.* Henry Holt, New York.

Feinberg, R. 1995a. Introduction: Theme and Variation in Pacific Island Seafaring. In *Seafaring in the Contemporary Pacific Islands: Studies in Continuity and Change*, edited by R. Feinberg, pp. 3–15. Northern Illinois University Press, DeKalb.

Feinberg, R. 1995b. Continuity and Change in Nukumanu Maritime Technology and Practice. In *Seafaring in the Contemporary Pacific Islands. Studies in Continuity and Change*, edited by R. Feinberg, pp. 159–195. Northern Illinois University Press, DeKalb.

Feinberg, R. 2008. Polynesian Representations of Geographical and Cosmological Space: Anuta, Solomon Islands. In *Canoes of the Grand Ocean*, edited by A. Di Piazza and E. Peartree, pp. 69–84. British Archaeological Reports International Series 1802. Archaeopress, Oxford.

Feinberg, R. 2020. People, Birds, Canoes, and Seafaring in the Pacific Islands. *Český lid* 107(3):335–350.

Feinberg, R., U. J. Dymon, P. Paiaki, P. Rangituteki, P. Nukuriaki, and M. Rollins. 2003. "Drawing the Coral Heads": Mental Mapping and Its Physical Representation in a Polynesian Community. *Cartographic Journal* 40(3):243–253.

Ferdon, E. N. 1979. A Possible Source of Origin of the Easter Island Boat-Shaped House. *Asian Perspectives* 22(1):1–8.

Fienup-Riordan, A. 1990. The Bird and the Bladder: The Cosmology of Central Yup'ik Seal Hunting. *Études Inuit Studies* 14(1–2):23–38.

Fienup-Riordan, A. 1994. *Boundaries and Passages: Rule and Ritual in Yup'ik Eskimo Oral Tradition.* University of Oklahoma Press, Norman.

Fienup-Riordan, A., and E. Carmack. 2011. "The Ocean Is Always Changing": Nearshore and Farshore Perspectives on Arctic Coastal Seas. *Oceanography* 24(3):266–279.

Fienup-Riordan, A., and A. Rearden. 2009. Cat tamarmeng ellangqertut/All Things Have Ancestors. In *Gifts from the Ancestors: Ancient Ivories of Bering Strait*, edited by W. W. Fitzhugh, J. Hollowell, and A. L. Crowell, pp. 226–239. Princeton University Art Museum, Princeton.

Filmer-Sankey, W., and T. Pestell. 2001. *Snape Anglo-Saxon Cemetery: Excavations and Surveys 1824–1992.* East Anglian Archaeology Report 95. Environment and Transport, Suffolk County Council, Suffolk.

Finamore, D., and S. D. Houston. 2010. *Fiery Pool: The Maya and the Mythic Sea.* Peabody Essex Museum and Yale University Press, New Haven.

Finkelberg, M. 2014. Boreas and Oreithyia: A Case-Study in Multichannel Transmission of Myth. In *Between Orality and Literacy: Communication and Adaption in Antiquity*, edited by R. Scodel, pp. 87–101. Mnemosyne: Bibliotheca Classica Batava, Supplementum, Vol. 367. Orality and Literacy in the Ancient World 10. Brill, Leiden.

Firth, R. 1946. *Malay Fishermen: Their Peasant Economy.* Kegan Paul, Trench, Trubner, London.

Firth, R. 1951. Notes on Some Tikopia Ornaments. *Journal of the Polynesian Society* 60(2/3):130–133.

Firth, R. 1967. Sea Creatures and Spirits in Tikopia Belief. In *Culture History: Essays in Honor of Kenneth P. Emory*, edited by G. A. Highland, R. W. Force, A. Howard, M. Kelly, and Y. H. Sinoto, pp. 539–564. Bernice P. Bishop Museum Special Publication 56. Bishop Museum Press, Honolulu, Hawai'i.

Firth, R. 1981. Figuration and Symbolism in Tikopia Fishing and Fish Use. *Journal de la société des océanistes* 37(72):219–226.

Fisken, M. 1994. Modifications of Whale Bones: Appendix D. In *Ozette Archaeological Project Research Reports, Vol. 2: Fauna*, edited by S. R. Samuels, pp. 359–377. Department of Anthropology, Washington State University, Pullman, Washington.

Fitzhugh, B. 2016. The Origins and Development of Arctic Maritime Adaptations in the Subarctic and Arctic Pacific. In *The Oxford Handbook of the Prehistoric Arctic*, edited by T. M. Friesen and O. K. Mason, pp. 253–278: Oxford University Press, New York.

Fitzhugh, W. W. 1976. Preliminary Culture History of Nain, Labrador: Smithsonian Fieldwork, 1975. *Journal of Field Archaeology* 3:123–142.

Fitzhugh, W. W. 1978. Maritime Archaic Cultures of the Central and Northern Labrador Coast. *Arctic Anthropology* 15(2):61–95.

Fitzhugh, W. W. 2009. Eagles, Beasts, and Gods: Art of the Old Bering Sea Hunting Complex. In *Gifts from the Ancestors: Ancient Ivories of Bering Strait*, edited by W. W. Fitzhugh, J. Hollowell, and A. L. Crowell, pp. 162–189. Princeton University Art Museum, Princeton.

Fitzhugh, W. W., J. Hollowell, and A. L. Crowell (editors). 2009. *Gifts from the Ancestors: Ancient Ivories of Bering Strait*. Princeton University Art Museum, Princeton.

Fitzpatrick-Nietschmann, J. 1980. Another Way of Dying: The Social and Cultural Context of Death in a Melanesian Community, Torres Strait. University Microfilms, Ann Arbor, Michigan.

Fladmark, K. R., D. E. Nelson, T. A. Brown, J. S. Vogel, and J. R. Southon. 1987. AMS Dating of Two Wooden Artifacts from the Northwest Coast. *Canadian Journal of Archaeology/Journal Canadien d'archéologie* 11:1–12.

Flatman, J. 2011. Places of Special Meaning: Westerdahl's Comet, "Agency," and the Concept of the "Maritime Cultural Landscape." In *The Archaeology of Maritime Landscapes*, edited by B. Ford, pp. 311–329. Springer, New York.

Flavel, J. 1796. *Navigation Spiritualized; or a New Compass for Seamen*. Edmund M. Blunt, Newburyport.

Fleisher, J., P. Lane, A. LaViolette, M. Horton, E. Pollard, E. Q. Morales, T. Vernet, A. Christie, and S. Wynne-Jones. 2015. When Did the Swahili Become Maritime? *American Anthropologist* 117(1):100–115.

Flemming, N. C. 1996. Sea Level, Neotectonics and Changes in Coastal Settlements: Threat and Response. In *The Sea and History*, edited by E. E. Rice, pp. 23–52. Sutton, Phoenix Mill.

Flom, G. T. 1925. Noa Words in North Sea Regions: A Chapter in Folklore and Linguistics. *Journal of American Folklore* 38(149):400–418.

Foley, J. C. H. 1990. *The Quetta*. Nairana Publications, Aspley, Queensland, Australia.

Forbes, T. R. 1953. The Social History of the Caul. *Yale Journal of Biology and Medicine* 25(6):495–508.

Forth, G. 2020. Classifying Mermaids: Observations on Local Naming and Classification of Dugongs (*Dugong dugon*) Among the Lio of Flores Island (Eastern Indonesia). *Journal of Ethnobiology* 40(1):56–69.

Forth, G. 2021. Rare Animals as Cryptids and Supernaturals: The Case of Dugongs on Flores Island. *Anthrozoös* 34(1):61–76.

Fowler, C. 2001. Personhood and Social Relations in the British Neolithic with a Study from the Isle of Man. *Journal of Material Culture* 6(2):137–163.

Fowler, C., and V. Cummings. 2003. Places of Transformation: Building Monuments from Water and Stone in the Neolithic of the Irish Sea. *Journal of the Royal Anthropological Institute* 9(1):1–20.

Fowles, J. 1978. *Islands*. Little, Brown, Boston.

Fox, C. E. 1924. *The Threshold of the Pacific: An Account of the Social Organization Magic and Religion of the People of San Cristoval in the Solomon Islands*. Kegan Paul, Trench, Trubner, London.

Fox, C. E., and F. H. Drew. 1915. Beliefs and Tales of San Cristoval (Solomon Islands). *Journal of the Royal Anthropological Institute of Great Britain and Ireland* 45:131–185, 187–228.

Frake, C. O. 1985. Cognitive Maps of Time and Tide Among Medieval Seafarers. *Man* 20(2):254–270.

Francfort, H.-P. 2013. The Bangudae Rock Art Panel: A Structural View. In *Bangudae: Petrogyph Panels in Ulsan, Korea, in the Context of World Rock Art*, edited by J. Kim, pp. 99–110. World Petroglyphs Research 1. Hollym, Morgan Hill, California.

Francis, P., and S. Self. 1983. The Eruption of Krakatau. *Scientific American* 249(5):172–187.

Frankel, H. 1978. *Canoes of Walomo.* Institute of Papua New Guinea Studies, Boroko.

Franklin, K. J. 1973. Other Language Groups in the Gulf District and Adjacent Areas. In *The Linguistic Situation in the Gulf District and Adjacent Areas, Papua New Guinea*, edited by K. Franklin, pp. 263–277. Pacific Linguistics Series C, No. 26. Department of Linguistics, Research School of Pacific Studies, Australian National University, Canberra.

Franklin, K. J., and C. L. Voorhoeve. 1973. Languages near the Intersection of the Gulf, Southern Highlands, and Western Districts. In *The Linguistic Situation in the Gulf District and Adjacent Areas, Papua New Guinea*, edited by K. Franklin, pp. 151–186. Pacific Linguistic Series C, No. 26. Department of Linguistics, Research School of Pacific Studies, Australian National University, Canberra.

Frazer, J. G. 1911. *The Golden Bough: A Study in Magic and Religion, Part 1: The Magic Art and the Evolution of Kings.* Vol. 1. 3rd ed. Macmillan, London.

Frazier, J. 2003. Prehistoric and Ancient Historic Interactions Between Humans and Marine Turtles. In *The Biology of Sea Turtles*, Vol. 2, edited by P. L. Lutz, J. A. Musick, and J. Wyneken, pp. 1–38. CRC Press, Boca Raton.

Frazier, J. G., V. Azzarà, O. Munoz, L. G. Marcucci, E. Badel, F. Genchi, M. Cattani, M. Tosi, and M. Delfino. 2018. Remains of Leatherback Turtles, *Dermochelys coriacea*, at Mid–Late Holocene Archaeological Sites in Coastal Oman: Clues of Past Worlds. *PeerJ* 6:e6123.

Freeman, M. M. R. 2005. "Just One More Time Before I Die": Securing the Relationship Between Inuit and Whalers in the Arctic Regions. In *Indigenous Use and Management of Marine Resources*, edited by N. Kishigami and J. M. Savelle, pp. 59–76. Senri Ethnological Studies 67. National Museum of Ethnology, Osaka.

Frénée, S. 2017. Pirates and Gallows at Execution Dock: Nautical Justice in Early Modern England. *Criminocorpuse.* http://criminocorpus.revues.org/3080.

Friel, I. 2012. How Much Did the Sea Matter in Medieval England (c. 1200–c. 1500)? In *Roles of the Sea in Medieval England*, edited by R. Gorski, pp. 167–186. Boydell, Woodbridge.

Frieman, C. 2008. Islandscapes and "Islandness": The Prehistoric Isle of Man in the Irish Seascape. *Oxford Journal of Archaeology* 27(2):135–151.

Frischer, B. 1984. Horace and the Monuments: A New Interpretation of the Archytas *Ode* (C. 1.28). *Harvard Studies in Classical Philology* 88:71–102.

Frost, D. 2022. "Nothing to Shew for His Tomb but a Wave": Storms, Shipwreck and the Human Cost of Global Trade in Seventeenth-Century Broadside Ballads. *Mariner's Mirror* 108(4):391–406.

Frost, H. 1969. The Stone-Anchors of Ugarit. *Ugaritica* 6:235–245.

Frost, H. 1991. Anchors Sacred and Profane: Ugarit-Ras Shamra, 1986: The Stone Anchors Revised and Compared. In *Ras Shamra-Ougarit, Vol. 6, Arts et industries de la Pierre*, edited by M. Yon, pp. 355–410. ERC, Paris.

Fujita, M., S. Yamasaki, C. Katagiri, I. Oshiro, K. Sano, T. Kurozumi, H. Sugawara, D. Kunikita, H. Matsuzaki, A. Kano, et al. 2016. Advanced Maritime Adaptation in the Western Pacific Coastal Region Extends Back to 35,000–30,000 Years Before Present. *Proceedings of the National Academy of Sciences* 113(40):11184-11189.

Furey, L., R. Phillipps, J. Emmitt, A. McAlister, and S. Holdaway. 2020. A Large Trolling Lure Shank from Ahuahu Great Mercury Island, New Zealand. *Journal of the Polynesian Society* 129(1):85–112.

Gadamus, L., and J. Raymond-Yakoubian. 2015. A Bering Strait Indigenous Framework for Resource Management: Respectful Seal and Walrus Hunting. *Arctic Anthropology* 52(2):87–101.

Gaffney, D. 2021. Pleistocene Water Crossings and Adaptive Flexibility Within the *Homo* Genus. *Journal of Archaeological Research* 29(2):255–326.

Galili, E., and B. Rosen. 2015a. Protecting the Ancient Mariners, Cultic Artifacts from the Holy Land Seas. *Archaeologia Maritima Mediterranea* 12:35–101.

Galili, E., and B. Rosen. 2015b. Marble Disc *Ophthalmoi* from Two Shipwrecks off the Israeli Coast. *International Journal of Nautical Archaeology* 44(1):208–213.

Galis, K. W. 1963. De Biak-Noemfoorse prauw. *Kultuurpatronen: Bulletin Ethnografisch Museum Delft* 5/6:121–142.

Gamble, C. 1992. Archaeology, History and the Uttermost Ends of the Earth—Tasmania, Tierra del Fuego and the Cape. *Antiquity* 66(252):712–720.

Ganguly, P., and A. Pal. 1963. Onge Harpoon and Spear. *Anthropos* 58(3/4):557–560.

Gardner, J. V., A. A. Armstrong, B. R. Calder, and J. Beaudoin. 2014. So, How Deep *Is* the Mariana Trench? *Marine Geodesy* 37(1):1–13.

Garwood, C. 2008. *Flat Earth: The History of an Infamous Idea*. Pan, London.

Gaspar, M. D., D. Klokler, and P. DeBlasis. 2014. Were Sambaqui People Buried in the Trash: Archaeology, Physical Anthropology, and the Evolution of the Interpretation of Brazilian Shell Mounds. In *The Cultural Dynamics of Shell-Matrix Sites*, edited by M. Roksandic, S. M. de Souza, S. Eggers, M. Burchell, and D. Klokler, pp. 91–100. University of New Mexico Press, Albuquerque.

Genda, H. 2016. Origin of Earth's Oceans: An Assessment of the Total Amount, History and Supply of Water. *Geochemical Journal* 50(1):27–42.

Gerbrands, A. A. 1967. *Wow-Ipits: Eight Asmat Woodcarvers of New Guinea*. Mouton, The Hague.

Geurtjens, H. 1956. Marind Astronomy. *Antiquity and Survival* 1:401–405.

Gianfrotta, P. A. 1980. Ancore "romane": Nuovi materiali per lo studio dei traffici marittimi. *Memoirs of the American Academy in Rome* 36:10.

Gibbs, M. 2006. Cultural Site Formation Processes in Maritime Archaeology: Disaster Response, Salvage and Muckelroy 30 Years On. *International Journal of Nautical Archaeology* 35(1):4–19.

Giles, A. R., S. M. Strachan, M. Doucette, G. S. Stadig, and Municipality of Pangnirtung. 2013. Adaptation to Aquatic Risks due to Climate Change in Pangnirtung, Nunavut. *Arctic* 66(2):207–217.

Gill, A. 1993. *Superstitions: Folk Magic in Hull's Fishing Community.* Hutton, Beverley, North Humberside, UK.

Gill, W. W. 1876a. *Myths and Songs from the South Pacific.* Henry S. King, London.

Gill, W. W. 1876b. *Life in the Southern Isles; or, Scenes and Incidents in the South Pacific and New Guinea.* Religious Tract Society, London.

Gillin, J. 1947. *Moche: A Peruvian Coastal Community.* Smithsonian Institution, Institute of Social Anthropology, Publication 3. Washington, DC.

Gillis, J. R. 2004. *Islands of the Mind: How the Human Imagination Created the Atlantic World.* Palgrave Macmillan, New York.

Gillis, J. R. 2007. Islands in the Making of an Atlantic Oceania, 1500–1800. In *Seascapes: Maritime Histories, Littoral Cultures, and Transoceanic Exchanges,* edited by J. H. Bentley, R. Bridenthal, and K. Wigen, pp. 21–37. University of Hawai'i Press, Honolulu.

Gillis, R. R. 2012. *The Human Shore: Seacoasts in History.* University of Chicago Press, Chicago.

Gilmore, D. D. 2003. *Monsters: Evil Beings, Mythical Beasts, and All Manner of Imaginary Terrors.* University of Pennsylvania Press, Philadelphia.

Gittinger, M. 1976. The Ship Textiles of South Sumatra: Functions and Design System. *Bijdragen tot de Taal-, Land- en Volkenkunde* 132(2/3):207–227.

Gjerde, J. M. 2020. Rock Art of Alta (Norway). In *Encyclopedia of Global Archaeology,* edited C. Smith, pp. 189–198. Springer, Cham, Switzerland.

Gjerde, J. M. 2021. The Earliest Boat Depiction in Northern Europe: Newly Discovered Early Mesolithic Rock Art at Valle, Northern Norway. *Oxford Journal of Archaeology* 40(2):136–152.

Glassow, M. A. 2005. Prehistoric Dolphin Hunting on Santa Cruz Island, California. In *The Exploitation and Cultural Importance of Sea Mammals,* edited by G. G. Monks, pp. 107–120. Oxbow, Oxford.

Glynn, R. 1981. Herakles, Nereus and Triton: A Study of Iconography in Sixth Century Athens. *American Journal of Archaeology* 85(2):121–132.

Godfrey, M. C. S. 1989. Shell Midden Chronology in Southwestern Victoria: Reflections of Change in Prehistoric Population and Subsistence? *Archaeology in Oceania* 24(2):65–69.

Goodrich, F. B. 1858. *Man upon the Sea, or a History of Maritime Adventure, Exploration and Discovery.* J. B. Lippincott, Philadelphia.

Gordon, T., and J. B. Haviland. 1979. *Milbi: Aboriginal Tales from Queensland's Endeavour River.* Told and illustrated by T. Gordon. Translated by J. B. Haviland. Australian National University Press, Canberra.

Göttlicher, A. 2004. A Newly Acquired Ancient Ship-Model in Kassel, Germany. *International Journal of Nautical Archaeology* 33(1):154–157.

Grana, L., and G. Prieto. 2021. Marine Diatom Remains as Bioindicators of the Uses of Pre-Hispanic Fishing Gear Recovered in Ritual Contexts at Huanchaco, North Coast of Peru. *Journal of Archaeological Science: Reports* 39:103167.

Grant, J. 1880. *The Mysteries of All Nations: Rise and Progress of Superstition, Laws Against and Trails of Witches, Ancient and Modern Delusions.* Reid and Son, Leith.

Grapard, A. G. 2018. Cults and Culture of the Sea: Historical and Geographical Perspectives. In *The Sea and the Sacred in Japan: Aspects of Maritime Religion,* edited by F. Rambelli, pp. xxv–xxix. Bloomsbury, London.

Gray, J. H. 1878. *China: A History of the Laws, Manners, and Customs of the People.* Vol. 2. Macmillan, London.

Green, A. R. W. 2003. *The Storm-God in the Ancient Near East.* Eisenbrauns, Indiana.

Green, N. 1988. Aboriginal Affiliations with the Sea in Western Australia. In *Traditional Knowledge of the Marine Environment in Northern Australia*, edited by F. Gray and L. Zann, pp. 19–29. Workshop Series 8. Great Barrier Reef Marine Park Authority, Townsville.

Greenwood, S. 2009. *The Anthropology of Magic.* Berg, Oxford.

Gregg, T. M., L. Mead, J. H. R. Burns, and M. Takabayashi. 2015. Puka mai he koʻa: The Significance of Corals in Hawaiian Culture. In *Ethnobiology of Corals and Coral Reefs*, edited by N. E. Narchi and L. L. Price, pp. 103–115. Springer, Cham, Switzerland.

Gregor, W. 1881. *Notes on the Folk-Lore of the North-East of Scotland.* Folklore Society, London.

Gregor, W. 1884. Fishermen's Folk-Lore. *Folk-Lore Journal* 2(12):353–357.

Gregor, W. 1885a. Some Folk-Lore of the Sea. *Folk-Lore Journal* 3(4):305–311.

Gregor, W. 1885b. Some Folk-Lore of the Sea. *Folk-Lore Journal* 3(2):180–185.

Gregor, W. 1885c. Some Folk-Lore of the Sea. *Folk-Lore Journal* 3(1):52–56.

Gregor, W. 1886. Some Folk-Lore of the Sea. *Folk-Lore Journal* 4(1):7–17.

Greiling, M. 2022. "Where Is the Ship Which from the Ceiling Hung?": Ghost Ships, the Ship Models Missing from Scotland's Churches. *Mariner's Mirror* 108(1):47–65.

Gudgeon, W. E. 1907. The Tohunga Maori. *Journal of the Polynesian Society* 16(2):63–91.

Gudgeon, W. E. 1909. On Matakite. *Journal of the Polynesian Society* 18(3):143–153.

Guenther, M. 2022. Therianthropes in a Cartesian and an Animistic Cosmology: Beyond-the-Pale Monsters Versus Being-in-the World Others. *Literatura Ludowa* 66(3):7–35.

Guerber, H. A. 1895. *Myths of Northern Lands.* American Book Company, New York.

Guérout, M., and R. Veccella. 2006. The Underwater Excavation of the Site Located in the Tupapaurau Pass in Moʻorea (Society Islands). *Bulletin of the Australasian Institute for Maritime Archaeology* 30:94–103.

Gunther, E. 1942. Reminiscences of a Whaler's Wife. *Pacific Northwest Quarterly* 33(1):65–69.

Gutchen, K. G. 2008. Affidavit of Kapua George Gutchen. Sworn on October 2008. Torres Strait Regional Seas Native Title Claim, Q6040 of 2001. Native Title Office, Torres Strait Regional Authority, Thursday Island, Queensland, Australia.

Guthrie, E. E. 1889. Superstitions of the Scottish Fishermen. *Folk-Lore Journal* 7(1):44–47.

Habu, J., and J. M. Savelle. 1994. Construction, Use, and Abandonment of a Thule Whale Bone House, Somerset Island, Arctic Canada. *Quaternary Research (Daiyonki-Kenkyu)* 33(1):1–18.

Haddon, A. C. 1890. The Ethnography of the Western Tribes of Torres Straits. *Journal of the Anthropological Institute of Great Britain and Ireland* 19:297–446.

Haddon, A. C. 1901. *Head-Hunters: Black, White and Brown.* Methuen, London.

Haddon, A. C. (editor). 1904. *Reports of the Cambridge Anthropological Expedition to Torres Straits, Vol. 5: Sociology, Magic and Religion of the Western Islanders.* Cambridge University Press, Cambridge.

Haddon, A. C. 1906. *Magic and Fetishism.* Archibald Constable, London.

Haddon, A. C. (editor). 1908. *Reports of the Cambridge Anthropological Expedition to Torres Straits, Vol. 6: Sociology, Magic and Religion of the Eastern Islanders.* Cambridge University Press, Cambridge.

Haddon, A. C. (editor). 1912. *Reports of the Cambridge Anthropological Expedition to Torres Straits, Vol. 4: Arts and Crafts.* Cambridge University Press, Cambridge.

Haddon, A. C. 1935. *Reports of the Cambridge Anthropological Expedition to Torres Straits, Vol. 1: General Ethnography.* Cambridge University Press, Cambridge.

Haddon, A. C. 1937. *Canoes of Oceania, Vol. 2: The Canoes of Melanesia, Queensland, and New Guinea.* Bernice P. Bishop Museum, Special Publication 28. The Museum, Honolulu, Hawai'i.

Hague, B. S., D. A. Jones, B. Trewin, D. Jakob, B. F. Murphy, D. J. Martin, and K. Braganza. 2021. ANCHORS: A Multi-Decadal Tide Gauge Dataset to Monitor Australian Relative Sea Level Changes. *Geoscience Data Journal* 9:256–272.

Haines, R., and R. Shlomowitz. 1998. Explaining the Modern Mortality Decline: What Can We Learn from Sea Voyages? *Social History of Medicine* 11(1):15–48.

Hale, H. M., and N. B. Tindale. 1933. Aborigines of Princess Charlotte Bay. *Records of the South Australian Museum* 5(1):63–116.

Hallam, S. J. 1987. Coastal Does Not Equal Littoral. *Australian Archaeology* 25(1):10–29.

Hallowell, A. I. 1960. Ojibwa Ontology, Behavior and World View. In *Culture in History: Essays in Honor of Paul Radin*, edited by S. Diamond, pp. 19–52. Columbia University Press, New York.

Halstad-McGuire, E. 2010. Sailing Home: Boat-Graves, Migrant Identities and Funerary Practices on the Viking Frontier. *At the Interface/Probing the Boundaries* 71:165–187.

Hamacher, D., G. M. Anderson, J. Barsa, D. Bosun, R. Day, S. Passi, and A. Tapim. 2022. *The First Astronomers: How Indigenous Elders Read the Stars.* Allen and Unwin, Sydney.

Hamell, G. R. 1986. Strawberries, Floating Islands, and Rabbit Captains: Mythical Realities and European Contact in the Northeast During the Sixteenth and Seventeenth Centuries. *Journal of Canadian Studies* 21(4):72–94.

Hamilton, A. 1908. *Fishing and Sea-Foods of the Ancient Maori.* Dominion Museum, Bulletin 2. John Mackay, Government Printer, Wellington, New Zealand.

Hammerton, J. A. (editor). 1931. *Manners and Customs of Mankind.* 4 vols. Amalgamated Press, London.

Han, J. 2013. The Bangudae Petroglyph Site and Perspectives for Its Inscription on the World Heritage List. In *Bangudae: Petrogyph Panels in Ulsan, Korea, in the Context of World Rock Art*, edited by J. Kim, pp. 139–159. World Petroglyphs Research 1. Hollym, Morgan Hill, California.

Hanlon, C. 2016. Under the Atlantic. In *Handbook of Transatlantic North American Studies*, edited by J. Straub, pp. 283–296. de Gruyter, Berlin/Boston.

Hansen, H. J., and C. B. Hansen. 1990. *Ships' Figureheads.* Schiffer, Pennsylvania.

Hansen, M. K. 2006. Beyond Seals: The Representation of Seals on Engraved Slate Plaquettes from the Magdalenian site Gönnersdorf (Central Rhineland, Germany). Masters dissertation in archaeology, University of Tromsø.

Haraway, D. 2007. *When Species Meet.* University of Minnesota Press, Minneapolis.

Hardy, K. 2017. Shell Middens. In *Molluscs in Archaeology: Methods, Approaches and Applications*, edited by M. J. Allen, pp. 259–272. Oxbow, Oxford.

Harley, B. 1994. *Church Ships: A Handbook of Votive and Commemorative Models.* Canterbury Press, Norwich.

Harper, M. 1999. British Migration and the Peopling of the Empire. In *The Oxford History of the British Empire, Vol. 3: The Nineteenth Century*, edited by A. Porter, pp. 75–87. Oxford University Press, Oxford.

Harris, J. R. 2001. The Protection of Sunken Warships as Gravesites at Sea. *Ocean and Coastal Law Journal* 7(1):75–129.

Harrison-Buck, E. 2012. Architecture as Animate Landscape: Circular Shrines in the Ancient Maya Lowlands. *American Anthropologist* 114(1):64–80.

Harritt, R. K. 2003. Re-examining Wales' Role in Bering Strait Prehistory: Some Preliminary Results of Recent Work. In *Indigenous Ways to the Present: Native Whaling in the Western Arctic*, edited by A. P. McCartney, pp. 25–67. Canadian Circumpolar Institute Press, Edmonton.

Hart, G. 2005. *The Routledge Dictionary of Egyptian Gods and Goddesses.* 2nd ed. Routledge, Oxon, England.

Harvey, G. 2006. *Animism: Respecting the Living World.* Columbia University Press, New York.

Haslam, M., J. Fujii, S. Espinosa, K. Mayer, K. Ralls, M. T. Tinker, and N. Uomini. 2019. Wild Sea Otter Mussel Pounding Leaves Archaeological Traces. *Scientific Reports* 9(1):4417.

Haslam, M., A. Hernandez-Aguilar, V. Ling, S. Carvalho, I. de La Torre, A. DeStefano, A. Du, B. Hardy, J. Harris, L. Marchant, T. Matsuzawa, et al. 2009. Primate archaeology. *Nature* 460(7253):339–344.

Hassan, J. 2003. *The Seaside, Health and the Environment in England and Wales Since 1800.* Routledge, Florence.

Hau'ofa, E. 1994. Our Sea of Islands. *Contemporary Pacific* 6(1):148–161.

Haussker, F. 2009. The Burial of the Missing Victims of Maritime Disasters: Fact and Fiction in Euripides' *Helen. Scripta Classica Israelica* 28:25–41.

Haviland, J. B., R. Hart, and T. Gordon. 1998. *Old Man Fog and the Last Aborigines of Barrow Point.* Smithsonian Institution Press, Washington, DC.

Hawkins, S., G. A. Zetika, R. Kinaston, Y. R. Firmando, D. M. Sari, Y. Suniarti, M. Lucas, P. Roberts, C. Reepmeyer, T. Maloney, et al. 2024. Earliest Known Funerary Rites in Wallacea After the Last Glacial Maximum. *Scientific Reports* 14:282.

Haworth, R. J., R. G. V. Baker, and P. J. Flood. 2004. A 6000 Year-Old Fossil Dugong from Botany Bay: Inferences About Changes in Sydney's Climate, Sea Levels and Waterways. *Australian Geographical Studies* 42(1):46–59.

Hayes, K. J. 1999. *Melville's Folk Roots.* Kent State University Press, Kent, Ohio.

Headrick, D. R., and P. Griset. 2001 Submarine Telegraph Cables: Business and Politics, 1838–1939. *Business History Review* 75(3):543–578.

Heaney, S. 1991. *Seeing Things: Poems.* Farrar, Straus and Giroux, New York.

Hedden, M. 2004. Passamaquoddy Shamanism and Rock Art in Machias Bay, Maine. In *The Rock Art of Eastern North America*, edited by C. Diaz-Granados and J. R. Duncan, pp. 319–343. University of Alabama Press, Tuscaloosa.

Heide, E. 2011. Holy Islands and the Otherworld: Places Beyond Water. In *Isolated Islands in Medieval Nature, Culture and Mind*, edited by T. Jørgensen and G. Jaritz, pp. 57–80. Central European University Press, Budapest.

Heizer, R. F. 1947. Petroglyphs from Southwestern Kodiak Island, Alaska. *Proceedings of the American Philosophical Society* 91(3):284–293.

Hellewell, E. R. 2015. An Investigation into the Placement of Disarticulated Human Remains into Shell Middens During Prehistory. PhD dissertation, University of York, England.

Helms, M. W. 1988. *Ulysses' Sail: An Ethnographic Odyssey of Power, Knowledge, and Geographical Distance.* Princeton University Press, Princeton.

Helms, S. W. 1975. Ship Graffiti in the Church of San Marco in Venice. *International Journal of Nautical Archaeology* 4(2):229–236.

Helskog, K. 1999. The Shore Connection: Cognitive Landscape and Communication with Rock Carvings in Northernmost Europe. *Norwegian Archaeological Review* 32(2):73–92.

Henderson, W. 1879. *Notes on the Folk-Lore of the Northern Counties of England and the Borders.* New ed. W. Satchell, Peyton, London.

Henningsen, H. 1952. Ship-Models in Danish Churches. *Mariner's Mirror* 38(4):294–300.

Henningsen, H. 1961. *Crossing the Equator: Sailors' Baptism and Other Initiation Rites.* Munksgaard, Copenhagen.

Henningsen, H. 1965. Coins for Luck Under the Mast. *Mariner's Mirror* 51(3):205–210.

Henry, T. 1928. *Ancient Tahiti.* Bernice P. Bishop Museum, Honolulu.

Henshilwood, C., F. d'Errico, M. Vanhaeren, K. van Niekerk, and Z. Jacobs. 2004. Middle Stone Age Shell Beads from South Africa. *Science* 304(5669):404–404.

Herel, A., and J. Philp. 2020. *Recording Kastom: Alfred Haddon's Journals from the Torres Strait and New Guinea, 1888 and 1898.* Sydney University Press, Sydney.

Herle, A., and S. Rouse (editors). 1998. *Cambridge and the Torres Strait: Centenary Essays on the 1898 Anthropological Expedition.* Cambridge University Press, Cambridge.

Heuvelmans, B. 1968. *In the Wake of the Sea-Serpents.* Rupert Hart-Davis, London.

Heuvelmans, B. 2006. *The Kraken and the Colossal Octopus: In the Wake of the Sea-Monsters.* Routledge, London.

Heyes, S. A. 2011. Cracks in the Knowledge: Sea Ice Terms in Kangiqsualujjuaq, Nunavik. *Canadian Geographer/Le géographe Canadien* 55(1):69–90.

Heywood, T. 1639. *A True Relation, of the Lives and Deaths of Two Most Famous English Pyrats, Purser, and Clinton who Lived in the Reigne of Queene Elizabeth.* Lo. Okes, London.

Hickey, F. R., and F. Yoringmal. 2013. Canoe Tales from the Archives. In *Melanesia: Art and Encounter*, edited by L. Bolton, N. Thomas, E. Bonshek, J. Adams, and B. Burt, pp. 256–259. British Museum Press, London.

Higham, C. 2011. The Bronze Age of Southeast Asia: New Insight on Social Change from Ban Non Wat. *Cambridge Archaeological Journal* 21(3):365–389.

Hill, B., and R. Hill. 1975. *Indian Petroglyphs of the Pacific Northwest.* University of Washington Press, Seattle.

Hill, E. 2011. Animals as Agents: Hunting Ritual and Relational Ontologies in Prehistoric Alaska and Chukotka. *Cambridge Archaeological Journal* 21(3):407–426.

Hill, E. 2012. The Nonempirical Past: Enculturated Landscapes and Other-than-Human Persons in Southwest Alaska. *Arctic Anthropology* 49(2):41–57.

Hill, E. 2017. The Archaeology and Ethnohistory of Walrus Ritual Around Bering Strait. *Études Inuit Studies* 41(1–2):73–99.

Hill, E. 2018a. Personhood and Agency in Eskimo Interactions with the Other-than-Human. In *Relational Identities and Other-than-Human Agency in Archaeology*, edited by E. Harrison-Buck and J. A. Hendon, pp. 29–50. University of Colorado Press, Denver.

Hill, E. 2018b. A Relational Geography of Humans and Animals on the Arctic Coast of Alaska. In *Relational Engagements of the Indigenous Americas: Alterity, Ontology, and Shifting Paradigms*, edited by M. R. Baltus and S. E. Baires, pp. 1–19. Lexington, Lanham.

Hill, E. 2022. Watercraft as Assemblage in the Western Arctic. In *Sacred Nature: Animism and Materiality in Ancient Religions*, edited by N. Laneri and A. Perdibon, pp. 17–32. Oxbow, Oxford.

Hilmi, N., T. Bambridge, A. Safa, B. Quinquis, and P. D'Arcy. 2016. Socioeconomic Significance of Fisheries in the Small Island Developing States: Natural Heritage or Commodity? In *Fisheries in the Pacific: The Challenges of Governance and Sustainability*, edited by E. Fache and S. Pauwels, pp. 175–197. Pacific-Credo, Marseille, France.

Hobart, M. 1978. The Path of the Soul: The Legitimacy of Nature in Balinese Conceptions of Space. In *Natural Symbols in South East Asia*, edited by G. B. Milner, pp. 5–28. School of Oriental and African Studies, University of London, London.

Hocart, A. M. 1922. The Cult of the Dead in Eddystone of the Solomons. *Journal of the Royal Anthropological Institute of Great Britain and Ireland* 52:71–112, 259–305.

Hocart, A. M. 1935. The Canoe and the Bonito in Eddystone Island. *Journal of the Royal Anthropological Institute of Great Britain and Ireland* 65:97–111.

Hocart, A. M. 1937. Fishing in Eddystone Island. *Journal of the Royal Anthropological Institute of Great Britain and Ireland* 67:33–41.

Hodder, I. 1999. *The Archaeological Process*. Blackwell, Oxford.

Hoeppe, G. 2000. When the Shark Bites the Stingray: The Night Sky in the Construction of the Manus World. *Anthropos* 95(1):23–36.

Hoffmann, S. M., D. Vickers, and M. Geymeier. 2022. Constellation Cetus: Whale or Monster? In *Astronomy in Culture: Cultures of Astronomy*, edited by S. M. Hoffmann and G. Wolfschmidt, pp. 287–340. Tredition, Hamburg; Open Science Technology, Berlin.

Höhler, C. 2021. Practices: Robots, Memories, Autonomy, and the Future. In *A Cultural History of the Sea in the Global Age*, Vol. 6, edited by F. Torma, pp. 21–44. Bloomsbury Academic, London.

Holbraad, M., and M. A. Pedersen. 2017. *The Ontological Turn: An Anthropological Exposition*. Cambridge University Press, Cambridge.

Hole, C. 1957. Notes on Some Folklore Survivals in English Domestic Life. *Folklore* 68(3):411–419.

Hole, C. 1967. Superstitions and Beliefs of the Sea. *Folklore* 78(3):184–189.

Holland, C. 1942. Some Superstitions of Sea-Faring Folk. *Navy League Journal* 2(4):11–15.

Hone, W. 1827. *The Every-Day Book*. Vol. 2. Hunt and Clarke, London.

Hoogervorst, T. G. 2012. Ethnicity and Aquatic Lifestyles: Exploring Southeast Asia's Past and Present Seascapes. *Water History* 4(3):245–265.

Hopman, M. G. 2012. *Scylla: Myth, Metaphor, Paradox.* Cambridge University Press, Cambridge.

Hopman, M. G. 2024. Scylla and Charybdis. In *The Oxford Handbook of Monsters in Classical Myth*, edited by D. Felton, pp. 165–179. Oxford University Press, Oxford.

Hornell, J. 1914. *The Sacred Chank of India: A Monograph of the Indian Conch (Turbinella Pyrum).* Madras Fisheries Bureau Bulletin 7. Government Press, Madras.

Hornell, J. 1923. Survivals of the Use of Oculi in Modern Boats. *Journal of the Royal Anthropological Institute of Great Britain and Ireland* 53(2):289–321.

Hornell, J. 1938. Boat Oculi Survivals: Additional Records. *Journal of the Royal Anthropological Institute of Great Britain and Ireland* 64(2):339–348.

Hornell, J. 1942. The Chank Shell Cult of India. *Antiquity* 16(6):113–133.

Hornell, J. 1943. The Prow of the Ship: Sanctuary of the Tutelary Deity. *Man* 43:121–128.

Horridge, A. 1982. *The Lashed-Lug Boat of the Eastern Archipelagoes.* Maritime Monographs and Reports 54. National Maritime Museum, Greenwich, London.

Hoson, O., G. Ogura, N. Ohtaishi, and S.-I. Oda. 2009. Are Ancient Dugong Bones Useful for Analysis? In *Proceedings of the 4th International Symposium on SEASTAR2000 and Asian Bio-Logging Science*, edited by N. Arai, pp. 35–40. Graduate School of Informatics, Kyoto University, Kyoto.

Hourihane, C. P., and J. J. Hourihane. 1979. The Kilnaruane Pillar Stone, Bantry, Co. Cork. *Journal of the Cork Historical and Archaeological Society* 84:65–73.

Housley, R. A. 1991. AMS Dates from the Late Glacial and Early Postglacial in North West Europe: A Review. In *The Late Glacial in Northwest Europe: Human Adaptation and Environmental Change at the End of the Pleistocene*, edited by N. Barton, A. J. Roberts, and D. A. Rose, pp. 25–39. CBA Research Report 77. Council for British Archaeology, London.

Howitt, A. W. 1904. *Native Tribes of South-East Australia.* Macmillan, London.

Hrdlička, A. 1941a. Exploration of Mummy Caves in the Aleutian Islands, Part 1: Previous Knowledge of Such Caves; Original Explorations. *Scientific Monthly* 52(1):5–23.

Hrdlička, A. 1941b. Exploration of Mummy Caves in the Aleutian Islands, Part 2: Further Exploration. *Scientific Monthly* 52(2):113–130.

Hrdlička, A. 1945. *The Aleutian and Commander Islands and Their Inhabitants.* Wistar Institute of Anatomy and Biology Press, Philadelphia.

Hughes, C. C. 1984. Saint Lawrence Island Eskimo. In *Handbook of North American Indians, Vol. 5: Arctic*, edited by D. Damas, pp. 262–277. Smithsonian Institution, Washington, DC.

Hui, T. Y. 2002. Between Heaven and the Deep Sea: The Religious Practice of Chinese Seafarers from the Eleventh to the Mid-Nineteenth Century. *East Asian History* 23:69–86.

Hunt, R. 1865. *Popular Romances of the West of England.* 1st series. John Camden Hotten, London.

Hunter-Anderson, R. L. 1981. Yapese Stone Fish Traps. *Asian Perspectives* 24:81–90.

Huntsman, J. W. 1963. A Study of the Whale Cult. MA dissertation, Brown University.

Hurwit, J. M. 1999. *The Athenian Acropolis: History, Mythology, and Archaeology from the Neolithic Era to the Present.* Cambridge University Press, Cambridge.

Hviding, E. 1995. Maritime Travel, Present and Past, in Marovo, Western Solomon Islands. In *Seafaring in the Contemporary Pacific Islands: Studies in Continuity and Change,* edited by R. Feinberg, pp. 90–113. Northern Illinois University Press, DeKalb.

Hviding, E. 1996. *Guardians of Marovo Lagoon: Practice, Place, and Politics in Maritime Melanesia.* University of Hawai'i Press, Honolulu.

Ikenga-Metuh, E. 1982. Religious Concepts in West African Cosmogonies: A Problem of Interpretation. *Journal of Religion in Africa* 13:11–24.

Ingersoll, K. A. 2016. *Waves of Knowing: A Seascape Epistemology.* Duke University Press, Durham.

Inglefield, J. N. [1795]. *Wonderful Escape from Shipwreck: An Account of the Loss of His Majesty's Ship Centaur.* Cheap Repository for Moral and Religious Tract, Bath.

Ingold, T. 1993. The Temporality of the Landscape. *World Archaeology* 25(2):152–174.

Ingold, T. 2000. *The Perception of the Environment: Essays on Livelihood, Dwelling and Skill.* Routledge, London.

Ingold, T. 2006. Rethinking the Animate, Re-Animating Thought. *Ethnos* 71 (1):9–20.

Irby, G. L. 2021. Knowledges: Knowledge of the Sea in Greco-Roman Antiquity; "Oceanography" and the Physics of Water. In *A Cultural History of the Sea in Antiquity,* Vol. 1, edited by M.-C. Beaulieu, pp. 19–41. Bloomsbury Academic, London.

Irwin, L. 1990. Divinity and Salvation: The Great Goddesses of China. *Asian Folklore Studies* 49(1):53–68.

Itoh, M. 2018. *The Japanese Culture of Mourning Whales: Whales Graves and Memorial Monuments in Japan.* Palgrave Macmillan, Singapore.

Ivens, W. G. 1927. *Melanesians of the South-East Solomon Islands.* Kegan Paul, Trench, Trubner, London.

Ivens, W. G. [1930]. *The Island Builders of the Pacific.* J. B. Lippincott, Philadelphia.

Iwasaki-Goodman, M., and M. Nomoto. 2001. Revitalizing the Relationship Between Ainu and Salmon: Salmon Rituals in the Present. *Senri Ethnological Studies* 59:27–46.

Jacobsen, S. B. 2003. How Old Is Planet Earth? *Science* 300(5625):1513–1514.

Jalland, P. 2002. *Australian Ways of Death: A Social and Cultural History, 1840–1918.* Oxford University Press, Melbourne.

James, B. 2019. Fish Traps of the Crocodile Islands: Windows on Another World. In *At Home on the Waves: Human Habitation of the Sea from the Mesolithic to Today,* edited by T. J. King and G. Robinson, pp. 174–200. Berghahn, New York.

Janssen, V., and S. McElroy. 2021. The Australian Height Datum Turns 50: Past, Present and Future. In *Proceedings of Association of Public Authority Surveyors Webinar Series 2021 (AWS2021),* pp. 3–27. APAS, Bathurst, Australia.

Jarvis, D. 2004. *Haunted Shores: True Ghost Stories of Newfoundland and Labrador.* Flanker, St. John's, Newfoundland.

Jarvis, D. 2017. *Haunted Ground: Ghost Stories from the Rock.* Flanker, St. John's, Newfoundland.

Javaux, E. J. 2019. Challenges in Evidencing the Earliest Traces of Life. *Nature* 572(7770):451–460.

Jeans, P. D. 2007. *Seafaring Lore and Legend*. International Marine / McGraw-Hill, Camden.

Jeffery, B. 2013. Reviving Community Spirit: Furthering the Sustainable, Historical and Economic Role of Fish Weirs and Traps. *Journal of Maritime Archaeology* 8(1):29–57.

J. E. M. 1873. A Colony of Heathens. *Journal of the Anthropological Institute of Great Britain and Ireland* 2:447–449.

Jenness, D. 1922. *Report of the Canadian Arctic Expedition, 1913–18, Vol. 12: The Life of the Copper Eskimos*. F. A. Acland, Ottawa.

Jensen, A. M. 2012. The Material Culture of Iñupiat Whaling: An Ethnographic and Ethnohistorical Perspective. *Arctic Anthropology* 49(2):143–161.

Jeon, H. 2013. Arts of Prehistoric and Ancient Korea and the Bangudae Petroglyphs. In *Bangudae: Petrogyph Panels in Ulsan, Korea, in the Context of World Rock Art*, edited by J. Kim, pp. 11–35. World Petroglyphs Research 1. Hollym, Morgan Hill, California.

Jerardino, A. 2016. On the Origins and Significance of Pleistocene Coastal Resource Use in Southern Africa with Particular Reference to Shellfish Gathering. *Journal of Anthropological Archaeology* 41:213–230.

Jochelson, W. 1904. The Mythology of the Koryak. *American Anthropologist* 6(4):413–425.

Jochelson, W. 1908. *The Koryak: Religion and Myths*. The Jesup North Pacific Expedition. Memoir of the American Museum of Natural History 6(1). E. J. Brill, Leiden and G. E. Stechert, New York.

Jochelson, W. 1925. *Archaeological Investigations in the Aleutian Islands*. Carnegie Institution of Washington, Washington.

Jochelson, W. 2002 [1933]. *History, Ethnology and Anthropology of the Aleut*. Anthropology of Pacific North America series. University of Utah Press, Salt Lake City.

Johannes, R. E. 1981. *Words of the Lagoon: Fishing and Marine Lore in the Palau District of Micronesia*. University of California Press, Berkeley.

Johannes, R. E., and J. W. MacFarlane. 1984. Traditional Sea Rights in the Torres Strait Islands. In *Maritime Institutions of the Western Pacific*, edited by K. Ruddle and T. Akimichi, pp. 253–66. Senri Ethnological Studies 17. National Museum of Ethnology, Osaka.

Johnson, J. R. 2023. Shadow of the Whale: West Coast Rituals Associated with Luring Whales. In *The History and Environmental Impacts of Hunting Deities: Supernatural Gamekeepers and Animal Masters*, edited by R. J. Chacon, pp. 201–226. Springer Nature, Cham, Switzerland.

Johnson, L. L. 2005. Aleut Sea-Mammal Hunting: Ethnohistorical and Archaeological Evidence. In *The Exploitation and Cultural Importance of Sea Mammals*, edited by G. G. Monks, pp. 39–61. Oxbow, Oxford.

Johnson, L. L. 2019. The Stone and Bone Artifacts from Asx̂aana-x̂ Cave, Islands of the Four Mountains, Alaska. *Quaternary Research* 91(3):1016–1027.

Johnston, P. F. 1985. *Ship and Boat Models in Ancient Greece*. Naval Institute Press, Annapolis.

Johnstone, P. 1964. The Bantry Boat. *Antiquity* 38(152):277–284.

Jokiel, P. L., C. Kelley, and K. Rodgers. 2019. Archaeology from a Submersible: Rare

Physical Evidence of Ancient Deepwater Bottom Fishing in Hawai'i. *Journal of Pacific Archaeology* 10(1):56–61.

Jolles, C. Z. 1995. Paul Silook's Legacy: The Ethnohistory of Whaling on St. Lawrence Island. In *Hunting the Largest Animals: Native Whaling in the Western Arctic and Subarctic*, edited by A. P. McCartney, pp. 221–252. Canadian Circumpolar Institute, University of Alberta, Edmonton.

Jolles, C. Z. 2003. When Whaling Folks Celebrate: A Comparison of Tradition and Experience in Two Bering Sea Whaling Communities. In *Indigenous Ways to the Present: Native Whaling in the Western Arctic*, edited by A. P. McCartney, pp. 307–339. Canadian Circumpolar Institute Press, Edmonton.

Jonaitis, A. 1981. *Tlingit Halibut Hooks: An Analysis of the Visual Symbols of a Rite of Passage*. Anthropological Papers of the American Museum of Natural History, Vol. 57(1). New York.

Jonaitis, A. 1999. *The Yuquot Whalers' Shrine*. University of Washington Press, Seattle.

Jones, A. 1998. Where Eagles Dare: Landscapes, Animals and the Neolithic of Orkney. *Journal of Material Culture* 3(3):301–324.

Jones, M. 2000. The Names Given to Ships in Fourteenth- and Fifteenth-Century England. *Nomina* 23:23–36.

Jones, M. 2016. Ship Names. In *The Oxford Handbook of Names and Naming*, edited by C. Hough, pp. 655–660. Oxford University Press, Oxford.

Jones, O., and P. Cloke. 2008. Non-Human Agencies: Trees in Place and Time. In *Material Agency: Towards a Non-Anthropocentric Approach*, edited by C. Knappett and L. Malafouris, pp. 79–96. Springer Science + Business Media, New York.

Jones, R. 1992. Philosophical Time Travellers. *Antiquity* 66(252):744–757.

Jones, W. 1871. *The Broad, Broad Ocean and Some of Its Inhabitants*. Frederick Warne, London.

Jones, W. 1898. *Credulities Past and Present*. New ed. Chatto and Windus, London.

Jordaan, R. E. 1984. The Mystery of Nyai Lara Kidul, Goddess of the Southern Ocean. *Archipel* 28:99–116.

Jordan, P. 2003. *Material Culture and Sacred Landscape: The Anthropology of the Siberian Khanty*. AltaMira Press, Walnut Creek.

Jousse, H., C. Guérin, A. Prieur, M. Faure, and J. Desse. 2002. Exploitation des ressources marines au cours des Ve–IVe millénaires: Le site à dugongs de l'île d'Akab (Umm al-Qaiwain, Émirats Arabes Unis). *Paléorient* 28/1:43–58.

Kalland, A. 2004. Japanese Perceptions of Whales and Dolphins. In *Wildlife in Asia: Cultural Perspectives*, edited by J. Knight, pp. 73–87. RoutledgeCurzon, London.

Kamakau, S. 1976 [1869–70]. *The Works of the People of Old: Na Hana a ka Po'e Kahiko*. Bishop Museum Press, Honolulu.

Kang, B. W. 2020. Reexamination of the Chronology of the Bangudae Petroglyphs and Whaling in Prehistoric Korea: A Different Perspective. *Journal of Anthropological Research* 76(4):480–506.

Kapitän, G. 1973. A Corinthian Shipwreck at Savelletri (Brindisi, Apulia, Italy). *International Journal of Nautical Archaeology* 2(1):185–186.

Kapitän, G. 1979. *Louteria* from the Sea. *International Journal of Nautical Archaeology* 8(2):97–120.

Kapitän, G. 1989. Archaeological Evidence for Rituals and Customs on Ancient Ships. In *Tropis I: International Symposium on Ship Construction in Antiquity at Athens*, edited by H. E. Tzalas, pp. 147–162. Hellenic Institute for the Preservation of Nautical Tradition, Piraeus.

Katayama, K. 1998. Auditory Exostoses Among Ancient Human Populations in the Circum-Pacific Area: Regional Variations in the Occurrence and Its Implications. *Anthropological Science* 106(4):285–296.

Kathirvel, M., and S. Srinivasagam. 1992. Taxonomy of the Mud Crab, *Scylla serrata* (Forskal), from India. In *The Mud Crab*, edited by C. A. Angell, pp. 127–141. Bay of Bengal Programme, Madras, India.

Kato, K. 2007. Prayers for the Whales: Spirituality and Ethics of a former Whaling Community—Intangible Cultural Heritage for Sustainability. *International Journal of Cultural Property* 14(3):283–313.

Kavanagh, E., and M. Bates. 2019. Semantics of the Sea: Stories and Science Along the Celtic Seaboard. *Internet Archaeology* 53. https://doi.org/10.11141/ia.53.8.

Kearney, A. 2025. Volumetric and Vertical Ecologies: The Cultural Depth and Breadth of Amphibiousness in Indigenous Sea Territories. In *Amphibious Concepts at the Edge of the Sea*, edited by J. Baumeister, I. C. Giurgiu, and D. A. Ottmann, pp. 191–211. Springer Nature, Singapore.

Kearney, A., M. O'Leary, and S. Platten. 2023. Sea Country: Plurality and Knowledge of Saltwater Territories in Indigenous Australian Contexts. *Geographical Journal* 189:104–116.

Keinan, G. 2002. The Effects of Stress and Desire for Control on Superstitious Behavior. *Personality and Social Psychology Bulletin* 28(1):102–108.

Keithahn, E. L. 1940. The Petroglyphs of Southeastern Alaska. *American Antiquity* 6(2):123–132.

Kelly, R. L. 2013. *The Lifeways of Hunter-Gatherers: The Foraging Spectrum.* 2nd ed. Cambridge University Press, Cambridge.

Kemp, J., and B. D'Olier. 2016. Early Navigation in the North Sea: The Use of the Lead and Line and Other Navigation Methods. *Journal of Navigation* 69(4):673–697.

Kemp, L. V. 2006. Ancient Stone Wall Fish Traps on the South Coast of South Africa: Documentation, Current Use, Ecological Effects and Management Implications. MSc dissertation, University of Cape Town, South Africa.

Kennedy, D. H. 1974. *Ship Names: Origins and Usages During 45 Centuries.* University Press of Virginia, Charlottesville.

Kesarkar-Gavankar, A., and M. Vicziany. 2023. Dariyadev: The Koli Sea God and the Fishing Environment in Mumbai. In *South Asian Goddesses and the Natural Environment*, edited by M. Vicziany and J. B. Bapat, pp. 108–131. Archaeopress, Oxford.

Kikiloi, K. 2003. A New Synthesis in Oceanic Domestication: The Symbiotic Development of *Loko I'a* in Precontact Oceania. *SPC Traditional Resource Management and Knowledge Information Bulletin* 15:3–10.

King, M. 1965. Fishing Rites at Be-Malai, Portuguese Timor. *Records of the South Australian Museum* 15:108–117.

Kingsford, C. L. 1908. *A Survey of London by John Stow, Reprinted from the Text of 1603*. 2 vols. Clarendon, Oxford.

Kirby, D., and M.-L. Hinkkanen. 2000. *The Baltic and the North Seas*. Routledge, London.

Kirch, P. V. 2000. *On the Road of the Winds: An Archaeological History of the Pacific Islands Before European Contact*. University of California Press, Berkeley.

Kirch, P. V., R. Mertz-Kraus, and W. D. Sharp. 2015. Precise Chronology of Polynesian Temple Construction and Use for Southeastern Maui, Hawaiian Islands Determined by 230Th Dating of Corals. *Journal of Archaeological Science* 53:166–177.

Kirksey, S. E., and S. Helmreich. 2010. The Emergence of Multispecies Ethnography. *Cultural Anthropology* 25(4):545–576.

Kishigami, N. 2013. Aboriginal Subsistence Whaling in Barrow, Alaska. In *Anthropological Studies of Whaling*, edited by N. Kishigami, H. Hamaguchi, and J. N. Savelle, pp. 101–120. Senri Ethnological Studies 84. National Museum of Ethnology, Osaka.

Kishigami, N., H. Hamaguchi, and J. N. Savelle. 2013. *Anthropological Studies of Whaling*. Senri Ethnological Studies 84. National Museum of Ethnology, Osaka.

Kjellgren, E. 2007. *Oceania: Art of the Pacific Islands in the Metropolitan Museum of Art*. Metropolitan Museum of Art, New York.

Kjellgren, E. 2014. *How to Read Oceanic Art*. Metropolitan Museum of Art, New York.

Klein, B., and G. Mackenthun. 2004. Introduction. In *Sea Changes: Historicizing the Ocean*, edited by B. Klein and G. Mackenthun, pp. 1–12. Routledge, New York.

Kleivan, I. 1984. West Greenland Before 1950. In *Handbook of North American Indians, Vol. 5: Arctic*, edited by D. Damas, pp. 595–621. Smithsonian Institution, Washington, DC.

Klokler, D. M. 2008. Food for Body and Soul: Mortuary Ritual in Shell Mounds (Laguna-Brazil). PhD dissertation, University of Arizona.

Klokler, D. 2014. A Ritually Constructed Shell Mound: Feasting at the Jabuticabeira II Site. In *The Cultural Dynamics of Shell-Matrix Sites*, edited by M. Roksandic, S. M. de Souza, S. Eggers, M. Burchell, and D. Klokler, pp. 151–162. University of New Mexico Press, Albuquerque.

Klokler, D. 2020. Fishing for "Lucky Stones": Symbolic Uses of Otoliths in Brazilian Shell Sites. *Journal of Anthropological Archaeology* 58:101167.

Knappert, J. 1992. *Pacific Mythology: An Encyclopedia of Myth and Legend*. Aquarian/Thorsons, London.

Knebel, W. 2003. *From the Old People: The Cape Alitak Petroglyphs*. Donning, Virginia Beach.

Knooihuizen, R. 2008. Fishing for Words: The Taboo Language of Shetland Fishermen and the Dating of Norn Language Death. *Transactions of the Philological Society* 106(1):100–113.

Kohn, E. 2013. *How Forests Think: Toward an Anthropology Beyond the Human*. University of California Press, Berkeley.

Kokkinou, A. 2014. Of Horses, Earthquakes, and the Sea: Poseidon and His Worshippers in Ancient Greece. In *Poseidon and the Sea: Myth, Cult, and Daily Life*, edited by S. D. Pevnick, pp. 51–63. Tampa Museum of Art in association with D. Giles, London.

Konrad, U., and G. Konrad. 1996. *Bis Pokumbu*: The Ancestor Pole Feast. In *Asmat: Myth and Ritual the Inspiration of Art*, edited by G. Konrad and U. Konrad, pp. 264–301. Erizzo Editrice, Venezia.

Kooijman, S., M. Dorren, L. Veeger, J. Verschueren, and R. Luyken. 1958. Report of the Investigation into the Problem of Depopulation Amongst the Marind-anim of Netherlands New Guinea. South Pacific Commission Population Studies S.18 Project. Noumea, New Caledonia.

Krause, F. 2017. Towards an Amphibious Anthropology of Delta Life. *Human Ecology* 45(3):403–408.

Krause, F., and M. Harris. 2021. Introduction: Life at Water's Edge. In *Delta Life: Exploring Dynamic Environments where Rivers Meet the Sea*, edited by F. Krause and M. Harris, pp. 1–24. Berghahn, New York.

Kristoffersen, S. 2010. Half Beast–Half Man: Hybrid Figures in Animal Art. *World Archaeology* 42(2):261–272.

Kroeber, A. L. 1948. *Anthropology*. George G. Harrap, London.

Krupnik, I. 1987. The Bowhead vs. the Gray Whale in Chukotkan Aboriginal Whaling. *Arctic* 40(1):16–32.

Krupnik, I. 1993. *Arctic Adaptations: Native Whalers and Reindeer Herders of Northern Eurasia*. University Press of New England, Hanover.

Krupnik, I. 2011. "How Many Eskimo Words for Ice?": Collecting Inuit Sea Ice Terminologies in the International Polar Year 2007–2008. *Canadian Geographer/Le géographe Canadien* 55(1):56–68.

Krupnik, I., and L. Müller-Wille. 2010. Franz Boas and Inuktitut Terminology for Ice and Snow: From the Emergence of the Field to the "Great Eskimo Vocabulary Hoax." In *SIKU: Knowing Our Ice*, edited by I. Krupnik, C. Aporta, S. Gearheard, G. J. Laidler, and L. K. Holm, pp. 377–400. Springer, Dordrecht.

Küchelmann, H. C. 2011. Whale Bones as Architectural Elements in and Around Bremen, Germany. In *Written in Bones: Studies on Technological and Social Contexts of Past Faunal Skeletal Remains*, edited by J. Baron and B. Kufel-Diakowska, pp. 207–223. Uniwersytet Wrocławski Instytut Archeologii, Wrocław.

Kwiatkowski, L., O. Torres, L. Bopp, O. Aumont, M. Chamberlain, J. Christian, J. P. Dunne, M. Gehlen, T. Ilyina, J. G. John, et al. 2020. Twenty-First Century Ocean Warming, Acidification, Deoxygenation, and Upper-Ocean Nutrient and Primary Production Decline from CMIP6 Model Projections. *Biogeosciences* 17(13):3439–3470.

Laade, W. 1969. Ethnographic Notes on the Murray Islanders, Torres Strait. *Zeitschrift für Ethnologie* 94:33–46.

Lady Wilde. 1890. *Ancient Cures, Charms, and Usages of Ireland: Contributions to Irish Lore*. Ward and Downey, London.

Lambert, W. G. 2007. Mesopotamian Creation Stories. In *Imagining Creation*, edited by M. J. Geller and M. Schipper, pp. 15–60. Brill, Leiden.

Lambert, W. G. 2013. *Babylonian Creation Myths*. Mesopotamian Civilizations 16. Eisenbrauns, Winona Lake.

Lambourn, E. 2021. Introduction: Charting a Cultural History of the Sea for the Medieval Age. In *A Cultural History of the Sea in the Medieval Age*, edited by E. Lambourn, pp. 1–26. Bloomsbury Academic, London.

Lancrenon, É., and D. Zanette. 2011. *Tridacna gigas: Objets de prestige en Mélanésie*. Au vent des îles, Tahiti.

Land, I. 2010. The Humours of Sailortown: Atlantic History Meets Subculture Theory. In *City Limits: Perspectives on the Historical European City*, edited by G. Clark, J. Owens, and G. T. Smith, pp. 325–347. McGill-Queen's University Press, Montreal.

Landtman, G. 1917. *The Folk-Tales of the Kiwai Papuans.* Finnish Society of Literature, Helsingfors.

Landtman, G. 1927. *The Kiwai Papuans of British New Guinea.* Macmillan, London.

Langdon, S. J. 2007. Sustaining a Relationship: Inquiry into the Emergence of a Logic of Engagement with Salmon Among the Southern Tlingits. In *Native Americans and the Environment: Perspectives on the Ecological Indian*, edited by M. E. Harkin and D. R. Lewis, pp. 233–273. University of Nebraska Press, Lincoln.

Langley, M. C., S. Kealy, and S. O'Connor. 2023. Sequins from the Sea: *Nautilus* Shell Bead Technology at Makpan, Alor Island, Indonesia. *Antiquity* 97(394):810–828.

Langley, M. C., S. O'Connor, and E. Piotto. 2016. 42,000-Year-Old Worked and Pigment-Stained Nautilus Shell from Jerimalai (Timor-Leste): Evidence for an Early Coastal Adaptation in ISEA. *Journal of Human Evolution* 97:1–16.

Lantis, M. 1938. The Alaskan Whale Cult and Its Affinities. *American Anthropologist* 40(3):438–464.

Lantis, M. 1947. *Alaskan Eskimo Ceremonialism.* Monographs of the American Ethnological Society 11. University of Washington Press, Seattle.

Larson, J. 2007. *Ancient Greek Cults: A Guide.* Routledge, New York.

Larson, M. A. 1995. And Then There Were None: The "Disappearance" of the *Qargi* in Northern Alaska. In *Hunting the Largest Animals: Native Whaling in the Western Arctic and Subarctic*, edited by A. P. McCartney, pp. 207–220. Canadian Circumpolar Institute, University of Alberta, Edmonton.

Larsson, C. 2022. The First Photograph of the Entire Globe: 50 Years On, Blue Marble Still Inspires. *The Conversation,* 7 December.

Larsson, L. 2003. Land, Water and Symbolic Aspects of the Mesolithic in Southern Scandinavia. *Before Farming* 4:1–14.

Lash, R. 2018a. Pebbles and *peregrinatio*: The Taskscape of Medieval Devotion on Inishark Island, Ireland. *Medieval Archaeology* 62(1):83–104.

Lash, R. 2018b. Enchantments of Stone: Confronting Other-than-Human Agency in Irish Pilgrimage Practices. *Journal of Social Archaeology* 18(3):284–305.

Lash, R., I. Kuijt, E. Alonzi, M. S. Chesson, and T. Burke. 2018. "Differing in Status, but One in Spirit": Sacred Space and Social Diversity at Island Monasteries in Connemara, Ireland. *Antiquity* 92(362):437–455.

Latour, B. 1993. *We Have Never Been Modern.* Harvard University Press, Cambridge, Massachusetts.

Laugrand, F., and J. Oosten. 2008. *The Sea Woman: Sedna in Inuit Shamanism and Art in the Eastern Arctic.* University of Alaska Press, Fairbanks.

Laugrand, F., and J. G. Oosten. 2013. "We're Back with Our Ancestors": Inuit Bowhead Whaling in the Canadian Eastern Arctic. *Anthropos* 108(2):431–444.

Laurenson, A. 1872–74. On Certain Beliefs and Phrases of Shetland fishermen. *Proceedings of the Society of Antiquaries of Scotland* 10:711–716.

Lawrence, D. H. 1923. *Studies in Classic American Literature*. Thomas Seltzer, New York.

Lawrence, R. M. 1898. *The Magic of the Horse-Shoe*. Gay and Bird, London.

Lawrie, M. 1970. *Myths and Legends of Torres Strait*. University of Queensland Press, St. Lucia.

Layard, J. n.d. Rites to Accompany the Manufacture of a Long-Distance Canoe. Cambridge Museum Collection.

Layard, J. 1942. *Stone Men of Malekula*. Chatto and Windus, London.

Leach, F. 2007. A Cache of Fishhooks from Serendipity Cave, Jackson Bay, New Zealand. In *Vastly Ingenious: The Archaeology of Pacific Material Culture in Honour of Janet M. Davidson*, edited by A. Anderson, K. Green, and F. Leach, pp. 79–95. Otago University Press, Dunedin.

Lean, V. S. 1903a. *Lean's Collectanea*. Vol. 2, Part 1. J. W. Arrowsmith, Bristol.

Lean, V. S. 1903b. *Lean's Collectanea*. Vol. 2, Part 2. J. W. Arrowsmith, Bristol.

Leary, J. C. 2013. Northsealand: A Study of the Effects, Perceptions of and Responses to Mesolithic Sea-Level Rise in the Southern North Sea and Channel/Manche. PhD dissertation, University of Manchester, UK.

Leather, M. 1977. *Saltwater Village*. Terence Dalton, Suffolk.

Lebatard, A.-E., D. L. Bourlès, R. Braucher, and A. Team. 2019. Absolute Dating of an Early Paleolithic Site in Western Africa Based on the Radioactive Decay of In Situ–Produced 10Be and 26Al. *Nuclear Instruments and Methods in Physics Research Section B: Beam Interactions with Materials and Atoms* 456:169–179.

Le Couteur, P. 2015. Slipping Off the Sealskin: Gender, Species, and Fictive Kinship in Selkie Folktales. *Gender Forum* 55:55–82.

Lee, G., and E. Stasack. 1999. *Spirit of Place: The Petroglyphs of Hawai'i*. Easter Island Foundation, Los Osos.

Lee, H. 1884. Sea Monster Unmasked. In *The Fisheries Exhibition Literature*, Vol. 3, pp. 318–440. International Fisheries Exhibition London 1883. William Clowes and Sons, London.

Lee, I. 1995. The Tradition of Christian Sea Symbolism in Medieval English Poetry and Milton. PhD dissertation, Oklahoma State University, Stillwater.

Lehman, J. S. 2013. Relating to the Sea: Enlivening the Ocean as an Actor in Eastern Sri Lanka. *Environment and Planning D: Society and Space* 31(3):485–501.

Lehn, W. H., and W. G. Rees. 1990. The Scoresby Ship Mirage of 1822. *Polar Record* 26(158):181–186.

Lenihan, D. J. 1991. The *Arizona* Revisited. *Natural History* 100(11):64–71.

Leon, B. C. 2005. Mesolithic and Neolithic Activity on Dalkey Island—A Reassessment. *Journal of Irish Archaeology* 14:1–21.

Léo Neto, N. A., R. A. Voeks, T. L. P. Dias, and R. Alves. 2012. Mollusks of Candomblé: Symbolic and Ritualistic Importance. *Journal of Ethnobiology and Ethnomedicine* 8(1):1–10.

Lepowsky, M. 1995. Voyaging and Cultural Identity in the Louisiade Archipelago of Papua New Guinea. In *Seafaring in the Contemporary Pacific Islands: Studies in Continuity and Change*, edited by R. Feinberg, pp. 34–54. Northern Illinois University Press, DeKalb.

Lerner, M. 1984. *The Flame and the Lotus: Indian and Southeast Asian Art from the Kronos Collections*. Metropolitan Museum of Art, New York.

Lessa, W. A. 1961. *Tales from Ulithi Atoll: A Comparative Study in Oceanic Folklore.* Folklore Studies 13. University of California Press, Berkeley.

Levinson, S. 2008. Landscape, Seascape and the Ontology of Places on Rossel Island, Papua New Guinea. *Language Sciences* 30:256–290.

Lewcock, R., and G. Brans. 1975. The Boat as an Architectural Symbol. In *Shelter, Sign and Symbol*, edited by P. Oliver, pp. 107–116. Barrie and Jenkins, London.

Lewis, D. 1970. Polynesian and Micronesian Navigation Techniques. *Journal of Navigation* 23(4):432–447.

Lewis, D. 1978. *The Voyaging Stars: Secrets of the Pacific Island Navigators.* Collins, Sydney.

Lewis, M. W. 1999. Dividing the Ocean Sea. *Geographical Review* 89(2):188–214.

Li, H., R. Wang, and H. Zhan. 2020. The Mechanism of Formation of Desert Mirages. *Physica scripta* 95(4):1–8.

Lincoln, M. 2014. *British Pirates and Society, 1680–1730.* Ashgate, London.

Lindenlauf, A. 2004. The Sea as a Place of No Return in Ancient Greece. *World Archaeology* 35(3):416–433.

Linder, E. 1986. The Khorsabad Wall Relief: A Mediterranean Seascape or River Transport of Timbers? *Journal of the American Oriental Society* 106(2):273–281.

Lindow, J. 2001. *Norse Mythology: A Guide to the Gods, Heroes, Rituals, and Beliefs.* Oxford University Press, Oxford.

Ling, J. 2013. *Rock Art and Seascapes in Uppland.* Swedish Rock Art Series 1. Oxbow, Oxford.

Ling, J. 2014. *Elevated Rock Art: Towards a Maritime Understanding of Rock Art in Northern Bohuslän, Sweden.* Oxbow, Oxford.

Linnaeus, C. 1735. *Systema naturae.* 1st ed. Stockholm.

Lipset, D. 2014. Living Canoes: Vehicles of Moral Imagination Among the Murik of Papua New Guinea. In *Vehicles: Cars, Canoes, and Other Metaphors of Moral Ambivalence*, edited by D. Lipset and R. Handler, pp. 21–47. Berghahn, New York.

Lobo, M. 2019. Affective Ecologies: Braiding Urban Worlds in Darwin, Australia. *Geoforum* 106:393–401.

Lockwood, W. B. 1955. Word Taboo in the Language of the Faroese Fishermen. *Transactions of the Philological Society* 54(1):1–24.

Losey, R. 2010. Animism as a Means of Exploring Archaeological Fishing Structures on Willapa Bay, Washington, USA. *Cambridge Archaeological Journal* 20(1):17–32.

Loveland, F. O. 1976. Tapirs and Manatees: Cosmological Categories and Social Process Among Rama Indians of Eastern Nicaragua. In *Frontier Adaptations in Lower Central America*, edited by M. Helms and F. O. Loveland, pp. 67–82. Institute for the Study of Human Issues, Philadelphia.

Lowe, C. 2003. The Magic of Place: Sama at Sea and on Land in Sulawesi, Indonesia. *Bijdragen tot de Taal-, Land-en Volkenkunde* 159(1):109–133.

Lowenstein, T. 1994. *Ancient Lands, Sacred Whales: The Inuit Hunt and Its Rituals.* Farrar, Straus and Giroux, New York.

Luby, E. M., and M. F. Gruber. 1999. The Dead Must Be Fed: Symbolic Meanings of the Shellmounds of the San Francisco Bay Area. *Cambridge Archaeological Journal* 9(1):95–108.

Lucier, C. V., and J. W. VanStone. 1995. *Traditional Beluga Drives of the Inupiat of Kotzebue Sound, Alaska.* Fieldiana Anthropology, New Series 25. Field Museum of Natural History, Chicago.

Luebbers, R. A. 1978. Meals and Menus: A Study of Change in Prehistoric Coastal Settlements in South Australia. PhD dissertation, Australian National University, Canberra.

Lummis, T. 1985. *Occupation and Society: The East Anglian Fishermen, 1880–1914.* Cambridge University Press, Cambridge.

Luncz, L. V., R. M. Wittig, and C. Boesch. 2015. Primate Archaeology Reveals Cultural Transmission in Wild Chimpanzees (*Pan troglodytes verus*). *Philosophical Transactions of the Royal Society B: Biological Sciences* 370(1682):20140348.

Lunde, P. 1992. Pillars of Hercules, Sea of Darkness. *Aramco World: Arab and Islamic Cultures and Connections* 43(3):6–17.

Lundy, D. 1974. The Rock Art of the Northwest Coast. PhD dissertation, Simon Fraser University, Vancouver, Canada.

Luomala, K. 1977. Porpoises and Taro in Gilbert Islands Myths and Customs. *Fabula* 18(1):201–211.

Lurker, M. 2004. *Routledge Dictionary of Gods and Goddesses, Devils and Demons.* Routledge, London.

Lydenberg, H. M. 1957. *Crossing the Line: Tales of the Ceremony During Four Centuries.* New York Public Library, New York.

Maaz, K., and D. Blau. 2012. *Fish Hooks of the Pacific Islands.* Daniel Blau, Munich, Germany.

MacCulloch, J. A. 1905. *The Misty Isle of Skye: Its Scenery, Its People, Its Story.* Oliphant Anderson and Ferrier, Edinburgh.

MacGregor, A. A. 1937. *The Peat-Fire Flame: Folk-Tales and Traditions of the Highlands and Islands.* Moray, Edinburgh.

Macintyre, K., and B. Dobson. 2017. The Conveyor of Souls: The Pied Cormorant. *Anthropology from the Shed* (blog). https://anthropologyfromtheshed.com/project/conveyor-souls-pied-cormorant/, accessed 20 August 2022.

Mack, J. 2011. *The Sea: A Cultural History.* Reaktion, London.

Mackenzie, D. A. 1923. *Myths of China and Japan.* Gresham, London.

MacKillop, J. 2004. *The Dictionary of Celtic Mythology.* Oxford University Press, Oxford.

Macknight, C. C. 1976. *The Voyage to Marege', Macassan Trepangers in Northern Australia.* Melbourne University Press, Melbourne.

MacLeod Banks, M. 1939. Folklore of the Net, Fishing-Line, Baiting and the Boat on the North-East Coast of Scotland. *Folklore* 50(4):342–348.

MacRae, D. 1880. *Notes About Gourock, Chiefly Historical.* Andrew Elliot, Edinburgh.

Maddock, K. 1978. Introduction. In *The Rainbow Serpent: A Chromatic Piece*, edited by I. R. Buchler and K. Maddock, pp. 1–21. Mouton, The Hague.

Magee, P. 2014. *The Archaeology of Prehistoric Arabia: Adaptation and Social Formation from the Neolithic to the Iron Age.* Cambridge University Press, Cambridge.

Magnus, O. 1555. *Historia de gentibus septentrionalibus.* Rome.

Magos, A. P. 1994. The Concept of *Mari-it* in Panaynon Maritime World View. In *Fishers of the Visayas. Visayas Maritime Anthropological Studies I*, edited by I. Ushijima and

C. N. Zayas, pp. 305–355. University of the Philippines College of Social Sciences and Philosophy, Quezon City.

Malakoff, D. 2008. Hawaiians of Skull Valley: What Were Polynesian Mormons Doing in 19th Century Utah? *Archaeology* 61(6):55–59.

Malindine, J. 2017. Northwest Coast Halibut Hooks: An Evolving Tradition of Form, Function, and Fishing. *Human Ecology* 45(1):53–65.

Malinowski, B. 1915. The Natives of Mailu: Preliminary Results of Robert Mond Research Work in British New Guinea. *Transactions and Proceedings of the Royal Society of South Australia* 39:494–706.

Malinowski, B. 1916. Baloma: The Spirits of the Dead in the Trobriand Islands. *Journal of the Royal Anthropological Institute of Great Britain and Ireland* 46:353–430.

Malinowski, B. 1918. Fishing in the Trobriand Islands. *Man* 18:87–92.

Malinowski, B. 1922. *Argonauts of the Western Pacific.* Routledge and Kegan Paul, London.

Malinowski, B. 1925. Magic, Science, and Religion. In *Science Religion and Reality*, edited by J. Needham, pp. 19–84. Macmillan, New York.

Malinowski, B. 1932. *The Sexual Life of Savages in North-Western Melanesia.* Routledge and Kegan Paul, London.

Malinowski, B. 1935. *Coral Gardens and Their Magic: A Study of the Methods of Tilling the Soil and of Agricultural Rites in the Trobriand Islands.* Vols. 1 and 2. George Allen and Unwin, London.

Malinowski, B. 1948. *Magic, Science and Religion and Other Essays.* Free Press, Glencoe, Illinois.

Malinowski, B. 1954. *Magic, Science and Religion and Other Essays.* Doubleday Anchor, New York.

Manas, J., B. David, L. Manas, J. Ash, and A. Shnukal. 2008. An Interview with Fr John Manas. *Memoirs of the Queensland Museum Cultural Heritage Series* 4(2):385–418.

Manguin, P.-Y. 2001. Shipshape Societies: Boat Symbolism and Political Systems in Insular Southeast Asia. *Techniques and Culture* 35–36:373–400.

Mansrud, A. 2017. Untangling Social, Ritual and Cosmological Aspects of Fishhook Manufacture in the Middle Mesolithic Coastal Communities of NE Skagerrak. *International Journal of Nautical Archaeology* 46(1):31–47.

Marcus, J. 2017. The Inca Conquest of Cerro Azul. *Ñawpa Pacha* 37(2):175–196.

Marean, C. W. 2024. The Origins and Significance of Coastal Resource Use in Human Evolution. In *Oxford Handbook of Island and Coastal Archaeology*, edited by S. Fitzpatrick and J. Erlandson. Oxford University Press, Oxford.

Marean, C. W., M. Bar-Matthews, J. Bernatchez, E. Fisher, P. Goldberg, A. I. R. Herries, Z. Jacobs, A. Jerardino, P. Karkanas, T. Minichillo, et al. 2007. Early Human Use of Marine Resources and Pigment in South Africa During the Middle Pleistocene. *Nature* 449(7164):905–908.

Marhadi, A., and L. Hatani. 2018. Ritual Process of Bajo People in Fishing Activities: Study of Bajo Society in Tiworo Islands Muna of Southeast Sulawesi. *Social Sciences* 13(3):619–636.

Mark, S. 2008. The Earliest Naval Ram. *International Journal of Nautical Archaeology* 37(2):253–272.

Marsden, P. R. V. 1965. The Luck Coin in Ships. *Mariner's Mirror* 51(1):33–34.

Marshall, G. de L. 2003. *Ships' Figure Heads in Australia.* Tangee, Kalamunda, Western Australia.

Martin, S. 1988. Eyre Peninsula and West Coast Aboriginal Fish Trap Survey. Report for South Australian Department of Environment and Planning, Adelaide.

Martinsson-Wallin, H., and J. Wehlin. 2017. Stones in the South: Decoding Bronze Age Ritual Practices on Gotland. *Current Swedish Archaeology* 25:227–256.

Marwick, E. W. 1975. *The Folklore of Orkney and Shetland.* B. T. Batsford, London.

Marx, P. A., and J.-R. Gisler. 2011. Athens NM Acropolis 923 and the Contest Between Athena and Poseidon for the Land of Attica. *Antike Kunst* 54:21–40.

Mason, O. K., and J. T. Rasic. 2019. Walrusing, Whaling and the Origins of the Old Bering Sea Culture. *World Archaeology* 51(3):454–483.

Mathews, R. H. 1904. Ethnological Notes on the Aboriginal Tribes of New South Wales and Victoria. *Journal and Proceedings of the Royal Society of New South Wales* 38:203–381.

Maude, H. C., and H. E. Maude (editors). 1994. *An Anthology of Gilbertese Oral Tradition.* Institute of Pacific Studies of the University of the South Pacific, Suva, Fiji.

Maury, M. F. 1855. *Physical Geography of the Sea.* Harper and Brothers, New York.

May, S. K., P. S. C. Taçon, D. Wesley, and M. Pearson. 2013. Painted Ships on a Painted Arnhem Land Landscape. *Great Circle* 35(2):83–102.

Mayer, C. E. 2020–2021. T-Shirts and Turtles: Art and Environmental Activism on Erub, Torres Strait. *Pacific Arts* 20(1):76–87.

Mazadiego, L. F., O. Puche, and A. M. Hervás. 2009. Water and Inca Cosmogony: Myths, Geology and Engineering in the Peruvian Andes. *Geological Society, London, Special Publications* 310(1):17–24.

McCartney, A. P. 1980. The Nature of Thule Eskimo Whale Use. *Arctic* 33(3):517–541.

McCarthy, E. 2015. Ship Carvers in Eighteenth- and Nineteenth-Century Britain. *Sculpture Journal* 24(2):179–194.

McCaughan, M. 1998. Voyagers in the Vault of Heaven: The Phenomenon of Ships in the Sky in Medieval Ireland and Beyond. *Material Culture Review* 48(1):170–180.

McCaughan, M. 2001. Symbolism of Ships and the Sea: From Ship of the Church to Gospel Trawler. *Folk Life* 40(1):54–61.

McCay, B. J. 2008. The Littoral and the Liminal: Challenges to the Management of the Coastal and Marine Commons. *MAST (Maritime Anthropology Studies)* 7(1):7–30.

McClanahan, T., H. Glaesel, J. Ruben, and R. Kiambo. 1997. The Effects of Traditional Fisheries Management on Fisheries Yields and the Coral-Reef Ecosystems of Southern Kenya. *Environmental Conservation* 24(2):105–120.

McConnel, U. 1930. The Rainbow-Serpent in North Queensland. *Oceania* 1(3):347–349.

McConnel, U. H. 1936. Totemic Hero-Cults in Cape York Peninsula, North Queensland, Part 2. *Oceania* 7(1):69–105.

McCullagh, R., and F. McCormick. 1991. The Excavation of Post-Medieval Burials from Braigh, Aignish, Lewis, 1989. *Post-Medieval Archaeology* 25(1):73–88.

McGee, W. J. 1898. The Seri Indians. *17th Annual Report of the Bureau of American Ethnology* 17(1):1–344.

McGhee, R. 1977. Ivory for the Sea Woman: The Symbolic Attributes of a Prehistoric Technology. *Canadian Journal of Archaeology/Journal Canadienne d'Archélogie* 1:141–149.

McGrail, S. 2010. The Global Origins of Seagoing Water Transport. In *The Global Origins and Development of Seafaring*, edited by A. Anderson, J. H. Barrett, and K. V. Boyle, pp. 95–107. McDonald Institute for Archaeological Research, Cambridge.

McKinnon, J., J. Mushynsky, and G. Cabrera. 2014. A Fluid Sea in the Mariana Islands: Community Archaeology and Mapping the Seascape of Saipan. *Journal of Maritime Archaeology* 9:59–79.

McKinnon, S. 1988. Tanimbar Boats. In *Islands and Ancestors: Indigenous Styles of Southeast Asia*, edited by J. P. Barbier and D. Newton, pp. 152–169. Prestel, Munich.

McKinnon, S. 1991. *From a Shattered Sun: Hierarchy, Gender, and Alliance in the Tanimbar Islands*. University of Wisconsin Press, Madison.

McMillan, A. D. 1999. *Since the Time of the Transformers: The Ancient Heritage of the Nuuchah-nulth, Ditidaht, and Makah*. University of British Columbia Press, Vancouver.

McMillan, A. D. 2019. Non-Human Whalers in Nuu-chah-nulth Art and Ritual: Reappraising Orca in Archaeological Context. *Cambridge Archaeological Journal* 29(2):309–326.

McMurdo, A. 1979. Excavation at a Petroglyph Site on Protection Island, British Columbia. In *CRARA '77: Papers from the Fourth Biennial Conference of the Canadian Rock Art Research Associates*, edited by D. Lundy, pp. 213–218. Heritage Record 8. British Columbia Provincial Museum, Victoria.

McNiven, I. J. 1992. Shell Middens and Mobility: The Use of Off-Site Faunal Remains, Queensland, Australia. *Journal of Field Archaeology* 19:495–508.

McNiven, I. J. 2004. Saltwater People: Spiritscapes, Maritime Rituals and the Archaeology of Australian Indigenous Seascapes. *World Archaeology* 35(3):329–349.

McNiven, I. J. 2008. Sentient Sea: Seascapes as Spiritscapes. In *Handbook of Landscape Archaeology*, edited by B. David and J. Thomas, pp. 149–157. Left Coast, Walnut Creek, California.

McNiven, I. J. 2010. Navigating the Human-Animal Divide: Marine Mammal Hunters and Rituals of Sensory Allurement. *World Archaeology* 42(2):215–230.

McNiven, I. J. 2013a. Between the Living and the Dead: Relational Ontologies and the Ritual Dimensions of Dugong Hunting Across Torres Strait. In *Archaeologies of Relationality: Humans, Animals, Things*, edited by C. Watts, pp. 97–116. Routledge, London.

McNiven, I. J. 2013b. Ritualized Middening Practices. *Journal of Archaeological Method and Theory* 20(4):552–587.

McNiven, I. J. 2015a. Precarious Islands: Kulkalgal Reef Island Settlement and High Mobility Across 700km of Seascape, Central Torres Strait and Northern Great Barrier Reef. *Quaternary International* 385:39–55.

McNiven, I. J. 2015b. Ascendancy of the Tudulgal, Central Torres Strait: Socio-political Manipulation and Domination of an Archipelago Polity. *Journal of Anthropological Archaeology* 39:164–80.

McNiven, I. J. 2015c. Canoes of Mabuyag and Torres Strait. *Memoirs of the Queensland Museum—Culture* 8(1):127–207.

McNiven, I. J. 2016a. The Ethnographic Echo: Archaeological Approaches to Writing Long-Term Histories of Indigenous Spiritual Beliefs and Ritual Practices. *Humanities Australia* 7:8–21.

McNiven, I. J. 2016b. Increase Rituals and Environmental Variability on Small Residential Islands of Torres Strait. *Journal of Island and Coastal Archaeology* 11:195–210.

McNiven, I. J. 2018a. Torres Strait Canoes as Social and Predatory Object-Beings. In *Relational Identities and Other-than-Human Agency in Archaeology,* edited by Eleanor Harrison-Buck and J. A. Hendon, pp. 167–196. University of Colorado Press, Denver.

McNiven, I. J. 2018b. Ritual Mutilation of Europeans on the Torres Strait Maritime Frontier. *Journal of Pacific History* 53(3):229–251.

McNiven, I. J. 2025a. More than the Sea: Review of Different Approaches to Seascapes Reveals Unique Transdisciplinary Conceptualizations and Contributions of Archaeology. *Journal of Island and Coastal Archaeology* 20(4):775–818.

McNiven, I. J. 2025b. Agentive Seas and Animate Canoes: Tangible and Intangible Dimensions of Marine Voyaging by the Marind-anim of Central-Southern New Guinea. In *Western New Guinea: Social, Biological, and Material Histories,* edited by D. Gaffney and M. Tolla, pp. 297–316. Terra Australis 58. Australian National University Press, Canberra.

McNiven, I. J., and A. C. Bedingfield. 2008. Past and Present Marine Mammal Hunting Rates and Abundances: Dugong (*Dugong dugon*) Evidence from Dabangai Bone Mound, Torres Strait. *Journal of Archaeological Science* 35:505–515.

McNiven, I. J., and L. M. Brady. 2012. Rock Art and Seascapes. In *Companion to Rock Art,* edited by J. McDonald and P. Veth, pp. 71–89. Wiley-Blackwell, West Sussex, UK.

McNiven, I. J., B. David, Goemulgau Kod, and J. Fitzpatrick. 2009. The Great *Kod* of Pulu: Mutual Historical Emergence of Ceremonial Sites and Social Groups in Torres Strait, NE Australia. *Cambridge Archaeological Journal* 19(3):291–317.

McNiven, I. J., and R. Feldman. 2003. Ritually Orchestrated Seascapes: Hunting Magic and Dugong Bone Mounds in Torres Strait, NE Australia. *Cambridge Archaeological Journal* 13(2):169–194.

McNiven, I. J., and L. Russell. 2023. *Innovation: Knowledge and Ingenuity.* First Knowledges series. Thames & Hudson, Port Melbourne; National Museum Australia, Canberra.

Mead, T. 1992. *Killers of Eden.* Dolphin, Sydney.

Meiggs, R. 1973. *Roman Ostia.* 2nd ed. Clarendon, Oxford.

Meiklejohn, C., D. C. Merrett, R. W. Nolan, M. P. Richards, and P. A. Mellars. 2005. Spatial Relationships, Dating and Taphonomy of the Human Bone from the Mesolithic Site of Cnoc Coig, Oronsay, Argyll, Scotland. *Proceedings of the Prehistoric Society* 71: 85–105.

Meilleur, B. A. 2019. Hawaiian Seascapes and Landscapes: Reconstructing Elements of a Polynesian Ecological Knowledge System. *Journal of the Polynesian Society* 128(3):305–336.

Meinardus, O. 1996–1997. Maritime Testimonies in Eastern Anatolia: Ani and Doğubayazit. *Revue des Études Arméniennes* 26:316–320.

Mellefont, J. 2000. Heirlooms and Tea Towels: Views of Ships' Gender in the Modern Maritime Museum. *Great Circle: Journal of the Australian Association for Maritime History* 22(1):5–16.

Melville, H. 1851. *Moby-Dick; or, The Whale.* Harper and Brothers, New York.

Melville, H. 1855. *White-Jacket; or the World in a Man-of-War.* Harper and Brothers, New York.

Memmott, P. 1982. Rainbows, Story Places, and Malkri Sickness in the North Wellesley Islands. *Oceania* 53(2):163–182.

Memmott, P. 1983. Social Structure and Use of Space Amongst the Lardil. In *Aborigines, Land and Land Rights,* edited by N. Peterson and M. Langton, pp. 33–65. Australian Institute of Aboriginal Studies, Canberra.

Memmott, P. 2007. *Gunyah Goondie+Wurley: The Aboriginal Architecture of Australia.* University of Queensland Press, St. Lucia.

Memmott, P., and D. Trigger. 1998. Marine Tenure in the Wellesley Islands Region, Gulf of Carpentaria. In *Customary Marine Tenure in Australia,* edited by N. Peterson and B. Rigsby, pp. 109–125. Oceania Monograph 48. University of Sydney, Sydney.

Méry, S., V. Charpentier, G. Auxiette, and E. Pelle. 2009. A Dugong Bone Mound: The Neolithic Ritual Site on Akab in Umm al-Quwain, United Arab Emirates. *Antiquity* 83(321):696–708.

Méry, S., and V. Charpentier. 2012. Akab Island: A Neolithic Sanctuary in the Gulf. In *Fifty Years of Emirates Archaeology: Proceedings of the Second International Conference on the Archaeology of the United Arab Emirates,* edited by D. T. Potts and P. Hellyer, pp. 69–77. Ministry of Cultural, Youth and Community Development, Abu Dhabi, United Arab Emirates.

Meyer, K. 1894. The Irish Mirabilia in the Norse "Speculum Regale." *Folklore* 5(4):299–316.

Michail, M. 2015. Ship Graffiti in Context: A Preliminary Study of Cypriot Patterns. In *Cypriot Cultural Details,* edited by I. Hadjikyriakos and M. G. Trentin, pp. 41–64. Oxbow, Oxford.

Michelet, M. J. 1861. *The Sea (La Mer).* Translated from French. Rudd and Carleton, New York.

Mikalson, J. D. 2010. *Ancient Greek Religion.* 2nd ed. John Wiley and Sons, West Sussex, UK.

Millar, R. M., W. Barras, and L. Bonnici. 2014. *Lexical Attrition in Scottish Fishing Communities.* Edinburgh University Press, Edinburgh.

Miller, A. G. 1977. The Maya and the Sea: Trade and Cult at Tancah and Tulum, Quintana Roo, Mexico. In *The Sea in the Pre-Columbian World,* edited by E. P. Benson, pp. 96–138. Dumbarton Oaks Research Library and Collections, Trustees for Harvard University, Washington, DC.

Miller, M. E., and M. O'Neal. 2010. The World of the Ancient Maya and the Worlds They Made. In *Fiery Pool: The Maya and the Mythic Sea,* edited by D. Finamore and S. D. Houston, pp. 24–37. Peabody Essex Museum and Yale University Press, New Haven.

Miller, O. 1993. *Fraser Island Legends.* Jacaranda, Milton, New South Wales.

Miller, R. 2003. The Early Medieval Seaman and the Church: Contacts Ashore. *Mariner's Mirror* 89(2):132–150.

Miller, R. W. H. 2010. Sea, Ship and Seaman in Early Christian Literature. *Mariner's Mirror* 96(4):418–429.

Miller, R. W. H. 2012. *One Firm Anchor: The Church and the Merchant Seafarer, an Introductory History.* Lutterworth, Cambridge.

Mills, B. J., and T. J. Fergusson. 2008. Animate Objects: Shell Trumpets and Ritual Networks in the Greater Southwest. *Journal of Archaeological Method and Theory* 15:338–361.

Minnegal, M. 1984a. Dugong Bones from Princess Charlotte Bay. *Australian Archaeology* 18:63–71.

Minnegal, M. 1984b. A Note on Butchering Dugong at Princess Charlotte Bay. *Australian Archaeology* 19:15–20.

Mithen, S. 2010. *To the Islands: An Archaeologist's Relentless Quest to Find the Prehistoric Hunter-Gatherers of the Hebrides.* Two Ravens, Isle of Lewis, Scotland.

Mobley, C. M., and W. M. McCallum. 2001. Prehistoric Intertidal Fish Traps from Central Southeast Alaska. *Canadian Journal of Archaeology/Journal Canadien d'Archéologie* 25(1/2):28–52.

Moerman, D. E. 1984. Common Property and the Common Good: Ecological Factors Among Peasant and Tribal Fishermen. In *The Fishing Culture of the World: Studies in Ethnology, Cultural Ecology and Folklore*, edited by B. Gunda, pp. 49–59. 2 vols. Akadémiai Kiadó, Budapest.

Mollat, M. 1975. Introduction. In *Ex-voto marins du Ponant offerts à Dieu et à ses Saints par les gens de la mer du Nord, de la Manche et de l'Atlantique*, edited by J. Lepage, E. Rieth, and D. Samson, pp. 11–17. Musées de la Marine, Palais de Chaillot, Paris.

Monberg, T. 1991. *Bellona Island: Beliefs and Rituals.* Pacific Islands Monograph Series 9. University of Hawai'i Press, Honolulu.

Monks, G. G. 2001. Quit Blubbering: An Examination of Nuu'chah'nulth (Nootkan) Whale Butchery. *International Journal of Osteoarchaeology* 11:136–149.

Monks, G. G., A. D. McMillan, and D. E. St. Claire. 2001. Nuu-Chah-Nulth Whaling: Archaeological Insights into Antiquity, Species Preferences, and Cultural Importance. *Arctic Anthropology* 38(1):60–81.

Moore, A. W. 1894. Water and Well-Worship in Man. *Folklore* 5(3):212–229.

Moore, D. R. 1984. *The Torres Strait Collections of A. C. Haddon.* British Museum Publications, London.

Mora, C., D. P. Tittensor, S. Adl, A. G. B. Simpson, and B. Worm. 2011. How Many Species Are There on Earth and in the Ocean? *PLoS Biology* 9(8):e1001127.

Morison, S. E. 1963. *Journals and Other Documents on the Life and Voyages of Christopher Columbus.* Heritage, New York.

Morphy, H. 1989. Introduction. In *Animals into Art*, edited by H. Morphy, pp. 1–17. Unwin Hyman, London.

Morphy, H., and J. Carty. 2015. Understanding Country. In *The BP Exhibition Indigenous Australia Enduring Civilisation*, edited by G. Sculthorpe, J. Carty, H. Morphy, M. Nugent, I. Coates, L. Bolton, and J. Jones, pp. 20–119. British Museum, London.

Morphy, H., and F. Morphy. 2006. Tasting the Waters: Discriminating Identities in the Waters of Blue Mud Bay. *Journal of Material Culture* 11(1/2):67–85.

Morphy, F., and H. Morphy. 2009. The Blue Mud Bay Case: Refractions Through Saltwater Country. *Dialogue (Academy of the Social Sciences in Australia)* 28(1):15–25.

Morriss, V. M. 2012. Islands in the Nile Sea: The Maritime Cultural Landscape of Thmuis, an Ancient Delta City. MA dissertation, Texas A&M University, College Station.

Morton, T. 2013. *Hyperobjects: Philosophy and Ecology After the End of the World.* University of Minnesota Press, Minneapolis.

Moss, R. 1925. *The Life After Death in Oceania and the Malay Archipelago.* Oxford University Press, Oxford.

Mountford, C. P. 1976. *Nomads of the Australian Desert.* Rigby, Adelaide.

Mountford, C. P. 1978. The Rainbow-Serpent Myths of Australia. In *The Rainbow Serpent: A Chromatic Piece*, edited by I. R. Buchler and K. Maddock, pp. 23–97. Mouton, The Hague.

Muckelroy, K. 1978. *Maritime Archaeology.* Cambridge University Press, Cambridge.

Mullen, P. B. 1969. The Function of Magic Folk Belief Among Texas Coastal Fishermen. *Journal of American Folklore* 82(325):214–225.

Müller, M. 1864. *Lectures on the Science of Language.* 2nd series. Longman, Green, Longman, Roberts and Green, London.

Müller, S. M. 2021. Conflicts: Underneath the Quiet Waves. In *A Cultural History of the Sea in the Global Age*, Vol. 6, edited by F. Torma, pp. 95–116. Bloomsbury Academic, London.

Müller-Wille, M. 1974. Boat-Graves in Northern Europe. *International Journal of Nautical Archaeology and Underwater Exploration* 3(2):187–204.

Mulville, J. 2002. The Role of Cetacea in Prehistoric and Historic Atlantic Scotland. *International Journal of Osteoarchaeology* 12(1):34–48.

Munn, N. 1977. The Spatiotemporal Transformations of Gawa Canoes. *Journal de la Société des Océanistes* 33(54):39–53.

Munn, N. D. 1986. *The Fame of Gawa: A Symbolic Study of Value Transformation in a Massim (Papua New Guinea) Society.* Cambridge University Press, Cambridge.

Murdock, J. 1892. Ethnological Results of the Point Barrow Expedition. In *Ninth Annual Report of the Bureau of Ethnology to the Secretary of the Smithsonian Institution 1887–'88*, pp. 19–441. US Government Printing Office, Washington, DC.

Murray, W. M. 1991. The Provenance and Date: The Evidence of the Symbols. In *The Athlit Ram*, edited by L. Casson and J. R. Steffy, pp. 51–66. Texas A&M University Press, College Station.

Murray, W. M., and P. M. Petsas. 1989. Octavian's Campsite Memorial for the Actian War. *Transactions of the American Philosophical Society* 79(4):1–172.

Musset, L. 2005. *The Bayeux Tapestry.* Translated by R. Rex. Boydell, Woodbridge, UK.

Mye, G. 2007. Affidavit of George Mye. Sworn on September 2007. Torres Strait Regional Seas Native Title Claim, Q6040 of 2001. Native Title Office, Torres Strait Regional Authority, Thursday Island, Queensland, Australia.

Mylona, D. 2015. From Fish Bones to Fishermen: Views from the Sanctuary of Poseidon at Kalaureia. In *Classical Archaeology in Context: Theory and Practice in Excavation in the Greek World*, edited by D. C. Haggis and C. M. Antonaccio, pp. 385–418. De Gruyter, Berlin.

Mylonopoulos, I. 2013. Springs, Sacred. In *The Encyclopedia of Ancient History*, Vol. 11, edited by R. S. Bagnall, K. Brodersen, C. B. Champion, A. Erskine, and S. R. Huebner, pp. 6367–6368, Blackwell/John Wiley and Sons, West Sussex, UK.

Nadel, J. H. 1984. Stigma and Separation: Pariah Status and Community Persistence in a Scottish Fishing Village. *Ethnology* 23(2):101–115.

Nadel-Klein, J. 2000. Granny Baited the Lines: Perpetual Crisis and the Changing Role of Women in Scottish Fishing Communities. *Women's Studies International Forum* 23(3):363–372.

Nadel-Klein, J. 2003. *Fishing for Heritage: Modernity and Loss Along the Scottish Coast.* Berg, Oxford.

Nagaoka, T. 1999. Hope Pukerane: A Study of Religious Sites in Roviana, New Georgia, Solomon Islands. MA dissertation, University of Auckland, New Zealand.

Nagaoka, T. 2000. *Hope* and Other Sacred Places in Kokorapa. Unpublished report, University of Auckland, New Zealand.

Nakata, M. 2007. *Disciplining the Savages: Savaging the Disciplines.* Aboriginal Studies Press, Canberra.

Narayana, A. C., R. Tatavarti, and M. Shakdwipe. 2005. Tsunami of 26 December 2004: Observations on Kerala coast. *Journal of the Geological Society of India* 65(2):239–246.

Naumann, N. 1974. Whale and Fish Cult in Japan: A Basic Feature of Ebisu Worship. *Asian Folklore Studies* 33(1):1–15.

Naumann, N. 2000. *Japanese Prehistory: The Material and Spiritual Culture of the Jomon Period.* Harrassowitz Verlag, Wiesbaden.

Neeser, R. W. 1921. *Ship Names of the United States Navy: Their Meaning and Origin.* Moffat, Yard, New York.

Neil, D. T. 2002. Cooperative Fishing Interactions Between Aboriginal Australians and Dolphins in Eastern Australia. *Anthrozoös* 15(1):3–18.

Neils, J. 1995. Les Femmes Fatales: Skylla and the Sirens in Greek Art. In *The Distaff Side: Representing the Female in Homer's "Odyssey,"* edited by B. Cohen, pp. 175–184. Oxford University Press, Oxford.

Nelson, E. W. 1899. The Eskimo About Bering Strait. In *Eighteenth Annual Report of the Bureau of American Ethnography to the Secretary of the Smithsonian Institution, 1896–97 (Part 1),* edited by J. W. Powell, pp. 3–518. US Government Printing Office, Washington, DC.

Nelson, R. K. 1969. *Hunters of the Northern Ice.* University of Chicago Press, Chicago.

Newman, S. E. 2016. Sharks in the Jungle: Real and Imagined Sea Monsters of the Maya. *Antiquity* 90(354):1522–1536.

Newman, S. P. 1998. Reading the Bodies of Early American Seafarers. *William and Mary Quarterly* 55(1):59–82.

Nicolini, B. 2005. Some Thoughts on the Magical Practice of the *Zār* Along the Red Sea in the Sudan. In *People of the Red Sea: Proceedings of Red Sea Project II,* edited by J. C. M. Starkey, pp. 157–162. British Archaeological Report S1395, Society for Arabian Studies Monographs 3. Archaeopress, Oxford.

Nietschmann, B. 1977. Torres Strait Islander Hunters and Environment. Work-in-progress Seminar by the Department of Human Geography, Research School of Pacific Studies, Australian National University. Copy of paper held by ANU Library.

Nietschmann, B. 1989. Traditional Sea Territories, Resources and Rights in Torres Strait. In *A Sea of Small Boats,* edited by J. Cordell, pp. 60–93. Cultural Survival Inc., Cambridge, MA.

Nietschmann, B., and J. Nietschmann. 1981. Good Dugong, Bad Dugong; Bad Turtle, Good Turtle. *Natural History* 90(5):54–63, 86–87.

Nimura, C. 2016. *Prehistoric Rock Art in Scandinavia: Agency and Environmental Change.* Swedish Rock Art Series 4. Oxbow, Oxford.

Nimura, C., P. Skoglund, and R. Bradley. 2020. Navigating Inland: Bronze Age Watercraft and the Lakes of Southern Sweden. *European Journal of Archaeology* 23(2):186–206.

NOAA (National Oceanic and Atmospheric Administration). 2001. Guidelines for Research, Exploration and Salvage of *RMS Titanic. Federal Register* 68(71):18905–18913.

Nolde, L. 2009. "Great Is Our Relationship with the Sea": Charting the Maritime Realm of the Sama of Southeast Sulawesi, Indonesia. *Explorations* 9:15–32.

Nordqvist, B. 2003. To Touch the Mind. In *Mesolithic on the Move: Papers Presented on the Sixth International Conference on the Mesolithic in Europe, Stockholm, 2000,* edited by L. Larsson, H. Kindgren, K. Knutsson, D. Loeffler, and A. Åkerlund, pp. 536–546. Oxbow, Oxford.

Norman, K., J. Inglis, C. Clarkson, J. T. Faith, J. Shulmeister, and D. Harris. 2018. An Early Colonisation Pathway into Northwest Australia 70–60,000 years ago. *Quaternary Science Reviews* 180:229–239.

Norton, P. 1976. *Ships' Figureheads.* Barre, New York.

Nothaft, C. P. E. 2011. Augustine and the Shape of the Earth: A Critique of Leo Ferrari. *Augustinian Studies* 42(1):33–48.

Nowak, T. J. 2001. A Preliminary Report on *Ophthalmoi* from the Tektas Burnu Shipwreck. *International Journal of Nautical Archaeology* 30(1):86–94.

Nuku, M. 2023. *Oceania: The Shape of Time.* Metropolitan Museum of Art, New York.

Nunn, P. 2003. Fished Up or Thrown Down: The Geography of Pacific Island Origin Myths. *Annals of the Association of American Geographers* 93(2):350–364.

Nunn, P. 2009. *Vanished Islands and Hidden Continents of the Pacific.* University of Hawai'i Press, Honolulu.

Nunn, P. 2018. *The Edge of Memory: Ancient Stories, Oral Tradition, and the Post-Glacial World.* Bloomsbury, London.

Nunn, P. 2020. In Anticipation of Extirpation: How Ancient Peoples Rationalized and Responded to Postglacial Sea Level Rise. *Environmental Humanities* 12(1):113–131.

Nunn, P. 2021. *Worlds in Shadow: Submerged Lands in Science, Memory and Myth.* Bloomsbury, London.

Nunn, P. 2022. *First a Wudd, and Syne a Sea*: Postglacial Coastal Change of Scotland Recalled in Ancient Stories. *Scottish Geographical Journal* 138(1–2):73–102.

Nunn, P., and R. Compatangelo-Soussignan. 2024. The Drowning of "Lyonesse": Early Legends of Land Submergence in Southwest Britain and Geoscience. *Folk Life: Journal of Ethnological Studies* 62(1):1–17.

Nunn, P., and M. Cook. 2022. Island Tales: Culturally-Filtered Narratives About Island Creation Through Land Submergence Incorporate Millennia-Old Memories of Postglacial Sea-Level Rise. *World Archaeology* 54(1):29–51.

Nunn, P., I. Ward, P. Stéphan, A. McCallum, W. R. Gehrels, G. Carey, A. Clarke, M. Cook, P. Geraghty, D. Guilfoyle, B. McNeair, G. Miller, E. Nakoro, D. Reynolds, and L. Stewart. 2022. Human Observations of Late Quaternary Coastal Change: Examples from Australia, Europe and the Pacific Islands. *Quaternary International* 638–639:212–224.

Nuttall, C. 2021. Seascape Dialogues: Human-Sea Interaction in the Aegean from Late Neolithic to Late Bronze Age. PhD dissertation, Uppsala University, Uppsala.

O'Connor, S., R. Ono, and C. Clarkson. 2011. Pelagic Fishing at 42,000 Years Before the Present and the Maritime Skills of Modern Humans. *Science* 334(6059):1117–1121.

O'Connor, S., S. C. Samper Carro, S. Hawkins, S. Kealy, J. Louys, and R. Wood. 2017. Fishing in Life and Death: Pleistocene Fish-Hooks from a Burial Context on Alor Island, Indonesia. *Antiquity* 91(360):1451–1468.

Offenberg, G. A. M., and J. Pouwer (editors). 2000. *Amoko. In the Beginning: Myths and Legends of the Asmat and Mimika Papuans.* Crawford House, Adelaide.

Ogundiran, A. 2002. Of Small Things Remembered: Beads, Cowries, and Cultural Translations of the Atlantic Experience in Yorubaland. *International Journal of African Historical Studies* 35(2/3):427–457.

Ogundiran, A. 2014. Cowries and Rituals of Self-Realization in the Yoruba Region, ca. 1600–1860. In *Materialities of Ritual in the Black Atlantic*, edited by A. Ogundiran and P. Saunders, pp. 68–86. Indiana University Press, Bloomington.

Okada, B. T. 1982. *Netsuke: Masterpieces from the Metropolitan Museum of Art.* Metropolitan Museum of Art, New York.

O'Leary, M., and R. L. Bland. 2013. Aleut Burial Mounds: *Ulaakan* and *Umqan. Alaska Journal of Anthropology* 11(1&2):139–168.

Oman, C. C. 1944. The English Folklore of Gervase of Tilbury. *Folklore* 55(1):2–15.

Oppenheim, M. (editor). 1913. *The Naval Tracts of Sir William Monson in Six Books.* Vol. 3. Publications of the Navy Records Society 43.

Orange, J. 1840. *Narrative of the Late George Vason of Nottingham: One of the First Missionaries Sent to the South Sea Islands by the London Missionary Society in the Ship Duff, Captain Wilson, 1796.* John Snow, London.

Orbell, M. 1996. *The Illustrated Encyclopedia of Māori Myth and Legend.* University of New South Wales Press, Sydney.

Orchard, T. J., and R. J. Wigen. 2016. Halibut Use on the Northwest Coast of North America: Reconciling Ethnographic, Ethnohistoric, and Archaeological Data. *Arctic Anthropology* 53(1):37–57.

Orme, N. 1983. *Early British Swimming, 55 BC–AD 1719, with the First Swimming Treatise in England, 1595.* University of Exeter Press, Exeter.

Oron, A. 2006. The Athlit Ram Bronze Casting Reconsidered: Scientific and Technical Re-Examination. *Journal of Archaeological Science* 33(1):63–76.

Orr, P. C. 1944. The Swordfish Man. *Santa Barbara Museum of Natural History Museum Leaflet* 19(3):33–34.

Ó Sabhain, P. S. 2019. The Centrality of the Galway Hooker to Dwelling in the Island and Coastal Communities of South West Conamara. PhD dissertation, National University of Ireland, Galway.

O'Sullivan, A. 2002. Living with the Dead Amongst Hunter-Gatherers. *Archaeology Ireland* 16(2):10–12.

Ōtō, T. 1963. The Taboos of Fishermen. In *Studies in Japanese folklore*, edited by R. M. Dorson, pp. 107–121. Indiana University Press, Bloomington.

Otway, C. 1841. *Sketches of Erris and Tyrawly.* William Curry, Dublin.

Owen, O., and M. Dalland. 1999. *Scar: A Viking Boat Burial on Sanday, Orkney.* Tuckwell, East Linton.

Paga, J., and M. M. Miles. 2016. The Archaic Temple of Poseidon at Sounion. *Hesperia: The Journal of the American School of Classical Studies at Athens* 85(4):657–710.

Paine, L. 2013. *The Sea and Civilization: A Maritime History of the World.* Alfred A. Knopf, New York.

Pakan, S. P. 2018. Waves Are Sleeping: Surf Tourism and Human-Waves Relationship in Siberut, Mentawai Islands. MSci dissertation, Wageningen University, Netherlands.

Pal, P. 1969. *The Art of Tibet.* The Asian Society, USA.

Palmer, J. B. 1961. Some Aspects of New Zealand Field Archaeology. *Journal of the Polynesian Society* 70(4):466–470.

Palmer, K. 1998. Customary Marine Tenure at Groote Eylandt. In *Customary Marine Tenure in Australia,* edited by N. Peterson and B. Rigsby, pp. 142–153. University of Sydney Oceania Publications, Sydney.

Pálsson, G. 1991. *Coastal Economies, Cultural Accounts: Human Ecology and Icelandic Discourse.* Manchester University Press, Manchester.

Pandya, V. 1993. *Above the Forest: A Study of Andamanese Ethnoanemology, Cosmology, and the Power of Ritual.* Oxford University Press, Delhi.

Pannell, S. 2000. In Wallace's Wake: The Devolution and Disappearance of Maritime Societies and Lifestyles in Eastern Indonesia. In *East of Wallace's Line: Studies of Past and Present Maritime Cultures of the Indo-Pacific Region,* edited by S. O'Connor and P. Veth, pp. 357–380. A. A. Balkema, Rotterdam.

Pannell, S. 2007. Of Gods and Monsters: Indigenous Sea Cosmologies, Promiscuous Geographies and the Depths of Local Sovereignty. In *A World of Water: Rain, Rivers and Seas in Southeast Asian Histories,* edited by P. Boomgaard, pp. 71–102. Koninklijk Instituut voor Taal-, Land- en Volkenkunde Press, Leiden, The Netherlands.

Papadopoulos, J. K., and D. Ruscillo. 2002. A *Ketos* in Early Athens: An Archaeology of Whales and Sea Monsters in the Greek World. *American Journal of Archaeology* 106(2):187–227.

Parer-Cook, E., and D. Parer. 1990. The Case of the Vanishing Mermaids. *GEO Australian Geographic Magazine* 12(3):16–35.

Parés, L. N. 2005. Transformations of the Sea and Thunder Voduns in the Gbe-Speaking Area and in the Bahian Jeje Candomblé. In *Africa and the Americas: Interconnections During the Slave Trade,* edited by J. C. Curto and R. Soulodre-La France, pp. 69–93. Africa World Press, Trenton, New Jersey.

Parker, A. J. 2001. Maritime Landscapes. *Landscapes* 1:22–41.

Parkinson, R. 1999. *Thirty Years in the South Seas: Land and People, Customs and Traditions in the Bismarck Archipelago and on the German Solomon Islands.* Edited by Dr. B. Ankermann, translated by J. Dennison. Translation edited by J. P. White. University of Hawai'i Press, Honolulu.

Parrinder, G. 1961. *West African Religion: A Study of the Beliefs and Practices of Akan, Ewe, Yoruba, Ibo, and Kindred Peoples.* Epworth, London.

Parry, J. H. 1974. *The Discovery of the Sea.* University of California Press, Berkeley.

Pasierowska, R. 2022. All Aboard the *King George* and *Happy Captive:* European Ship-Naming Practices in the Trans-Atlantic Slave Trade, 1750–1755. *International Journal of Maritime History* 34(1):183–195.

Patarino, V. V. 2002. "One Foot in Sea and One on Shore": The Religious Culture of English Sailors, 1550–1688. PhD dissertation, University of Colorado, Boulder.

Patton, A. K., and J. M. Savelle. 2006. The Symbolic Dimensions of Whale Bone Use in Thule Winter Dwellings. *Études Inuit Studies* 30(2):137–161.

Patton, K. C. 2007. *The Sea Can Wash Away All Evils: Modern Marine Pollution and the Ancient Cathartic Ocean.* Columbia University Press, New York.

Pattrick, P., M. Minguzzi, N. Weidberg, and F. Porri. 2022. Ecological Value of the Earliest Human Manipulated Coastal Habitats: Preliminary Insights into the Nursery Function of a Pre-Colonial Stonewalled Fish Trap in South Africa. *Regional Studies in Marine Science* 52(2022):102266.

Paulin, C., with M. Fenwick. 2016. *Te Matau a Māui: Fish-Hooks, Fishing and Fisheries in New Zealand.* University of Hawaiʻi Press, Honolulu.

Pauwelussen, A. P. 2017. Amphibious Anthropology: Engaging with Maritime Worlds in Indonesia. PhD dissertation, Wageningen University, The Netherlands.

Payne, R., and D. Webb. 1971. Orientation by Means of Long Range Acoustic Signaling in Baleen Whales. *Annals of the New York Academy of Sciences* 188(1):110–141.

Pearson, M. 2014. Oceanic History. In *A Companion to Global Historical Thought*, edited by P. Duara, V. Murthy, and A. Sartori, pp. 337–350. John Wiley & Sons, Oxford.

Pearson, M. N. 2006. Littoral Society: The Concept and the Problems. *Journal of World History* 17(4):353–373.

Peden, A. E., D. Demant, M. S. Hagger, and K. Hamilton. 2018. Personal, Social, and Environmental Factors Associated with Lifejacket Wear in Adults and Children: A Systematic Literature Review. *PLoS ONE* 13(5):e0196421.

Pelly, D. F. 2001. *Sacred Hunt: A Portrait of the Relationship Between Seals and Inuit.* Duncan and McIntyre, Vancouver.

Pelly, U. 1977. Symbolic Aspects of the Bugis Ship and Shipbuilding. *Journal of the Steward Anthropological Society* 8(2):87–106.

Penny, S. 2016. Crossing the Line: A Rite of Passage on HMS *Terrible. Performance Research* 21(2):32–37.

Petersen, E. B. 1989. Vænget Nord: Excavation, Documentation and Interpretation of a Mesolithic Site at Vedbæk, Denmark. In *The Mesolithic in Europe: Papers Presented at the Third International Symposium, Edinburgh 1985*, edited by C. Bonsall, pp. 325–330. John Donald, Edinburgh.

Petersen, R. 1984. East Greenland Before 1950. In *Handbook of North American Indians. Volume 5. Arctic*, edited by D. Damas, pp. 622–639. Smithsonian Institution, Washington, DC.

Peterson, N., and B. Rigsby. 1998. Introduction. In *Customary Marine Tenure in Australia*, edited by N. Peterson and B. Rigsby, pp. 1–22. Oceania Monograph 48. University of Sydney, Sydney.

Pétillon, J.-M. 2008. First Evidence of a Whale-Bone Industry in the Western European Upper Paleolithic: Magdalenian Artifacts from Isturitz (Pyrénées-Atlantiques, France). *Journal of Human Evolution* 54(5):720–726.

Pétillon, J.-M. 2013. Circulation of Whale-Bone Artifacts in the Northern Pyrenees During the Late Upper Paleolithic. *Journal of Human Evolution* 65(5):525–543.

Pevnick, S. D. (editor). 2014. *Poseidon and the Sea: Myth, Cult, and Daily Life.* Tampa Museum of Art in association with D. Giles, London.

Pfeffer, M. T. 1995. Distribution and Design of Pacific Octopus Lures: The Hawaiian Octopus Lure in Regional Context. *Hawaiian Archaeology* 4:47–56.

Phillipps, W. J. 1948. Ika-whenua: The Mauri of the Whales on Mahia Peninsula. *Journal of the Polynesian Society* 57(1):41–45.

Piddington, R. 1932. Totemic System of the Karadjeri Tribe. *Oceania* 2(4):373–400.

Piggott, J. 1969. *Japanese Mythology.* Paul Hamlyn, London.

Pillsbury, J. 1996. The Thorny Oyster and the Origins of Empire: Implications of Recently Uncovered Spondylus Imagery from Chan, Peru. *Latin American Antiquity* 7(4):313–340.

Pinney, C. 2018. *The Waterless Sea: A Curious History of Mirages.* Reaktion, London.

Pinney, C. 2021. Representations: The Struggle for Maritime Empiricism; Optics and Mirage in the Arctic. In *A Cultural History of the Sea in the Age of Enlightenment*, Vol. 4, edited by M. Cohen, pp. 155–176. Bloomsbury Academic, London.

Plomley, N. J. B. (editor). 1966. *Friendly Mission: The Tasmanian Journals and Papers of George Augustus Robinson, 1829–1834.* Tasmanian Historical Research Association, Hobart.

Poggie, J. J., Jr., and C. Gersuny. 1972. Risk and Ritual: An Interpretation of Fishermen's Folklore in a New England Community. *Journal of American Folklore* 85(335):66–72.

Poggie, J. J., Jr., and R. B. Pollnac. 1988. Danger and Rituals of Avoidance Among New England Fishermen. *MAST: Maritime Anthropological Studies* 1(1):66–78.

Poggie, J. J., Jr., R. B. Pollnac, and C. Gersuny. 1976. Risk as a Basis for Taboos Among Fishermen in Southern New England. *Journal for the Scientific Study of Religion* 15(3):257–262.

Polehampton, A. 1862. *Kangaroo Land.* Richard Bentley, London.

Pollard, E. 2008. Inter-Tidal Causeways and Platforms of the 13th- to 16th-Century City-State of Kilwa Kisiwani, Tanzania. *International Journal of Nautical Archaeology* 37(1):98–114.

Pollard, T. 1999. The Drowned and the Saved: Archaeological Perspectives on the Sea as Grave. In *The Loved Body's Corruption: Archaeological Contributions to the Study of Human Mortality*, edited by J. Downes and T. Pollard, pp. 30–51. Cruithne, Glasgow.

Polunin, N. V. C. 1984. Do Traditional Marine "Reserves" Conserve? A View of Indonesian and New Guinean Evidence. In *Maritime Institutions of the Western Pacific*, edited by K. Ruddle and T. Akimichi, pp. 267–283. Senri Ethnological Studies 17. National Museum of Ethnology, Osaka.

Pontoppidan, E. 1755. *The Natural History of Norway.* A. Linde, London.

Porter, R. P. 1893. *Report on Population and Resources of Alaska at the Eleventh Census: 1890.* US Government Printing Office, Washington, DC.

Potts, D. T. 1990. *The Arabian Gulf in Antiquity, Vol. 1: From Prehistory to the Fall of the Achaemenid Empire.* Clarendon, Oxford.

Pouwer, J. 2000. "We-Humans" Betwixt and Between: A Guide to the Myths. In *Amoko: In the Beginning: Myths and Legends of the Asmat and Mimika Papuans*, edited by G. A. M. Offenberg and J. Pouwer, pp. 22–54. Crawford House, Adelaide.

Powell, A. W. B. 1958. The Canoes of Geelvink Bay, Dutch New Guinea. *Records of the Auckland Institute and Museum* 5(1/2):111–115.

Powell, E. A. 2020. Remembering the Shark Hunters. *Archaeology* 73(2):42–47.

Powell, G. E. J., and E. Magnusson. 1866. *Icelandic Legends (Collected by Jón Arnason)*. Longmans, Green, London.

Praet, I. 2015. *Animism and the Question of Life*. Routledge, London.

Prajudi, R. H. 2016. A Conversation with the Sea in Ancient Hinterland Architecture in Indonesia. In *International Seminar on Vernacular Settlements: Conversations with the Sea; People, Place and Ideas of Maritime Vernacular Settlements,* pp. 1–12. Universitas Hasanuddin, Makassar.

Prieto, G. 2018. The Temple of the Fishermen: Early Ceremonial Architecture at Gramalote, a Residential Settlement of the Second Millennium B.C., North Coast of Peru. *Journal of Field Archaeology* 43(3):200–221.

Prins, A. H. J. 1970. Maritime Art in an Islamic context: Oculus and Therion in Lamu Ships. *Mariner's Mirror* 56:327–339.

Pryor, F. 2001. *The Flag Fen Basin: Archaeology and Environment of a Fenland Landscape*. English Heritage, London.

Przyluski, J. 1931. Varuna, God of the Sea and the Sky. *Journal of the Royal Asiatic Society of Great Britain and Ireland* 3:613–622.

Puhvel, M. 1963. The Seal in the Folklore of Northern Europe. *Folklore* 74(1):326–333.

Pukui, M. K., S. Elbert, and E. Mookini. 1974. *Place Names of Hawaii*. University of Hawaiʻi Press, Honolulu.

Pulak, C. 1998. The Uluburun Shipwreck: An Overview. *International Journal of Nautical Archaeology* 27(3):188–224.

Pulsford, R. L. 1975 Ceremonial Fishing for Tuna by the Motu of Pari. *Oceania* 46(2):107–113.

Pulvertaft, D. 2018. The Colour Schemes of British Warship Figureheads, 1727–1900. *Mariner's Mirror* 104(2):192–210.

Pulvertaft, D. 2022. The Figurehead of HMS *Seringapatam*. *Mariner's Mirror* 108(4):469–471.

Pungetti, G. 2022. Seascape Contexts and Concepts. In *Routledge Handbook of Seascapes,* edited by G. Pungetti, pp. 3–22. Routledge, London.

Pykles, B. C., and J. S. Reeves. 2021. Hawaiian Latter-day Saints in the Utah Desert: The Negotiation of Identity at Iosepa. *Historical Archaeology* 55(4):501–510.

Qu, F. 2017. Ivory Versus Antler: A Reassessment of Binary Structuralism in the Study of Prehistoric Eskimo Cultures. *Arctic Anthropology* 54(1):90–109.

Quarcoopome, E. N. 1991. Self-Decoration and Religious Power in Dangme Culture. *African Arts* 24(3):56–65, 96.

Quarcoopome, N. O. 1994. Thresholds and Thrones: Morphology and Symbolism of Dangme Public Altars. *Journal of Religion in Africa* 24:339–357.

Quigley, C. 1955. Certain Considerations on the Origin and Diffusion of Oculi. *American Neptune* 15(3):191–198.

Quigley, C. 1958. The Origin and Diffusion of Oculi: A Rejoinder. *American Neptune* 18(1):25–58.

Quigley, K. 2021. Islands and Shores: The Pelagic Picturesque. In *A Cultural History of the Sea in the Age of Enlightenment*, Vol. 4, edited by M. Cohen, pp. 113–133. Bloomsbury Academic, London.

Quinn, J. 2014. Mythologizing the Sea: The Nordic Sea-Deity Rán. In *Nordic Mythologies: Interpretations, Intersections, and Institutions*, edited by T. R. Tangherlini, pp. 71–99. North Pinehurst, Berkeley.

Quinnell, M., and I. Miller. 2011. Torres Strait Islander Material Culture Collections in the Queensland Museum, 1873–2011. In *The Torres Strait Islands*, edited by Stephanie Kennard, Rebecca Mutch, and Michelle Ryan, pp. 221–249. Queensland Art Gallery / Gallery of Modern Art, Brisbane.

Raab, L. M., K. Bradford, and A. Yatsko. 1994. Advances in Southern Channel Islands Archaeology: 1983 to 1993. *Journal of California and Great Basin Anthropology* 16(2):243–270.

Raban, A., and Y. Kahanov. 2003. Clay Models of Phoenician Vessels in the Hecht Museum at the University of Haifa, Israel. *International Journal of Nautical Archaeology* 32(1):61–72.

Radcliffe-Brown, A. R. 1922. *The Andaman Islanders: A Study in Social Anthropology.* Cambridge University Press, Cambridge.

Radcliffe-Brown, A. R. 1926. The Rainbow-Serpent Myth of Australia. *Journal of the Royal Anthropological Institute of Great Britain and Ireland* 56:19–25.

Radcliffe-Brown, A. R. 1930. The Rainbow-Serpent Myth in South-East Australia. *Oceania* 1(3):342–347.

Radcliffe-Brown, A. R. 1958 [1939]. Taboo. In *Reader in Comparative Religion: An Anthropological Approach*, edited by W. A. Lessa and E. Z. Vogt, pp. 99–111. Row, Peterson, Evanston, Illinois.

Radić, I. 1991. Three More *Louteria* Finds in the Eastern Adriatic. *International Journal of Nautical Archaeology* 20(2):155–160.

Raffan, J. 2011. One World to Another. In *Bill Reid and the Haida Canoe*, edited by Martine J. Reid, pp. 135–145. Harbour Publishing, Madeira Park, British Columbia.

Rainey, F. G. 1947. The Whale Hunters of Tigara. *Anthropological Papers of the American Museum of Natural History* 41(2):231–283.

Ramos-Muñoz, J., J. J. Cantillo-Duarte, D. Bernal-Casasola, A. Barrena-Tocino, S. Domínguez-Bella, E. Vijande-Vila, I. Clemente-Conte, I. Gutiérrez-Zugasti, M. Soriguer-Escofet, and S. Almisas-Cruz. 2016. Early Use of Marine Resources by Middle/Upper Pleistocene Human Societies: The Case of Benzú Rockshelter (Northern Africa). *Quaternary International* 407:6–15.

Rankin, L. K. 2008. Un-Caching Hunter-Gatherer Culture in Labrador: From Daily Life to Long Term History. *North Atlantic Archaeology* 1:117–156.

Rappoport, A. S. 1928. *Superstitions of Sailors.* Stanley Paul, London.

Rasmussen, K. 1927. *Across Arctic America: Narrative of the Fifth Thule Expedition.* G. P. Putman's Sons, New York.

Rasmussen, K. 1929. *The Intellectual Culture of the Iglulik Eskimos: Report of the Fifth Thule Expedition, 1921–1924.* Vol. 7.1. Gyldendalske Boghandel, Nordisk Forlag, Copenhagen.

Rasmussen, K. 1931. *The Netsilik Eskimos: Social Life and Spiritual Culture; Report of the Fifth Thule Expedition, 1921–1924.* Vol. 8. Gyldendalske Boghandel, Nordisk Forlag, Copenhagen.

Raven, M. M. 1990. The Point of No Diminishing Returns: Hunting and Resource Decline on Boigu Island, Torres Strait. PhD dissertation, University of California, Davis.

Ravenstein, E. G. (editor). 1898. *A Journal of The First Voyage of Vasco da Gama, 1497–1499.* Hakluyt Society, London.

Read, T. W., with Gunditjmara. 2007. *Gunditjmara Country.* Hawker Brownlow Education, Heatherton, Victoria.

Redford, D. (editor). 2014. *Maritime History and Identity: The Sea and Culture in the Modern World.* I. B. Tauris, London.

Rediker, M. 1981. "Under the Banner of King Death": The Social World of Anglo-American Pirates, 1716 to 1726. *William and Mary Quarterly* 38(2):203–227.

Rediker, M. 1987. *Between the Devil and the Deep Blue Sea: Merchant Seamen, Pirates and the Anglo-American Maritime World, 1700–1750.* Cambridge University Press, Cambridge.

Reed, A., and I. Hames. 2023. *Myths and Legends of Fiji and Rotuma: Students Edition.* Reed Publishing, Auckland.

Reed, A. W. 1967. *Treasury of Maori Folklore.* A. H. and A. W. Reed, Wellington.

Reeves, R. R. 2002. The Origins and Character of "Aboriginal Subsistence" Whaling: A Global Review. *Mammal Review* 32(2):71–106.

Reid, J. L. 2015. *The Sea Is My Country: The Maritime World of the Makahs, an Indigenous Borderlands People.* Yale University Press, New Haven.

Reid, K. 2011. Ocean Funerals: The Sea and Victorian Cultures of Death. *Journal for Maritime Research* 13(1):37–54.

Reid, M. J. 2011. Homeward: Bill Reid and the Haida Canoe. In *Bill Reid and the Haida Canoe*, edited by M. J. Reid, pp. 41–126. Harbour Publishing, Madeira Park, British Columbia.

Renfrew, C. 1985. *The Archaeology of Cult: The Sanctuary at Phylakopi.* British School of Archaeology at Athens, London.

Resink, G. J. 1997. Kanjeng Ratu Kidul: The Second Divine Spouse of the Sultans of Ngayogyakarta. *Asian Folklore Studies* 56(2):313–316.

Revolon, S. 2018. Iridescence as Affordance: On Artefacts and Light Interference in the Renewal of Life Among the Owa (Eastern Solomon Islands). *Oceania* 88(1):31–40.

Rich, S. A. 2013. Ship Timber as Symbol? Dendro-Provenancing and Contextualizing Ancient Cedar Ship Remains from the Eastern Mediterranean / Near East. PhD dissertation, Katholieke Universiteit Leuven, Belgium.

Rich, S. A. 2021. *Shipwreck Hauntography: Underwater Ruins and the Uncanny.* Amsterdam University Press, Amsterdam.

Richards, R. 2012. *Head Hunters Black and White: Three Collectors in the Western Solomon Islands 1893 to 1914, and the Diary of Graham Officer, Collector of Museum Objects in the Solomon Islands in 1901 for Museum Victoria in Melbourne.* Paremata, Wellington.

Rick, T. C., and J. M. Erlandson (editors). 2008. *Human Impacts on Ancient Marine Ecosystems: A Global Perspective.* University of California Press, Berkeley.

Ricklis, R. A. 2012a. Chronology at Buckeye Knoll. In *Archaeology and Bioarchaeology of the Buckeye Knoll Site (41VT98), Victoria County, Texas: Final Report, Vol. 1*, edited by R. A. Ricklis, R. A. Weinstein, and D. C. Wells, pp. 147–161. Coastal Environments, Corpus Christi, Texas.

Ricklis, R. A. 2012b. Mortuary Artifacts. In *Archaeology and Bioarchaeology of the Buckeye Knoll Site (41VT98), Victoria County, Texas: Final Report, Vol. 2*, edited by R. A. Ricklis, R. A. Weinstein, and D. C. Wells, pp. 591–653. Coastal Environments, Corpus Christi, Texas.

Ricklis, R. A. 2012c. Sociocultural Implications. In *Archaeology and Bioarchaeology of the Buckeye Knoll Site (41VT98), Victoria County, Texas: Final Report, Vol. 2*, edited by R. A. Ricklis, R. A. Weinstein, and D. C. Wells, pp. 655–677. Coastal Environments, Corpus Christi, Texas.

Ridpath, I., and W. Tirion. 2006. *The Monthly Sky Guide*. 7th ed. Cambridge University Press, Cambridge.

Riesenberg, S. H. 1972. The Organisation of Navigational Knowledge on Puluwat. *Journal of the Polynesian Society* 81(1):19–56.

Rigsby, B., and A. Chase. 1998. The Sandbeach People and Dugong Hunters of Eastern Cape York Peninsula: Property in Land and Sea Country. In *Customary Marine Tenure in Australia*, edited by N. Peterson and B. Rigsby, pp. 192–218. University of Sydney Oceania Publications, Sydney.

Rinder, F. 1895. Fragments of Caithness Folk-Lore. *Scottish Review* 26:49–63.

Ririmasse, M. N. R. 2010. Boat Symbolism and Social Identity in the Southeast Moluccas. *Naditira Widya* 4(2):245–256.

Ritvo, H. 1997. *The Platypus and the Mermaid and Other Figments of the Classifying Imagination*. Harvard University Press, Cambridge, Massachusetts.

Rivard, D. A. 2009. *Blessing the World: Ritual and Lay Piety in Medieval Religion*. Catholic University of America Press, Washington, DC.

Rix, D., and C. Cormick. 2024. *Warra Wai: How Indigenous Australians Discovered Captain Cook and What They Tell About the Coming of the Ghost People*. Scribner, Cammeray, New South Wales, Australia.

Roberts, A., and C. Mountford. 1969. *The Dawn of Time: Australian Aboriginal Myths*. Rigby, Adelaide.

Roberts, A., and C. Mountford. 1971. *The First Sunrise: Australian Aboriginal Myths*. Rigby, Adelaide.

Robins, R. P., E. C. Stock, and D. S. Trigger. 1998. Saltwater People, Saltwater Country: Geomorphological, Anthropological and Archaeological Investigations of the Coastal Lands in the Southern Gulf of Carpentaria Country of Queensland. *Memoirs of the Queensland Museum Cultural Heritage Series* 1(1):75–125.

Robinson, R., P. Mumbulla, and B. Bancroft. 1997. *The Whalers*. Angus and Robinson, Sydney.

Rodgers, S. 1984. Feminine Power at Sea. *Royal Anthropological Institute News* 64:2–4.

Rodrigues, A. S. L., L. K. Horwitz, S. Monsarrat, and A. Charpentier. 2016. Ancient Whale Exploitation in the Mediterranean: Species Matters. *Antiquity* 90(352):928–938.

Roe, M. 2022. Community Voices and the Capture of Seascape Values. In *Routledge Handbook of Seascapes*, edited by G. Pungetti, pp. 492–506. Routledge, London.

Roe, P. G. 1991. The Petroglyphs of Maisabel: A Study in Methodology. In *Proceedings of the Twelfth Congress of the International Association for Caribbean Archaeology*, edited by L. S. Robinson, pp. 317–370. Cayenne, French Guiana.

Roelse, A., H. W. Granger, and J. W. Graham. 1975. *The Adjustment of the Australian Levelling Survey 1970–1971*. Technical Report 12. 2nd ed. Department of Minerals and Energy, Canberra, Australia.

Rogers, A. J. 2024. Aquaculture in the Ancient World: Ecosystem Engineering, Domesticated Landscapes, and the First Blue Revolution. *Journal of Archaeological Research* 32(3):427–491.

Rogers, D. B. 1929. *Prehistoric Man of the Santa Barbara Coast*. Santa Barbara Museum of Natural History, Santa Barbara, California.

Roldán, A. L. 1992. Looking at Anthropology from a Biological Point of View: A. C. Haddon's Metaphors on Anthropology. *History of the Human Sciences* 5(4):21–32.

Roller, D. W. 2006. *Through the Pillars of Herakles: Greco-Roman Exploration of the Atlantic*. Routledge, New York.

Romero Recio, M. 2021. Religious Practices at Sea in Antiquity. In *A Cultural History of the Sea in Antiquity*, Vol. 1, edited by M.-C. Beaulieu, pp. 43–58. Bloomsbury Academic, London.

Romm, J. S. 1992. *The Edges of the Earth in Ancient Thought: Geography, Exploration, and Fiction*. Princeton University Press, Princeton.

Roos Jacobs, I., L. M. Brady, J. Bradley, and A. Kearney. 2025. The Seascape in Stone: Archaeological and Cosmological Assessment of Maritime Motifs in Yanyuwa "Rock Art." *Journal of Social Archaeology* 25(2):179–202.

Rosen, N. 1989. Chalk Iconography in Olokun Worship. *African Arts* 22(3):44–53, 88.

Ross, K., and M. Oxenham. 2017. The Distribution of Unworked Molluscs, with Special Reference to Unionidae (Freshwater Mussels), in Mainland Southeast Asian Mortuary Contexts. *Journal of Indo-Pacific Archaeology* 41:1–12.

Ross, M. 1994. The Knife Against the Wave: A Uniquely Irish Legend of the Supernatural? *Folklore* 105(1–2): 83–88.

Ross, M. 1998. Anchors in a Three-Decker World. *Folklore* 109(1–2):63–75.

Rostworowski de Diez Canseco, M. 1977. Coastal Fishermen, Merchants, and Artisans in Pre-Hispanic Peru. In *The Sea in the Pre-Columbian World*, edited by E. P. Benson, pp. 167–186. Dumbarton Oaks Research Library and Collections, Trustees for Harvard University, Washington, DC.

Roth, W. E. 1903. *Superstition, Magic, and Medicine*. North Queensland Ethnography Bulletin 5. Government Printer, Brisbane.

Roth, W. E. 1907. North Queensland Ethnography Bulletin 9: Burial Ceremonies, and Disposal of the Dead. *Records of the Australian Museum* 6(5):365–403.

Roughsey, D. 1971. *Moon and Rainbow: The Autobiography of an Aboriginal*. A. H. and A. W. Reed, Sydney.

Rouja, P. M. 1998. Fishing for Culture: Toward an Aboriginal Theory of Marine Resource Use Among the Bardi Aborigines of One Arm Point, Western Australia. PhD dissertation, Durham University.

Rowe, C., I. J. McNiven, B. David, T. Richards, and M. Leavesley. 2013. Holocene Pollen Records from Caution Bay, Southern Mainland Papua New Guinea. *Holocene* 23(8):1130–1142.

Rowe, T. 1763. Pretences of Witchcraft to Control Winds. *Gentleman's Magazine*, January 33:12–15.

Rowland, M. J., and S. Ulm. 2011. Indigenous Fish Traps and Weirs of Queensland. *Queensland Archaeological Research* 14:1–58.

Royal Australian Navy. 1986. *HMAS Vampire Decommissioning Service.* 4-page program.

Rozwadowski, H. M. 1996. Fathoming the Ocean: Discovery and Exploration of the Deep Sea, 1840–1880. PhD dissertation, University of Pennsylvania.

Rozwadowski, H. M. 2005. *Fathoming the Ocean: Discovery and Exploration of the Deep Sea.* Belknap Press of Harvard University Press, Cambridge, Massachusetts.

Rozwadowski, H. M. 2021. Travelers: Vertical and Horizontal Voyaging on and in the Nonhuman Ocean. In *A Cultural History of the Sea in the Global Age*, Vol. 6, edited by F. Torma, pp. 139–159. Bloomsbury Academic, London.

Ruddle, K., and T. Akimichi. 1984. Introduction. In *Maritime Institutions of the Western Pacific*, edited by K. Ruddle and T. Akimichi, pp. 1–9. Senri Ethnological Studies 17. National Museum of Ethnology, Osaka.

Rudolf, W. 2011. The Spiritual Islescape of the Anglo-Saxons. In *The Sea and Englishness in the Middle Ages: Maritime Narratives, Identity and Culture*, edited by S. I. Sobecki, pp. 31–57. D. S. Brewer, Cambridge.

Ruitenbeek, K. 1999. Mazu, the Patroness of Sailors, in Chinese Pictorial Art. *Artibus Asiae* 58(3/4):281–329.

Russell, A. 1909. Orkney Folk-Lore. *Notes and Queries* Series 10, 12(312):483–484.

Russell, J. B. 1989. The Flat Error: The Modern Distortion of Medieval Geography. *Mediaevalia* 15:337–353.

Russell, J. B. 2001. *Inventing the Flat Earth: Columbus and Modern Historians.* Praeger, New York.

Russell, L. 2012. *Roving Mariners: Australian Aboriginal Whalers and Sealers in the Southern Oceans, 1790–1870.* State University of New York Press, Albany.

Russell, N. 2012. *Social Zooarchaeology: Humans and Animals in Prehistory.* Cambridge University Press, Cambridge.

Ryan, A. 2012. *Where Land Meets Sea: Coastal Explorations of Landscape, Representation and Spatial Experience.* Ashgate, Surrey, England.

Rybníček, M., P. Kočár, B. Muigg, J. Peška, R. Sedláček, W. Tegel, and T. Kolář. 2020. World's Oldest Dendrochronologically Dated Archaeological Wood Construction. *Journal of Archaeological Science* 115:105082.

Rybska, E. 2014. Symbolism of Shells in World Culture. *Edukacja biologiczna i środowiskowa* 1:19–28.

Sabo, G., III, and D. R. Sabo. 1985. Belief Systems and the Ecology of Sea Mammal Hunting Among the Baffinland Eskimo. *Arctic Anthropology* 22(2):77–86.

Sackey, J. A. 2019. *Marine Kingdom: What You Should Know Overcoming Satanic Kingdom.* Fresh Fire Worldwide Ministries, Merrifield, Virginia.

Safer, J. F., and F. M. Gill. 1982. *Spirals from the Sea: An Anthropological Look at Shells.* Clarkson N. Potter, New York.

Sahlins, M. 1981. *Historical Metaphors and Mythical Realities: Structure in the Early History of the Sandwich Islands Kingdom*. University of Michigan Press, Ann Arbor.

Saladin d'Anglure, B. 1984. Inuit of Quebec. In *Handbook of North American Indians, Vol. 5: Arctic*, edited by D. Damas, pp. 476–507. Smithsonian Institution, Washington, DC.

Salls, R. A., L. M. Raab, and K. G. Bradford. 1993. A San Clemente Island Perspective on Coastal Residential Structures and the Emergence of Sedentism. *Journal of California and Great Basin Anthropology* 15(2):176–194.

Salm, S. J., and T. Falola. 2002. *Culture and Customs of Ghana*. Greenwood, Westport, Connecticut.

Salmen-Hartley, J., and I. McKechnie. 2023. An Examination of Indigenous Halibut Fishing Technology on the Northwest Coast of North America. *Arctic Anthropology* 59(1):87–105.

Salmi, A.-K., T. Äikäs, and S. Lipkin. 2011. Animating Rituals at Sámi Sacred Sites in Northern Finland. *Journal of Social Archaeology* 11(2):212–235.

Salvador, R. B., and B. M. Tomotani. 2014. The Kraken: When Myth Encounters Science. *História, Ciências, Saúde-Manguinhos* 21(3):971–994.

Salvatori, S. 2007. The Prehistoric Graveyard of Ra's al-Hamra 5, Muscat, Sultanate of Oman, Part 1: 1981–1985 Excavations Report. *Journal of Oman Studies* 14:5–57.

Samper-Carro, S. C., S. O'Connor, Mahirta, S. Kealy, and C. Shipton. 2022. Talking Dead: New Burials from Tron Bon Lei (Alor Island, Indonesia) Inform on the Evolution of Mortuary Practices from the Terminal Pleistocene to the Holocene in Southeast Asia. *PloS ONE* 17(8):e0267635.

Samson, A. V. M. 2006. Offshore Finds from the Bronze Age in North-Western Europe: The Shipwreck Scenario Revisited. *Oxford Journal of Archaeology* 25(4):371–388.

Samson, J. 2023. Blue Continent to Blue Pacific. In *The Cambridge History of the Pacific Ocean, Vol. 2: The Pacific Ocean Since 1800*, edited by A. P. Hattori and J. Samson, pp. 132–163. Cambridge University Press, Cambridge.

Sanderson, S. 1996. Introduction. In *The People of the Sea: Celtic Tales of the Seal-Folk*, by D. Thomson, pp. vii–ix. Canongate, Edinburgh.

Sanderson, S. F. 1973. Singing for a Fish: A Study in Custom and Belief. *Béaloideas* 39/41:287–297.

Sapir, E. 1959. Indian Legends from Vancouver Island. *Journal of American Folklore* 72(284):106–114.

Sarkar, S. R. 1974. Socio-Economic Aspects of Onge Fishing. *Anthropos* 69(3/4):568–589.

Sather, C. A. 1997. *The Bajau Laut: Adaptation, History, and Fate in a Maritime Fishing Society of Southeastern Sabah*. Oxford University Press, Kuala Lumpur.

Savelle, J. M. 1997. The Role of Architectural Utility in the Formation of Zooarchaeological Whale Bone Assemblages. *Journal of Archaeological Science* 24(10):869–885.

Savelle, J. M. 2005. The Development of Indigenous Whaling: Prehistoric and Historic Contexts. In *Indigenous Use and Management of Marine Resources*, edited by N. Kishigami and J. M. Savelle, pp. 53–58. Senri Ethnological Studies 67. National Museum of Ethnology, Osaka.

Savelle, J. M., and N. Kishigami. 2013. Anthropological Research on Whaling: Prehistoric, Historic and Current Contexts. In *Anthropological Studies of Whaling*, edited by N.

Kishigami, H. Hamaguchi, and J. N. Savelle, pp. 1–48. Senri Ethnological Studies 84. National Museum of Ethnology, Osaka.

Savelle, J. M., and A. Vadnais. 2011. Releasing the Soul: Zooarchaeological Evidence for a Whale Cult Among the Prehistoric Thule Inuit in Canada. *Bulletin of the National Museum of Ethnology* 36(1):93–112.

Scarre, C. 2002. A Pattern of Islands: The Neolithic Monuments of North-West Brittany. *European Journal of Archaeology* 5(1):24–41.

Schneider, K. 2012. *Saltwater Sociality: A Melanesian Island Ethnography.* Berghahn, New York.

Scoresby-Jackson, R. E. 1861. *The Life of William Scoresby.* T. Nelson and Sons, London.

Scott, C. 1989. Knowledge Construction Among Cree Hunters: Metaphors and Literal Understanding. *Journal de la Société des Américanistes* 75:193–208.

Scott, C., and M. Mulrennan. 1999. Land and Sea Tenure at Erub, Torres Strait: Property, Sovereignty and the Adjudication of Cultural Continuity. *Oceania* 70(2):146–176.

Scott, C. H. 2004. "Our Feet Are on the Land, but Our Hands Are in the Sea": Knowing and Caring for Marine Territory at Erub, Torres Strait. In *Woven Histories, Dancing Lives: Torres Strait Islander Identity, Culture and History*, edited by R. Davis, pp. 259–270. Aboriginal Studies Press, Canberra.

Scott, M. W. 2013. "Heaven on Earth" or Satan's "Base" in the Pacific? Internal Christian Politics in the Dialogic Construction of the Makiran Underground Army. In *Christian Politics in Oceania*, edited by M. Tomlinson and D. McDougall, pp.49–77. Berghahn, Oxford.

Scott, M. W. 2021. How the Missionary Got His *Mana*: Charles Elliot Fox and the Power of Name-Exchange in Solomon Islands. *Oceania* 91(1):106–127.

Sébillot, P. 1882. *Traditions et superstitions de la Haute-Bretagne.* Maisonneuve, Paris.

Seely, P. H. 1991. The Firmament and the Water Above, Part 1: The Meaning of *Raqia* in Gen 1:6–8. *Westminster Theological Journal* 53:227–240.

Seely, P. H. 1992. The Firmament and the Water Above, Part 2: The Meaning of "The Water Above the Firmament" in Gen 1:6–8. *Westminster Theological Journal* 54:31–47.

Seersholm, F. V., M. W. Pedersen, M. J. Søe, H. Shokry, S. S. T. Mak, A. Ruter, M. Raghavan, W. Fitzhugh, K. H. Kjær, E. Willerslev, et al. 2016. DNA Evidence of Bowhead Whale Exploitation by Greenlandic Paleo-Inuit 4,000 Years Ago. *Nature Communications* 7:13389.

Sehasseh, E. M., P. Fernandez, S. Kuhn, M. Stiner, S. Mentzer, D. Colarossi, A. Clark, F. Lanoe, M. Pailes, D. Hoffmann, et al. 2021. Early Middle Stone Age Personal Ornaments from Bizmoune Cave, Essaouira, Morocco. *Science Advances* 7(39):eabi8620.

Sekerci, Y., and S. Petrovskii. 2015. Mathematical Modelling of Plankton–Oxygen Dynamics Under the Climate Change. *Bulletin of Mathematical Biology* 77:2325–2353.

Seligmann, C. G. 1910. *The Melanesians of British New Guinea.* Cambridge University Press, Cambridge.

Semple, E. C. 1911. *Influences of Geographic Environment on the Basis of Ratzel's System of Anthropo-Geography.* Henry Holt, New York.

Semple, E. C. 1927. The Templed Promontories of the Ancient Mediterranean. *Geographical Review* 17(3):353–386.

Shaw, J., C. L. Amos, D. A. Greenberg, C. T. O'Reilly, D. R. Parrott, and E. Patton. 2010. Catastrophic Tidal Expansion in the Bay of Fundy, Canada. *Canadian Journal of Earth Sciences* 47(8):1079–1091.

Shearar, C. 2000. *Understanding Northwest Coast Art: A Guide to Crests, Beings and Symbols.* Douglas and McIntyre, University of Washington Press, Seattle.

Shepard, K. 1940. *The Fish-Tailed Monster in Greek and Etruscan Art.* Privately printed, New York.

Sheppard, P. J. 2021. *Tomoko*: Raiding Canoes of the Western Solomon Islands. *Technical Reports of the Australian Museum Online* 34:231–244.

Sheppard, P. J., and R. Walter. 2014. Shell Valuables and History in Roviana and Vella Lavella. In *The Things We Value: Culture and History in Solomon Islands*, edited by B. Burt and L. Bolton, pp. 32–45. Sean Kingston, Canon Pyon.

Sheppard, P. J., R. Walter, and T. Nagaoka. 2000. The Archaeology of Head-Hunting in Roviana Lagoon, New Georgia. *Journal of the Polynesian Society* 109(1):9–37.

Sherbondy, J. 1998. Andean Irrigation in History. In *Searching for Equity: Conceptions of Justice and Equity in Peasant Irrigation*, edited by R. Boelens and G. Davila, pp. 210–214. Royal Van Gorcum, Assen.

Shlomowitz, R., and J. McDonald. 1991. Babies At Risk on Immigrant Voyages to Australia in the Nineteenth Century. *Economic History Review* 44(1):86–101.

Shoemaker, N. 2014. *Living with Whales: Documents and Oral Histories of Native New England Whaling History.* University of Massachusetts Press, Amherst.

Sibeko, O. 2020. Bottled Seawater: A Sea Inland. Master of Fine Arts dissertation, University of the Witwatersrand, Johannesburg, South Africa.

Silver, C. 1987. "East of the Sun and West of the Moon": Victorians and Fairy Brides. *Tulsa Studies in Women's Literature* 6(2):283–298.

Silverblatt, I. 1987. *Moon, Sun, and Witches: Gender Ideologies and Class in Inca and Colonial Peru.* Princeton University Press, Princeton.

Simek, R. 1996. *Heaven and Earth in the Middle Ages: The Physical World before Columbus.* Translated by A. Hall. Boydell, Woodbridge.

Simon, E. 2014. Poseidon in Ancient Greek Religion, Myth, and Art. In *Poseidon and the Sea: Myth, Cult, and Daily Life*, edited by S. D. Pevnick, pp. 37–49. Tampa Museum of Art in association with D. Giles, London.

Simonett, H. 2016. Of Human and Non-Human Birds: Indigenous Music Making and Sentient Ecology in Northwestern Mexico. In *Current Directions in Ecomusicology: Music, Nature, Environment*, edited by A. S. Allen and K. Dawe, pp. 99–108. Routledge, New York.

Simpson, E. B. 1908. *Folk Lore in Lowland Scotland.* J. M. Dent, London.

Simpson, P. 2012. *Guidebook to the Constellations: Telescopic Sights, Tales and Myths.* Springer, New York.

Singh, N. P. 2003. *With the Gods and the Sea: The True Story of a Family's Survival in the Pacific.* Verand, Blackheath, New South Wales, Australia.

Skaarup, J. 1995 Stone-Age Burials in Boats. In *The Ship as Symbol in Prehistoric and Medieval Scandinavia*, edited by O. Crumlin-Pedersen and B. M. Thye, pp. 51–58. Studies in Archaeology and History. National Museum, Copenhagen.

Skeat, W. W. 1900. *Malay Magic: Being an Introduction to the Folklore and Popular Religion of the Malay Peninsula*. Macmillan, London.

Skelly, R., B. David, I. J. McNiven, and B. Barker. 2011. The Ritual Dugong Bone Mounds of Koey Ngurtai, Torres Strait, Australia: Investigating Their Construction. *International Journal of Osteoarchaeology* 21:32–54.

Skinner, H. D. 1930. Review of *Pacific Island Records: Fish Hooks* by Harry Beasley. *American Anthropologist* 32(2):309–312.

Skoglund, P. 2008. Stone Ships: Continuity and Change in Scandinavian Prehistory. *World Archaeology* 40(3):390–406.

Small, C., and R. J. Nicholls. 2003. A Global Analysis of Human Settlement in Coastal Zones. *Journal of Coastal Research* 19(3):584–599.

Smidt, D. 2006. Korwar area. In *Shadows of New Guinea: Art from the Great Island of Oceania in the Barbier-Mueller Collections*, edited by P. Peltier and F. Morin, pp. 30–49, 393–398. Musée Barbier-Mueller, Geneva.

Smith, A. B., and J. Kinahan. 1984. The Invisible Whale. *World Archaeology* 16(1):89–97.

Smith, H. I. 1909. Archeological Remains on the Coast of Northern British Columbia and Southern Alaska. *American Anthropologist* 11(4):595–600.

Smith, I. 2007. Metal Pa Kahawai—Post-Contact Fishing Lure Form in Northern New Zealand. In *Vastly Ingenious: The Archaeology of Pacific Material Culture in Honour of Janet M. Davidson*, edited by A. Anderson, K. Green, and F. Leach, pp. 69–78. Otago University Press, Dunedin.

Smith, K. L. 1995. Tom and Ellen Lopp and the Natives of Wales, 1890–1902. *Alaskan History* 10(2):36–46.

Smith, M. 1996. *Bunyips and Bigfoots: In Search of Australia's Mystery Animals*. Millennium, Alexandria, New South Wales.

Smith, M. E. (editor). 1977. *Those Who Live from the Sea*. West Publishing, St. Paul.

Smith, R. 1991. *One Foot in the Sea*. John Donald, Edinburgh.

Smyth, D. 1990. Aboriginal Maritime Culture in the Cairns Section of the Great Barrier Reef Marine Park. Unpublished report to the Great Barrier Reef Marine Park Authority, Cairns, Australia.

Smyth, G. 2023. *Serpent, Siren, Maelstrom and Myth: Sea Stories and Folktales from Around the World*. British Library, London.

Sognnes, K. 1994. Ritual Landscapes: Toward a Reinterpretation of Stone Age Rock Art in Trøndelag, Norway. *Norwegian Archaeological Review* 27(1):29–50.

Somerville, A. T. P. 2017. Where Oceans Come From. *Comparative Literature* 69(1):25–31.

Sonne, B. 1986. Toornaarsuk, An Historical Proteus. *Arctic Anthropology* 23(1/2):199–219.

Southon, M., and the Kaurareg Tribal Elders 1998. The Sea of Waubin: The Kaurareg and Their Marine Environment. In *Customary Marine Tenure in Australia*, edited by N. Peterson and B. Rigsby, pp. 219–229. University of Sydney Oceania Publications, Sydney.

Spencer, M. 1992. The Wreck of the *Catterthun*. *Australian Geographic* 11:100–115.

Spencer, R. F. 1959. *The North Alaskan Eskimo: A Study in Ecology and Society*. Smithsonian Institution Bureau of American Ethnology Bulletin 171. US Government Printing Office, Washington, DC.

Spooner, B. C. 1961. Cloud Ships over Cornwall. *Folklore* 72(1):323–329.

Spriggs, M. 1986. Landscape, Land Use, and Political Transformation in Southern Melanesia. In *Island Societies: Archaeological Approaches to Evolution and Transformation*, edited by P. V. Kirch, pp. 6–19. Cambridge University Press, Cambridge.

Stacey, N. 2007. *Boats to Burn: Bajo Fishing Activity in the Australian Fishing Zone.* Australian National University Press, Canberra.

Stair, J. B. n.d. [c. 1897]. *Old Samoa or Flotsam and Jetsam from the Pacific Ocean.* Religious Tract Society, Oxford.

Staley, D. P., and O. K. Mason. 2004. A Punuk Whale Bone Grave from Sivuqaq, St. Lawrence Island: Evidence of High Social Standing, AD 775–1020. *Alaska Journal of Anthropology* 2(1–2):126–136.

Stallard, A. J. 2010. Origins of the Idea of Antipodes: Errors, Assumptions, and a Bare Few Facts. *Terrae Incognitae* 42(1):34–51.

Stammers, M. 2004. *End of Voyages: The Afterlife of a Ship.* Tempus, Gloucestershire.

Stanbury, P., and J. Clegg. 1996. *A Field Guide to Aboriginal Rock Engravings with Special Reference to Those Around Sydney.* Oxford University Press, Oxford.

Standen, V. G., B. T. Arriaza, and C. M. Santoro. 1997. External Auditory Exostosis in Prehistoric Chilean Populations: A Test of the Cold Water Hypothesis. *American Journal of Physical Anthropology* 103(1):119–129.

Starkey, L. J. 2017. Why Sea Monsters Surround the Northern Lands: Olaus Magnus's Conception of Water. *Preternature: Critical and Historical Studies on the Preternatural* 6(1):31–62.

Stasch, R. 1996. Killing as Reproductive Agency: Dugong, Pigs, and Humanity Among the Kiwai, Circa 1900. *Anthropos* 91(4/6):359–379.

St. Clair, S. 1971. *Folklore of the Ulster People.* Mercier, Cork.

St. Claire, D. E. 1991. Barkley Sound Tribal Territories. In *Between Ports Alberni and Renfrew: Notes on Westcoast Peoples*, edited by E. Y. Arima, D. St. Claire, L. Clamhouse, J. Edgar, C. Jones, and J. Thomas, pp. 13–202. Canadian Museum of Civilization, Mercury Series, Canadian Ethnology Service Paper 121. Ottawa.

Steenstrup, J. 1857. Oplysninger om Atlanterhavets colossale Blaeksprutter. *Førhandlinger ved de Skandinaviske Naturforskeres* 7:182–185.

Steffian, A. F., M. E. Odell, and P. G. Saltonstall. 2023. Cupules and Cut Lines: An Expanded View of Kodiak Alutiiq Petroglyphs. *Alaska Journal of Anthropology* 21(1&2):1–23.

Steinberg, P. E. 2001. *The Social Construction of the Ocean.* Cambridge University Press, Cambridge.

Stensrud, A. B. 2020. Sentient Springs and Sources of Life: Water, Climate Change and World-Making Practices in the Andes. In *Sacred Waters: A Cross-Cultural Compendium of Hallowed Springs and Holy Wells*, edited by C. Ray, pp. 368–377. Routledge, London.

Stewart, D. J. 2005. Burial at Sea: Separating and Placing the Dead During the Age of Sail. *Mortality* 10(4):276–285.

Stewart, D. J. 2007. Gravestones and Monuments in the Maritime Cultural Landscape: Research Potential and Preliminary Interpretations. *International Journal of Nautical Archaeology* 36(1): 112–124.

Stewart, D. J. 2011. *The Sea Their Graves: An Archaeology of Death and Remembrance in Maritime Culture*. University of Florida Press, Gainesville.

Stewart, H. 1977. *Indian Fishing: Early Methods on the Northwest Coast*. University of Washington Press, Seattle.

Stojanovic, V. 2015. The Kilnaruane High Cross: Iconography, Site, and Potential Pilgrimage Round in Bantry, County Cork. MA dissertation, University of Guelph, Ontario.

Stow, D. 2017. *Oceans: A Very Short Introduction*. Oxford University Press, Oxford.

Strasser, T. F., C. Runnels, K. Wegmann, E. Panagopoulou, F. McCoy, C. Digregorio, P. Karkanas, and N. Thompson. 2011. Dating Palaeolithic Sites in Southwestern Crete, Greece. *Journal of Quaternary Science* 26(5):553–560.

Strauss, A. E. 1987. Magic and Ritual on the Open Ocean. *Archaeology of Eastern North America* 15:125–136.

Streuding, J. H. 2014. Success at Sea: Maritime Votive Offerings and Naval Dedications in Antiquity. Master's dissertation, Texas A&M University, College Station.

Stringer, C. B., J. C. Finlayson, R. Nick, E. Barton, Y. Fernández-Jalvo, I. Cáceres, R. C. Sabin, E. J. Rhodes, A. P. Currant, J. Rodríguez-Vidal, et al. 2008. Neanderthal Exploitation of Marine Mammals in Gibraltar. *Proceedings of the National Academy of Sciences* 105(38):14319–14324.

Strongman, L. 2008. "When Earth and Sky Almost Meet": The Conflict Between Traditional Knowledge and Modernity in Polynesian Navigation. *Journal of World Anthropology: Occasional Papers* 3(2):48–110.

Stuhlfauth, G. 1942. Das schiff als symbol der altchristlichen kunst. *Rivista di archeologia cristiana* 19:111–141.

Suby, J. A., and R. A. Guichón. 2014. General Considerations About the Bioarchaeological Contexts in Patagonian Coast Shell Middens. In *The Cultural Dynamics of Shell-Matrix Sites*, edited by M. Roksandic, S. M. de Souza, S. Eggers, M. Burchell, and D. Klokler, pp. 189–196. University of New Mexico Press, Albuquerque.

Sudo, K., O. Hoson, K. Ishigaki, A. Nakamori, A. Shimabukuro, S. Nakagun, Y. Taishi, R. Masuda, and N. Ohtaishi. 2015. Historical Decrease of the Dugong Population and Its Management Vision Around the Ryukyu Archipelago, Japan. In *IWMC 2015 Abstracts: Vth International Wildlife Management Congress, July 26–30 2015, Sapporo, Japan*, p. 237.

Sullivan, P. 1998. Salt Water, Fresh Water and Yawuru Social Organisation. In *Customary Marine Tenure in Australia*, edited by N. Peterson and B. Rigsby, pp. 96–108. Oceania Monograph 48. University of Sydney, Sydney.

Swanton, J. R. 1905. *Part 1: The Haida of Queen Charlotte Islands*. Memoirs of the American Museum of Natural History 8. E. J. Brill, Leiden and G. E. Stechert, London.

Swanton, J. R. 1909. *Tlingit Myths and Texts*. Smithsonian Institution Bureau of American Ethnology, Bulletin 39. US Government Printing Office, Washington, DC.

Swinton, N. 1985. The Inuit Sea Goddess. MA dissertation, Department of Art History, Concordia University, Montreal, Quebec.

Symmons-Symonolewicz, K. 1960. The Origin of Malinowski's Theory of Magic. *Polish Review* 5(4):36–44.

Synge, J. M. 1907. *The Aran Islands*. Maunsel, Dublin; Elkin Mathews, London.

Szabados, M. 2008. Understanding Sea Level Change. *ACSM Bulletin* 236:10–14.

Szabó, K. A., P. Piper, and G. Barker. 2008. Sailing Between Worlds: The Symbolism of Death in Northwest Borneo. In *Islands of Inquiry: Colonisation, Seafaring and the Archaeology of Maritime Landscapes*, edited by G. Clark, F. Leach, and S. O'Connor, pp. 149–169. Australian National University Press, Canberra.

Szabo, V. 2018. Northern Seas, Marine Monsters, and Perceptions of the Premodern North Atlantic in the Longue Durée. In *Visions of North in Premodern Europe*, edited by D. Jorgensen, and V. Langum, pp. 145–182. Brepols, Turnhout, Belgium.

Taçon, P. S. C., S. K. May, R. Lamilami, F. McKeague, I. G. Johnston, A. Jalandoni, D. Wesley, I. D. Sanz, L. M. Brady, D. Wright, and J. Goldhahn. 2020. Maliwawa Figures—A Previously Undescribed Arnhem Land Rock Art Style. *Australian Archaeology* 86(3):208–225.

Taçon, P. S. C., M. Wilson, and C. Chippindale. 1996. Birth of the Rainbow Serpent in Arnhem Land Rock Art and Oral History. *Archaeology in Oceania* 31(3):103–124.

Tambiah, S. J. 1983. On Flying Witches and Flying Canoes: The Coding of Male and Female Values. In *The Kula: New Perspectives on Massim Exchange*, edited by J. W. Leach and E. Leach, pp. 171–200. Cambridge University Press, Cambridge.

Tambiah, S. J. 1990. *Magic, Science, Religion, and the Scope of Rationality.* Cambridge University Press, Cambridge.

Tanner, A. 1979. *Bringing Home Animals: Religious Ideology and Mode of Production of the Mistassini Cree Hunters.* E. Hurst, London.

Tape, W. 1985. The Topology of Mirages. *Scientific American* 252(6):120–129.

Taranto, T., D. Jacobs, and B. Long. 1997. *Torres Strait Atlas.* CSIRO, Cleveland.

Tarlow, S. 2011. *Ritual, Belief and the Dead in Early Modern Britain and Ireland.* Cambridge University Press, Cambridge.

Taube, K. A. 2010. Where Earth and Sky Meet: The Sea in Ancient and Contemporary Maya Cosmology. In *Fiery Pool: The Maya and the Mythic Sea*, edited by D. Finamore and S. D. Houston, pp. 202–219. Peabody Essex Museum and Yale University Press, New Haven.

Taylor, D. A. 1992. *Documenting Maritime Folklore: An Introductory Guide.* Publications of the American Folklife Centre 18. Library of Congress, Washington, DC.

Taylor, J. G. 1984. Historical Ethnography of the Labrador Coast. In *Handbook of North American Indians, Vol. 5: Arctic*, edited by D. Damas, pp. 508–521. Smithsonian Institution, Washington, DC.

Taylor, J. G. 1985. The Arctic Whale Cult in Labrador. *Études Inuit Studies* (1985):121–132.

Taylor, L. 1990. The Rainbow Serpent as Visual Metaphor in Western Arnhem Land. *Oceania* 60(4):329–344.

Taylor, R. 1855. *Te Ika a Maui, or New Zealand and its Inhabitants, Illustrating the Origin, Manners, Customs, Mythology, Religion, Rites, Songs, Proverbs, Fables, and Language of the Natives. Together with the Geology, Natural History, Productions, and Climate of the Country; Its State as Regards Christianity; Sketches of the Principal Chiefs, and Their Present Position.* Wertheim and Macintosh, London.

Tcherkézoff, S. 1999. Who Said the 17th–18th Centuries Papālagi/Europeans Were "Sky-Bursters"? A Eurocentric Projection onto Polynesia. *Journal of the Polynesian Society* 108(4):417–425.

Tennent, J. E. 1852. Stone-Pillar Worship Still Existing in Ireland. *Notes and Queries* 5(119):121–122.

Tent, J. 2023. The Flag-Waving Names of Ocean Liners. *Mariner's Mirror* 109(3):342–358.

Tent, J., and P. Geraghty. 2001. Exploding Sky or Exploded Myth? The Origin of Papālagi. *Journal of the Polynesian Society* 110(2):171–214.

Tenazas, R. C. P. 1973. The Boat-Coffin Burial Complex in the Philippines and Its Relation to Similar Practices in Southeast Asia. *Philippine Quarterly of Culture and Society* 1(1):19–25.

Teske, T. (editor). 1987. *Darnley Island of Torres Strait*. Far Northern Schools Development Unit, Cairns.

Theodoropoulou-Polychroniadis, Z. 2015. *Sounion Revisited: The Sanctuaries of Poseidon and Athena at Sounion in Attica*. Oxbow, Oxford.

Thomas, T. 2013. Sensory Efficacy in the Art of New Georgia. In *Melanesia: Art and Encounter*, edited by L. Bolton, N. Thomas, E. Bonshek, J. Adams, and B. Burt, pp. 199–208. British Museum Press, London.

Thomas, T. 2014. Shrines in the Landscape of New Georgia. In *Monuments and People in the Pacific*, edited by H. Martinsson-Wallin and T. Thomas, pp. 47–76. Studies in Global Archaeology 20. Department of Archaeology and Ancient History, Uppsala University, Uppsala.

Thomsen, A. 2015. Riding for Poseidon: Terracotta Figurines from the Sanctuary of Poseidon. *Hesperia Supplements* 48:109–118.

Thomson, D. 1996 [1954]. *The People of the Sea: Celtic Tales of the Seal-Folk*. Canongate, Edinburgh.

Thomson, D. F. 1933. The Hero Cult, Initiation and Totemism on Cape York. *Journal of the Royal Anthropological Institute of Great Britain and Ireland* 63:453–537.

Thomson, D. F. 1934a. Notes on a Hero Cult from the Gulf of Carpentaria, North Queensland. *Journal of the Royal Anthropological Institute of Great Britain and Ireland* 64:217–235.

Thomson, D. F. 1934b. The Dugong Hunters of Cape York. *Journal of the Royal Anthropological Institute of Great Britain and Ireland* 64:237–262.

Thorpe, B. 1851. *Northern Mythology, Comprising the Principal Popular Traditions and Superstitions of Scandinavia, North Germany, and The Netherlands*. Vol. 1. Edward Lumley, London.

Thorpe, B. 1852. *Northern Mythology, Comprising the Principal Popular Traditions and Superstitions of Scandinavia, North Germany, and The Netherlands*. Vol. 3. Edward Lumley, London.

Thurston, E., and K. Rangachari. 1909. *Castes and Tribes of Southern India*. Vols. 1–7. Government Press, Madras.

Thye, B. M. 1995. Early Christian Ship Symbols. In *The Ship as Symbol in Prehistoric and Medieval Scandinavia*, edited by O. Crumlin-Pedersen and B. M. Thye, pp. 186–196. Studies in Archaeology and History. National Museum, Copenhagen.

Tiboni, F. 2006. Animal-Shaped Figureheads and the Evolution of a "Keel-Post-Stem" Structure in Nuragic Bronze Models and Boats Between the 9th and 7th Centuries BC. *International Journal of Nautical Archaeology* 35(1):141–144.

Tiley, S. 2023. Iconic Resources, Prestige, and Conservation on Boigu Island of the Torres Strait, Australia. In *The History and Environmental Impacts of Hunting Deities: Supernatural Gamekeepers and Animal Masters*, edited by R. J. Chacon, pp. 189–200. Springer Nature, Cham, Switzerland.

Tilley, C. 1999. The Metaphorical Transformation of Wala Canoes. In *Metaphor and Material Culture*, edited by C. Tilley, pp. 102–132. Blackwell, Oxford.

Tindale, N. B. 1962. Geographical Knowledge of the Kaiadilt People of Bentinck Island, Queensland. *Records of the South Australian Museum* 14(2):259–296.

Tindale, N. B. 1977. Further Report on the Kaiadilt People of Bentinck Island, Gulf of Carpentaria Queensland. In *Sunda and Sahul: Prehistoric Studies in Southeast Asia, Melanesia and Australia*, edited by J. Allen, J. Golson, and R. Jones, pp. 187–204. Academic Press, New York.

Tindale, N. B., and B. G. Maegraith. 1931. Traces of an Extinct Aboriginal Population on Kangaroo Island. *Records of the South Australian Museum* 4:275–289.

Titcomb, M., and M. K. Pukui. 1952. *Native Use of Fish in Hawaii*. Memoir 29. Supplement to the Journal of the Polynesian Society. Avery, New Plymouth, New Zealand.

Tjiputra, J. F., J. Negrel, and A. Olsen. 2023. Early Detection of Anthropogenic Climate Change Signals in the Ocean Interior. *Scientific Reports* 13(1):3006.

Tommaseo, M., G. Hauser, and A. Vienna. 1997. Auditory Hyperostosis and the Environment: An Update. *International Journal of Anthropology* 12:29–42.

Toomer, G. J. (editor). 1998. *Ptolemy's Almagest*. Princeton University Press, Princeton.

Torrente, F. 2015. Ancestral Fishing Techniques and Rites on 'Anaa Atoll, Tuamotu Islands, French Polynesia. *SPC Traditional Marine Resource Management and Knowledge Information Bulletin* 35:18–25.

Torreon, L. C., and A. S. Tiempo. 2021. Ritual Practices in Fishing. *Asia Pacific Journal of Management and Sustainable Development* 9(1):12–18.

Toynbee, J. M. C. 1996. *Death and Burial in the Roman World*. Johns Hopkins University Press, Baltimore.

Trigger, D. S. 1987. Inland, Coast and Islands: Traditional Aboriginal Society and Material Culture in a Region of the Southern Gulf of Carpentaria. *Records of the South Australian Museum* 21(2):69–84.

Trinkaus, E., M. Samsel, and S. Villotte. 2019. External Auditory Exostoses Among Western Eurasian Late Middle and Late Pleistocene Humans. *PLoS ONE* 14(8):e0220464.

Troncoso, A., F. Armstrong, and M. Basile. 2018. Rock Art in Central and South America: Social Settings and Regional Diversity. In *Oxford Handbook of the Archaeology and Anthropology of Rock Art*, edited by B. David and I. J. McNiven, pp. 273–314. Oxford University Press, Oxford.

Trubitt, M. B. D. 2003. The Production and Exchange of Marine Shell Prestige Goods. *Journal of Archaeological Research* 11(3):243–277.

Tuggle, D., and M. Tomonari-Tuggle. 1999. The Petroglyphs of Kahalu'u, Kona, Hawai'i. *Rapa Nui Journal* 13(1):3–13.

Turner, D. H. 2000. From Here into Eternity: Power and Transcendence in Australian Aboriginal Music. In *Indigenous Religious Musics*, edited by K. Ralls-Macleod and G. Harvey, pp. 35–55. Ashgate, Aldershot, England.

Turner, E. 1994. Behind Inupiaq Reincarnation: Cosmological Cycling. In *Amerindian Rebirth: Reincarnation Belief Among North American Indians and Inuit*, edited by A. C. Mills and R. Slobodin, pp. 67–81. University of Toronto Press, Toronto.

Turner, L. M. 1894. Ethnology of the Ungava District, Hudson Bay Territory. In *Eleventh Annual Report of the Bureau of American Ethnology to the Secretary of the Smithsonian Institution 1888–'90*, edited by J. W. Powell, pp. 159–350. US Government Printing Office, Washington, DC.

Turner, V. 1967. Betwixt and Between: The Liminal Period in Rites de Passage. In *The Forest of Symbols: Aspects of Ndembu Ritual*, pp. 93–111. Cornell University Press, New York.

Turner, V. 1979. Frame, Flow and Reflection: Ritual and Drama as Public Liminality. *Japanese Journal of Religious Studies* 6(4):465–499.

Turner, V. 2009 [1969]. *The Ritual Process: Structure and Anti-Structure*. AldineTransaction, New Brunswick.

Tylor, E. B. 1871. *Primitive Culture: Researches into the Development of Primitive Mythology, Philosophy, Religion, Art, and Custom*. Vols. 1 and 2. John Murray, London.

Tyrrell, M. 2007. Sentient Beings and Wildlife Resources: Inuit, Beluga Whales and Management Regimes in the Canadian Arctic. *Human Ecology* 35(5):575–586.

Uimonen, P., and H. Masimbi. 2021. Spiritual Relationality in Swahili Ocean Worlds. *Kritisk etnografi: Swedish Journal of Anthropology* 4(2):35–50.

Urry, J. 1982. From Zoology to Ethnology: A. C. Haddon's Conversion to Anthropology. *Canberra Anthropology* 5:58–85.

Urwin, C., J. J. Bradley, I. J. McNiven, L. Russell, and L. Yulianti Farid. 2023. Re-Assessing Regional Chronologies for Island Southeast Asian Voyaging to Aboriginal Australia. *Archaeology in Oceania* 58(3):245–274.

Urwin, C., I. J. McNiven, S. Clarke, L. Macquarie, and T. Whap. 2016. Hearing the Evidence: Using Archaeological Data to Analyse the Long-Term Impacts of Dugong (*Dugong dugon*) Hunting on Mabuyag, Torres Strait, over the Past 1000 Years. *Australian Archaeology* 82(3):201–217.

US Environmental Protection Agency. 2025. Burial at Sea. https://www.epa.gov/ocean-dumping/burial-sea.

Valientes, E. A. 2019. The Archaeology and Meaning of the Boat-Shaped Stone Markers in Vuhus Island, Batanes Province, Northern Philippines. *Hukay* 21:1–25.

van Baal, J. 1966. *Dema: Description and Analysis of Marind-Anim Culture (South New Guinea)*. Martinus Nijhoff, The Hague.

van Baaren, T. P. 1968. *Korwars and Korwar Style: Art and Ancestor Worship in North-West New Guinea*. Mouton, Paris.

van den Hurk, Y., F. Sikström, L. Amkreutz, M. Bleasdale, A. Borvon, B. Ephrem, C. Fernández-Rodríguez, H. M. B. Gibbs, L. Jonsson, A. Lehouck, et al. 2023. The Prelude to Industrial Whaling: Identifying the Targets of Ancient European Whaling Using Zooarchaeology and Collagen Mass-Peptide Fingerprinting. *Royal Society Open Science* 10(9):230741.

Van de Noort, R. 2011. *North Sea Archaeologies: A Maritime Biography, 10,000 BC to AD 1500*. Oxford University Press, Oxford.

van Duzer, C. 2013. *Sea Monsters and Medieval and Renaissance Maps.* British Library, London.

van Dyke, R. M., K. E. Primeau, K. Throgmorton, and D. E. Witt. 2024. Seashells and Sound Waves: Modelling Soundscapes in Chacoan Great-House Communities. *Antiquity* 98(399):1–18.

van Gennep, A. 1960. *The Rites of Passage.* University of Chicago Press, Chicago.

van Ginkel, R. 1990. Fishermen, Taboos, and Ominous Animals: A Comparative Perspective. *Anthrozoös* 4(2):73–81.

van Ginkel, R. 2013. The Cultural Seascape, Cosmology and the Magic of Liminality. In *Coastal Cultures: Liminality and Leisure*, edited by P. Gilchrist, T. Carter, and D. Burdsey, pp. 45–64. LSA Publications 126. Leisure Studies Association, Eastbourne.

Vanhaeren, M., F. d'Errico, I. Billy, and F. Grousset. 2004. Tracing the Source of Upper Palaeolithic Shell Beads by Strontium Isotope Dating. *Journal of Archaeological Science* 31(10):1481–1488.

Vanhaeren, M., F. d'Errico, C. Stringer, S. L. James, J. A. Todd, and H. K. Mienis. 2006. Middle Paleolithic Shell Beads in Israel and Algeria. *Science* 312(5781):1785–1788.

Vanhaeren, M., F. d'Errico, K. L. van Niekerk, C. S. Henshilwood, and R. M. Erasmus. 2013. Thinking Strings: Additional Evidence for Personal Ornament Use in the Middle Stone Age at Blombos Cave, South Africa. *Journal of Human Evolution* 64(6):500–517.

van Hasselt, J. L. 1876. Die nuforesen, äusserliches Vorkommen, Kleider, Verzierungen, Waffen, Häuser. *Zeitschrift für Ethnologie* 8:134–139, 169–202.

Vatter, E. 1932. *Ata kiwan: Unbekannte bergvölker im tropischem Holland.* Bibliographisches Institut, Leipzig.

Vaughan, I. M. 1922. Ships and Saints. *Dublin Review* 171(342):84–89.

Vavouranakis, G. 2011. Introduction. In *The Seascape in Aegean Prehistory*, edited by G. Vavouranakis, pp. 13–29. Monograph 14. Danish Institute at Athens, Athens.

Veniaminov, I. 1984. *Notes on the Islands of the Unalaska District.* Translated by Lydia T. Black and R. H. Geoghegan. Limestone Press, Kingston, Canada.

Verhart, L. B. M. 2004. The Implications of Prehistoric Finds on and off the Dutch Coast. In *Submarine Prehistoric Archaeology of the North Sea: Research Priorities and Collaboration with Industry*, edited by N. C. Flemming, pp. 57–61. CBA Research Report 141. Council for British Archaeology/English Heritage, York.

Vermeule, E. 1979. *Aspects of Death in Early Greek Art and Poetry.* University of California Press, Berkeley.

Vermeule, E., and S. Chapman. 1971. A Protoattic Human Sacrifice? *American Journal of Archaeology* 75(3):285–293.

Villotte, S., S. S., and C. J. Knüsel. 2014. External Auditory Exostoses and Aquatic Activities During the Mesolithic and the Neolithic in Europe: Results from a Large Prehistoric Sample. *Anthropologie* 52(1):73–90.

Viveiros de Castro, E. 1998. Cosmological Deixis and Amerindian Perspectivism. *Journal of the Royal Anthropological Institute* 4:469–488.

Vogiatzakis, I. N., M. Zomeni, and A. M. Mannion. 2017. Characterizing Islandscapes: Conceptual and Methodological Challenges Exemplified in the Mediterranean. *Land* 6(1):1–14.

von Brandt, A. 1984. The Fishery of Lan Yu (Botel Tobago): An Old Fishing Culture. In *The Fishing Culture of the World: Studies in Ethnology, Cultural Ecology and Folklore*, edited by B. Gunda, pp. 469–527. 2 vols. Akadémiai Kiadó, Budapest.

von Busch, P. 1985. New Finds of Boat Graffiti. In *Postmedieval Boat and Ship Archaeology*, edited by C. O. Cederlund, pp. 365–368. BAR International Series 256. Oxford.

von Ehrenheim, H., P. Klingborg, and A. Frejman. 2019. Water at Ancient Greek Sanctuaries: Medium of Divine Presence or Commodity for Mortal Visitors? *Journal of Archaeology and Ancient History* 26:1–31.

von Hardenberg, W. G. 2021. Making a Stable Sea: The Littorals of Eighteenth-Century Europe and the Origins of a Spatial Concept. *Isis* 112(1):130–140.

Voorhoeve, C. L. 1986. We, People of One Canoe, They, People of Wood: Two Asmat Origin Myths. *IRIAN: Bulletin of Irian Jaya* 14:79–125.

Wachsmann, S. 1998. *Seagoing Ships and Seamanship in the Bronze Age Levant*. Texas A&M University Press, College Station.

Wagner, G., K. Hilbert, D. Bandeira, M. C. Tenório, and M. M. Okumura. 2011. Sambaquis (Shell Mounds) of the Brazilian Coast. *Quaternary International* 239(1–2):51–60.

Wahab, M. R. A., Z. Ramli, M. A. A. Samad, N. S. M. Supian, M. U. M. Nasir, and S. S. Masdey. 2018. Ancient Maritime Symbols in Malay Traditional Boat in the East Coast, Peninsular Malaysia. *Planning Malaysia* 16(1):372–380.

Waite, D. 1990. *Mon* Canoes of the Western Solomon Islands. In *Art and Identity in Oceania*, edited by A. Hanson and L. Hanson, pp. 44–66. Crawford House, Bathurst.

Waite, D. 2000. An Artefact/Image Text of Head-Hunting Motifs. *Journal of the Polynesian Society* 109(1):115–144.

Waite, D. 2021. Canoe Carvings from Western Solomon Islands: The Operative Efficacy of Simultaneous Visual Presences. *Pacific Arts* 21(1):76–106.

Wallace, J. 1693. *A Description of the Isles of Orkney*. John Reid, Edinburgh.

Walsh, M. J. K. 2008. "On of the Princypalle Havenes of the See": The Port of Famagusta and the Ship Graffiti in the Church of St George of the Greeks, Cyprus. *International Journal of Nautical Archaeology* 37(1):115–129.

Walter, R., H. Buckley, C. Jacomb, and E. Matisoo-Smith. 2017. Mass Migration and the Polynesian Settlement of New Zealand. *Journal of World Prehistory* 30:351–376.

Walter, R., and P. Sheppard. 2000. Nusa Roviana: The Archaeology of a Melanesian Chiefdom. *Journal of Field Archaeology* 27(3):295–318.

Walter, R., T. Thomas, and P. Sheppard. 2004. Cult Assemblages and Ritual Practice in Roviana Lagoon, Solomon Islands. *World Archaeology* 36(1):142–157.

Ward, E. 1707. *The Wooden World Dissected, in the Character of a Ship of War*. H. Meere, London.

Wardwell, A. 1986. *Ancient Eskimo Ivories of the Bering Strait*. Hudson Hills Press, New York.

Watanabe, H. 1972. *The Ainu Ecosystem: Environment and Group Structure*. University of Tokyo Press, Tokyo.

Watanabe, H. 1994. The Animal Cult of Northern Hunter-Gatherers: Patterns and Their Ecological Implications. In *Circumpolar Religion and Ecology: An Anthropology of the North*, edited by T. Irimoto and T. Yamada, pp. 47–67. University of Tokyo Press, Tokyo.

Watanabe, Y. 2013. Beluga Hunting Practices of the Indigenous People in Kamchatka: Characterization of Sea Mammal Hunting in Northeastern Asia. In *Anthropological Studies of Whaling*, edited by N. Kishigami, H. Hamaguchi, and J. N. Savelle, pp. 177–194. Senri Ethnological Studies 84. National Museum of Ethnology, Osaka.

Waterhouse, J. H. L. 2005 [1928]. *The Roviana and English Dictionary*. New ed., edited by L. Parkinson. Shepp, Sydney.

Waterman, T. T. 1920. *The Whaling Equipment of the Makah Indians*. University of Washington Publications in Anthropology 1(1). University of Washington Press, Seattle.

Waugh, A. 1960. The Folklore of the Merfolk. *Folklore* 71(2):73–84.

Wax, M., and R. Wax. 1963. The Notion of Magic. *Current Anthropology* 4(5):495–518.

Weeks, L., H. David-Cuny, A. Avanzini, S. Lischi, F. Genchi, F. Caputo, Y. Y. Al Ali, and M. Boraik. 2019. Worked and Decorated Shell Discs from Southern Arabia and the Wider Near East. *Arabian Archaeology and Epigraphy* 30(2):213–238.

Wehlin, J. 2010. Approaching the Gotlandic Bronze Age from Sea: Future Possibilities from a Maritime Perspective. In *Baltic Prehistoric Interactions and Transformations: The Neolithic to the Bronze Age*, edited by H. Martinsson-Wallin, pp. 89–110. Gotland University Press, Visby.

Weisler, M. I., K. D. Collerson, Y.-X. Feng, J.-X. Zhao, and K.-F. Yu. 2006. Thorium-230 Coral Chronology of a Late Prehistoric Hawaiian Chiefdom. *Journal of Archaeological Science* 33(2):273–282.

Weisler, M. I., Q. Hua, and J.-x. Zhao. 2009. Late Holocene 14C Marine Reservoir Corrections for Hawai'i Derived from U-series Dated Archaeological Coral. *Radiocarbon* 51(3):955–968.

Weisler, M. I., M. Mihaljević, and A. J. Rogers. 2019. Sea Urchins: Improving Understanding of Prehistoric Subsistence, Diet, Foraging Behavior, Tool Use, and Ritual Practices in Polynesia. *Journal of Island and Coastal Archaeology* 15(4):547–575.

Weisler, M. I., and A. J. Rogers. 2021. Ritual Use of Limpets in Late Hawaiian Prehistory. *Journal of Field Archaeology* 46(1):52–61.

Welch, D. J., A. Røkkum, T. A. Jefferson, N. Higa, and J. R. McNeill 2010. An Anthropological Study of the Significance of the Dugong in Okinawa Culture. Revised Report. Prepared for Commandant US Marine Corps, Washington, DC.

Wescoat, B. D. 2005. Buildings for Votive Ships on Delos and Samothrace. In *Architecture and Archaeology in the Cyclades*, edited by M. Yeroulanou and M. Stamatopoulou, pp. 153–172. BAR International Series 1455. Archaeopress, Oxford.

Wesley, D., J. F. McKinnon, and J. T. Raupp. 2012. Sails Set in Stone: A Technological Analysis of Non-Indigenous Watercraft Rock Art Paintings in North Western Arnhem Land. *Journal of Maritime Archaeology* 7(2):245–269.

Westerdahl, C. 1992. The Maritime Cultural Landscape. *International Journal of Nautical Archaeology* 21(1):5–14.

Westerdahl, C. 2002. The Ritual Landscape at Sea. In *Maritime Archäologie heute. Maritime Archaeology Today*, edited by K. Krüger and C. O. Cederlund, pp. 51–72. 3rd International Marine Archaeological Conference of the Baltic Sea Area, 2001. Ingo Koch Verlag, Rostock.

Westerdahl, C. 2005a. Seal on Land, Elk at Sea: Notes on and Applications of the Ritual Landscape at the Seaboard. *International Journal of Nautical Archaeology* 34(1):2–23.

Westerdahl, C. 2005b. Maritime Cosmology and Archaeology. *Deutsches Schifffahrtsarchiv* 2:7–54.

Westerdahl, C. 2010. "Horses Are Strong at Sea": The Liminal Aspect of the Maritime Cultural Landscape. In *The Global Origins and Development of Seafaring*, edited by A. Anderson, J. Barrett, and K. Boyle, pp. 275–287. McDonald Institute Monographs. McDonald Institute for Archaeological Research, Cambridge.

Westerdahl, C. 2011a. The Binary Relationship of Sea and Land. In *The Archaeology of Maritime Landscapes*, edited by B. Ford, pp. 291–310. Springer, New York.

Westerdahl, C. 2011b. The Maritime Cultural Landscape. In *The Oxford Handbook of Maritime Archaeology*, edited by A. Catsambis, B. Ford, and D. L. Hamilton, pp. 733–762. Oxford University Press, Oxford.

Westerdahl, C. 2013. Medieval Carved Ship Images Found in Nordic Churches: The Poor Man's Votive Ships? *International Journal of Nautical Archaeology* 42(2):337–347.

Westerdahl, C. 2014. Spiritscapes of the North: Traces of the Fear of the Drowned in Maritime Landscapes? In *Med hjärta och hjärna: En vänbok till Professor Elisabeth Arwill-Nordbladh*, edited by H. Alexandersson, A. Andreeff, and A. Bünz, pp. 483–503. GOTARC Series A. Gothenburg Archaeological Studies 5. University of Gothenburg, Göteborg.

Westerdahl, C. 2015. Contrasts of the Maritime Environment—Possible Implications in Prehistory—A Very Short Course of Cognition in the Ancient Maritime Cultural Landscape. In *Ritual Landscapes and Borders within Rock Art Research: Papers in Honour of Professor Kalle Sognnes*, edited by H. Stebergløkken, R. Berge, E. Lindgaard, and H. V. Stuedal, pp. 141–154. Archaeopress, Oxford.

Westropp, T. J. 1911. Part 2: History and Archaeology. *Proceedings of the Royal Irish Academy. Section A: Mathematical and Physical Sciences* 31:2.1–2.78.

Westropp, T. J. 1922. A Study of the Folklore on the Coasts of Connacht, Ireland (continued). *Folklore* 33(4):389–397.

Westropp, T. J. 1923. A Study of the Folklore on the Coasts of Connacht, Ireland (continued). *Folklore* 34(4):333–349.

Whalen, M. E. 2013. Wealth, Status, Ritual, and Marine Shell at Casas Grandes, Chihuahua, Mexico. *American Antiquity* 78(4):624–639.

Wharton, W. J. L. (editor). 1893. *Captain Cook's Journal During his First Voyage Round the World Made in H.M. Bark "Endeavour" 1768–71*. A literal transcription of the original MSS. Elliot Stock, London.

Wheeler, G. C. 1914. An Account of the Death Rites and Eschatology of the People of the Bougainville Strait (Western Solomon Islands). *Archiv für Religionswissenschaft* 17:64–112.

Whitaker, I. 1986. North Atlantic Sea-Creatures in the *King's Mirror* (Konungs Skuggsjá). *Polar Record* 23(142):3–13.

White, J. 2017. *Tides: The Science and Spirit of the Ocean*. Trinity University Press, San Antonio.

White, N. I., and W. D. Hand. 1970. *The Frank C. Brown Collection of North Carolina Folklore, Vol. 7: Popular Beliefs and Superstitions from North Carolina, Part 2.* Duke University Press, Durham.

White, N. J., I. D. Haigh, J. A. Church, T. Koen, C. S. Watson, T. R. Pritchard, P. J. Watson, R. J. Burgette, K. L. McInnes, Z.-J. You, X. Zhang, and P. Tregoning. 2014. Australian Sea Levels—Trends, Regional Variability and Influencing Factors. *Earth-Science Reviews* 136:155–174.

White, T. H. 1959. *The Godstone and the Blackymor.* P. G. Putnam's Sons, New York.

Whitridge, P. 1999. The Prehistory of Inuit and Yupik Whale Use. *Revista deArqueolog'ia Americana* 16:99–154.

Whitridge, P. 2002. Social and Ritual Determinants of Whale Bone Transport at a Classic Thule Winter Site in the Canadian Artic. *International Journal of Osteoarchaeology* 12(1):65–75.

Whitridge, P. 2004. Landscapes, Houses, Bodies, Things: "Place" and the Archaeology of Inuit Imaginaries. *Journal of Archaeological Method and Theory* 11(2):213–250.

Wigen, K. 2006. Introduction. *American Historical Review* 111(3):717–721.

Wilbert, J. 1977. Navigators of the Winter Sun. In *The Sea in the Pre-Columbian World*, edited by E. P. Benson, pp. 16–46. Dumbarton Oaks Research Library and Collections, Trustees for Harvard University, Washington, DC.

Wilbert, J. 1993. *Mystic Endowment: Religious Ethnography of the Warao Indians.* Harvard University Press, Cambridge, Massachusetts.

Wilkinson, T. T. 1869. Scarborough Folk-Lore. *Notes and Queries* Series 4, 4(85):131–132.

Willerslev, R. 2007. *Soul Hunters: Hunting, Animism, and Personhood among the Siberian Yukaghirs.* University of California Press, Berkeley.

Williams, F. E. 1932. Trading Voyages from the Gulf of Papua. *Oceania* 3(2):139–166.

Williams, F. E. 1940a. *Drama of Orokolo: The Social and Ceremonial Life of the Elema.* Oxford University Press, London.

Williams, F. E. 1940b. Natives of Lake Kutubu, Papua. *Oceania* 11(2):121–157.

Williams, F. E. 1976. Bull-Roarers in the Papuan Gulf. In *"The Vailala Madness" and Other Essays*, edited by E. Schwimmer, pp. 73–122. University of Queensland Press, St. Lucia.

Williams, G. M. 2003. *Handbook of Hindu Mythology.* ABC-CLIO, Santa Barbara.

Williams, H. 1981. A Ship of Actium on a Roman Lamp. *International Journal of Nautical Archaeology and Underwater Exploration* 10(1):23–27.

Williams, H. 1989. Figureheads on Greek and Roman Ships. In *Tropis I: International Symposium on Ship Construction in Antiquity at Athens*, edited by H. E. Tzalas, pp. 293–297. Hellenic Institute for the Preservation of Nautical Tradition, Piraeus.

Williams, T. 1858. *Fiji and the Fijians.* Vol. 1. Edited by G. S. Rowe. Alexander Heylin, London.

Willis, S., and E. Holliday. 2022. *Triggering Death: Quantifying the True Human Cost of Global Fishing.* Report. Fish Safety Foundation, New Zealand.

Willson, M. 2016. *Seawomen of Iceland: Survival on the Edge.* University of Washington Press, Seattle.

Wilson, L. 1993. *Kerkar Lu: Contemporary Artefacts of the Torres Strait Islanders.* Queensland Department of Education, Brisbane.

Winchester, S. 2001. In the Eye of the Whirlpool: From the Mythical Charybdis to the Monster Maelstrom, These Watery Gyres Thrill and Chill Us. *Smithsonian* 32(5):84–94.

Wing, E. S. 1977. Factors Influencing Exploitation of Marine Resources. In *The Sea in the Pre-Columbian World*, edited by E. P. Benson, pp. 47–64. Dumbarton Oaks Research Library and Collections, Trustees for Harvard University, Washington, DC.

Wohlers, J. F. H. 1874. The Mythology and Traditions of the Maori in New Zealand. *Transactions of the New Zealand Institute* 7:3–53.

Woodford, C. M. 1890. *A Naturalist Among the Head-Hunters.* George Philip and Son, London.

Woodworth, P. L. 2017. Differences Between Mean Tide Level and Mean Sea Level. *Journal of Geodesy* 91(1):69–90.

Woolmer, M. 2012. "Ornamental" Horns on Phoenician Warships. *Levant* 44(2):238–252.

World Health Organization. 2014. *Global Report on Drowning: Preventing a Leading Killer.* World Health Organization, Geneva.

Wright, D., B. Stephenson, P. S. C. Taçon, R. N. Williams, A. Fogel, S. Sutton, and S. Ulm. 2016. Exploring Ceremony: The Archaeology of a Men's Meeting House ("*Kod*") on Mabuyag, Western Torres Strait. *Cambridge Archaeological Journal* 26(4):721–740.

Yeo, K. S. 2021. *Divine Custody: A History of Singapore's Oldest Teochew Temple.* National University of Singapore Press, Singapore.

Yesner, D. R. 1980. Maritime Hunter-Gatherers: Ecology and Prehistory. *Current Anthropology* 21(6):727–750.

Younker, R. W., and R. M. Davidson. 2011. The Myth of the Solid Heavenly Dome: Another Look at the Hebrew (*Rāqîaʿ*). *Andrews University Seminary Studies* 1:125–147.

Zazzaro, C., H. Liebner, A. Soriente, G. Ferraioli, and A. G. Purnawibawa. 2022. The Construction of an Historical Boat in South Sulawesi (Indonesia): The Padewakang. *Journal of Maritime Archaeology* 17(4):507–557.

Zegwaard, Rev. G. A. 1959. Headhunting Practices of the Asmat of Netherlands New Guinea. *American Anthropologist* 61(6):1020–1041.

Zender, M. 2010. The Music of Shells. In *Fiery Pool: The Maya and the Mythic Sea*, edited by D. Finamore and S. D. Houston, pp. 83–85. Peabody Essex Museum and Yale University Press, New Haven.

Zerner, C. 1994a. Tracking Sasi: The Transformation of a Central Moluccan Reef Management Institution in Indonesia. In *Collaborative and Community-Based Management of Coral Reefs: Lessons from Experience*, edited by A. T. White, L. Z. Hale, Y. Renard, and L. Cortesi, pp. 19–32. Kumarian, West Hartford, Connecticut.

Zerner, C. 1994b. Transforming Customary Law and Coastal Management Practices in the Maluku Islands, Indonesia, 1870–1992. In *Natural Connections: Perspectives in Community-based Conservation*, edited by D. Western, R. M. Wright, and S. C. Strum, pp. 80–112. Island Press, Washington, DC.

Zerner, C. 2003. Sounding the Makassar Strait: The Poetics and Politics of an Indonesian Marine Environment. In *Culture and the Question of Rights: Forests, Coasts, and Seas in Southeast Asia*, edited by C. Zerner, pp. 56–108. Duke University Press, Durham.

Zimmerman, M. R. 1998. Alaskan and Aleutian Mummies. In *Mummies, Disease and Ancient Cultures*, edited by A. Cockburn, E. Cockburn, and T. A. Reyman, pp. 138–153. Cambridge University Press, Cambridge.

INDEX

Ian J. McNiven is professor of Indigenous archaeology at Monash Indigenous Studies Centre, Monash University. He is coeditor of *The Oxford Handbook of the Archaeology of Indigenous Australia and New Guinea.*

Society and Ecology in Island and Coastal Archaeology

Edited by Victor D. Thompson and Scott M. Fitzpatrick

The settlement and occupation of islands, coastlines, and archipelagoes can be traced deep into the human past. From the voyaging and seafaring peoples of the Oceania to the Mesolithic fisher-hunter-gatherers of coastal Ireland, to coastal salt production among Maya traders, the range of variation found in these societies over time is boundless. Yet, they share a commonality that links them all together—their dependence upon seas, coasts, and estuaries for life and prosperity. Thus, in all these cultures there is a fundamental link between society and the ecology of islands and coasts. Books in this series explore the nature of humanity's relationship to these environments from a global perspective. Topics in this series would range from edited volumes to single case studies covering the archaeology of initial migrations, seafaring, insularity, trade, societal complexity and collapse, early village life, aquaculture, and historical ecology, among others along islands and coasts.

The Powhatan Landscape: An Archaeological History of the Algonquian Chesapeake, by Martin D. Gallivan (2016; first paperback edition, 2018)

An Archaeology of Abundance: Reevaluating the Marginality of California's Islands, edited by Kristina M. Gill, Mikael Fauvelle, and Jon M. Erlandson (2019)

Maritime Communities of the Ancient Andes, edited by Gabriel Prieto and Daniel H. Sandweiss (2019)

The Archaeology of Human-Environmental Dynamics on the North American Atlantic Coast, edited by Leslie Reeder-Myers, John A. Turck, and Torben C. Rick (2019)

Historical Ecology and Archaeology in the Galapagos Islands: A Legacy of Human Occupation by Peter W. Stahl, Fernando J. Astudillo, Ross W. Jamieson, Diego Quiroga, and Florencio Delgado (2020)

The Archaeology of Island Colonization: Global Approaches to Initial Human Settlement, edited by Matthew F. Napolitano, Jessica H. Stone, and Robert J. DiNapoli (2021)

Human Behavioral Ecology and Coastal Environments, edited by Heather B. Thakar and Carola Flores Fernandez (2023)

Fisher-Hunter-Gatherer Complexity in North America, edited by Christina Perry Sampson (2023)

Sustainability in Ancient Island Societies: An Archaeology of Human Resilience, edited by Scott M. Fitzpatrick, Jon M. Erlandson, and Kristina M. Gill (2024)

Intertidal Shipwrecks: Management of a Historic Resource in an Unmanageable Environment, edited by Jennifer E. Jones, Calvin H. Mires, and Daniel Zwick (2025)

The Archaeology of Seafaring in Small-Scale Societies: Negotiating Watery Worlds, edited by Alberto García-Piquer, Mikael Fauvelle, and Colin Grier (2026)

Sentient Seas: Archaeologies of Seascapes and Maritime Rituals, by Ian J. McNiven (2026)